Dear MyCopy Customer,

This Springer book is a monochrome print version of the eBook to which your library gives you access via SpringerLink. It is available to you at a subsidized price since your library subscribes to at least one Springer eBook subject collection.

Please note that MyCopy books are only offered to library patrons with access to at least one Springer eBook subject collection. MyCopy books are strictly for individual use only.

You may cite this book by referencing the bibliographic data and/or the DOI (Digital Object Identifier) found in the front matter. This book is an exact but monochrome copy of the print version of the eBook on SpringerLink.

Charalambos D. Aliprantis
Donald J. Brown · Owen Burkinshaw

Existence and Optimality of Competitive Equilibria

With 38 Figures

Springer-Verlag Berlin Heidelberg GmbH

Professor Charalambos D. Aliprantis, Department of Mathematical Sciences, IUPUI, 1125 East 38th Street, Indianapolis, IN 46205, USA

Professor Donald J. Brown, Department of Economics, Stanford University, Stanford, CA 94305, USA

Professor Owen Burkinshaw, Department of Mathematical Sciences, IUPUI, 1125 East 38th Street, Indianapolis, IN 46205, USA

DOI 10.1007/978-3-662-21893-8

Library of Congress Cataloging-in-Publication Data
Aliprantis, Charalambos D.
Existence and optimality of competitive equilibria / Charalambos D. Aliprantis, Donald J. Brown, and Owen Burkinshaw.
Bibliography: p.
Includes index.

1. Equilibrium (Economics)-Mathematical models. 2. Economics, Mathematical. I. Brown, Donald J., 1937- . II. Burkinshaw, Owen. III. Title.
HB145.A438 1989
339.5-dc19

Originally published by Springer-Verlag Berlin Heidelberg New York in 1989
MyCopy version of the original edition 1989

To Bernadette, Claire, and Dionisi
CDA

To Betty and Vanessa
DJB

To Betty and Mary
OB

As soon as an equilibrium state is defined for a model of an economy, the fundamental question of its existence is raised.

Gerard Debreu

If a set of prices can be found which equates supply and demand, then the resulting situation is optimal.

Kenneth J. Arrow

PREFACE

This monograph is a systematic exposition of the authors' research on general equilibrium models with an infinite number of commodities. It is intended to serve both as a graduate text on aspects of general equilibrium theory and as an introduction, for economists and mathematicians working in mathematical economics, to current research in a frontier area of general equilibrium theory. To this end, we have provided two introductory chapters on the basic economic model and the mathematical framework. The exercises at the end of each section complement the main exposition.

Chapter one is a concise but substantiative discussion of the questions of existence and optimality of competitive equilibria in the Walrasian general equilibrium model of an economy with a finite number of households, firms and commodities. Our extension of this model to economies with an infinite number of commodities constitutes the core material of this book and begins in chapter three. Readers familiar with the Walrasian general equilibrium model as exposited in [13], [23] or [52] may treat chapter one as a handy reference for the main economic concepts and notions that are used throughout the book.

Chapter two is an introduction to the theory of topological Riesz spaces. These spaces are the mathematical structures we use to model economies with an infinite number of commodities. Chapter two should be readily accessible to readers familiar with the duality theory of locally convex spaces, say at the level of [31], [33], [58] or [62]. Comprehensive discussions of the theory of topological Riesz spaces can be found in the books [6], [8] and [63].

In chapters three and four we again address the questions of the existence and optimality of Walrasian equilibria for economies with a finite number of households and firms, but with an infinite number of commodities. In particular, chapter three is concerned with pure exchange economies and chapter four considers production economies.

The final chapter, chapter five, is our most original and significant contribution to the literature on economies with an infinite number of commodities. Building upon the analysis of the previous chapters we address the questions of existence and optimality of a competitive equilibrium in the overlapping generations model. This is an intertemporal model of exchange where there are a countable number of generations each finitely lived. Hence, formally this is an economic model with both an infinite (countable) number of agents (households) and an infinite number of commodities. Chapter five may be read immediately after chapter three.

C. D. ALIPRANTIS, D. J. BROWN, AND O. BURKINSHAW November, 1988

ACKNOWLEDGMENTS

The first chapter of this monograph is an outgrowth of the lectures delivered by the first and third authors at the IUPUI Math Economics seminar during the academic years 1984–87. We would like to express our sincere thanks to the participants of the seminar Paul Carlin, Subir Chakrabarti, Mike Gleeson, Bob Sandy, and Gang Yi for their comments and contributions during the discussions. The financial support received by these authors from the National Science Foundation is also greatly appreciated.

The second author learned to appreciate the beauty and significance of the Walrasian general equilibrium model during his long tenure as a member of the Cowles Foundation for Research in Economics at Yale University. The Cowles Foundation is unique in its unqualified support of basic research in economic theory and the author is pleased to acknowledge this support. Financial support for his research has been provided, in part, by grants and fellowships from the California Institute of Technology, the Indiana University Institute for Advanced Study, Johns Hopkins University, the National Science Foundation, and Yale University.

The monograph was composed by the authors on a Macintosh Plus microcomputer using the typesetting system TEXTURES. We express with pleasure our gratitude to E. Spyropoulos for his help during the composition process.

CONTENTS

CHAPTER 5: THE OVERLAPPING GENERATIONS MODEL

CHAPTER 1:

THE ARROW–DEBREU MODEL

One of the two central paradigms in modern general equilibrium theory is the Walrasian general equilibrium model of an economy with a finite number of commodities and a finite number of households and firms, as formulated by K. J. Arrow and G. Debreu [12].

In this chapter, we shall investigate the existence and optimality of Walrasian (or competitive) equilibrium in the Arrow–Debreu model. Two existence proofs are presented. The first one uses the classical notions of demand and supply functions. In this case, a price vector is an equilibrium price vector if at these prices supply equals demand. However, supply and demand functions need not be defined, even for strictly positive prices, in economies having an infinite number of commodities; see Example 3.6.1 on page 168 and Exercise 6 on page 176. Our second existence proof of a Walrasian equilibrium is independent of the notions of supply and demand functions. The argument of this proof, which combines the core equivalence theorem of G. Debreu and H. E. Scarf [24] with H. E. Scarf's core existence theorem for balanced games [60], does generalize to economies with infinite dimensional commodity spaces as first demonstrated by B. Peleg and M. E. Yaari [53] for the commodity space $\mathcal{R}_\infty$.

In the classical Arrow–Debreu model only a finite number of commodities are exchanged, produced or consumed. It is useful to think of physical commodities such as steel or wheat or apples that are available at different times or in different locations or in different states of the world as different commodities. We suppose that there are ℓ such commodities. Inputs for production are negatively signed and outputs of production are positively signed. Any two commodity bundles can be added to produce a new commodity bundle and any scalar multiple of a commodity bundle is a commodity bundle. Hence, it is natural to view the commodity space E as the finite dimensional vector space $\mathcal{R}^\ell$.

The terms at which good j can be exchanged in the market for good i is defined by the ratio of the prices $\frac{p_i}{p_j}$, where p_i and p_j are nonnegative real numbers and $p_j > 0$. That is, $\frac{p_i}{p_j}$ is the amount of good j that can be exchanged for a unit amount of good i at prices $\mathbf{p} = (p_1, p_2, \ldots, p_\ell)$. Given a price vector $\mathbf{p} = (p_1, p_2, \ldots, p_\ell)$ and a commodity vector $\mathbf{x} = (x_1, x_2, \ldots, x_\ell)$, the "value" of $\mathbf{x}$ at prices $\mathbf{p}$ is given by $\mathbf{p}\cdot\mathbf{x} = \sum_{i=1}^{\ell} p_i x_i$. Hence, each price vector defines a linear functional on the commodity space E and we define the price space as the dual space of E, denoted by E'. For the case $E = \mathcal{R}^\ell$, we see that $E' = \mathcal{R}^\ell$.

In addition to the linear structure of the commodity space, we impose a topology on E such that the linear operations of vector addition and scalar multiplication are continuous. In the finite dimensional case this enables us to show (under some additional hypotheses) that the supply and demand functions depend continuously on prices—and thus, capturing the economic intuition that a "small" change in prices results in a "small" change in demand and supply. In later chapters we require the commodity space to be a topological vector space E and the price space to be the topological dual E', i.e., the space of continuous linear functionals on E. This formal duality between commodities and price was introduced by G. Debreu [22].

The behavioral assumption that consumers prefer more to less has important implications for equilibrium analysis. One consequence is that equilibrium prices must be positive. The natural partial ordering on $\mathcal{R}^\ell$ makes precise the notion that commodity bundle $\mathbf{x}$ "has more" than commodity bundle $\mathbf{y}$, i.e., $\mathbf{x} > \mathbf{y}$. The Euclidean space $\mathcal{R}^\ell$ together with the natural partial ordering is an ordered vector space. Partially ordered vector spaces were used explicitly in equilibrium analysis for the first time by D. M. Kreps [41]. In this chapter, we use the natural order structure of $\mathcal{R}^\ell$ to formulate the notions of monotone preferences—agents who prefer more to less—and positive linear functionals—positive prices. Later, we restrict our attention to Riesz spaces (or vector lattices) as models of the commodity and the price spaces. That is, we require $\langle E, E'\rangle$ the dual pair of topological vector spaces that define the commodity and price spaces to be dual topological Riesz spaces. This Riesz space duality between commodities and prices—introduced by C. D. Aliprantis and D. J. Brown [1]—is the central theme of this monograph.

1.1. PREFERENCES AND UTILITY FUNCTIONS

The basic tenet of economic theory is that economic agents are rational in the sense that they know their own interests and act in a way to maximize their own welfare. This assumption is made precise by hypothesizing an opportunity set for the individual over which it is assumed that the agent can make consistent pairwise choices. One consistency requirement is that if she chooses a over b and b over c, then she will choose a over c. Formally, we suppose the opportunities comprise some (non-empty) set X and individual tastes or preferences are represented by a binary relation on X. In this section, we shall discuss the basic properties of preferences in a general setting with particular emphasis on preferences defined on subsets of finite dimensional commodity spaces.

We begin our discussion by recalling some basic properties of binary relations. Recall that a **binary relation** on a (non-empty) set X is a non-empty subset $\succeq$ of $X \times X$. The membership $(x, y) \in \succeq$ is usually written as $x \succeq y$. A binary relation

$\succeq$ on a set X is said to be:

1. **Reflexive**; whenever $x \succeq x$ holds for all $x \in X$.
2. **Complete**; whenever for each pair x, y of elements of X either $x \succeq y$ or $y \succeq x$ holds.
3. **Transitive**; whenever $x \succeq y$ and $y \succeq z$ imply $x \succeq z$.

Definition 1.1.1. *A preference relation on a set is a reflexive, complete and transitive relation on the set.*

Let $\succeq$ be a preference relation on a set X. The notation $x \succeq y$ is read "the bundle x is at least as good as the bundle y" or that "x is no worse than y." The notation $x \succ y$ (read "x is preferred to y" or that "x is better than y") means that $x \succeq y$ and $y \not\succeq x$. When $x \succeq y$ and $y \succeq x$ both hold at the same time, then we write $x \sim y$ and say that "x is indifferent to y." If x is an element of X, then the set $\{y \in X\colon\ y \succ x\}$ is called *the better than set of* x and the set $\{y \in X\colon\ x \succ y\}$ is called *the worse than set of* x. Analogous names are given to the sets $\{y \in X\colon\ y \succeq x\}$ and $\{y \in X\colon\ x \succeq y\}$.

When X has a topological structure (i.e., X is a topological space), the continuity of preferences is defined as follows.

Definition 1.1.2. *A preference relation* $\succeq$ *on a topological space* X *is said to be*

a) **upper semicontinuous**, *if for each* $x \in X$ *the set* $\{y \in X\colon\ y \succeq x\}$ *is closed;*
b) **lower semicontinuous**, *if for each* $x \in X$ *the set* $\{y \in X\colon\ x \succeq y\}$ *is closed; and*
c) **continuous**, *whenever* $\succeq$ *is both upper and lower semicontinuous, i.e., whenever for each* $x \in X$ *the sets*

$$\{y \in X\colon\ y \succeq x\} \qquad \text{and} \qquad \{z \in X\colon\ x \succeq z\}$$

are both closed.

Since the complements of the sets $\{y \in X\colon\ y \succ x\}$ and $\{z \in X\colon\ x \succ z\}$ are $\{z \in X\colon\ x \succeq z\}$ and $\{y \in X\colon\ y \succeq x\}$ respectively, it should be immediate that a preference relation $\succeq$ on a topological space X is continuous if and only if for each $x \in X$ the sets

$$\{y \in X\colon\ y \succ x\} \qquad \text{and} \qquad \{z \in X\colon\ x \succ z\}$$

are both open.

The continuous preferences are characterized as follows.

Theorem 1.1.3. *For a preference relation $\succeq$ on a topological space X the following statements are equivalent.*

a) *The preference $\succeq$ is continuous.*
b) *The preference $\succeq$ (considered as a subset of $X \times X$) is closed in $X \times X$.*
c) *If $x \succ y$ holds in X, then there exist disjoint neighborhoods U_x and U_y of x and y respectively, such that $a \in U_x$ and $b \in U_y$ imply $a \succ b$.*

Proof. (a) $\Longrightarrow$ (c) Let $x \succ y$. We have two cases.

I. There exists some $z \in X$ such that $x \succ z \succ y$. In this case, the two neighborhoods $U_x = \{a \in X\colon\ a \succ z\}$ and $U_y = \{b \in X\colon\ z \succ b\}$ satisfy the desired properties.
II. There is no $z \in X$ satisfying $x \succ z \succ y$. In this case, take $U_x = \{a \in X\colon\ a \succ y\}$ and $U_y = \{b \in X\colon\ x \succ b\}$

(c) $\Longrightarrow$ (b) Let $\{(x_\alpha, y_\alpha)\}$ be a net of $\succeq$ satisfying $(x_\alpha, y_\alpha) \longrightarrow (x, y)$ in $X \times X$. If $y \succ x$ holds, then there exist two neighborhoods U_x and U_y of x and y respectively, such that $a \in U_x$ and $b \in U_y$ imply $b \succ a$. In particular, for all sufficiently large α, we must have $y_\alpha \succ x_\alpha$, which is a contradiction. Hence, $x \succeq y$ holds, and so (x, y) belongs to $\succeq$. That is, $\succeq$ is a closed subset of $X \times X$.

(b) $\Longrightarrow$ (a) Let $\{y_\alpha\}$ be a net of $\{y \in X\colon\ y \succeq x\}$ satisfying $y_\alpha \longrightarrow z$ in X. Then the net $\{(y_\alpha, x)\}$ of $\succeq$ satisfies $(y_\alpha, x) \longrightarrow (z, x)$ in $X \times X$. Since $\succeq$ is closed in $X \times X$, we see that $(z, x) \in \succeq$. Thus, $z \succeq x$ holds, proving that the set $\{y \in X\colon\ y \succeq x\}$ is a closed set.

In a similar fashion, we can show that the set $\{y \in X\colon\ x \succeq y\}$ is a closed set for each $x \in X$, and the proof of the theorem is complete. ■

Throughout this book we shall employ the symbol $\mathcal{R}$ to indicate the set of real numbers. Any function $u\colon X \longrightarrow \mathcal{R}$ defines a preference relation on X by saying that

$$x \succeq y \qquad \text{if and only if} \qquad u(x) \geq u(y).$$

In this case $x \succ y$ is, of course, equivalent to $u(x) > u(y)$.

A function $u\colon X \longrightarrow \mathcal{R}$ is said to be a **utility function** representing a preference relation $\succeq$ on a set X whenever $x \succeq y$ holds if and only if $u(x) \geq u(y)$. The utility functions are not uniquely determined. For instance, if a function u represents a preference relation, then so do the functions $u + c$, u^3, u^5 and e^u.

When can a preference relation be represented by a utility function? The next theorem tells us that a very general class of preference relations can be represented by utility functions. The proof of the next theorem can be found in [32, p. 53].

Theorem 1.1.4. *Every continuous preference on a topological space with a countable base of open sets can be represented by a continuous utility function.*

Convexity is used to express the behavioral assumption that the more an agent has of commodity i, the less willing she is to exchange a unit of commodity j for an additional unit of commodity i, i.e., convexity represents the notion of diminishing marginal rate of substitution. Several convexity properties of preference relations are defined next.

Definition 1.1.5. *A preference relation* $\succeq$ *defined on a convex subset* X *of a vector space is said to be:*

a) **Convex**; *whenever* $y \succeq x$ *and* $z \succeq x$ *in* X *and* $0 < \alpha < 1$ *imply* $\alpha y + (1-\alpha)z \succeq x$.

b) **Strictly Convex**; *whenever* $y \succeq x$, $z \succeq x$ *and* y *different than* z *imply* $\alpha y + (1-\alpha)z \succ x$ *for all* $0 < \alpha < 1$.

It should be clear that a preference relation $\succeq$ defined on a convex set X is convex if and only if the set $\{y \in X\colon\ y \succeq x\}$ is convex for each $x \in X$.

A utility function that gives rise to a convex preference is referred to as a *quasi-concave function*. Similarly, a utility function that gives rise to a strictly convex preference is known as a *strictly quasi-concave function*. Their definition is as follows.

Definition 1.1.6. *A function* $u\colon C \longrightarrow \mathcal{R}$ *defined on a non-empty convex subset* C *of a vector space is said to be:*

1. **Quasi-concave**; *whenever for each* $x, y \in C$ *with* $x \neq y$ *and each* $0 < \alpha < 1$ *we have*

$$u(\alpha x + (1-\alpha)y) \geq \min\{u(x), u(y)\}\,.$$

2. **Strictly quasi-concave**; *whenever for each pair* $x, y \in C$ *with* $x \neq y$ *and each* $0 < \alpha < 1$ *we have*

$$u(\alpha x + (1-\alpha)y) > \min\{u(x), u(y)\}\,.$$

3. **Concave**; *whenever for each* $x, y \in C$ *with* $x \neq y$ *and each* $0 < \alpha < 1$ *we have*

$$u(\alpha x + (1-\alpha)y) \geq \alpha u(x) + (1-\alpha)u(y)\,.$$

4. **Strictly concave**; *whenever for each* $x, y \in C$ *with* $x \neq y$ *and each* $0 < \alpha < 1$ *we have*

$$u(\alpha x + (1-\alpha)y) > \alpha u(x) + (1-\alpha)u(y)\,.$$

The concavity properties can also be expressed in terms of convex combinations. For instance, it can be shown easily by mathematical induction that a function

$u: C \longrightarrow \mathcal{R}$ defined on a convex subset of vector space is quasi-concave if and only if

$$u\Big(\sum_{i=1}^{n} \alpha_i x_i\Big) \geq \min\{u(x_i)\colon\ i = 1, \ldots, n\}$$

holds for each convex combination $\sum_{i=1}^{n} \alpha_i x_i$ of elements of C. Similar statements hold true for the other concavity properties.

A function $u: C \longrightarrow \mathcal{R}$ defined on a convex subset C of a vector space is said to be **convex** whenever $-u$ is concave, i.e., whenever for each $x, y \in C$ and each $0 < \alpha < 1$ we have

$$u\big(\alpha x + (1-\alpha)y\big) \leq \alpha u(x) + (1-\alpha)u(y)\,.$$

Similarly, a function u is said to be **strictly convex** whenever $-u$ is strictly concave.

Every concave function is quasi-concave. Indeed, if $u: C \longrightarrow \mathcal{R}$ is a concave function and $x, y \in C$ and $0 < \alpha < 1$, then put $m = \min\{u(x), u(y)\}$ and note that

$$u(\alpha x + (1-\alpha)y) \geq \alpha u(x) + (1-\alpha)u(y) \geq \alpha m + (1-\alpha)m = m\,.$$

The converse is false. For instance, the function $u: [0, \infty) \longrightarrow \mathcal{R}$ defined by the formula $u(x) = x^2$ is quasi-concave (in fact, strictly quasi-concave) but it is not a concave function (why?). In a similar manner, we can establish that a strictly concave function is strictly quasi-concave.

The concave twice differentiable functions are precisely the ones having non-positive second derivatives. The details follow.

Theorem 1.1.7. *Let (a, b) be an open interval of $\mathcal{R}$ and let $f: (a, b) \longrightarrow \mathcal{R}$ be a twice differentiable function. Then f is concave (resp. convex) if and only if $f''(x) \leq 0$ (resp. $f''(x) \geq 0$) holds for all $x \in (a, b)$.*

Proof. Assume first that $f: (a, b) \longrightarrow \mathcal{R}$ is a concave function and let $x \in (a, b)$. Pick h small enough such that $x+h$ and $x-h$ both belong to (a, b). Using Taylor's second order formula we have

$$f(x+h) - f(x) = f'(x)h + \tfrac{1}{2}f''(x)h^2 + o(h^2)$$

and

$$f(x-h) - f(x) = -f'(x)h + \tfrac{1}{2}f''(x)h^2 + o(h^2)\,.$$

Thus,

$$\frac{f(x+h) - 2f(x) + f(x-h)}{h^2} = f''(x) + \frac{o(h^2)}{h^2}\,,$$

and so

$$f''(x) = \lim_{h \to 0} \frac{f(x+h) - 2f(x) + f(x-h)}{h^2}\,. \qquad (\star)$$

Since, $f(x+h)-2f(x)+f(x-h) = 2[\frac{1}{2}f(x+h)+\frac{1}{2}f(x-h)-f(\frac{1}{2}(x+h)+\frac{1}{2}(x-h))] \leq 0$ holds, it follows from $(\star)$ that $f''(x) \leq 0$.

Now assume that $f''(x) \leq 0$ holds for all x. Fix s and t in (a, b) such that $s < t$, and let $0 < \alpha < 1$. Put $r = \alpha s + (1-\alpha)t$. By the Mean Value Theorem there exist ζ, ξ and τ satisfying $s < \zeta < r < \tau < t$ and $\zeta < \xi < \tau$ such that

$$\begin{aligned}\alpha f(s) + (1-\alpha)f(t) - f(r) &= \alpha[f(s) - f(r)] + (1-\alpha)[f(t) - f(r)] \\ &= \alpha f'(\zeta)(s-r) + (1-\alpha)f'(\tau)(t-r) \\ &= \alpha f'(\zeta)(1-\alpha)(s-t) + (1-\alpha)f'(\tau)\alpha(t-s) \\ &= \alpha(1-\alpha)(t-s)[f'(\tau) - f'(\zeta)] \\ &= \alpha(1-\alpha)(t-s)(\tau-\zeta)f''(\xi) \leq 0\,.\end{aligned}$$

That is, $f(r) \geq \alpha f(s) + (1-\alpha)f(t)$ holds, which shows that f is a concave function.

The above proof also shows that if $f''(x) < 0$ holds for all $x \in (a, b)$, then f is strictly concave. ■

The following theorem characterizes the quasi-concave and strictly quasi-concave functions.

Theorem 1.1.8. *For a convex subset C of a vector space and a function $u: C \longrightarrow \mathcal{R}$ the following statements hold.*

a) *The function u is quasi-concave if and only if the preference relation defined by u is convex.*

b) *The function u is strictly quasi-concave if and only if the preference relation defined by u is strictly convex.*

Proof. We shall prove (a) and leave the identical arguments for proving (b) to the reader. Assume first that u is a quasi-concave function and let $x \succeq y$ and $z \succeq y$ hold in C (i.e., $u(x) \geq u(y)$ and $u(z) \geq u(y)$) and let $0 < \alpha < 1$. Since u is quasi-concave, we have

$$u(\alpha x + (1-\alpha)z) \geq \min\{u(x), u(z)\} \geq u(y)\,,$$

which means that $\alpha x + (1-\alpha)z \succeq y$.

Now assume that the preference relation defined by u is convex and let $x, y \in C$. Without loss of generality, we can suppose that $u(x) \geq u(y)$ (i.e., $x \succeq y$). From $x \succeq y$ and $y \succeq y$ and the convexity of $\succeq$, we see that $\alpha x + (1-\alpha)y \succeq y$. Therefore,

$$u(\alpha x + (1-\alpha)y) \geq u(y) = \min\{u(x), u(y)\}\,,$$

and the proof of the theorem is finished. ■

We now turn our attention to monotonicity properties of preferences. Usually, in such a case the preference is defined on a subset of a (partially) ordered vector space.

An *ordered vector space* E is a real vector space E together with an order relation $\geq$ that satisfies the following two properties connecting the algebraic and order structures.

i) If $x \geq y$ holds in E, then $x + z \geq y + z$ also holds for all $z \in E$; and
ii) If $x \geq y$ holds in E, then $\alpha x \geq \alpha y$ also holds for all $\alpha \geq 0$.

The symbol $x > y$ is used to designate that $x \geq y$ and $x \neq y$ both hold. The set $E^+ = \{x \in E\colon\ x \geq 0\}$ is known as the *positive cone* of E and its elements are referred to as the positive vectors.

The important example for this chapter will be the ordered vector space $E = \mathcal{R}^\ell$. The ordering is defined by $\mathbf{x} = (x_1, x_2, \ldots, x_\ell) \geq \mathbf{y} = (y_1, y_2, \ldots, y_\ell)$ if and only if $x_i \geq y_i$ holds for all $i = 1, 2, \ldots, \ell$. The positive cone of $\mathcal{R}^\ell$ is denoted by $\mathcal{R}^\ell_+$. Clearly,

$$\mathcal{R}^\ell_+ = \{\mathbf{x} = (x_1, x_2, \ldots, x_\ell)\colon\ x_i \geq 0 \text{ holds for all } i = 1, 2, \ldots, \ell\}.$$

Note that $\mathbf{x} > \mathbf{y}$ holds in $\mathcal{R}^\ell$ if and only if $x_i \geq y_i$ holds for all i and $x_i > y_i$ holds for at least one i.

Definition 1.1.9. *A preference relation $\succeq$ on a non-empty subset X of an ordered vector space is said to be:*
a) **Monotone**; *whenever $x, y \in X$ and $x > y$ imply $x \succeq y$; and*
b) **Strictly monotone**; *whenever $x, y \in X$ and $x > y$ imply $x \succ y$.*

A strictly monotone preference is clearly monotone. However, a monotone preference need not be strictly monotone. For example, consider the preference on $\mathcal{R}^2_+$ defined by the utility function $u(x, y) = xy$. Clearly, $(x_1, y_1) > (x_2, y_2)$ implies

$$u(x_1, y_1) = x_1 y_1 \geq x_2 y_2 = u(x_2, y_2).$$

On the other hand note that $(2, 0) > (1, 0)$ and $(2, 0) \not\succ (1, 0)$ hold.

The level curves of a strictly monotone quasi-concave function are "convex to the origin." Recall that a *level curve* of a function $u\colon C \longrightarrow \mathcal{R}$ is any set of the form $\{x \in C\colon\ u(x) = c\}$, where c is any fixed real number—in economics the level curves are known, of course, as **indifference curves**. Intuitively, a curve is said to be "convex to the origin" whenever its graph has the shape shown in Figure 1.1-1.

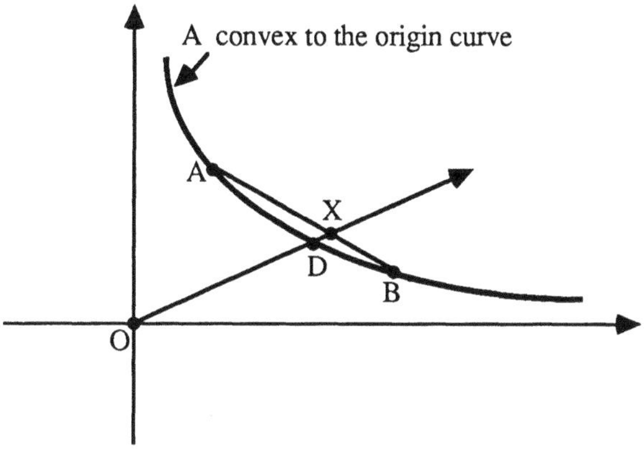

Fig. 1.1-1

Mathematically, a "convex to the origin" curve is described by saying that if A and B are any two points on the curve, then a ray passing through the origin O and any point X of the line segment AB will meet the curve at most at one point D between O and X, see Figure 1.1-1. The notion of diminishing marginal rate of substitution is clearly seen by observing the slopes at points A and B.

Theorem 1.1.10. *Let $u: C \longrightarrow \mathcal{R}$ be a function defined on a convex subset C of the positive cone of some ordered vector space. If u is strictly monotone and quasi-concave, then its level curves are convex to the origin.*

Proof. Assume that $x, y \in C$ satisfy $u(x) = u(y) = c$ and let $z = \alpha x + (1-\alpha)y$ for some $0 < \alpha < 1$. Since u is quasi-concave, we see that

$$u(z) \geq \min\{u(x), u(y)\} = c.$$

Since u is strictly monotone, we see that the ray $\{\lambda z\colon\ \lambda \geq 0\}$ cannot meet the level set $\{a \in C\colon\ u(a) = c\}$ at any point outside the line segment joining 0 and z. This shows that the level curves of u are convex to the origin. ■

We continue our discussion with the introduction of the extremely desirable bundles.

Definition 1.1.11. *Let $\succeq$ be a preference relation defined on a subset X of a vector space E. Then a vector $v \in E$ is said to be an* **extremely desirable bundle** *(or* **vector***) for $\succeq$ whenever*
1. *$x + \alpha v \in X$ holds for all $x \in X$ and all $\alpha > 0$; and*
2. *$x + \alpha v \succ x$ holds for all $x \in X$ and all $\alpha > 0$.*

Note that if $v > 0$ is an extremely desirable bundle then so is λv for each $\lambda > 0$. It was mentioned before that quite often preferences are represented by utility functions. The next theorem is an important representation theorem for preferences defined on the positive cone of a finite dimensional vector space.

Theorem 1.1.12. *For a continuous preference $\succeq$ defined on the positive cone $\mathcal{R}^\ell_+$ of some $\mathcal{R}^\ell$ the following statements hold.*

1. *If $\succeq$ is convex, monotone with an extremely desirable bundle, then $\succeq$ can be represented by a continuous, monotone and quasi-concave utility function.*
2. *If $\succeq$ is strictly convex, strictly monotone with an extremely desirable bundle, then $\succeq$ can be represented by a continuous, strictly monotone and strictly quasi-concave utility function.*

Proof. We shall prove (1) and leave the identical proof of part (2) for the reader. So, let $\succeq$ be a continuous, convex and monotone preference relation having an extremely desirable bundle v. Replacing v by $e = v+(1,1,\dots,1)$, we see (by the monotonicity of $\succeq$) that e is also extremely desirable. Thus, we can assume that there exists an extremely desirable bundle $e = (e_1, e_2, \dots, e_\ell)$ satisfying $e_i > 0$ for each i.

Now for each $x \in \mathcal{R}^\ell_+$, we put

$$u(x) = \inf\{\alpha > 0\colon\ \alpha e \succeq x\}.$$

Since all components of e are positive, there exists some $\alpha > 0$ such that $\alpha e > x$, and so by the monotonicity $\alpha e \succeq x$ must hold for some $\alpha > 0$. Thus, $u(x)$ is well defined.

We claim that $x \sim u(x)e$. Since the set $\{y \in \mathcal{R}^\ell_+\colon\ y \succeq x\}$ is closed, it easily follows that $u(x)e \succeq x$ holds. On the other hand, if $u(x) > 0$, then for all $\varepsilon > 0$ sufficiently small we must have $x \succeq (u(x) - \varepsilon)e$, and so by letting $\varepsilon \to 0$, we see that $x \succeq u(x)e$ also holds. Consequently, if $u(x) > 0$, then $u(x)e \sim x$. If $u(x) = 0$, then from $x \geq 0$ and the monotonicity of $\succeq$, we infer that $x \succeq 0 = u(x)e$. That is, $x \sim u(x)e$ is also true in this case.

Now observe that if $\alpha \geq 0$ and $\beta \geq 0$, then $\alpha e \succeq \beta e$ if and only if $\alpha \geq \beta$. Indeed, if $\alpha e \succeq \beta e$, then $\beta > \alpha$ implies $\beta e = \alpha e + (\beta - \alpha)e \succ \alpha e$, which is impossible. In particular, the above show that for each x in $\mathcal{R}^\ell_+$ there exists exactly one scalar—the number $u(x)$—such that $x \sim u(x)e$. The geometrical meaning of $u(x)$ is shown in Figure 1.1-2. Now it should be clear that the function $u\colon \mathcal{R}^\ell_+ \longrightarrow \mathcal{R}$ defined above is a utility function representing $\succeq$. The continuity of u follows from the identities

$$\{x \in \mathcal{R}^\ell_+\colon\ u(x) \leq r\} = \{x \in \mathcal{R}^\ell_+\colon\ x \preceq re\}$$

and

$$\{x \in \mathcal{R}^\ell_+\colon\ u(x) \geq r\} = \{x \in \mathcal{R}^\ell_+\colon\ x \succeq re\}$$

and the continuity of $\succeq$. ■

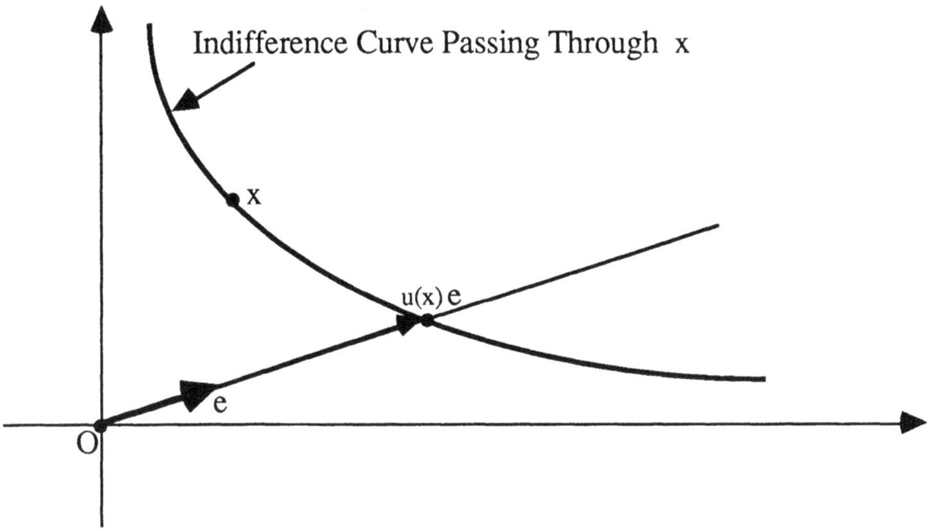

Fig. 1.1-2

EXERCISES

1. Consider the relation $\succeq$ on $\mathcal{R}_+^\ell$ defined by $\mathbf{x} \succeq \mathbf{y}$ whenever $\mathbf{x} \geq \mathbf{y}$, i.e., whenever
$$\succeq = \{(\mathbf{x}, \mathbf{y}) \in \mathcal{R}_+^\ell \times \mathcal{R}_+^\ell : \ \mathbf{x} \geq \mathbf{y}\}.$$
Describe the properties of $\succeq$ and show that in general $\succeq$ is not a preference relation. Under what condition is $\succeq$ a preference relation?

2. Formulate and prove the n-dimensional analogue of Theorem 1.1.7.

3. If a function $f\colon(a,b) \longrightarrow \mathcal{R}$ satisfies $f''(x) < 0$ for all $x \in (a,b)$, then show that f is strictly concave.

4. Show that the function $f\colon[0,\infty) \longrightarrow \mathcal{R}$ defined by $f(x) = x^2$ is strictly quasi-concave but it fails to be a concave function.

5. Show that a function $u\colon C \longrightarrow \mathcal{R}$—where C is a convex subset of a vector space—is quasi-concave if and only if
$$u\Big(\sum_{i=1}^{n} \alpha_i x_i\Big) \geq \min\{u(x_i)\colon \ i = 1, \ldots, n\}$$
holds for each convex combination $\sum_{i=1}^{n} \alpha_i x_i$ of C.
State and prove similar results for functions with the other concavity properties described in Definition 1.1.6.

6. Let $\succeq$ be a preference relation defined on a topological space X. If $u: X \longrightarrow \mathcal{R}$ is a utility function representing $\succeq$ (i.e., $x \succeq y \iff u(x) \geq u(y)$) and $\succeq$ is continuous, is then the utility function u necessarily continuous?

7. Prove statement (b) of Theorem 1.1.8.

8. Prove statement (2) of Theorem 1.1.12.

9. Consider the five preference relations on $\mathcal{R}^2_+$ defined by the utility functions

$$u_1(x,y) = x + y\,, \quad u_2(x,y) = xy\,, \quad u_3(x,y) = \sqrt{x} + \sqrt{y}\,,$$

$$u_4(x,y) = y(1+x) \quad \text{and} \quad u_5(x,y) = (x+1)(y+2)\,.$$

Describe the properties of these preference relations and sketch the shape of their indifference curves.

10. Consider the two preferences on $\mathcal{R}^2_+$ defined by the utility functions

$$u_1(x,y) = x \quad \text{and} \quad u_2(x,y) = y\,.$$

Describe the properties of these preference relations and sketch the shape of their indifference curves.

11. Does the utility function $u(x,y,z) = x^2 + y^2 + z^2$ on $\mathcal{R}^3_+$ represent a convex preference? Also, sketch the indifference curves of u.

12. Let C be a non-empty convex subset of a vector space and let $u: C \longrightarrow \mathcal{R}$ be a function. Show that u is a concave function if and only if the set

$$\{(x,\alpha) \in C \times \mathcal{R}\colon\ \alpha \leq u(x)\}$$

is a convex set.

13. Is every continuous quasi-concave utility function on $\mathcal{R}^\ell_+$ necessarily monotone? *Answer*: No. Example: $u(x_1,\ldots,x_\ell) = e^{-(x_1^2+\cdots+x_\ell^2)}$

14. For each $i = 1,\ldots,m$ let $u_i: C \longrightarrow \mathcal{R}$ be a utility function—where C is a convex subset of a vector space. If $\lambda_i > 0$, $i = 1,\ldots,m$, are fixed positive real numbers, then the function $V: \mathcal{R}^m \longrightarrow \mathcal{R}$ defined by

$$V(u_1,\ldots,u_m) = \sum_{i=1}^m \lambda_i u_i$$

is known as a *Social Welfare Function*. Consider the function $U: C^m \longrightarrow \mathcal{R}$ defined by $U(x_1,\ldots,x_m) = V(u_1(x_1),\ldots,u_m(x_m)) = \sum_{i=1}^m \lambda_i u_i(x_i)$.

a) If each u_i is concave, then show that U is also concave.

b) If each u_i is concave and at least one u_i is strictly concave, then show that U is likewise strictly concave.

c) If each u_i is quasi-concave, is U necessarily quasi-concave?

15. For each $i = 1, \ldots, m$ let $u_i: C \longrightarrow \mathcal{R}$ be a utility function—where C is a convex subset of a vector space. If each u_i is quasi-concave, then show that the function $V: C^m \longrightarrow \mathcal{R}$ defined by

$$V(x_1, \ldots, x_m) = \min\{u_1(x_1), \ldots, u_m(x_m)\}$$

is a quasi-concave function. If all the u_i are concave, is V necessarily a concave function?

16. Let $\succeq$ be a monotone preference on $\mathcal{R}^\ell_+$. If $\succeq$ has an extremely desirable bundle, then show that every $w \in \operatorname{Int}(\mathcal{R}^\ell_+)$ is also an extremely desirable bundle—and so $\succeq$ is strictly monotone on $\operatorname{Int}(\mathcal{R}^\ell_+)$.
[HINT: If $\mathbf{v}$ is an extremely desirable bundle for $\succeq$ and $\mathbf{w} \in \operatorname{Int}(\mathcal{R}^\ell_+)$, then pick some $\alpha > 0$ such that $\mathbf{w} - \alpha\mathbf{v} \geq 0$, and note that for each $\mathbf{x} \in \mathcal{R}^\ell_+$ we have $\mathbf{x} + \mathbf{w} = \mathbf{x} + (\mathbf{w} - \alpha\mathbf{v}) + \alpha\mathbf{v} \succeq \mathbf{x} + \alpha\mathbf{v} \succ \mathbf{x}$.]

17. If a preference $\succeq$ on $\mathcal{R}^\ell_+$ is continuous, convex and strictly monotone, then show that $\mathbf{x} \succ \mathbf{y}$ in $\mathcal{R}^\ell_+$ implies $\alpha\mathbf{x} + (1-\alpha)\mathbf{y} \succ \mathbf{y}$ for each $0 < \alpha \leq 1$.

18. If $f: (a, b) \longrightarrow \mathcal{R}$ is a concave function, then show that f has a right- and left-hand derivative at each point $x \in (a, b)$.

1.2. MAXIMAL ELEMENTS

Let $\succeq$ be a preference relation on a set X and let A be a non-empty subset of X. Then we say that an element $a \in A$ is a **maximal element** for $\succeq$ on A whenever there is no element $b \in A$ satisfying $b \succ a$. Since $\succeq$ (as a preference relation) is complete, note that an element $a \in A$ is a maximal element if and only if $a \succeq x$ holds for each $x \in A$. It may happen that $\succeq$ need not have any maximal elements on a given set A. The next few results describe some basic properties of maximal elements.

Theorem 1.2.1. *For a preference relation $\succeq$ on a set X and a non-empty subset A of X the following statements hold.*

1. *All maximal elements of A for $\succeq$ lie in the same indifference set; and*
2. *If $X = \mathcal{R}^\ell_+$ and $\succeq$ has a strictly desirable bundle, then no interior point of A can be a maximal element.*

Proof. (1) Let a be a maximal element for $\succeq$ on A. If $b \in A$ is another maximal element, then $a \succeq b$ and $b \succeq a$ both hold, and so $a \sim b$. This means that the maximal elements of A for $\succeq$ lie in the same indifference set.

(2) Let v be an extremely desirable bundle for $\succeq$ and let a be an interior point of A. Then for some sufficiently small $\alpha > 0$ we must have $a + \alpha v \in A$. Now the relation $a + \alpha v \succ a$ shows that a cannot be a maximal element for $\succeq$ on A. ∎

Recall that a preference relation $\succeq$ on a topological space X is said to be **upper semicontinuous** whenever for each $x \in X$ the set $\{y \in X\colon\ y \succeq x\}$ is a closed set. Remarkably, upper semicontinuous preference relations on compact topological spaces always have maximal elements. The details are included in the next theorem. (Keep in mind that for terminology concerning topological concepts we follow J. L. Kelley's book [38].)

Theorem 1.2.2. *The set of all maximal elements of an upper semicontinuous preference relation on a compact topological space is non-empty and compact.*

Proof. Let $\succeq$ be an upper semicontinuous preference on a compact topological space X. For each $x \in X$ let $C_x = \{y \in X\colon\ y \succeq x\}$. Since $\succeq$ is upper semicontinuous, the (non-empty) set C_x is closed—and hence compact. Now note that the set of all maximal elements of $\succeq$ is the compact set $\bigcap_{x\in X} C_x$. We shall show that $\bigcap_{x\in X} C_x \neq \emptyset$.

To this end, let $x_1, x_2, \ldots, x_n \in X$. Since $\succeq$ is a complete binary relation, the set $\{x_1, x_2, \ldots, x_n\}$ is completely ordered. We can assume that $x_1 \succeq x_2 \succeq \cdots \succeq x_n$. This implies $C_{x_1} \subseteq C_{x_2} \subseteq \cdots \subseteq C_{x_n}$, and so $\bigcap_{i=1}^n C_{x_i} = C_{x_1} \neq \emptyset$. Thus the collection of closed sets $\{C_x\colon\ x \in X\}$ has the finite intersection property. By the compactness of X, the set $\bigcap_{x\in X} C_x$ is non-empty. ∎

When does a preference relation have a unique maximal element on a set? The next result provides an answer.

Theorem 1.2.3. *For an upper semicontinuous convex preference $\succeq$ on a convex compact subset X of a topological vector space, the following statements hold.*

a) *The set of all maximal elements of $\succeq$ in X is a non-empty, convex and compact.*
b) *If, in addition, $\succeq$ is strictly convex, then $\succeq$ has exactly one maximal element in X.*

Proof. (a) By Theorem 1.2.2, we know that the set of all maximal elements of $\succeq$ is non-empty and compact. To see that this set is also convex, let a and b be two maximal elements of $\succeq$ in X and let $0 < \alpha < 1$. Then $\alpha a + (1-\alpha)b \in X$ and by the convexity of $\succeq$, we see that $\alpha a + (1-\alpha)b \succeq a$. On the other hand, by the maximality of a, we have $a \succeq \alpha a + (1-\alpha)b$ and therefore, $\alpha a + (1-\alpha)b$ is also a maximal element of $\succeq$.

(b) Assume that $\succeq$ is also strictly convex. If a and b are two distinct maximal elements, then $\frac{1}{2}a + \frac{1}{2}b \in X$ and $\frac{1}{2}a + \frac{1}{2}b \succ a$ must hold (why?), contrary to the maximality property of a. This shows that $\succeq$ has exactly one maximal element in X. The geometrical meaning of the maximal element is shown in Figure 1.2-1. ■

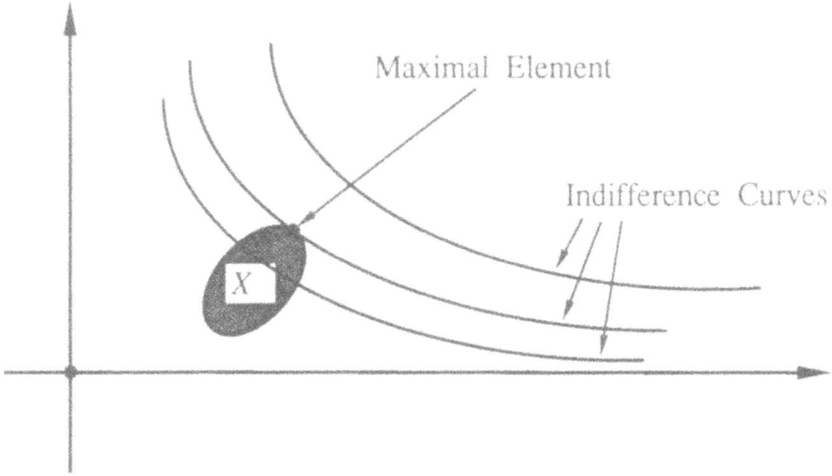

Fig. 1.2-1

The next results deal with maximal elements of preference relations on topological vector spaces. They are not needed for this chapter but they will be employed later.

Lemma 1.2.4. *Let $\langle X, X' \rangle$ be a dual pair, let C be a non-empty, convex and weakly closed subset of X and let $f: C \longrightarrow \mathcal{R}$ be a quasi-concave function. If f is Mackey upper semicontinuous, then f is also weakly upper semicontinuous.*

Proof. Assume that the function f and the non-empty convex set C satisfy the hypotheses of the theorem. Fix some $x \in C$ and let $K = \{y \in C\colon\ f(y) \geq f(x)\}$.

Since the function f is quasi-concave, the set K is clearly convex. Also, by the Mackey upper semicontinuity of f, we see that K is also Mackey-closed. By a classical result of Functional Analysis (see, for instance, Theorem 2.3.4 or [8, Theorem 9.13, p. 137]), it follows that K is also weakly closed. Therefore, the function f is also weakly upper semicontinuous. ■

Combining Theorems 1.2.2 and 1.2.3 with the preceding lemma, we have the following useful consequences.

Corollary 1.2.5. *Consider a dual pair $\langle X, X' \rangle$ and let C be a non-empty, convex, and weakly compact subset of X. If $f: C \longrightarrow \mathcal{R}$ is a Mackey-continuous quasi-concave function, then the set of maximal elements of the preference relation defined by f, i.e., the set*

$$\{x \in C\colon\ f \text{ attains its maximum on } C \text{ at } x\},$$

is non-empty, convex, and weakly compact.

Corollary 1.2.6. *Let $\langle X, X' \rangle$ be a dual pair and let C be a non-empty, convex, and weakly compact subset of X. If $f: C \longrightarrow \mathcal{R}$ is a Mackey-continuous strictly quasi-concave function, then the preference relation defined by f has exactly one maximal element.*

EXERCISES

1. Consider the convex compact set $C = \{(x, y) \in \mathcal{R}^2_+\colon\ x + 2y \leq 2\}$ as shown in Figure 1.2-2. Find the unique maximal element in C for the utility functions:
   a) $u(x, y) = x^2 y$;
   b) $u(x, y) = (x + 2)y$; and
   b) $u(x, y) = \min\{x, y\}$.

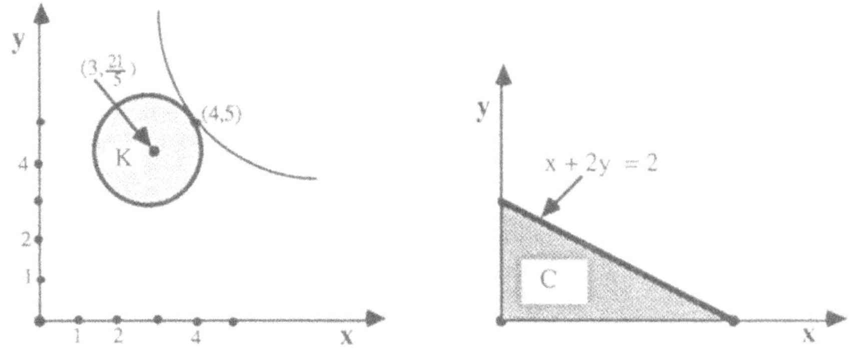

Fig. 1.2-2

2. Consider the disk $K = \{ (x,y) \in \mathcal{R}^2\colon\ (x-3)^2 + (y - \frac{21}{5})^2 \leq \frac{41}{25} \}$ as shown in Figure 1.2-2. Find the unique maximal element in K for the utility function $u(x,y) = xy$. *Answer*: (4,5)

3. Consider the utility function $u\colon \mathcal{R}^2_+ \longrightarrow \mathcal{R}$ defined by

$$u(x,y) = \min\{ x^2y,\ xy \}\,.$$

   a) Describe the indifference curves of u;
   b) Show that u is a continuous, monotone and quasi-concave utility function; and
   c) Find the unique maximal element for the utility function u in the convex compact set $C = \{(x,y) \in \mathcal{R}^2_+\colon\ x^2 + y^2 \leq 1\}$. *Answer*: $(\frac{\sqrt{3}}{3}, \frac{\sqrt{6}}{3})$

4. Let $\succeq$ be a preference relation on a set X and let A be a non-empty subset of X. Show that an element $a \in A$ is a maximal element if and only if $a \succeq x$ holds for all $x \in A$.

5. Fix a vector $\mathbf{0} < \mathbf{p} \in \mathcal{R}^\ell_+$ and define the utility function $u\colon \mathcal{R}^\ell_+ \longrightarrow \mathcal{R}$ by

$$u(\mathbf{x}) = \mathbf{p}\cdot\mathbf{x} = \sum_{i=1}^{\ell} p_i x_i\,.$$

If C is the convex hull of a finite number of vectors $\mathbf{x}_1, \ldots, \mathbf{x}_m$ of $\mathcal{R}^\ell_+$, i.e.,

$$C = \Big\{ \sum_{i=1}^{m} \alpha_i \mathbf{x}_i\colon\ \alpha_i \geq 0 \text{ for all } i \text{ and } \sum_{i=1}^{m} \alpha_i = 1 \Big\}\,,$$

then show that at least one of the $\mathbf{x}_i$ is a maximal element in C for u.

6. Let (X, Σ, μ) be a finite measure space and let $1 < p,\ q < \infty$ satisfy $\frac{1}{p} + \frac{1}{q} = 1$. Consider the utility function $u\colon L_p^+(X, \Sigma, \mu) \longrightarrow \mathcal{R}$ defined by

$$u(f) = \int_X \sqrt{f}\, d\mu\,.$$

   a) Show that u is well defined, i.e., show that $f \in L_p^+(X, \Sigma, \mu)$ implies $\sqrt{f}$ in $L_1^+(X, \Sigma, \mu)$.
   b) Show that u is strictly concave, strictly monotone and norm continuous.
   c) Show that the utility function u has a unique maximal element in the convex set

$$B = \{ f \in L_p^+(X, \Sigma, \mu)\colon\ \|f\|_p \leq 1 \}\,.$$

   d) Find the unique maximal element of u in B. *Answer*: $[\mu(X)]^{-\frac{1}{p}}\cdot\mathbf{1}$

7. Let $\succeq$ be a preference relation on a topological space that is represented by a utility function u. If $x_\alpha \longrightarrow x$ in X implies $\limsup_\alpha u(x_\alpha) \leq u(x)$, then show that the preference relation $\succeq$ is upper semicontinuous.

8. Let $\langle X, X' \rangle$ be a dual pair, let C be a non-empty, convex and weakly closed subset of X and let $u: C \longrightarrow \mathcal{R}$ be a quasi-concave Mackey-continuous function. Show that $x_\alpha \xrightarrow{w} x$ in C implies $\limsup_\alpha u(x_\alpha) \leq u(x)$.
[HINT: Let $x_\alpha \xrightarrow{w} x$ in C and assume that $\limsup_\alpha u(x_\alpha) > u(x)$. Pick some $\varepsilon > 0$ such that $\limsup_\alpha u(x_\alpha) > u(x) + \varepsilon > u(x)$. By passing to a subnet, we can suppose that $\lim_\alpha u(x_\alpha)$ exists. Since $u(C)$ is a connected set (i.e., an interval of $\mathcal{R}$), there exists some $z \in C$ with $u(x) + \varepsilon > u(z) > u(x)$. Clearly, $u(x_\alpha) > u(z)$ holds for all α sufficiently large. Now use the weak upper semicontinuity of u (see Theorem 1.2.4) to infer that $u(x) \geq u(z) > u(x)$, a contradiction.]

1.3. DEMAND FUNCTIONS

Preferences and utility functions are not observable in the market place. What we do observe are agents making transactions at market prices, i.e., demanding and supplying commodities at these prices. This suggests an alternative primitive formulation of economic behavior in terms of demand functions. In this section, we derive demand functions from utility maximization subject to a budget constraint. Consequently, the demand functions satisfy certain restrictions which play a critical role in equilibrium analysis.

Before starting our discussion in this section, let us introduce some standard notation. Boldface letters will denote vectors. For instance, the boldface letter $\mathbf{x}$ will represent the vector $\mathbf{x} = (x_1, x_2, \ldots, x_\ell)$ and $\mathbf{p}$ the vector $\mathbf{p} = (p_1, p_2, \ldots, p_\ell)$. The symbol $\mathbf{x} \gg \mathbf{0}$ means that $x_i > 0$ holds for each i, i.e., all components of $\mathbf{x}$ are positive real numbers. Similarly, the notation $\mathbf{x} \gg \mathbf{y}$ means that $x_i > y_i$ holds for each i. Any vector $\mathbf{x}$ that satisfies $\mathbf{x} \gg \mathbf{0}$ is called a **strictly positive vector**.

Now fix a vector $\mathbf{p} \in \mathcal{R}^\ell_+$—which we shall call a *price*. The **budget set** for $\mathbf{p}$ corresponding to a vector $\omega \in \mathcal{R}^\ell_+$ is the set

$$\mathcal{B}_\omega(\mathbf{p}) = \{\mathbf{x} \in \mathcal{R}^\ell_+ \colon \ \mathbf{p}\cdot\mathbf{x} \le \mathbf{p}\cdot\omega\}\,.$$

A *budget set* for $\mathbf{p}$ is any set of the form $\mathcal{B}_\omega(\mathbf{p})$. The *budget line* of a budget set $\mathcal{B}_\omega(\mathbf{p})$ is the set $\{\mathbf{x} \in \mathcal{B}_\omega(\mathbf{p})\colon\ \mathbf{p}\cdot\mathbf{x} = \mathbf{p}\cdot\omega\}$. Recall that the dot product $\mathbf{p}\cdot\mathbf{x}$ of two vectors is defined by

$$\mathbf{p}\cdot\mathbf{x} = p_1x_1 + p_2x_2 + \cdots + p_\ell x_\ell = \sum_{i=1}^{\ell} p_i x_i\,.$$

It is well known that the function $(\mathbf{p},\mathbf{x}) \longmapsto \mathbf{p}\cdot\mathbf{x}$—from $\mathcal{R}^\ell_+ \times \mathcal{R}^\ell_+$ into $\mathcal{R}$—is (jointly) continuous. An immediate consequence of the continuity of the dot product function $(\mathbf{p},\mathbf{x}) \longmapsto \mathbf{p}\cdot\mathbf{x}$ is that all budget sets are closed.

When does a price have bounded budget sets? It turns out that either all budget sets for a price are bounded or else all are unbounded. The condition for boundedness or unboundedness of the budget sets is included in the next theorem.

Theorem 1.3.1. *For a price* $\mathbf{p} \in \mathcal{R}^\ell_+$ *the following statements hold.*

1. *All budget sets for* $\mathbf{p}$ *are bounded if and only if* $\mathbf{p} \gg \mathbf{0}$.
2. *All budget sets for* $\mathbf{p}$ *are unbounded if and only if* $\mathbf{p}$ *has at least one component equal to zero.*

Proof. We establish (1) and leave the identical proof of (2) for the reader. To this end, assume first that every budget set for a price $\mathbf{p}$ is bounded. Then, we claim that $p_i > 0$ holds for each i. Indeed, if some $p_i = 0$, then the vectors $n\mathbf{e}_i$ $(i = 1, \ldots, \ell)$—where $\mathbf{e}_i$ denotes the standard unit vector in the ith direction—belong to every budget set (since $\mathbf{p}\cdot\mathbf{e}_i = 0$), proving that every budget set is unbounded.

Now assume that $\mathbf{p} \gg \mathbf{0}$ and let $\omega \in \mathcal{R}^\ell_+$. Put $r = \min\{p_1, p_2, \ldots, p_\ell\} > 0$. If $\mathbf{x} \in \mathcal{B}_\omega(\mathbf{p})$, then for each i we have

$$0 \le p_i x_i \le \sum_{k=1}^{\ell} p_k x_k = \mathbf{p} \cdot \mathbf{x} \le \mathbf{p} \cdot \omega\,,$$

and therefore

$$0 \le x_i \le \frac{\mathbf{p} \cdot \mathbf{x}}{p_i} \le \frac{\mathbf{p} \cdot \omega}{r} < \infty$$

holds for each $i = 1, 2, \ldots, \ell$. This shows that the budget set $\mathcal{B}_\omega(\mathbf{p})$ is bounded. ■

Since all budget sets are closed (and compactness in a finite dimensional vector space is equivalent to closedness and boundedness), the first part of Theorem 1.3.1 can be restated as follows: *All budget sets for a price* $\mathbf{p}$ *are compact if and only if* $\mathbf{p} \gg \mathbf{0}$. In particular, from this conclusion and Theorem 1.2.3, we have the following result.

Theorem 1.3.2. *For a price* $\mathbf{p} \gg \mathbf{0}$ *and a continuous preference* $\succeq$ *on* $\mathcal{R}^\ell_+$ *the following statements hold.*

1. *If* $\succeq$ *is also convex, then on every budget set for* $\mathbf{p}$ *the preference* $\succeq$ *has at least one maximal element.*
2. *If* $\succeq$ *is strictly convex, then on every budget set for* $\mathbf{p}$ *the preference* $\succeq$ *has exactly one maximal element.*
3. *If* $\succeq$ *has an extremely desirable bundle and is strictly convex, then on every budget set for* $\mathbf{p}$ *the preference* $\succeq$ *has exactly one maximal element lying on the budget line.*

The geometrical interpretation of part (3) of the preceding theorem is depicted in Figure 1.3-1.

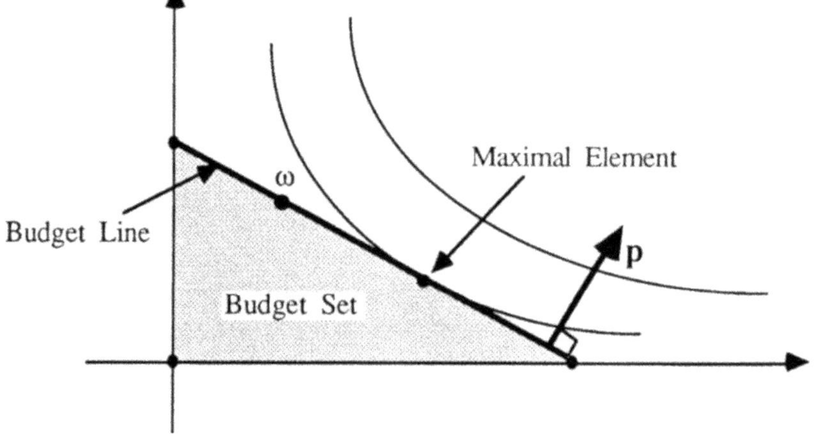

Fig. 1.3-1

For the rest of the discussion in this section all preference relations will be assumed defined on some $\mathcal{R}^\ell_+$. You should keep in mind that the interior of $\mathcal{R}^\ell_+$ is precisely the set of all strictly positive vectors and the boundary of $\mathcal{R}^\ell_+$ consists of all vectors of $\mathcal{R}^\ell_+$ having at least one component equal to zero.

Theorem 1.3.3. *For a price $\mathbf{p} \in \partial\mathcal{R}^\ell_+$ and a preference relation $\succeq$ on $\mathcal{R}^\ell_+$ the following statements hold.*

1. *If $\succeq$ is strictly monotone, then $\succeq$ does not have any maximal element in any budget set for $\mathbf{p}$.*
2. *If $\succeq$ is strictly monotone on $\mathrm{Int}(\mathcal{R}^\ell_+)$ such that everything in the interior is preferred to anything on the boundary and if an element $\omega \in \mathcal{R}^\ell_+$ satisfies $\mathbf{p}\cdot\omega > 0$, then $\succeq$ does not have any maximal element in $\mathcal{B}_\omega(\mathbf{p})$.*

Proof. Let $\mathbf{p} = (p_1, p_2, \ldots, p_\ell) \in \mathcal{R}^\ell_+$ be a price having at least one component zero. We can assume that $p_1 = 0$.

(1) Suppose that $\succeq$ is strictly monotone and let $\mathbf{x}$ be a vector in some budget set $\mathcal{B}_\omega(\mathbf{p})$. Then, $\mathbf{y} = (x_1 + 1, x_2, \ldots, x_\ell) \in \mathcal{B}_\omega(\mathbf{p})$ and $\mathbf{y} > \mathbf{x}$. The strict monotonicity of $\succeq$ implies $\mathbf{y} \succ \mathbf{x}$. This shows that $\succeq$ does not have a maximal element in $\mathcal{B}_\omega(\mathbf{p})$.

(2) Now assume that $\succeq$ satisfies the stated properties and that $\mathbf{p}\cdot\omega > 0$. From $\mathbf{p}\cdot\omega > 0$, it follows that the budget set $\mathcal{B}_\omega(\mathbf{p})$ contains strictly positive elements and so if $\succeq$ has a maximal element in $\mathcal{B}_\omega(\mathbf{p})$, then this element must be strictly positive. However, if $\mathbf{x}$ is any strictly positive element in $\mathcal{B}_\omega(\mathbf{p})$, then $\mathbf{y} = (x_1+1, x_2, \ldots, x_\ell)$ is also a strictly positive element in $\mathcal{B}_\omega(\mathbf{p})$ satisfying $\mathbf{y} > \mathbf{x}$. Since $\succeq$ is strictly monotone on $\mathrm{Int}(\mathcal{R}^\ell_+)$, we see that $\mathbf{y} \succ \mathbf{x}$ must hold, which shows that $\succeq$ does not have a maximal element in $\mathcal{B}_\omega(\mathbf{p})$. ■

Now consider a continuous strictly convex preference relation $\succeq$ on some $\mathcal{R}^\ell_+$ having an extremely desirable bundle. Also, let $0 < \omega \in \mathcal{R}^\ell_+$ be a fixed vector—referred to as *the initial endowment*. Then, by Theorem 1.3.2(3), for each price $\mathbf{p} \in \mathrm{Int}(\mathcal{R}^\ell_+)$ the preference relation $\succeq$ has exactly one maximal element in the budget set $\mathcal{B}_\omega(\mathbf{p})$. This maximal element is called **the demand vector** of the preference $\succeq$ at prices $\mathbf{p}$ and will be denoted by $\mathbf{x}_\omega(\mathbf{p})$. If, in a given situation, ω is fixed and clarity is not at stake, then the subscript ω will be dropped and the demand vector $\mathbf{x}_\omega(\mathbf{p})$ will be denoted simply by $\mathbf{x}(\mathbf{p})$. Thus, in this case, a function

$$\mathbf{x}_\omega : \mathrm{Int}(\mathcal{R}^\ell_+) \longrightarrow \mathcal{R}^\ell_+$$

is defined by saying that $\mathbf{x}_\omega(\mathbf{p})$ is the demand vector of $\succeq$ at prices $\mathbf{p}$. The function $\mathbf{x}_\omega(\cdot)$ is known as the **demand function** corresponding to the preference $\succeq$. Two important properties of the demand function should be noted immediately.

1) Since [by Theorem 1.3.2(3)], $\mathbf{x}_\omega(\mathbf{p})$ lies on the budget line, for each $\mathbf{p} \in \mathrm{Int}(\mathcal{R}^\ell_+)$ we always have $\mathbf{p}\cdot\mathbf{x}_\omega(\mathbf{p}) = \mathbf{p}\cdot\omega$.
2) The demand function is a homogeneous function of degree zero, i.e., for each $\lambda > 0$ and each $\mathbf{p} \gg 0$ we have $\mathbf{x}_\omega(\mathbf{p}) = \mathbf{x}_\omega(\lambda\mathbf{p})$.
   This follows immediately from the budget identity $\mathcal{B}_\omega(\lambda\mathbf{p}) = \mathcal{B}_\omega(\mathbf{p})$.

Observe that a continuous preference $\succeq$ on $\mathcal{R}^\ell_+$ need not be strictly convex in order for the demand function $\mathbf{x}_\omega(\cdot)$ to be defined. The hypothesis of strict convexity may be relaxed. For example, the preference relation on $\mathcal{R}^2_+$ defined by the utility function $u(x,y) = xy$ is strictly monotone on $\text{Int}(\mathcal{R}^2_+)$ but not strictly convex on $\mathcal{R}^2_+$. For each price $\mathbf{p} \gg \mathbf{0}$ the preference relation defined by this utility function has exactly one maximal element in the budget set $\mathcal{B}_\omega(\mathbf{p})$. Therefore, it is easy to check that the demand function $\mathbf{x}_\omega(\cdot)$ for this preference is well defined and satisfies the above two properties.

Our immediate objective is to study the properties of the demand functions. Since the demand functions are defined for certain preferences, let us give a name to these preferences that will be useful in the economic analysis in this chapter.

Definition 1.3.4. *A continuous preference relation $\succeq$ on some $\mathcal{R}^\ell_+$ is said to be a* **neoclassical preference** *whenever either*

1) *$\succeq$ is strictly monotone and strictly convex; or else*
2) *$\succeq$ is strictly monotone and strictly convex on* $\text{Int}(\mathcal{R}^\ell_+)$, *and everything in the interior is preferred to anything on the boundary.*

The next example illustrates how neoclassical preferences arise from common utility functions.

Example 1.3.5. We exhibit two neoclassical preferences defined by utility functions u_1 and u_2. Preference $\succeq_1$ will satisfy condition (1) but not condition (2) of Definition 1.3.4, and preference $\succeq_2$ will satisfy condition (2) but not condition (1). Preferences such as (1) typically have demands on the boundary of $\mathcal{R}^\ell_+$, but preferences of type (2) always have demands on the interior of $\mathcal{R}^\ell_+$.

(1) Consider the utility function defined on $\mathcal{R}^2_+$ by the function

$$u_1(x,y) = \sqrt{x} + \sqrt{y}.$$

Then the utility function is continuous, strictly monotone, and strictly convex on $\mathcal{R}^2_+$. However, this utility function does not have the property that everything in the interior of $\mathcal{R}^2_+$ is preferred to anything on the boundary. Since the element $(1,0) \in \partial\mathcal{R}^2_+$ is clearly preferred to $(\frac{1}{9}, \frac{1}{9})$ which is in the interior.

(2) Now consider the preference defined by the formula

$$u_2(x,y) = xy.$$

This utility function is strictly convex and strictly monotone on $\text{Int}(\mathcal{R}^2_+)$ however, it is not strictly convex on the boundary $\partial\mathcal{R}^2_+$ since every vector on the boundary is indifferent to the origin. For this very reason, $\mathbf{x} \in \partial\mathcal{R}^2_+$ and $\mathbf{y} \in \text{Int}(\mathcal{R}^2_+)$ imply $\mathbf{y} \succ \mathbf{x}$, i.e., everything in the interior is preferred to anything on the boundary. ■

It should be noted that strictly positive vectors are always extremely desirable vectors for neoclassical preferences. Our immediate objective is to study the properties of the demand functions that correspond to neoclassical preferences. The next theorem is the first step in establishing the continuity of demand functions.

Theorem 1.3.6. *Let $\succeq$ be a neoclassical preference on some $\mathcal{R}^\ell_+$ and let ω and $\mathbf{p}$ in $\mathcal{R}^\ell_+$ satisfy $\mathbf{p}\cdot\omega > 0$. If a sequence $\{\mathbf{p}_n\}$ of $\mathrm{Int}(\mathcal{R}^\ell_+)$ satisfies $\mathbf{p}_n \longrightarrow \mathbf{p}$ and $\mathbf{x}_\omega(\mathbf{p}_n) \longrightarrow \mathbf{x}$, then we have:*

a) $\mathbf{p} \gg \mathbf{0}$, *i.e.*, $\mathbf{p} \in \mathrm{Int}(\mathcal{R}^\ell_+)$;
b) $\mathbf{x} \in \mathcal{B}_\omega(\mathbf{p})$; *and*
c) $\mathbf{x} = \mathbf{x}_\omega(\mathbf{p})$.

Proof. From $\mathbf{p}_n \cdot \mathbf{x}_\omega(\mathbf{p}_n) = \mathbf{p}_n \cdot \omega$ and the continuity of the dot product, it follows that $\mathbf{p}\cdot\mathbf{x} = \mathbf{p}\cdot\omega$, and so $\mathbf{x} \in \mathcal{B}_\omega(\mathbf{p})$. Next, we claim that $\mathbf{x}$ is a maximal element for $\succeq$ in $\mathcal{B}_\omega(\mathbf{p})$. To see this, let $\mathbf{y} \in \mathcal{B}_\omega(\mathbf{p})$. Then $\mathbf{p}\cdot\mathbf{y} \le \mathbf{p}\cdot\omega$ holds, and so (since $\mathbf{p}\cdot\omega > 0$) for each $0 < \lambda < 1$, we have $\mathbf{p}\cdot(\lambda\mathbf{y}) < \mathbf{p}\cdot\omega$. From $\mathbf{p}_n \longrightarrow \mathbf{p}$ and the continuity of the dot product, we see that there exists some n_0 satisfying $\mathbf{p}_n\cdot(\lambda\mathbf{y}) < \mathbf{p}_n\cdot\omega = \mathbf{p}_n\cdot\mathbf{x}_\omega(\mathbf{p}_n)$ for all $n \ge n_0$. Thus, $\mathbf{x}_\omega(\mathbf{p}_n) \succeq \lambda\mathbf{y}$ holds for all $n \ge n_0$, and this (in view of the continuity of $\succeq$) implies $\mathbf{x} \succeq \lambda\mathbf{y}$ for all $0 < \lambda < 1$. Letting $\lambda \uparrow 1$ (and using the continuity of $\succeq$ once more), we see that $\mathbf{x} \succeq \mathbf{y}$. This shows that $\mathbf{x}$ is a maximal element in $\mathcal{B}_\omega(\mathbf{p})$.

Now a glance at Theorem 1.3.3 reveals that $\mathbf{p} \gg \mathbf{0}$ must hold, in which case Theorem 1.3.2(2) guarantees that $\mathbf{x} = \mathbf{x}_\omega(\mathbf{p})$, and the proof of the theorem is finished. ■

To obtain the continuity of the demand functions we need the Closed Graph Theorem for continuous functions.

Lemma 1.3.7. (The Closed Graph Theorem) *Let $f\colon X \longrightarrow Y$ be a function between two topological spaces with Y Hausdorff and compact. Then f is continuous if and only if its graph $G_f = \{(x, f(x))\colon\ x \in X\}$ is a closed subset of $X \times Y$.*

Proof. If f is continuous, then its graph G_f is clearly a closed subset of $X \times Y$.

For the converse, assume that G_f is a closed subset of $X \times Y$. Let $\{x_\alpha\}$ be a net of X satisfying $x_\alpha \longrightarrow x$. We have to show that $f(x_\alpha) \longrightarrow f(x)$. To this end, assume by way of contradiction that $f(x_\alpha) \not\to f(x)$. Then there exist an open neighborhood V of $f(x)$ and a subnet $\{y_\lambda\}$ of $\{x_\alpha\}$ satisfying $f(y_\lambda) \notin V$ for each λ. Since Y is a compact topological space, there exists a subnet $\{z_\sigma\}$ of $\{y_\lambda\}$ (and hence, a subnet of $\{x_\alpha\}$) with $f(z_\sigma) \longrightarrow u$ in Y. Clearly, $u \notin V$ and so $u \ne f(x)$. On the other hand, we have $(z_\sigma, f(z_\sigma)) \longrightarrow (x, u)$ in $X \times Y$, and by the closedness of G_f, we infer that $u = f(x) \in V$, which is impossible. This contradiction shows that the function f is continuous at x, and hence continuous everywhere on X. ■

If Y is not compact, then the closedness of the graph G_f need not imply the continuity of f. For instance, the function $f\colon \mathcal{R} \longrightarrow \mathcal{R}$ defined by

$$f(x) = \begin{cases} \frac{1}{x}, & \text{if } x \ne 0; \\ 0, & \text{if } x = 0. \end{cases}$$

has a closed graph but it is not continuous. It is, also interesting to know that there are examples of functions with closed graphs that are discontinuous at every point. To construct such an example, consider $X = \mathcal{R}$ with the Euclidean topology and $Y = \mathcal{R}$ with the discrete topology (i.e., every subset is open). Then the function $f: X \longrightarrow Y$ defined by $f(x) = x$ has a closed graph but fails to be continuous at any point of X.

We are now ready to establish the continuity of the demand functions. Intuitively, the continuity of a demand function expresses the fact that "small changes in the price vector result in small changes in the demand vector." The geometrical meaning of this statement is depicted in Figure 1.3-2.

Theorem 1.3.8. *Every demand function corresponding to a neoclassical preference is continuous.*

Proof. Let $\succeq$ be a neoclassical preference on some $\mathcal{R}^\ell_+$ and let $\omega \in \mathcal{R}^\ell_+$ be fixed. For simplicity, we shall denote the demand function $\mathbf{x}_\omega(\cdot)$ by

$$\mathbf{x}(\cdot) = \big(x_1(\cdot), x_2(\cdot), \ldots, x_\ell(\cdot)\big)\,.$$

Now, let $\mathbf{p} \gg \mathbf{0}$ be fixed. Note first that $\mathbf{p}$ is in the interior of a "box" $[\mathbf{r}, \mathbf{s}]$ with $\mathbf{r} \gg \mathbf{0}$.* Let $r = \min\{r_1, r_2, \ldots, r_\ell\} > 0$. If $\mathbf{q} = (q_1, q_2, \ldots, q_\ell) \in [\mathbf{r}, \mathbf{s}]$, then we have

$$q_i x_i(\mathbf{q}) \le \sum_{k=1}^{\ell} q_k x_k(\mathbf{q}) = \mathbf{q} \cdot \mathbf{x}(\mathbf{q}) = \mathbf{q} \cdot \omega \le \mathbf{s} \cdot \omega\,,$$

and consequently

$$x_i(\mathbf{q}) \le \frac{\mathbf{s} \cdot \omega}{q_i} \le \frac{\mathbf{s} \cdot \omega}{r} = M < \infty \qquad (\star)$$

holds for each $i = 1, 2, \ldots, \ell$. This implies that the function $\mathbf{x}(\cdot)$ is bounded on $[\mathbf{r}, \mathbf{s}]$, and so the set $Y = \overline{\mathbf{x}([\mathbf{r}, \mathbf{s}])}$—where bar denotes closure—is a compact subset of $\mathcal{R}^\ell_+$. To show that $\mathbf{x}(\cdot)$ is continuous at $\mathbf{p}$, it suffices to establish that $\mathbf{x}: [\mathbf{r}, \mathbf{s}] \longrightarrow Y$ is continuous. By Lemma 1.3.7, it suffices to show that the function $\mathbf{x}: [\mathbf{r}, \mathbf{s}] \longrightarrow Y$ has a closed graph.

To this end, let a sequence $\{\mathbf{q}_n\} \subseteq [\mathbf{r}, \mathbf{s}]$ satisfy $\mathbf{q}_n \longrightarrow \mathbf{q}$ and $\mathbf{x}(\mathbf{q}_n) \longrightarrow \mathbf{x}$. By Theorem 1.3.6, it follows that $\mathbf{x} = \mathbf{x}(\mathbf{q})$. This shows that the function $\mathbf{x}: [\mathbf{r}, \mathbf{s}] \longrightarrow Y$ has a closed graph, and the proof of the theorem is finished. ∎

---

* The "box" $[\mathbf{r}, \mathbf{s}]$ is the set $[\mathbf{r}, \mathbf{s}] = \{\mathbf{x} \in \mathcal{R}^\ell: \ \mathbf{r} \le \mathbf{x} \le \mathbf{s}\}$. In mathematical terminology, a "box" is known as an **order interval**.

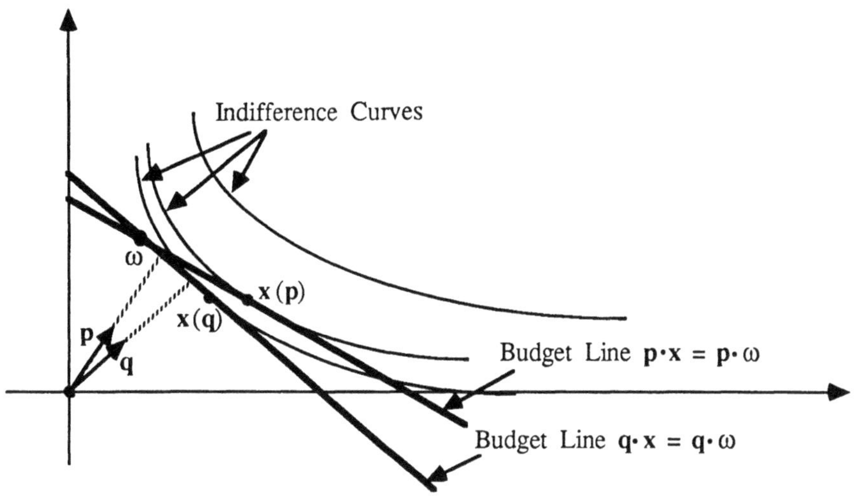

As the price vector **p** changes to **q** the demand vector **x**(**p**) changes to **x** (**q**)

Fig. 1.3-2

Now let us give an economic interpretation of the discussion so far. The vector space $\mathcal{R}^\ell_+$ can be thought of as representing the commodity space of our economy–where, of course, the number ℓ represents the number of available commodities. A preference relation can be thought of as representing the "taste" of a consumer and the vector ω as her initial endowment. The vector $\mathbf{p} = (p_1, p_2, \ldots, p_\ell)$ represents the prevailing prices—p_i is the price (usually per unit) of commodity i. Then the demand vector $\mathbf{x}(\mathbf{p})$ represents the commodity bundle that maximizes the consumer's utility function subject to her budget constraint. If $\mathbf{x}_\omega(\mathbf{p}) = \mathbf{x}(\mathbf{p}) = (x_1(\mathbf{p}), x_2(\mathbf{p}), \ldots, x_\ell(\mathbf{p}))$ is the demand vector, then the real number

$$\sum_{i=1}^{\ell} x_i(\mathbf{p})$$

represents the total number of units of goods demanded by the individual—for a vector $\mathbf{x} = (x_1, x_2, \ldots, x_\ell)$ the number $\sum_{i=1}^{\ell} |x_i|$ is called the ℓ_1*-norm* of the vector and is denoted by $\|\mathbf{x}\|_1$, i.e., $\|\mathbf{x}\|_1 = \sum_{i=1}^{\ell} |x_i|$. Thus, the number $\|\mathbf{x}(\mathbf{p})\|_1$ is the aggregate number of units of goods demanded by the consumer.

As prices go to the boundary, some goods become (relatively) cheap and consequently demand for some commodities must become "very large." The details of this statement are given in the next theorem.

Theorem 1.3.9. *Consider a neoclassical preference* $\succeq$ *on* $\mathcal{R}^\ell_+$, *a vector* $\omega \in \mathcal{R}^\ell_+$ *and denote by* $\mathbf{x}(\cdot) = \big(x_1(\cdot), x_2(\cdot), \ldots, x_\ell(\cdot)\big)$ *the demand function corresponding to* $\succeq$. *Also, assume that a sequence* $\{\mathbf{p}_n\}$ *of strictly positive vectors satisfies*

$$\mathbf{p}_n = (p_1^n, p_2^n, \ldots, p_\ell^n) \longrightarrow \mathbf{p} = (p_1, p_2, \ldots, p_\ell)\,.$$

Then, we have:

1) *If* $p_i > 0$ *holds for some* i, *then the sequence* $\{x_i(\mathbf{p}_n)\}$*—the* i^{th} *components of the demand sequence* $\{\mathbf{x}(\mathbf{p}_n)\}$*—is a bounded sequence.*
2) *If* $\mathbf{p} \in \partial\mathcal{R}^\ell_+$ *and* $\mathbf{p}\cdot\omega > 0$, *then*

$$\lim_{n\to\infty} \|\mathbf{x}(\mathbf{p}_n)\|_1 = \lim_{n\to\infty} \sum_{i=1}^{\ell} x_i(\mathbf{p}_n) = \infty\,.$$

Proof. Assume that $\{\mathbf{p}_n\}$ is a sequence of strictly positive prices satisfying the hypotheses of the theorem. Pick some $\mathbf{q} \gg \mathbf{0}$ such that $\mathbf{p}_n \leq \mathbf{q}$ holds for all n.

(1) Assume that $p_i > 0$ holds for some i. From $\mathbf{p}_n \gg \mathbf{0}$ and $\lim_{n\to\infty} p_i^n = p_i$, we infer that there exists some $\delta > 0$ such that $p_i^n > \delta$ holds for each n. Now note that the inequality

$$p_i^n x_i(\mathbf{p}_n) \leq \sum_{k=1}^{\ell} p_k^n x_k(\mathbf{p}_n) = \mathbf{p}_n\cdot\mathbf{x}(\mathbf{p}_n) = \mathbf{p}_n\cdot\omega \leq \mathbf{q}\cdot\omega\,,$$

implies that

$$x_i(\mathbf{p}_n) \leq \frac{\mathbf{q}\cdot\omega}{p_i^n} \leq \frac{\mathbf{q}\cdot\omega}{\delta} < \infty$$

holds for each n. Therefore, $\{x_i(\mathbf{p}_n)\}$ is a bounded sequence.

(2) If $\{\mathbf{x}(\mathbf{p}_n)\}$ has a bounded subsequence, then by passing to a subsequence (and relabelling), we can assume that $\mathbf{x}(\mathbf{p}_n) \longrightarrow \mathbf{x}$ holds in $\mathcal{R}^\ell_+$. In such a case, Theorem 1.3.6 implies that $\mathbf{p} \gg \mathbf{0}$ must hold, which contradicts $\mathbf{p} \in \partial\mathcal{R}^\ell_+$, and our conclusion follows. ∎

Part (2) of the preceding theorem asserts that when prices drop to zero, then the demand collectively tends to infinity. However, it should be noted that when the individual price of a commodity drops to zero, the demand for that particular commodity does not necessarily tend to infinity. For a clarification of this important point see Exercise 5 of this section.

EXERCISES

1. Show that a function $f\colon X \longrightarrow \mathcal{R}^\ell$—where X is a topological space—is continuous if and only if

a) f has a closed graph; and
b) for each $x \in X$ there exist a neighborhood V_x of x and some real number $M_x > 0$ such that $\|f(y)\|_1 \le M_x$ holds for each $y \in V_x$.

2. Find the demand function for the preference relation on $\mathcal{R}^2_+$ represented by the utility function $u(x,y) = \sqrt{x} + \sqrt{y}$ and having initial endowment $\omega = (1,2)$. *Answer:* $\mathbf{x}(\mathbf{p}) = \frac{p_1+2p_2}{p_1+p_2}\left(\frac{p_2}{p_1}, \frac{p_1}{p_2}\right)$

3. Find the demand function for the preference relation on $\mathcal{R}^3_+$ represented by the utility function $u(x,y,z) = \min\{x,y,z\}$ and having an initial endowment $\omega = (1,2,3)$. *Answer:* $\mathbf{x}(\mathbf{p}) = \frac{p_1+2p_2+3p_3}{p_1+p_2+p_3}(1,1,1)$

4. Consider the preference relation $\succeq$ on $\mathcal{R}^\ell_+$ represented by a *Cobb–Douglas utility function*

$$u(x_1, x_2, \ldots, x_\ell) = x_1^{\alpha_1} \cdot x_2^{\alpha_2} \cdots x_\ell^{\alpha_\ell},$$

where $0 < \alpha_j < 1$ for each j and $\sum_{j=1}^{\ell} \alpha_j = 1$.
a) Show that $\succeq$ is a neoclassical preference, and
b) Find the demand function of $\succeq$ for an arbitrary initial endowment $\omega > \mathbf{0}$. *Answer:* $\mathbf{x}(\mathbf{p}) = \mathbf{p}\cdot\omega\left(\frac{\alpha_1}{p_1}, \frac{\alpha_2}{p_2}, \ldots, \frac{\alpha_\ell}{p_\ell}\right)$

5. In Theorem 1.3.9 we saw that if $\{\mathbf{p}_n\} \subseteq \mathrm{Int}(\mathcal{R}^\ell_+)$ satisfies $\mathbf{p}_n \longrightarrow \mathbf{p} \in \partial\mathcal{R}^\ell_+$ and $\mathbf{p}\cdot\omega > 0$, then the collective demand $\|\mathbf{x}(\mathbf{p}_n)\|_1 = \sum_{i=1}^{\ell} x_i(\mathbf{p}_n)$ converges to infinity. This exercise shows that although the demand collectively tends to infinity, the demand for any single commodity can be bounded in spite of the fact that the prices for that commodity may converge to zero.

Consider the preference relation on $\mathcal{R}^3_+$ represented by the utility function

$$u(x,y,z) = \sqrt{x} + \sqrt{y} + y + \tfrac{z}{1+z},$$

and let $\omega = (1,1,1)$.
a) Show that u is a strictly monotone, strictly concave and continuous utility function.
b) If $(x,y,z) \in \mathcal{R}^3_+$ and $z > 0$, then show that

$$(x, y+z, 0) \succ (x,y,z).$$

c) If a price $\mathbf{p} = (p_1,p_2,p_3) \gg \mathbf{0}$ satisfies $p_2 = p_3$, then show that the demand bundle $\mathbf{x}_\omega(\mathbf{p}) = \big(x(\mathbf{p}), y(\mathbf{p}), z(\mathbf{p})\big)$ satisfies $z(\mathbf{p}) = 0$.
d) Consider the sequence $\{\mathbf{p}_n\} \subseteq \mathrm{Int}(\mathcal{R}^\ell_+)$ of prices defined by $\mathbf{p}_n = (1, \frac{1}{n}, \frac{1}{n})$ and note that $\mathbf{p}_n \longrightarrow (1,0,0)$. If $\mathbf{x}_\omega(\mathbf{p}_n) = \big(x(\mathbf{p}_n), y(\mathbf{p}_n), z(\mathbf{p}_n)\big)$ is the demand sequence, then show that $z(\mathbf{p}_n) = 0$ holds for each n—and hence, the demand for the third commodity remains bounded in spite of the fact that the prices of the third commodity converge to zero.
e) Show that $\lim_{n\to\infty} y(\mathbf{p}_n) = \infty$.

6. For this exercise $\succeq$ will denote a continuous and convex preference relation on $\mathcal{R}^\ell_+$ having an extremely desirable bundle. Also, let $\mathbf{0} < \omega \in \mathcal{R}^\ell_+$ be a fixed vector. Consider the *demand correspondence* (i.e., the set valued function) $\mathbf{x}\colon \mathrm{Int}(\mathcal{R}^\ell_+) \longrightarrow 2^{\mathcal{R}^\ell_+}$ defined by

$$\mathbf{x}(\mathbf{p}) = \{\mathbf{x} \in \mathcal{B}_\omega(\mathbf{p})\colon\ \mathbf{x} \succeq \mathbf{y} \ \text{holds for all} \ \mathbf{y} \in \mathcal{B}_\omega(\mathbf{p})\}\,, \quad \mathbf{p} \in \mathrm{Int}(\mathcal{R}^\ell_+)\,.$$

Note that if the preference $\succeq$ is strictly convex, then the demand correspondence coincides with the demand function. Establish the following properties for the demand correspondence.

a) For each $\mathbf{p} \gg \mathbf{0}$ the set $\mathbf{x}(\mathbf{p})$ is non-empty, convex and compact, i.e., the demand function is non-empty, convex-valued and compact-valued.
b) For each $\mathbf{y} \in \mathbf{x}(\mathbf{p})$, we have $\mathbf{p} \cdot \mathbf{y} = \mathbf{p} \cdot \omega$.
c) The demand correspondence is homogeneous of degree zero, that is, $\mathbf{x}(\mathbf{p}) = \mathbf{x}(\lambda\mathbf{p})$ holds for each $\mathbf{p} \gg \mathbf{0}$ and each $\lambda > 0$.
d) If $\{\mathbf{p}_n\} \subseteq \mathrm{Int}(\mathcal{R}^\ell_+)$ satisfies $\mathbf{p}_n \longrightarrow \mathbf{p} \gg \mathbf{0}$, then there exists a bounded subset B of $\mathcal{R}^\ell_+$ such that $\mathbf{x}(\mathbf{p}_n) \subseteq B$ holds for each n.
[HINT: Repeat the proof of Theorem 1.3.9(1).]
e) If $\{\mathbf{p}_n\} \subseteq \mathrm{Int}(\mathcal{R}^\ell_+)$ satisfies $\mathbf{p}_n \longrightarrow \mathbf{p} \in \partial\mathcal{R}^\ell_+ \setminus \{\mathbf{0}\}$ and a sequence $\{\mathbf{y}_n\}$ of $\mathcal{R}^\ell_+$ satisfies $\mathbf{y}_n \in \mathbf{x}_n(\mathbf{p}_n)$ for each n, then $\lim_{n\to\infty} \|\mathbf{y}_n\|_1 = \infty$.
[HINT: Mimic the proof of Theorem 1.3.9(2).]
f) If $\mathbf{p}_n \longrightarrow \mathbf{p}$ holds in $\mathrm{Int}(\mathcal{R}^\ell_+)$ and $\mathbf{y}_n \in \mathbf{x}(\mathbf{p}_n)$ for each n, then there exists a subsequence $\{\mathbf{z}_n\}$ of the sequence $\{\mathbf{y}_n\}$ such that $\mathbf{z}_n \longrightarrow \mathbf{z} \in \mathbf{x}(\mathbf{p})$.
[HINT: Invoke part (d) and the arguments of the proof of Theorem 1.3.6.]
g) The demand correspondence has a closed graph, i.e., the set

$$\mathbf{G} = \{(\mathbf{p}, \mathbf{y}) \in \mathrm{Int}(\mathcal{R}^\ell_+) \times \mathcal{R}^\ell_+\colon\ \mathbf{y} \in \mathbf{x}(\mathbf{p})\}$$

is a closed subset of $\mathrm{Int}(\mathcal{R}^\ell_+) \times \mathcal{R}^\ell_+$.

1.4. EXCHANGE ECONOMIES

In the pure theory of international trade, we consider several countries exchanging goods on international markets at fixed terms of trade. This model is the genesis of the exchange economies that we discuss in this and the next two sections. Here, we shall prove the existence of prices—terms of trade—which clear all markets. Such prices are called equilibrium prices. In Section 1.6, we shall examine the ability of competitive markets to efficiently allocate resources.

The symbol $\mathcal{P}$ will denote the set of all preferences on $\mathcal{R}_+^\ell$. We start our discussion with a general definition of exchange economies with a finite dimensional commodity space.

Definition 1.4.1. *An* **exchange economy** $\mathcal{E}$ *is a function from a non-empty set* A *(called the set of agents or consumers) into* $\mathcal{R}_+^\ell \times \mathcal{P}$, *i.e.,*

$$\mathcal{E}: A \longrightarrow \mathcal{R}_+^\ell \times \mathcal{P}.$$

If $\mathcal{E}: A \longrightarrow \mathcal{R}_+^\ell \times \mathcal{P}$ is an economy, then the value $\mathcal{E}_i = (\omega_i, \succeq_i)$ represents the characteristics of agent i; the element ω_i is called his initial endowment and $\succeq_i$ his preference or taste. If $\mathbf{p}$ is any price vector, then the non-negative real number $\mathbf{p} \cdot \omega_i$ is called *the income* of agent i at prices $\mathbf{p}$ and is denoted by w_i, i.e., $w_i = \mathbf{p} \cdot \omega_i$. When A is a finite set, the vector $\omega = \sum_{i \in A} \omega_i$ is called the *total* (or the *aggregate* or the *social*) *endowment* of the economy.

In this section, we shall study an important class of exchange economies—the neoclassical exchange economies. Their definition is as follows.

Definition 1.4.2. *A* **neoclassical exchange economy** *is an exchange economy* $\mathcal{E}: A \longrightarrow \mathcal{R}_+^\ell \times \mathcal{P}$ *such that:*

1) *The set* A *of agents is finite;*
2) *Each agent* i *has a non-zero initial endowment* ω_i *(i.e.,* $\omega_i > 0$*) and his preference relation* $\succeq_i$ *is neoclassical; and*
3) *The total endowment* $\omega = \sum_{i \in A} \omega_i$ *is strictly positive, i.e.* $\omega \gg 0$ *holds.*

For the rest of our discussion in this section $\mathcal{E}$ will always indicate a neoclassical exchange economy. In this case, each agent i has a neoclassical preference $\succeq_i$, and hence, by the discussion in Section 1.3, each agent i has a demand function $\mathbf{x}_i\colon \text{Int}(\mathcal{R}^\ell_+) \longrightarrow \mathcal{R}^\ell_+$. The aggregate demand minus the total endowment is known as the excess demand function.

Definition 1.4.3. *If $\mathcal{E}$ is a neoclassical exchange economy, then* **the excess demand function** *for the economy $\mathcal{E}$ is the function $\zeta\colon \text{Int}(\mathcal{R}^\ell_+) \longrightarrow \mathcal{R}^\ell$ defined by*

$$\zeta(\mathbf{p}) = \sum_{i\in A} \mathbf{x}_i(\mathbf{p}) - \sum_{i\in A} \omega_i = \sum_{i\in A} \mathbf{x}_i(\mathbf{p}) - \omega\,.$$

In component form the excess demand function will be denoted as

$$\zeta(\cdot) = \big(\zeta_1(\cdot), \zeta_2(\cdot), \ldots, \zeta_\ell(\cdot)\big)\,.$$

The basic properties of the excess demand function are described in the next theorem.

Theorem 1.4.4. *The excess demand function ζ of a neoclassical exchange economy satisfies the following properties.*

1) *ζ is homogeneous of degree zero, i.e., $\zeta(\lambda\mathbf{p}) = \zeta(\mathbf{p})$ holds for all $\mathbf{p} \gg \mathbf{0}$ and all $\lambda > 0$.*
2) *ζ is continuous.*
3) *ζ satisfies Walras' Law, i.e., $\mathbf{p}\cdot\zeta(\mathbf{p}) = 0$ holds for all $\mathbf{p} \gg \mathbf{0}$.*
4) *If a sequence $\{\mathbf{p}_n\}$ of strictly positive prices satisfies*

$$\mathbf{p}_n = (p^n_1, p^n_2, \ldots, p^n_\ell) \longrightarrow \mathbf{p} = (p_1, p_2, \ldots, p_\ell)$$

and $p_k > 0$ holds for some k, then the sequence $\{\zeta_k(\mathbf{p}_n)\}$ of the kth components of $\{\zeta(\mathbf{p}_n)\}$ is bounded.

5) *If $\mathbf{p}_n \gg \mathbf{0}$ holds for each n and $\mathbf{p}_n \longrightarrow \mathbf{p} \in \partial\mathcal{R}^\ell_+ \setminus \{\mathbf{0}\}$, then there exists at least one k such that $\limsup_{n\to\infty} \zeta_k(\mathbf{p}_n) = \infty$.*

Proof. (1) The desired conclusion follows from the fact that $\mathbf{x}_i(\lambda\mathbf{p}) = \mathbf{x}_i(\mathbf{p})$ holds for all $\mathbf{p} \gg \mathbf{0}$, all $\lambda > 0$ and all $i \in A$.

(2) The continuity of the excess demand function follows immediately from Theorem 1.3.8.

(3) If $\mathbf{p} \gg \mathbf{0}$, then we have

$$\mathbf{p}\cdot\zeta(\mathbf{p}) = \mathbf{p}\cdot\sum_{i\in A}[\mathbf{x}_i(\mathbf{p}) - \omega_i] = \sum_{i\in A}[\mathbf{p}\cdot\mathbf{x}_i(\mathbf{p}) - \mathbf{p}\cdot\omega_i] = \sum_{i\in A} 0 = 0\,.$$

Finally, note that the validity of (4) and (5) can be established easily by invoking Theorem 1.3.9. ■

We now define the notion of an equilibrium price vector for a neoclassical exchange economy.

Definition 1.4.5. *A strictly positive price* $\mathbf{p}$ *is said to be an* **equilibrium price** *for a neoclassical exchange economy whenever*

$$\zeta(\mathbf{p}) = \mathbf{0}.$$

Does every neoclassical exchange economy have an equilibrium price? The celebrated Arrow–Debreu theorem says yes! The rest of the section is devoted to establishing this result.

Since the excess demand function ζ is homogeneous of degree zero (in other words, $\zeta(\lambda\mathbf{p}) = \zeta(\mathbf{p})$ holds for all $\lambda > 0$), we see that a strictly positive price $\mathbf{p}$ is an equilibrium price if and only if $\zeta(\lambda\mathbf{p}) = \mathbf{0}$ holds for all $\lambda > 0$. In other words, if $\mathbf{p}$ is an equilibrium price, then the whole half-ray $\{\lambda\mathbf{p}\colon\ \lambda > 0\}$ consists of equilibrium prices. This means that the search for equilibrium prices can be confined to sets that contain at least one element from each half-ray. The two most commonly employed normalizations of prices are the two sets

$$\Delta = \{\mathbf{p} \in \mathcal{R}^\ell_+\colon\ p_1 + p_2 + \cdots + p_\ell = 1\}$$

and

$$S_{\ell-1} = \{\mathbf{p} \in \mathcal{R}^\ell_+\colon\ (p_1)^2 + (p_2)^2 + \cdots + (p_\ell)^2 = 1\}.$$

Their geometrical meaning is shown in Figure 1.4-1; notice that each half-ray determined by a positive vector $\mathbf{p}$ intersects both sets. In this chapter, we shall work exclusively with the "simplex" Δ.

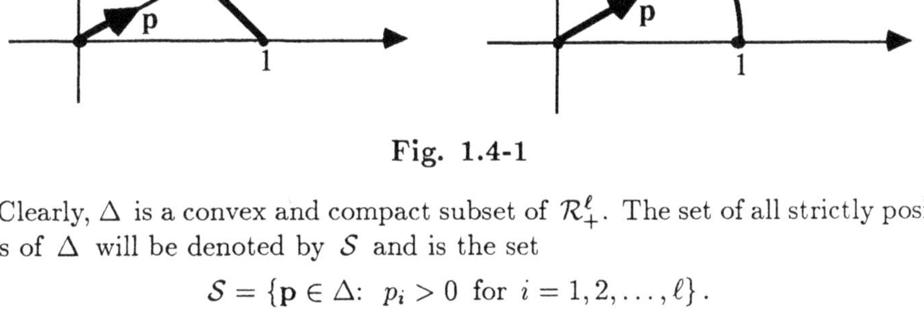

Fig. 1.4-1

Clearly, Δ is a convex and compact subset of $\mathcal{R}^\ell_+$. The set of all strictly positive prices of Δ will be denoted by $\mathcal{S}$ and is the set

$$\mathcal{S} = \{\mathbf{p} \in \Delta\colon\ p_i > 0 \text{ for } i = 1, 2, \ldots, \ell\}.$$

Now we can consider the excess demand function ζ as a function from $\mathcal{S}$ into $\mathcal{R}^\ell_+$. According to Theorem 1.4.4, the function $\zeta: \mathcal{S} \longrightarrow \mathcal{R}^\ell_+$ has the following characteristic properties.

Theorem 1.4.6. *If $\zeta(\cdot) = \big(\zeta_1(\cdot), \zeta_2(\cdot), \ldots, \zeta_\ell(\cdot)\big)$ is the excess demand function for a neoclassical exchange economy, then*
1. *ζ is continuous on $\mathcal{S}$;*
2. *ζ satisfies Walras' Law, i.e., $\mathbf{p} \cdot \zeta(\mathbf{p}) = 0$ holds for each $\mathbf{p} \in \mathcal{S}$;*
3. *$\{\mathbf{p}_n\} \subseteq \mathcal{S}$, $\mathbf{p}_n \longrightarrow \mathbf{p} = (p_1, \ldots, p_\ell)$ and $p_k > 0$ imply that the sequence $\{\zeta_k(\mathbf{p}_n)\}$ of the kth components of $\{\zeta(\mathbf{p}_n)\}$ is bounded; and*
4. *$\mathbf{p}_n \longrightarrow \mathbf{p} \in \partial\mathcal{S}$ with $\{\mathbf{p}_n\} \subseteq \mathcal{S}$ imply $\lim_{n\to\infty} \|\zeta(\mathbf{p}_n)\|_1 = \infty$.*

To establish that every neoclassical exchange economy has an equilibrium price, we shall invoke a fixed point theorem due to S. Kakutani [36]. For convenience, we recall a few things about correspondences. A *correspondence* (or a *multivalued function*) between two sets X and Y is any function $\phi: X \longrightarrow 2^Y$, i.e., the value $\phi(x)$ is a subset of Y for each x. As usual, 2^Y denotes the set of all subsets of Y. The *graph* of a correspondence $\phi: X \longrightarrow 2^Y$ is the subset of $X \times Y$ defined by

$$G_\phi = \{(x, y) \in X \times Y:\ x \in X \text{ and } y \in \phi(x)\}.$$

If X and Y are topological spaces, then a correspondence $\phi: X \longrightarrow 2^Y$ is said to have a *closed graph* whenever its graph G_ϕ is a closed subset of $X \times Y$. A point $x \in X$ is said to be a *fixed point* for a correspondence $\phi: X \longrightarrow 2^X$ whenever $x \in \phi(x)$ holds. The fixed point theorem of S. Kakutani can be stated now as follows; for a proof see [32, p. 201].

Theorem 1.4.7. (Kakutani) *Let C be a non-empty, compact and convex subset of some $\mathcal{R}^\ell$. If $\phi: C \longrightarrow 2^C$ is a non-empty and convex-valued correspondence with closed graph, then ϕ has a fixed point, i.e., there exists some $x \in C$ with $x \in \phi(x)$.*

We are now ready to establish a general result that will guarantee the existence of equilibrium prices for every neoclassical exchange economy. The proof of the next theorem is a slight modification of the proof of Proposition 6.3 in [32].

Theorem 1.4.8. *For a function $\zeta(\cdot) = \big(\zeta_1(\cdot), \zeta_2(\cdot), \ldots, \zeta_\ell(\cdot)\big)$ from $\mathcal{S}$ into $\mathcal{R}^\ell$ assume that:*
1) *ζ is continuous;*
2) *ζ satisfies Walras' Law, i.e., $\mathbf{p} \cdot \zeta(\mathbf{p}) = 0$ holds for each $\mathbf{p} \in \mathcal{S}$;*
3) *$\{\mathbf{p}_n\} \subseteq \mathcal{S}$, $\mathbf{p}_n \longrightarrow \mathbf{p} = (p_1, \ldots, p_\ell)$ and $p_i > 0$ imply that the sequence $\{\zeta_i(\mathbf{p}_n)\}$ of the ith components of $\{\zeta(\mathbf{p}_n)\}$ is bounded; and*
4) *$\mathbf{p}_n \longrightarrow \mathbf{p} \in \partial\mathcal{S}$ with $\{\mathbf{p}_n\} \subseteq \mathcal{S}$ imply $\lim_{n\to\infty} \|\zeta(\mathbf{p}_n)\|_1 = \infty$.*

Then, there exists at least one vector $\mathbf{p} \in \mathcal{S}$ satisfying $\zeta(\mathbf{p}) = \mathbf{0}$.

Proof. Let $\zeta: \mathcal{S} \longrightarrow \mathcal{R}^\ell$ be a function satisfying the four properties of the theorem. As usual, ζ will be written in component form as $\zeta(\cdot) = \big(\zeta_1(\cdot), \zeta_2(\cdot), \ldots, \zeta_\ell(\cdot)\big)$.

For each $\mathbf{p} \in \mathcal{S}$, we define a subset $\Lambda(\mathbf{p})$ of $\{1, 2, \ldots, \ell\}$ by

$$\Lambda(\mathbf{p}) = \big\{k \in \{1, 2, \ldots, \ell\}\colon\ \zeta_k(\mathbf{p}) = \max\{\zeta_i(\mathbf{p})\colon\ i = 1, 2, \ldots, \ell\}\big\}.$$

That is, when $\mathbf{p} \in \mathcal{S}$, the set $\Lambda(\mathbf{p})$ consists of all those commodities which have the greatest excess demand. Clearly, $\Lambda(\mathbf{p}) \neq \emptyset$. For $\mathbf{p} \in \Delta \setminus \mathcal{S} = \partial\mathcal{S}$, let

$$\Lambda(\mathbf{p}) = \big\{k \in \{1, 2, \ldots, \ell\}\colon\ p_k = 0\big\}.$$

Clearly, $\Lambda(\mathbf{p}) \neq \emptyset$ holds in this case too.

Now we define a correspondence $\phi\colon \Delta \longrightarrow 2^\Delta$ by the formula

$$\phi(\mathbf{p}) = \{\mathbf{q} \in \Delta\colon\ q_k = 0 \text{ for all } k \notin \Lambda(\mathbf{p})\}.$$

Since $\Lambda(\mathbf{p}) \neq \emptyset$, it easily follows that $\phi(\mathbf{p}) \neq \emptyset$ for all $\mathbf{p} \in \Delta$. Moreover, note that $\phi(\mathbf{p})$ is a convex and compact subset of Δ—in fact, $\phi(\mathbf{p})$ is a *face* of Δ. In addition, note that if $\Lambda(\mathbf{p}) = \{1, 2, \ldots, \ell\}$, then $\phi(\mathbf{p}) = \Delta$.

Thus, we have defined a correspondence $\phi\colon \Delta \longrightarrow 2^\Delta$ which is non-empty, compact, and convex-valued. We claim that ϕ has also a closed graph.

To establish that ϕ has a closed graph, assume that $\mathbf{p}_n \longrightarrow \mathbf{p}$ in Δ, $\pi_n \longrightarrow \pi$ in Δ and $\pi_n \in \phi(\mathbf{p}_n)$ for each n. We have to show that $\pi \in \phi(\mathbf{p})$. We distinguish two cases.

CASE I: $\mathbf{p} \in \mathcal{S}$.

In this case, we can assume that $\mathbf{p}_n \gg \mathbf{0}$ holds for each n. Now let $k \notin \Lambda(\mathbf{p})$. This means that $\zeta(\mathbf{p}) < \max\{\zeta_i(\mathbf{p})\colon\ i = 1, 2, \ldots, \ell\}$. Since ζ is continuous at $\mathbf{p}$, there exists some m such that

$$\zeta_k(\mathbf{p}_n) < \max\{\zeta_i(\mathbf{p}_n)\colon\ i = 1, 2, \ldots, \ell\}$$

holds for all $n \geq m$, and therefore $k \notin \Lambda(\mathbf{p}_n)$ holds for all $n \geq m$. Now from the relation $\pi_n = (\pi_1^n, \pi_2^n, \ldots, \pi_\ell^n) \in \phi(\mathbf{p}_n)$, we see that $\pi_k^n = 0$ for all $n \geq m$. In view of $\pi_n \longrightarrow \pi$, we have $\lim_{n\to\infty} \pi_k^n = \pi_k$, and so $\pi_k = 0$. In other words, $\pi_k = 0$ holds for all $k \notin \Lambda(\mathbf{p})$, and so $\pi \in \phi(\mathbf{p})$.

CASE II: $\mathbf{p} \in \Delta \setminus \mathcal{S} = \partial\mathcal{S}$.

Without loss of generality, we can suppose that $\mathbf{p} = (0, 0, \ldots, 0, p_{r+1}, \ldots, p_\ell)$, where $1 \leq r < \ell$ and $p_i > 0$ holds for each $i = r+1, r+2, \ldots, \ell$. In this case we distinguish two subcases.

CASE IIa: *There exists a subsequence of* $\{\mathbf{p}_n\}$ *(which we can assume it to be* $\{\mathbf{p}_n\}$ *itself) lying in* $\mathcal{S}$.

In this case, note that $\Lambda(\mathbf{p}) = \{1, 2, \ldots, r\}$, and so

$$\phi(\mathbf{p}) = \{\mathbf{q} \in \Delta\colon\ q_i = 0 \text{ for } i = r+1, r+2, \ldots, \ell\}.$$

Now from our hypothesis, it follows that the sequence $\{\zeta_i(\mathbf{p}_n)\}$ is bounded for each $i = r+1, \ldots, \ell$ and that $\lim_{n\to\infty} \|\zeta(\mathbf{p}_n)\|_1 = \infty$. Therefore, there exists some n_0

such that $\Lambda(\mathbf{p}_n) \subseteq \{1, 2, \ldots, r\}$ holds for each $n \geq n_0$. The latter and $\pi_n \in \phi(\mathbf{p}_n)$ imply $\pi_n \in \phi(\mathbf{p})$ for all $n \geq n_0$. Consequently, $\pi = \lim_{n\to\infty} \pi_n \in \phi(\mathbf{p})$.

CASE IIb: *No subsequence of* $\{\mathbf{p}_n\}$ *lies in* $\mathcal{S}$.

In this case, we can assume $\{\mathbf{p}_n\} \subseteq \partial\mathcal{S}$ and $\mathbf{p} = (0, \ldots, 0, p_{r+1}, \ldots, p_\ell)$. Since $\lim_{n\to\infty} p_i^n = p_i$ holds for each $i = 1, \ldots, \ell$, we infer that there exists some m such that $\Lambda(\mathbf{p}_n) \subseteq \{1, \ldots, r\}$ holds for all $n \geq m$. From $\pi_n \in \phi(\mathbf{p}_n)$, it follows that $\pi_i^n = 0$ for all $n \geq m$ and all $i = r+1, r+2, \ldots, \ell$. This (in view of $\pi_n \longrightarrow \pi$) implies that $\pi_i = 0$ for $i = r+1, \ldots, \ell$, and so $\pi \in \phi(\mathbf{p})$.

Thus, we have established that the correspondence ϕ has a closed graph. Now, by Kakutani's fixed point theorem (Theorem 1.4.7), ϕ has a fixed point, say $\mathbf{p}$, i.e., $\mathbf{p} \in \phi(\mathbf{p})$. We claim that $\mathbf{p}$ is an equilibrium price.

To see this, note first that $\mathbf{p} \notin \partial\mathcal{S}$. Indeed, if $\mathbf{p} \in \partial\mathcal{S}$, then we have $p_k = 0$ for each $k \in \Lambda(\mathbf{p})$ and, since $\mathbf{p} \in \phi(\mathbf{p})$, we have $p_k = 0$ for all $k \notin \Lambda(\mathbf{p})$, which implies that $\mathbf{p} = \mathbf{0} \notin \Delta$, a contradiction. Thus, $\mathbf{p} \in \mathcal{S}$, i.e., $\mathbf{p} \gg \mathbf{0}$.

Next, put $m = \max\{\zeta_i(\mathbf{p})\colon i = 1, 2, \ldots, \ell\}$, and note that $p_i > 0$ for all $i = 1, \ldots, \ell$ and $\mathbf{p} \in \phi(\mathbf{p})$ imply that $\Lambda(\mathbf{p}) = \{1, 2, \ldots, \ell\}$. This means that $\zeta_i(\mathbf{p}) = m$ holds for each i. On the other hand, using Walras' Law, we see that

$$m = \Big(\sum_{i=1}^{\ell} p_i\Big)m = \sum_{i=1}^{\ell} p_i m = \sum_{i=1}^{\ell} p_i \zeta_i(\mathbf{p}) = \mathbf{p}\cdot\zeta(\mathbf{p}) = 0,$$

and this implies that $\zeta(\mathbf{p}) = \mathbf{0}$. The proof of the theorem is now complete. ■

A special form of the Arrow–Debreu theorem can be stated as follows.

Theorem 1.4.9. (Arrow–Debreu) *Every neoclassical exchange economy has an equilibrium price, i.e., there exists at least one price* $\mathbf{p} \gg \mathbf{0}$ *satisfying* $\zeta(\mathbf{p}) = \mathbf{0}$.

Proof. The conclusion follows immediately by observing that (by Theorem 1.4.6) any excess demand function satisfies the hypotheses of Theorem 1.4.8. ■

It should be emphasized that the proof of the preceding result is non constructive. It guarantees the existence of equilibrium prices but it does not provide any method of computing them. A constructive proof of the existence was first given by H. E. Scarf. An exposition of the constructive approach to equilibrium analysis can be found in his monograph [61]. As a matter of fact, it is very difficult to predict where the equilibrium prices lie on the simplex even in very simple cases. The next example illustrates this point.

Example 1.4.10. Consider an economy having $\mathcal{R}^2$ as commodity space and three agents—i.e., $A = \{1, 2, 3\}$—with the following characteristics:

Agent 1: Initial endowment $\omega_1 = (1, 2)$ and utility function $u_1(x, y) = xy$.

Agent 2: Initial endowment $\omega_2 = (1, 1)$ and utility function $u_2(x, y) = x^2 y$.

Agent 3: Initial endowment $\omega_3 = (2, 3)$ and utility function $u_3(x, y) = xy^2$.

Note that the preferences represented by the above utility functions are all neoclassical—and all are only strictly monotone on $\mathrm{Int}(\mathcal{R}^{\ell}_{+})$. The total endowment is the vector $\omega = \omega_1 + \omega_2 + \omega_3 = (4, 6)$.

Next, we shall determine the demand functions $\mathbf{x}_1(\cdot)$, $\mathbf{x}_2(\cdot)$ and $\mathbf{x}_3(\cdot)$. To this end, let $\mathbf{p} = (p_1, p_2) \gg \mathbf{0}$ be fixed.

The first agent maximizes the utility function $u_1(x, y) = xy$ subject to the budget constraint $p_1x + p_2y = p_1 + 2p_2$. Employing Lagrange multipliers, we see that at the maximizing point we must have $\nabla u = (y, x) = \lambda\mathbf{p}$. This leads us to the system of equations

$$y = \lambda p_1\,, \qquad x = \lambda p_2 \qquad \text{and} \qquad p_1x + p_2y = p_1 + 2p_2\,.$$

Solving the above system, we obtain

$$\mathbf{x}_1(\mathbf{p}) = \left(\tfrac{p_1+2p_2}{2p_1}, \tfrac{p_1+2p_2}{2p_2}\right).$$

The second agent maximizes the utility function $u_2(x, y) = x^2y$ subject to $p_1x + p_2y = p_1 + p_2$. Using Lagrange multipliers again, we obtain the system

$$2xy = \lambda p_1\,, \qquad x^2 = \lambda p_2 \qquad \text{and} \qquad p_1x + p_2y = p_1 + p_2\,.$$

Solving the system, we obtain

$$\mathbf{x}_2(\mathbf{p}) = \left(\tfrac{2p_1+2p_2}{3p_1}, \tfrac{p_1+p_2}{3p_2}\right).$$

Finally, for the third agent we have the system

$$y^2 = \lambda p_1\,, \qquad 2xy = \lambda p_2 \qquad \text{and} \qquad p_1x + p_2y = 2p_1 + 3p_2\,,$$

from which we get

$$\mathbf{x}_3(\mathbf{p}) = \left(\tfrac{2p_1+3p_2}{3p_1}, \tfrac{4p_1+6p_2}{3p_2}\right).$$

Therefore, $\mathbf{x}_1(\mathbf{p}) + \mathbf{x}_2(\mathbf{p}) + \mathbf{x}_3(\mathbf{p}) = \left(\tfrac{11p_1+16p_2}{6p_1}, \tfrac{13p_1+20p_2}{6p_2}\right)$ and so

$$\zeta(\mathbf{p}) = \left(\tfrac{11p_1+16p_2}{6p_1}, \tfrac{13p_1+20p_2}{6p_2}\right) - (4, 6) = \left(-\tfrac{13p_1-16p_2}{6p_1}, \tfrac{13p_1-16p_2}{6p_2}\right).$$

Clearly, $\zeta(\mathbf{p}) = \mathbf{0}$ holds if and only if $13p_1 - 16p_2 = 0$. Taking into account that $p_1 + p_2 = 1$, we infer that an equilibrium price is

$$\mathbf{p}_{eq} = \left(\tfrac{16}{29}, \tfrac{13}{29}\right) \approx (0.45, 0.55)\,.$$

The equilibrium half-ray is "close" to the bisector line $p_2 = p_1$; see Figure 1.4-2. ■

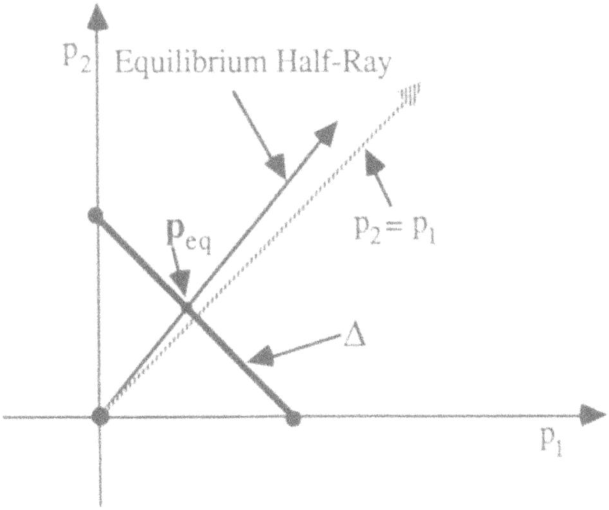

Fig. 1.4-2

EXERCISES

1. Consider an exchange economy with commodity space $\mathcal{R}^2$ having three consumers with the following characteristics:
Consumer 1. Initial endowment $(1,2)$ and utility function $u_1(x,y) = \sqrt{x} + \sqrt{y}$.
Consumer 2. Initial endowment $(3,4)$ and utility function $u_2(x,y) = \min\{x,y\}$.
Consumer 3. Initial endowment $(1,1)$ and utility function $u_3(x,y) = ye^x$.
Find the excess demand function and the equilibrium prices for this exchange economy. *Answer*: If $t = \frac{p_2}{p_1}$, then $\zeta(\mathbf{p}) = \left(\frac{3t^2+t-2}{1+t}, -\frac{3t^2+t-2}{t(1+t)}\right)$.

2. Consider the function $\zeta\colon \mathrm{Int}(\mathcal{R}^\ell_+) \longrightarrow \mathcal{R}^2$ defined by

$$\zeta(\mathbf{p}) = \left(-\frac{p_2}{p_1+p_2}, \frac{p_1}{p_1+p_2}\right).$$

a) Show that ζ is homogeneous of degree zero.
b) Show that ζ is continuous.
c) Show that ζ satisfies Walras' Law.
d) Can ζ be the excess demand function for a neoclassical exchange economy with commodity space $\mathcal{R}^2$?

3. For this exercise ω denotes a fixed strictly positive vector of $\mathcal{R}^\ell$. Fix two non-zero vectors $\mathbf{a}$ and $\mathbf{b}$ in $\mathcal{R}^\ell_+$ and define the function $\zeta\colon \mathrm{Int}(\mathcal{R}^\ell_+) \longrightarrow \mathcal{R}^\ell_+$ by

$$\zeta(\mathbf{p}) = \frac{\mathbf{p}\cdot\mathbf{a}}{\mathbf{p}\cdot\omega}\mathbf{b} - \frac{\mathbf{p}\cdot\mathbf{b}}{\mathbf{p}\cdot\omega}\mathbf{a}.$$

a) Show that ζ is homogeneous of degree zero.
b) Show that ζ is a continuous function.
c) Show that ζ satisfies Walras' Law.
d) Show that ζ cannot be the excess demand function of a neoclassical exchange economy with commodity space $\mathcal{R}^\ell_+$.
e) Does ζ have an equilibrium price?

4. If $\zeta(\cdot)$ is the excess demand function for a neoclassical exchange economy and some price $\mathbf{p} \gg \mathbf{0}$ satisfies either $\zeta(\mathbf{p}) \geq \mathbf{0}$ or $\zeta(\mathbf{p}) \leq \mathbf{0}$, then show that $\zeta(\mathbf{p}) = \mathbf{0}$ holds.

5. This exercise presents another proof of the Arrow–Debreu theorem in a more general context. Consider an exchange economy with a finite number of consumers each of whom has a continuous and convex preference with an extremely desirable vector. In this case—as we saw in Exercise 6 of Section 1.3—the demand $\mathbf{x}_i(\cdot)$ is a non-empty, convex-valued and compact-valued correspondence.

Define the *excess demand correspondence* $\zeta\colon \mathrm{Int}(\mathcal{R}^\ell_+) \longrightarrow 2^{\mathcal{R}^\ell}$ by

$$\zeta(\mathbf{p}) = \sum_{i=1}^{m} \mathbf{x}_i(\mathbf{p}) - \sum_{i=1}^{m} \omega_i = \sum_{i=1}^{m} \mathbf{x}_i(\mathbf{p}) - \omega\,.$$

A price $\mathbf{p}$ is said to be an **equilibrium price** whenever $\mathbf{0} \in \zeta(\mathbf{p})$. Prove that the excess demand correspondence has an equilibrium price by establishing the validity of the following statements.

a) The excess demand correspondence is non-empty, convex- and compact-valued.
b) For each $\mathbf{z} \in \zeta(\mathbf{p})$, we have $\mathbf{p} \cdot \mathbf{z} = 0$.
c) If $\{\mathbf{p}_n\} \subseteq \mathrm{Int}(\mathcal{R}^\ell_+)$ satisfies $\mathbf{p}_n \longrightarrow \mathbf{p} \in \partial\mathcal{R}^\ell_+ \setminus \{\mathbf{0}\}$ and $\mathbf{z}_n \in \zeta(\mathbf{p}_n)$ for each n, then $\lim_{n\to\infty} \|\mathbf{z}_n\|_1 = \infty$.
[HINT: Use Exercise 6(e) of Section 1.3.]
d) If $\mathbf{p}_n \longrightarrow \mathbf{p}$ holds in $\mathrm{Int}(\mathcal{R}^\ell_+)$ and $\mathbf{z}_n \in \zeta(\mathbf{p}_n)$ for each n, then there exists a subsequence $\{\mathbf{y}_n\}$ of the sequence $\{\mathbf{z}_n\}$ such that $\mathbf{y}_n \longrightarrow \mathbf{y} \in \zeta(\mathbf{p})$.
e) For each $0 < \varepsilon < 1$ there exists a closed ball B_ε such that $\zeta(\mathbf{p}) \subseteq B_\varepsilon$ holds for each $\mathbf{p} \gg \mathbf{0}$ satisfying $\varepsilon \leq p_i \leq 1$ for all i.
[HINT: Use Exercise 6(d) of Section 1.3.]
f) For each $0 < \varepsilon \leq \frac{1}{\ell}$, let $S_\varepsilon = \{\mathbf{p} \in S\colon\ p_i \geq \varepsilon \text{ for all } i\}$ and then pick some closed ball B_ε such that $\zeta(\mathbf{p}) \subseteq B_\varepsilon$ holds for each $\mathbf{p} \in S_\varepsilon$. Also, for $\mathbf{z} \in B_\varepsilon$, let

$$\psi_\varepsilon(\mathbf{z}) = \big\{\mathbf{p} \in S_\varepsilon\colon\ \mathbf{p} \cdot \mathbf{z} = \max_{\mathbf{q} \in S_\varepsilon} \mathbf{q} \cdot \mathbf{z}\big\}\,.$$

Now define the correspondence $\phi_\varepsilon\colon S_\varepsilon \times B_\varepsilon \longrightarrow S_\varepsilon \times B_\varepsilon$ by

$$\phi_\varepsilon(\mathbf{p}, \mathbf{z}) = \psi_\varepsilon(\mathbf{z}) \times \zeta(\mathbf{p})\,.$$

The correspondence ϕ_ε satisfies the hypotheses of Kakutani's fixed point theorem (Theorem 1.4.7). If $(\mathbf{p}, \mathbf{z})$ is a fixed point for ϕ_ε, i.e., if $(\mathbf{p}, \mathbf{z}) \in \phi_\varepsilon(\mathbf{p}, \mathbf{z})$, then

$$\mathbf{z} \in \zeta(\mathbf{p}) \quad \text{and} \quad \mathbf{q} \cdot \mathbf{z} \leq \mathbf{p} \cdot \mathbf{z} = 0 \quad \text{for all} \quad \mathbf{q} \in S_\varepsilon\,.$$

g) For each n there exists—by part (f)—some price $\mathbf{p}_n \in S$ and some vector $\mathbf{z}_n \in \zeta(\mathbf{p}_n)$ satisfying

$$\mathbf{q} \cdot \mathbf{z}_n \leq 0 \quad \text{for all} \quad \mathbf{q} \in S_{\frac{1}{n+\ell}}\,.$$

By passing to a subsequence (and relabelling), we can assume without loss of generality that $\mathbf{p}_n \longrightarrow \mathbf{p} \in \Delta$. The sequence $\{\mathbf{z}_n\}$ is bounded (why?) and so by passing to a subsequence again, we can assume that $\mathbf{z}_n \longrightarrow \mathbf{z}$. Then, $\mathbf{p} \gg \mathbf{0}$ and $\mathbf{z} \in \zeta(\mathbf{p})$ hold. To finish the proof notice that $\mathbf{z} = \mathbf{0}$ also holds.

1.5. OPTIMALITY IN EXCHANGE ECONOMIES

In this section—and throughout this monograph—we shall be concerned with two notions of optimality; Pareto optimality and the core. In a neoclassical exchange economy, any redistribution of the social endowment to agents is called an *allocation*. An allocation is Pareto optimal if there is no other allocation that each individual prefers to the given allocation. Pareto optimal allocations need not be individually rational. That is, an individual may prefer her initial endowment to the commodity bundle she receives in a Pareto optimal allocation; for instance, giving the social endowment to a single individual results in a Pareto optimal allocation that is not individually rational in an economy with at least two agents.

A stronger notion of optimality is the cooperative game theoretic notion of the core. The idea is simple: No allocation is sustainable as an "equilibrium allocation" if agents are free to cooperate and bargain among themselves and a coalition of agents can obtain for themselves a redistribution of their initial endowments that each member of the coalition prefers to the commodity bundle she receives in the given allocation. The core is the set of allocations that cannot be improved upon in this way. Clearly, every core allocation is an individually rational Pareto optimal allocation.

In this section we shall deal exclusively with the study of allocations in exchange economies with a finite number of consumers. Accordingly, the set $A = \{1, \ldots, m\}$ will denote the set of consumers of an arbitrary exchange economy with a finite number of consumers. The initial endowment of each consumer i will be denoted by ω_i. The letter ω will denote the total endowment, i.e., $\omega = \sum_{i=1}^{m} \omega_i \gg \mathbf{0}$.

An **allocation** is an m-tuple $(\mathbf{x}_1, \mathbf{x}_2, \ldots, \mathbf{x}_m)$ of vectors of $\mathcal{R}_+^\ell$ such that

$$\sum_{i=1}^{m} \mathbf{x}_i = \omega .$$

That is, an allocation is a redistribution of the total endowment ω among the m consumers of the economy.

We start our discussion by stating some basic properties of allocations.

Definition 1.5.1. *An allocation* $(\mathbf{x}_1, \mathbf{x}_2, \ldots, \mathbf{x}_m)$ *is said to be:*

a) **Individually Rational**, *if* $\mathbf{x}_i \succeq_i \omega_i$ *holds for each consumer* i*;*

b) **Weakly Pareto Optimal**, *if there is no allocation* $(\mathbf{y}_1, \mathbf{y}_2, \ldots, \mathbf{y}_m)$ *such that* $\mathbf{y}_i \succ_i \mathbf{x}_i$ *holds for each consumer* i*; and*

c) **Pareto Optimal**, *whenever there is no allocation* $(\mathbf{y}_1, \mathbf{y}_2, \ldots, \mathbf{y}_m)$ *such that* $\mathbf{y}_i \succeq_i \mathbf{x}_i$ *holds for each consumer* i *and* $\mathbf{y}_i \succ_i \mathbf{x}_i$ *holds for at least one consumer* i.

Clearly, every Pareto optimal allocation is weakly Pareto optimal. The converse is true when preferences are continuous and strictly monotone.

Theorem 1.5.2. *If the consumers in an exchange economy have continuous and strictly monotone preferences, then an allocation is Pareto optimal if and only if it is weakly Pareto optimal.*

Proof. Assume that preferences are continuous and strictly monotone. For $m = 1$ the result is trivial. So, assume $m > 1$. Let $(\mathbf{x}_1, \mathbf{x}_2, \ldots, \mathbf{x}_m)$ be a weakly Pareto optimal allocation.

Now suppose that an allocation $(\mathbf{y}_1, \mathbf{y}_2, \ldots, \mathbf{y}_m)$ satisfies $\mathbf{y}_i \succeq_i \mathbf{x}_i$ for each i and $\mathbf{y}_k \succ_k \mathbf{x}_k$ for some k. By the continuity of the preference $\succeq_k$, there exists some $0 < \alpha < 1$ such that $(1-\alpha)\mathbf{y}_k \succ_k \mathbf{x}_k$. Now if we let $\mathbf{z}_i = \mathbf{y}_i + \frac{\alpha}{m-1}\mathbf{y}_k$ whenever $i \neq k$ and $\mathbf{z}_k = (1-\alpha)\mathbf{y}_k$, then $(\mathbf{z}_1, \mathbf{z}_2, \ldots, \mathbf{z}_m)$ is an allocation. Moreover, by the strict monotonicity of the preferences, we see that $\mathbf{z}_i \succ_i \mathbf{x}_i$ holds for all i, contradicting the weak Pareto optimality of $(\mathbf{x}_1, \mathbf{x}_2, \ldots, \mathbf{x}_m)$. This implies that $(\mathbf{x}_1, \mathbf{x}_2, \ldots, \mathbf{x}_m)$ is a Pareto optimal allocation. ■

We shall employ the symbol $\mathcal{A}$ to denote the set of all allocations, i.e.,

$$\mathcal{A} = \Big\{(\mathbf{x}_1, \mathbf{x}_2, \ldots, \mathbf{x}_m)\colon\ \mathbf{x}_i \geq \mathbf{0} \text{ for all } i = 1, 2, \ldots, m \text{ and } \sum_{i=1}^{m} \mathbf{x}_i = \omega\Big\}.$$

Clearly, $\mathcal{A}$ is a convex, closed and bounded subset (and hence, a convex and compact) subset of $(\mathcal{R}^\ell)^m$. The set of all individually rational allocations will be denoted by $\mathcal{A}_r$, i.e.,

$$\mathcal{A}_r = \{(\mathbf{x}_1, \mathbf{x}_2, \ldots, \mathbf{x}_m) \in \mathcal{A}\colon\ \mathbf{x}_i \succeq_i \omega_i \text{ for } i = 1, 2, \ldots, m\}.$$

Since $(\omega_1, \omega_2, \ldots, \omega_m) \in \mathcal{A}_r$, the set $\mathcal{A}_r$ is always non-empty.

If each preference $\succeq_i$ is continuous, then clearly $\mathcal{A}_r$ is a closed subset of $(\mathcal{R}^\ell)^m$ and hence $\mathcal{A}_r$ is a compact set. In case each preference $\succeq_i$ is convex and continuous, then the set $\mathcal{A}_r$ is a (non-empty) convex and compact subset of $(\mathcal{R}^\ell)^m$.

Continuity of preferences suffices to guarantee the existence of individually rational Pareto optimal allocations.

Theorem 1.5.3. *If in an exchange economy with a finite number of consumers each consumer has a continuous preference, then individually rational Pareto optimal allocations always exist.*

Proof. We shall denote allocations by lower case letters; for instance, $x \in \mathcal{A}$ means that $x = (\mathbf{x}_1, \mathbf{x}_2, \ldots, \mathbf{x}_m) \in \mathcal{A}$.

Start by introducing an equivalence relation $\sim$ on $\mathcal{A}_r$ by saying that $x \sim y$ whenever $\mathbf{x}_i \sim_i \mathbf{y}_i$ holds for each $i = 1, 2, \ldots, m$. You should stop and check that $\sim$ is indeed an equivalence relation on $\mathcal{A}_r$. For simplicity, we shall denote the set of all equivalence classes by $\mathcal{A}_r$ again (instead of $\mathcal{A}_r/\!\sim$).

Next, we define an order relation $\succeq$ on $\mathcal{A}_r$ by saying that $x \succeq y$ whenever $\mathbf{x}_i \succeq_i \mathbf{y}_i$ holds for each i. Since $\mathcal{A}_r$ now represents the equivalence classes, it is easy to verify that $\succeq$ is indeed an order relation.

Recall that a (non-empty) subset $\mathcal{C}$ of $\mathcal{A}_r$ is said to be a *chain* whenever every two elements of $\mathcal{C}$ are comparable, i.e., whenever $x, y \in \mathcal{C}$ implies either $x \succeq y$ or $y \succeq x$. Now let $\mathcal{C}$ be an arbitrary chain of $\mathcal{A}_r$. Then, we claim that $\mathcal{C}$ is bounded from above in $\mathcal{A}_r$, i.e., we claim that there exists some $x \in \mathcal{A}_r$ such that $x \succeq c$ holds for each $c \in \mathcal{C}$. To see this, we distinguish two cases.

CASE I: *There exists some $c_0 \in \mathcal{C}$ satisfying $c_0 \succeq c$ for each $c \in \mathcal{C}$.*

In this case, our claim is obvious.

CASE II: *For each $c \in \mathcal{C}$ there exists some $x \in \mathcal{C}$ such that $x \succ c$.*

In this case, the set $\mathcal{C}$ under $\succeq$ is a directed set, and so if we define $x_\alpha = \alpha$ for $\alpha \in \mathcal{C}$, then $\{x_\alpha\colon\ \alpha \in \mathcal{C}\}$ is a net of the compact set $\mathcal{A}_r$. Let $x \in \mathcal{A}_r$ be an accumulation point of the net $\{x_\alpha\colon\ \alpha \in \mathcal{C}\}$. Then, we claim that $x \succeq c$ holds for each $c \in \mathcal{C}$. To see this, let $c \in \mathcal{C}$ be fixed and note that for each $\alpha \succeq c$, we have $x_\alpha = \alpha \succeq c$. Since (by the continuity of preferences) the set

$$\{y \in \mathcal{A}_r\colon\ y \succeq c\} = \{y \in \mathcal{A}_r\colon\ \mathbf{y}_i \succeq_i \mathbf{c}_i \text{ for all } i = 1, 2, \ldots, m\}$$

is closed, we easily infer that $x \succeq c$ must hold for each $c \in \mathcal{C}$. Thus, $x \in \mathcal{A}_r$ is an upper bound for $\mathcal{C}$.

Now by Zorn's Lemma there exists a maximal element $x \in \mathcal{A}_r$ for $\succeq$. Since $y \in \mathcal{A}$ and $y \succeq x$ imply $y \in \mathcal{A}_r$, we see that there is no other $y \in \mathcal{A}$ satisfying $y \succ x$, and this shows that x is an individually rational Pareto optimal allocation. The proof of the theorem is now complete. ■

We now turn our attention to a very important class of allocations—the core allocations. To understand this concept, we need the idea of "improving upon an allocation." A *coalition* S of consumers is simply a non-empty subset of $A = \{1, \ldots, m\}$. We say that a coalition S **improves upon** an allocation $(\mathbf{x}_1, \mathbf{x}_2, \ldots, \mathbf{x}_m)$ whenever there exists another allocation $(\mathbf{y}_1, \mathbf{y}_2, \ldots, \mathbf{y}_m)$ such that

a) $\sum_{i \in S} \mathbf{y}_i = \sum_{i \in S} \omega_i$; and

b) $\mathbf{y}_i \succ_i \mathbf{x}_i$ holds for each $i \in S$.

That is, a coalition S improves upon an allocation if the consumers in S can redistribute their total endowment $\sum_{i \in S} \omega_i$ amongst themselves in such a way that each one of them becomes better off.

The allocations that cannot be improved upon by any coalition are known as *core allocations*.

Definition 1.5.4. *A* **core allocation** *is an allocation that cannot be improved upon by any coalition.*

The set of all core allocations of an economy $\mathcal{E}$ *is called the* **core** *of the economy and is denoted by* Core($\mathcal{E}$).

It should be noted that at a core allocation there is no incentive for agents to form coalitions and bargain for a redistribution of the social endowment.

Theorem 1.5.5. *Every core allocation is individually rational and weakly Pareto optimal.*

Proof. Let $(\mathbf{x}_1, \mathbf{x}_2, \ldots, \mathbf{x}_m)$ be a core allocation. To see that $(\mathbf{x}_1, \mathbf{x}_2, \ldots, \mathbf{x}_m)$ is individually rational, note that if $\omega_k \succ_k \mathbf{x}_k$ holds for some k, then the coalition S consisting of the $\mathrm{k^{th}}$ consumer alone (i.e., $S = \{k\}$) can improve upon the allocation. Hence, $\mathbf{x}_i \succeq_i \omega_i$ must hold for each i.

To see that $(\mathbf{x}_1, \mathbf{x}_2, \ldots, \mathbf{x}_m)$ is also weakly Pareto optimal, let $(\mathbf{y}_1, \mathbf{y}_2, \ldots, \mathbf{y}_m)$ be another allocation satisfying $\mathbf{y}_i \succ_i \mathbf{x}_i$ for each i. This means that the grand coalition $A = \{1, \ldots, m\}$ can improve upon the allocation, which is impossible. Hence, the allocation $(\mathbf{x}_1, \mathbf{x}_2, \ldots, \mathbf{x}_m)$ is also weakly Pareto optimal. ■

The best way to illustrate the various optimality properties of allocations is by employing *Edgeworth's Box*. Consider a two consumer exchange economy with commodity space $\mathcal{R}^2$. The total endowment is $\omega = \omega_1 + \omega_2$. We consider the first consumer with commodity space the xy-plane and the second consumer with commodity space the st-plane as shown in Figure 1.5-1. The point B—the origin of the st-plane—corresponds to the point ω in the xy-plane and the point A—the origin of the xy-plane—corresponds to the point ω in the st-plane. An allocation is an arbitrary point in the box determined by the x, y, s and t axis—referred to as **Edgeworth's Box**.

An arbitrary Pareto optimal allocation corresponds to a point Q in the box for which the indifference curves of the two consumers are tangent. The set of all Pareto optimal allocations—known as the **Contract Curve**—is represented in Figure 1.5-1 by the boldface curve joining the points A and B. If P denotes the initial allocation, then the points inside the shaded lens correspond to the individually rational allocations. The points on the Contract Curve inside the darkened lens correspond to the core allocations (which in this case coincide with the set of all individually rational Pareto optimal allocations). As we shall see later, the Walrasian equilibria lie on the core part of the Contract Curve.

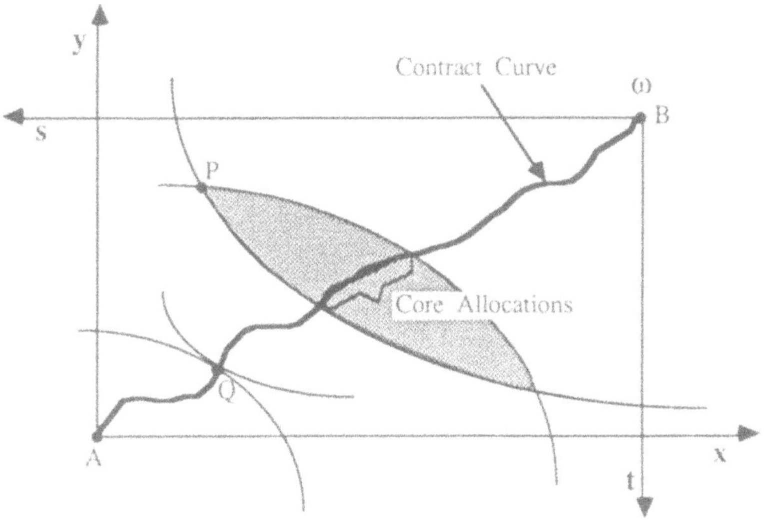

Fig. 1.5-1

To prove the existence of core allocations, we must introduce the notion of an n-person cooperative game with nontransferable utility—which we shall simply refer to as an n-person game. As we shall see, every exchange economy defines such a game. Moreover, each payoff vector in the core of the associated n-person game corresponds to a core allocation in the exchange economy. H. E. Scarf [60] showed that balanced n-person games have a non-empty core and concluded from this that neoclassical exchange economies have a non-empty core. In order to establish Scarf's core existence theorem, we need some preliminary discussion.

Fix a finite set of players $N = \{1, 2, \ldots, n\}$ and let $\mathcal{N}$ denote the set of all coalitions of N, i.e., $\mathcal{N} = \{S \subseteq N\colon\ S \neq \emptyset\}$. An *n-person game* is simply a non-empty correspondence $V\colon \mathcal{N} \longrightarrow 2^{\mathcal{R}^n}$, i.e., an n-person game is a non-empty set valued function from the set of all coalitions into the collection of all subsets of $\mathcal{R}^n$. The set $V(S)$ can be thought of as the set consisting of all payoff vectors that coalition S can attain for its members. As usual, a coalition S can *improve upon* a payoff vector $\mathbf{x} \in V(N)$ whenever there is a payoff vector $\mathbf{y} \in V(S)$ such that $y_i > x_i$ holds for all $i \in S$. The core of the game is then defined to be the set of all vectors of $V(N)$ that no coalition can improve upon. In mathematical terminology, the core is defined as follows.

Definition 1.5.6. *The* **core** *of an n-person game V is the set*

$$\mathrm{Core}(V) = V(N) \setminus \bigcup_{S \in \mathcal{N}} \mathrm{Int}V(S) = \bigcap_{S \in \mathcal{N}} \left[V(N) \setminus \mathrm{Int}V(S) \right].$$

We continue by introducing the notion of *balancedness* for an n-person game—which is due to O. N. Bondareva [17]. Recall that the symbol χ_S denotes the characteristic function of S, i.e., the function $\chi_S: \mathcal{N} \longrightarrow \mathcal{R}$ defined by $\chi_S(k) = 1$ if $k \in S$ and $\chi_S(k) = 0$ if $k \notin S$.

Definition 1.5.7. *A (non-empty) family $\mathcal{B}$ of $\mathcal{N}$ is said to be* **balanced** *whenever there exist non-negative weights $\{w_S\colon\ S \in \mathcal{B}\}$ satisfying*

$$\sum_{S \in \mathcal{B}} w_S \chi_S = \chi_N \,.$$

Equivalently, a family $\mathcal{B}$ of coalitions is balanced whenever there exist non-negative scalars $\{w_S\colon\ S \in \mathcal{B}\}$ such that

$$\sum_{\substack{S \in \mathcal{B} \\ i \in S}} w_S = 1$$

holds for each $i = 1, 2, \ldots, n$. Unfortunately, it is not easy to check whether or not a given family of coalitions is balanced. For instance, if $N = \{1, 2, 3\}$, then the families

$$\mathcal{B}_1 = \big\{\{1\}, \{2\}, \{3\}\big\} \qquad \text{and} \qquad \mathcal{B}_2 = \big\{\{1,2\}, \{2,3\}, \{1,3\}\big\}$$

are both balanced—for $\mathcal{B}_1$ take weights $\{1, 1, 1\}$ and for $\mathcal{B}_2$ take $\{\frac{1}{2}, \frac{1}{2}, \frac{1}{2}\}$—while the family $\mathcal{B}_3 = \big\{\{1\}, \{1,2\}, \{1,3\}\big\}$ is not balanced.

Definition 1.5.8. (Bondareva) *An n-person game V is said to be* **balanced** *whenever every balanced family $\mathcal{B}$ of coalitions satisfies*

$$\bigcap_{S \in \mathcal{B}} V(S) \subseteq V(N) \,.$$

We are now ready to state and prove the fundamental result of H. E. Scarf [60] concerning the existence of core allocations for certain balanced games. The elegant proof below is due to R. Vohra [66].

Theorem 1.5.9. (Scarf) *If V is a balanced n-person game such that*

a) *each $V(S)$ is closed,*

b) *each* $V(S)$ *is comprehensive from below, i.e.,* $\mathbf{x} \leq \mathbf{y}$ *and* $\mathbf{y} \in V(S)$ *imply* $\mathbf{x} \in V(S)$,
c) $\mathbf{x} \in \mathcal{R}^n$, $\mathbf{y} \in V(S)$ *and* $x_i = y_i$ *for all* $i \in S$ *imply* $\mathbf{x} \in V(S)$, *and*
d) *each* $V(S)$ *is bounded from above in* $\mathcal{R}^S$, *i.e., for each coalition* S *there exists some* $M_S > 0$ *satisfying* $x_i \leq M_S$ *for all* $\mathbf{x} \in V(S)$ *and all* $i \in S$,

then the n-person game has a non-empty core.

Proof. Consider an n-person game V that satisfies the hypotheses of our theorem. Since every "translation" of V satisfies the same properties as V (see Exercise 6 at the end of this section), replacing V by an appropriate translation, we can assume without loss of generality that $0 \in \text{Int}V(S)$ holds for each coalition S.

Next, fix some constant $c > 0$ such that for each coalition S and each $\mathbf{x} \in V(S)$ we have $x_i < c$ for all $i \in S$, and then consider the set

$$W = \Big[\bigcup_{S \in \mathcal{N}} V(S)\Big] \bigcap (-\infty, c]^n .$$

Clearly, W is a closed, comprehensive from below (i.e., $W - \mathcal{R}^n_+ = W$ holds), bounded from above in $\mathcal{R}^n$ by $\mathbf{c} = (c, c, \ldots, c)$ and contains a ball about zero; see Figure 1.5-2. In particular, the boundary ∂W of W is contained in W, i.e., $\partial W \subseteq W$ holds.

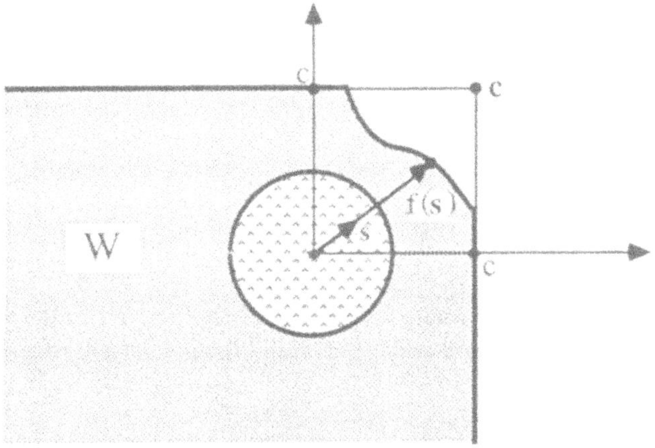

Fig. 1.5-2

The following property $(\star)$ of the set W will be employed in the proof.

If $\mathbf{x} \in \partial W$ *and* $x_r = 0$ *for some* r, *then* $x_i = c$ *also holds for some* i. $(\star)$

To see this, assume $x_r = 0$ and $x_i < c$ for each i. Since $0 \in \text{Int}V(\{r\})$, there exists some $\mathbf{y} \in V(\{r\})$ with $0 < y_r < c$. From property (c), we see that the vector $\mathbf{z}$ with $z_i = c$ for $i \neq r$ and $z_r = y_r$ belongs to $V(\{r\})$ (and hence to W) and satisfies $z_i > x_i$ for all i. This implies, $\mathbf{x} \in \text{Int}W$, a contradiction.

Now, let Δ denote the $n-1$ closed simplex. Then, we claim that for each $\mathbf{s} \in \Delta$ there exists exactly one $\alpha > 0$ such that $\alpha\mathbf{s} \in \partial W$. Indeed, if $\alpha\mathbf{s}$, $\beta\mathbf{s} \in \partial W$ satisfy $\alpha > \beta > 0$, then $\alpha\mathbf{s} > \beta\mathbf{s}$. If $s_i > 0$ holds for each i, then $\alpha s_i > \beta s_i$ for each i, and so $\beta\mathbf{s}$ is an interior point of W, a contradiction. On the other hand, if $s_i = 0$ holds for some i, then by property $(\star)$, there exists some r with $\beta s_r = c$, and so $\alpha s_r > \beta s_r = c$ which implies $\alpha\mathbf{s} \notin W$, a contradiction. Thus, there exists at most one $\alpha > 0$ with $\alpha\mathbf{s} \in \partial W$. To see that there exists such an $\alpha > 0$, let $\alpha = \sup\{\beta > 0\colon\ \beta\mathbf{s} \in W\}$, and note that $\alpha\mathbf{s} \in \partial W \cap \mathcal{R}^n_+$.

Thus, a function $f\colon \Delta \longrightarrow \partial W \cap \mathcal{R}^n_+$ can be defined by the formula

$$f(\mathbf{s}) = \alpha\mathbf{s}, \ \text{ where } \alpha = \sup\{\beta > 0\colon\ \beta\mathbf{s} \in W\}.$$

It turns out that the function f is continuous. To see this, it suffices (by Theorem 1.3.7) to show that f has a closed graph. So, let $\mathbf{s}_m \to \mathbf{s}$ in Δ and $f(\mathbf{s}_m) \to \mathbf{y}$ in $\mathcal{R}^n$. Write $f(\mathbf{s}_m) = \alpha_m\mathbf{s}_m \in \partial W$. Then, $\alpha_m = \|\alpha_m\mathbf{s}_m\|_1 = \|f(\mathbf{s}_m)\|_1 \to \|\mathbf{y}\|_1$, and so $f(\mathbf{s}_m) = \alpha_m\mathbf{s}_m \to \|\mathbf{y}\|_1\mathbf{s} = \mathbf{y}$. Since ∂W is a closed set, we see that $\mathbf{y} = \|\mathbf{y}\|_1\mathbf{s} \in \partial W$. By the above discussion, $f(\mathbf{s}) = \mathbf{y}$, and so f has a closed graph.

For each coalition S let $\mathbf{e}_S$ denote the vector of $\mathcal{R}^n$ whose i[th] coordinate is 1 if $i \in S$ and 0 otherwise, and let $|S|$ denote the number of elements of S. Define a correspondence $\psi\colon \Delta \longrightarrow 2^\Delta$ by

$$\psi(\mathbf{s}) = \left\{\frac{\mathbf{e}_S}{|S|}\colon\ S \in \mathcal{N} \ \text{ and } \ f(\mathbf{s}) \in V(S)\right\}.$$

Since $f(\mathbf{s}) \in \partial W \subseteq \bigcup_{S\in\mathcal{N}} V(S)$, it follows immediately that $\psi(\mathbf{s})$ is a non-empty subset of Δ. In addition, ψ has a closed graph. To see this, let $\mathbf{s}_m \to \mathbf{s}$ in Δ, $\mathbf{y}_m \in \psi(\mathbf{s}_m)$ for all m and $\mathbf{y}_m \to \mathbf{y}$ in $\mathcal{R}^n$. Since the range of ψ (i.e., the set $\bigcup_{\mathbf{s}\in\Delta}\psi(\mathbf{s})$) is a finite set, we see that the sequence $\{\mathbf{y}_m\}$ must be eventually constant. Hence, there exists some m_0 such that $\mathbf{y}_m = \mathbf{y}$ holds for all $m \geq m_0$, and so $\mathbf{y} \in \psi(\mathbf{s}_m)$ for all $m \geq m_0$. Therefore, there exists some coalition S such that $\mathbf{y} = \frac{\mathbf{e}_S}{|S|}$ and $f(\mathbf{s}_m) \in V(S)$ for all $m \geq m_0$. Since f is continuous and $V(S)$ is a closed set, we infer that $f(\mathbf{s}) \in V(S)$. Therefore, $\mathbf{y} \in \psi(\mathbf{s})$, and so ψ has a closed graph. The latter conclusion easily implies that the convex hull correspondence of ψ, i.e., the correspondence $\mathbf{s} \mapsto \mathrm{co}\psi(\mathbf{s})$, has likewise a closed graph; see Exercise 7 at the end of this section.

Now define the function $g\colon \Delta \times \Delta \longrightarrow \Delta$ by

$$g(\mathbf{s},\mathbf{t}) = \left(\frac{s_1+(t_1-\frac{1}{n})^+}{1+\sum_{i=1}^n(t_i-\frac{1}{n})^+}, \frac{s_2+(t_2-\frac{1}{n})^+}{1+\sum_{i=1}^n(t_i-\frac{1}{n})^+}, \ldots, \frac{s_n+(t_n-\frac{1}{n})^+}{1+\sum_{i=1}^n(t_i-\frac{1}{n})^+}\right),$$

where, as usual, $r^+ = \max\{r, 0\}$ for each real number r. Clearly, g is a continuous function. Finally, consider the correspondence $\phi\colon \Delta \times \Delta \longrightarrow 2^{\Delta\times\Delta}$ defined by

$$\phi(\mathbf{s},\mathbf{t}) = \{g(\mathbf{s},\mathbf{t})\} \times \mathrm{co}\psi(\mathbf{s}).$$

Note that ϕ is non-empty and convex-valued and has a closed graph. Thus, by Kakutani's fixed point theorem (Theorem 1.4.7), ϕ has a fixed point, say $(\mathbf{s},\mathbf{t})$. That is, the point $(\mathbf{s},\mathbf{t}) \in \Delta \times \Delta$ satisfies

$$\mathbf{s} = g(\mathbf{s},\mathbf{t}) \quad \text{and} \quad \mathbf{t} \in \mathrm{co}\psi(\mathbf{s}).$$

Keep in mind that $\mathbf{t} \in \text{co}\psi(\mathbf{s})$ means that $\mathbf{t}$ is a convex combination of the form

$$\mathbf{t} = \sum_{S \in \mathcal{T}} \lambda_S \frac{\mathbf{e}_S}{|S|}, \quad \text{where} \quad \mathcal{T} = \{S \in \mathcal{N}\colon\ f(\mathbf{s}) \in V(S)\}. \tag{$\star\star$}$$

From $\mathbf{s} = g(\mathbf{s}, \mathbf{t})$, we see that

$$s_i\Big[\sum_{i=1}^{n} (t_i - \tfrac{1}{n})^+\Big] = \big(t_i - \tfrac{1}{n}\big)^+ \quad \text{for} \quad i = 1, \dots, n. \tag{$\star\star\star$}$$

We shall prove that $t_i = \frac{1}{n}$ holds for each i. For this, it suffices to show that $\big(t_i - \frac{1}{n}\big)^+ = 0$ holds for each i—indeed, if this is the case, then $t_i \le \frac{1}{n}$ must hold for each i and the equalities follow from $1 = \sum_{i=1}^n t_i \le \sum_{i=1}^n \frac{1}{n} = 1$.

In order to establish that $t_i = \frac{1}{n}$ holds for each i, assume by way of contradiction that $\sum_{i=1}^n \big(t_i - \frac{1}{n}\big)^+ > 0$. From ($\star\star\star$), we see that

$$I = \{i \in N\colon\ s_i > 0\} = \{i \in N\colon\ t_i > \tfrac{1}{n}\}$$

and

$$J = \{i \in N\colon\ s_i = 0\} = \{i \in N\colon\ t_i \le \tfrac{1}{n}\}.$$

Note that both coalitions I and J are non-empty. Indeed, from $\sum_{i=1}^n \big(t_i - \frac{1}{n}\big)^+ > 0$, it follows that $\big(t_i - \frac{1}{n}\big)^+ > 0$ for some i, i.e., $t_i > \frac{1}{n}$ for some i, and so $I \ne \emptyset$. On the other hand, if $t_i > \frac{1}{n}$ holds for each i, then $1 = \sum_{i=1}^n t_i > \sum_{i=1}^n \frac{1}{n} = 1$ should also hold, which is absurd, and so $J \ne \emptyset$. Clearly, $\mathbf{x} = f(\mathbf{s}) \in \partial W$. Now for $i \in I$ (i.e., for $t_i > \frac{1}{n} > 0$), it follows from ($\star\star$) that there exists some coalition S with $i \in S$ and $\mathbf{x} = f(\mathbf{s}) \in V(S)$, and so by the choice of the constant c, we must have $x_i < c$. For $r \in J$ (i.e, for $s_r = 0$), it follows—in view of $\mathbf{x} = f(\mathbf{s}) = \alpha\mathbf{s}$—that $x_r = 0$. However, this contradicts ($\star$), and hence $\mathbf{t} = \sum_{S \in \mathcal{T}} \lambda_S \frac{\mathbf{e}_S}{|S|} = \big(\frac{1}{n}, \frac{1}{n}, \dots, \frac{1}{n}\big) = \frac{1}{n}\mathbf{e}_{\mathcal{N}}$ holds.

Letting $w_S = n\lambda_S$, the latter expression for $\mathbf{t}$ implies that

$$\sum_{S \in \mathcal{T}} w_S \chi_S = \chi_N\,.$$

Consequently, the family $\mathcal{T} = \{S \in \mathcal{N}\colon\ f(\mathbf{s}) \in V(S)\}$—see ($\star\star$)—is a balanced family. Since the game is balanced, we infer that $\bigcap_{S \in \mathcal{T}} V(S) \subseteq V(N)$, and therefore the vector $\mathbf{x} = f(\mathbf{s}) \in V(N)$. To finish the proof, we shall establish that the vector $\mathbf{x}$ belongs to Core(V).

To see this, assume by way of contradiction that there exists some coalition S such that $\mathbf{x} \in \text{Int}V(S)$. Since $\mathbf{x} \in V(N)$, it follows from the choice of c that $x_i < c$ holds for each i. Now an easy argument shows that $\mathbf{x} \in \text{Int}W$, contrary to $\mathbf{x} = f(\mathbf{s}) \in \partial W$. Thus, $\mathbf{x} \notin \text{Int}V(S)$ for each coalition S, and consequently $\mathbf{x} \in \text{Core}(V)$. The proof of the theorem is now complete. ■

We are now ready to demonstrate that exchange economies have core allocations. The result is due to H. E. Scarf [60].

Theorem 1.5.10. (Scarf) *Every exchange economy whose consumers' preferences are represented by continuous and quasi-concave utility functions has a non-empty compact core.*

Proof. Consider an exchange economy with m consumers such that the preference of each consumer $\succeq_i$ is represented by a continuous quasi-concave utility function u_i. The proof consists of two steps.

STEP I: *The core is non-empty.*

To establish this claim, we define an m-person game V by

$$V(S) = \Big\{(x_1, \ldots, x_m) \in \mathcal{R}^m\colon \text{ There exists an allocation } (\mathbf{y}_1, \ldots, \mathbf{y}_m) \text{ with } \sum_{i\in S} \mathbf{y}_i = \sum_{i\in S} \omega_i \text{ and } x_i \le u_i(\mathbf{y}_i) \text{ for each } i \in S\Big\}.$$

We claim that the m-person game V satisfies the properties listed in Theorem 1.5.9.

To see this, note that properties (b) and (c) are trivially true and (d) follows immediately from the fact that each utility function u_i (as a continuous function) is bounded on the compact set $[\mathbf{0}, \omega]$. The closedness of the sets $V(S)$ needs some checking.

Assume that a sequence $\{(x_1^n, \ldots, x_m^n)\} \subseteq V(S)$ satisfies $(x_1^n \ldots, x_m^n) \longrightarrow (x_1, \ldots, x_m)$ in $\mathcal{R}^m$. For each n pick some allocation $(\mathbf{y}_1^n, \ldots, \mathbf{y}_m^n)$ such that $\sum_{i\in S} \mathbf{y}_i^n = \sum_{i\in S} \omega_i$ and $x_i^n \le u_i(\mathbf{y}_i^n)$ for each $i \in S$. Since the set $\mathcal{A}$ of all allocations is a compact set, we can assume (by passing to a subsequence and relabelling) that $(\mathbf{y}_1^n, \ldots, \mathbf{y}_m^n) \longrightarrow (\mathbf{y}_1, \ldots, \mathbf{y}_m) \in \mathcal{A}$. Clearly, $\sum_{i\in S} \mathbf{y}_i = \sum_{i\in S} \omega_i$ and by the continuity of the utility functions, we see that $x_i \le u_i(\mathbf{y}_i)$ for each $i \in S$. This shows that $(x_1, \ldots, x_m) \in V(S)$, and so every set $V(S)$ is a closed set.

Next, we show that the m-person game V is balanced. To this end, let $\mathcal{B}$ be a balanced family of coalitions with weights $\{\lambda_S\colon\ S \in \mathcal{B}\}$, and let $(x_1, \ldots, x_m)$ belong to $\bigcap_{S\in\mathcal{B}} V(S)$. We have to show that $(x_1, \ldots, x_m) \in V(\{1, \ldots, m\})$.

To see this, put $\mathcal{B}_i = \{S \in \mathcal{B}\colon\ i \in S\}$ and let $S \in \mathcal{B}$. Since $(x_1, \ldots, x_m)$ belongs to $V(S)$, there exists an allocation $(\mathbf{y}_1^S, \ldots, \mathbf{y}_m^S)$ satisfying $\sum_{i\in S} \mathbf{y}_i^S = \sum_{i\in S} \omega_i$ and $x_i \le u_i(\mathbf{y}_i^S)$ for all $i \in S$. Now let

$$\mathbf{y}_i = \sum_{S\in\mathcal{B}_i} \lambda_S \mathbf{y}_i^S, \quad \text{for} \quad i = 1, 2, \ldots, m.$$

Since each $\mathbf{y}_i$ is a convex combination, it follows from the quasi-concavity of u_i that $x_i \le u_i(\mathbf{y}_i)$ holds for each i. Moreover, we have

$$\begin{aligned}\sum_{i=1}^m \mathbf{y}_i &= \sum_{i=1}^m \sum_{S\in\mathcal{B}_i} \lambda_S \mathbf{y}_i^S = \sum_{S\in\mathcal{B}} \lambda_S \Big(\sum_{i\in S} \mathbf{y}_i^S\Big) = \sum_{S\in\mathcal{B}} \lambda_S \Big(\sum_{i\in S} \omega_i\Big)\\ &= \sum_{i=1}^m \Big(\sum_{S\in\mathcal{B}_i} \lambda_S\Big)\omega_i = \sum_{i=1}^m \omega_i = \omega,\end{aligned}$$

which proves that $(x_1, \ldots, x_m) \in V(\{1, \ldots, m\})$, as desired.

Now, Theorem 1.5.9 guarantees that the m-person game has a non-empty core. Pick $(x_1, \ldots, x_m) \in \text{Core}(V)$ and let $(\mathbf{x}_1, \ldots, \mathbf{x}_m)$ be an allocation satisfying $x_i \leq u_i(\mathbf{x}_i)$ for each i. To finish the proof of this step, we shall establish that $(\mathbf{x}_1, \ldots, \mathbf{x}_m)$ is a core allocation for the economy.

For this, assume by way of contradiction that there is an allocation $(\mathbf{y}_1, \ldots, \mathbf{y}_m)$ and a coalition S satisfying $\sum_{i \in S} \mathbf{y}_i = \sum_{i \in S} \omega_i$ and $u_i(\mathbf{y}_i) > u_i(\mathbf{x}_i) \geq x_i$ for each $i \in S$. The latter, coupled with the continuity of the utility functions, shows that $(x_1, \ldots, x_m)$ belongs to $\text{Int}V(S)$ which contradicts

$$(x_1, \ldots, x_m) \in \text{Core}(V) = V(N) \setminus \bigcup_{S \in \mathcal{N}} \text{Int}V(S).$$

Hence, $(\mathbf{x}_1, \ldots, \mathbf{x}_m)$ is a core allocation.

STEP II: *The core is a compact set.*

Denote by $\mathcal{C}$ the (non-empty) set of all core allocations. Clearly, $\mathcal{C}$ is a subset of the compact set $\mathcal{A}$, and hence the closure of $\mathcal{C}$ is also a compact set. To see that $\mathcal{C}$ is closed, let $(\mathbf{x}_1, \ldots, \mathbf{x}_m)$ be an allocation lying in the closure of $\mathcal{C}$, and assume by way of contradiction that there exist an allocation $(\mathbf{y}_1, \ldots, \mathbf{y}_m)$ and a coalition S of consumers satisfying

$$\sum_{i \in S} \mathbf{y}_i = \sum_{i \in S} \omega_i \quad \text{and} \quad \mathbf{y}_i \succ_i \mathbf{x}_i \quad \text{for all} \quad i \in S.$$

For each $i \in S$, the set of allocations

$$U_i = \{(\mathbf{z}_1, \ldots, \mathbf{z}_m) \in \mathcal{A}\colon\ \mathbf{z}_i \succeq_i \mathbf{y}_i\}$$

is a closed subset of $(\mathcal{R}^\ell)^m$. Thus, the set $U = \bigcup_{i \in S} U_i$ is a closed subset of $(\mathcal{R}^\ell)^m$, and so its complement U^c is open. From $(\mathbf{x}_1, \ldots, \mathbf{x}_m) \in U^c$, we see that $U^c \cap \mathcal{C} \neq \emptyset$. Now if $(\mathbf{z}_1, \ldots, \mathbf{z}_m) \in U^c \cap \mathcal{C}$, then we have

$$\sum_{i \in S} \mathbf{y}_i = \sum_{i \in S} \omega_i \quad \text{and} \quad \mathbf{y}_i \succ_i \mathbf{z}_i \quad \text{for all} \quad i \in S,$$

which contradicts the fact that $(\mathbf{z}_1, \ldots, \mathbf{z}_m)$ is a core allocation. Hence, $(\mathbf{x}_1, \ldots, \mathbf{x}_m)$ belongs to $\mathcal{C}$, and so $\mathcal{C}$ is closed. The proof of the theorem is now complete. ■

EXERCISES

1. This exercise presents an alternate proof of the existence of individually rational Pareto optimal allocations (Theorem 1.5.3).

Assume that in an exchange economy with a finite number of consumers each preference $\succeq_i$ is represented by a continuous utility function u_i. Fix m positive real numbers $\lambda_1, \lambda_2, \ldots, \lambda_m$ and consider the function $U: (\mathcal{R}^\ell_+)^m \longrightarrow \mathcal{R}$ defined by

$$U(\mathbf{x}_1, \mathbf{x}_2, \ldots, \mathbf{x}_m) = \sum_{i=1}^{m} \lambda_i u_i(\mathbf{x}_i).$$

a) Show that U has a maximal element in $\mathcal{A}_r$—the non-empty compact set of all individually rational allocations.

b) Show that every maximal element of U in $\mathcal{A}_r$ is an individually rational Pareto optimal allocation—and hence, individually rational Pareto optimal allocations exist.

2. This exercise demonstrates the existence of individually rational weakly Pareto optimal allocations. Consider an exchange economy with a finite number of agents such that each preference $\succeq_i$ is represented by a continuous utility function u_i. Define the function $V: (\mathcal{R}^\ell_+)^m \longrightarrow \mathcal{R}$ by

$$V(\mathbf{x}_1, \mathbf{x}_2, \ldots, \mathbf{x}_m) = \min\{u_1(\mathbf{x}_1), u_2(\mathbf{x}_2), \ldots, u_m(\mathbf{x}_m)\}.$$

a) Show that V is a continuous function.

b) Show that V has a maximal element in the non-empty compact set $\mathcal{A}_r$ of all individually rational allocations.

c) Show that every maximal element of V in $\mathcal{A}_r$ is an individually rational weakly Pareto optimal allocation—and hence, individually rational weakly Pareto optimal allocations exist.

d) Show that if each u_i is concave, then V is likewise concave.

e) If each u_i is quasi-concave is V likewise quasi-concave?

3. If V is an n-person game and $V(N)$ is closed, then show that Core(V) is a closed set. If Core(V) is a closed set, is $V(N)$ necessarily a closed set?

4. Consider the 3-person game $V: \mathcal{N} \longrightarrow \mathcal{R}^3$ defined by

$$\begin{aligned} V(\{1\}) = V(\{1,2\}) &= \{(x,y,z) \in \mathcal{R}^3:\ x \le 1\}, \\ V(\{2\}) = V(\{2,3\}) &= \{(x,y,z) \in \mathcal{R}^3:\ y \le 1\}, \\ V(\{3\}) = V(\{1,3\}) &= \{(x,y,z) \in \mathcal{R}^3:\ z \le 1\}, \ \text{and} \\ V(\{1,2,3\}) &= \{(x,y,z) \in \mathcal{R}^3:\ x^2 + y^2 + z^2 \le 3\}. \end{aligned}$$

Find the core of the game. *Answer*: Core(V) $= \{(1,1,1)\}$

5. Consider the 2-person game $V:\mathcal{N} \longrightarrow \mathcal{R}^2$ defined by

$$V(\{1\}) = \{(x,y) \in \mathcal{R}^2\colon\ x \le 1\}\,,$$
$$V(\{2\}) = \{(x,y) \in \mathcal{R}^2\colon\ y \le \tfrac{1}{2}\}\,,\ \text{ and}$$
$$V(\{1,2\}) = \big\{(x,y) \in \mathcal{R}^2\colon\ x < 4 \ \text{ and } \ y \le \tfrac{x-3}{x-4}\big\}\,.$$

a) Show that V is a balanced game satisfying the hypotheses of Scarf's theorem (Theorem 1.5.9)—and hence its core is non-empty.
b) Determine the core of the game.
Answer: $\text{Core}(V) = \Big\{(x, \tfrac{x-3}{x-4})\colon\ 1 \le x \le 2\Big\}$

6. Let V be an n-person game. If $\mathbf{a} \in \mathcal{R}^n$ is a fixed vector, then define the $\mathbf{a}$-*translate n-person game* $V_\mathbf{a}$ *of* V by

$$V_\mathbf{a}(S) = \mathbf{a} + V(S)\,.$$

Establish the following properties of the translate games of V.
a) If some $V(S)$ is a closed set, then $V_\mathbf{a}(S)$ is likewise a closed set.
b) If some $V(S)$ is comprehensive from below (i.e., if $V(S) - \mathcal{R}^n_+ = V(S)$), then $V_\mathbf{a}(S)$ is also comprehensive from below.
c) Assume that for some coalition S the set $V(S)$ satisfies the following property: $\mathbf{x} \in V(S)$, $\mathbf{y} \in \mathcal{R}^n$ and $x_i = y_i$ for each $i \in S$ imply $\mathbf{y} \in V(S)$. Then $V_\mathbf{a}(S)$ satisfies the same property.
d) The n-person game V is balanced if and only if the n-person game $V_\mathbf{a}$ is balanced.
e) $\text{Core}(V_\mathbf{a}) = \mathbf{a} + \text{Core}(V)$—and so, conclude that the n-person game $V_\mathbf{a}$ has a non-empty core if and only if the n-person game V has a non-empty core.

7. Prove the following result regarding correspondences that was invoked in the proof of Theorem 1.5.9. Assume that $\mathcal{F}$ is a non-empty finite subset of $\mathcal{R}^n$ and that $\psi\colon \Delta \longrightarrow \mathcal{F}$ is a non-empty valued correspondence. If ψ has a closed graph, then show that its convex hull correspondence $\mathbf{s} \mapsto \text{co}\psi(\mathbf{s})$ likewise has a closed graph.
[HINT: Let $\mathbf{s}_m \longrightarrow \mathbf{s}$ in Δ, $\mathbf{y}_m \longrightarrow \mathbf{y}$ in $\mathcal{R}^n$ and $\mathbf{y}_m \in \text{co}\psi(\mathbf{s}_m)$ for each m. Since $\mathcal{F}$ is a finite set, there exists a subset Φ of $\mathcal{F}$ such that $\psi(\mathbf{s}_m) = \Phi$ holds for infinitely many m. On the other hand, if $\mathbf{a} \in \psi(\mathbf{s}_m)$ holds for infinitely many m, then it follows from the closedness of ψ that $\mathbf{a} \in \psi(\mathbf{s})$. This implies $\mathbf{y}_m \in \text{co}\Phi \subseteq \text{co}\psi(\mathbf{s})$ for infinitely many m, and hence $\mathbf{y} \in \text{co}\psi(\mathbf{s})$.]

1.6. OPTIMALITY AND DECENTRALIZATION

The classical intuition, that decentralized competitive markets produce out of the self-interested behavior of economic agents an optimal distribution of resources, dates back at least to Adam Smith's "invisible hand." This intuition is made precise in the two welfare theorems of K. J. Arrow [11] and G. Debreu [22].

If market prices are equilibrium prices, i.e., prices at which all markets clear, then the quantities demanded by households, at these prices, constitute an allocation. Such allocations are called Walrasian (or competitive) equilibria. Competitive allocations are realized in a decentralized and non-cooperative manner, since each consumer's demand derives from utility maximization subject only to her budget constraint—without knowledge of the demands or concern for the tastes of other consumers. In this setting, prices serve as signals of scarcity and agents interact with the market rather than with each other as in the bargaining, implicit in both the core and Pareto optimality. It is therefore quite surprising that every competitive allocation is Pareto optimal (the first welfare theorem) and that every Pareto optimal allocation can be achieved in a decentralized fashion as a competitive allocation—subject to income transfers—(the second welfare theorem). Here we have used Arrow's formulation of the welfare theorems for economies with a finite number of agents and commodities. An equivalent formulation for economies with a finite number of agents but with an infinite dimensional commodity space can be found in G. Debreu's pioneering paper [22].

What about the core? Here the results are even more striking. Every Walrasian allocation is in the core (a stronger version of the first welfare theorem) and "in the limit" only core allocations are Walrasian. The latter theorem is called a core equivalence theorem in the economics literature, and was originally proven by F. Y. Edgeworth [26] for an exchange economy with two goods and identical agents. Edgeworth's model is the first economic model that uses a potential infinity of consumers to express the notion of perfect competition, where each household has a negligible influence in determining equilibrium prices. An extensive discussion of Edgeworth's notion of optimally allocating resources by bargaining and cooperation between individuals and Walras' concept of efficiently allocating resources by a decentralized price system can be found in [32].

Edgeworth's construction was elegantly extended by G. Debreu and H. E. Scarf [24] to arbitrary exchange economies, using the notion of replicas of a given economy which formalizes the idea of "in the limit." H. E. Scarf in his paper [60] on the nonemptiness of the core for an n-person game observed that his result together with the Debreu–Scarf core equivalence theorem provides a new proof of the existence of Walrasian equilibria—a proof independent of the notions of demand and supply functions. The major results of this section are the welfare theorems and H. E. Scarf's proof of the existence of Walrasian equilibria in exchange economies.

Definition 1.6.1. *An allocation* $(\mathbf{x}_1, \ldots, \mathbf{x}_m)$ *in an exchange economy is said to be:*

a) *A* **Walrasian** *(or a* **competitive***)* **equilibrium***; whenever there exists some price* $\mathbf{p} \neq \mathbf{0}$ *such that* $\mathbf{x}_i \in \mathcal{B}_i(\mathbf{p}) = \{\mathbf{x} \in \mathcal{R}^\ell_+ \colon\ \mathbf{p}\cdot\mathbf{x} \leq \mathbf{p}\cdot\omega_i\}$ *and*

$$\mathbf{x} \succ_i \mathbf{x}_i \quad \textit{implies} \quad \mathbf{p}\cdot\mathbf{x} > \mathbf{p}\cdot\omega_i\,,$$

or equivalently, whenever $\mathbf{x}_i$ *is a maximal element in the budget set* $\mathcal{B}_i(\mathbf{p})$ *for each* i.

b) *A* **quasiequilibrium***; whenever there exists some price* $\mathbf{p} \neq \mathbf{0}$ *such that*

$$\mathbf{x} \succeq_i \mathbf{x}_i \quad \textit{implies} \quad \mathbf{p}\cdot\mathbf{x} \geq \mathbf{p}\cdot\omega_i\,.$$

Any non-zero price satisfying (b) above is referred to as a price *supporting the quasiequilibrium.* If every consumer has an extremely desirable bundle, then a Walrasian equilibrium is necessarily a quasiequilibrium. To see this, assume that each consumer i has an extremely desirable bundle $\mathbf{v}_i$ and let $(\mathbf{x}_1, \ldots, \mathbf{x}_m)$ be a Walrasian equilibrium. Pick some price $\mathbf{p} \neq \mathbf{0}$ such that $\mathbf{x} \succ_i \mathbf{x}_i$ implies $\mathbf{p}\cdot\mathbf{x} > \mathbf{p}\cdot\omega_i$. Then, $\mathbf{x} \succeq_i \mathbf{x}_i$ implies $\mathbf{x} + \varepsilon\mathbf{v}_i \succ_i \mathbf{x}_i$ and so

$$\mathbf{p}\cdot\mathbf{x} + \varepsilon\mathbf{p}\cdot\mathbf{v}_i = \mathbf{p}\cdot(\mathbf{x} + \varepsilon\mathbf{v}_i) > \mathbf{p}\cdot\omega_i$$

holds for all $\varepsilon > 0$. This implies $\mathbf{p}\cdot\mathbf{x} \geq \mathbf{p}\cdot\omega_i$, which shows that $(\mathbf{x}_1, \ldots, \mathbf{x}_m)$ is a quasiequilibrium.

As the next example shows, a quasiequilibrium need not be a Walrasian equilibrium.

Example 1.6.2. Consider the exchange economy with commodity space $\mathcal{R}^2$ and two consumers with the following characteristics.

Consumer 1: Initial endowment $\omega_1 = (\frac{1}{2}, 0)$ and utility function $u_1(x,y) = x + y$.

Consumer 2: Initial endowment $\omega_2 = (\frac{1}{2}, 1)$ and utility function $u_2(x,y) = y$.

Clearly, the bundle $(1,1)$ is extremely desirable by both consumers. We claim that the allocation $(\mathbf{x}_1, \mathbf{x}_2)$, where

$$\mathbf{x}_1 = (1,0) \quad \text{and} \quad \mathbf{x}_2 = (0,1)\,,$$

is a quasiequilibrium. To see this, consider the price $\mathbf{p} = (0,1)$ and note that

1) $u_1(\mathbf{x}) = u_1(x,y) \geq u_1(1,0)$ implies $\mathbf{p}\cdot\mathbf{x} = y \geq 0 = \mathbf{p}\cdot\omega_1$; and
2) $u_2(\mathbf{x}) = u_2(x,y) = y \geq u_2(0,1) = 1$ implies $\mathbf{p}\cdot\mathbf{x} = y \geq \mathbf{p}\cdot\omega_2 = 1$.

Therefore, $(\mathbf{x}_1, \mathbf{x}_2)$ is a quasiequilibrium.

However, $(\mathbf{x}_1, \mathbf{x}_2)$ is not a Walrasian equilibrium. To establish this claim, assume by way of contradiction that there exists some non-zero price $\mathbf{p} = (p_1, p_2)$ such that $\mathbf{x} \succ_i \mathbf{x}_i$ implies $\mathbf{p}\cdot\mathbf{x} > \mathbf{p}\cdot\omega_i$. In particular, $u_2(x,y) = y > u_2(0,1) = 1$ implies $p_2 y > \frac{p_1}{2} + p_2$. It follows that $p_2 \geq \frac{p_1}{2} + p_2$ and so $p_1 \leq 0$. On the other hand, we have $(1,0) \succ_1 \omega_1$ and $\mathbf{p}\cdot(1,0) = p_1 > \mathbf{p}\cdot\omega_1 = \frac{1}{2}p_1$, which is a contradiction. Hence, $(\mathbf{x}_1, \mathbf{x}_2)$ is not a Walrasian equilibrium. ■

A Walrasian equilibrium is always a Pareto optimal allocation. This result is known as the first welfare theorem and is due to K. J. Arrow [11].

Theorem 1.6.3. (Arrow) *If in an exchange economy preferences are strictly convex, then every Walrasian equilibrium allocation is Pareto optimal.*

Proof. Let $(\mathbf{x}_1, \ldots, \mathbf{x}_m)$ be a Walrasian equilibrium allocation with respect to a price $\mathbf{p}$. Assume that there is another allocation $(\mathbf{y}_1, \ldots, \mathbf{y}_m)$ such that $\mathbf{y}_i \succeq_i \mathbf{x}_i$ holds for all i and $\mathbf{y}_i \succ_i \mathbf{x}_i$ for at least one i. Clearly, $\mathbf{p}\cdot\mathbf{y}_i > \mathbf{p}\cdot\omega_i \geq \mathbf{p}\cdot\mathbf{x}_i$ holds for at least one i. From $\omega = \sum_{i=1}^m \mathbf{x}_i = \sum_{i=1}^m \mathbf{y}_i$, we have

$$\mathbf{p}\cdot\omega = \sum_{i=1}^{m} \mathbf{p}\cdot\mathbf{x}_i = \sum_{i=1}^{m} \mathbf{p}\cdot\mathbf{y}_i\,.$$

Therefore, $\mathbf{p}\cdot\mathbf{y}_k < \mathbf{p}\cdot\mathbf{x}_k$ must hold for at least one k and thus $\mathbf{y}_k \neq \mathbf{x}_k$. It then follows from the strict convexity of the preferences that $\frac{1}{2}\mathbf{y}_k + \frac{1}{2}\mathbf{x}_k \succ_k \mathbf{x}_k$ holds. Therefore, we have

$$\tfrac{1}{2}\mathbf{p}\cdot\mathbf{y}_k + \tfrac{1}{2}\mathbf{p}\cdot\mathbf{x}_k > \mathbf{p}\cdot\omega_k \geq \mathbf{p}\cdot\mathbf{x}_k.$$

From this, we see $\frac{1}{2}\mathbf{p}\cdot\mathbf{y}_k > \frac{1}{2}\mathbf{p}\cdot\mathbf{x}_k$ holds and so, we have $\mathbf{p}\cdot\mathbf{y}_k > \mathbf{p}\cdot\mathbf{x}_k$, which is impossible. Therefore, the allocation $(\mathbf{x}_1, \ldots, \mathbf{x}_m)$ is Pareto optimal. ■

The above proof of the first welfare theorem is deceptively simple and seems to depend only on the definitions of Walrasian equilibrium and Pareto optimality; but this proof does not carry over to the overlapping generations model which has a countable infinity of households.

The basic distinction between Walrasian equilibria and quasiequilibria is the income each agent has at the supporting prices. At a quasiequilibrium some agents may have zero income at the supporting prices. If at a quasiequilibrium every agent has positive income, then the quasiequilibrium is, in fact, a Walrasian equilibrium (why?).

Two basic properties of supporting prices are included in the next result.

Theorem 1.6.4. *For a price* $\mathbf{p}$ *supporting a quasiequilibrium* $(\mathbf{x}_1, \ldots, \mathbf{x}_m)$ *the following statements hold:*

a) $\mathbf{p}\cdot\mathbf{x}_i = \mathbf{p}\cdot\omega_i$ *for each* i*; and*
b) *if one preference is monotone, then* $\mathbf{p} \geq \mathbf{0}$.

Proof. Let $(\mathbf{x}_1, \ldots, \mathbf{x}_m)$ be a quasiequilibrium in an exchange economy supported by a price $\mathbf{p}$.

(a) Observe that $\mathbf{x}_i \succeq_i \mathbf{x}_i$ implies $\mathbf{p}\cdot\mathbf{x}_i \geq \mathbf{p}\cdot\omega_i$ for each i. From

$$\sum_{i=1}^{m} \mathbf{x}_i = \sum_{i=1}^{m} \omega_i = \omega\,,$$

we see that $\sum_{i=1}^{m} \mathbf{p}\cdot\mathbf{x}_i = \sum_{i=1}^{m} \mathbf{p}\cdot\omega_i$, and so $\mathbf{p}\cdot\mathbf{x}_i = \mathbf{p}\cdot\omega_i$ must hold for each i.
(b) Assume that $\succeq_1$ is monotone. To see that the price $\mathbf{p}$ is a positive vector, let $\mathbf{x}\geq\mathbf{0}$. Then, by the monotonicity of $\succeq_1$, we have $\mathbf{x}_1+\mathbf{x}\succeq_1\mathbf{x}_1$, and therefore $\mathbf{p}\cdot\mathbf{x}_1+\mathbf{p}\cdot\mathbf{x}=\mathbf{p}\cdot(\mathbf{x}_1+\mathbf{x})\geq\mathbf{p}\cdot\omega_1$. Since, from part (a) we have $\mathbf{p}\cdot\mathbf{x}_1=\mathbf{p}\cdot\omega_1$, it follows that $\mathbf{p}\cdot\mathbf{x}\geq 0$. ■

In terms of supportability properties, the Walrasian equilibria in exchange economies with strictly monotone preferences are characterized as follows.

Theorem 1.6.5. *If in an exchange economy preferences are strictly monotone, then for an allocation* $(\mathbf{x}_1,\ldots,\mathbf{x}_m)$ *and a non-zero price* $\mathbf{p}$ *the following statements are equivalent:*
1) *Each* $\mathbf{x}_i$ *is a maximal element in the budget set*

$$\mathcal{B}_i(\mathbf{p})=\{\mathbf{x}\in\mathcal{R}^{\ell}_{+}\colon\ \mathbf{p}\cdot\mathbf{x}\leq\mathbf{p}\cdot\omega_i\}\,.$$

2) $\mathbf{p}\gg\mathbf{0}$ *and* $\mathbf{x}\succ_i\mathbf{x}_i$ *implies* $\mathbf{p}\cdot\mathbf{x}>\mathbf{p}\cdot\omega_i$.
3) $\mathbf{x}\succ_i\mathbf{x}_i$ *implies* $\mathbf{p}\cdot\mathbf{x}\geq\mathbf{p}\cdot\omega_i$.
4) $\mathbf{x}\succeq_i\mathbf{x}_i$ *implies* $\mathbf{p}\cdot\mathbf{x}\geq\mathbf{p}\cdot\omega_i$.

Proof. Let $(\mathbf{x}_1,\ldots,\mathbf{x}_m)$ be an allocation and let $\mathbf{p}$ be a non-zero price.
$(1)\Longrightarrow(2)$ Let $\mathbf{x}\succ_i\mathbf{x}_i$. Since $\mathbf{x}_i$ is a maximal element in the budget set $\mathcal{B}_i(\mathbf{p})$, it follows that $\mathbf{p}\cdot\mathbf{x}>\mathbf{p}\cdot\omega_i$. Theorem 1.3.3(1) shows that $\mathbf{p}\gg\mathbf{0}$ holds.
$(2)\Longrightarrow(3)$ Obvious.
$(3)\Longrightarrow(4)$ Let $\mathbf{x}\succeq_i\mathbf{x}_i$. Since the preference of each consumer is strictly monotone, we see that $\mathbf{x}+\varepsilon\omega\succ_i\mathbf{x}_i$ holds. Therefore $\mathbf{p}\cdot\mathbf{x}+\varepsilon\mathbf{p}\cdot\omega=\mathbf{p}\cdot(\mathbf{x}+\varepsilon\omega)>\mathbf{p}\cdot\omega_i$ holds for each $\varepsilon>0$, and so $\mathbf{p}\cdot\mathbf{x}\geq\mathbf{p}\cdot\omega_i$.
$(4)\Longrightarrow(1)$ Observe that $\mathbf{x}_i\succeq_i\mathbf{x}_i$ implies $\mathbf{p}\cdot\mathbf{x}_i\geq\mathbf{p}\cdot\omega_i$ for each i. From

$$\sum_{i=1}^{m}\mathbf{x}_i=\sum_{i=1}^{m}\omega_i=\omega\,,$$

we see that $\sum_{i=1}^{m}\mathbf{p}\cdot\mathbf{x}_i=\sum_{i=1}^{m}\mathbf{p}\cdot\omega_i$, and so $\mathbf{p}\cdot\mathbf{x}_i=\mathbf{p}\cdot\omega_i$ must hold for each i. Therefore, by Theorem 1.6.4, we have $\mathbf{p}>\mathbf{0}$.

Now fix some i such that $\mathbf{p}\cdot\omega_i>0$. Then, we claim that $\mathbf{x}_i$ is a maximal element in the budget set $\mathcal{B}_i(\mathbf{p})$. To see this, assume by way of contradiction that there exists some $\mathbf{x}\in\mathcal{B}_i(\mathbf{p})$ (i.e., $\mathbf{p}\cdot\mathbf{x}\leq\mathbf{p}\cdot\omega_i$) satisfying $\mathbf{x}\succ_i\mathbf{x}_i$. Since the set $\{\mathbf{y}\in\mathcal{R}^{\ell}_{+}\colon\ \mathbf{y}\succ_i\mathbf{x}_i\}$ is open in $\mathcal{R}^{\ell}_{+}$, $\mathbf{x}\succ_i\mathbf{x}_i$ and $\lim_{\varepsilon\uparrow 1}\varepsilon\mathbf{x}=\mathbf{x}$, there exists some $0<\varepsilon<1$ such that $\varepsilon\mathbf{x}\succ_i\mathbf{x}_i$. Therefore, $\mathbf{p}\cdot(\varepsilon\mathbf{x})\geq\mathbf{p}\cdot\omega_i$. On the other hand, from $\mathbf{p}\cdot\omega_i>0$ and $\mathbf{p}\cdot\mathbf{x}\leq\mathbf{p}\cdot\omega_i$, we see that

$$\mathbf{p}\cdot\omega_i>\varepsilon(\mathbf{p}\cdot\omega_i)\geq\varepsilon(\mathbf{p}\cdot\mathbf{x})=\mathbf{p}\cdot(\varepsilon\mathbf{x})\geq\mathbf{p}\cdot\omega_i\,,$$

which is impossible. Thus, $\mathbf{x}_i$ is maximal in $\mathcal{B}_i(\mathbf{p})$.

Now, by Theorem 1.3.3(1), we see that $\mathbf{p}\gg\mathbf{0}$ must hold, and so by the above conclusion each $\mathbf{x}_i$ is a maximal element in $\mathcal{B}_i(\mathbf{p})$ and the proof of the theorem is finished. ■

The Arrow–Debreu theorem (Theorem 1.4.9) can now be restated as follows.

Theorem 1.6.6. (Arrow–Debreu) *Every neoclassical exchange economy has a Walrasian equilibrium.*

A strong form of the first welfare theorem is given next.

Theorem 1.6.7. *Every Walrasian equilibrium is a core allocation—and hence, it is also weakly Pareto optimal.*

Proof. Let $(\mathbf{x}_1, \ldots, \mathbf{x}_m)$ be a Walrasian equilibrium in some exchange economy and let $\mathbf{p}$ be a price such that $\mathbf{x} \succ_i \mathbf{x}_i$ implies $\mathbf{p} \cdot \mathbf{x} > \mathbf{p} \cdot \omega_i$. We shall establish that $(\mathbf{x}_1, \ldots, \mathbf{x}_m)$ is a core allocation. To this end, assume by way of contradiction that there exist an allocation $(\mathbf{y}_1, \ldots, \mathbf{y}_m)$ and a coalition S such that

a) $\sum_{i \in S} \mathbf{y}_i = \sum_{i \in S} \omega_i$; and
b) $\mathbf{y}_i \succ_i \mathbf{x}_i$ for each $i \in S$.

Then, $\mathbf{p} \cdot \mathbf{y}_i > \mathbf{p} \cdot \omega_i$ must hold for each $i \in S$, and consequently

$$\mathbf{p} \cdot \Big(\sum_{i \in S} \mathbf{y}_i\Big) = \sum_{i \in S} \mathbf{p} \cdot \mathbf{y}_i > \sum_{i \in S} \mathbf{p} \cdot \omega_i = \mathbf{p} \cdot \Big(\sum_{i \in S} \omega_i\Big),$$

which contradicts (a). Therefore, $(\mathbf{x}_1, \ldots, \mathbf{x}_m)$ is a core allocation. ■

We continue our discussion with the notion of "supportability" of allocations by prices.

Definition 1.6.8. *An allocation* $(\mathbf{x}_1, \ldots, \mathbf{x}_m)$ *in an exchange economy is said to be* **supported** *by a non-zero price* $\mathbf{p}$ *whenever*

$$\mathbf{x} \succeq_i \mathbf{x}_i \quad \textit{implies} \quad \mathbf{p} \cdot \mathbf{x} \geq \mathbf{p} \cdot \mathbf{x}_i \,.$$

When preferences are monotone, supporting prices are always positive prices. Indeed, if $(\mathbf{x}_1, \ldots, \mathbf{x}_m)$ is an allocation supported by a price $\mathbf{p}$ and $\mathbf{x} \geq \mathbf{0}$, then $\mathbf{x}_1 + \mathbf{x} \succeq_1 \mathbf{x}_1$ holds and so $\mathbf{p} \cdot (\mathbf{x}_1 + \mathbf{x}) = \mathbf{p} \cdot (\mathbf{x}_1 + \mathbf{x}) \geq \mathbf{p} \cdot \mathbf{x}_1$, from which it follows that $\mathbf{p} \cdot \mathbf{x} \geq 0$, i.e., $\mathbf{p} \geq \mathbf{0}$.

The name "supporting price" comes from the mathematical terminology, according to which a linear functional f on a vector space E is said to *support* a subset A of E at some point $a \in A$ whenever

$$f(x) \geq f(a) \quad \text{holds for all } x \in A \,.$$

The geometrical meaning of supporting functionals is shown in Figure 1.6-1.

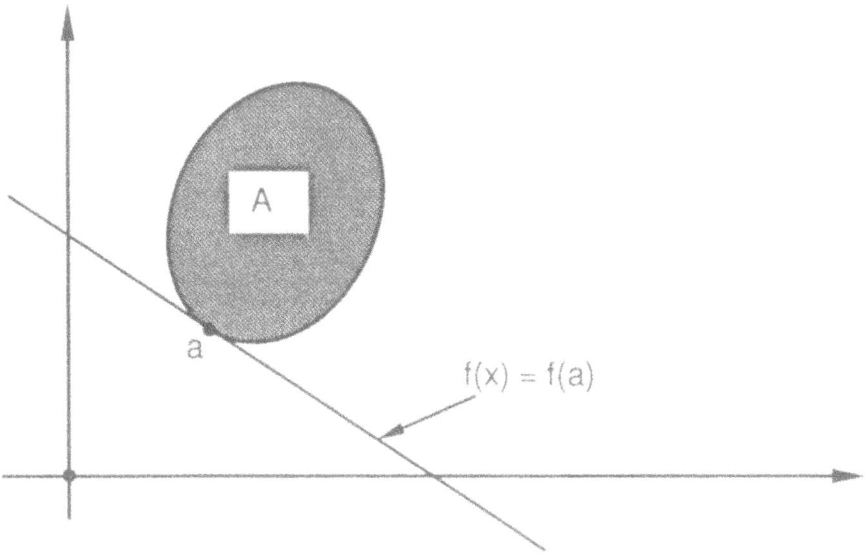

Fig. 1.6-1

Therefore, a price $\mathbf{p}$ supports an allocation $(\mathbf{x}_1, \ldots, \mathbf{x}_m)$ if and only if $\mathbf{p}$ as a functional on $\mathcal{R}^\ell$ supports each "better set" $\{\mathbf{x} \in \mathcal{R}^\ell_+ : \ \mathbf{x} \succeq_i \mathbf{x}_i\}$ at the point $\mathbf{x}_i$.

Our next objective is to establish that (under appropriate hypotheses) an allocation is Pareto optimal if and only if it can be supported by a price—Debreu's formulation of the welfare theorems. The validity of this statement can be "derived" intuitively from Edgeworth's box. If $\mathbf{x}$ is an allocation, then $\mathbf{x}$ is Pareto optimal if and only if the indifference curves passing through $\mathbf{x}$ are (for "smooth" preferences) tangent to each other at $\mathbf{x}$—and so they are supported by the common price $\mathbf{p}$; see Figure 1.6.2.

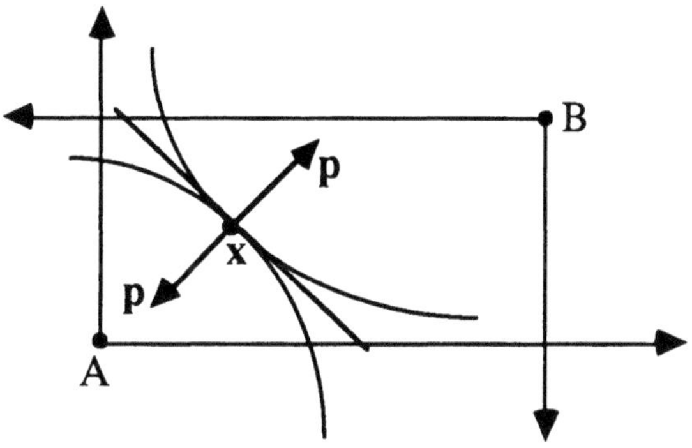

Fig. 1.6-2

Theorem 1.6.9. *If an allocation is supported by a price* $\mathbf{p}$ *satisfying* $\mathbf{p} \cdot \omega \neq 0$, *then the allocation is weakly Pareto optimal.*

Proof. Assume that an allocation $(\mathbf{x}_1, \ldots, \mathbf{x}_m)$ is supported by a price $\mathbf{p}$ that satisfies $\mathbf{p} \cdot \omega \neq 0$. Also, suppose by way of contradiction that there exists another allocation $(\mathbf{z}_1, \ldots, \mathbf{z}_m)$ satisfying $\mathbf{z}_i \succ_i \mathbf{x}_i$ for each i.

By the supportability of $\mathbf{p}$, we get $\mathbf{p} \cdot \mathbf{z}_i \geq \mathbf{p} \cdot \mathbf{x}_i$, and from

$$\mathbf{p} \cdot \omega = \sum_{i=1}^{m} \mathbf{p} \cdot \mathbf{z}_i = \sum_{i=1}^{m} \mathbf{p} \cdot \mathbf{x}_i ,$$

we infer that $\mathbf{p} \cdot \mathbf{z}_i = \mathbf{p} \cdot \mathbf{x}_i$ holds for each i. Now, by the continuity of the preferences, there exists some $0 < \delta < 1$ satisfying $\delta \mathbf{z}_i \succ_i \mathbf{x}_i$ for each i. As above, it follows that $\delta \mathbf{p} \cdot \mathbf{z}_i = \mathbf{p} \cdot \mathbf{x}_i$ and so $\mathbf{p} \cdot \mathbf{z}_i = \delta \mathbf{p} \cdot \mathbf{z}_i$ holds for each i. The latter implies $\mathbf{p} \cdot \mathbf{z}_i = 0$ for each i and consequently $\mathbf{p} \cdot \omega = \sum_{i=1}^{m} \mathbf{p} \cdot \mathbf{z}_i = 0$, a contradiction. This contradiction shows that the allocation $(\mathbf{x}_1, \ldots, \mathbf{x}_m)$ is weakly Pareto optimal. ■

For the converse of Theorem 1.6.9, we need a condition that insures that no bundle is maximal. A preference $\succeq$ defined on a topological space X is said to be:

1) **locally non-satiated**, whenever for each $x \in X$ and each neighborhood V of x there exists at least one bundle $y \in V$ with $y \succ x$; and
2) **non-satiated**, whenever for each $x \in X$ there exists some $z \in X$ such that $z \succ x$.

Note that a locally non-satiated preference is necessarily non-satiated (and, of course, a non-satiated preference can be defined on an arbitrary set).

Theorem 1.6.10. *If in an exchange economy each preference is strictly convex and non-satiated, then every weakly Pareto optimal allocation—and hence, every Pareto optimal allocation—is supported by a non-zero price.*

Proof. Consider an exchange economy whose consumers have strictly convex and non-satiated preferences, and let $(\mathbf{x}_1, \ldots, \mathbf{x}_m)$ be a weakly Pareto optimal allocation.

For each i let

$$F_i = \{\mathbf{x} \in E^+ \colon\ \mathbf{x} \succ_i \mathbf{x}_i\} .$$

By non-satiation, each F_i is non-empty. Also, by the strict convexity, each F_i is a convex set. Now consider the convex set

$$F = F_1 + F_2 + \cdots + F_m - \omega ,$$

where $\omega = \sum_{i=1}^{m} \omega_i$ is the total endowment, and note that $\mathbf{0} \notin F$. Indeed, if $\mathbf{0} \in F$, then there exist $\mathbf{z}_i \succ_i \mathbf{x}_i \,(i = 1, \ldots, m)$ such that $0 = \sum_{i=1}^{m} \mathbf{z}_i - \omega$ holds, contradicting the fact that the allocation $(\mathbf{x}_1, \ldots, \mathbf{x}_m)$ is weakly Pareto optimal. Now by the finite dimensional version of the separation theorem (for a proof see Exercise 6 of section 2.3), there exists some non-zero price $\mathbf{p} \neq \mathbf{0}$ such that $\mathbf{p} \cdot \mathbf{y} \geq 0$ holds for each $\mathbf{y} \in F$.

To finish the proof, we shall show that the price $\mathbf{p}$ supports the allocation $(\mathbf{x}_1, \ldots, \mathbf{x}_m)$. To this end, assume that $\mathbf{x} \succeq_r \mathbf{x}_r$ holds for some r. For each i there exists (by the non-satiatedness) some $\mathbf{z}_i \in E^+$ such that $\mathbf{z}_i \succ_i \mathbf{x}_i$. By the strict convexity of the preference relations, for each $0 < t < 1$ we have

$$t\mathbf{z}_i + (1-t)\mathbf{x}_i \succ_i \mathbf{x}_i \text{ for } i \neq r \text{ and } t\mathbf{z}_r + (1-t)\mathbf{x} \succ_r \mathbf{x}_r,$$

and so $\sum_{i\neq r}[t\mathbf{z}_i + (1-t)\mathbf{x}_i] + t\mathbf{z}_r + (1-t)\mathbf{x} - \omega \in F$ holds for each $0 < t < 1$. The latter implies

$$t\sum_{i\neq r}\mathbf{p}\cdot\mathbf{z}_i + (1-t)\sum_{i\neq r}\mathbf{p}\cdot\mathbf{x}_i + t\mathbf{p}\cdot\mathbf{z}_r + (1-t)\mathbf{p}\cdot\mathbf{x} \geq \mathbf{p}\cdot\omega$$

for all $0 < t < 1$. Letting $t \to 0$, we obtain

$$\sum_{i\neq r}\mathbf{p}\cdot\mathbf{x}_i + \mathbf{p}\cdot\mathbf{x} \geq \mathbf{p}\cdot\omega = \sum_{i\neq r}\mathbf{p}\cdot\mathbf{x}_i + \mathbf{p}\cdot\mathbf{x}_r,$$

or $\mathbf{p}\cdot\mathbf{x} \geq \mathbf{p}\cdot\mathbf{x}_r$. This shows that $\mathbf{p}$ supports the allocation $(\mathbf{x}_1, \ldots, \mathbf{x}_m)$. ■

Let us illustrate the various optimality notions with a concrete example.

Example 1.6.11. Consider the exchange economy with commodity space $\mathcal{R}^2$ and two consumers having the following characteristics.

Consumer 1: Initial endowment $\omega_1 = (\frac{3}{2}, \frac{1}{2})$ and utility function $u_1(x,y) = xy$.

Consumer 2: Initial endowment $\omega_2 = (\frac{3}{2}, \frac{3}{2})$ and utility function $u_2(x,y) = x^2y$.

The total endowment is $\omega = \omega_1 + \omega_2 = (3,2)$. Consider now the two consumers corresponding to the corners of the Edgeworth box; see Figure 1.6-3. In the xy-plane consumer 1 (whom we shall call consumer A) has utility function

$$u_A(x,y) = xy.$$

Consumer 2—whom we shall call consumer B—has a utility function in the st-plane given by $u_2(s,t) = s^2t$. Given that $s = 3 - x$ and $t = 2 - y$, we see that the utility function of consumer B in the xy-plane is given by

$$u_B(x,y) = (3-x)^2(2-y).$$

Clearly, a point (x,y) inside the box will give rise to a Pareto optimal allocation if and only if $\nabla u_A = \lambda \nabla u_B$ holds. Thus, the points that correspond to Pareto optimal allocations must satisfy the equation

$$(y,x) = -\lambda\big(2(3-x)(2-y), (3-x)^2\big).$$

The latter equation is equivalent to $\frac{y}{x} = \frac{2(2-y)}{3-x}$. Solving for y, we obtain

$$y = \frac{4x}{x+3}, \quad 0 \leq x \leq 3,$$

which is the equation of the Contract Curve; see Figure 1.6-3.

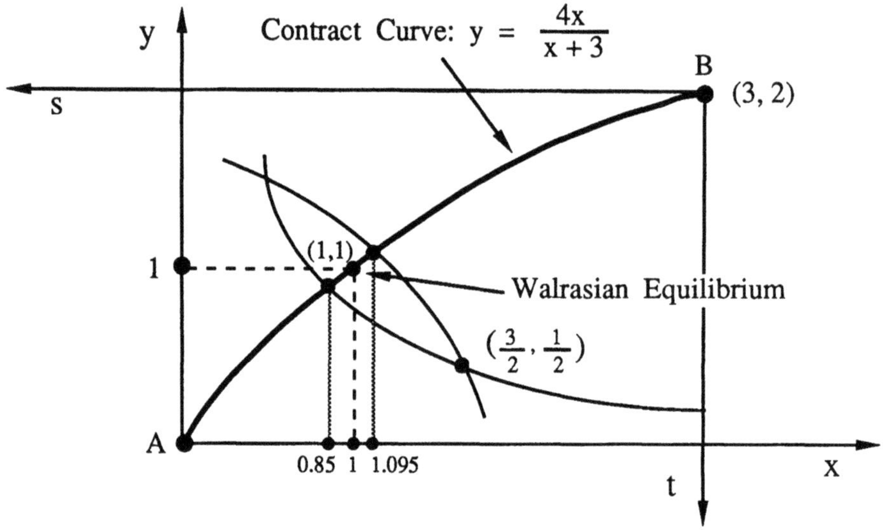

Fig. 1.6-3

The core consists of all points of the contract curve lying inside the lens shown in Figure 1.6-3. To describe the core, note first that the indifference curve of consumer A passing through $(\frac{3}{2}, \frac{1}{2})$ is given by the equation $xy = \frac{3}{2} \cdot \frac{1}{2} = \frac{3}{4}$ or $y = \frac{3}{4x}$. This curve meets the contract curve $y = \frac{4x}{x+3}$ when $\frac{3}{4x} = \frac{4x}{x+3}$ or equivalently when $16x^2 - 3x - 9 = 0$. Solving the quadratic yields

$$x = \frac{3 + \sqrt{585}}{32} = 0.84958 \cdots \approx 0.850 \,.$$

Now the indifference curve of consumer B passing through $(\frac{3}{2}, \frac{1}{2})$ satisfies the equation $(3-x)^2(2-y) = (3-\frac{3}{2})^2(2-\frac{1}{2}) = \frac{27}{8}$ (in the xy-plane). Hence, this curve meets the contract curve when $(3-x)^2(2-\frac{4x}{x+3}) = \frac{27}{8}$ or equivalently when $(3-x)^3 = \frac{27}{16}(x+3)$. Letting $x = 3 - t$, we see that t satisfies the equation $t = 6 - \frac{16}{27}t^3$. The (approximate) solution of this equation is $t \approx 1.904764 \approx 1.905$, and so $x \approx 1.095$. Thus, the core consists of all points of the form $(x, \frac{4x}{x+3})$, where (approximately) $0.850 \le x \le 1.095$; see Figure 1.6-3.

Finally, notice that a straightforward computation shows that the allocation

$$\mathbf{x}_1 = (1,1) \quad \text{and} \quad \mathbf{x}_2 = (2,1)$$

is a Walrasian equilibrium supported by the price $\mathbf{p} = (1,1)$. ■

And now we turn our attention to replica economies with the objective of establishing the Debreu–Scarf core equivalence theorem.

Definition 1.6.12. (Debreu–Scarf) *If $\mathcal{E}$ is an exchange economy with m consumers and r is any positive integer, then the r-***fold replica economy** *$\mathcal{E}_r$ of $\mathcal{E}$ is a new exchange economy with rm consumers—indexed by (i,j), $i=1,\ldots,m$; $j=1,\ldots,r$—such that each consumer (i,j) has*

a) *a preference $\succeq_{ij}$ equal to $\succeq_i$; and*
b) *an initial endowment ω_{ij} equal to ω_i (i.e., $\omega_{ij}=\omega_i$), and so the total endowment of the replica economy $\mathcal{E}_r$ is*

$$\sum_{j=1}^{r}\sum_{i=1}^{m}\omega_{ij}=r\omega\,.$$

Clearly, $\mathcal{E}_1=\mathcal{E}$. The consumers of the form (i,j), $j=1,\ldots,r$, are known as consumers of *type* i. Thus, the r-fold replica economy $\mathcal{E}_r$ is a new economy consisting of r consumers from each type i. A geometrical diagram for the consumers of the replica economies is shown in Figure 1.6-4.

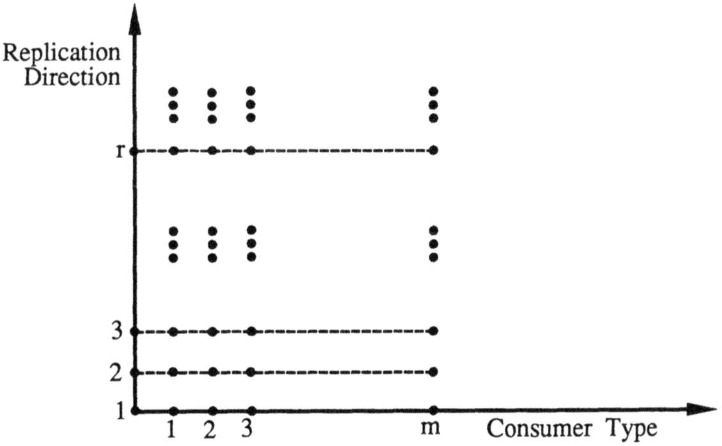

Fig. 1.6-4

Every allocation $(\mathbf{x}_1,\ldots,\mathbf{x}_m)$ of an exchange economy $\mathcal{E}$ gives rise to a natural allocation

$$(\mathbf{x}_{11},\ldots,\mathbf{x}_{1r},\mathbf{x}_{21},\ldots,\mathbf{x}_{2r},\ldots,\mathbf{x}_{m1},\ldots,\mathbf{x}_{mr})$$

for the r-fold replica economy $\mathcal{E}_r$ by letting

$$\mathbf{x}_{ij}=\mathbf{x}_i \quad \text{for } j=1,\ldots,r \text{ and } i=1,\ldots,m\,.$$

Any such allocation is called an **equal treatment allocation** for $\mathcal{E}_r$. In this manner, every allocation of $\mathcal{E}$ can be considered as an allocation for every r-fold replica economy $\mathcal{E}_r$. It is easy to see that every Walrasian equilibrium of our original exchange economy is also a Walrasian equilibrium for every r-fold replica economy $\mathcal{E}_r$—and hence, it also belongs to the core of every r-fold replica economy.

Our next objective is to show that these are the only allocations in our original economy that belong to the core of every replica economy—these allocations are called **Edgeworth equilibria**. To accomplish this, we need two simple lemmas.

Lemma 1.6.13. *Let $\succeq$ be a continuous, convex and strictly monotone preference defined on some $\mathcal{R}^\ell_+$. If $\mathbf{x}_1, \ldots, \mathbf{x}_n$ are positive vectors in $\mathcal{R}^\ell_+$ such that $\mathbf{x}_i \succeq \mathbf{y}$ holds for each i and $\mathbf{x}_i \succ \mathbf{y}$ holds for at least one i, then $\sum_{i=1}^n \alpha_i \mathbf{x}_i \succ \mathbf{y}$ holds for each convex combination with positive weights.*

Proof. Let $\succeq$ be a continuous, convex and strictly monotone preference on some $\mathcal{R}^\ell_+$. Also, let $\mathbf{x}_1, \ldots, \mathbf{x}_n$ be vectors in $\mathcal{R}^\ell_+$ satisfying $\mathbf{x}_i \succeq \mathbf{y}$ for each i and $\mathbf{x}_k \succ \mathbf{y}$. Fix $0 < \alpha_i < 1$ $(i = 1, \ldots, n)$ such that $\sum_{i=1}^n \alpha_i = 1$.

Since $\lim_{\varepsilon \uparrow 1} \varepsilon \mathbf{x}_k = \mathbf{x}_k$, it follows from the continuity of $\succeq$ that there exists some $0 < \varepsilon < 1$ such that $\varepsilon \mathbf{x}_k \succ \mathbf{y}$. Now by the convexity of $\succeq$, we see that

$$\alpha_k(\varepsilon \mathbf{x}_k) + \sum_{\substack{i=1 \\ i \neq k}}^n \alpha_i \mathbf{x}_i \succeq \mathbf{y}\,.$$

On the other hand, note that

$$\sum_{i=1}^n \alpha_i \mathbf{x}_i = \alpha_k \mathbf{x}_k + \sum_{\substack{i=1 \\ i \neq k}}^n \alpha_i \mathbf{x}_i > \alpha_k(\varepsilon \mathbf{x}_k) + \sum_{\substack{i=1 \\ i \neq k}}^n \alpha_i \mathbf{x}_i\,.$$

Therefore, from the strict monotonicity of $\succeq$, we infer that

$$\sum_{i=1}^n \alpha_i \mathbf{x}_i \succ \alpha_k(\varepsilon \mathbf{x}_k) + \sum_{\substack{i=1 \\ i \neq k}}^n \alpha_i \mathbf{x}_i \succeq \mathbf{y}\,,$$

and our conclusion follows. ■

Lemma 1.6.14. *In an exchange economy with continuous and strictly monotone preferences, a coalition S improves upon an allocation $(\mathbf{x}_1, \ldots, \mathbf{x}_m)$ if and only if there exists a set of positive vectors $\{\mathbf{y}_i \in \mathcal{R}^\ell_+ \colon\ i \in S\}$ such that*

a) *$\sum_{i \in S} \mathbf{y}_i \leq \sum_{i \in S} \omega_i$; and*
b) *$\mathbf{y}_i \succeq_i \mathbf{x}_i$ for each $i \in S$ and $\mathbf{y}_i \succ_i \mathbf{x}_i$ holds for at least one $i \in S$.*

Proof. Assume that a coalition S and a set of positive vectors $\{\mathbf{y}_i \in \mathcal{R}^\ell_+ \colon\ i \in S\}$ satisfy properties (a) and (b) of the lemma. We can suppose that $S = \{1, \ldots, r\}$.

If $r = 1$, then $\mathbf{y}_1 \succ_1 \mathbf{x}_1$ and the coalition $S = \{1\}$ improves upon $(\mathbf{x}_1, \ldots, \mathbf{x}_m)$ with the allocation $(\omega_1, \ldots, \omega_m)$. Now assume that $r \geq 2$. Fix $k \in S$ with $\mathbf{y}_k \succ_k \mathbf{x}_k$

and then pick some $0 < \varepsilon < 1$ such that $\varepsilon\mathbf{y}_k \succ_k \mathbf{x}_k$. Now consider the allocation $(\mathbf{z}_1, \ldots, \mathbf{z}_m)$ defined by

$$\mathbf{z}_i = \begin{cases} \omega_i & \text{if } i \notin S; \\ \varepsilon\mathbf{y}_k + \sum_{i \in S} \omega_i - \sum_{i \in S} \mathbf{y}_i & \text{if } i = k; \\ \mathbf{y}_i + \frac{1-\varepsilon}{r-1}\mathbf{y}_k & \text{if } i \in S \text{ and } i \neq k. \end{cases}$$

Then the allocation $(\mathbf{z}_1, \ldots, \mathbf{z}_m)$ satisfies

i) $\sum_{i \in S} \mathbf{z}_i = \sum_{i \in S} \omega_i$; and
ii) $\mathbf{z}_i \succ_i \mathbf{x}_i$ for each $i \in S$.

The above show that if the coalition S satisfies properties (a) and (b), then S improves upon the allocation $(\mathbf{x}_1, \ldots, \mathbf{x}_m)$, and the proof is finished. ■

And now we are ready to establish the existence of Edgeworth equilibria, i.e., to establish that there are allocations that belong to the core of every replica economy.

Theorem 1.6.15. (Debreu–Scarf) *If in an exchange economy $\mathcal{E}$ preferences are represented by continuous, quasi-concave and strictly monotone utility functions, then there are allocations of $\mathcal{E}$ that belong to the core of every r-fold replica economy.*

Proof. Let $\mathcal{E}$ be an exchange economy with continuous, convex and strictly monotone preferences. As usual, an allocation $(\mathbf{x}_1, \ldots, \mathbf{x}_m)$ of $\mathcal{E}$ will be considered as an allocation for each r-fold replica economy $\mathcal{E}_r$ by assigning the bundle $\mathbf{x}_i$ to each consumer of type i. For each n, let

$$\mathcal{C}_n = \{(\mathbf{x}_1, \ldots, \mathbf{x}_m) \in \mathcal{A}\colon\ (\mathbf{x}_1, \ldots, \mathbf{x}_m) \in \text{Core}(\mathcal{E}_n)\}.$$

The sets $\mathcal{C}_n$ have the following properties.

1. *Each $\mathcal{C}_n$ is non-empty.*

Note first that in the n-fold replica economy $\mathcal{E}_n$ the consumers' characteristics satisfy all assumptions of Theorem 1.5.10, and hence $\text{Core}(\mathcal{E}_n) \neq \emptyset$. Let

$$(\mathbf{x}_{11}, \ldots, \mathbf{x}_{1n}, \mathbf{x}_{21}, \ldots, \mathbf{x}_{2n}, \ldots, \mathbf{x}_{m1}, \ldots, \mathbf{x}_{mn})$$

be a core allocation for $\mathcal{E}_n$. Then we claim that

$$\mathbf{x}_{ij} \sim_i \mathbf{x}_{ik} \quad \text{for } j,\ k = 1, \ldots, n \text{ and } i = 1, \ldots, m,$$

i.e., no consumer prefers his bundle to that of another consumer of the same type.

To see this, note first that (by rearranging the consumers of each type), we can suppose that $\mathbf{x}_{ij} \succeq_i \mathbf{x}_{i1}$ holds for all i and j. Put

$$\mathbf{y}_{i1} = \tfrac{1}{n}\sum_{j=1}^{n} \mathbf{x}_{ij}, \quad i = 1, \ldots, m.$$

Then $\sum_{i=1}^{n} \mathbf{y}_{i1} = \sum_{i=1}^{n} \omega_i = \omega$, and by the convexity of preferences, we have $\mathbf{y}_{i1} \succeq_i \mathbf{x}_{i1}$ for each i. Now assume by way of contradiction that there exists some

$k\,(1 \le k \le m)$ and some $r\,(1 \le r \le n)$ with $\mathbf{x}_{kr} \succ_k \mathbf{x}_{k1}$. The latter, in view of Lemma 1.6.13, implies $\mathbf{y}_{k1} \succ_k \mathbf{x}_{k1}$. Now if each consumer $(i,1)$ gets the bundle $\mathbf{y}_{i1}$, then by Lemma 1.6.14 the coalition $\{(i,1)\colon\ i = 1,\ldots,m\}$ improves upon the original allocation of $\mathcal{E}_n$, which is impossible. This contradiction establishes the validity of our claim.

Next, note that by the convexity of preferences we have $\mathbf{y}_{i1} \succeq_i \mathbf{x}_{ij}$ for all $j = 1,\ldots,n$. Now an easy argument shows that $(\mathbf{y}_{11}, \mathbf{y}_{21}, \ldots, \mathbf{y}_{m1}) \in \mathcal{C}_n$, and thus $\mathcal{C}_n$ is non-empty.

2. *Each* $\mathcal{C}_n$ *is a compact set.*

By Theorem 1.5.10 we know that $\mathrm{Core}(\mathcal{E}_n)$ is a compact set. This easily implies that $\mathcal{C}_n$ is likewise a compact set.

3. *For each* n *we have* $\mathcal{C}_{n+1} \subseteq \mathcal{C}_n$.

This inclusion follows immediately by observing that if an allocation of $\mathcal{E}$ cannot be improved upon in the $(n+1)$-fold replica economy, then it cannot also be improved upon in the n-fold replica economy.

Now note that since the set of all allocations $\mathcal{A}$ of $\mathcal{E}$ is a compact set and the sequence $\{\mathcal{C}_n\}$ has the finite intersection property, it follows that $\bigcap_{n=1}^{\infty} \mathcal{C}_n \neq \emptyset$. Finally, to complete the proof note that that set of all allocations of $\mathcal{E}$ that belong to the core of every replica economy is precisely the set $\bigcap_{n=1}^{\infty} \mathcal{C}_n$. ■

As mentioned before, a Walrasian equilibrium in an exchange economy is also a Walrasian equilibrium for its replica economies. In particular, every Walrasian equilibrium lies in the core of every replica economy. Remarkably, the converse of the latter statement is also true. This characterization of the Walrasian equilibria is due to G. Debreu and H. E. Scarf [24]—which is also known as the Debreu–Scarf core equivalence theorem. The characterization provides another way of proving the existence of Walrasian equilibria and is stated next.

Theorem 1.6.16. (Debreu–Scarf) *An allocation in an exchange economy with continuous, convex and strictly monotone preferences is a Walrasian equilibrium if and only if it is an Edgeworth equilibrium.*

Proof. Let $\mathcal{E}$ be an exchange economy with continuous, convex and strictly monotone preferences. Also, let $(\mathbf{x}_1,\ldots,\mathbf{x}_m)$ be an allocation of $\mathcal{E}$ that belongs to the core of every r-fold replica economy of $\mathcal{E}$. We have to show that $(\mathbf{x}_1,\ldots,\mathbf{x}_m)$ is a Walrasian equilibrium.

For each i define the sets

$$F_i = \{\mathbf{x} \in \mathcal{R}^{\ell}_{+}\colon\ \mathbf{x} \succ_i \mathbf{x}_i\} \quad \text{and} \quad G_i = F_i - \omega_i\,.$$

The strict monotonicity of preferences implies that each F_i is non-empty. By Lemma 1.6.13, we know that each F_i is also convex. Therefore, each G_i is non-empty and convex. Now denote by G the convex hull of $\bigcup_{i=1}^{m} G_i$, i.e.,

$$G = \mathrm{co}\Big(\bigcup_{i=1}^{m} G_i\Big) = \Big\{\sum_{i=1}^{m} \lambda_i \mathbf{y}_i\colon\ \mathbf{y}_i \in G_i,\ \lambda_i \ge 0 \text{ for each } i \text{ and } \sum_{i=1}^{m} \lambda_i = 1\Big\}\,.$$

We claim that $\mathbf{0}$ does not belong to the convex set G.

To see this, assume by way of contradiction that $\mathbf{0} \in G$. Then, there exist $\mathbf{y}_i \in G$ and $\lambda_i \geq 0$ $(i = 1, \ldots, m)$ such that

$$\sum_{i=1}^{m} \lambda_i = 1 \quad \text{and} \quad \sum_{i=1}^{m} \lambda_i \mathbf{y}_i = \mathbf{0}. \tag{$\star$}$$

Put $S = \{i\colon\ \lambda_i > 0\}$ and note that $S \neq \emptyset$. Next, for each i pick some $\mathbf{v}_i \in \mathcal{R}^\ell_+$ such that $\mathbf{v}_i \succ_i \mathbf{x}_i$ and $\mathbf{y}_i = \mathbf{v}_i - \omega_i$. From $(\star)$, it follows that $\sum_{i=1}^m \lambda_i \mathbf{v}_i = \sum_{i=1}^m \lambda_i \omega_i$ or

$$\sum_{i \in S} \lambda_i \mathbf{v}_i = \sum_{i \in S} \lambda_i \omega_i. \tag{$\star\star$}$$

Now if n is a positive integer, denote by n_i the smallest integer greater than or equal to $n\lambda_i$, that is, $0 \leq n_i - n\lambda_i < 1$—and, of course, $i \in S$ implies $n_i \leq n$. Since for each $i \in S$ we have $\lim_{n\to\infty} \frac{n\lambda_i}{n_i} = 1$ and $\mathbf{v}_i \succ_i \mathbf{x}_i$, there exists (by the continuity of preferences) some n large enough satisfying

$$\mathbf{z}_i = \tfrac{n\lambda_i}{n_i} \mathbf{v}_i \succ_i \mathbf{x}_i \quad \text{for each} \quad i \in S. \tag{$\star\star\star$}$$

Taking into account $(\star\star)$, we see that

$$\sum_{i \in S} n_i \mathbf{z}_i = \sum_{i \in S} n\lambda_i \mathbf{v}_i = \sum_{i \in S} n\lambda_i \omega_i \leq \sum_{i \in S} n_i \omega_i.$$

The preceding inequality, coupled with $(\star\star\star)$ and Lemma 1.6.14, shows that the allocation $(\mathbf{x}_1, \ldots, \mathbf{x}_m)$ can be improved upon in the n-fold replica of the economy $\mathcal{E}$, which is a contradiction. Hence, $\mathbf{0} \notin G$.

Now by the separation theorem for finite dimensional vector spaces (see, for example Exercise 6 of Section 2.3), there exists some non-zero price $\mathbf{p} \in \mathcal{R}^\ell_+$ such that $\mathbf{p} \cdot \mathbf{g} \geq 0$ holds for all $\mathbf{g} \in G$. In particular, if $\mathbf{x} \succ_i \mathbf{x}_i$, then $\mathbf{x} - \omega_i \in G$, and so $\mathbf{p} \cdot \mathbf{x} \geq \mathbf{p} \cdot \omega_i$ holds. Now a glance at statement (4) of Theorem 1.6.5 reveals that indeed $(\mathbf{x}_1, \ldots, \mathbf{x}_m)$ is a Walrasian equilibrium, and the proof of the theorem is complete. ■

As an immediate consequence of the preceding result and Theorem 1.6.15, we have another existence proof—due to H. E. Scarf [60]—of Walrasian equilibria.

Corollary 1.6.17. (Scarf) *If preferences in an exchange economy can be represented by continuous, quasi-concave and strictly monotone utility functions, then the economy has Walrasian equilibria.*

EXERCISES

1. Assume that in an exchange ecconomy every consumer has an extremely desirable bundle. Show that an allocation $(\mathbf{x}_1, \ldots, \mathbf{x}_m)$ is a Walrasian equilibrium with respect to some price $\mathbf{p} > \mathbf{0}$ if and only if $\mathbf{x} \succ_i \mathbf{x}_i$ implies $\mathbf{p} \cdot \mathbf{x} > \mathbf{p} \cdot \omega_i$.

2. Consider the exchange economy described in Example 1.6.11. Show that the allocation $(\mathbf{x}_1, \mathbf{x}_2)$, where $\mathbf{x}_1 = (1,1)$ and $\mathbf{x}_2 = (2,1)$, is a Walrasian equilibrium supported by the price $\mathbf{p} = (1,1)$.

3. Show that in an exchange economy every quasiequilibrium is a weakly Pareto optimal allocation.

4. Show that every preference with an extremely desirable bundle defined on $\mathcal{R}^\ell_+$ is locally non-satiated. Also, give an example of a monotone locally non-satiated preference on some $\mathcal{R}^\ell_+$ which is not strictly monotone.
[HINT: For the second case consider the preference on $\mathcal{R}^2_+$ defined by the utility function $u(x,y) = x$.]

5. If in an exchange economy preferences are convex and the total endowment is extremely desirable by each consumer, then show that every weakly Pareto optimal allocation can be supported by a price.
[HINT: Let $(\mathbf{x}_1, \ldots, \mathbf{x}_m)$ be a weakly Pareto optimal allocation, define the convex set $F_i = \{\mathbf{x} \in E^+ \colon \mathbf{x} \succeq_i \mathbf{x}_i\}$ and consider the convex set

$$F = F_1 + F_2 + \cdots + F_m - \omega .$$

Then $-\frac{1}{n}\omega \notin F$ (why?) and so by the separation theorem there exists some price $\mathbf{p}_n \in \mathcal{R}^\ell$ with $\|\mathbf{p}_n\|_1 = 1$ such that $-\frac{1}{n}\mathbf{p}_n \cdot \omega \leq \mathbf{p} \cdot \mathbf{z}$ holds for all $\mathbf{z} \in F$. If $\mathbf{p}$ is a limit point of the sequence $\{\mathbf{p}_n\}$, then $\mathbf{p}$ is a non-zero price satisfying $\mathbf{p} \cdot \mathbf{z} \geq 0$ for each $\mathbf{z} \in F$. To see that the price $\mathbf{p}$ supports $(\mathbf{x}_1, \ldots, \mathbf{x}_m)$, note that $\mathbf{x} \succeq_i \mathbf{x}_i$ implies $\mathbf{x} - \mathbf{x}_i \in F$.]

6. Consider the neoclassical exchange economy with commodity space $\mathcal{R}^2$ and two consumers with the following characteristics.
Consumer 1: Initial endowment $\omega_1 = (2,1)$ and utility function $u_1(x,y) = (y+1)e^x$.
Consumer 2: Initial endowment $\omega_2 = (2,3)$ and utility function $u_2(x,y) = xy$.
   a) Find the individual demand functions.
   Answer: $\mathbf{x}_1(\mathbf{p}) = \left(\frac{t+2}{t}, t-1\right)$, $\mathbf{x}_2(\mathbf{p}) = \left(\frac{2t+3}{2t}, \frac{2t+3}{2}\right)$; $t = \frac{p_1}{p_2}$
   b) Find the excess demand function. *Answer*: $\zeta(\mathbf{p}) = \left(\frac{7-4t}{t}, \frac{4t-7}{2}\right)$
   c) Find the Walrasian equilibria. *Answer*: $\left(\left(\frac{15}{7}, \frac{3}{4}\right), \left(\frac{13}{7}, \frac{13}{4}\right)\right)$
   d) Draw the Edgeworth box for this economy and find the equation of the contract curve. *Answer*: $y = \frac{x}{5-x}$

e) Find and draw the core allocations in the Edgeworth box.
Answer: Core $= \{(x, \frac{x}{5-x}) \colon x_0 \leq x \leq \frac{17-\sqrt{39}}{5}\}$, where x_0 satisfies the equation $5e^{x_0} = 2e^2(5 - x_0)$.

f) Show that every allocation in the contract curve is supported by prices.

7. Consider an exchange economy with m consumers each of whom has a preference relation represented by a continuous, quasi-concave and strictly monotone utility function. Show that an allocation is a Walrasian equilibrium if and only if it belongs to the core of every $2n$-fold replica economy.

8. Verify that every Walrasian equilibrium is an Edgeworth equilibrium, i.e., that it belongs to the core of every replica economy.

9. Consider an exchange economy with m consumers each of whom has the same initial endowment ω and the same continuous, strictly quasi-concave and strictly monotone utility function.

a) Show that the sets of all individually rational allocations, of all Walrasian equilibria and of all core allocations coincide.

b) If $(\mathbf{x}_1, \ldots, \mathbf{x}_m)$ is a core allocation, then show that $\mathbf{x}_i \sim \omega$ holds for each i.

10. If an allocation is a Pareto (resp. weakly Pareto) optimal in an exchange economy with strictly convex preferences, then show that it is also a Pareto (resp. weakly Pareto) optimal allocation in every replica economy.

1.7. PRODUCTION ECONOMIES

Firms (or producers) constitute the most important sector of modern market economies. In the Arrow–Debreu model, the technological capabilities of a firm is represented as a subset of the commodity space, called the production set of the firm. A vector in the production set is called a production plan, where the negative components of the vector correspond to inputs and the positive components to outputs. For instance, in an economy with four commodities, the production plan $(-1, 2, -3, 1)$ expresses the fact that the firm needs 1 unit of commodity one and 3 units of commodity three to produce 2 units of commodity two and 1 unit of commodity four. Production sets are a significant generalization of production functions.

In general, a firm will have many ways of producing a certain combination of outputs from inputs. We are particularly interested in efficient plans. A production plan $\mathbf{y}$ is efficient for the production set Y if there is no other plan $\mathbf{x}$ in Y such that $\mathbf{x} > \mathbf{y}$. Clearly, the family of efficient production plans lie on the boundary of Y. The principal behavioral assumption we shall make regarding firms is that they are price-taking profit maximizers. Hence, our firms treat prices as a given and choose plans in their production sets which maximize profits. If prices are strictly positive and a profit maximizing plan exists, then it is easy to see that this plan is efficient.

The critical technological assumption regarding firms is that their production sets are convex. This expresses the notion of constant or diminishing returns to scale, i.e., doubling of inputs in a given plan produces a plan with no more than twice the outputs of the original plan. We also assume that every plan must use at least one input and the firm can shut down without cost, i.e., the zero vector is in the firm's production set. It is easy to construct technologies satisfying all of our assumptions, where there are no profit maximizing plans for a given vector of strictly positive prices. For example, if production takes place in $\mathcal{R}^2$ and the technology is given by the set $Y = \{(x, y)\colon\ x \leq 0 \text{ and } -x \leq y\}$, then there is no profit maximizing production plan at prices $\mathbf{p} = (1, 2)$. This is an example of a constant returns to scale technology.

Analogous to the notion of demand functions, we would like to define the notion of a supply function. The supply function specifies how much of each commodity the firm will sell as outputs and how much of each commodity the firm will buy as inputs, at prices $\mathbf{p}$. If this function is to be defined for all strictly positive prices, then it is sufficient to assume that the production set of the firm is bounded from above. There is no economic justification for such an assumption, but we shall make it to simplify the analysis in this introductory chapter and address the general case in Chapter 4.

Under the above assumptions on technology and our maintained hypothesis on households, we prove the existence of an equilibrium price, i.e., prices at which supply equals demand. At equilibrium prices, households are maximizing utility subject to their budget constraints; firms are maximizing profits relative to their technology;

and all markets clear. In Chapter 4, we shall establish the First Welfare Theorem, which asserts that the resulting distribution of resources in a production economy at equilibrium prices is Pareto optimal. Another approach, more general than the one presented in this section, can be found in W. Neuefeind [51]. He proves the existence of equilibrium prices where the domain of the supply function need not be the whole interior of the price simplex, hence he is able to replace the "bounded from above" assumption on technology with more acceptable economic assumptions such as free disposal. For yet another existence proof, using only the Brower fixed point theorem, we refer the reader to the works of L. W. McKenzie [48, 49].

We begin the discussion with the definition of a production set.

Definition 1.7.1. *A non-empty subset Y of a some finite dimensional $\mathcal{R}^\ell$ is said to be a* **production set** *whenever*

1) *Y is closed;*
2) *Y is convex;*
3) *$\mathcal{R}^\ell_+ \cap Y = \{\mathbf{0}\}$; and*
4) *Y is bounded from above, i.e., there exists some $\mathbf{a} \in \mathcal{R}^\ell_+$ satisfying $\mathbf{y} \le \mathbf{a}$ for all $\mathbf{y} \in Y$.*

Some examples of production sets are shown in Figure 1.7-1.

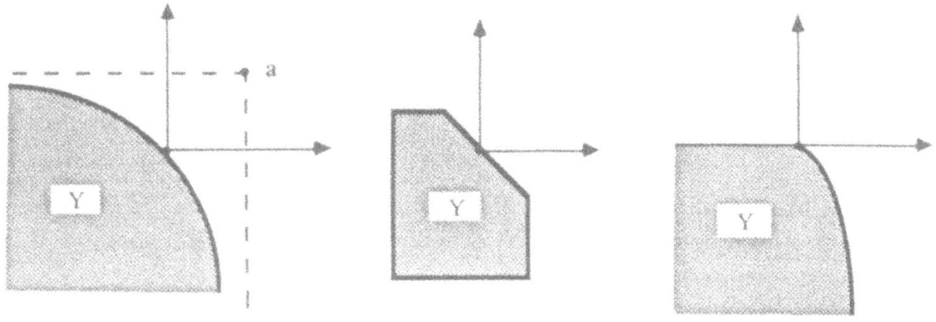

Fig. 1.7-1

Definition 1.7.2. *If Y is a production set and $\mathbf{p} \gg \mathbf{0}$ is a strictly positive price, then* **the profit function** *at prices $\mathbf{p}$ is the function $\wp: Y \longrightarrow \mathcal{R}$ defined by*

$$\wp(\mathbf{y}) = \mathbf{p} \cdot \mathbf{y}, \quad \mathbf{y} \in Y.$$

Since the dot product is a continuous function it should be obvious that every profit function is continuous. It turns out that every profit function attains a maximum value. The details follow.

Theorem 1.7.3. *If Y is a production set and $\mathbf{p}$ is a strictly positive price, then there exists at least one production plan that maximizes the profit function. That is, there exists some $\mathbf{y}_0 \in Y$ satisfying $\mathbf{p}\cdot\mathbf{y} \le \mathbf{p}\cdot\mathbf{y}_0$ for all $\mathbf{y} \in Y$.*

Proof. Let Y be a production plan and let $\mathbf{p}$ be a strictly positive price. Since $\mathbf{0} \in Y$, we see that

$$\sup\{\mathbf{p}\cdot\mathbf{y}\colon\ \mathbf{y} \in Y\} = \sup\{\mathbf{p}\cdot\mathbf{y}\colon\ \mathbf{y} \in Y \text{ and } \mathbf{p}\cdot\mathbf{y} \ge 0\}.$$

Let $\mathbf{A} = \{\mathbf{y} \in Y : \mathbf{p}\cdot\mathbf{y} \ge 0\}$. The set $\mathbf{A}$ is represented by the darkened region of the production set shown in Figure 1.7-2.

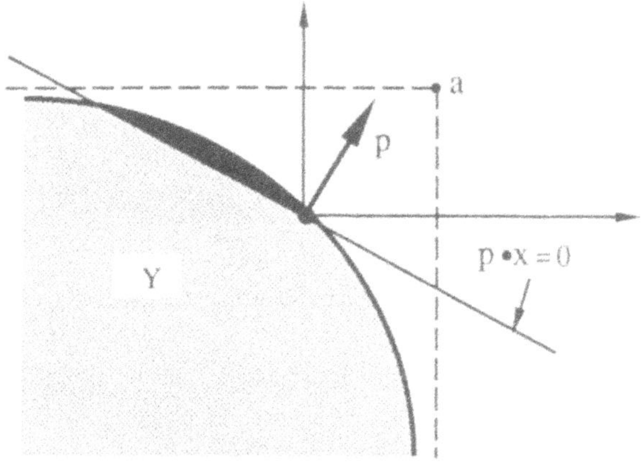

Fig. 1.7-2

We shall show that $\mathbf{A}$ is compact. Obviously, $\mathbf{A}$ is closed and hence, we need only show that it is bounded. Since $\mathbf{Y}$ is bounded from above and contains $\mathbf{0}$, the proof reduces to showing that the negative components of the production plans in $\mathbf{A}$ are bounded from below.

Put $p = \min\{p_1, p_2, \ldots, p_\ell\} > 0$, and let $\mathbf{y} \in Y$ satisfy $\mathbf{p}\cdot\mathbf{y} \ge 0$. Let

$$I = \{k\colon\ y_k \ge 0\} \quad \text{and} \quad J = \{k\colon\ y_k < 0\}.$$

Now if $y_k < 0$, then we have

$$py_k \ge p_k y_k \ge \sum_{j\in J} p_j y_j \ge -\sum_{i\in I} p_i y_i \ge -\sum_{r=1}^{\ell} p_r a_r = -\mathbf{p}\cdot\mathbf{a},$$

and so $y_k \ge -\frac{\mathbf{p}\cdot\mathbf{a}}{p}$ holds for all $k = 1, \ldots, \ell$. Thus, the closed set $\{\mathbf{y} \in Y\colon\ \mathbf{p}\cdot\mathbf{y} \ge 0\}$ is bounded from below, and hence it is a compact set. This implies that some production plan maximizes the profit function. ■

Now consider a production set Y and let $\mathbf{p} \gg \mathbf{0}$ be a strictly positive price. It is easy to see that the profit function $\wp$ is increasing—in the sense that $\mathbf{x} > \mathbf{y}$ implies $\wp(\mathbf{x}) = \mathbf{p} \cdot \mathbf{x} > \mathbf{p} \cdot \mathbf{y} = \wp(\mathbf{y})$. In particular, it follows that no interior points of Y can be profit maximizers. That is, the profit maximizing production plans must lie on the boundary of Y. More precisely, the profit maximizing production plans must lie in a very specific part of the boundary of Y known as *the efficiency frontier* of Y. Its precise definition is as follows. (Recall that the set $\mathbf{y} + \mathcal{R}^\ell_+$ is the set of all vectors greater than or equal to $\mathbf{y}$.)

Definition 1.7.4. *If Y is a production set, then the* **efficiency frontier** $\mathbf{Eff}(Y)$ *of Y is the set*

$$\mathbf{Eff}(Y) = \{\mathbf{y} \in Y\colon\ (\mathbf{y} + \mathcal{R}^\ell_+) \cap Y = \{\mathbf{y}\}\}.$$

The profit maximizing production plans lie in $\mathbf{Eff}(Y)$. Note that $\mathbf{Eff}(Y)$ is always non-empty—by the very definition of the production set we have $\mathbf{0} \in \mathbf{Eff}(Y)$. It may happen that $\mathbf{Eff}(Y) = \{\mathbf{0}\}$; for instance, $\mathbf{Eff}(-\mathcal{R}^\ell_+) = \{\mathbf{0}\}$. In Figure 1.7-3, we indicate the geometrical meaning of the efficiency frontier for two production sets.

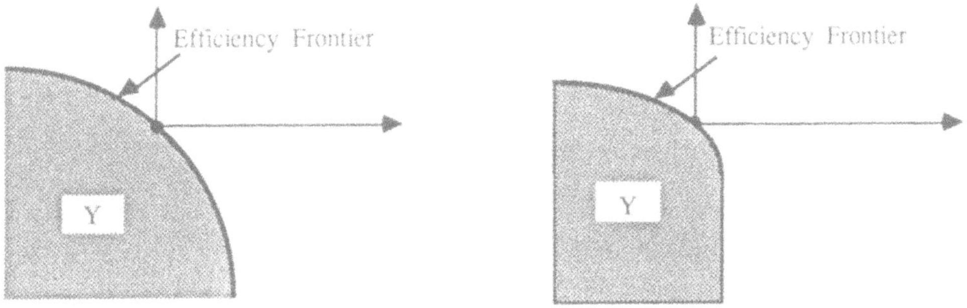

Fig. 1.7-3

Consider again a production set Y and let $\mathbf{p} \gg \mathbf{0}$. By Theorem 1.7.3, we know that the profit function $\wp(\mathbf{y}) = \mathbf{p} \cdot \mathbf{y}$ attains a maximum on Y. By the preceding discussion, the profit maximizers must lie in the efficiency frontier set $\mathbf{Eff}(Y)$. *When does the profit function have a unique maximizer?* To answer this question, note first that the set of maximizers for $\wp$, i.e., the set

$$\{\mathbf{z} \in \mathbf{Eff}(Y)\colon\ \mathbf{p} \cdot \mathbf{y} \le \mathbf{p} \cdot \mathbf{z} \text{ for all } \mathbf{y} \in Y\}$$

is non-empty and convex. This implies that when the production set Y is "strictly convex," then there exists exactly one profit maximizing vector in $\mathbf{Eff}(Y)$. A convex subset X of a finite dimensional vector space is said to be **strictly convex** whenever for each $x, y \in X$ with $x \neq y$ and for all $0 < \alpha < 1$ it follows that $\alpha x + (1-\alpha)y$ is in the relative interior of X. That is, a convex set X is strictly convex if the boundary of X contains no line segments. In Figure 1.7-1, the set to the left is strictly convex, while the other two sets are not strictly convex.

Therefore, when Y is strictly convex, every profit function has exactly one maximizing production plan in $\mathbf{Eff}(Y)$. We shall call such production sets strictly convex.

Definition 1.7.5. *A production set is said to be a* **strictly convex** *whenever the efficiency frontier contains no line segments.*

Every production set whose efficiency frontier is the "level curve" of a strictly concave function is automatically strictly convex. To see this, consider a production set Y whose efficiency frontier coincides with the level curve of a strictly concave function g on Y, say $\mathbf{Eff}(Y) = \{\mathbf{x} \in Y \colon\ g(\mathbf{x}) = 0\}$. Recall that g is *strictly concave* whenever for each $\mathbf{x}, \mathbf{y} \in Y$ with $\mathbf{x} \neq \mathbf{y}$ and each $0 < \alpha < 1$, we have

$$g(\alpha\mathbf{x} + (1-\alpha)\mathbf{y}) < \alpha g(\mathbf{x}) + (1-\alpha)g(\mathbf{y}).$$

The above inequality shows that if $\mathbf{x}, \mathbf{y} \in \mathbf{Eff}(Y)$, then $a\mathbf{x} + (1-\alpha)\mathbf{y} \notin \mathbf{Eff}(Y)$ holds for each $0 < \alpha < 1$ and so $\mathbf{Eff}(Y)$ contains no line segments.

If a firm's technology is given by a close convex cone, which is the representation of constant returns to scale technology, then its technology is not strictly convex. For a strictly convex production set, its profit function has a unique maximizing production plan for each strictly positive price.

Theorem 1.7.6. *If Y is a strictly convex production set, then every profit function has a unique maximizer in Y, i.e., for each $\mathbf{p} \gg \mathbf{0}$ there exists a unique $\mathbf{z} \in Y$ satisfying $\mathbf{p} \cdot \mathbf{y} \leq \mathbf{p} \cdot \mathbf{z}$ for all $\mathbf{y} \in Y$.*

In case the efficiency frontier of a production set is the level surface of a smooth strictly concave function g, then the unique profit maximizer can be found by using Lagrange multipliers, where as usual the gradient ∇g must be parallel to $\mathbf{p}$, i.e., $\nabla g = \lambda \mathbf{p}$; see Figure 1.7-4.

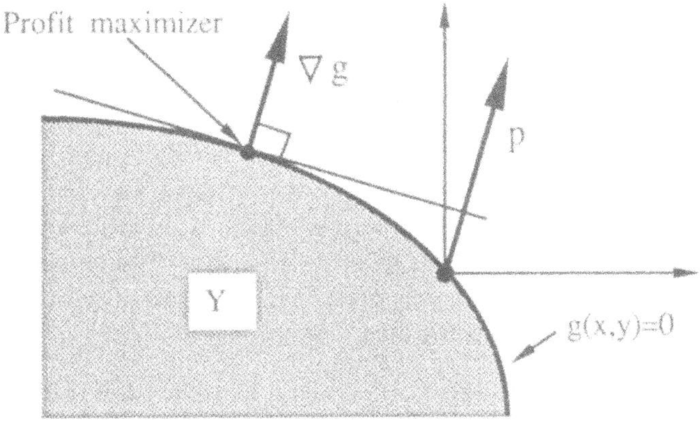

Fig. 1.7-4

Now consider a strictly convex production set Y. Then for each $\mathbf{p} \gg \mathbf{0}$ there exists exactly one production plan $\mathbf{y}(\mathbf{p})$ in Y that maximizes the profit function $\wp(\mathbf{y}) = \mathbf{p} \cdot \mathbf{y}$. In other words, every strictly convex production set Y defines a function

$$\mathbf{y}\colon \mathrm{Int}(\mathcal{R}^\ell_+) \longrightarrow \mathcal{R}^\ell,$$

which is known as the **supply** function corresponding to the production set Y. As expected, the supply function behaves quite well.

Theorem 1.7.7. *The supply function corresponding to a strictly convex production set is*

1) *homogeneous of degree zero;*
2) *bounded from above; and*
3) *continuous.*

Proof. Let Y be a strictly convex production set and let $\mathbf{y}\colon \mathrm{Int}(\mathcal{R}^\ell_+) \longrightarrow \mathcal{R}^\ell$ be its supply function.

(1) Note that an element $\mathbf{z} \in Y$ maximizes the function $\wp(\mathbf{y}) = \mathbf{p} \cdot \mathbf{y}$, $\mathbf{y} \in Y$ if and only if it also maximizes the function $\wp_\lambda(\mathbf{y}) = (\lambda\mathbf{p}) \cdot \mathbf{y} = \lambda(\mathbf{p} \cdot \mathbf{y})$, $\mathbf{y} \in Y$ for each $\lambda > 0$. This implies that $\mathbf{y}(\lambda\mathbf{p}) = \mathbf{y}(\mathbf{p})$ holds for all $\lambda > 0$.

(2) If $\mathbf{y} \le \mathbf{a}$ holds for all $\mathbf{y} \in Y$, then clearly $\mathbf{y}(\mathbf{p}) \le \mathbf{a}$ also holds for all $\mathbf{p} \gg \mathbf{0}$.

(3) Fix some $\mathbf{a} \in \mathcal{R}^\ell_+$ such that $\mathbf{y} \le \mathbf{a}$ holds for each $\mathbf{y} \in Y$. We shall establish first that the supply function $\mathbf{y}(\cdot)$ is bounded on the "boxes" of $\mathrm{Int}(\mathcal{R}^\ell_+)$. To this end, let $[\mathbf{r}, \mathbf{s}]$ be a box with $\mathbf{r} = (r_1, r_2, \ldots, r_\ell) \gg 0$. Put $r = \min\{r_1, r_2, \ldots, r_\ell\} > 0$. Now let $\mathbf{r} \le \mathbf{p} \le \mathbf{s}$. Clearly, $\mathbf{p} \cdot \mathbf{y}(\mathbf{p}) \ge 0$. Now if some component $y_i(\mathbf{p})$ of $\mathbf{y}(\mathbf{p})$ satisfies $y_i(\mathbf{p}) < 0$, then we have

$$r y_i(\mathbf{p}) \ge r_i y_i(\mathbf{p}) \ge \sum_{\substack{1\le j\le \ell \\ y_j(\mathbf{p})<0}} r_j y_j(\mathbf{p}) \ge -\sum_{\substack{1\le j\le \ell \\ y_j(\mathbf{p})\ge 0}} r_j y_j(\mathbf{p}) \ge -\sum_{j=1}^{\ell} r_j a_j = -\mathbf{r} \cdot \mathbf{a}\,.$$

Hence, $y_j(\mathbf{p}) \geq -\frac{\mathbf{r}\cdot\mathbf{a}}{r}$ holds for all $j = 1, 2, \ldots, \ell$, and so $\mathbf{y}(\cdot)$ is bounded on $[\mathbf{r}, \mathbf{s}]$. This conclusion, coupled with the Closed Graph Theorem (Lemma 1.3.7), reveals that the supply function $\mathbf{y}(\cdot)$ is continuous if and only if it has a closed graph.

To see that $\mathbf{y}(\cdot)$ has a closed graph, let $\mathbf{p}_n \longrightarrow \mathbf{p}$ in $\mathrm{Int}(\mathcal{R}^\ell_+)$ and $\mathbf{y}(\mathbf{p}_n) \longrightarrow \mathbf{y}$ in $\mathcal{R}^\ell$. Since Y is a closed set, we see that $\mathbf{y} \in Y$. On the other hand, if $\mathbf{z} \in Y$ is arbitrary, then from the inequality $\mathbf{p}_n\cdot\mathbf{y}(\mathbf{p}_n) \geq \mathbf{p}_n\cdot\mathbf{z}$ and the joint continuity of the dot product, we infer that $\mathbf{p}\cdot\mathbf{y} \geq \mathbf{p}\cdot\mathbf{z}$. Since $\mathbf{z}$ is arbitrary, the latter shows that $\mathbf{y}$ maximizes profit on Y at prices $\mathbf{p}$. Hence, by the uniqueness of the profit maximizing vector, we infer that $\mathbf{y} = \mathbf{y}(\mathbf{p})$. This shows that $\mathbf{y}(\cdot)$ has a closed graph and the proof of the theorem is finished. ■

The supply functions exhibit the following boundary behavior.

Theorem 1.7.8. *Consider a supply function* $\mathbf{y}(\cdot) = \big(y_1(\cdot), y_2(\cdot), \ldots, y_\ell(\cdot)\big)$ *corresponding to a strictly convex production set* Y *and let a sequence* $\{\mathbf{p}_n\}$ *of strictly positive prices satisfy*

$$\mathbf{p}_n = (p_1^n, p_2^n, \ldots, p_\ell^n) \longrightarrow \mathbf{p} = (p_1, p_2, \ldots, p_\ell)\,.$$

If $p_r > 0$ *holds for some* r, *then the sequence of real numbers* $\{y_r(\mathbf{p}_n)\}$*—the* r^{th} *component sequence of the supply sequence* $\{\mathbf{y}(\mathbf{p}_n)\}$*—is a bounded sequence.*

Proof. Assume that the supply function $\mathbf{y}(\cdot)$ and the sequence $\{\mathbf{p}_n\}$ of strictly positive prices satisfy the hypotheses of the theorem. Pick some $\mathbf{a} \in \mathcal{R}^\ell_+$ such that $\mathbf{y} \leq \mathbf{a}$ holds for all $\mathbf{y} \in Y$.

Then $y_r(\mathbf{p}_n) \leq a_r$ holds for all n, and so the sequence $\{y_r(\mathbf{p}_n)\}$ is bounded from above. To see that $\{y_r(\mathbf{p}_n)\}$ is also bounded from below fix some $\delta > 0$ and some $M > 0$ such that $p_r^n > \delta$ and $\mathbf{p}_n\cdot\mathbf{a} \leq M$ hold for all n. Now for $y_r(\mathbf{p}_n) < 0$, we have

$$\begin{aligned}
\delta y_r(\mathbf{p}_n) &\geq p_r^n y_r(\mathbf{p}_n) \\
&\geq \sum_{\substack{1\leq j\leq \ell \\ y_j(\mathbf{p}_n)<0}} p_j^n y_j(\mathbf{p}_n) \\
&\geq -\sum_{\substack{1\leq j\leq \ell \\ y_j(\mathbf{p}_n)\geq 0}} p_j^n y_j(\mathbf{p}_n) \\
&\geq -\sum_{j=1}^{\ell} p_j^n a_j \\
&= -\mathbf{p}_n\cdot\mathbf{a} \\
&\geq -M\,,
\end{aligned}$$

and so $y_r(\mathbf{p}_n) \geq -\frac{M}{\delta}$ holds for all n, as desired. ■

And now we are ready to describe the notion of a neoclassical private ownership production economy.

Definition 1.7.9. *A* **neoclassical private ownership production economy** $\mathcal{E}$ *is a 4-tuple*

$$\Big(\mathcal{R}^\ell, \{(\omega_i, \succeq_i): 1 \le i \le m\}, \{Y_j: 1 \le j \le k\}, \{\theta_{ij}: 1 \le i \le m;\ 1 \le j \le k\}\Big),$$

the components of which have the following interpretation:

1. $\mathcal{R}^\ell$ *is the commodity space, i.e., there are* ℓ *commodities in the economy.*
2. *There are* m *consumers indexed by* i *such that each consumer has an initial endowment* $\omega_i > \mathbf{0}$ *and a neoclassical preference* $\succeq_i$. *The total endowment is assumed to be strictly positive, i.e.,* $\omega = \sum_{i=1}^m \omega_i \gg \mathbf{0}$.
3. *There are* k *producers indexed by* j *such that the* j^{th} *producer is characterized by a strictly convex production set* Y_j.
4. *The economy is a private ownership economy. That is, the firms are owned by the consumers. The real number* θ_{ij} *represents consumer* i*'s share of producer* j*'s profit. It is assumed that* $0 \le \theta_{ij} \le 1$ *holds for all* i *and all* j *and* $\sum_{i=1}^m \theta_{ij} = 1$ *for all* $j = 1, \ldots, k$.

It is interesting to note that every neoclassical exchange economy can be considered as a neoclassical private ownership production economy with any number of producers having the strictly convex production sets $\{\mathbf{0}\}$ or $-\mathcal{R}^\ell_+$.

The supply function of the jth producer in a neoclassical private ownership production economy will be denoted by $\mathbf{y}_j(\cdot)$. Now from property (4) above, we see that the *income* of the ith consumer at prices $\mathbf{p} \gg \mathbf{0}$ is given by the formula

$$w_i(\mathbf{p}) = \mathbf{p} \cdot \omega_i + \sum_{j=1}^k \theta_{ij} \mathbf{p} \cdot \mathbf{y}_j(\mathbf{p}).$$

Since $\omega_i > \mathbf{0}$, it follows that $w_i(\mathbf{p}) > 0$ holds for each $\mathbf{p} \gg \mathbf{0}$. Thus, the income of consumer i is a function $w_i: \text{Int}(\mathcal{R}^\ell_+) \longrightarrow (0, \infty)$. It turns out that income functions are continuous.

Theorem 1.7.10. *In a neoclassical private ownership production economy, the income function of each consumer* $w_i: \text{Int}(\mathcal{R}^\ell_+) \longrightarrow (0, \infty)$, *defined by*

$$w_i(\mathbf{p}) = \mathbf{p} \cdot \omega_i + \sum_{j=1}^k \theta_{ij} \mathbf{p} \cdot \mathbf{y}_j(\mathbf{p}),$$

is continuous.

Proof. The desired conclusion follows immediately from the continuity of the supply functions $\mathbf{y}_j(\cdot)$ (Theorem 1.7.7) and the joint continuity of the dot product. ■

The budget set of the ith consumer is the closed convex set

$$\mathcal{B}_i(\mathbf{p}) = \{\mathbf{x} \in \mathcal{R}^\ell_+ : \ \mathbf{p}\cdot\mathbf{x} \le w_i(\mathbf{p})\}\,.$$

Since each consumer shares part of each producer's profit, each consumer's budget set is "larger" than the set $\{\mathbf{x} \in \mathcal{R}^\ell_+ : \ \mathbf{p}\cdot\mathbf{x} \le \mathbf{p}\cdot\omega_i\}$; see Figure 1.7-5.

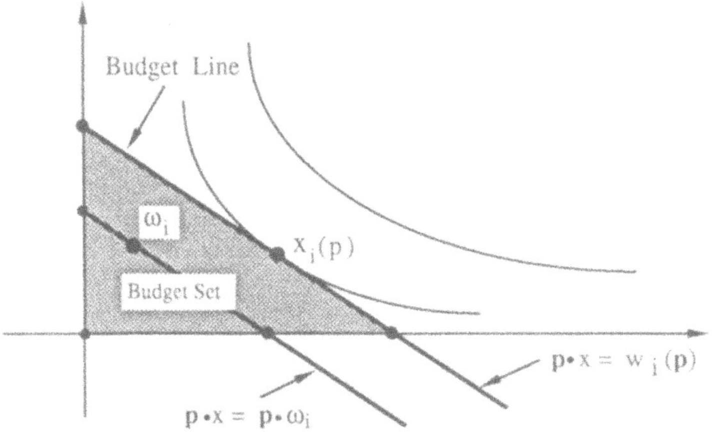

Fig. 1.7-5

When $\mathbf{p} \gg \mathbf{0}$, every budget set is bounded. To see this, fix $\mathbf{p} \gg \mathbf{0}$ and i, and note that for each $\mathbf{x} \in \mathcal{B}_i(\mathbf{p})$ and each $r = 1, 2, \ldots, \ell$, we have

$$0 \le x_r = \frac{p_r x_r}{p_r} \le \frac{\mathbf{p}\cdot\mathbf{x}}{p_r} \le \frac{w_i(\mathbf{p})}{p_r} < \infty\,,$$

and from this it follows that $\mathcal{B}_i(\mathbf{p})$ is a bounded set. Consequently, $\mathcal{B}_i(\mathbf{p})$ is a (non-empty) convex and compact subset of $\mathcal{R}^\ell$. By Theorem 1.3.2, for each $\mathbf{p} \gg 0$ there exists exactly one maximal element in $\mathcal{B}_i(\mathbf{p})$ for $\succeq_i$. This maximal element is called the **demand** of consumer i at prices $\mathbf{p}$ and is denoted by $\mathbf{x}_i(\mathbf{p})$. As in the exchange case, we can easily prove that $\mathbf{x}_i(\mathbf{p})$ lies on the budget line, i.e., it satisfies $\mathbf{p}\cdot\mathbf{x}_i(\mathbf{p}) = w_i(\mathbf{p})$; see Figure 1.7-5. Thus, each consumer i has a **demand function** $\mathbf{x}_i\colon \mathrm{Int}(\mathcal{R}^\ell_+) \longrightarrow \mathcal{R}^\ell$. It is important to note that demand functions of production economies behave as in the exchange case. We gather their properties in the next result which is the analogue of Theorem 1.3.9.

Theorem 1.7.11. *If $\mathbf{x}_i(\cdot) = \big(x^i_1(\cdot), x^i_2(\cdot), \ldots, x^i_\ell(\cdot)\big)$ is a demand function of the ith consumer in a neoclassical private ownership production economy, then:*

1. *$\mathbf{x}_i(\cdot)$ is homogeneous of degree zero;*
2. *$\mathbf{x}_i(\cdot)$ is continuous; and*
3. *$\{\mathbf{p}_n\} \subseteq \mathrm{Int}(\mathcal{R}^\ell_+)$, $\mathbf{p}_n \longrightarrow \mathbf{p} = (p_1, p_2, \ldots, p_\ell)$ and $p_r > 0$ imply that the sequence of real numbers $\{x^i_r(\mathbf{p}_n)\}$ is bounded.*

Proof. Let $\mathbf{x}_i(\cdot) = \big(x_1^i(\cdot), x_2^i(\cdot), \ldots, x_\ell^i(\cdot)\big)$ be a demand function for some consumer i in a neoclassical private ownership production economy.

(1) The zero degree homogeneity of $\mathbf{x}(\cdot)$ follows immediately from the identity $\mathcal{B}_i(\lambda\mathbf{p}) = \mathcal{B}_i(\mathbf{p})$.

(2) First note that $\mathbf{x}_i$ is bounded on the boxes of $\mathrm{Int}(\mathcal{R}_+^\ell)$. This, in connection with Lemma 1.3.7, shows that $\mathbf{x}_i$ is continuous if and only if $\mathbf{x}_i\colon \mathrm{Int}(\mathcal{R}_+^\ell) \longrightarrow \mathcal{R}^\ell$ has a closed graph.

To see that $\mathbf{x}_i$ has a closed graph, assume that $\mathbf{p}_n \longrightarrow \mathbf{p}$ in $\mathrm{Int}(\mathcal{R}_+^\ell)$ and $\mathbf{x}_i(\mathbf{p}_n) \longrightarrow \mathbf{x}$ in $\mathcal{R}^\ell$. From $\mathbf{p}_n{\cdot}\mathbf{x}_i(\mathbf{p}_n) = w_i(\mathbf{p}_n)$ and the continuity of the income and dot product functions, we infer that $\mathbf{p}\cdot\mathbf{x} = w_i(\mathbf{p})$, and so $\mathbf{x} \in \mathcal{B}_i(\mathbf{p})$. Thus, in order to show that $\mathbf{x} = \mathbf{x}(\mathbf{p})$ holds, it suffices to establish that $\mathbf{x}$ is a maximal element for $\succeq_i$ in $\mathcal{B}_i(\mathbf{p})$.

To this end, let $\mathbf{z} \in \mathcal{B}_i(\mathbf{p})$. We have to show that $\mathbf{x} \succeq_i \mathbf{z}$ holds. From $\mathbf{z} \in \mathcal{B}_i(\mathbf{p})$, it follows that $\mathbf{p}\cdot\mathbf{z} \le w_i(\mathbf{p})$ holds, and so (since $w_i(\mathbf{p}) > 0$) for each $0 < \lambda < 1$, we have $\mathbf{p}{\cdot}\lambda\mathbf{z} < w_i(\mathbf{p})$. From the continuity of the income and dot product functions, we see that there exists some n_0 such that $\mathbf{p}_n\cdot(\lambda\mathbf{z}) < w_i(\mathbf{p}_n)$ holds for all $n \ge n_0$. Hence, $\mathbf{x}_i(\mathbf{p}_n) \succeq_i \lambda\mathbf{z}$ holds for all $n \ge n_0$ and so $\mathbf{x} = \lim_{n\to\infty}\mathbf{x}_i(\mathbf{p}_n) \succeq_i \lambda\mathbf{z}$ for all $0 < \lambda < 1$. Letting $\lambda \uparrow 1$ and using the continuity of $\succeq_i$ once more, we conclude that $\mathbf{x} \succeq_i \mathbf{z}$, as desired.

(3) Fix $\delta > 0$ and $M > 0$ such that $p_r^n > \delta$ and $\mathbf{p}_n{\cdot}(\omega_i + \mathbf{a}) < M$ hold for each n. Then note that

$$\begin{aligned}
0 \le x_r^i(\mathbf{p}_n) &= \frac{p_r^n x_r^i(\mathbf{p}_n)}{p_r^n} < \frac{p_r^n x_r^i(\mathbf{p}_n)}{\delta} \le \frac{\mathbf{p}_n{\cdot}\mathbf{x}_i(\mathbf{p}_n)}{\delta}\\
&= \frac{\mathbf{p}_n{\cdot}\omega_i + \sum_{j=1}^k \theta_{ij}\mathbf{p}_n{\cdot}\mathbf{y}_j(\mathbf{p}_n)}{\delta} \le \frac{\mathbf{p}_n{\cdot}\omega_i + \sum_{j=1}^k \theta_{ij}\mathbf{p}_n{\cdot}\mathbf{a}}{\delta}\\
&= \frac{\mathbf{p}_n{\cdot}\omega_i + \mathbf{p}_n{\cdot}\mathbf{a}}{\delta} = \frac{\mathbf{p}_n{\cdot}(\omega_i + \mathbf{a})}{\delta} < \frac{M}{\delta},
\end{aligned}$$

holds for each n, and the desired conclusion follows. ■

The next result describes an important boundary behavior of the demand and supply functions.

Theorem 1.7.12. *Consider a neoclassical private ownership production economy and let $\{\mathbf{p}_n\}$ be a sequence of strictly positive prices satisfying $\mathbf{p}_n \longrightarrow \mathbf{p} \in \partial\mathcal{R}_+^\ell\setminus\{\mathbf{0}\}$. Then there exists at least one $1 \le r \le \ell$ such that either*

1) $\limsup_{n\to\infty} x_r^i(\mathbf{p}_n) = \infty$ *holds for some consumer i, or*
2) $\limsup_{n\to\infty} y_r^j(\mathbf{p}_n) = -\infty$ *holds for some producer j.*

Proof. Assume that $\{\mathbf{p}_n\} \subseteq \mathrm{Int}(\mathcal{R}_+^\ell)$ satisfies $\mathbf{p}_n \longrightarrow \mathbf{p} \in \partial\mathcal{R}_+^\ell \setminus \{\mathbf{0}\}$. Suppose by way of contradiction that the sequences $\{\mathbf{x}_i(\mathbf{p}_n)\}$ and $\{\mathbf{y}_j(\mathbf{p}_n)\}$ are bounded for each $i = 1, 2, \ldots, m$ and each $j = 1, 2, \ldots, k$. Then—by passing to an appropriate subsequence and relabelling—we can assume without loss of generality that

$$\mathbf{x}_i(\mathbf{p}_n) \longrightarrow \mathbf{x}_i \quad\text{and}\quad \mathbf{y}_j(\mathbf{p}_n) \longrightarrow \mathbf{y}_j$$

hold for each $i = 1, 2, \ldots, m$ and each $j = 1, 2, \ldots, k$.

From $\mathbf{p}_n \cdot \mathbf{x}_i(\mathbf{p}_n) = \mathbf{p}_n \cdot \omega_i + \sum_{j=1}^{k} \theta_{ij} \mathbf{p}_n \cdot \mathbf{y}_j(\mathbf{p}_n)$, we obtain that

$$\mathbf{p} \cdot \mathbf{x}_i = \mathbf{p} \cdot \omega_i + \sum_{j=1}^{k} \theta_{ij} \mathbf{p} \cdot \mathbf{y}_j$$

holds for each $i = 1, 2, \ldots, m$. Since $\mathbf{p} > \mathbf{0}$ and $\omega = \sum_{i=1}^{m} \omega_i \gg \mathbf{0}$, there exists some i such that $\mathbf{p} \cdot \omega_i > 0$. Now put $w_i = \mathbf{p} \cdot \omega_i + \sum_{j=1}^{k} \theta_{ij} \mathbf{p} \cdot \mathbf{y}_j$ and note that $w_i \geq \mathbf{p} \cdot \omega_i > 0$. (For this we have to observe that $\mathbf{p}_n \cdot \mathbf{y}_j(\mathbf{p}_n) \geq 0$ implies $\mathbf{p} \cdot \mathbf{y}_j \geq 0$.)

Next, consider the set

$$\mathcal{B} = \{\mathbf{x} \in \mathcal{R}_+^\ell \colon \ \mathbf{p} \cdot \mathbf{x} \leq w_i\}.$$

Clearly, $\mathbf{x}_i \in \mathcal{B}$. Since $w_i > 0$ holds, an easy argument—like the one in the proof of Theorem 1.3.3(2)—shows that $\succeq_i$ does not have any maximal element in $\mathcal{B}$. To obtain a contradiction, we shall establish that the element $\mathbf{x}_i$ is a maximal element for $\succeq_i$ in $\mathcal{B}$.

To this end, let $\mathbf{z} \in \mathcal{B}$, i.e., $\mathbf{p} \cdot \mathbf{z} \leq w_i$. From $w_i > 0$, we see that $\mathbf{p} \cdot (\lambda \mathbf{z}) < w_i$ holds for all $0 < \lambda < 1$. By the continuity of the dot product, we see that there exists some n_0 satisfying

$$\mathbf{p}_n \cdot (\lambda \mathbf{z}) < \mathbf{p}_n \cdot \omega_i + \sum_{j=1}^{k} \theta_{ij} \mathbf{p}_n \cdot \mathbf{y}_j(\mathbf{p}_n)$$

for all $n \geq n_0$. Consequently, $\lambda \mathbf{z} \in \mathcal{B}_i(\mathbf{p}_n)$ holds for all $n \geq n_0$, and so $\mathbf{x}_i(\mathbf{p}_n) \succeq_i \lambda \mathbf{z}$ for each $n \geq n_0$. From the continuity of $\succeq_i$, it follows that $\mathbf{x}_i \succeq_i \lambda \mathbf{z}$ for all $0 < \lambda < 1$. Letting $\lambda \uparrow 1$ and using the continuity of $\succeq_i$ once more, we see that $\mathbf{x}_i \succeq_i \mathbf{z}$ holds for all $\mathbf{z} \in \mathcal{B}$, and this contradiction completes the proof of the theorem. ■

We can now define the excess demand function for a neoclassical private ownership production economy.

Definition 1.7.13. *If $\mathcal{E}$ is a neoclassical private ownership production economy, then the* **excess demand function** $\zeta \colon \mathrm{Int}(\mathcal{R}_+^\ell) \longrightarrow \mathcal{R}^\ell$ *is the function defined by*

$$\zeta(\mathbf{p}) = \sum_{i=1}^{m} \mathbf{x}_i(\mathbf{p}) - \sum_{j=1}^{k} \mathbf{y}_j(\mathbf{p}) - \sum_{i=1}^{m} \omega_i = \sum_{i=1}^{m} \mathbf{x}_i(\mathbf{p}) - \sum_{j=1}^{k} \mathbf{y}_j(\mathbf{p}) - \omega .$$

Here are the basic properties of the excess demand function. They are the same as the ones in the exchange case (Theorem 1.4.4).

Theorem 1.7.14. *The excess demand function ζ of a neoclassical private ownership production economy satisfies the following properties.*

1) *ζ is homogeneous of degree zero, i.e., $\zeta(\lambda \mathbf{p}) = \zeta(\mathbf{p})$ holds for all $\mathbf{p} \gg \mathbf{0}$ and all $\lambda > 0$.*
2) *ζ is bounded from below.*
3) *ζ is continuous.*
4) *ζ satisfies Walras' Law, i.e., $\mathbf{p} \cdot \zeta(\mathbf{p}) = 0$ holds for all $\mathbf{p} \gg \mathbf{0}$.*
5) *If a sequence $\{\mathbf{p}_n\}$ of strictly positive prices satisfies*

$$\mathbf{p}_n = (p_1^n, p_2^n, \ldots, p_\ell^n) \longrightarrow \mathbf{p} = (p_1, p_2, \ldots, p_\ell)$$

and $p_i > 0$ holds for some i, then the sequence $\{\zeta_i(\mathbf{p}_n)\}$ of the ith components of $\{\zeta(\mathbf{p}_n)\}$ is bounded.

6) *If $\mathbf{p}_n \gg \mathbf{0}$ holds for each n and $\mathbf{p}_n \longrightarrow \mathbf{p} \in \partial \mathcal{R}_+^\ell \setminus \{\mathbf{0}\}$, then*

$$\lim_{n\to\infty} \|\zeta(\mathbf{p}_n)\|_1 = \infty .$$

Proof. (1) The proof follows immediately from Theorems 1.7.7 and 1.7.11.

(2) This follows immediately by observing that since each production set Y_j is bounded from above, each set $-Y_j$ is bounded from below.

(3) The continuity of the excess demand function follows immediately from Theorems 1.7.7 and 1.7.11.

(4) For each $\mathbf{p} \gg \mathbf{0}$, we have

$$\begin{aligned}
\mathbf{p}\cdot\zeta(\mathbf{p}) &= \mathbf{p}\cdot\Big(\sum_{i=1}^m \mathbf{x}_i(\mathbf{p}) - \sum_{j=1}^k \mathbf{y}_j(\mathbf{p}) - \sum_{i=1}^m \omega_i\Big)\\
&= \mathbf{p}\cdot\Big(\sum_{i=1}^m \Big[\mathbf{x}_i(\mathbf{p}) - \sum_{j=1}^k \theta_{ij}\mathbf{y}_j(\mathbf{p}) - \omega_i\Big]\Big)\\
&= \sum_{i=1}^m \Big[\mathbf{p}\cdot\mathbf{x}_i(\mathbf{p}) - \sum_{j=1}^k \theta_{ij}\mathbf{p}\cdot\mathbf{y}_j(\mathbf{p}) - \mathbf{p}\cdot\omega_i\Big]\\
&= \sum_{i=1}^m 0\\
&= 0 .
\end{aligned}$$

(5) This is a consequence of Theorems 1.7.8 and 1.7.11.

(6) Since each function $-\mathbf{y}_j(\cdot)$ is bounded from below, the conclusion follows immediately from Theorem 1.7.12. ■

The notion of an equilibrium price is now defined as in the exchange case. We say that a strictly positive price $\mathbf{p}$ is **an equilibrium price** for a neoclassical private ownership production economy whenever the excess demand vanishes at $\mathbf{p}$, i.e., whenever $\zeta(\mathbf{p}) = \mathbf{0}$ holds.

At an equilibrium price $\mathbf{p}$ the equation $\zeta(\mathbf{p}) = \mathbf{0}$ expresses the fact that supply equals demand at prices $\mathbf{p}$. The Arrow–Debreu theorem gives sufficient conditions for a production economy to have at least one equilibrium price.

Theorem 1.7.15. (Arrow–Debreu) *Every neoclassical private ownership production economy has an equilibrium price.*

Proof. By Theorem 1.7.14, we know that the excess demand function $\zeta: S \longrightarrow \mathcal{R}^\ell$ of a neoclassical private ownership production economy satisfies all hypotheses of Theorem 1.4.8. Hence, there exists some $\mathbf{p} \gg \mathbf{0}$ such that $\zeta(\mathbf{p}) = \mathbf{0}$. ■

The above result implies immediately the corresponding theorem for neoclassical exchange economies. Again, it should be pointed out that the proof of this theorem is non constructive, and we refer the reader to Scarf's monogram [61] for a constructive proof of existence. The final example of this section illustrates the difficulty in computing equilibrium prices even for a simple production economy.

Example 1.7.16. Consider the neoclassical private ownership production economy having

1) Commodity space $\mathcal{R}^2$;
2) Two consumers with characteristics:
   Consumer 1: Initial endowment $\omega_1 = (1,2)$ and utility function $u_1(x,y) = xy$,
   Consumer 2: Initial endowment $\omega_2 = (2,2)$ and utility function $u_2(x,y) = x^2y$;
3) One producer with production set

$$Y = \Big\{(x,y)\colon\ x < 1 \text{ and } y \le \tfrac{x}{x-1}\Big\}\ ; \text{ and}$$

4) Shares $\theta_{11} = \theta_{21} = \frac{1}{2}$.

The production set is shown in Figure 1.7-6. The efficiency frontier in this case coincides with the boundary of Y and is the set

$$\mathbf{Eff}(Y) = \Big\{(x,y)\colon\ x < 1 \text{ and } y = \tfrac{x}{x-1}\Big\}\,.$$

First, a price vector $\mathbf{p} = (p_1, p_2) \gg \mathbf{0}$ is announced. Then the producer chooses a plan which will maximize her profit function. This is the production plan (x,y) in the efficiency frontier whose normal line has slope $\frac{p_2}{p_1}$; see Figure 1.7-6. Differentiating $y = \frac{x}{x-1}$, we see that $y' = -\frac{1}{(x-1)^2}$ and so the normal line has slope $(x-1)^2$. Therefore, the profit maximizing production plan (x,y) satisfies $(x-1)^2 = \frac{p_2}{p_1}$. Introducing the parameter

$$t = \sqrt{\frac{p_2}{p_1}} > 0\,,$$

we see that $x = 1 - t$ and $y = 1 - \frac{1}{t}$. Thus, the supply function is

$$\mathbf{y}(\mathbf{p}) = (1 - t, 1 - \tfrac{1}{t}), \quad \text{where} \quad t = \sqrt{\tfrac{p_2}{p_1}}.$$

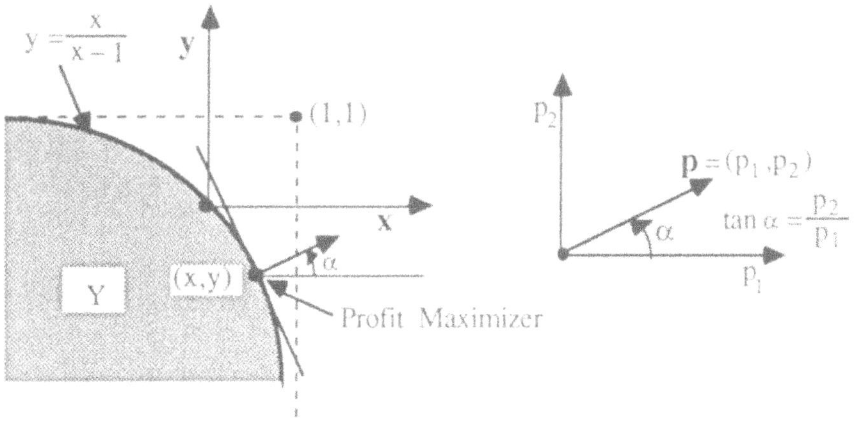

Fig. 1.7-6

Now let us look at the decision of the first consumer. Her income is

$$w_1(\mathbf{p}) = \mathbf{p} \cdot \omega_1 + \tfrac{1}{2}\mathbf{p} \cdot \mathbf{y}(\mathbf{p}) = p_1 + 2p_2 + \tfrac{1}{2}p_1(1 - t) + \tfrac{1}{2}p_2(1 - \tfrac{1}{t}).$$

She maximizes her utility function $u_1(x, y) = xy$ subject to her budget constraint $p_1x + p_2y = w_1(\mathbf{p})$. Using Lagrange multipliers, we see that at her utility maximizer bundle (x, y) we must have $p_1x = p_2y$. Thus, $w_1(\mathbf{p}) = p_1x + p_2y = 2p_1x = 2p_2y$, and so

$$x = \tfrac{w_1(\mathbf{p})}{2p_1} = \tfrac{3}{4} + \tfrac{5}{4}t^2 - \tfrac{1}{2}t \qquad \text{and} \qquad y = \tfrac{w_1(\mathbf{p})}{2p_2} = \tfrac{5}{4} + \tfrac{3}{4t^2} - \tfrac{1}{2t}.$$

Consequently, the demand function for consumer one is:

$$\mathbf{x}_1(\mathbf{p}) = \left(\tfrac{3}{4} + \tfrac{5}{4}t^2 - \tfrac{1}{2}t, \tfrac{5}{4} + \tfrac{3}{4t^2} - \tfrac{1}{2t}\right).$$

The second consumer is next. Her income is

$$w_2(\mathbf{p}) = \mathbf{p} \cdot \omega_2 + \tfrac{1}{2}\mathbf{p} \cdot \mathbf{y}(\mathbf{p}) = 2p_1 + 2p_2 + \tfrac{1}{2}p_1(1 - t) + \tfrac{1}{2}p_2(1 - \tfrac{1}{t}),$$

and she maximizes her utility function $u_2(x, y) = x^2y$ subject to her budget constraint $p_1x + p_2y = w_2(\mathbf{p})$. At the maximizing bundle, the Lagrange Multiplier Method guarantees that $p_1x = 2p_2y$, and so $w_2(\mathbf{p}) = p_1x + p_2y = \frac{3}{2}p_1x = 3p_2y$. This implies

$$x = \tfrac{2w_2(\mathbf{p})}{3p_1} = \tfrac{5}{3} + \tfrac{5}{3}t^2 - \tfrac{2}{3}t \qquad \text{and} \qquad y = \tfrac{w_2(\mathbf{p})}{3p_2} = \tfrac{5}{6} + \tfrac{5}{6t^2} - \tfrac{1}{3t}.$$

The above show that the demand function of the second consumer is:

$$\mathbf{x}_2(\mathbf{p}) = \left(\tfrac{5}{3} + \tfrac{5}{3}t^2 - \tfrac{2}{3}t, \tfrac{5}{6} + \tfrac{5}{6t^2} - \tfrac{1}{3t}\right).$$

The excess demand function for this production economy is now given by the formula

$$\zeta(\mathbf{p}) = \mathbf{x}_1(\mathbf{p}) + \mathbf{x}_2(\mathbf{p}) - \mathbf{y}(\mathbf{p}) - \omega_1 - \omega_2 = \left(\tfrac{35t^2-2t-19}{12}, -\tfrac{35t^2-2t-19}{12t^2}\right).$$

Consequently, $\zeta(\mathbf{p}) = \mathbf{0}$ if and only if $35t^2 - 2t - 19 = 0$. Solving the quadratic and taking into account that $t > 0$, we get

$$t = \tfrac{1+\sqrt{666}}{35} \approx 0.766\,.$$

Since $\frac{p_2}{p_1} = t^2 \approx 0.587$, we see that the equilibrium prices are given by the formula

$$\mathbf{p}_{eq} = p_1(1, t^2) \approx p_1(1, 0.587), \quad p_1 > 0\,.$$

Figure 1.7-7 illustrates the half-line of equilibrium prices in the price plane. ■

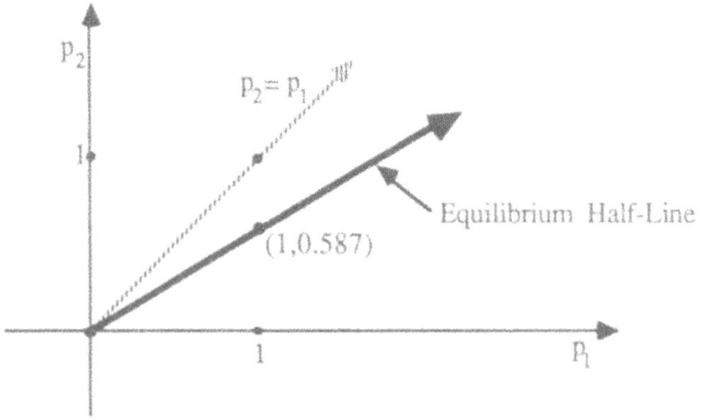

Fig. 1.7-7

EXERCISES

1. Consider the production set $Y = \{(x, y) \in \mathcal{R}^2\colon\ x \leq a \text{ and } y \leq 1 - e^x\}$, where $a \geq 0$ is a fixed real number.
   a) Sketch the production set Y and show that it is a strictly convex production set.

b) Find the equation of the efficiency frontier. *Answer*: $y = 1 - e^x\,,\ x \le a$

c) Find the supply function for the production set Y.
Answer: $\mathbf{y}(\mathbf{p}) = \left(-\ln(\frac{p_2}{p_1}), 1 - \frac{p_1}{p_2}\right)$ if $\frac{p_2}{p_1} \ge e^{-a}$ and $\mathbf{y}(\mathbf{p}) = (a, 1 - e^a)$ if $\frac{p_2}{p_1} < e^{-a}$

2. Consider the neoclassical private ownership production economy with commodity space $\mathcal{R}^2$ having two consumers and two producers with the following characteristics.
Consumer 1: Initial endowment $\omega_1 = (1,3)$ and utility function $u_1(x,y) = xy$.
Consumer 2: Initial endowment $\omega_2 = (2,3)$ and utility function $u_2(x,y) = xy^2$.
Producer 1: Production set $Y_1 = \{(x,y) \in \mathcal{R}^2\colon\ x < 1 \text{ and } y \le \frac{x}{x-1}\}$.
Producer 2: Production set $Y_2 = \{(x,y) \in \mathcal{R}^2\colon\ x < 1 \text{ and } y \le g(x)\}$, where

$$g(x) = \begin{cases} 1 - e^x, & \text{if } x \le 0\,;\\ \ln(1-x), & \text{if } 0 < x < 1\,. \end{cases}$$

Shares: $\theta_{11} = \frac{1}{3}$, $\theta_{12} = \frac{2}{3}$, $\theta_{21} = \frac{2}{3}$ and $\theta_{22} = \frac{1}{3}$.

a) Find the supply functions of the producers. *Answer*: If $t = \sqrt{\frac{p_2}{p_1}}$, then

$$\mathbf{y}_1(\mathbf{p}) = \left(1 - t, 1 - \tfrac{1}{t}\right) \quad\text{and}\quad \mathbf{y}_2(\mathbf{p}) = \begin{cases} \left(-2\ln t, 1 - \frac{1}{t^2}\right), & \text{if } t \ge 1\,;\\ \left(1 - t^2, 2\ln t\right), & \text{if } 0 < t < 1\,. \end{cases}$$

b) Find the demand functions of the consumers. *Answer*:

$$\mathbf{x}_1(\mathbf{p}) = \begin{cases} \left(\frac{6t^2 - t - 2\ln t + 1}{3}, \frac{6t^2 - t - 2\ln t + 1}{3t^2}\right), & \text{if } t \ge 1\,,\\ \left(\frac{4t^2 - t + 2t^2\ln t + 3}{3}, \frac{4t^2 - t + 2t^2\ln t + 3}{3t^2}\right), & \text{if } 0 < t < 1\,; \end{cases}$$

$$\mathbf{x}_2(\mathbf{p}) = \begin{cases} \left(\frac{12t^2 - 4t - 2\ln t + 7}{9}, \frac{2(12t^2 - 4t - 2\ln t + 7)}{9t^2}\right), & \text{if } t \ge 1\,,\\ \left(\frac{10t^2 - 4t + 2t^2\ln t + 9}{9}, \frac{2(10t^2 - 4t + 2t^2\ln t + 9)}{9t^2}\right), & \text{if } 0 < t < 1\,. \end{cases}$$

c) Find the excess demand function. *Answer*:

$$\zeta(\mathbf{p}) = \begin{cases} \left(\frac{30t^2 + 2t + 10\ln t - 26}{9}, -\frac{30t^2 + 2t + 10\ln t - 26}{9t^2}\right), & \text{if } t \ge 1\,;\\ \left(\frac{31t^2 + 2t + 8t^2\ln t - 27}{9}, -\frac{31t^2 + 2t + 8t^2\ln t - 27}{9t^2}\right), & \text{if } 0 < t < 1\,. \end{cases}$$

d) Find the equilibrium prices for the production economy.
Answer: $t \approx 0.91208$; $\mathbf{p}_{eq} \approx p_1(1, 0.8319)$, $p_1 > 0$

3. Is the efficiency frontier of an arbitrary production set necessarily closed?

4. This exercise presents another proof of the Arrow–Debreu theorem for production economies in a more general context. Consider a production economy with m consumers and k producers. Each consumer has a continuous convex preference with an extremely desirable vector and each producer is characterized by a production set. For each $\mathbf{p} \gg \mathbf{0}$ we put

$$\mathbf{x}_i(\mathbf{p}) = \{\mathbf{z} \in \mathcal{B}_i(\mathbf{p})\colon\ \mathbf{z} \succeq_i \mathbf{x} \text{ for all } \mathbf{x} \in \mathcal{B}_i(\mathbf{p})\}$$

and

$$\mathbf{y}_j(\mathbf{p}) = \{\mathbf{z} \in Y_j\colon\ \mathbf{p}\cdot\mathbf{y} \le \mathbf{p}\cdot\mathbf{z} \ \text{ for all } \ \mathbf{y} \in Y_j\}$$

and then define the *excess demand correspondence* $\zeta\colon \mathrm{Int}(\mathcal{R}^\ell_+) \longrightarrow \mathcal{R}^\ell$ by

$$\zeta(\mathbf{p}) = \sum_{i=1}^{m} \mathbf{x}_i(\mathbf{p}) - \sum_{j=1}^{k} \mathbf{y}_j(\mathbf{p}) - \omega\,.$$

a) Show that for each $\mathbf{p} \gg \mathbf{0}$ the sets $\mathbf{x}_i(\mathbf{p})$ and $\mathbf{y}_j(\mathbf{p})$ are all non-empty, convex and compact.
b) Show that the excess demand correspondence is non-empty, convex-valued and compact-valued.
c) Show that for each $\mathbf{z} \in \zeta(\mathbf{p})$ we have $\mathbf{p}\cdot\mathbf{z} = 0$.
d) If $\{\mathbf{p}_n\} \subseteq \mathrm{Int}(\mathcal{R}^\ell_+)$ satisfies $\mathbf{p}_n \longrightarrow \mathbf{p} \in \partial\mathcal{R}^\ell_+ \setminus \{0\}$ and $\mathbf{z}_n \in \zeta(\mathbf{p}_n)$ holds for for each n, then show that $\lim_{n\to\infty} \|\mathbf{z}_n\|_1 = \infty$.
e) Show that if $\mathbf{p}_n \longrightarrow \mathbf{p}$ holds in $\mathrm{Int}(\mathcal{R}^\ell_+)$ and $\mathbf{z}_n \in \zeta(\mathbf{p}_n)$ for each n, then there exists a subsequence $\{\mathbf{y}_n\}$ of the sequence $\{\mathbf{z}_n\}$ and some $\mathbf{y} \in \zeta(\mathbf{p})$ such that $\mathbf{y}_n \longrightarrow \mathbf{y}$.
f) Show that ζ has an equilibrium price, i.e., show that there exists some $\mathbf{p} \gg \mathbf{0}$ such that $\mathbf{0} \in \zeta(\mathbf{p})$.
[HINT: Mimic the arguments of Exercise 5 of Section 1.4.]

5. Consider a neoclassical private ownership production economy whose *aggregate production set* $Y = Y_1 + \cdots + Y_k$ is a cone. If $\{\mathbf{y}_n\} \subseteq Y$ satisfies $\mathbf{y}_n^- \to \mathbf{0}$, then show that $\mathbf{y}_n^+ \to \mathbf{0}$.
[HINT: Any equilibrium price $\mathbf{p}$ satisfies $\mathbf{p} \gg \mathbf{0}$ and $0 \ge \mathbf{p}\cdot(\mathbf{y}_n^+ - \mathbf{y}_n^-)$.]

6. This exercise presents another proof—due to C. D. Aliprantis and D. J. Brown [1]—of the Arrow–Debreu theorem. Let

$$\Delta = \{\mathbf{p} \in \mathcal{R}^\ell_+\colon\ p_1 + p_2 + \ldots + p_\ell = 1\} \qquad \text{and} \qquad S = \{\mathbf{p} \in \Delta\colon\ \mathbf{p} \gg 0\}\,,$$

and consider a function $\zeta\colon S \longrightarrow \mathcal{R}^\ell$ such that:
a) ζ is continuous;
b) $\mathbf{p}\cdot\zeta(\mathbf{p}) = 0$ holds for each $\mathbf{p} \in S$; and
c) if a sequence $\{\mathbf{p}_n\}$ of S satisfies $\mathbf{p}_n \longrightarrow \mathbf{p} \in \Delta \setminus S$, then there exists a price $\mathbf{q} \in S$ with $\limsup_{n\to\infty} \mathbf{q}\cdot\zeta(\mathbf{p}_n) > 0$.

1. Using Theorem 1.7.14 show that the excess demand function ζ of a neoclassical private ownership production economy satisfies the above three properties.
2. Define the *revealed preference relation* $\mathfrak{R}$ on S by $\mathbf{p}\,\mathfrak{R}\,\mathbf{q}$ if $\mathbf{p}\cdot\zeta(\mathbf{q}) > 0$ holds. Show that the revealed preference relation satisfies the following properties.
   α) $\mathfrak{R}$ is irreflexive, i.e., $\mathbf{p}\,\mathfrak{R}\,\mathbf{p}$ is false for each $\mathbf{p} \in S$;
   β) $\mathfrak{R}$ is convex, i.e., for each $\mathbf{p} \in S$ the set $\{\mathbf{q} \in S\colon\ \mathbf{q}\,\mathfrak{R}\,\mathbf{p}\}$ is a convex

set; and

γ) $\Re$ is upper-semicontinuous, i.e., $\{\mathbf{q} \in S\colon \ \mathbf{p}\,\Re\,\mathbf{q}\}$ is open in S for each price $\mathbf{p} \in S$.

3. If C is the convex hull of a finite subset of S, then show that there exists a price $\mathbf{p} \in C$ such that $\mathbf{q}\cdot\zeta(\mathbf{p}) \le 0$ holds for each $\mathbf{q} \in C$.
   [HINT: For each $\mathbf{q} \in C$ consider the compact set $F(\mathbf{p}) = \{\mathbf{p} \in C\colon \ \mathbf{p}\cdot\zeta(\mathbf{q}) \le 0\}$. If $\mathbf{q}_1, \ldots, \mathbf{q}_r \in C$, then we claim that $\operatorname{co}\{\mathbf{q}_1, \ldots, \mathbf{q}_r\} \subseteq \bigcup_{i=1}^r F(\mathbf{q}_i)$. Indeed, if $\mathbf{p} = \sum_{i=1}^r \lambda_i \mathbf{q}_i$ is a convex combination and $\mathbf{p} \notin \bigcup_{i=1}^r F(\mathbf{q}_i)$, then $\mathbf{p}_i\,\Re\,\mathbf{p}$ holds for each i, and so by the convexity of $\Re$, we see that $\mathbf{p}\,\Re\,\mathbf{p}$, contrary to the irreflexivity of $\Re$. Now by K. Fan's [27] generalization of the classical Knaster-Kuratowski-Mazurkiewicz theorem [40], it follows that $\bigcap_{\mathbf{q}\in C} F(\mathbf{q}) \neq \emptyset$. If $\mathbf{p} \in \bigcap_{\mathbf{q}\in C} F(\mathbf{q})$, then $\mathbf{q}\cdot\zeta(\mathbf{p}) \le 0$ holds for all $\mathbf{q} \in C$.]
4. Show that there exists a price $\mathbf{p} \in S$ satisfying $\zeta(\mathbf{p}) = \mathbf{0}$.
   [HINT: Let $\mathcal{F}$ denote the collection of all finite subsets of S. For each $\alpha \in \mathcal{F}$ let C_α denote the convex hull of α. Clearly, C_α is a compact subset of S and $\bigcup_{\alpha\in\mathcal{F}} C_\alpha = S$. The collection $\{C_\alpha\colon \ \alpha \in \mathcal{F}\}$ is directed upwards by inclusion. By part (3) for each α there exists some price $\mathbf{p}_\alpha \in C_\alpha$ satisfying $\mathbf{q}\cdot\zeta(\mathbf{p}_\alpha) \le 0$ for all $\mathbf{q} \in C_\alpha$. Now consider the net $\{\mathbf{p}_\alpha\colon \ \alpha \in \mathcal{F}\}$ and note that by passing to a subnet, we can assume that $\mathbf{p}_\alpha \to \mathbf{p}$ holds in Δ. If $\mathbf{p} \in \Delta \setminus S$, then by our assumption (c), there exists some $\mathbf{q} \in S$ satisfying $\limsup_\alpha \mathbf{q}\cdot\zeta(\mathbf{p}_\alpha) > 0$. However, if $\mathbf{q} \in C_\beta$, then $\mathbf{q} \in C_\alpha$ for all $\alpha \supseteq \beta$ and so $\mathbf{q}\cdot\zeta(\mathbf{p}_\alpha) \le 0$ for all $\alpha \supseteq \beta$, which is a contradiction. So, $\mathbf{p} \in S$. Finally, to see that $\zeta(\mathbf{p}) = \mathbf{0}$ fix $\mathbf{q} \in S$, and use assumption (a) to infer that $\mathbf{q}\cdot\zeta(\mathbf{p}) = \lim_\alpha \mathbf{q}\cdot\zeta(\mathbf{p}_\alpha) \le 0$ holds. Since $\mathbf{p} \in S$ is arbitrary, conclude that $\zeta(\mathbf{p}) = \mathbf{0}$.]

CHAPTER 2:

RIESZ SPACES OF COMMODITIES AND PRICES

G. Debreu's proposal in [22] that the commodity space E and price space E' for economies with an infinite number of commodities be viewed as dual topological vector spaces $\langle E, E' \rangle$ was refined in [16] by T. F. Bewley in his seminal study of the existence of equilibrium prices in capital markets. He required that $\langle E, E' \rangle$ be a dual pair of locally convex spaces and introduced the Mackey topology for the given pairing as the appropriate locally convex topology for equilibrium analysis on infinite dimensional commodity spaces.

As noted earlier, D. M. Kreps [41] considered ordered locally convex spaces and their dual spaces as commodity-price dual spaces in his study of arbitrage in financial markets. We shall refine the duality of D. M. Kreps by supposing that $\langle E, E' \rangle$ are dual topological Riesz spaces. The lattice operations in a Riesz space were originally motivated by consideration of option pricing in financial markets—see D. J. Brown and S. A. Ross's paper [19] for a discussion of this motivation—but C. D. Aliprantis and D. J. Brown first recognized in [1] that the commodity and price spaces of all the current equilibrium models were dual topological Riesz spaces.

The equilibrium analysis in this book will be conducted within the framework of dual topological Riesz spaces. Accordingly, this chapter discusses briefly the properties of these spaces that are necessary for our investigations. We assume the reader is familiar with the standard theory of topological vector spaces (and, in particular, with the theory of locally convex spaces) as it is exposited in the books [31, 33, 58, 62]. For detail accounts of the theory of Riesz spaces the reader can consult the monographs [6, 8, 42, 63, 70].

When working with infinite dimensional vector spaces as commodity spaces one should keep in mind the following six basic structural differences between these spaces and their finite dimensional counterparts.

1. *Non-uniqueness of the topology.* While a finite dimensional vector space admits only one (Hausdorff) linear topology, an arbitrary infinite dimensional vector space admits many linear topologies.
2. *Multiplicity of dual spaces.* A finite dimensional vector space has only one dual while an infinite dimensional vector space can have several "duals."

3. *Lack of joint continuity of the evaluation map.* While in the finite dimensional case the evaluation map $(\mathbf{x}, \mathbf{p}) \longmapsto \mathbf{p} \cdot \mathbf{x}$ is jointly continuous, in the infinite dimensional case the evaluation map is no longer jointly continuous.
4. *Non-compactness of the order intervals.* The "boxes" of a finite dimensional vector space are always compact while their counterparts in an infinite dimensional topological Riesz space need not even be weakly compact.
5. *Empty interior of the positive cone.* The positive cone of a finite dimensional vector space always has interior points while the positive cone of an arbitrary topological Riesz space need not have interior points.
6. *Loss of properness.* A monotone preference on the positive cone of a finite dimensional vector space is automatically uniformly proper—see Section 3.2 for the definition—while on an infinite dimensional Riesz space such a claim is not true.

2.1. PARTIALLY ORDERED VECTOR SPACES

A **partially ordered vector space** is a real vector space E equipped with an order relation $\geq$ (i.e., equipped with a reflexive, antisymmetric and transitive relation $\geq$) which is compatible with the algebraic structure in the sense that

a) $x \geq y$ implies $x + z \geq y + z$ for all $z \in E$; and
b) $x \geq y$ implies $\alpha x \geq \alpha y$ for all $\alpha \geq 0$.

In a partially ordered vector space E any vector satisfying $x \geq 0$ is called a *positive vector*. The notation $x > 0$ means $x \geq 0$ and $x \neq 0$. The set of positive vectors is referred to as the *positive cone* of E and is denoted by E^+, i.e.,

$$E^+ = \{x \in E \colon x \geq 0\}.$$

The positive cone E^+ satisfies the following properties:

1) $E^+ + E^+ \subseteq E^+$;
2) $\alpha E^+ \subseteq E^+$ for each $\alpha \geq 0$; and
3) $E^+ \cap (-E^+) = \{0\}$.

The order relations of a (real) vector space E that make E a partially ordered vector space correspond in a one-to-one fashion with the convex cones of E. A non-empty subset C of E is said to be a *convex cone* whenever

i) $C + C \subseteq C$;
ii) $\alpha C \subseteq C$ for each $\alpha \geq 0$; and
iii) $C \cap (-C) = \{0\}$.

It is easy to see that if C is a convex cone of a vector space E, then the relation $\geq$ on E defined by

$$x \geq y \quad \text{whenever} \quad x - y \in C$$

is an order relation that makes E a partially ordered vector space having the additional property that $E^+ = C$.

A **Riesz space** (or a **vector lattice**) is a partially ordered vector space E which is at the same time a lattice. That is, a partially ordered vector space E is said to be a Riesz space whenever for every pair of vectors x and y the supremum (least upper bound) and infimum (greatest lower bound) of the set $\{x, y\}$ exist in E. Using standard lattice theory notation, the supremum and infimum of the set $\{x, y\}$ will be denoted by $x \vee y$ and $x \wedge y$, respectively. In other words,

$$x \vee y = \sup\{x, y\} \qquad \text{and} \qquad x \wedge y = \inf\{x, y\}.$$

Keep in mind that in a partially ordered vector space E an element $z \in E$ is said to be the *supremum* of a non-empty subset A of E (in symbols, $z = \sup A$) whenever

α) $a \leq z$ holds for each $a \in A$; and

β) whenever $a \leq b$ holds for all $a \in A$ and some $b \in E$, then $z \leq b$.

The geometrical meanings of $x \vee y$ and $x \wedge y$ are shown in Figure 2.1-1.

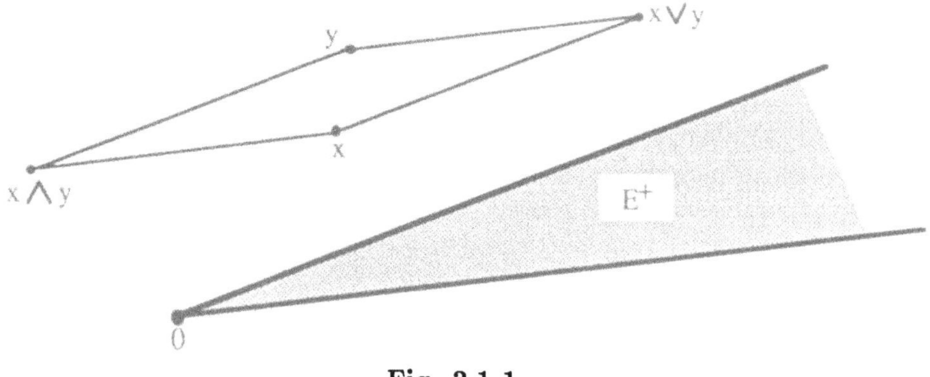

Fig. 2.1-1

Unless otherwise specified, the letter E will be employed to indicate an arbitrary Riesz space. With each element $x \in E$, we associate its *positive part* x^+, its *negative part* x^- and its *absolute value* $|x|$ defined by the formulas

$$x^+ = x \vee 0, \quad x^- = (-x) \vee 0 \quad \text{and} \quad |x| = x \vee (-x).$$

The following important identities hold:

$$x = x^+ - x^- \quad \text{and} \quad |x| = x^+ + x^-.$$

The absolute value function satisfies the *triangle inequality*, i.e., for each pair of vectors x and y in a Riesz space, we have

$$|x + y| \leq |x| + |y|.$$

More lattice identities are included in the next result.

Theorem 2.1.1. *If x, y, z are elements in a Riesz space, then we have*

1) $(-x) \vee (-y) = -(x \wedge y)$ *and* $(-x) \wedge (-y) = -(x \vee y)$;
2) $x \vee y = \frac{1}{2}(x + y + |x - y|)$ *and* $x \wedge y = \frac{1}{2}(x + y - |x - y|)$;
3) $x \vee y + x \wedge y = x + y$;
4) $x + y \vee z = (x + y) \vee (x + z)$ *and* $x + y \wedge z = (x + y) \wedge (x + z)$;
5) $\alpha(x \vee y) = (\alpha x) \vee (\alpha y)$ *and* $\alpha(x \wedge y) = (\alpha x) \wedge (\alpha y)$ *for all* $\alpha \geq 0$;
6) $x = (x - y)^+ + x \wedge y$.

To indicate how one can prove the above lattice identities, let us establish, for example, the validity of the first identity of (4). So, let $x, y, z \in E$. Put $a = x + y \vee z$ and $b = (x + y) \vee (x + z)$. To show that $a = b$ holds, it suffices to establish that $b \leq a$ and $a \leq b$ both hold.

From $a = x + y \vee z$, we get $y \vee z = a - x$ and so $y \leq a - x$ and $z \leq a - x$. Thus, $x + y \leq x + (a - x) = a$ and $x + z \leq a$. Hence, $b = (x + y) \vee (x + z) \leq a$. On the other hand, from $b = (x + y) \vee (x + z)$, it follows that $x + y \leq b$, and $x + z \leq b$, or $y = (x + y) - x \leq b - x$ and $z \leq b - x$. Thus, $y \vee z \leq b - x$ and so $a = x + y \vee z \leq b$ also holds.

A useful lattice inequality is stated in the next result.

Theorem 2.1.2. *If x, y and z are positive elements in a Riesz space, then*

$$x \wedge (y + z) \leq x \wedge y + x \wedge z .$$

Proof. Let $a = x \wedge (y + z)$, where x, y and z are three positive elements in a Riesz space. Then $a \leq x$ and $a \leq y + z$ both hold. Since $y \geq 0$, we see that $a \leq y + x$, and so $a \leq (y + x) \wedge (y + z)$. From Theorem 2.1.1(4), it follows that

$$a \leq (y + x) \wedge (y + z) = y + x \wedge z .$$

Since $a \leq x \leq x + x \wedge z$ is obviously true, using Theorem 2.1.1(4) once more, we get

$$x \wedge (y + z) = a \leq (x + x \wedge y) \wedge (z + x \wedge y) = x \wedge z + x \wedge y ,$$

as claimed. ■

The next theorem describes an important property of Riesz spaces known as the *Riesz Decomposition Property*.

Theorem 2.1.3. (The Riesz Decomposition Property) *Assume that x, y_1 and y_2 are three positive elements in a Riesz space satisfying $0 \leq x \leq y_1 + y_2$. Then there exist positive elements x_1 and x_2 such that*

$$0 \leq x_1 \leq y_1, \quad 0 \leq x_2 \leq y_2 \quad \textit{and} \quad x = x_1 + x_2 .$$

Proof. Let three positive elements x, y_1 and y_2 of a Riesz space satisfy the inequality $0 \leq x \leq y_1 + y_2$. Put $x_1 = x \wedge y_1$ and $x_2 = x - x \wedge y_1$. Clearly, $0 \leq x_1 \leq x$ and $x = x_1 + x_2$ hold. On the other hand, note that

$$\begin{aligned} x_2 &= x - x \wedge y_1 = x + (-x) \vee (-y_1) \\ &= (x - x) \vee (x - y_1) \leq 0 \vee (y_1 + y_2 - y_1) = y_2 , \end{aligned}$$

and the proof is finished. ■

A subset A of a Riesz space E is said to be a **solid set** whenever $|y| \leq |x|$ and $x \in A$ imply $y \in A$. Every solid set A is a balanced (or circled) set, i.e., $x \in A$ implies $\lambda x \in A$ for each $|\lambda| \leq 1$. The **solid hull** $\mathrm{sol}(A)$ of an arbitrary subset is the smallest solid set (with respect to inclusion) that contains A and is precisely the set

$$\mathrm{sol}(A) = \{y \in E\colon \text{There exists some } x \in A \text{ with } |y| \leq |x|\}\,.$$

As usual, the **convex hull** $\mathrm{co}(A)$ of a subset A of a vector space X is the smallest convex set that contains A (with respect to inclusion) and it consists of all convex combinations of A, i.e.,

$$\mathrm{co}(A) = \Big\{x \in X\colon \exists\, a_i \in A,\ \lambda_i > 0\ (i = 1, \ldots, n) \text{ with } \sum_{i=1}^{n} \lambda_i = 1 \text{ and } x = \sum_{i=1}^{n} \lambda_i a_i\Big\}.$$

Theorem 2.1.4. *In a Riesz space the convex hull of a solid set is likewise a solid set.*

Proof. Let A be a solid subset of a Riesz space and assume that $|y| \leq |\alpha x_1 + \beta x_2|$ holds with $0 < \alpha, \beta < 1$, $\alpha + \beta = 1$ and $x_1, x_2 \in A$. We shall show that $y \in \mathrm{co}(A)$.

Put $y_1 = [y \vee (-\alpha|x_1|)] \wedge (\alpha|x_1|)$ and note that $|y_1| \leq \alpha|x_1| \leq |x_1|$. From the solidness of A, we infer that $\alpha^{-1}y_1 \in A$. Next let $y_2 = y - y_1$, and note that

$$\begin{aligned} y_2 &= y - [y \vee (-\alpha|x_1|)] \wedge (\alpha|x_1|) \\ &= y + \big\{-[y \vee (-\alpha|x_1|)]\big\} \vee (-\alpha|x_1|) \\ &= y + \big[(-y) \wedge (\alpha|x_1|)\big] \vee (-\alpha|x_1|) \\ &= \big[0 \wedge (y + \alpha|x_1|)\big] \vee (y - \alpha|x_1|)\,. \end{aligned}$$

On the other hand, the triangle inequality implies $|y| \leq \alpha|x_1| + \beta|x_2|$, and consequently $-\alpha|x_1| - \beta|x_2| \leq y \leq \alpha|x_1| + \beta|x_2|$. Therefore,

$$\begin{aligned} -\beta|x_2| = (-\beta|x_2|) \wedge 0 &\leq (y + \alpha|x_1|) \wedge 0 \\ &\leq y_2 \leq 0 \vee (y - \alpha|x_1|) \leq \beta|x_2|\,, \end{aligned}$$

and so, by the solidness of A, we get $\beta^{-1}y_2 \in A$. Therefore,

$$y = y_1 + y_2 = \alpha(\alpha^{-1}y_1) + \beta(\beta^{-1}y_2) \in \mathrm{co}(A)\,.$$

Now the proof of the solidness of $\mathrm{co}(A)$ can be completed by induction. ∎

We remark that the solid hull of a convex set is not necessarily a convex set. A vector subspace F of a Riesz space E is said to be a **Riesz subspace** whenever for each pair $x, y \in F$ the elements $x \vee y$ and $x \wedge y$ both belong to F. Clearly, every Riesz subspace with the induced ordering is a Riesz space in its own right. A vector subspace which is at the same time a solid set is referred to as an **ideal**. Every ideal is necessarily a Riesz subspace—this follows immediately from the identities in part (2) of Theorem 2.1.1.

Every non-empty subset S of a Riesz space is contained in a smallest ideal called the *ideal generated by the set* S. This ideal is precisely the set

$$A = \Big\{ x \in E\colon\ \exists\ x_i \in S \text{ and } \lambda_i > 0\ (i = 1, \ldots, n) \text{ with } |x| \le \sum_{i=1}^{n} \lambda_i |x_i| \Big\}.$$

In case a set consists of a single element, say x, then the ideal generated by x is known as a *principal ideal* and is precisely the set

$$A_x = \{ y \in E\colon\ \exists\ \lambda > 0 \text{ such that } |y| \le \lambda |x| \}.$$

We shall encounter principal ideals quite often in our economic analysis.

Two Riesz spaces E and F are said to be **Riesz isomorphic** whenever there exists a *lattice isomorphism*—also known as a Riesz isomorphism—from E onto F. That is, E and F are Riesz isomorphic whenever there exists a one-to-one onto linear operator $T\colon E \longrightarrow F$ satisfying

$$T(x \vee y) = T(x) \vee T(y) \quad \text{and} \quad T(x \wedge y) = T(x) \wedge T(y)$$

for all x, $y \in E$. From the point of view of Riesz space theory two Riesz isomorphic Riesz spaces are considered as identical objects.

A Riesz space E is said to be **Archimedean** whenever $0 \le nx \le y$ for each n and some x, $y \in E$ implies $x = 0$. In this monograph, we shall deal exclusively with Archimedean Riesz spaces. Accordingly, the phrase "Riesz space" will be synonymous with "Archimedean Riesz space."

A special class of examples of Riesz spaces is provided by the function spaces. A **function space** is a vector space E of real-valued functions defined on a non-empty set Ω such that for each pair f, $g \in E$ their pointwise maximum and minimum functions, defined by

$$(f \vee g)(x) = \max\{f(x), g(x)\} \quad \text{and} \quad (f \wedge g)(x) = \min\{f(x), g(x)\}, \quad x \in \Omega,$$

belong to E. Under the pointwise ordering $\ge$ (i.e., $f \ge g$ holds if $f(x) \ge g(x)$ for each $x \in \Omega$) every function space is clearly a Riesz space. Here are some examples of function spaces.

1) $\mathcal{R}^\ell$ — the Euclidean ℓ-dimensional space;
2) $C(\Omega)$ — the continuous real-valued function on a topological space Ω;
3) $C_b(\Omega)$ — the continuous bounded real-valued function on a topological space Ω;
4) $\mathcal{R}^\Omega$ — the real-valued functions defined on a non-empty set Ω;
5) $\ell_\infty(\Omega)$ — the bounded real-valued functions defined on a non-empty set Ω; and
6) ℓ_p — the real sequences $(x_1, x_2, \ldots)$ such that $\sum_{i=1}^{\infty} |x_i|^p < \infty$ $(0 < p < \infty)$.

The $L_p(\mu)$ spaces are also Riesz spaces under the ordering $f \ge g$ whenever $f(x) \ge g(x)$ holds for μ-almost all x.

It is important to know that every principal ideal of an Archimedean Riesz space can be represented as a function space; details of such representations can be found in the book by W. A. J. Luxemburg and A. C. Zaanen [42]. That is, if A_x is a principal ideal of an Archimedean Riesz space, then there exists a function space E which is lattice isomorphic to A_x. An immediate consequence of this result—due to A. I. Yudin—is that any lattice identity (or inequality) which is true in the real number system is automatically true in any Archimedean Riesz space. To demonstrate this point, let us establish the following lattice identity:

$$|x-y| = x \vee y - x \wedge y \qquad (\star)$$

If x and y are real numbers, then either $x \geq y$ (in which case we have $|x-y| = x-y$, $x \vee y = x$ and $x \wedge y = y$) or $x < y$ (in which case $|x-y| = y-x$, $x \vee y = y$ and $x \wedge y = x$). Now let x, y belong to an arbitrary Riesz space E. Since x and y belong to a principal ideal A_z (for example, let $z = |x| + |y|$) and A_z is a Riesz subspace of E, it follows from the representation theorem that $(\star)$ is true in any Archimedean Riesz space—in fact, it is true in any Riesz space. To test your understanding of the above useful remark, verify the validity of the lattice identities listed in Theorem 2.1.1.

A Riesz space E is said to be **Dedekind** (or **order**) **complete** whenever every non-empty subset of E which is (order) bounded from above has a supremum (least upper bound). Recall that if A is a non-empty subset of E, then

1) A is said to be *bounded from above*, whenever there exists some $x \in E$ such that $a \leq x$ holds for each $a \in A$; and
2) A has a *supremum*, whenever A has a least upper bound (written symbolically as $u = \sup A$) in the sense that
   a) u is an upper bound of A; and
   b) for every other upper bound v of A we have $u \leq v$.

The Riesz spaces $\mathcal{R}^{\Omega}$, $\ell_\infty(\Omega)$, $L_p(\mu)$ and ℓ_p are all Dedekind complete Riesz spaces. The Riesz space $C[0,1]$ is not a Dedekind complete Riesz space.

Now let $\{x_\alpha\}$ be a net in a Riesz space. The symbol $x_\alpha \uparrow$ means that $\alpha \geq \beta$ implies $x_\alpha \geq x_\beta$. The symbolism $x_\alpha \uparrow x$ means that $x_\alpha \uparrow$ and $x = \sup\{x_\alpha\}$ both hold. The symbols $x_\alpha \downarrow$ and $x_\alpha \downarrow x$ are defined similarly. The notation $x_\alpha \uparrow\leq x$ means that $x_\alpha \uparrow$ and $x_\alpha \leq x$ for each α. It is easy to see that a Riesz space is Dedekind complete if and only if $0 \leq x_\alpha \uparrow\leq x$ in E implies the existence of the supremum $\sup\{x_\alpha\}$.

EXERCISES

1. If x is an element in a Riesz space, then show that $x = x^+ - x^-$.

2. If in a Riesz space we have $x = y - z$, $x \geq 0$, $y \geq 0$ and $y \wedge z = 0$, then show that $y = x^+$ and $z = x^-$.

3. For three elements x y and z in a Riesz space establish the following inequalities

$$|x \vee y - z \vee y| \leq |x - y| \quad \text{and} \quad |x \wedge y - z \wedge y| \leq |x - y|.$$

4. Show that in a Riesz space $|x| \wedge |y| = 0$ if and only if $|x + y| = |x| + |y|$.

5. If x and y are elements of a Riesz space, then show that the

$$|x| \vee |y| = \tfrac{1}{2}(|x + y| + |x - y|) \quad \text{and} \quad |x| \wedge |y| = \tfrac{1}{2}\big|\,|x + y| - |x - y|\,\big|.$$

6. Consider the plane $\mathcal{R}^2$ with the lexicographic ordering, i.e., with the ordering $(x_1, y_1) \geq (x_2, y_2)$ whenever either $x_1 > x_2$ or else $x_1 = x_2$ and $y_1 \geq y_2$. Show that:
   a) The plane $\mathcal{R}^2$ with the lexicographic ordering is a linearly ordered vector space—and hence, it is a Riesz space; and
   b) The lexicographic plane is not an Archimedean Riesz space.

7. Let E denote the vector space of all differentiable functions defined on $(0, 1)$. Show that under the pointwise ordering E is a partially ordered vector space but it fails to be a function space.

8. Let A be a nonempty subset of a Riesz space E. If $\sup A$ exists, then for each x in E show that $\sup(x \wedge A) = x \wedge \sup A$. Similarly, if $\inf A$ exists, then show that $\inf(x \vee A) = x \vee \inf A$.

9. Describe the principal ideal in $\mathcal{R}_\infty$ (the Riesz space of all real-valued sequences) generated by the sequence $(1, 1, 1, \ldots)$.

10. Give an example of a convex subset of the Riesz space $\mathcal{R}^2$ whose solid hull is not convex.

11. Show that the Riesz space $C[0, 1]$ is not Dedekind complete.

12. Show that the Riesz spaces $L_p[0, 1]$ $(0 < p \leq \infty)$ are all Dedekind complete Riesz spaces.

13. Use math induction to establish the following stronger version of the Riesz Decomposition Property for a Riesz space E. If $|x| \leq |y_1 + \cdots + y_n|$, then there exist elements $x_1, \ldots, x_n \in E$ satisfying $x = x_1 + \cdots + x_n$ and $|x_i| \leq |y_i|$ for each i.

14. A positive nonzero element x of a Riesz space E is called an *atom* whenever $0 \leq y \leq x$, $0 \leq z \leq x$ and $y \wedge z = 0$ imply either $y = 0$ or $z = 0$. Show that the commodity space $C[0, 1]$ does not contain any atoms. Also, describe the atoms of the Riesz spaces ℓ_p $(0 < p \leq \infty)$.

2.2. POSITIVE LINEAR FUNCTIONALS

In this section, we shall discuss the basic properties of positive linear functionals on Riesz spaces; the details can be found in the books [6, 8, 63, 70]. A positive linear functional should be interpreted as representing the concept of a price in our economic analysis.

Let E be a Riesz space. Any set of the form

$$[x,y]=\{z\in E\colon\ x\leq z\leq y\}$$

is called an *order interval* of E. The subsets of the order intervals are known as *order bounded sets*. A linear functional $\phi\colon E\longrightarrow\mathcal{R}$ is said to be *order bounded* whenever ϕ maps order intervals of E onto order bounded subsets of $\mathcal{R}$.

A *positive linear functional* $\phi\colon E\longrightarrow\mathcal{R}$ is a linear functional such that $x\geq 0$ implies $\phi(x)\geq 0$. It should be clear that every positive linear functional is necessarily order bounded. The positive linear functionals correspond precisely to the additive functions from E^+ into $\mathcal{R}^+$. That is, if a function $\phi\colon E^+\longrightarrow\mathcal{R}^+$ is *additive* (i.e., if $\phi(x+y)=\phi(x)+\phi(y)$ holds for each $x,\ y\in E^+$), then ϕ defines a positive linear functional (which we shall denote by ϕ again) $\phi\colon E\longrightarrow\mathcal{R}$ by the formula

$$\phi(x)=\phi(x^+)-\phi(x^-).$$

In other words, a positive linear functional is completely characterized by its action on E^+.

The set of all order bounded linear functionals forms a vector space—referred to as the **order dual** of E and is denoted by $E^\sim$. The relation $\phi\geq\psi$ whenever $\phi(x)\geq\psi(x)$ for all $x\in E^+$ is an order relation that makes $E^\sim$ a partially ordered vector space. It turns out that the partially ordered vector space $E^\sim$ is a Riesz space. Its lattice operations are given by

$$\phi\vee\psi(x)=\sup\{\phi(y)+\psi(z)\colon\ y,\ z\in E^+\ \text{ and }\ y+z=x\}$$

and

$$\phi\wedge\psi(x)=\inf\{\phi(y)+\psi(z)\colon\ y,\ z\in E^+\ \text{ and }\ y+z=x\},$$

for all $\phi,\ \psi\in E^\sim$ and all $x\in E^+$. In particular, for each $\phi\in E^\sim$ and each $x\in E^+$ we have

$$|\phi|(x)=\sup\{|\phi(y)|\colon\ |y|\leq x\}.$$

Consequently, the absolute value of an order bounded linear functional functional ϕ satisfies the inequality

$$|\phi(x)|\leq|\phi|(|x|),\quad x\in E.$$

In addition, the order dual $E^\sim$ is always a Dedekind complete Riesz space. It is possible for $E^\sim$ to be the trivial Riesz space. For instance, if $E=L_p[0,1]$ for $0<p<1$, then $E^\sim=\{0\}$.

A net $\{x_\alpha\}$ in a Riesz space is said to be *order convergent* to some element x, in symbols $x_\alpha \xrightarrow{o} x$, whenever there exists another net $\{y_\alpha\}$ with the same indexed set satisfying $|x_\alpha - x| \le y_\alpha$ for each α and $y_\alpha \downarrow 0$; the latter properties are written symbolically as $|x_\alpha - x| \le y_\alpha \downarrow 0$. A subset A of a Riesz space is said to be *order closed* whenever $\{x_\alpha\} \subseteq A$ and $x_\alpha \xrightarrow{o} x$ imply $x \in A$. An order closed ideal is known as a **band**.

Two vectors x and y in a Riesz space are said to be *disjoint* (in symbols $x \perp y$) whenever $|x| \wedge |y| = 0$ holds. Notice that in a function space two functions are disjoint if and only if they have disjoint supports. Two non-empty subsets A and B are said to be disjoint—in symbols, $A \perp B$—whenever $a \perp b$ holds for all $a \in A$ and $b \in B$. The *disjoint complement* of a non-empty subset D of a Riesz space E—denoted by D^d—is the set consisting of all vectors that are disjoint to every vector of D, i.e.,

$$\begin{aligned} D^d &= \{x \in E\colon\ x \perp y \ \text{ for all } \ y \in D\} \\ &= \{x \in E\colon\ |x| \wedge |y| = 0 \ \text{ for all } \ y \in D\}\,. \end{aligned}$$

The disjoint complement D^d is always a band of E. We have $D \cap D^d = \{0\}$.

A band B of a Riesz space is said to be a *projection band* whenever $B \oplus B^d = E$ holds. When E is Dedekind complete every band is a projection band—a result due to F. Riesz.

Theorem 2.2.1. (F. Riesz) *In a Dedekind complete Riesz space every band is a projection band.*

In general, not every band in a Riesz space is a projection band. However, if E is Dedekind complete, then Theorem 2.2.1 shows that for every band B in E, the space can be written as a direct sum $E = B \oplus B^d$. A Riesz space in which every band is a projection band is called a Riesz space with the *projection property*.

We now turn our attention to the concept of order continuity. In economics this concept is often associated with the economic intuition of impatience.

Definition 2.2.2. *A function $f\colon E \longrightarrow F$ between two Riesz spaces is said to be* **order continuous** *whenever $x_\alpha \xrightarrow{o} x$ in E implies $f(x_\alpha) \xrightarrow{o} f(x)$ in F.*

The algebraic and lattice operations of a Riesz space are all order continuous functions. That is, the functions

1) $(x,y) \longmapsto x + y$, from $E \times E$ into E;
2) $(\alpha,x) \longmapsto \alpha x$, from $\mathcal{R} \times E$ into E;
3) $(x,y) \longmapsto x \vee y$, from $E \times E$ into E;
4) $(x,y) \longmapsto x \wedge y$, from $E \times E$ into E;
5) $x \longmapsto x^+$, from E into E;

6) $x \longmapsto x^-$, from E into E; and
7) $x \longmapsto |x|$, from E into E;

are all order continuous.

The vector space of all order continuous order bounded linear functionals on a Riesz space E is denoted by $E_n^\sim$, i.e.,

$$\begin{aligned} E_n^\sim &= \{\phi \in E^\sim\colon\ \phi \text{ is order continuous}\} \\ &= \{\phi \in E^\sim\colon\ x_\alpha \xrightarrow{o} x \text{ in } E \text{ implies } \phi(x_\alpha) \xrightarrow{o} \phi(x)\}, \end{aligned}$$

and is called the **order continuous dual** of E. It turns out (by a theorem of T. Ogasawara) that $E_n^\sim$ is a band of $E^\sim$, and so by Theorem 2.2.1 the order continuous dual $E_n^\sim$ is a projection band. Thus,

$$E^\sim = E_n^\sim \oplus (E_n^\sim)^d .$$

The linear functionals of $E_n^\sim$ are known as *singular functionals*.

With every order bounded linear functional $\phi \in E^\sim$ we associate two important ideals of E. Its *null ideal* N_ϕ, defined by

$$N_\phi = \{x \in E\colon\ |\phi|(|x|) = 0\},$$

and its *carrier* C_ϕ, defined by

$$C_\phi = (N_\phi)^d = \{x \in E\colon\ |x| \wedge |y| = 0 \text{ for all } y \in N_\phi\}.$$

If ϕ is order continuous, then N_ϕ is a band of E.

Theorem 2.2.3. (Nakano) *For two order continuous linear functionals $\phi, \psi \in E_n^\sim$ the following statements are equivalent:*

a) $\phi \perp \psi$;
b) $C_\phi \subseteq N_\psi$;
c) $C_\psi \subseteq N_\phi$;
d) $C_\phi \perp C_\psi$.

Riesz spaces with an abundance of order continuous linear functionals will play a crucial role in our economic analysis.

Definition 2.2.4. *A Riesz space E is said to be a* **normal Riesz space** *whenever*

1. *E is Dedekind complete; and*
2. *$E_n^\sim$ separates the points of E, i.e., for each $x \neq 0$ there exists some $\phi \in E_n^\sim$ with $\phi(x) \neq 0$.*

A Riesz subspace F of a Riesz space E is said to be **order dense** in E whenever for each $0 < x \in E$ there exists some vector $y \in F$ satisfying $0 < y \leq x$, or equivalently, whenever for each $x \in E^+$ there exists a net $\{y_\alpha\}$ of F satisfying $0 \leq y_\alpha \uparrow x$ in E. In $\mathcal{R}^{[0,1]}$ the Riesz subspace $\ell_\infty[0,1]$—all bounded real-valued functions on $[0,1]$—is an order dense Riesz subspace while the Riesz subspace $C[0,1]$ is not order dense. An ideal A in a Riesz space E is order dense if and only if $A^d = \{0\}$, i.e., if and only if $x \perp a$ for each $a \in A$ implies $a = 0$.

Every singular linear functional on a normal Riesz space has an order dense null ideal.

Theorem 2.2.5. *If E is a normal Riesz space and ϕ is a singular linear functional on E (i.e., $\phi \in (E_n^\sim)^d$), then its null ideal N_ϕ is order dense in E.*

Proof. Assume that $\phi \in (E_n^\sim)^d$ and let $x \in C_\phi$. If $\psi \in E_n^\sim$, then $\psi \perp \phi$ and from this it follows that $C_\phi \subseteq N_\psi$. Thus, $|\psi|(|x|) = 0$ and in view of $|\psi(x)| \leq |\psi|(|x|)$, we see that $\psi(x) = 0$ for all $\psi \in E_n^\sim$. Since $E_n^\sim$ separates the points of E, we infer that $x = 0$ and so $C_\phi = \{0\}$. Therefore, $(N_\phi)^d = C_\phi = \{0\}$, and hence N_ϕ is order dense in E. ■

Finally, we close the section by mentioning that a positive linear functional ϕ on a Riesz space is said to be **strictly positive** whenever $x > 0$ implies $\phi(x) > 0$. Notice that every positive linear functional ϕ is strictly positive on its carrier C_ϕ.

EXERCISES

1. Use the Riesz Decomposition Property to show that for any pair of positive elements x and y in a Riesz space we have $[0,x] + [0,y] = [0, x+y]$.

2. Show that the algebraic and lattice operations of a Riesz space are all order continuous functions.

3. Show that $\ell_\infty(\Omega)$ is an order dense Riesz subspace of $\mathcal{R}^\Omega$. Also, show that $C[0,1]$ is a Riesz subspace of $\mathcal{R}^{[0,1]}$ which is not order dense.

4. Show that the disjoint complement of a non-empty set is a band.

5. Show that an ideal A of a Riesz space is order dense if and only if $A^d = \{0\}$.

6. Show that a Riesz subspace F of an Archimedean Riesz space E is order dense if and only if for each $x \in E^+$ there exists a net $\{x_\alpha\}$ of F^+ satisfying $x_\alpha \uparrow x$ in E.

7. Let E be a Riesz space. If the order dual $E^\sim$ separates the points E, then show that E is an Archimedean Riesz space.

8. Consider the commodity space $C[0,1]$ and the two positive prices φ and ψ in $E^\sim$ defined by $\varphi(f) = f(0)$ and $\psi(f) = \int_0^1 f(t)\,dt$. Show that the linear functionals satisfy $\varphi \perp \psi$.

9. Let E be a Riesz space and consider two positive prices $0 \leq f \leq g \in E^\sim$. Show that their carriers satisfy $C_f \subseteq C_g$.

10. Consider a Riesz space E and a positive price $0 \leq f \in E^\sim$. Show that

$$f(x \vee y) = \sup\{g(x) + h(y)\colon\ f = g + h \ \text{ and } \ 0 \leq h, g \in E^\sim\},$$

and

$$f(x \wedge y) = \inf\{g(x) + h(y)\colon\ f = g + h \ \text{ and } \ 0 \leq h, g \in E^\sim\},$$

hold for all $x, y \in E$.

2.3. TOPOLOGICAL RIESZ SPACES

In this section, we shall discuss the properties of Riesz spaces when they are equipped with linear topologies "compatible" with their algebraic and lattice structures. The most useful and natural linear topologies on a Riesz space are the locally solid topologies; a detail account of locally solid topologies can be found in [6]. Recall that a *linear topology* on a vector space is any topology that makes both algebraic operations

a) $(x,y) \longmapsto x+y$ from $E \times E$ into E, and
b) $(\alpha, x) \longmapsto \alpha x$ from $\mathcal{R} \times E$ into E

continuous functions.

A linear topology τ on a Riesz space E is said to be **locally solid**—and (E,τ) is called a *locally solid Riesz space*—whenever τ has a base at zero consisting of solid sets. Recall that the functions

1) $(x,y) \longmapsto x \vee y$ from $E \times E$ into E,
2) $(x,y) \longmapsto x \wedge y$ from $E \times E$ into E,
3) $x \longmapsto x^+$ from E into E,
4) $x \longmapsto x^-$ from E into E, and
5) $x \longmapsto |x|$ from E into E,

are referred to collectively as the *lattice operations* of E. If τ is a linear topology on E, then either all lattice operations are uniformly continuous functions or else all fail to be uniformly continuous. The locally solid topologies on a Riesz space E are precisely the linear topologies on E that make the lattice operations uniformly continuous.

Theorem 2.3.1. *A linear topology on a Riesz E space is locally solid if and only if it makes the lattice operations of E uniformly continuous.*

The first important property of locally solid Riesz spaces is described in the next result. Recall that the *topological dual* of a topological vector space is the vector space consisting of all continuous linear functionals.

Theorem 2.3.2. *The topological dual of a locally solid Riesz space is an ideal of its order dual—and hence, it is a Dedekind complete Riesz space in its own right.*

If (E,τ) is a locally solid Riesz space, then its topological dual will be denoted by $(E,\tau)'$, or simply by E'. According to Theorem 2.3.2 the topological dual E' is an ideal of the order dual $E^\sim$.

Among the important locally solid topologies are the locally convex-solid ones. A locally solid topology τ on a Riesz space E is said to be a *locally convex-solid topology*—and (E,τ) is called a *locally convex-solid Riesz space*—whenever τ is also locally convex. From Theorem 2.1.4, it should be clear that a linear topology on a Riesz space is locally convex-solid if and only if it has a base at zero consisting of solid and convex sets.

A seminorm q on a Riesz space E is said to be a *lattice seminorm* whenever $|x| \le |y|$ in E implies $q(x) \le q(y)$. The locally convex-solid topologies on a Riesz space E are precisely the locally convex topologies on E that are generated by families of lattice seminorms. A *Fréchet lattice* is a complete metrizable locally convex-solid Riesz space—the Riesz space $\mathcal{R}_\infty$ of all real-valued sequences with the product topology is a Fréchet lattice.

A *dual system* $\langle X, X'\rangle$ is a pair of vector spaces X and X' together with a bilinear function $(x, x') \longmapsto \langle x, x'\rangle$, from $X \times X'$ into $\mathcal{R}$, satisfying the two properties

1) If $\langle x, x'\rangle = 0$ for all $x' \in X'$, then $x = 0$; and
2) If $\langle x, x'\rangle = 0$ for all $x \in X$, then $x' = 0$.

Now consider a dual system $\langle X, X'\rangle$. A locally convex topology τ on X is said to be *consistent* (or *compatible*) with the dual system $\langle X, X'\rangle$ whenever $(X,\tau)' = X'$ holds, i.e., whenever a linear functional $f\colon X \longrightarrow \mathcal{R}$ belongs to the topological dual of (X,τ) if and only if there exists (exactly one) $x' \in X'$ such that $f(x) = \langle x, x'\rangle$ holds for each $x \in X$. From the theory of locally convex spaces we know that a locally convex topology τ on X is consistent with $\langle X, X'\rangle$ if and only if τ is finer than the weak topology $\sigma(X, X')$ and coarser than the Mackey topology $\tau(X, X')$, i.e., if and only if

$$\sigma(X, X') \subseteq \tau \subseteq \tau(X, X')$$

holds. The weak topology $\sigma(X, X')$—denoted simply by w—is also known as the topology of *pointwise convergence*. The *weak topology* $\sigma(X, X')$ is the locally convex topology on X that is generated by the family of seminorms $\{p_{x'}\colon\ x' \in X'\}$, where $p_{x'}(x) = |\langle x, x'\rangle|$ for each $x \in X$ and each $x' \in X'$. Accordingly, a net $\{x_\alpha\}$ of X satisfies $x_\alpha \xrightarrow{w} x$ if and only if $\langle x_\alpha, x'\rangle \to \langle x, x'\rangle$ holds in $\mathcal{R}$ for each $x' \in X'$. The locally convex topology $\sigma(X', X)$ on X' is defined in a similar manner—as usual, $\sigma(X', X)$ is called the *weak* topology* and is denoted by w^*. The *Mackey topology* $\tau(X, X')$ is the locally convex topology on X of uniform convergence on the $\sigma(X', X)$-compact, convex and balanced subsets of X'. That is, a net $\{x_\alpha\}$ of X satisfies $x_\alpha \xrightarrow{\tau(X,X')} x$ if and only if for each $\sigma(X', X)$-compact, convex and balanced subset A of X' we have

$$\sup\{|\langle x_\alpha - x, x'\rangle|\colon\ x' \in A\} \longrightarrow 0\,.$$

An important theorem associated with dual systems is the so-called separation theorem—the finite dimensional version of which will be discussed in Exercise 6 at the end of this section. The separation theorem will be employed quite extensively in our economic analysis; for a proof see, for example, [8, Theorem 9.10, p. 136].

Theorem 2.3.3. (The Separation Theorem) *Let $\langle X, X'\rangle$ be a dual system and let A and B be two non-empty disjoint convex sets. If for some consistent locally convex topology on X one of the convex sets A or B has a non-empty interior, then there exists some non-zero $x' \in X'$ satisfying*

$$\langle a, x'\rangle \ge \langle b, x'\rangle$$

for all $a \in A$ and all $b \in B$.

Recall that a subset A of a topological vector space is said to be *topologically bounded* (or simply *bounded*) whenever for each neighborhood V of zero there exists some $\lambda > 0$ such that $A \subseteq \lambda V$ holds. Another important property of the dual system is described in the next result.

Theorem 2.3.4. *If $\langle X, X' \rangle$ is a dual system, then all consistent locally convex topologies on X have*

a) *the same closed convex sets; and*
b) *the same bounded sets.*

We now turn our attention to topological Riesz spaces. A **Riesz dual system** $\langle E, E' \rangle$ is a dual system such that

1) E is a Riesz space;
2) E' is an ideal of the order dual $E^\sim$ separating the points of E; and
3) the duality function $\langle \cdot, \cdot \rangle$ is the natural one, i.e.,

$$\langle x, x' \rangle = x'(x)$$

holds for all $x \in E$ and all $x' \in E'$.

If (E, τ) is a locally convex-solid Riesz space, then (by Theorem 2.3.2) the dual system $\langle E, E' \rangle$ is a Riesz dual system. Here are a few examples of Riesz dual systems.

a) $\langle L_p(\mu), L_q(\mu) \rangle$, $1 < p,\ q < \infty$; $\frac{1}{p} + \frac{1}{q} = 1$;
b) $\langle \ell_p, \ell_q \rangle$, $1 \le p,\ q \le \infty$; $\frac{1}{p} + \frac{1}{q} = 1$;
c) $\langle L_\infty(\mu), L_1(\mu) \rangle$ and $\langle L_1(\mu), L_\infty(\mu) \rangle$, μ a σ-finite measure; and
d) $\langle C(\Omega), \mathrm{ca}(\Omega) \rangle$, Ω a Hausdorff compact topological space.

With each Riesz dual system $\langle E, E' \rangle$ there are two important consistent locally convex-solid topologies on E; the absolute weak topology $|\sigma|(E, E')$ and the absolute Mackey topology $|\tau|(E, E')$. The ***absolute weak topology*** $|\sigma|(E, E')$ on E, denoted also by $|w|$, is the locally convex-solid topology on E of uniform convergence on the order intervals of E' and is generated by the family of lattice seminorms $\{q_{x'}\}_{x' \in E'}$, where $q_{x'}(x) = |x'|(|x|)$ for each $x \in E$ and each $x' \in E'$. In other words, $x_\alpha \xrightarrow{|w|} x$ holds in E if and only if $|x'|(|x_\alpha - x|) \to 0$ holds in $\mathcal{R}$ for each $x' \in E'$. The ***absolute Mackey topology*** $|\tau|(E, E')$ is the locally convex-solid topology on E of uniform convergence on the $\sigma(E', E)$-compact, convex and solid subsets of E'. We have the following inclusions

$$\sigma(E, E') \subseteq |\sigma|(E, E') \subseteq |\tau|(E, E') \subseteq \tau(E, E').$$

A locally convex-solid topology τ on E is consistent with the Riesz dual system $\langle E, E' \rangle$ if and only if $|\sigma|(E, E') \subseteq \tau \subseteq |\tau|(E, E')$ holds.

Now let $\langle E, E' \rangle$ be a Riesz dual system. Then every element x of E defines an order bounded linear functional $\hat{x}$ on E' via the formula

$$\hat{x}(x') = x'(x), \quad x' \in E'.$$

Thus, a mapping $x \longmapsto \hat{x}$ can be defined from E into $(E')^{\sim}$. It turns out that this mapping is a lattice isomorphism (into), and so the Riesz space E can be identified with a Riesz subspace of $(E')^{\sim}$. In addition, each x acts as an order continuous linear functional on E', and therefore E can be also identified with a Riesz subspace of $(E')^{\sim}_n$. The mapping $x \longmapsto \hat{x}$ is called the *natural embedding* of E into $(E')^{\sim}$ (or $(E')^{\sim}_n$).

Definition 2.3.5. *A linear topology τ on a Riesz space is said to be* **order continuous** *whenever $x_\alpha \xrightarrow{o} 0$ implies $x_\alpha \xrightarrow{\tau} 0$.*

A Fréchet lattice with order continuous topology is referred to as an *order continuous Fréchet lattice*. Order continuous topologies will play an important role in this monograph. The consistent order continuous locally convex-solid topologies of a Riesz dual system are characterized as follows; for a proof see [8, pp. 168–170].

Theorem 2.3.6. *For a Riesz dual system $\langle E, E' \rangle$ the following statements are equivalent.*

1) *The Riesz space E is Dedekind complete and the weak topology $\sigma(E, E')$ is order continuous.*
2) *The Riesz space E is Dedekind complete and every consistent locally convex-solid topology on E is order continuous.*
3) *Every order interval of E is weakly compact.*
4) *The Riesz space E is an ideal of $(E')^{\sim}_n$ —and hence, an ideal of $(E')^{\sim}$ too.*

The concept of a symmetric Riesz dual system will be employed quite often in our economic analysis and is introduced next.

Definition 2.3.7. *A Riesz dual system is said to be* **symmetric** *whenever it satisfies the equivalent statements of Theorem 2.3.6.*

Observe that if $\langle E, E' \rangle$ is a symmetric Riesz dual system, then $\langle E', E \rangle$ is likewise a symmetric Riesz dual system—and this justifies the employed terminology. Here are some examples of Riesz dual systems.

a) $\langle L_p(\mu), L_q(\mu) \rangle$, $1 < p, q < \infty$; $\frac{1}{p} + \frac{1}{q} = 1$;

b) $\langle L_\infty(\mu), L_1(\mu) \rangle$, μ a σ-finite measure;

c) $\langle \ell_p, \ell_q \rangle$, $1 \le p, q \le \infty$ $\frac{1}{p} + \frac{1}{q} = 1$;

d) $\langle c_0, \ell_1 \rangle$; and

e) $\langle \phi, \mathcal{R}_\infty \rangle$, where ϕ is the Riesz space of all eventually zero sequences.

The Riesz dual system $\langle C[0,1], \mathrm{ca}[0,1]\rangle$ is not a symmetric Riesz dual system. From Theorem 2.3.6 it should be immediate that if E is a normal Riesz space, then the Riesz dual system $\langle E, (E)_n^\sim \rangle$ is a symmetric Riesz dual system.

Now let us mention a few very important mathematical points that will play a crucial role in our study. Consider a Riesz dual system $\langle E, E'\rangle$ and let $\omega \in E^+$ be a fixed vector—think of ω as the vector representing the social endowment. As mentioned before, the order intervals of E need not be weakly compact—weak compactness in E will always mean $\sigma(E,E')$-compactness. In particular, the weak compactness of the order interval $[0,\omega]$—inside of which all economic activity takes place and is the equivalent of Edgeworth's box—will be of great importance to our economic analysis.

In general, for an arbitrary ω the order interval $[0,\omega]$ may or may not be weakly compact. For example, in the Riesz dual system $\langle \ell_\infty, \ell'_\infty\rangle$ ($\ell'_\infty =$ the norm dual of ℓ_∞) if $\omega = (\alpha_1, \alpha_2, \ldots)$ satisfies $\lim_{n\to\infty} \alpha_n = 0$, then $[0,\omega]$ is weakly compact (in fact norm compact), while if $\omega = (1,1,1,\ldots)$, then $[0,\omega]$ is not weakly compact. The Riesz dual system $\langle L_\infty, L'_\infty\rangle$ (where $L_\infty = L_\infty[0,1]$ and L'_∞ is the norm dual of L_∞) does not have any weakly compact order intervals. Reason: Let $0 < \omega \in L_\infty$. Pick a measurable set A of positive measure and some $\varepsilon > 0$ with $\omega \geq \varepsilon\chi_A$, and then select a disjoint sequence $\{A_n\}$ of measurable subsets of A of positive measure. If $f_n = \varepsilon\chi_{A_n} \in [0,\omega]$, then the sequence $\{f_n\}$ is a disjoint sequence satisfying $\|f_n\|_\infty = \varepsilon$ for each n, and so $\{f_n\}$ is not convergent to zero. This implies that $[0,\omega]$ is not weakly compact; see [8, Corollary 18.3, p. 309].

Now let us discuss a few properties of the weak closure $\overline{A_\omega}$ of A_ω. Recall that the ideal A_ω generated by ω is the Riesz subspace

$$A_\omega = \{x \in E\colon\ \exists\ \lambda > 0 \text{ such that } |x| \leq \lambda\omega\}.$$

The band B_ω generated by ω (i.e., the smallest band that contains ω) is the ideal given by

$$B_\omega = \{x \in E\colon\ |x| \wedge n\omega \uparrow |x|\}.$$

Clearly, $A_\omega \subseteq B_\omega$. Since every band is τ-closed [6, Theorem 5.6, p. 35], it follows that $\overline{A_\omega} \subseteq B_\omega$. The vector space $\overline{A_\omega}$ coincides with the τ-closure of A_ω, which shows that $\overline{A_\omega}$ is also an ideal. The ideal $\overline{A_\omega}$ is the set

$$\overline{A_\omega} = \{x \in E\colon\ |x| \wedge n\omega \xrightarrow{\tau} |x|\}.$$

If τ is order continuous (equivalently, if the Riesz dual system is symmetric), then clearly $\overline{A_\omega} = B_\omega$. However, in general $\overline{A_\omega}$ does not coincide with B_ω. For instance, in $\langle \ell_\infty, \ell'_\infty\rangle$ if $\omega = (1, \frac{1}{2}, \frac{1}{3}, \ldots)$, then $\overline{A_\omega} \subseteq c_0 \neq \ell_\infty = B_\omega$.

Two basic properties dealing with the weak compactness of the order interval $[0,\omega]$ are included in the next result.

Theorem 2.3.8. *For a Riesz dual system $\langle E, E'\rangle$ and some element $\omega \in E^+$ the following statements hold.*

1. *If $[0,\omega]$ is weakly compact, then the topology τ is order continuous on $\overline{A_\omega}$.*
2. *If E is Dedekind complete and τ is order continuous on $\overline{A_\omega}$, then $[0,\omega]$ is weakly compact.*

Proof. (1) Assume that $[0,\omega]$ is weakly compact. Let $x_\alpha \downarrow 0$ in $\overline{A_\omega}$, and let V and W be two solid τ-neighborhoods of zero satisfying $W+W \subseteq V$. We can assume that there exists some $0 \le x \in \overline{A_\omega}$ satisfying $0 \le x_\alpha \le x$ for all α. Pick some $0 \le y \in A_\omega$ with $x - y \in W$, and note that the order interval $[0,y]$ is weakly compact. Since $x_\alpha \wedge y \downarrow 0$ holds in $[0,y]$, it follows that $x_\alpha \wedge y \xrightarrow{w} 0$, and so $x_\alpha \wedge y \xrightarrow{\tau} 0$; see [6, Theorem 9.8, p. 63]. Pick some α_0 with $x_\alpha \wedge y \in W$ for all $\alpha \ge \alpha_0$. If $\alpha \ge \alpha_0$, then from the lattice identity $v = (v-w)^+ + v \wedge w$ we obtain

$$0 \le x_\alpha = (x_\alpha - y)^+ + x_\alpha \wedge y \le (x-y)^+ + x_\alpha \wedge y \in W + W \subseteq V\,,$$

and so $x_\alpha \in V$ for all $\alpha \ge \alpha_0$. Therefore, $x_\alpha \xrightarrow{\tau} 0$ so that τ is order continuous on $\overline{A_\omega}$.

(2) Let E be Dedekind complete and let τ be order continuous on $\overline{A_\omega}$. Let $\big(\overline{A_\omega}\big)'$ denote $\big(\overline{A_\omega},\tau\big)'$ and consider $\overline{A_\omega}$ equipped with the topology τ.

The Dedekind completeness of E implies that $\overline{A_\omega}$ (as an ideal of E) is Dedekind complete, and so the Riesz dual system $\langle \overline{A_\omega}, (\overline{A_\omega})'\rangle$ is symmetric; see [8, Theorem 11.13, p. 170]. In particular, the order interval $[0,\omega]$ is $\sigma\big(A_\omega, (\overline{A_\omega})'\big)$-compact. Since $(\overline{A_\omega})'$ consists precisely of the restrictions of the functionals of E' to A_ω, it follows that the order interval $[0,\omega]$ is $\sigma(E,E')$-compact. ∎

Finally, we shall close this section with a characterization of the strictly positive elements. Recall that a vector $e > 0$ in a locally convex-solid Riesz space (E,τ) is said to be *strictly positive* (or a *quasi-interior point*), in symbols $e \gg 0$, whenever $0 < \phi \in E'$ implies $\phi(e) > 0$. Equivalently, a vector $e > 0$ is strictly positive whenever e acts as a strictly positive linear functional on E'.

Theorem 2.3.9. *For a Riesz dual system $\langle E, E'\rangle$ and a positive element $0 < e \in E$ the following statements are equivalent.*

1) *The element e is strictly positive, i.e., $0 < \phi \in E'$ implies $0 < \phi(e)$.*
2) *For each $x \in E^+$ we have $x \wedge ne \xrightarrow{w} x$.*
3) *The principal ideal A_e is weakly dense in E.*

EXERCISES

1. If $\langle E, E'\rangle$ is a Riesz dual system, then show that the positive cone E^+ is weakly closed.

2. Consider the Riesz dual system $\langle \ell_\infty, \ell'_\infty \rangle$. If $\omega = (\alpha_1, \alpha_2, \ldots) \in \ell_\infty$ satisfies $\lim_{n\to\infty} \alpha_n = 0$, then show that the order interval $[0, \omega]$ is norm compact—and hence, $[0, \omega]$ is also weakly compact.

3. Consider a Riesz dual system $\langle E, E' \rangle$ and let $0 \le f \in E'$. For each $x \in E$ show that
$$f(x^+) = \sup\{g(x)\colon\ 0 \le g \le f \ \text{ and } \ g \in E'\}.$$

4. Let $\langle E, E' \rangle$ be a Riesz dual system and let x be an element of E. Show that x is a positive element (i.e., $x \in E^+$) if and only if $f(x) \ge 0$ holds for all $0 \le f \in E'$.

5. The two non-empty convex subsets
$$A = \{(x, y) \in \mathcal{R}^2\colon\ x > 0 \ \text{ and } \ y > \tfrac{1}{x}\} \quad \text{and} \quad B = \{(x, y) \in \mathcal{R}^2\colon\ y \le 0\}$$
of $\mathcal{R}^2$ are disjoint. Find a hyperplane that separates them.

6. This exercise presents a direct proof of the separation theorem in finite dimensional vector spaces. The theorem is stated as follows.
(**The separation theorem for finite dimensional vector spaces**) *Every pair A and B of non-empty disjoint convex subsets of some $\mathcal{R}^\ell$ vector space, can be separated by a hyperplane, i.e., there exist some non-zero vector $\mathbf{p} \in \mathcal{R}^\ell$ and some constant c such that*
$$\mathbf{p} \cdot \mathbf{a} \le c \le \mathbf{p} \cdot \mathbf{b}$$
holds for all $\mathbf{a} \in A$ and all $\mathbf{b} \in B$.
The geometrical interpretation of the separation is shown in Figure 2.3-1.

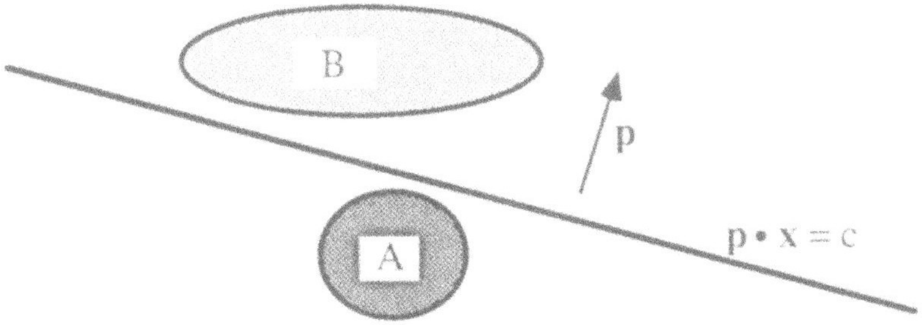

Fig. 2.3-1

Establish the validity of the separation theorem by proving the following statements. For our discussion here the Euclidean norm of an arbitrary vector $\mathbf{v} \in \mathcal{R}^\ell$ will be denoted by $\|\mathbf{v}\|$, i.e., $\|\mathbf{v}\| = \left(\sum_{i=1}^{\ell} v_i^2\right)^{\frac{1}{2}}$.

a) *If C is a non-empty closed convex subset of some $\mathcal{R}^\ell$, then there exists exactly one vector $\mathbf{x}_0 \in C$ which is closest to the origin, i.e., there exists exactly one vector $\mathbf{x}_0 \in C$ satisfying*
$$\|\mathbf{x}_0\| \le \|\mathbf{x}\| \quad \textit{for all} \quad \mathbf{x} \in C.$$

[HINT: Let $d = \inf\{\|\mathbf{x}\|\colon\ \mathbf{x} \in C\}$ and then select a sequence $\{\mathbf{x}_n\}$ of C such that $\lim_{n\to\infty} \|\mathbf{x}_n\| = d$. From

$$\left\|\frac{\mathbf{x}_m - \mathbf{x}_n}{2}\right\|^2 = \frac{\|\mathbf{x}_n\|^2}{2} + \frac{\|\mathbf{x}_m\|^2}{2} - \left\|\frac{\mathbf{x}_n + \mathbf{x}_m}{2}\right\|^2$$
$$\leq \frac{\|\mathbf{x}_n\|^2}{2} + \frac{\|\mathbf{x}_m\|^2}{2} - d^2 \longrightarrow \frac{d^2}{2} + \frac{d^2}{2} - d^2 = 0\,,$$

we see that $\{\mathbf{x}_n\}$ is a Cauchy sequence. If $\lim_{n\to\infty} \mathbf{x}_n = \mathbf{x}_0 \in C$, then $\|\mathbf{x}_0\| = d$.

To see that $\mathbf{x}_0$ is uniquely determined, assume that another vector $\mathbf{z} \in C$ satisfies $\|\mathbf{x}_0\| = \|\mathbf{z}\| = d$. Define the sequence $\{\mathbf{x}_n\}$ of C by $\mathbf{x}_{2n} = \mathbf{x}_0$ and $\mathbf{x}_{2n+1} = \mathbf{z}$ and note that by the above discussion $\lim_{n\to\infty} \mathbf{x}_n$ exists in $\mathcal{R}^\ell$. This implies $\mathbf{z} = \mathbf{x}_0$. The geometrical meaning of the vector $\mathbf{x}_0$ is shown in Figure 2.3-2.]

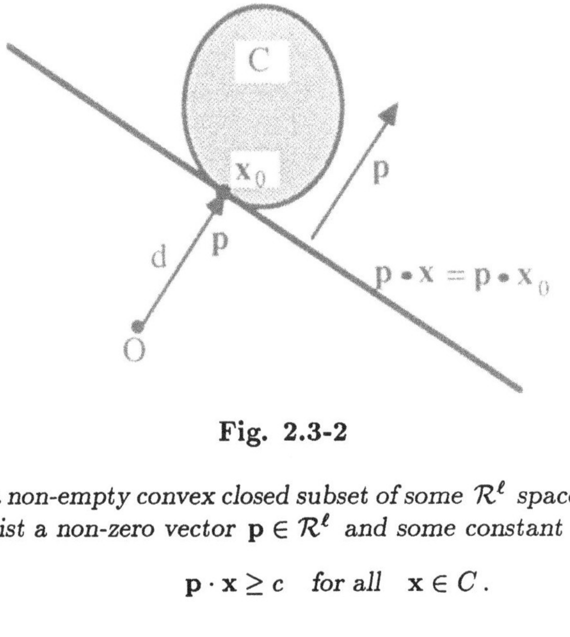

Fig. 2.3-2

b) *If C is a non-empty convex closed subset of some $\mathcal{R}^\ell$ space and $\mathbf{0} \notin C$, then there exist a non-zero vector $\mathbf{p} \in \mathcal{R}^\ell$ and some constant $c > 0$ satisfying*

$$\mathbf{p}\cdot\mathbf{x} \geq c \quad \textit{for all} \quad \mathbf{x} \in C\,.$$

[HINT: Let $\mathbf{x}_0$ be the unique element satisfying $\|\mathbf{x}_0\| = \min\{\|\mathbf{x}\|\colon\ \mathbf{x} \in C\}$ and let $\mathbf{p} = \mathbf{x}_0 \neq \mathbf{0}$ and $c = \mathbf{p}\cdot\mathbf{p} = \|\mathbf{p}\|^2 > 0$. Pick $\mathbf{x} \in C$ and assume by way of contradiction that $\mathbf{p}\cdot\mathbf{x} = \mathbf{x}_0\cdot\mathbf{x} < c = \mathbf{x}_0\cdot\mathbf{x}_0$, or $\mathbf{x}_0\cdot(\mathbf{x}_0 - \mathbf{x}) > 0$. Now for each $0 < \alpha < 1$, we have $\alpha\mathbf{x} + (1-\alpha)\mathbf{x}_0 \in C$ and

$$\|\mathbf{x}_0\|^2 - \|\alpha\mathbf{x} + (1-\alpha)\mathbf{x}_0\|^2 = \|\mathbf{x}_0\|^2 - \|\alpha(\mathbf{x} - \mathbf{x}_0) + \mathbf{x}_0\|^2$$
$$= \alpha[2\mathbf{x}_0\cdot(\mathbf{x}_0 - \mathbf{x}) - \alpha\|\mathbf{x} - \mathbf{x}_0\|^2\,]\,.$$

In view of $\mathbf{x}_0\cdot(\mathbf{x}_0 - \mathbf{x}) > 0$, there is $0 < \alpha < 1$ so that

$$\alpha[2\mathbf{x}_0\cdot(\mathbf{x}_0 - \mathbf{x}) - \alpha\|\mathbf{x} - \mathbf{x}_0\|^2] > 0\,.$$

This implies $\|\alpha\mathbf{x}+(1-\alpha)\mathbf{x}_0\| < \|\mathbf{x}_0\|$, a contradiction.]

c) *If C is a convex subset of some $\mathcal{R}^\ell$ and $\mathbf{0} \notin C$, then there exists a non-zero vector $\mathbf{p} \in \mathcal{R}^\ell$ such that $\mathbf{p}\cdot\mathbf{x} \geq 0$ holds for all $\mathbf{x} \in C$.*

[HINT: If $\mathbf{0} \notin \overline{C}$, then the conclusion follows immediately from the previous part. If $\mathbf{0} \in \overline{C}$, then note that $\mathbf{0} \in \partial\overline{C}$ (why?). Pick a sequence $\{\mathbf{y}_n\}$ of $\mathcal{R}^\ell$ with $\mathbf{y}_n \notin \overline{C}$ for each n and $\lim_{n\to\infty}\mathbf{y}_n = \mathbf{0}$. By the previous part, for each n there exists some $\mathbf{p}_n \in \mathcal{R}^\ell$ with $\|\mathbf{p}_n\| = 1$ satisfying $\mathbf{p}_n\cdot\mathbf{y}_n \leq \mathbf{p}_n\cdot\mathbf{x}$ for each $\mathbf{x} \in C$. If $\mathbf{p}$ is a limit point of $\{\mathbf{y}_n\}$, then $\mathbf{p}\cdot\mathbf{x} \geq 0$ holds for each $\mathbf{x} \in C$.]

d) *Complete the proof of the separation theorem.*

[HINT: Note that $\mathbf{0} \notin B - A$.]

7. For the Riesz dual system $\langle \ell_1, \ell_\infty\rangle$ show that the absolute weak topology and the norm topology on ℓ_1 coincide.

8. Let $\langle E, E'\rangle$ be a dual system and let Y be a closed vector subspace. If $x \notin \overline{Y}$, then show there exists a continuous linear functional f such that $f(x) \neq 0$ and $f(y) = 0$ for all $y \in Y$.

9. If $\langle X, X'\rangle$ is a dual system and $f \in X'$ is a non-zero linear functional, then show that f maps Mackey-open sets onto open subsets of $\mathcal{R}$.

10. Let $\langle X, X'\rangle$ be a dual system and let C be a closet convex subset of X. If $x \notin C$, then show that there exists some $f \in X'$ satisfying $f(x) \notin \overline{f(C)}$.

2.4. BANACH LATTICES

A special class of locally convex-solid Riesz spaces is provided by the class of Banach lattices. A norm $\|\cdot\|$ on a Riesz space is said to be a **lattice norm** whenever it satisfies the condition that $|x| \leq |y|$ implies $\|x\| \leq \|y\|$. A Riesz space equipped with a lattice norm is referred to as a *normed Riesz space*. A **Banach lattice** is a complete normed Riesz space. In other words, a Banach lattice is a Banach space which is at the same time a Riesz space and its norm is a lattice norm. Here are some familiar examples of Banach lattices.

1) The $\mathcal{R}^n$ spaces with the Euclidean norm

$$\|\mathbf{x}\| = \sqrt{\sum_{i=1}^{n}(x_i)^2}\,.$$

2) The $L_p(\mu)$ spaces with the L_p-norm

$$\|f\|_p = \left(\int |f|^p \, d\mu\right)^{\frac{1}{p}}, \quad 1 \leq p < \infty\,.$$

3) The $L_\infty(\mu)$ spaces with the essential sup norm

$$\|f\|_\infty = \operatorname{ess\,sup} |f|\,.$$

4) The ℓ_p spaces with the ℓ_p-norm

$$\|\mathbf{x}\|_p = \left(\sum_{n=1}^{\infty} |x_n|^p\right)^{\frac{1}{p}}, \quad 1 \leq p < \infty\,.$$

5) The ℓ_∞ space with the sup norm

$$\|\mathbf{x}\|_\infty = \sup\{|x_n|\colon\ n = 1, 2, \ldots\}\,.$$

6) The $C(\Omega)$ spaces—Ω Hausdorff and compact—with the sup norm

$$\|f\|_\infty = \sup\{|f(x)|\colon\ x \in \Omega\}\,.$$

7) The ca(Ω) spaces—all regular Borel measures on a compact Hausdorff topological space—with the total variation norm

$$\|\mu\| = |\mu|(\Omega)\,.$$

Every positive linear functional on a Banach lattice is necessarily continuous. Since the norm dual of a Banach lattice is (by Theorem 2.3.2) an ideal of its order dual, it follows that the norm and order duals of a Banach lattice coincide. We state this property as a theorem.

Theorem 2.4.1. *The norm and order duals of a Banach lattice E coincide, i.e., $E' = E^{\sim}$ holds. Moreover, the norm dual of a Banach lattice is a Dedekind complete Banach lattice.*

Remarkably, for a given Riesz space E there is at most one lattice norm (up to an equivalence) that makes E a Banach lattice. Two classes of Banach lattices arise naturally in many contexts. They are the AL- and AM-spaces and they are introduced next.

Definition 2.4.2. *A Banach lattice E is said to be*
1) *an* **AL-space,** *whenever $\|x + y\| = \|x\| + \|y\|$ for all $x, y \in E^+$; and*
2) *an* **AM-space,** *whenever $\|x \vee y\| = \max\{\|x\|, \|y\|\}$ for all $x, y \in E^+$.*

The Banach lattices that can be considered simultaneously as AM- and AL-spaces (under, of course, two equivalent lattice norms) are the finite dimensional spaces. An AM-space E is said to have a *unit* whenever there exists an element $e > 0$—called the *unit*—such that for each $x \in E$ there exists some $\lambda > 0$ satisfying $|x| \leq \lambda e$. If an AM-space has a unit e, then the formula

$$\|x\|_\infty = \inf\{\lambda > 0\colon\ |x| \leq \lambda e\}, \quad x \in E, \tag{$\star$}$$

defines a lattice norm on E which is equivalent to the norm of E. Unless otherwise stated, every AM-space with unit will be assumed to be equipped with the lattice norm defined by ($\star$).

The AL- and AM-spaces are in "duality" to each other.

Theorem 2.4.3. *For a Banach lattice E the following statements hold.*
1) *E is an AL-space if and only if its norm dual E' is an AM-space.*
2) *E is an AM-space if and only if its norm dual E' is an AL-space.*

The norm dual of an AL-space is always an AM-space with unit. Typical examples of AM-spaces are provided by the $C(\Omega)$ Banach lattices (Ω Hausdorff and compact) and of AL-spaces by the $L_1(\mu)$ Banach lattices. We have the following representation theorems for AL- and AM-spaces.

Theorem 2.4.4. (Kakutani) *A Banach lattice is an AL-space if and only if it is lattice isometric to some concrete $L_1(\mu)$ space.*

Theorem 2.4.5. (Kakutani–Bohnenblust–M. Krein–S. Krein) *A Banach lattice E is an AM-space with unit if and only if it is lattice isometric to some $C(\Omega)$ Banach lattice for a (unique up to a homeomorphism) Hausdorff compact topological space Ω.*

A Banach lattice E is said to have *order continuous norm* whenever $x_\alpha \downarrow 0$ in E implies $\|x_\alpha\| \downarrow 0$, or equivalently, whenever the locally convex-solid topology generated by the norm is order continuous. The L_p-spaces for $1 \le p < \infty$ and the ca(Ω) spaces have order continuous norms. The Banach lattices ℓ_∞, $L_\infty[0,1]$ and $C[0,1]$ (all with their sup norms) do not have order continuous norms (why?). An immediate consequence of Theorem 2.4.4 is that every AL-space has order continuous norm—the claim follows immediately from the representation theorem and the Lebesgue dominated convergence theorem.

As formula ($\star$) indicates the AM-spaces are intimately related to principal ideals. Before discussing this connection, let us introduce the class of uniformly complete Riesz spaces.

A sequence $\{x_n\}$ in a Riesz space E is said to *converge e-uniformly* (where $0 < e \in E$ is an arbitrary fixed vector) to an element x whenever for each $\varepsilon > 0$ there exists some n_0 (depending upon ε) such that $|x_n - x| \le \varepsilon e$ holds for all $n \ge n_0$. Likewise a sequence $\{x_n\}$ of a Riesz space is said to be *e-uniformly Cauchy* whenever for each $\varepsilon > 0$ there exists some n_0 satisfying $|x_n - x_m| \le \varepsilon e$ for all $n, m \ge n_0$. A Riesz space is said to be **uniformly complete** whenever every e-uniformly Cauchy sequence—where $e > 0$ is arbitrary—is e-uniformly convergent. Every Dedekind complete Riesz space is uniformly complete but a uniformly complete Riesz space need not be Dedekind complete—C[0,1] is uniformly complete but fails to be Dedekind complete. Every Banach lattice is a uniformly complete Riesz space.

And now we come to the connection between AM-spaces and principal ideals.

Theorem 2.4.6. *If x is an element in a uniformly complete Riesz space, then the principal ideal A_x under the lattice norm*

$$\|y\|_\infty = \inf\{\lambda > 0\colon\ |y| \le \lambda |x|\}, \quad y \in A_x$$

is an AM-space with unit $|x|$.

It should be kept in mind that for an AM-space E with unit e the order interval $[-e, e]$ coincides with the closed unit ball of E, i.e., we have

$$\{x \in E\colon\ \|x\| \le 1\} = [-e, e].$$

EXERCISES

1. If E is a normed Riesz space, then show that $\|x^+ - y^+\| \le \|x - y\|$ holds for all vectors $x, y \in E$.

2. If A is an ideal in a Banach lattice E, then show that the norm closure of A is also an ideal.

3. Consider the Riesz space $C[0,1]$ equipped with the norm $\|f\| = \int_0^1 |f(t)|\,dt$. Show that $C[0,1]$ under this norm is a normed Riesz space but not a Banach lattice.
[HINT: The space $C[0,1]$ is dense in $L_1[0,1]$.]

4. Show that every reflexive Banach lattice has order continuous norm. Also, give an example of a Banach lattice with order continuous norm which is not a reflexive Banach lattice.

5. Assume that a sequence $\{x_n\}$ in a Banach lattice E satisfies $x_n \leq x_{n+1}$ for all n, i.e., $x_n \uparrow$. If $\lim_{n\to\infty} x_n = x$ holds in E, then show that the vector x is the least upper bound of the set $\{x_n\}$.
[HINT: The lattice operations are continuous and $(x_n - x_{n+m})^+ = 0$.]

6. Consider the function $\phi\colon \mathcal{R}_\infty \longrightarrow [0,\infty]$ defined by $\phi(\mathbf{x}) = \sum_{i=1}^{\infty} 2^{-i}|x_i|$ for each $\mathbf{x} = (x_1, x_2, \ldots) \in \mathcal{R}_\infty$. If $E = \{\mathbf{x} \in \mathcal{R}_\infty\colon\ \phi(\mathbf{x}) < \infty\}$, then show that E is a Riesz space and ϕ is a lattice norm on E.

7. If a sequence $\{x_n\}$ in a Banach lattice E is norm convergent to the bundle x, then show there exists a subsequence $\{y_n\}$ of $\{x_n\}$ and a bundle $v \in E^+$ such that $|y_n - x| \leq \frac{1}{n}v$ holds for all n.

8. If E is a Banach lattice and $0 < x \in E$, then show that there exists a positive linear functional f in E' of norm one such that $f(x) = \|x\|$.

9. If x is a positive vector in a Banach lattice E, then show that

$$\|x\| = \sup\{f(x)\colon\ 0 \leq f \in E' \ \text{ and } \ \|f\| = 1\}.$$

10. Consider a Banach lattice E and let $0 \leq f \in E'$. Let A be an ideal and suppose that a linear functional $g\colon A \longrightarrow \mathcal{R}$ satisfies $0 \leq g(x) \leq f(x)$ for all $x \in A^+$. Then show that g can be extended to a positive linear functional on E such that $0 \leq g \leq f$ holds.

11. Show that every Dedekind complete Riesz space is a uniformly complete Riesz space. Also, present an example of a uniformly complete Riesz space which is not Dedekind complete.

CHAPTER 3:

MARKETS WITH INFINITELY MANY COMMODITIES

We have defined commodities as physical goods which may differ in the location or time at which they are produced or consumed, or in the state of the world in which they become available. If we allow an infinite variation in any of these contingencies, then we are naturally led to consider economies with infinitely many commodities.

T. F. Bewley's 1972 paper [16] is the seminal article on the existence of Walrasian equilibria in economies with a finite number of agents and infinitely many commodities. Equally important for our research is a little noticed 1970 paper by B. Peleg and M. E. Yaari [53] on the existence of competitive equilibria in an exchange economy with a countable number of commodities. A comparison of these two disparate approaches to the existence problem, in economies with infinite dimensional commodity spaces, is an excellent introduction to the merits of a Riesz space analysis of general equilibrium models.

The Peleg–Yaari model is a model of an intertemporal infinite horizon economy in discrete time—where the state of the world is known; agents are assumed to have perfect foresight regarding prices; there are a finite number of agents and a countable number of time periods; and in each period a single perishable good is available for consumption. Distinguishing between consumption today and consumption tomorrow, gives rise to a countable number of commodities. Hence, the commodity space is $\mathcal{R}_\infty$ and each agent's consumption set is $\mathcal{R}_\infty^+$, where she has a preference relation and an initial endowment. The intended interpretation of this model is a decentralized model of economic growth and agents are thought to be national economies.

Agents are assumed to be impatient in the sense of I. Fisher [28], i.e., they prefer present consumption to future consumption. This behavioral assumption on tastes is captured by requiring each agent's preference to be continuous in the product topology. In addition, preferences are assumed to be strictly convex and strictly monotone. Prices in this model should correspond to interest rates between periods; hence, in the Peleg–Yaari model, prices are defined as nonnegative sequences of real numbers that give finite valuation to the social endowment. It follows from the assumption of strict monotonicity of preferences that equilibrium interest rates are positive in each period—and thus are never in the dual space of $\mathcal{R}_\infty$.

Assuming perfect foresight, the notion of competitive equilibrium in the Peleg–Yaari model is the same as that in the Arrow–Debreu model of Chapter 1. The Peleg–Yaari proof follows that of H. E. Scarf—they first show that the core is nonempty; then they prove that Edgeworth equilibria exist; and finally they demonstrate the existence of prices that support an Edgeworth equilibrium as a Walrasian equilibrium. The last part of their argument is much more delicate than the similar step in the Debreu-Scarf paper [24], since $\mathcal{R}^+_\infty$ has empty interior in the product topology which prevents the straightforward application of the separating hyperplane theorem. The fact that the economically interesting topologies on a commodity space E typically give rise to an empty interior for E^+ is the essential difference between the standard Arrow–Debreu model and the general equilibrium models which are the principal concern of this monograph.

In contrast to the Peleg–Yaari model, T. F. Bewley formulates his model in terms of a dual pair of locally convex spaces $\langle E, E'\rangle$ which correspond, respectively, to the commodity and price spaces. For the economic situation considered by Peleg and Yaari, Bewley's model specializes to the dual pair $\langle \ell_\infty, \mathrm{ba}\rangle$. Agents' consumption sets are ℓ^+_∞ and preferences are strictly convex and strictly monotone. Bewley also assumes that agents are impatient by requiring preferences to be lower semicontinuous with respect to the Mackey topology for the dual pairing $\langle \ell_\infty, \ell_1\rangle$.

The Hewitt–Yosida representation theorem states that every linear functional in ba can be expressed as the sum of a linear functional in ℓ_1 and a purely finitely additive linear functional. Purely finitely additive functionals cannot be interpreted as defining interest rates between periods. Hence, Bewley's proof of existence is in two parts. First, he demonstrates the existence of a Walrasian equilibrium with supporting prices in ba. Then, using the impatience assumption he shows that the ℓ_1 part of the supporting prices is nontrivial and supports the given allocation as a competitive allocation. To prove the existence of a Walrasian equilibrium with prices in ba, Bewley restricts agents' characteristics to the finite dimensional subspaces of ℓ_∞ that contain the initial and total endowments. For each of the standard Arrow–Debreu exchange economies, there is a Walrasian equilibrium by the Arrow–Debreu existence theorem. Finally, he extracts a convergent subnet from this net of allocations and prices. The limit is the desired equilibrium allocation and price.

To compare the two models, we first observe that ℓ_∞ is a linear subspace of $\mathcal{R}_\infty$. Invoking the Riesz space structure of $\mathcal{R}_\infty$, much more is true. That is, ℓ_∞ is a principal ideal of $\mathcal{R}_\infty$. For our purposes, a more interesting principal ideal of $\mathcal{R}_\infty$ is A_ω, where ω is the total endowment of the agents in the Peleg–Yaari model. Restricting the preferences of agents in the Peleg–Yaari model to A_ω and noting that A_ω and ℓ_∞ are both AM-spaces, we might expect (by Bewley's theorem) that this restricted economy has a Walrasian equilibrium with respect to the duality $\langle A_\omega, A'_\omega\rangle$. This conjecture is true, but our proof does not follow Bewley's limiting argument. Instead, we shall use Scarf's argument for demonstrating the existence of Walrasian equilibria in the Arrow–Debreu model.

First, the order interval $[0, x]$ of $\mathcal{R}_\infty$ is weakly compact for each $x \in \mathcal{R}^+_\infty$ and—as first observed by Peleg and Yaari—this is sufficient to prove the existence of core allocations. Each agent's consumption in a core allocation lies in A_ω; and recalling that $A_\omega = \bigcup_{n=1}^{\infty}[-n\omega, n\omega]$, we see that each agent's consumption in a core allocation for each replica economy is also in A_ω. Hence, Edgeworth equilibria—if they exist—have their consumptions in A_ω. Assuming that agents have convex and strictly monotone preferences, the existence of Edgeworth equilibria follows from the weak compactness of the order interval $[-\omega, \omega]$ and the equal treatment property. To complete the proof, we notice that the positive cone of A_ω has non-empty interior. Hence, the separating hyperplane argument used in the Debreu–Scarf paper to construct prices supporting an Edgeworth equilibrium as a quasiequilibrium can be applied in this case. Of course, these prices lie in A'_ω. The only remaining question is the nature of the supporting prices. It is not difficult to show that they are order continuous and therefore correspond to the ℓ_1-type prices. It is now a small step to show that the allocation and supporting prices constitute an equilibrium in the sense of Peleg and Yaari.

The above comparison of the two models of T. F. Bewley and B. Peleg and M. E. Yaari, abstracted to Riesz spaces, suggests a new means of proving the existence of core allocations, Edgeworth equilibria, and Walrasian equilibria in a large class of exchange economies with a finite number of agents and infinitely many commodities. Our proof of the existence of a Walrasian equilibrium for these exchange economies in [2] consists of two steps. First, we restrict agents' characteristics to A_ω, the principal ideal generated by the total endowment, and prove the existence of a competitive equilibrium for the exchange economy with the commodity-price space duality $\langle A_\omega, A'_\omega \rangle$— here we use H. E. Scarf's argument for existence, generalized to the Riesz space setting. Then, when possible, we extend the supporting prices in A'_ω to prices in E' which support the allocation as a Walrasian equilibrium in E. That this is not always possible is seen in the Peleg–Yaari model where $E = \mathcal{R}_\infty$ and the supporting prices define a strictly positive linear functional in ℓ_1. For an important class of preferences, the uniformly proper preferences introduced by A. Mas-Colell in [46], the supporting prices in A'_ω can be extended to equilibrium prices in E'—as first shown by N. C. Yannelis and W. R. Zame [69]. Uniform properness is an interesting property in its own right and was introduced to compensate for the empty interior of the positive cone in economically interesting commodity spaces. There are no uniformly proper and strictly monotone preferences on $\mathcal{R}_\infty^+$. In this case, the best result is the existence of Walrasian equilibria with respect to the commodity-price duality $\langle A_\omega, A'_\omega \rangle$.

It is important to notice that demand functions need not exist in economies with infinite dimensional commodity spaces—see Example 3.6.1 and Exercise 6 on page 176. Hence, the proof of existence in the standard Arrow–Debreu model (see Theorem 1.4.9) cannot be extended to the infinite dimensional case.

3.1. THE ECONOMIC MODELS

From this point on we shall employ the mathematics from the theory of Riesz spaces as was discussed briefly in Chapter 2. However, for a complete account of the theory of Riesz spaces the interested reader should consult the books [6, 8, 42, 63, 70].

Two very important characteristics of the economic models in this chapter are the following.

1. The commodity-price duality will be described by a Riesz dual system $\langle E, E' \rangle$. The Riesz space E is the commodity space and the Riesz space E' is the price space. As usual, the evaluation $\langle x, p \rangle$ will be denoted by $p \cdot x$, i.e.,

$$p \cdot x = \langle x, p \rangle$$

for all $x \in E$ and all $p \in E'$.

2. There are m consumers indexed by i such that:
   a) Each consumer i has E^+ as her consumption set.
   b) Each consumer i has an initial endowment $\omega_i > 0$. The total endowment will be denoted by ω, i.e.,

$$\omega = \sum_{i=1}^{m} \omega_i .$$

   c) The preferences of each consumer i are represented by a monotone quasi-concave utility function $u_i: E^+ \longrightarrow \mathcal{R}$. Monotonicity means, of course, that $x > y$ in E^+ implies $u_i(x) \geq u_i(y)$.
   d) There is a locally convex-solid topology τ on E consistent with the dual system $\langle E, E' \rangle$ for which every utility function u_i is τ-continuous. (Equivalently, all utility functions are continuous for the absolute Mackey topology $|\tau|(E, E')$—the finest locally convex-solid topology on E consistent with the dual system $\langle E, E' \rangle$.) In particular, note that each utility function u_i is Mackey—i.e., $\tau(E, E')$—continuous.

The above properties will characterize our exchange economies in this chapter. Formally, we have the following definition.

Definition 3.1.1. *An* **exchange economy** $\mathcal{E}$ *is a 2-tuple*

$$\mathcal{E} = \big(\langle E, E' \rangle, \{(\omega_i, u_i)\colon\ i = 1, \ldots, m\}\big),$$

where the components of $\mathcal{E}$ *satisfy properties* (**1**) *and* (**2**) *above.*

A **pure exchange economy** *is an exchange economy with the additional property that* u_i *is strictly monotone for each* i.

3.2. PROPER AND MYOPIC PREFERENCES

The basic properties of preferences and utility functions were discussed in Chapter 1. In this section, we shall discuss a very special property of preference relations—known as *properness*—that will play an important role in our study. In the infinite dimensional case, this property compensates for the absence of interior points in the positive cone. It was introduced by A. Mas-Colell [46] and its definition follows.

Definition 3.2.1. (Mas-Colell) *Let E be a Riesz space, τ a linear topology on E and $\succeq$ a preference relation on E^+.*

1) *The preference relation $\succeq$ is said to be τ-**proper** at some point $x \in E^+$ whenever there exists some $v > 0$ and some τ-neighborhood V of zero such that $x - \alpha v + z \succeq x$ in E^+ with $\alpha > 0$ implies $z \notin \alpha V$.*
2) *The preference relation $\succeq$ is said to be **uniformly τ-proper** whenever there exists some $v > 0$ and some τ-neighborhood V of zero such that for any arbitrary $x \in E^+$ satisfying $x - \alpha v + z \succeq x$ in E^+ with $\alpha > 0$ we have $z \notin \alpha V$.*

*Any vector v that satisfies property (2) will be referred to as a vector of uniform properness for $\succeq$. If clarity requires v to be indicated, then we shall say that $\succeq$ is a v-**uniformly τ-proper preference**.*

It should be noted immediately that if a monotone preference is v-uniformly τ-proper, then it is also w-uniformly τ-proper for each $w \geq v$. A uniformly proper preference expresses the economic intuition that any loss along the direction determined by a vector of uniform properness cannot be recovered by a "small" bundle. Vectors of uniform properness are always extremely desirable bundles.

Lemma 3.2.2. *Every vector of uniform properness for a uniformly proper preference is extremely desirable.*

Proof. Let E be a Riesz space, τ a linear topology on E, $\succeq$ a uniformly τ-proper preference on E^+ and $v > 0$ a vector of uniform properness for $\succeq$.

To see that v is extremely desirable, assume by way of contradiction that for some $x \in E^+$ and some $\alpha > 0$ we have $x \succeq x + \alpha v$. Then from

$$x = (x + \alpha v) - \alpha v + 0 \succeq x + \alpha v$$

and the uniform properness of $\succeq$, it follows that $0 \notin \alpha V$, which is impossible. Hence, $x + \alpha v \succ x$ holds for all $\alpha > 0$ and all $x \in E^+$. ■

If $\succeq$ is a preference and $x \in E^+$, then—as usual—the set $\{y \in E^+ \colon y \succeq x\}$ will be denoted by $P(x)$, that is, $P(x) = \{y \in E^+ \colon y \succeq x\}$. The notion of uniform properness has been characterized by A. Mas-Colell [46] as follows.

Theorem 3.2.3. (Mas-Colell) *Let τ be a locally convex topology on a Riesz space E and let $\succeq$ be a preference on E^+. Then $\succeq$ is uniformly τ-proper if and only if there exists a non-empty τ-open convex cone Γ such that*

a) $\Gamma \cap (-E^+) \neq \emptyset$; *and*
b) $(x+\Gamma) \cap P(x) = \emptyset$ *for all* $x \in E^+$.

Proof. Assume that $\succeq$ is uniformly τ-proper, and let $v > 0$ be a vector of uniform properness corresponding to some open, convex, τ-neighborhood V of zero. Consider the non-empty τ-open convex cone

$$\Gamma = \{\, w \in E\colon\ \exists\ \alpha > 0 \text{ and } y \in V \text{ with } w = \alpha(y-v)\,\}.$$

The geometrical meaning of Γ is shown in Figure 3.2-1.

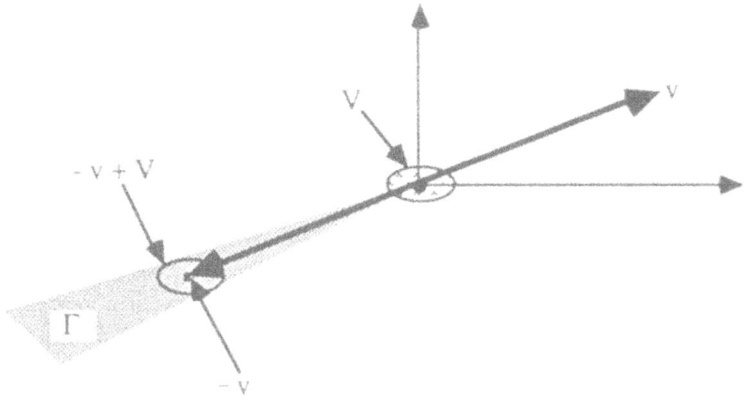

Fig. 3.2-1

From $-v \in \Gamma$, we see that $\Gamma \cap (-E^+) \neq \emptyset$. Now let $x \in E^+$. If $z \in (x+\Gamma) \cap P(x)$, then pick $\alpha > 0$ and $y \in V$ with

$$z = x + \alpha(y-v) = x - \alpha v + \alpha y \succeq x,$$

and so by the uniform τ-properness we have $\alpha y \notin \alpha V$, i.e., $y \notin V$, which is impossible. Consequently, $(x+\Gamma) \cap P(x) = \emptyset$ for all $x \in E^+$.

For the converse assume that there exists a non-empty τ-open convex cone Γ satisfying (a) and (b). Pick some $w \in \Gamma \cap (-E^+)$ and some τ-open neighborhood V of zero with $w + V \subseteq \Gamma$. Put $v = -w > 0$, and let $x - \alpha v + z \succeq x$ in E^+ with $\alpha > 0$. If $z \in \alpha V$, then $z = \alpha y$ for some $y \in V$ and so

$$x - \alpha v + z = x + \alpha(y-v) = x + \alpha(w+y) \in (x+\Gamma) \cap P(x) = \emptyset,$$

which is impossible. Thus, $x - \alpha v + z \succeq x$ in E^+ with $\alpha > 0$ implies $z \notin \alpha V$. ■

The preceding theorem allows us to give a geometrical interpretation of properness in terms of the open convex cone Γ. Figure 3.2-2 illustrates the geometrical property of the cone Γ; the translate of the cone Γ at any point $x \in E^+$ does not intersect the better set of x.

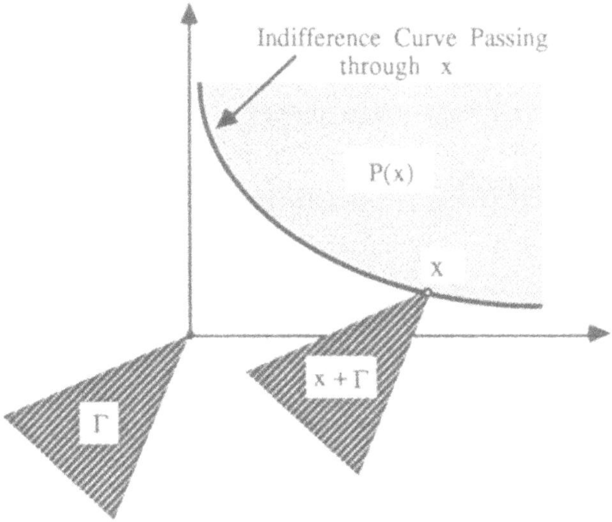

Fig. 3.2-2

The property of uniform properness is a strong condition for preferences. Also, S. F. Richard and W. R. Zame [57] have shown that a uniformly proper preference can be extended to a preference on a closed convex set with a non-empty interior containing the positive cone E^+.

On an AM-space with unit, a monotone preference with an extremely desirable bundle is automatically uniformly norm proper.

Theorem 3.2.4. *If a monotone preference on the positive cone of an AM-space with unit has an extremely desirable bundle, then it is uniformly norm proper.*

Proof. Let E be an AM-space with unit and let $\succeq$ be a monotone preference on E^+ having an extremely desirable bundle $v > 0$. Observe that if $w \in \text{Int}(E^+)$, then $x + w \succ x$ holds for all $x \in E^+$. Indeed, if $w \in \text{Int}(E^+)$, then pick some $\alpha > 0$ with $w - \alpha v \in E^+$ and note that for $x \in E^+$ we have

$$x + w = x + \alpha v + (w - \alpha v) \succeq x + \alpha v \succ x\,.$$

Now consider the non-empty open convex cone $\Gamma = -\text{Int}(E^+)$. Clearly, we have $\Gamma \cap (-E^+) \neq \emptyset$. On the other hand, if $x \in E^+$, then we claim that

$$(x + \Gamma) \cap \{\, y \in E^+ \colon\ y \succeq x \,\} = \emptyset\,.$$

Indeed, if this is not the case, then there exists some $w \in \text{Int}(E^+)$ with $x - w \geq 0$ and $x - w \succeq x$, and so we must have $x = (x - w) + w \succ x - w \succeq x$, which is impossible. Therefore,

$$(x + \Gamma) \cap \{\, y \in E^+ \colon y \succeq x \,\} = \emptyset$$

holds for all $x \in E^+$, and hence by Theorem 3.2.3 the preference relation $\succeq$ is uniformly norm proper. ■

An immediate consequence of Theorem 3.2.4 is the following.

Corollary 3.2.5. *If a monotone preference relation on the positive cone of some $\mathcal{R}^\ell$ space has an extremely desirable bundle, then it is uniformly proper.*

We continue by exhibiting a class of uniformly proper preferences. Fix a non-zero positive linear functional p in E' (i.e., $0 < p \in E'$) and consider the preference relation $\succeq$ on E^+ defined by the utility function

$$u(x) = p \cdot x\,, \quad x \in E^+\,.$$

Clearly, the preference $\succeq$ is convex, monotone and continuous for every locally convex topology on E consistent with the duality $\langle E, E'\rangle$. The preference $\succeq$ is also uniformly proper for any locally convex topology on E consistent with the duality $\langle E, E'\rangle$. To see this, consider the non-empty, open (for the consistent locally convex topologies) and convex cone

$$\Gamma = \{x \in E\colon\ p \cdot x < 0\}\,.$$

Then $\Gamma \cap (-E^+) \neq \emptyset$ and $(x + \Gamma) \cap \{y \in E^+\colon\ y \succeq x\} = \emptyset$ holds for each $x \in E^+$. The uniform properness of $\succeq$ now follows immediately from Theorem 3.2.3.

The next result presents a characterization of the uniformly proper preferences in terms of an approximation property.

Theorem 3.2.6. *Let (E, τ) be a Hausdorff locally convex-solid Riesz space and let $\succeq$ be a preference on E^+. If A is a τ-dense ideal of E, then $\succeq$ is uniformly τ-proper if and only if there exist a τ-neighborhood V of zero and some $0 < v \in A$ such that*

$$x - \alpha v + z \succeq x \ \text{ in } \ E^+ \ \text{ with } \ \alpha > 0 \ \text{ implies } \ z \notin \alpha V\,.$$

Proof. Assume that $\succeq$ is uniformly τ-proper. Pick a τ-neighborhood W of zero and some $0 < w \in E$ such that

$$x - \alpha w + z \succeq x \ \text{ in } \ E^+ \ \text{ with } \ \alpha > 0 \ \text{ implies } \ z \notin \alpha W. \qquad (\star)$$

Choose a convex solid τ-neighborhood V of zero with $w \notin V$ and $V + V \subseteq W$. Since the ideal A is τ-dense in E, there exists some $v \in A$ with $w - v \in V$. Replacing v by $w \wedge v^+$ and taking into account the inequality $|w - w \wedge v^+| \leq |w - v|$, we can assume that $0 < v \leq w$ holds. Now we claim that

$$x - \alpha v + z \succeq x \ \text{ in } \ E^+ \ \text{ with } \ \alpha > 0 \ \text{ implies } \ z \notin \alpha V\,.$$

Indeed, if $x - \alpha v + z \succeq x$ holds in E^+ with $\alpha > 0$, then from $(\star)$ and the relation

$$x - \alpha w + [z - \alpha(v - w)] = x - \alpha v + z \succeq x,$$

we see that $z - \alpha(v - w) \notin \alpha W$. On the other hand, if $z \in \alpha V$, then we have

$$z - \alpha(v - w) \in \alpha V + \alpha V = \alpha(V + V) \subseteq \alpha W\,,$$

which is impossible. Hence, $z \notin \alpha V$, and the proof of the theorem is finished. ■

In other words, the preceding theorem tells us that a uniformly τ-proper preference has at least one vector of uniform properness in every τ-dense ideal of E. In particular, as we shall see next, this implies that the strictly positive vectors must be necessarily vectors of uniform properness for any uniformly proper preference.

Theorem 3.2.7. *Let $\langle E, E' \rangle$ be a Riesz dual system and let τ be a consistent locally convex-solid topology on E. If $\succeq$ is a uniformly τ-proper preference on E^+, then every strictly positive element of E is a vector of uniform τ-properness for $\succeq$.*

Proof. Let $\langle E, E' \rangle$, τ and $\succeq$ satisfy the hypotheses of the theorem. Also, let e be a strictly positive element of E. Then the ideal A_e is τ-dense in E—in fact, we have $e \gg 0$ if and only if A_e is τ-dense in E. To see this, assume by way of contradiction that A_e is not τ-dense in E. Then, by the classical separation theorem, there exists a non-zero price $p \in E'$ (i.e., $|p| > 0$) which vanishes on the ideal A_e. Therefore, we must have

$$\begin{aligned} 0 < |p| \cdot e &= \sup\{p \cdot x\colon\ x \in E \text{ and } |x| \le e\} \\ &= \sup\{p \cdot x\colon\ x \in A_e \text{ and } |x| \le e\} = 0\,, \end{aligned}$$

which is impossible. Hence, A_e is τ-dense in E.

Now by Theorem 3.2.6 there exists some $0 < v \in A_e$ of uniform τ-properness for $\succeq$. Pick some $\lambda > 0$ satisfying $0 < v \le \lambda e$ and note that λe is a vector of uniform τ-properness for $\succeq$. This implies that e itself is a vector of uniform τ-properness for $\succeq$, as claimed. ■

Impatience is an important feature of intertemporal choice behavior and plays an essential role in the existence proofs of Bewley and Peleg–Yaari. Characterizations of impatience in terms of the continuity of utility functions can be found in [18], [54] and [65]. In the sequel, we shall present an order-theoretic definition of impatience that subsumes the notions in these papers. Every utility function which is continuous in an order continuous topology is myopic (or impatient) in our sense. (Recall that a net $\{x_\alpha\}$ in a Riesz space is said to be *order convergent* to some element x, in symbols $x_\alpha \xrightarrow{o} x$, whenever there exists another net $\{y_\alpha\}$ with the same indexed set such that $y_\alpha \downarrow 0$ and $|x_\alpha - x| \le y_\alpha$ holds for each α.)

Definition 3.2.8. *An order continuous utility function $u\colon E^+ \longrightarrow \mathcal{R}$ will be referred to as a* **myopic utility function**, *i.e., a function $u\colon E^+ \longrightarrow \mathcal{R}$ is said to be myopic whenever $x_\alpha \xrightarrow{o} x$ in E^+ implies $u(x_\alpha) \longrightarrow u(x)$.*

As mentioned above, myopia (i.e., order continuity) should be interpreted as a mathematical notion that captures the economic intuition of impatience; for more about this economic intuition see [10, 18, 54].

Note that if a utility function $u: E^+ \longrightarrow \mathcal{R}$ is continuous for an order continuous locally solid topology τ (i.e., $x_\alpha \xrightarrow{o} x$ implies $x_\alpha \xrightarrow{\tau} x$), then u is automatically myopic. Also, in case E is a Fréchet lattice, then every myopic utility function $u: E^+ \to \mathcal{R}$ is continuous. This follows immediately from the fact that in a Fréchet lattice every topologically convergent sequence has an order convergent subsequence; see Exercise 8 at the end of this section.

A myopic utility function is not necessarily topologically continuous and a topologically continuous utility function need not be myopic. The next two examples clarify the situation.

Example 3.2.9. *(A myopic utility function which is not topologically continuous)* Let $E = \ell_1$ and let τ be the order continuous locally convex-solid topology induced on E by the ℓ_2-norm. Now consider the utility function $u: E^+ \longrightarrow \mathcal{R}$ defined by

$$u(\mathbf{x}) = \sum_{i=1}^{\infty} x_i, \quad \mathbf{x} = (x_1, x_2, \dots) \in E^+ .$$

Clearly, u is strictly monotone and concave and, moreover, we claim that it is also myopic. To see the latter, let $\mathbf{x}_\alpha \xrightarrow{o} \mathbf{x}$ in E^+, where $\mathbf{x}_\alpha = (x_1^\alpha, x_2^\alpha, \dots)$ and $\mathbf{x} = (x_1, x_2, \dots)$. Pick a net $\{ \mathbf{y}_\alpha \}$ of E^+ such that $|\mathbf{x}_\alpha - \mathbf{x}| \le \mathbf{y}_\alpha$ for each α and $\mathbf{y}_\alpha \downarrow \mathbf{0}$. From

$$|u(\mathbf{x}_\alpha) - u(\mathbf{x})| \le \sum_{i=1}^{\infty} |x_i^\alpha - x_i| \le \sum_{i=1}^{\infty} y_i^\alpha = \|\mathbf{y}_\alpha\|_1$$

and $\|\mathbf{y}_\alpha\|_1 \downarrow 0$, we see that $u(\mathbf{x}_\alpha) \longrightarrow u(\mathbf{x})$, and so u is order continuous.

Now we claim that the utility function is not τ-continuous. To see this, for each n pick some $k_n > n$ with $\sum_{i=n}^{k_n} \frac{1}{i} > 1$ and let

$$\mathbf{x}_n = \left(\tfrac{1}{n}, \tfrac{1}{n+1}, \dots, \tfrac{1}{k_n}, 0, 0, \dots\right), \quad n = 1, 2, \dots .$$

Then $\{ \mathbf{x}_n \}$ is a sequence of E^+ satisfying $\lim_{n\to\infty} \|\mathbf{x}_n\|_2 = 0$ (i.e., $\mathbf{x}_n \xrightarrow{\tau} \mathbf{0}$). On the other hand, the inequalities

$$u(\mathbf{x}_n) = \sum_{i=n}^{k_n} \tfrac{1}{i} > 1 > 0 = u(\mathbf{0}),$$

show that $u(\mathbf{x}_n) \not\to 0$, and hence u is not τ-continuous. ■

Example 3.2.10. *(A topologically continuous utility function which is not myopic)* Let $\{r_0, r_1, r_2, \dots\}$ be an enumeration of the rational numbers in $[0,1]$ with $r_0 = 0$. Consider the Riesz space C[0,1] and define $u: (C[0,1])^+ \longrightarrow \mathcal{R}$ by

$$u(x) = \sum_{i=0}^{\infty} 2^{-i} \sqrt{x(r_i)} .$$

It is easy to see that u is $\|\cdot\|_\infty$-continuous, strictly monotone and strictly concave. In addition, we claim that u fails to be order continuous. To see this, consider the sequence $\{x_n\}$ of continuous functions defined by

$$x_n(t) = \begin{cases} 1 - nt & \text{for } 0 \le t \le \frac{1}{n}, \\ 0 & \text{for } \frac{1}{n} \le t \le 1. \end{cases}$$

Clearly, $0 \le x_{n+1} \le x_n$ holds for all n, and the constant function zero is the only positive continuous function less than every x_n. Therefore, we have $x_n \downarrow 0$. However, $u(x_n) \ge x_n(0) = 1 > u(0) = 0$ holds. Therefore, $u(x_n)$ does not converge to $u(0)$ and hence, u is not a myopic utility function. ■

The myopic utility functions have the following interesting continuity property.

Theorem 3.2.11. *If $u: E^+ \longrightarrow \mathcal{R}$ is a myopic utility function, then on every principal ideal of E the utility function u is $\|\cdot\|_\infty$-continuous.*

Proof. Let $x \in E^+$, and let $\{y_n\}$ be a sequence of A_x such that $\|y - y_n\|_\infty \longrightarrow 0$. Put

$$\varepsilon_n = \sup\{\, \|y_i - y\|_\infty \colon i \ge n \,\}$$

and note that $\varepsilon_n \downarrow 0$ and that $|y_n - y| \le \varepsilon_n x$ for all n. Since $\varepsilon_n x \downarrow 0$ holds in E (keep in mind that E is assumed to be an Archimedean Riesz space), it follows that $y_n \xrightarrow{o} y$ in E, and so by the order continuity of u, we see that $u(y_n) \longrightarrow u(y)$. ■

Our next result presents a useful continuity property of the myopic quasi-concave utility functions.

Theorem 3.2.12. *Let E be a normal Riesz space, let $a \in E^+$ and let $\{x_n\}$ be a sequence of $[0, a]$. If x is a $\sigma(E, E_n^\sim)$-accumulation point of $\{x_n\}$ and a utility function $u: E^+ \longrightarrow \mathcal{R}$ is monotone, quasi-concave and myopic, then*

$$u(x) \ge \liminf_{n\to\infty} u(x_n)\,.$$

Proof. Assume that E, $\{x_n\}$, x and $u: E^+ \longrightarrow \mathcal{R}$ satisfy the hypotheses of the theorem. Fix $\varepsilon > 0$. Let N_ϕ denote the null ideal, and let C_ϕ denote the carrier ideal of $\phi \in E_n^\sim$.

Next consider the ideal

$$C = \bigcup_{\phi \in E_n^\sim} C_\phi\,,$$

and note that C is order dense in E. To see this, let $0 \le z \in C^d$. Then $z \perp C_\phi$ holds and so $z \in C_\phi^d = N_\phi$ for all ϕ. Thus, $\phi(z) = 0$ for all $\phi \in E_n^\sim$ and since $E_n^\sim$ separates the points of E, we see that $z = 0$. Therefore, C is order dense in E.

Now by the order continuity of u and an easy inductive argument, it follows that there exist sequences $\{y_n\}$ of E^+ and $\{\phi_n\}$ of $(E_n^\sim)^+$ such that

a) $y_n \in C_{\phi_n}$ and $0 \le y_n \le x_n$ for all n;
b) $\phi_k(x_n - y_n) < 2^{-n}$ for $1 \le k \le n$; and
c) $u(y_n) > u(x_n) - \varepsilon$.

Since x is a $\sigma(E, E_n^{\sim})$-accumulation point of the convex hull of $\{x_k\colon\ k \geq n\}$, it is also a $|\sigma|(E, E_n^{\sim})$-accumulation point of the convex hull of $\{x_k\colon\ k \geq n\}$. Thus, for each n there exists some $\zeta_n \in \mathrm{co}\{\, x_k\colon\ k \geq n\}$ satisfying

$$\phi_k(|x - \zeta_n|) < 2^{-n} \text{ for } 1 \leq k \leq n\,.$$

Write ζ_n as a convex combination $\zeta_n = \sum_{i=1}^{m_n} \lambda_i^n x_{n_i}$, where $n_i \geq n$ for $1 \leq i \leq m_n$, and then put

$$z_n = \sum_{i=1}^{m_n} \lambda_i^n y_{n_i}\,.$$

From (b) and

$$|x - z_n| \leq |x - \zeta_n| + |\zeta_n - z_n| = |x - \zeta_n| + \sum_{i=1}^{m_n} \lambda_i^n (x_{n_i} - y_{n_i})\,,$$

we see that

$$\phi_k(|x - z_n|) < 2^{-n} + 2^{-n} = 2^{1-n} \quad \text{for} \quad 1 \leq k \leq n\,. \tag{1}$$

Taking into account that u is quasi-concave, it follows from (c) that

$$\begin{aligned} u(z_n) &\geq \min\{\, u(y_{n_i})\colon\ 1 \leq i \leq m_n \,\} \\ &\geq \min\{\, u(x_{n_i})\colon\ 1 \leq i \leq m_n \,\} - \varepsilon\,, \end{aligned}$$

and consequently

$$u(z_n) \geq \inf\{\, u(x_k)\colon\ k \geq n \,\} - \varepsilon \quad \text{for all} \quad n\,. \tag{2}$$

Our next goal is to establish that the sequence $\{z_n\}$ is order convergent. For each n write $E = N_{\phi_n} \oplus C_{\phi_n}$, and then let h_n be the projection of x onto C_{ϕ_n}. Put $h = \sup\{\, h_n \,\} \leq x$, and we claim that $z_n \xrightarrow{o} h$.

To see this, note first that from

$$0 \leq \phi_k(x - h) \leq \phi_k(x - h_k) = 0\,,$$

we have $\phi_k(x - h) = 0$ for all k. Thus, from (**1**) and the inequality

$$|h - z_n| = |x - z_n - (x - h)| \leq |x - z_n| + x - h\,,$$

it follows that

$$\phi_k(|h - z_n|) < 2^{1-n} \quad \text{for} \quad 1 \leq k \leq n\,. \tag{3}$$

Put $f_n = \sup\{|h - z_k|\colon\ k \geq n\}$, and note that $|h - z_n| \leq f_n$ holds for all n. Thus, in order to establish that $z_n \xrightarrow{o} h$ it suffices to show that $f_n \downarrow 0$. To this end, let $0 \leq f \leq f_n$ hold for all n. Then from (**3**), we have

$$\phi_m(f) \leq \phi_m(f_n) \leq \sum_{k=n}^{\infty} \phi_m(|h - z_k|) \leq \sum_{k=n}^{\infty} 2^{1-k} = 2^{2-n}$$

for all $n \geq m$, and so $\phi_m(f) = 0$ for all m, i.e., $f \in N_{\phi_m}$ for all m. Therefore, $f \perp C_{\phi_m}$ for all m. This implies $f \perp h$ and $f \perp y_n$ for all n, and hence $f \perp z_n$ for all n. In turn, the latter implies $f \perp |h - z_n|$ for all n, and so $f \perp f_1$. From $0 \leq f \leq f_1$, we infer that $f = 0$. Thus, $f_n \downarrow 0$, and hence $z_n \xrightarrow{o} h$ holds.

Now by the order continuity of u, we see that $u(h) = \lim_{n\to\infty} u(z_n)$. A glance at (**2**) reveals that

$$u(h) = \lim_{n\to\infty} u(z_n) \geq \liminf_{n\to\infty} u(x_n) - \varepsilon\,.$$

In view of $0 \leq h \leq x$ and the monotonicity of u, we have $u(x) \geq u(h)$, and so

$$u(x) \geq \liminf_{n\to\infty} u(x_n) - \varepsilon$$

holds. Since $\varepsilon > 0$ is arbitrary, the latter implies $u(x) \geq \liminf_{n\to\infty} u(x_n)$, and the proof of the theorem is finished. ■

EXERCISES

1. If a preference relation is v-uniformly τ-proper, then show that is also w-uniformly τ-proper for each $w \geq v$.

2. Let $(x_1, \ldots, x_m)$ be an allocation, and let p be a non-zero price such that each preference relation $\succeq_i$ satisfies $x \succeq_i x_i$ implies $p\cdot x \geq p\cdot \omega_i = p\cdot x_i$. Then show that each preference relation $\succeq_i$ is τ-proper at x_i.
[HINT: Choose a τ-neighborhood V of zero such that $|p\cdot y| < 1$ holds for all $y \in V$. Then choose some $v \in E^+$ with $p\cdot v = 1$ and note that $x_i - \alpha v + z \succeq_i x_i$ implies $z \notin \alpha V$.]

3. Let τ be a (Hausdorff) locally convex topology on a Riesz space E. Show that a preference $\succeq$ on E^+ is τ-proper at some point $x \in E^+$ if and only if there exists some non-empty τ-open convex cone Γ such that
a) $\Gamma \bigcap (-E^+) \neq \emptyset$; and
b) $(x + \Gamma) \bigcap \{y \in E^+\colon\ y \succeq x\} = \emptyset$.
Use this conclusion to present an alternate proof of Exercise 1.

4. Let $\succeq$ be a monotone uniformly τ-proper preference. If $\mathcal{U}$ denotes the (non-empty) set of all vectors of uniform properness for $\succeq$, then show that
a) $\mathcal{U}$ is a convex subcone of E^+;
b) $\mathcal{U} + E^+ = \mathcal{U}$; and
c) $\mathcal{U}$ has a non-empty interior relative to E^+.

5. Consider the Riesz dual system $\langle \ell_p, \ell_q\rangle$, $1 \leq p,\, q \leq \infty$; $\frac{1}{p} + \frac{1}{q} = 1$, and let τ be a consistent locally convex-solid topology on ℓ_p. If $\succeq$ is a uniformly τ-proper preference on ℓ_p^+ and $(v_1, v_2, \ldots)$ is a vector of uniform τ-properness for $\succeq$, then show that there exists some n such that the vector $(v_1, v_2, \ldots, v_n, 0, 0, 0, \ldots)$ is also a vector of uniform τ-properness for $\succeq$.

6. The preference relation considered in this problem was introduced by A. Mas-Colell [46]. For each n let $u_n\colon \mathcal{R} \longrightarrow \mathcal{R}$ be the continuous function defined by

$$u_n(t) = \begin{cases} 2^n t, & \text{if } t \le \frac{1}{2^{2n}}, \\ \frac{1}{2^n} - \frac{1}{2^{2n}} + t, & \text{if } t > \frac{1}{2^{2n}}, \end{cases}$$

and consider the utility function $U: \ell_1^+ \longrightarrow \mathcal{R}$ defined by

$$U(x_1, x_2, \ldots) = \sum_{n=1}^{\infty} u_n(x_n).$$

a) Show that U is a strictly monotone, concave and weakly continuous (and hence norm continuous) utility function.
b) Show that the preference $\succeq$ represented by the utility function U is not uniformly norm proper.
[HINT: Assume that $\succeq$ is uniformly norm proper. Then, by Theorem 3.2.7, the strictly positive vector $\mathbf{v} = (\frac{1}{2^3}, \frac{1}{2^5}, \ldots, \frac{1}{2^{2n+1}}, \ldots)$ must be a vector of uniform norm properness for $\succeq$. To obtain a contradiction note that $\mathbf{v} - 2^{-\ell}\mathbf{v} + 2^{-2\ell}\mathbf{e}_\ell \succ \mathbf{v}$ holds for each ℓ, where $\mathbf{e}_\ell$ denotes the sequence having its ℓth component equal to one and every other equal to zero.]

7. Consider the Riesz space C[0,1] and define $u: (C[0,1])^+ \longrightarrow \mathcal{R}$ by

$$u(x) = \int_0^1 \sqrt{x(t)}\, dt.$$

Then show that the utility function u is strictly monotone, strictly concave, $\|\cdot\|_\infty$-continuous and that it fails to be myopic.
[HINT: To show that the utility function u is not myopic use [8, Exercise 15, p. 199].]

8. If $x_n \xrightarrow{\tau} x$ holds in a Fréchet lattice, then show that there exists a subsequence $\{x_{k_n}\}$ of $\{x_n\}$ such that $x_{k_n} \xrightarrow{o} x$. Use this result to conclude that every myopic utility function defined on the positive cone of a Fréchet lattice is topologically continuous.
[HINT: Assume that $x_n \xrightarrow{\tau} x$ holds in a Fréchet lattice. Pick a sequence $\{V_n\}$ of τ-neighborhoods of zero that form a base at zero such that $V_{n+1} + V_{n+1} \subseteq V_n$ holds for each n. Now pick a subsequence $\{x_{k_n}\}$ of $\{x_n\}$ such that $n|x_{k_n} - x| \in V_n$ holds for each n. By the τ-completeness, the element $y = \sum_{n=1}^{\infty} n|x_{k_n} - x|$ exists in the Fréchet lattice. Now note that $|x_{k_n} - x| \le \frac{1}{n}y$ holds for each n.]

9. Let $\langle E, E' \rangle$ be a symmetric Riesz dual system. If a utility function $u: E^+ \to \mathcal{R}$ is weakly continuous on the order bounded subsets of E^+, then show that u is a myopic utility function.
[HINT: Since $\langle E, E' \rangle$ is a symmetric Riesz dual system, the absolute weak topology $|\sigma|(E, E')$ is order continuous, and so order convergence in E implies $|\sigma|(E, E')$-convergence (and hence weak convergence). Since an order convergent net is eventually order bounded (why?), it follows that the utility function u is necessarily a myopic utility function.]

3.3. EDGEWORTH EQUILIBRIA AND THE CORE

In this section, we shall see that the existence of core and Edgeworth equilibrium allocations follow from the weak compactness of the order interval $[0,\omega]$. In fact, we shall present an example of a two person exchange economy with infinitely many commodities where agents' preferences are continuous, strictly convex and strictly monotone, and yet the core is empty. In this example the order interval $[0,\omega]$ defined by the total endowment is not weakly compact.

We begin our discussion by exploring the relationship between the weak compactness of the order interval $[0,\omega]$ and the weak compactness of the set of all allocations. An **allocation** in an exchange economy is an m-tuple $(x_1,\dots,x_m)$ such that $x_i \in E^+$ for each i and $\sum_{i=1}^m x_i = \sum_{i=1}^m \omega_i = \omega$. The set of all allocations will be denoted by $\mathcal{A}$, i.e.,

$$\mathcal{A} = \{(x_1,\dots,x_m)\colon\ x_i \in E^+ \text{ for each } i \text{ and } \sum_{i=1}^m x_i = \omega\}.$$

Since E^+ is convex and weakly closed and $(\omega_1,\dots,\omega_m)$ belongs to $\mathcal{A}$, it is easy to see that $\mathcal{A}$ is a non-empty, convex and weakly closed subset of E^m. When the order interval $[0,\omega]$ is weakly compact, it turns out that $\mathcal{A}$ is also a weakly compact subset of E^m.

Theorem 3.3.1. *If the order interval $[0,\omega]$ is weakly compact, then the set $\mathcal{A}$ of all allocations in an exchange economy is a non-empty, convex and weakly compact subset of E^m.*

Proof. Let $\{(x_1^\alpha,\dots,x_m^\alpha)\}$ be a net of $\mathcal{A}$. Since $0 \le x_i^\alpha \le \omega$ holds for each i and all α, we see that for each i the net $\{x_i^\alpha\}$ lies in the weakly compact set $[0,\omega]$. This implies that every subnet of the net $\{x_i^\alpha\}$ has a weakly convergent subnet in $[0,\omega]$. Thus, by passing to an appropriate subnet, we see that the net $\{(x_1^\alpha,\dots,x_m^\alpha)\}$ has a weakly convergent subnet to some $(x_1,\dots,x_m)$ in E^m. Clearly, $x_i \in E^+$ holds for each i, and from $\sum_{i=1}^m x_i^\alpha = \omega$ for each α, we infer that $\sum_{i=1}^m x_i = \omega$, i.e., $(x_1,\dots,x_m) \in \mathcal{A}$. Thus, every net of $\mathcal{A}$ has a weakly convergent subnet in $\mathcal{A}$, and so $\mathcal{A}$ is a weakly compact subset of E^m. ■

For pure exchange economies the converse of the preceding theorem is also true.

Theorem 3.3.2. *If an exchange economy has at least two consumers, then the order interval $[0,\omega]$ is weakly compact if and only if the set $\mathcal{A}$ of all allocations is a weakly compact subset of E^m.*

Proof. The "only if" part follows immediately from Theorem 3.3.1. For the "if" part assume that $m \ge 2$ holds and that $\mathcal{A}$ is weakly compact.

If $\{x_\alpha\}$ is a net of $[0,\omega]$, then consider the allocation net $\{(x_\alpha, \omega - x_\alpha, 0,\dots,0)\}$, and note that—since $\mathcal{A}$ is weakly compact—the net $\{x_\alpha\}$ must have a weakly convergent subnet in $[0,\omega]$. Thus, $[0,\omega]$ is a weakly compact set, as desired. ■

The notion of improving upon an allocation by a coalition is defined as before. We say that a coalition S **improves upon** an allocation $(x_1, \ldots, x_m)$ whenever there exists another allocation $(y_1, \ldots, y_m)$ such that

a) $\sum_{i \in S} y_i = \sum_{i \in S} \omega_i$; and

b) $y_i \succ_i x_i$ holds for each $i \in S$.

The allocations that cannot be improved upon by any coalition are known as *core allocations*.

Definition 3.3.3. *A* **core allocation** *is an allocation that cannot be improved upon by any coalition.*

Repeating the proofs of Theorems 1.5.5 and 1.6.7, we have the following two results.

Theorem 3.3.4. *Every core allocation is individually rational and weakly Pareto optimal.*

Theorem 3.3.5. *Every Walrasian equilibrium is a core allocation.*

The next basic result tells us that when the order interval $[0, \omega]$ is weakly compact core allocations always exist.

Theorem 3.3.6. *If in an exchange economy the order interval $[0, \omega]$ is weakly compact, then the core of the economy is a non-empty weakly compact subset of E^m.*

Proof. The proof follows line by line the arguments of the proof of Theorem 1.5.10. In that proof, we defined the m-person game by

$$V(S) = \{(\xi_1, \ldots, \xi_m) \in \mathcal{R}^m\colon \text{ There exists an allocation } (y_1, \ldots, y_m) \text{ with}$$
$$\sum_{i \in S} y_i = \sum_{i \in S} \omega_i \text{ and } \xi_i \le u_i(y_i) \text{ for each } i \in S\},$$

and verified that it satisfied all the hypotheses of Scarf's theorem (Theorem 1.5.9). Assumptions (b) and (c) of Scarf's theorem are trivially true and (d) follows from the fact that each utility function u_i is monotone and hence bounded on $[0, \omega]$. The only property that requires special attention in this case is the closedness of the sets $V(S)$. Everything else can be proved exactly as in the proof of Theorem 1.5.10.

So, in order to complete the proof, we must establish that each $V(S)$ is closed. To this end, let a net $\{(\xi_1^\alpha, \ldots, \xi_m^\alpha)\}$ of some $V(S)$ satisfy $(\xi_1^\alpha, \ldots, \xi_m^\alpha) \to (\xi_1, \ldots, \xi_m)$ in $\mathcal{R}^m$. For each α pick an allocation $(y_1^\alpha, \ldots, y_m^\alpha)$ satisfying $\xi_i^\alpha \le u_i(y_i^\alpha)$ for each $i \in S$ and $\sum_{i \in S} y_i^\alpha = \sum_{i \in S} \omega_i$. Since $0 \le y_i^\alpha \le \omega$ holds for all i and all α, and $[0, \omega]$ is weakly compact, we can assume (by passing to an appropriate subnet) that $y_i^\alpha \xrightarrow{w} y_i$ holds for all i. Clearly, $(y_1, \ldots, y_m)$ is an allocation and

$\sum_{i\in S} y_i = \sum_{i\in S}\omega_i$ holds. On the other hand, since (by Theorem 1.2.4) each utility function is weakly upper semicontinuous, it follows from Exercise 8 on page 18 that

$$\xi_i = \limsup_\alpha \xi_i^\alpha \le \limsup_\alpha u_i(y_i^\alpha) \le u(y_i)$$

for each $i \in S$. Therefore, $(\xi_1, \ldots, \xi_m) \in V(S)$, and so each $V(S)$ is closed, as desired. ■

The next example shows that if the order interval $[0, \omega]$ is not weakly compact, then the core of the economy may be empty. The example is due to the authors [4]. An example of this type has also been presented by A. Araujo [10].

Example 3.3.7. In what follows the symbol $L_p\,(1 \le p \le \infty)$ will denote $L_p[0,1]$. We consider a two consumer exchange economy with the following characteristics. Its Riesz dual system will be either $\langle C[0,1], \mathrm{ca}[0,1]\rangle$ or $\langle L_p, L_q\rangle\,(1 \le p, q \le \infty$; and $\frac{1}{p} + \frac{1}{q} = 1)$. The consumers' initial endowments are $\omega_1 = \omega_2 = \mathbf{1}$, where $\mathbf{1}$ denotes the constant function one on $[0,1]$. Each consumer has the positive cone as hers consumption set and their preferences are represented by the utility functions

$$u_1(x) = \int_0^{\frac{1}{2}} \sqrt{x(t)}\,dt + \frac{1}{2}\int_{\frac{1}{2}}^1 \sqrt{x(t)}\,dt \quad \text{and} \quad u_2(x) = \frac{1}{2}\int_0^{\frac{1}{2}} \sqrt{x(t)}\,dt + \int_{\frac{1}{2}}^1 \sqrt{x(t)}\,dt\,.$$

It is easy to see that the utility functions are strictly monotone and strictly concave—and so, by Theorem 3.2.4, they are also uniformly proper with respect to the Riesz dual system $\langle C[0,1], \mathrm{ca}[0,1]\rangle$. The order interval $[0,\omega]$ (where $\omega = \omega_1 + \omega_2 = \mathbf{2} \gg 0$) is $\sigma(L_p, L_q)$-compact but it is not $\sigma(C[0,1], \mathrm{ca}[0,1])$-compact.

We claim that the pure exchange economy with respect to the Riesz dual system $\langle C[0,1], \mathrm{ca}[0,1]\rangle$ has an empty core—and so, since in this case the core allocations coincide with the individually rational Pareto optimal allocations (why?), the economy does not have any individually rational Pareto optimal allocation. The proof of this claim will be accomplished with a number of steps.

1. *The utility functions are continuous for both the $\|\cdot\|_1$-norm and the Mackey topology $\tau(L_\infty, L_1)$. In particular, they are continuous for the sup norm and all the L_p-norms.*

Let a net $\{x_\alpha\} \subseteq L_\infty^+$ satisfy $x_\alpha \xrightarrow{\tau(L_\infty, L_1)} x$. Since $[-\mathbf{1}, \mathbf{1}]$ is a convex, circled and $\sigma(L_1, L_\infty)$-compact subset of L_1, it follows that

$$\begin{aligned} V = [-\mathbf{1},\mathbf{1}]^\circ &= \Big\{x \in L_\infty\colon \Big|\int_0^1 x(t)y(t)\,dt\Big| \le 1 \quad \text{for all} \quad y \in [-\mathbf{1},\mathbf{1}]\Big\} \\ &= \Big\{x \in L_\infty\colon \int_0^1 |x(t)|\,dt \le 1\Big\} \end{aligned}$$

is a $\tau(L_\infty, L_1)$-neighborhood of zero. From this, we see that

$$\|x_\alpha - x\|_1 = \int_0^1 |x_\alpha(t) - x(t)|\,dt \longrightarrow 0\,.$$

Thus, if a net $\{x_\alpha\}$ converges to x for the Mackey topology $\tau(L_\infty, L_1)$, then it also converges to x for the L_1-norm.

Next, let us show that the utility functions are continuous for the L_1-norm. So, assume that $\|x_\alpha - x\|_1 \longrightarrow 0$ holds in L_1^+. If $f = \chi_{[0,\frac{1}{2}]} + \frac{1}{2}\chi_{(\frac{1}{2},1]}$, then we have

$$\begin{aligned} |u_1(x_\alpha) - u_1(x)| &\le \int_0^{\frac{1}{2}} \big|\sqrt{x_\alpha(t)} - \sqrt{x(t)}\big|\,dt + \frac{1}{2}\int_{\frac{1}{2}}^1 \big|\sqrt{x_\alpha(t)} - \sqrt{x(t)}\big|\,dt \\ &= \int_0^1 f(t)\big|\sqrt{x_\alpha(t)} - \sqrt{x(t)}\big|\,dt \le \int_0^1 f(t)\sqrt{|x_\alpha(t) - x(t)|}\,dt \\ &\le \sqrt{\frac{5}{8}} \cdot \Big(\int_0^1 |x_\alpha(t) - x(t)|\,dt\Big)^{\frac{1}{2}} \longrightarrow 0\,, \end{aligned}$$

where the last inequality holds by virtue of Hölder's inequality. So, $u_1(x_\alpha) \to u_1(x)$, and similarly $u_2(x_\alpha) \longrightarrow u_2(x)$.

2. *Let (x_1, x_2) be an allocation with respect to L_1 satisfying $x_1 > 0$ and $x_2 > 0$. Then there exist two constants $0 \le a \le 2$ and $0 \le b \le 2$ with $a \ne b$ such that the allocation (x_1^*, x_2^*), given by*

$$x_1^* = a\chi_{[0,\frac{1}{2}]} + b\chi_{(\frac{1}{2},1]} \qquad \text{and} \qquad x_2^* = (2-a)\chi_{[0,\frac{1}{2}]} + (2-b)\chi_{(\frac{1}{2},1]}\,,$$

satisfies $x_1^* \succeq_1 x_1$ and $x_2^* \succeq_2 x_2$.

To establish this claim, let (x_1, x_2) be an allocation with respect to L_1 with $x_1 > 0$ and $x_2 > 0$. Put $a = 2\int_0^{\frac{1}{2}} x_1(t)\,dt$ and $b = 2\int_{\frac{1}{2}}^1 x_1(t)\,dt$, and note that $0 \le a \le 2$ and $0 \le b \le 2$ both hold. Let x_1^* and x_2^* be defined as above. Now using Hölder's inequality, we obtain

$$\int_0^{\frac{1}{2}} \sqrt{x_1(t)}\,dt \le \frac{1}{\sqrt{2}}\Big[\int_0^{\frac{1}{2}} x_1(t)\,dt\Big]^{\frac{1}{2}} = \frac{\sqrt{a}}{2} \qquad \text{and} \qquad \int_{\frac{1}{2}}^1 \sqrt{x_1(t)}\,dt \le \frac{\sqrt{b}}{2}\,.$$

Thus, $u_1(x_1) = \int_0^{\frac{1}{2}} \sqrt{x_1(t)}\,dt + \frac{1}{2}\int_{\frac{1}{2}}^1 \sqrt{x_1(t)}\,dt \le \frac{\sqrt{a}}{2} + \frac{\sqrt{b}}{4} = u_1(x_1^*)$, i.e., $x_1^* \succeq_1 x_1$. Also,

$$\begin{aligned} u_2(x_2) &= \frac{1}{2}\int_0^{\frac{1}{2}} \sqrt{2 - x_1(t)}\,dt + \int_{\frac{1}{2}}^1 \sqrt{2 - x_1(t)}\,dt \\ &\le \frac{1}{2\sqrt{2}}\Big(\int_0^{\frac{1}{2}} [2 - x_1(t)]\,dt\Big)^{\frac{1}{2}} + \frac{1}{\sqrt{2}}\Big(\int_{\frac{1}{2}}^1 [2 - x_1(t)]\,dt\Big)^{\frac{1}{2}} \\ &= \frac{1}{2\sqrt{2}}\Big(1 - \frac{a}{2}\Big)^{\frac{1}{2}} + \frac{1}{\sqrt{2}}\Big(1 - \frac{b}{2}\Big)^{\frac{1}{2}} = \frac{1}{4}\sqrt{2-a} + \frac{1}{2}\sqrt{2-b} = u_2(x_2^*)\,, \end{aligned}$$

and so $x_2^* \succeq_2 x_2$.

Next, we will verify that we can choose a and b with $a \neq b$. So, assume that $a = b$. In this case, we have $x_1^* = a$ and $x_2^* = 2 - a$. From $x_1^* \succeq_1 x_1 > 0$ and $x_2^* \succeq_2 x_2 > 0$, we see that $0 < a < 2$. By the symmetry of the situation, we can also assume that $0 < a \leq 1$. Then we claim that the allocation (y_1, y_2), given by

$$y_1 = \tfrac{3}{2}a\chi_{[0,\frac{1}{2}]} + \tfrac{1}{2}a\chi_{(\frac{1}{2},1]} \qquad \text{and} \qquad y_2 = (2 - \tfrac{3}{2}a)\chi_{[0,\frac{1}{2}]} + (2 - \tfrac{1}{2}a)\chi_{(\frac{1}{2},1]},$$

satisfies $y_1 \succ_1 x_1^*$ and $y_2 \succ_2 x_2^*$ (and hence, $y_1 \succ_1 x_1$ and $y_2 \succ_2 x_2$). Indeed, note that

$$u_1(y_1) = \frac{1}{2}\sqrt{\frac{3a}{2}} + \frac{1}{4}\sqrt{\frac{a}{2}} = \frac{2\sqrt{3}+1}{4\sqrt{2}}\sqrt{a} > \frac{3}{4}\sqrt{a} = u_1(x_1^*).$$

On the other hand, we see that

$$u_2(y_2) = \frac{1}{4}\sqrt{2 - \frac{3a}{2}} + \frac{1}{2}\sqrt{2 - \frac{a}{2}} = \frac{1}{4\sqrt{2}}(\sqrt{4-3a} + 2\sqrt{4-a}),$$

and a direct calculation shows that $u_2(y_2) > \frac{3}{4}\sqrt{2-a} = u_2(x_2^*)$. The proof of step 2 is now complete.

3. *Assume that (x_1, x_2) is an allocation with $0 < x_i \in C[0,1]$, $i = 1,2$. Then there exists an allocation (y_1, y_2) with $y_i \succ_i x_i$ and $y_i \in C[0,1]$ for $i = 1,2$. In other words, the economy with Riesz dual system $\langle C[0,1], \mathrm{ca}[0,1]\rangle$ has no core allocations.*

To see this, let (x_1, x_2) be an allocation with $0 < x_i \in C[0,1]\,(i = 1,2)$. By part (2) there exist two constants $0 \leq a \leq 2$ and $0 \leq b \leq 2$ with $a \neq b$ such that the allocation (x_1^*, x_2^*), given by

$$x_1^* = a\chi_{[0,\frac{1}{2}]} + b\chi_{(\frac{1}{2},1]} \qquad \text{and} \qquad x_2^* = (2-a)\chi_{[0,\frac{1}{2}]} + (2-b)\chi_{(\frac{1}{2},1]},$$

satisfies $x_1^* \succeq_1 x_1$ and $x_2^* \succeq_2 x_2$. Since x_1^* and x_2^* are not continuous functions, we see that $x_1^* \neq x_1$ and $x_2^* \neq x_2$. Thus, by the strict concavity of the utility functions, we obtain that the allocation (ψ_1, ψ_2), given by $\psi_1 = \frac{1}{2}(x_1 + x_1^*)$ and $\psi_2 = \frac{1}{2}(x_2 + x_2^*)$, satisfies $\psi_1 \succ_1 x_1$ and $\psi_2 \succ_2 x_2$.

Now since $C[0,1]$ is $\|\cdot\|_1$-dense in L_1, there exists a sequence $\{z_n\} \subseteq C[0,1]$ satisfying $0 \leq z_n \leq \mathbf{2}$ for each n and $\lim_{n\to\infty} \|\psi_1 - z_n\|_1 = 0$ (and consequently $\lim_{n\to\infty} \|\psi_2 - (\mathbf{2} - z_n)\|_1 = 0$). By virtue of the $\|\cdot\|_1$-continuity of the utility functions (part 1), there exists some n so that the allocation $(z_n, \mathbf{2} - z_n)$ satisfies $z_n \succ_1 x_1$ and $\mathbf{2} - z_n \succ_2 x_2$. Therefore, the economy has no core allocations. ■

The r-fold replica economy of an exchange economy is introduced precisely as in Definition 1.6.12. That is, the ***r-fold replica economy*** $\mathcal{E}_r$ of an exchange economy $\mathcal{E}$ is a new exchange economy having the following characteristics.

1. The commodity-price duality of $\mathcal{E}_r$ is described by the Riesz dual system $\langle E, E' \rangle$, the same Riesz dual system as that of $\mathcal{E}$.
2. The economy $\mathcal{E}_r$ has rm consumers indexed by (i,j), $(i = 1,\ldots,m;\ j = 1,\ldots,k)$ such that each consumer (i,j) has
   a) a preference $\succeq_{ij}$ equal to $\succeq_i$; and
   b) an initial endowment ω_{ij} equal to ω_i (i.e., $\omega_{ij} = \omega_i$), and so the total endowment of the r-fold replica economy $\mathcal{E}_r$ is

$$\sum_{j=1}^{r}\sum_{i=1}^{m}\omega_{ij} = r\omega\,.$$

The consumers of the form (i,j), $j = 1,\ldots,r$, are known as consumers of *type* i—the "clones" of consumer i. As in the finite dimensional case, every allocation $(x_1,\ldots,x_m)$ of an exchange economy $\mathcal{E}$ gives rise—by letting $x_{ij} = x_i$—to an allocation of any r-fold replica economy of $\mathcal{E}$. These type of allocations are referred to as *equal treatment allocations*.

As we have seen before, the classical Debreu–Scarf theorem (Theorem 1.6.16) asserts that in the finite dimensional case an allocation is (under certain conditions) a Walrasian equilibrium if and only if it belongs to the core of its replica economies. The purpose of the last part of this section is to isolate the latter property and study its general behavior. To do this, we repeat the name we have given to these allocations.

Definition 3.3.8. *An allocation in an exchange economy is said to be an* **Edgeworth equilibrium** *whenever it belongs to the core of every r-fold replica of the economy.*

The notion of Edgeworth equilibrium is a "price free" concept. By this we mean that the concept is intrinsically related to the commodity space E rather than to the price space E'. Specifically, if a Riesz subspace F contains the order interval $[0,\omega]$ (the "part" of the space that contains the consumption vectors assigned to each agent in any allocation), then by considering the utility functions restricted to F, it is not difficult to see that an allocation is an Edgeworth equilibrium with respect to E if and only if it is an Edgeworth equilibrium with respect to F.

Example 3.3.7 shows that in general Edgeworth equilibria need not exist. However, if the order interval $[0,\omega]$ is weakly compact, then Edgeworth equilibria always exist.

Theorem 3.3.9. *If in a pure exchange economy the order interval $[0,\omega]$ is weakly compact, then the economy has an Edgeworth equilibrium.*

Proof. The proof follows line by line the proof of Theorem 1.6.15 which is the corresponding result for finite dimensional commodity spaces—instead of Theorem 1.5.10 invoke Theorem 3.3.6. ■

In order to study the various relationships between Edgeworth equilibria and quasiequilibria, we need a simple result from the theory of Riesz spaces.

Lemma 3.3.10. *Let (E, τ) be a locally convex-solid Riesz space, and let two nets $\{x_\alpha\}$ and $\{y_\alpha\}$ satisfy $0 \le x_\alpha \le y_\alpha + x$ for all α and some $x \in E^+$. If $y_\alpha \xrightarrow{\tau} 0$ and the order interval $[0, x]$ is weakly compact, then the net $\{x_\alpha\}$ has a weakly convergent subnet.*

Proof. From $y_\alpha \xrightarrow{\tau} 0$, it follows that $|y_\alpha| \xrightarrow{\tau} 0$. By the Riesz Decomposition Property, we can write $x_\alpha = w_\alpha + v_\alpha$ with $0 \le w_\alpha \le |y_\alpha|$ and $0 \le v_\alpha \le x$ for all α. Then $w_\alpha \xrightarrow{\tau} 0$, and since $[0, x]$ is weakly compact, we see that the net $\{v_\alpha\}$ has a weakly convergent subnet. Therefore, the net $\{x_\alpha\}$ likewise has a weakly convergent subnet. ∎

Now let $(x_1, \ldots, x_m)$ be an allocation in an exchange economy. Then we define the two sets

$$F_i = \{x \in X_i\colon\ x \succeq_i x_i\} \qquad \text{and} \qquad G_i = F_i - \omega_i = \{x \in E\colon\ x + \omega_i \succeq_i x_i\}.$$

Clearly, the sets F_i and G_i are non-empty, convex and weakly closed for each i. (For our discussion you should keep in mind that the weak and τ topologies have the same convex and closed sets (Theorem 2.3.4). In particular, you should keep in mind that the weak and τ closures of any convex set coincide.) We shall denote by $\mathbf{G}$ the convex hull of the set $\bigcup_{i=1}^m G_i$, i.e.,

$$\mathbf{G} = \mathrm{co}\bigcup_{i=1}^{m} G_i = \left\{\sum_{i=1}^{m} \lambda_i y_i\colon\ y_i \in G_i \text{ and } \lambda_i \ge 0 \text{ for each } i \text{ and } \sum_{i=1}^{m} \lambda_i = 1\right\}.$$

A basic property of the non-empty convex set $\mathbf{G}$ is described in the next result. This property for a special case is due to B. Peleg and M. E. Yaari [53].

Lemma 3.3.11. *Consider an exchange economy such that the total endowment is extremely desirable by each consumer and the order interval $[0, \omega]$ is weakly compact. If $(x_1, \ldots, x_m)$ is an Edgeworth equilibrium and $\varepsilon > 0$, then $0 \notin \varepsilon\omega + \overline{\mathbf{G}}$.*

Proof. Let $\varepsilon > 0$ be fixed, and assume by way of contradiction that $0 \in \varepsilon\omega + \overline{\mathbf{G}}$. Since $\mathbf{G}$ is convex, we see that the weak closure of $\mathbf{G}$ coincides with the τ-closure of $\mathbf{G}$. Thus, there exists a net $\{y_\alpha\}$ of $\mathbf{G}$ with $\varepsilon\omega + y_\alpha \xrightarrow{\tau} 0$, and so $y_\alpha \xrightarrow{\tau} -\varepsilon\omega$.

Write $y_\alpha = \sum_{i=1}^m \lambda_i^\alpha y_i^\alpha$ with $y_i^\alpha \in G_i$, $\lambda_i^\alpha \ge 0$ $(i = 1, \ldots, m)$ and $\sum_{i=1}^m \lambda_i^\alpha = 1$. By passing to an appropriate subnet, we can assume that $\lim_\alpha \lambda_i^\alpha = \lambda_i \ge 0$ holds in $\mathcal{R}$ for each i. Clearly, $\sum_{i=1}^m \lambda_i = 1$ holds. Put $S = \{s \in \{1, \ldots, m\}\colon\ \lambda_s > 0\}$, and note that $S \ne \emptyset$. Also, we can suppose that there exists some $\lambda > 0$ satisfying $\lambda_s^\alpha \ge \lambda$ for all $s \in S$ and all α.

Now for each i let $v_i^\alpha = y_i^\alpha + \omega_i$. Then clearly $v_i^\alpha \in F_i$, and so $v_i^\alpha \ge 0$. We claim that for each $s \in S$ the net $\{v_s^\alpha\}$ has a weakly convergent subnet in E. To see this, fix $s \in S$ and note that

$$0 \leq \lambda_s^\alpha v_s^\alpha \leq \sum_{i=1}^m \lambda_i^\alpha v_i^\alpha = \sum_{i=1}^m \lambda_i^\alpha (y_i^\alpha + \omega_i) = \sum_{i=1}^m \lambda_i^\alpha y_i^\alpha + \sum_{i=1}^m \lambda_i^\alpha \omega_i$$
$$= y_\alpha + \sum_{i=1}^m \lambda_i^\alpha \omega_i \leq y_\alpha + \omega \leq y_\alpha + \varepsilon\omega + \omega .$$

Hence,

$$0 \leq v_s^\alpha \leq \frac{1}{\lambda_s^\alpha}(y_\alpha + \varepsilon\omega) + \frac{1}{\lambda_s^\alpha}\omega \leq \frac{1}{\lambda_s^\alpha}(y_\alpha + \varepsilon\omega) + \frac{1}{\lambda}\omega$$

holds in E, and so by Lemma 3.3.10 the net $\{v_s^\alpha\}$ has a weakly convergent subnet. Consequently, by passing to an appropriate subnet, we can assume that $v_s^\alpha \xrightarrow{w} v_s$ holds in E for each $s \in S$. Since each F_s is weakly closed, we infer that $v_s \in F_s$ (i.e., $v_s \succeq_s x_s$) holds for each $s \in S$. From

$$y_\alpha = \sum_{i=1}^m \lambda_i^\alpha (v_i^\alpha - \omega_i) \geq \sum_{s\in S} \lambda_s^\alpha v_s^\alpha - \sum_{i=1}^m \lambda_i^\alpha \omega_i \xrightarrow{w} \sum_{s\in S} \lambda_s v_s - \sum_{s\in S} \lambda_s \omega_s$$

(and the fact that E^+ is weakly closed), by taking weak limits, we infer that

$$-\varepsilon\omega = \lim_a y_\alpha \geq \sum_{s\in S} \lambda_s v_s - \sum_{s\in S} \lambda_s \omega_s .$$

Therefore,

$$\sum_{s\in S} \lambda_s (v_s + \varepsilon\omega) \leq \sum_{s\in S} \lambda_s \omega_s . \tag{$\star$}$$

Now for a positive integer n denote by n_s the smallest integer greater than or equal to $n\lambda_s$ (i.e., $0 \leq n_s - n\lambda_s < 1$). From $n\lambda_s \leq n$, we see that $n_s \leq n$ holds for each s. Since $\lim_{n\to\infty} \frac{n\lambda_s}{n_s} = 1$ and $v_s + \varepsilon\omega \succ_s x_s$ hold for each $s \in S$, we can choose (by the τ-continuity of the utility functions) n large enough so that

$$z_s = \tfrac{n\lambda_s}{n_s}(v_s + \varepsilon\omega) \succ_s x_s , \quad s \in S . \tag{$\star\star$}$$

(Here we use that ω is strictly desirable by each consumer.) Taking into account ($\star$), we get

$$\sum_{s\in S} n_s z_s = \sum_{s\in S} n\lambda_s (v_s + \varepsilon\omega) \leq \sum_{s\in S} n\lambda_s \omega_s \leq \sum_{s\in S} n_s \omega_s .$$

The latter inequality, coupled with ($\star\star$) shows that the allocation $(x_1, \ldots, x_m)$ can be improved upon by a coalition in the n-fold replica of the economy, which is a contradiction. Hence, $0 \notin \varepsilon\omega + \overline{\mathbf{G}}$ must hold, as claimed. ■

EXERCISES

1. Show that the notion of Edgeworth equilibrium is a "price free" concept. That is, show that if $\langle F, F' \rangle$ is a dual system (which is not necessarily a Riesz dual system) such that F is a Riesz subspace of E containing the order interval $[0, \omega]$, then show that an allocation is an Edgeworth equilibrium with respect to $\langle E, E' \rangle$ if and only if it is an Edgeworth equilibrium with respect to $\langle F, F' \rangle$. (For the the economy with dual system $\langle F, F' \rangle$ we consider each preference $\succeq_i$ restricted to F^+.)

2. If an exchange economy has one consumer with a strictly convex preference and initial endowment ω, then show that (ω) is an Edgeworth equilibrium.

3. Prove Theorems 3.3.4, 3.3.5 and 3.3.9.

4. Show that the assumption of monotonicity of preferences in Theorem 3.3.6 is superfluous. That is, show that if in an exchange economy the order interval $[0, \omega]$ is weakly compact and each utility function $u_i \colon E^+ \longrightarrow \mathcal{R}$ is quasi-concave and Mackey-continuous, then the core of the economy is a non-empty weakly compact subset of E^m.

5. Show that the order interval $[\mathbf{0}, \mathbf{1}]$ of $C[0,1]$ is not $\sigma(C[0,1], \mathrm{ca}[0,1])$-compact.

3.4. WALRASIAN EQUILIBRIA AND QUASIEQUILIBRIA

In addition to the notions of Walrasian equilibrium and quasiequilibrium (introduced in the finite dimensional case in Section 1.6), we shall present in this section a notion of approximate quasiequilibrium. The latter equilibrium notion originated with the paper of B. Peleg and M. E. Yaari [53] and permits a characterization of Edgeworth equilibria in terms of a family of approximate quasiequilibria. The material in this section originates in our paper on Edgeworth equilibria [2].

The notions of Walrasian equilibrium and quasiequilibrium are defined as in the finite dimensional case (Definition 1.6.1).

Definition 3.4.1. *An allocation* $(x_1, \ldots, x_m)$ *in an exchange economy is said to be:*

a) *A* **Walrasian** *(or a* **competitive***)* **equilibrium***; whenever there exists a non-zero price* $p \in E'$ *such that* $x_i \in \mathcal{B}_i(p)$ *and*

$$x \succ_i x_i \text{ implies } p \cdot x > p \cdot \omega_i\,,$$

or equivalently, whenever x_i *is a maximal element in the budget set* $\mathcal{B}_i(p) = \{x \in E^+ \colon\ p \cdot x \leq p \cdot \omega_i\}$ *for each* i.

b) *A* **quasiequilibrium***; whenever there exists a non-zero price* $p \in E'$ *such that*

$$x \succeq_i x_i \text{ implies } p \cdot x \geq p \cdot \omega_i\,.$$

Every price satisfying property (b) above is known as a price *supporting the quasiequilibrium.* If every consumer has an extremely desirable bundle, then a Walrasian equilibrium is necessarily a quasiequilibrium; see the discussion after Definition 1.6.1. Supportability by prices is defined as in the finite dimensional case (Definition 1.6.8).

Definition 3.4.2. *An allocation* $(x_1, \ldots, x_m)$ *in an exchange economy is said to be* **supported** *by a non-zero price* $p \in E'$ *whenever*

$$x \succeq_i x_i \text{ implies } p \cdot x \geq p \cdot x_i\,.$$

The phrase "the allocation $(x_1,\ldots,x_m)$ is supported by the price p" is synonymous to the phrase "the price p supports the allocation $(x_1,\ldots,x_m)$." Two basic properties of supporting prices are included in the next result whose proof is similar to that of Theorem 1.6.4.

Theorem 3.4.3. *For a price $p \in E'$ supporting a quasiequilibrium $(x_1,\ldots,x_m)$ the following statements hold:*
a) *$p \cdot x_i = p \cdot \omega_i$ for each i; and*
b) *if for some i the preference relation $\succeq_i$ is monotone, then $p \geq 0$.*

Recall that a price $\mathbf{p}$ on some $\mathcal{R}^\ell$ space is said to be strictly positive whenever every component of $\mathbf{p}$ is a positive number. A price $\mathbf{p}$ is, of course, strictly positive if and only if $\mathbf{x} > \mathbf{0}$ implies $\mathbf{p} \cdot \mathbf{x} > 0$. The latter property is taken to be the definition of strict positivity in the infinite dimensional case. Thus, a price $p \in E'$ is said to be **strictly positive**—in symbols $p \gg 0$—whenever $x > 0$ implies $p \cdot x > 0$. Similarly, a positive vector $0 < x \in E$ is said to be **strictly positive**—in symbols $x \gg 0$—whenever $p > 0$ implies $p \cdot x > 0$.

With these definitions in mind, Theorem 1.6.5 is also valid in our setting. We state it below for future reference; for a proof repeat the proof of Theorem 1.6.5.

Theorem 3.4.4. *For an allocation $(x_1,\ldots,x_m)$ and a non-zero price $p \in E'$ in a pure exchange economy with $\omega \gg 0$ the following statements are equivalent:*
1) *Each x_i is a maximal element in the budget set $\mathcal{B}_i(p) = \{x \in E^+ \colon\ p \cdot x \leq p \cdot \omega_i\}$.*
2) *$p \gg 0$ and $x \succ_i x_i$ implies $p \cdot x > p \cdot \omega_i$.*
3) *$x \succ_i x_i$ implies $p \cdot x \geq p \cdot \omega_i$.*
4) *$x \succeq_i x_i$ implies $p \cdot x \geq p \cdot \omega_i$.*

Let us illustrate next the Walrasian equilibrium concept with an interesting example due to L. E. Jones [35].

Example 3.4.5. (Jones) Consider an exchange economy with Riesz dual system $\langle L_p[0,1], L_q[0,1]\rangle$, $1 \leq p, q \leq \infty$; $\frac{1}{p} + \frac{1}{q} = 1$, having two consumers with initial endowments $\omega_1 = \omega_2 = \frac{1}{2}\chi_{[0,1]}$ and preferences represented by the utility functions

$$u_1(x) = \int_0^1 tx(t)\,dt \qquad \text{and} \qquad u_2(x) = \int_0^1 (1-t)x(t)\,dt\,.$$

Clearly, both utility functions are strictly monotone, concave (in fact, linear) and weakly continuous. The total endowment of the economy is $\omega = \omega_1 + \omega_2 = \mathbf{1}$, which is clearly a strictly positive vector.

Now consider the allocation (x_1, x_2) given by $x_1 = \chi_{[0,\frac{1}{2}]}$ and $x_2 = \chi_{(\frac{1}{2},1]}$. A direct computation shows that

$$u_1(x_1) = u_2(x_2) = \tfrac{1}{8}\,.$$

In addition, we have the following properties.

1. *The allocation (x_1, x_2) is a Walrasian equilibrium supported by the strictly positive price $0 \ll \mathbf{p} \in L_q[0,1]$ defined by $\mathbf{p}(t) = \max\{t, 1-t\}$. (Recall that any function $\mathbf{p} \in L_q[0,1]$ defines a price by the formula $\mathbf{p} \cdot x = \int_0^1 \mathbf{p}(t)x(t)\,dt$.)*

   To see this, note first that we have

$$\mathbf{p} \cdot x_1 = \mathbf{p} \cdot x_2 = \mathbf{p} \cdot \omega_1 = \mathbf{p} \cdot \omega_2 = \tfrac{1}{8}.$$

Now observe that $x \succeq_1 x_1$ implies

$$\mathbf{p} \cdot x = \int_0^1 \mathbf{p}(t)x(t)\,dt \geq \int_0^{\frac{1}{2}} tx(t)\,dt = u_1(x)$$
$$\geq u_1(x_1) = \int_0^{\frac{1}{2}} t\,dt = \int_0^1 \mathbf{p}(t)x_1(t)\,dt = \mathbf{p} \cdot x_1 = \mathbf{p} \cdot \omega_1 .$$

Similarly, $x \succeq_2 x_2$ implies $\mathbf{p} \cdot x \geq \mathbf{p} \cdot \omega_2$.

2. *Aside from a scalar multiple, the price $\mathbf{p}$ defined in part (1) above is the only price that supports (x_1, x_2) as a Walrasian equilibrium.*

   To see this, let $0 \ll \mathbf{s} \in L_q[0,1]$ be a price that supports (x_1, x_2) as a Walrasian equilibrium—note that by Theorem 3.4.4 any such a price must be strictly positive. Clearly, $\mathbf{s} \cdot x_1 = \mathbf{s} \cdot \omega_1 = \mathbf{s} \cdot \omega_2 = \mathbf{s} \cdot x_2$. Now for each Lebesgue measurable subset A of $[0,1]$ with positive Lebesgue measure, we have $\frac{\mathbf{s} \cdot x_1}{\mathbf{s} \cdot \chi_A} \chi_A \in \mathcal{B}_1(\mathbf{s})$, and consequently $x_1 \succeq_1 \frac{\mathbf{s} \cdot x_1}{\mathbf{s} \cdot \chi_A} \chi_A$, or $u_1(x_1) \geq u_1\big(\frac{\mathbf{s} \cdot x_1}{\mathbf{s} \cdot \chi_A} \chi_A\big) = \frac{\mathbf{s} \cdot x_1}{\mathbf{s} \cdot \chi_A} \int_A t\,dt$. In particular, it follows that $\mathbf{s} \cdot \chi_A \geq \frac{\mathbf{s} \cdot x_1}{u_1(x_1)} \int_A t\,dt = 8(\mathbf{s} \cdot x_1) \int_A t\,dt$, or

$$\int_A \mathbf{s}(t)\,dt \geq 8(\mathbf{s} \cdot x_1) \int_A t\,dt$$

holds for each Lebesgue measurable subset A of $[0,1]$ with positive Lebesgue measure. This implies that

$$\mathbf{s}(t) \geq 8(\mathbf{s} \cdot x_1)t$$

for almost all t. Similarly, we have $\mathbf{s}(t) \geq 8(\mathbf{s} \cdot x_2)(1-t)$ for almost all t in $[0,1]$.

Next, we claim that $\mathbf{s}(t) = 8(\mathbf{s} \cdot x_1)t$ holds for almost all $t \in [\frac{1}{2}, 1]$. To verify this, assume by way of contradiction that $\mathbf{s}(t) > 8(\mathbf{s} \cdot x_1)t$ holds for all t in some Lebesgue measurable subset of $[\frac{1}{2}, 1]$ of positive Lebesgue measure. Then, we have

$$\mathbf{s} \cdot x_1 = \mathbf{s} \cdot x_2 = \int_{\frac{1}{2}}^1 \mathbf{s}(t)\,dt > 8(\mathbf{s} \cdot x_1) \int_{\frac{1}{2}}^1 t\,dt = 8(\mathbf{s} \cdot x_1)\tfrac{1}{8} = \mathbf{s} \cdot x_1 ,$$

which is impossible. Hence, $\mathbf{s}(t) = 8(\mathbf{s} \cdot x_1)t$ holds for almost all t in $[\frac{1}{2}, 1]$. Similarly, $\mathbf{s}(t) = 8(\mathbf{s} \cdot x_2)(1-t) = 8(\mathbf{s} \cdot x_1)(1-t)$ holds for almost all t in $[0, \frac{1}{2}]$, and so

$$\mathbf{s}(t) = 8(\mathbf{s} \cdot x_1)\max\{t, 1-t\} = 8(\mathbf{s} \cdot x_1)\mathbf{p}(t)$$

holds for almost all t in $[0,1]$, as claimed. ■

We are now ready to bring to our attention the notion of properness—which was discussed in Section 3.2—in order to establish an infinite dimensional analogue of the Debreu–Scarf core equivalence theorem (Theorem 1.6.16). First, we shall show that in the presence of uniform properness an Edgeworth equilibrium is necessarily a quasiequilibrium.

Theorem 3.4.6. *If in an exchange economy preferences are uniformly τ-proper, then every Edgeworth equilibrium is a quasiequilibrium.*

Proof. Consider an exchange economy with uniformly τ-preferences, and suppose that $(x_1, \ldots, x_m)$ is an Edgeworth equilibrium. As before, we define

$$F_i = \{x \in E^+ \colon\ x \succeq_i x_i\} \qquad \text{and} \qquad G_i = F_i - \omega_i = \{x \in E \colon\ x + \omega_i \succeq_i x_i\},$$

and let $\mathbf{G} = \operatorname{co} \bigcup_{i=1}^m G_i$.

By the uniform τ-properness of the preferences, for each i there exists a convex, solid, open τ-neighborhood V_i of zero and some $v_i > 0$ such that $x - \alpha v_i + z \succeq_i x$ in E^+ with $\alpha > 0$ imply $z \notin \alpha V_i$. Put $V = \bigcap_{i=1}^m V_i$ and $v = v_1 + \cdots + v_m$.

Next, consider the set

$$\Gamma = \{\alpha w \colon\ \alpha > 0 \text{ and } w \in E \text{ satisfies } w + v \in \tfrac{1}{2}V\},$$

and note that Γ is a non-empty, convex, τ-open cone of E. We claim that $\Gamma \cap \mathbf{G} = \emptyset$.

To see this, assume by way of contradiction that $\Gamma \cap \mathbf{G} \neq \emptyset$. Let $a \in \Gamma \cap \mathbf{G}$. Write

$$a = \sum_{i=1}^m \lambda_i (z_i - \omega_i), \text{ with } \lambda_i \geq 0 \text{ and } z_i \succeq_i x_i \text{ for each } i \text{ and } \sum_{i=1}^m \lambda_i = 1; \text{ and}$$

$a = \alpha w$ for some $\alpha > 0$ and some $w \in E$ with $w + v \in \frac{1}{2}V$.

Since for each i there exists a sequence $\{r_n^i\}$ of strictly positive rational numbers with $r_n^i \downarrow_n \lambda_i$, we can choose rational numbers $\frac{n_i}{n}$ (n_i and n positive integers) such that

$$\Big[\tfrac{1}{\alpha} \sum_{i=1}^m \tfrac{n_i}{n}(z_i - \omega_i) - w\Big] + (w + v) \in \tfrac{1}{2}V + \tfrac{1}{2}V = V.$$

Consequently,

$$\sum_{i=1}^m n_i z_i - \sum_{i=1}^m n_i \omega_i + \alpha n v \in \alpha n V. \qquad (\star)$$

Next, put

$$y = \sum_{i=1}^m n_i \omega_i - \alpha n v \qquad \text{and} \qquad z = \sum_{i=1}^m n_i z_i \geq 0.$$

From $z - y = z + \alpha n v - \sum_{i=1}^m n_i \omega_i \leq z + \alpha n v$, it follows that

$$(y-z)^- = (z-y)^+ \leq z + \alpha n v = \sum_{i=1}^{m} (n_i z_i + \alpha n v_i).$$

Therefore, by the Riesz Decomposition Property, there exist $w_i \in E^+ (i = 1, \ldots, m)$ with $0 \leq w_i \leq n_i z_i + \alpha n v_i$ and $\sum_{i=1}^{m} w_i = (y-z)^-$. Now let

$$y_i = z_i + \tfrac{\alpha n}{n_i} v_i - \tfrac{1}{n_i} w_i = \tfrac{1}{n_i}(n_i z_i + \alpha n v_i - w_i) \geq 0,$$

and note that $y_i \succ_i z_i$ holds for each i. Indeed, if this is not true, then we must have $z_i = y_i - \frac{\alpha n}{n_i} v_i + \frac{1}{n_i} w_i \succeq_i y_i$, which (in view of the properness) implies $\frac{1}{n_i} w_i \notin \frac{\alpha n}{n_i} V$, or $w_i \notin \alpha n V$. On the other hand, from

$$0 \leq w_i \leq (y-z)^- \leq |y-z| = \Big| \sum_{i=1}^{m} n_i (z_i - \omega_i) + \alpha n v \Big|$$

and ($\star$), we see that $w_i \in \alpha n V$, which contradicts $w_i \notin \alpha n V$. Thus, $y_i \succ_i z_i$ holds for all i.

From $y_i \succ_i z_i \succeq_i x_i$ and

$$\sum_{i=1}^{m} n_i y_i = \sum_{i=1}^{m} n_i z_i + \alpha n \sum_{i=1}^{m} v_i - \sum_{i=1}^{m} w_i = z + \alpha n v - (y-z)^-$$
$$\leq z + \alpha n v + y - z = y + \alpha n v = \sum_{i=1}^{m} n_i \omega_i,$$

we see that there exists a coalition in some replica of the economy which can improve upon the allocation $(x_1, \ldots, x_m)$. However, the latter is a contradiction, and hence $\Gamma \cap \mathbf{G} = \emptyset$.

Finally, since $\Gamma \cap \mathbf{G} = \emptyset$ and Γ is τ-open, it follows from the classical separation theorems (see Theorem 2.3.3) that there exists some $p \neq 0$ satisfying $p \cdot g \geq p \cdot w$ for all $g \in \mathbf{G}$ and all $w \in \Gamma$. Since $w \in \Gamma$ implies $\alpha w \in \Gamma$ for all $\alpha > 0$, we see that $p \cdot g \geq 0$ holds for each $g \in \mathbf{G}$. Thus, if $x \succeq_i x_i$, then $x - \omega_i \in \mathbf{G}$, and so $p \cdot (x - \omega_i) = p \cdot x - p \cdot \omega_i \geq 0$ implies $p \cdot x \geq p \cdot \omega_i$. This shows that the allocation $(x_1, \ldots, x_m)$ is a quasiequilibrium, and the proof of the theorem is finished. ■

An immediate consequence of the preceding result and Theorem 3.3.9 is the following result of A. Mas-Colell [46].

Corollary 3.4.7. (Mas-Colell) *If in a pure exchange economy preferences are uniformly τ-proper and the order interval $[0, \omega]$ is weakly compact, then the economy has quasiequilibria.*

In terms of the notion of properness, the Debreu–Scarf theorem (Theorem 1.6.16) can be formulated as follows.

Theorem 3.4.8. *In a pure exchange economy with uniformly τ-proper preferences and strictly positive total endowment an allocation is an Edgeworth equilibrium if and only if it is a Walrasian equilibrium.*

Proof. As mentioned before, a Walrasian equilibrium is always an Edgeworth equilibrium. On the other hand, in this case, every Edgeworth equilibrium is (by Theorem 3.4.6) a quasiequilibrium which in turn is (by Theorem 3.4.4) a Walrasian equilibrium. ■

An immediate consequence of the preceding theorem and Theorem 3.3.9 is the following existence result.

Corollary 3.4.9. *If in a pure exchange economy preferences are uniformly τ-proper, the total endowment is strictly positive and the order interval $[0, \omega]$ is weakly compact, then the economy has a Walrasian equilibrium.*

We continue our discussion with the introduction of the notion of an approximate quasiequilibrium. As we shall see, it is important that the social income is non-zero. This leads us to normalize prices with respect to the social income.

Definition 3.4.10. *An allocation $(x_1, \ldots, x_m)$ in an exchange economy is said to be an* **approximate quasiequilibrium** *whenever for each $\varepsilon > 0$ there exists some price $p \in E'$ (depending upon ε) such that:*
1. *$p \cdot \omega = 1$ (and so $p \neq 0$ holds); and*
2. *$x \succeq_i x_i$ implies $p \cdot x \geq p \cdot \omega_i - \varepsilon$.*

A non-empty subset X of a Riesz space E is said to be **comprehensive from above** whenever $x \geq y$ in E and $y \in X$ imply $x \in X$, or equivalently, whenever $X + E^+ = X$ holds. Similarly, a non-empty subset X of a Riesz space E is said to be **comprehensive from below** whenever $X - E^+ = X$ holds. It is easy to check that a non-empty set X is comprehensive from above if and only if its complement $E \setminus X$ is comprehensive from below (and vice-versa). The positive cone E^+ is a comprehensive from above set. Figure 3.4-1 shows the geometrical interpretation of "comprehensiveness."

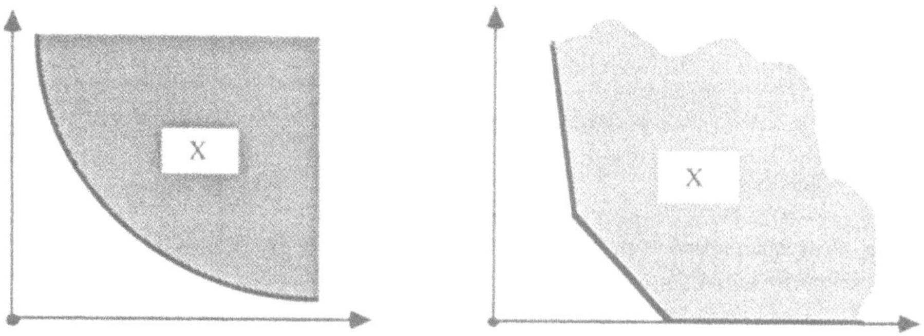

Two comprehensive from above sets

Fig. 3.4-1

Quite often the prices that satisfy property (2) of Definition 3.4.10 are positive prices. This can be seen from the following result.

Theorem 3.4.11. *Let $\succeq$ be a monotone preference relation defined on a comprehensive from above subset X of a Riesz space E, and let p be a linear functional on E. Assume that there exists some real constant c and some fixed $x_0 \in X$ such that*

$$x \succeq x_0 \quad \text{in} \quad X \quad \text{implies} \quad p \cdot x \geq c\,.$$

Then p is a positive linear functional, i.e., $x \geq 0$ implies $p \cdot x \geq 0$.

Proof. Assume that X, $\succeq$, p, x_0 and c satisfy the hypotheses of the theorem and let $x \geq 0$. Then $x_0 + \delta^{-1}x \in X$ and $x_0 + \delta^{-1}x \geq x_0$ and so by the monotonicity of $\succeq$, we see that $x_0 + \delta^{-1}x \succeq x_0$ holds in X for all $\delta > 0$. Hence, $p \cdot (x_0 + \delta^{-1}x) \geq c$ holds for all $\delta > 0$. This implies $p \cdot x \geq \delta(c - p \cdot x_0)$ for all $\delta > 0$, from which it follows that $p \cdot x \geq 0$. ■

From Theorem 3.4.4, we see that in a pure exchange economy with a strictly positive total endowment every quasiequilibrium is an approximate quasiequilibrium. In many cases, every Edgeworth equilibrium is an approximate quasiequilibrium. The details are included in the next theorem.

Theorem 3.4.12. *If in an exchange economy ω is extremely desirable by each consumer and the order interval $[0, \omega]$ is weakly compact, then every Edgeworth equilibrium is an approximate quasiequilibrium.*

Proof. Consider an exchange economy satisfying the properties of the theorem, let $(x_1, \ldots, x_m)$ be an Edgeworth equilibrium and let $\varepsilon > 0$. We have to show that there exists some price $p \in E'$ with $p \cdot \omega = 1$ and such that $x \succeq_i x_i$ in E^+ implies $p \cdot x \geq p \cdot \omega - \varepsilon$.

To this end, start by observing that, by Lemma 3.3.11, we know $0 \notin \varepsilon\omega + \overline{\mathbf{G}}$. Since $\varepsilon\omega + \overline{\mathbf{G}}$ is a weakly closed convex set, it follows from the classical separation theorem (strict separation form) that there exists some $p \in E'$ satisfying

$$p \cdot (y + \varepsilon\omega) > 0 \quad \text{for all} \quad y \in \mathbf{G}\,. \tag{$\star$}$$

We claim that $p \cdot \omega > 0$. Indeed, from $x_i - \omega_i \in G_i$, we see that $0 = \sum_{i=1}^{m} \frac{1}{m}(x_i - \omega_i)$ belongs to $\mathbf{G}$, and so $p \cdot \omega = \frac{1}{\varepsilon} p \cdot (0 + \varepsilon\omega) > 0$.

Replacing p by $\frac{p}{p \cdot \omega}$, we can assume that ($\star$) holds for a price p with $p \cdot \omega = 1$. Now if $x \succeq_i x_i$ holds in E^+, then $x - \omega_i \in G_i \subseteq \mathbf{G}$, and so from ($\star$) we get $p \cdot (x - \omega_i + \varepsilon\omega) > 0$. This implies

$$p \cdot x \geq p \cdot \omega_i - \varepsilon\,,$$

as desired. Also, note that—by Theorem 3.4.11—the price p is a positive price. ■

And now let us take a closer look at the ideal generated by ω. Recall that

$$A_\omega = \{x \in E\colon\ \exists\ \lambda > 0 \ \text{with} \ |x| \leq \lambda\omega\}\,.$$

As mentioned before, the "economic activity" of our agents is confined to the order interval $[0, \omega]$. In particular, note that if $(x_1, \ldots, x_m)$ is an allocation, then each x_i belongs to A_ω.

On A_ω the $\|\cdot\|_\infty$-norm is defined by the formula

$$\|x\|_\infty = \inf\{\lambda > 0\colon\ |x| \leq \lambda\omega\}\,, \quad x \in A_\omega\,.$$

The $\|\cdot\|_\infty$-norm is a lattice norm and so A_ω with the topology generated by the $\|\cdot\|_\infty$-norm is a locally convex-solid Riesz space. In case the order interval $[0, \omega]$ is weakly compact, $(A_\omega, \|\cdot\|_\infty)$ is in fact a Banach lattice. Clearly, for each $x \in A_\omega$ we have

$$|x| \leq \|x\|_\infty \cdot \omega\,. \tag{$\star\star$}$$

This inequality implies that the $\|\cdot\|_\infty$-closed unit ball of A_ω coincides with the order interval $[-\omega, \omega]$. Therefore, if A'_ω denotes the norm dual of $(A_\omega, \|\cdot\|_\infty)$, then $A'_\omega = A^\sim_\omega$ holds. In particular, the restrictions of the functionals of E' to A_ω belong to A'_ω.

There is one more important property regarding the ideal A_ω. If q is a lattice seminorm on E, then from $(\star\star)$ it follows that $q(x) \leq q(\omega)\|x\|_\infty$ holds for all $x \in A_\omega$. In other words, every lattice seminorm of E is $\|\cdot\|_\infty$-continuous on A_ω. In particular, each utility function is $\|\cdot\|_\infty$-continuous on A_ω.

The above discussion leads us to the following remarkable conclusion: *If $\mathcal{E}$ is an exchange economy with Riesz dual system $\langle E, E'\rangle$, then the characteristics of $\mathcal{E}$—when restricted to A_ω—define a new exchange economy with Riesz dual system $\langle A_\omega, A'_\omega\rangle$.* In other words, underlying every exchange economy with Riesz dual system $\langle E, E'\rangle$, there is an exchange economy with the same preferences and the same endowments and with $\langle A_\omega, A'_\omega\rangle$ as the commodity-price duality.

The new exchange economy with respect to the Riesz dual system $\langle A_\omega, A'_\omega\rangle$ plays a very important role that will be clarified in the next few results.

Theorem 3.4.13. *If $(x_1, \ldots, x_m)$ is an approximate quasiequilibrium for an exchange economy, then there exists a positive linear functional p on A_ω such that*
1. *$p \cdot \omega = 1$; and*
2. *$x \succsim_i x_i$ in A^+_ω implies $p \cdot x \geq p \cdot \omega_i$.*

In other words, every approximate quasiequilibrium is a quasiequilibrium with respect to the economy whose preferences and endowments are the same as the original ones and with commodity-price duality defined by the Riesz dual system $\langle A_\omega, A'_\omega\rangle$.

Proof. Let $(x_1, \ldots, x_m)$ be an approximate quasiequilibrium for an exchange economy. For each n pick some $0 \leq p_n \in E'$ with $p_n \cdot \omega = 1$ and such that

$$x \succsim_i x_i \text{ in } E^+ \text{ implies } p_n \cdot x \geq p_n \cdot \omega_i - \tfrac{1}{n}\,. \tag{$\star\star\star$}$$

The condition $p_n \cdot \omega = 1$ tells us that each p_n restricted to $(A_\omega, \|\cdot\|_\infty)$ has norm one. Let p be a $\sigma(A'_\omega, A_\omega)$-accumulation point of the sequence $\{p_n\}$ (where each p_n is now considered restricted to A_ω). Then, $p \cdot \omega = 1$ and from $(\star\star\star)$ we see that $x \succsim_i x_i$ in A^+_ω implies $p \cdot x \geq p \cdot \omega_i$.

This shows that the allocation $(x_1, \ldots, x_m)$ is a quasiequilibrium for the exchange economy whose preferences and endowments are the original ones and whose Riesz dual system is $\langle A_\omega, A'_\omega \rangle$. ■

From Theorem 3.4.4 and the preceding result we have the following consequence. (Keep in mind that ω is a strictly positive element in A_ω.)

Corollary 3.4.14. *If in an exchange economy each preference is strictly monotone on A_ω^+, then every approximate quasiequilibrium is a Walrasian equilibrium with respect to the economy whose preferences and endowments are the same as the original ones and with commodity-price duality defined by the Riesz dual system $\langle A_\omega, A'_\omega \rangle$.*

Now we continue our discussion with the introduction of one more equilibrium concept—the extended quasiequilibrium. In what follows, the symbol $\overline{A_\omega}$ will denote the weak closure of the ideal A_ω, which is, of course, the same as the τ-closure of A_ω. The set $\overline{A_\omega}$ is an ideal of E.

Definition 3.4.15. *An allocation $(x_1, \ldots, x_m)$ in an exchange economy is said to be an* **extended quasiequilibrium** *whenever there exists a function $\pi\colon (\overline{A_\omega})^+ \longrightarrow [0, \infty]$ (called an extended price supporting the allocation) such that:*

a) $\pi(\omega) = 1$;

b) *π is additive, i.e., $\pi(x+y) = \pi(x) + \pi(y)$ holds for all $x, y \in (\overline{A_\omega})^+$; and*

c) *$x \succeq_i x_i$ in $(\overline{A_\omega})^+$ implies $\pi(x) \geq \pi(\omega_i)$.*

Let $(x_1, \ldots, x_m)$ be an allocation in an exchange economy supported by an extended price π. Then the price π satisfies the following properties.

1. *π is monotone, i.e., $0 \leq y \leq x$ in $\overline{A_\omega}$ implies $\pi(y) \leq \pi(x)$.*

Indeed, if $0 \leq y \leq x$ holds, then from $x = (x - y) + y$ and the additivity of π, we see that

$$\pi(y) \leq \pi(x-y) + \pi(y) = \pi(x).$$

2. *π is finite on A_ω^+, i.e., $\pi(x) < \infty$ holds for each $x \in A_\omega^+$.*

If $x \in A_\omega^+$, then pick some positive integer n with $0 \leq x \leq n\omega$, and note that by (a) and the additivity of π we have

$$\pi(x) \leq \pi(n\omega) = \pi(\underbrace{\omega + \cdots + \omega}_{n \text{ terms}}) = \underbrace{\pi(\omega) + \cdots + \pi(\omega)}_{n \text{ terms}} = n\pi(\omega) = n < \infty .$$

3. *π defines a positive linear functional on A_ω.*

This follows immediately from a classical result of L. V. Kantorovič; see [8, Theorem 1.7, p. 7]. The formula defining π on A_ω is given by

$$\pi(x) = \pi(x^+) - \pi(x^-), \quad x \in A_\omega .$$

The notions of extended quasiequilibrium and quasiequilibrium on the ideal A_ω coincide. The details are included in the next result.

Theorem 3.4.16. *If in an exchange economy the total endowment is extremely desirable by each consumer, then an allocation is a quasiequilibrium on A_ω if and only if it is an extended quasiequilibrium.*

Moreover, if $0 < p \in A'_\omega$ supports a quasiequilibrium on A_ω, then the formula

$$\pi(x) = \sup\{p \cdot (x \wedge n\omega)\colon\ n = 1, 2, \dots\}, \quad x \in (\overline{A_\omega})^+,$$

defines an extended price that supports the allocation as an extended quasiequilibrium.

Proof. Consider an exchange economy such that the total endowment is extremely desirable by each consumer and let $(x_1, \dots, x_m)$ be an allocation.

Assume first that $(x_1, \dots, x_m)$ is a quasiequilibrium on A_ω supported by a price $0 < p \in A'_\omega$. Since $p \cdot \omega > 0$ must hold (why?), replacing p by $\frac{p}{p \cdot \omega}$, we can assume that $p \cdot \omega = 1$ holds. Next, consider the formula defining $\pi(x)$ in the statement of the theorem and note that $\pi(x) = p \cdot x$ holds for all $x \in A^+_\omega$, and so $\pi(\omega) = p \cdot \omega = 1$.

To see that π is additive, let $x, y \in (\overline{A_\omega})^+$. Then, from the lattice inequality $(x + y) \wedge n\omega \le x \wedge n\omega + y \wedge n\omega$ (see Theorem 2.1.2), we infer that

$$p \cdot \big((x + y) \wedge n\omega\big) \le p \cdot (x \wedge n\omega) + p \cdot (y \wedge n\omega) \le \pi(x) + \pi(y),$$

and consequently

$$\pi(x + y) \le \pi(x) + \pi(y).$$

On the other hand, the lattice inequality $x \wedge n\omega + y \wedge \ell\omega \le (x + y) \wedge (n + \ell)\omega$ implies $p \cdot (x \wedge n\omega) + p \cdot (y \wedge \ell\omega) \le p \cdot [(x + y) \wedge (n + \ell)\omega] \le \pi(x + y)$ for all n and ℓ, from which it follows that

$$\pi(x) + \pi(y) \le \pi(x + y).$$

Hence $\pi(x + y) = \pi(x) + \pi(y)$ holds, i.e., π is additive.

Now let $y \succeq_i x_i$ in $(\overline{A_\omega})^+$, and let $\varepsilon > 0$. Then $y + \varepsilon\omega \succ_i x_i$ holds in E^+. Since $y \wedge n\omega + \varepsilon\omega \xrightarrow{\tau} y + \varepsilon\omega$ (remember that $\overline{A_\omega}$ is also the τ-closure of A_ω), there exists some ℓ with $y \wedge \ell\omega + \varepsilon\omega \succ_i x_i$ in A^+_ω. It follows that

$$\pi(y) + \varepsilon \ge p \cdot (y \wedge \ell\omega) + \varepsilon = p \cdot (y \wedge \ell\omega + \varepsilon\omega) \ge p \cdot \omega_i = \pi(\omega_i)$$

holds. Since $\varepsilon > 0$ is arbitrary, we infer that $\pi(y) \ge \pi(\omega_i)$.

Conversely, assume that the formula $\pi(x) = \sup\{p \cdot (x \wedge n\omega)\colon\ n = 1, 2, \dots\}$ is an extended price that supports the allocation $(x_1, \dots, x_m)$. Then, according to Kantorovič's theorem [8, Theorem 1.7, p. 7], π extended by the formula $\pi(x) = \pi(x^+) - \pi(x^-)$ defines a positive linear functional on A_ω with $\pi(\omega) = 1$ such that

$$x \succeq_i x_i \quad \text{in} \quad A^+_\omega \quad \text{implies} \quad \pi(x) \ge \pi(\omega_i).$$

That is, the allocation $(x_1, \dots, x_m)$ is a quasiequilibrium in A_ω, and the proof of the theorem is finished. ■

And now we come to one of the major results in this section. It asserts that the notions of Edgeworth equilibrium, approximate quasiequilibrium and extended quasiequilibrium coincide.

Theorem 3.4.17. *Assume that in an exchange economy the total endowment ω is extremely desirable by each consumer and that preferences are strictly monotone on A_ω^+. If the order interval $[0, \omega]$ is weakly compact, then for an allocation the following statements are equivalent.*

1. *The allocation is an Edgeworth equilibrium.*
2. *The allocation is an approximate quasiequilibrium.*
3. *The allocation is an extended quasiequilibrium.*
4. *The allocation is a Walrasian equilibrium for an economy with the same preferences and endowments and with commodity-price duality defined by the Riesz dual system $\langle A_\omega, A'_\omega \rangle$.*

Proof. (1) $\Longrightarrow$ (2) This is Theorem 3.4.12.

(2) $\Longrightarrow$ (3) This follows from Theorems 3.4.13 and 3.4.16.

(3) $\Longrightarrow$ (4) By Theorem 3.4.16 the allocation is a quasiequilibrium with respect to the Riesz dual system $\langle A_\omega, A'_\omega \rangle$. Now the implication follows immediately from Theorem 3.4.4.

(4) $\Longrightarrow$ (1) By Theorem 3.3.5 the allocation is in the core of every n-fold replica of the economy with Riesz dual system $\langle A_\omega, A'_\omega \rangle$. Since the allocations in E coincide with those in A_ω, the latter shows that the allocation is in the core of every n-fold replica of the economy with Riesz dual system $\langle E, E' \rangle$. That is, the allocation is an Edgeworth equilibrium. ■

If the order interval $[0, \omega]$ is not weakly compact, then there is no guarantee that Edgeworth equilibria exist. However, in this case, we have the following companion of Theorem 3.4.17 that characterizes the Edgeworth equilibria—which it is the generalization to the infinite dimensional setting of the classical result of G. Debreu and H. E. Scarf (Theorem 1.6.16).

Theorem 3.4.18. *If in an exchange economy each preference is strictly monotone on A_ω^+, then for an allocation the following statements are equivalent.*

1. *The allocation is an Edgeworth equilibrium.*
2. *The allocation is an Edgeworth equilibrium with respect to $\langle A_\omega, A'_\omega \rangle$.*
3. *The allocation is an approximate quasiequilibrium with respect to $\langle A_\omega, A'_\omega \rangle$.*
4. *The allocation is a quasiequilibrium with respect to $\langle A_\omega, A'_\omega \rangle$.*
5. *The allocation is a Walrasian equilibrium with respect to $\langle A_\omega, A'_\omega \rangle$.*
6. *The allocation is an extended quasiequilibrium.*

Proof. (1) $\Longrightarrow$ (2) Obvious.

(2) $\Longrightarrow$ (3) Fix an Edgeworth equilibrium $(x_1, \ldots, x_m)$ with respect to the Riesz dual system $\langle A_\omega, A'_\omega \rangle$. Let $\varepsilon > 0$ and keep in mind that preferences are automatically $\|\cdot\|_\infty$-continuous on A_ω^+. Put $F_i = \{x \in A_\omega^+ \colon x \succsim_i x_i\}$, $G_i = F_i - \omega_i$, and let $\mathbf{G}$ be the convex hull of $\bigcup_{i=1}^m G_i$. Pick some n with $n\omega > x_1$ and note that by the strong

monotonicity of preferences on A_ω^+, we have $n\omega \succ_1 x_1$. Since $n\omega$ is an $\|\cdot\|_\infty$-interior point of A_ω^+ and the preference $\succeq_1$ is $\|\cdot\|_\infty$-continuous, it follows that $n\omega$ is an $\|\cdot\|_\infty$-interior point of F_1. From $\varepsilon\omega + F_1 - \omega_1 \subseteq \varepsilon\omega + \mathbf{G}$, we infer that $\varepsilon\omega + \mathbf{G}$ has $\|\cdot\|_\infty$-interior points.

Since the allocation $(x_1, \ldots, x_m)$ is an Edgeworth equilibrium with respect to A_ω, a repetition of the proof of Theorem 1.6.16 shows that $0 \notin \varepsilon\omega + \mathbf{G}$. Thus, by the classical separation theorem (see Theorem 2.3.3), there exists a non-zero price $p \in A'_\omega$ satisfying $p\cdot(\varepsilon\omega + g) \geq 0$ for all $g \in \mathbf{G}$. From Theorem 3.4.11, it follows that $p \geq 0$. On the other hand, $p \cdot \omega = 0$ implies $p = 0$ (why?), which is a contradiction. Thus $p \cdot \omega > 0$, and so replacing p by $\frac{p}{p\cdot\omega}$, we can assume that $p \cdot \omega = 1$. Now if $x \succeq_i x_i$ holds in A_ω^+, then $x - \omega_i \in \mathbf{G}$, and so $p \cdot (\varepsilon\omega + x - \omega_i) \geq 0$, from which it follows that

$$p \cdot x \geq p \cdot \omega_i - \varepsilon .$$

Therefore, $(x_1, \ldots, x_m)$ is an approximate quasiequilibrium with respect to the Riesz dual system $\langle A_\omega, A'_\omega \rangle$.

(3) $\Longrightarrow$ (4) This is Theorem 3.4.13.

(4) $\Longrightarrow$ (5) It follows immediately from Theorem 3.4.4.

(5) $\Longrightarrow$ (6) It follows immediately from Theorem 3.4.16.

(6) $\Longrightarrow$ (1) By Theorem 3.4.16, we know that the allocation is a quasiequilibrium with respect to A_ω and so by Theorem 3.4.4 it is also a Walrasian equilibrium with respect to A_ω. Now to complete the proof of the theorem proceed as in the proof of the implication (4) $\Longrightarrow$ (1) of Theorem 3.4.17. ■

An immediate consequence of the preceding theorem is the following remarkable result.

Corollary 3.4.19. *If in a pure exchange economy the order interval $[0, \omega]$ is weakly compact, then the economy has a Walrasian equilibrium with respect to the Riesz dual system $\langle A_\omega, A'_\omega \rangle$.*

Proof. Consider a pure exchange economy with the order interval $[0, \omega]$ weakly compact. By Theorem 3.3.9 this economy has an Edgeworth equilibrium which by Theorem 3.4.18 it must be a Walrasian equilibrium with respect to the Riesz dual system $\langle A_\omega, A'_\omega \rangle$. ■

The total endowment ω need not be in general a strictly positive element of E. However, ω is always a strictly positive element of the ideal $\overline{A_\omega}$. Thus, if $(\overline{A_\omega})'$ denotes the topological dual of $(\overline{A_\omega}, \tau)$—which consists precisely of the restrictions of the linear functionals of E' on $\overline{A_\omega}$ (why?)—the preceding two results can be formulated as follows.

Theorem 3.4.20. *If an exchange economy is a pure exchange economy with respect to the Riesz dual system $\langle \overline{A_\omega}, (\overline{A_\omega})' \rangle$ and preferences are uniformly τ-proper on $\overline{A_\omega}$, then an allocation is an Edgeworth equilibrium if and only if it is a Walrasian equilibrium with respect to the Riesz dual system $\langle \overline{A_\omega}, (\overline{A_\omega})' \rangle$.*

In particular, in this case, if the order interval $[0,\omega]$ *is also weakly compact, then the economy has a Walrasian equilibrium with respect to the Riesz dual system* $\langle \overline{A_\omega}, (\overline{A_\omega})' \rangle$.

The supporting prices enjoy several important order and topological continuity properties. Two of them are stated in the next result.

Theorem 3.4.21. *Assume that in an exchange economy the total endowment is extremely desirable by each consumer. If a linear functional* $0 \le p \in A'_\omega$ *supports an allocation* $(x_1, \ldots, x_m)$ *on* A_ω *(i.e.,* $x \succeq_i x_i$ *in* A^+_ω *implies* $p \cdot x \ge p \cdot x_i$*), then the following statements hold.*

1) *The linear functional* p *is* τ*-continuous on* $[0,\omega]$*; and*
2) *If, in addition,* $[0,\omega]$ *is weakly compact, then* p *is order continuous on* A_ω*, i.e.,* $v_\alpha \downarrow 0$ *in* A_ω *implies* $p \cdot v_\alpha \downarrow 0$ *in* $\mathcal{R}$.

Proof. (1) Assume that a net $\{y_\alpha\}$ satisfies $0 \le y_\alpha \le x_i$ and $y_\alpha \xrightarrow{\tau} 0$. Fix $\varepsilon > 0$. From $x_i - y_\alpha + \varepsilon\omega \xrightarrow{\tau} x_i + \varepsilon\omega \succ_i x_i$, we see that there exists some α_0 such that $x_i - y_\alpha + \varepsilon\omega \succ_i x_i$ holds for all $\alpha \ge \alpha_0$. Thus,

$$p \cdot (x_i - y_\alpha + \varepsilon\omega) = p \cdot x_i - p \cdot y_\alpha + \varepsilon p \cdot \omega \ge p \cdot x_i$$

holds for all $\alpha \ge \alpha_0$, and so $0 \le p \cdot y_\alpha \le \varepsilon p \cdot \omega$ for all $\alpha \ge \alpha_0$, i.e., $\lim_\alpha p \cdot y_\alpha = 0$.

Next, suppose that a net $\{y_\alpha\}$ satisfies $0 \le y_\alpha \le \omega = \sum_{i=1}^m x_i$ for each α and $y_\alpha \xrightarrow{\tau} 0$. Then, by the Riesz Decomposition Property, we can write $y_\alpha = \sum_{i=1}^m y^i_\alpha$ with $0 \le y^i_\alpha \le x_i$ for all α and all i. From $0 \le y^i_\alpha \le y_\alpha$, we see that $y^i_\alpha \xrightarrow{\tau} 0$ for each i. Thus,

$$\lim_\alpha p \cdot y_\alpha = \lim_\alpha \sum_{i=1}^m p \cdot y^i_\alpha = 0\,.$$

Finally, let $\{y_\alpha\} \subseteq [0,\omega]$ satisfy $y_\alpha \xrightarrow{\tau} y$. Then, we have $(y_\alpha - y)^+ \xrightarrow{\tau} 0$ and $(y_\alpha - y)^- \xrightarrow{\tau} 0$, and so by the above

$$p \cdot y_\alpha - p \cdot y = p \cdot (y_\alpha - y) = p \cdot [(y_\alpha - y)^+] - p \cdot [(y_\alpha - y)^-] \longrightarrow 0\,.$$

(2) Let $v_\alpha \downarrow 0$ hold in A_ω. Without loss of generality, we can suppose $0 \le v_\alpha \le \omega$ holds for all α. Since $[0,\omega]$ is weakly compact, the net $\{v_\alpha\}$ has a weakly convergent subnet, and from $v_\alpha \downarrow 0$, it follows that $v_\alpha \xrightarrow{w} 0$. The latter implies $v_\alpha \xrightarrow{\tau} 0$; see [6, Theorem 9.8, p. 63]. Now from part (1), we see that $p \cdot v_\alpha \downarrow 0$ holds in $\mathcal{R}$. ■

The above theorem tells us that every price supporting an allocation on the ideal A_ω is automatically τ-continuous on the order interval $[0,\omega]$. Remarkably, if preferences are ω-uniformly τ-proper, then any price supporting an allocation on A_ω is, in fact, τ-continuous on A_ω. This interesting result is due to N. C. Yannelis and W. R. Zame [69].

Theorem 3.4.22. (Yannelis-Zame) *Assume that an allocation in an exchange economy is supported on A_ω by a price $0 < p \in A'_\omega$. If preferences are uniformly τ-proper on A_ω, then the price p is τ-continuous on A_ω.*

Proof. Let $(x_1, \ldots, x_m)$ be an allocation in an exchange economy supported on A_ω by a price $0 < p \in A'_\omega$ and assume that the preferences are uniformly τ-proper on A_ω. Since every vector of A^+_ω is bounded by a multiple of ω, it follows that ω is a vector of uniform properness. Pick a convex, solid τ-neighborhood V of zero such that $x - \alpha\omega + z \succeq_i x$ in A^+_ω with $\alpha > 0$ implies $z \notin \alpha V$.

Next, consider the Minkowski functional ρ of V, i.e., the seminorm $\rho\colon E \to [0, \infty)$ defined by

$$\rho(y) = \inf\{\, \lambda > 0\colon\ y \in \lambda V \,\}, \quad y \in E.$$

Clearly, ρ is a τ-continuous lattice seminorm on E. Now let $0 \le z \le \omega = \sum_{i=1}^m x_i$. By the Riesz Decomposition Property we can write $z = \sum_{i=1}^m z_i$ with $0 \le z_i \le x_i$ for each i. Let $\alpha_i = \rho(z_i)$, and let $\varepsilon > 0$ be fixed. Put $y_i = x_i + (\alpha_i + \varepsilon)\omega - z_i \ge 0$, and note that $x_i = y_i - (\alpha_i + \varepsilon)\omega + z_i \ge 0$. If $y_i - (\alpha_i + \varepsilon)\omega + z_i \succeq_i y_i$ holds, then by the uniform τ-properness of $\succeq_i$ on A_ω, we see that $z_i \notin (\alpha_i + \varepsilon)V$, contrary to $\rho(z_i) = \alpha_i$. Therefore, $y_i \succ_i y_i - (\alpha_i + \varepsilon)\omega + z_i = x_i$ holds, and so by the supportability of the allocation by p on A_ω, we obtain that

$$p \cdot y_i \ge p \cdot x_i = p \cdot [y_i - (\alpha_i + \varepsilon)\omega + z_i] = p \cdot y_i - (\alpha_i + \varepsilon)p \cdot \omega + p \cdot z_i.$$

Hence, $p \cdot z_i \le (\alpha_i + \varepsilon)p \cdot \omega$ holds for each i and all $\varepsilon > 0$, and so

$$p \cdot z_i \le \alpha_i p \cdot \omega = (p \cdot \omega)\rho(z_i) \le (p \cdot \omega)\rho(z).$$

This implies

$$p \cdot z = \sum_{i=1}^m p \cdot z_i \le \Big(\sum_{i=1}^m p \cdot \omega\Big)\rho(z) = m(p \cdot \omega)\rho(z)$$

for all z with $0 \le z \le \omega$. Now if $z \in A_\omega$ is arbitrary, then pick some $\lambda > 0$ such that $|z| \le \lambda\omega$ and note that

$$|p \cdot z| \le p \cdot |z| = \lambda p \cdot \big(\tfrac{1}{\lambda}|z|\big) \le \lambda m(p \cdot \omega)\rho\big(\tfrac{1}{\lambda}|z|\big) = m(p \cdot \omega)\rho(z)\,.$$

The above inequality shows that the price p is τ-continuous on A_ω. ■

EXERCISES

1. Show that a non-empty subset X of a Riesz space E is comprehensive from above (i.e., $X + E^+ = X$ holds) if and only if its complement $E \setminus X$ is comprehensive from below (i.e., if and only if $E \setminus X - E^+ = E \setminus X$ holds).

2. Show that every quasiequilibrium is necessarily an approximate quasiequilibrium.

3. Prove Theorems 3.4.3 and 3.4.4.

4. Show that if in an exchange economy every consumer has an extremely desirable bundle, then every Walrasian equilibrium is a quasiequilibrium.

5. If in a pure exchange economy the total endowment is strictly positive, then show that every allocation supported by prices is Pareto optimal.

6. Consider an exchange economy with Riesz dual system $\langle L_p[0,1], C^1[0,1]\rangle$, where $1 \le p \le \infty$ and $C^1[0,1]$ is the vector space of all continuously differentiable functions on $[0,1]$, having two consumers with the following characteristics.
Consumer 1: Initial endowment $\omega_1 = \frac{1}{2}\chi_{[0,1]}$ and utility function

$$u_1(x) = \int_0^1 tx(t)\,dt\,.$$

Consumer 2: Initial endowment $\omega_2 = \frac{1}{2}\chi_{[0,1]}$ and utility function

$$u_2(x) = \int_0^1 (1-t)x(t)\,dt\,.$$

a) Show that the allocation $(\chi_{[0,\frac{1}{2}]}, \chi_{(\frac{1}{2},1]})$ is an Edgeworth equilibrium.
b) Show that the allocation $(\chi_{[0,\frac{1}{2}]}, \chi_{(\frac{1}{2},1]})$ is not a Walrasian equilibrium with respect to the dual system $\langle L_p[0,1], C^1[0,1]\rangle$.
c) Show that the allocation $(\chi_{[0,\frac{1}{2}]}, \chi_{(\frac{1}{2},1]})$ is a Walrasian equilibrium with respect to the dual system $\langle L_p[0,1], C[0,1]\rangle$.
[HINT: Use Example 3.4.5.]

7. Consider an exchange economy with m consumers having Riesz dual system $\langle L_p(T,\Sigma,\mu), L_q(T,\Sigma,\mu)\rangle$—where $1 \le p,\, q \le \infty$; $\frac{1}{p} + \frac{1}{q} = 1$ and (T,Σ,μ) is a finite measure space—and total endowment $\omega = \mathbf{1}$ (the constant function one). Assume that for each i there exists some function $0 < f_i \in L_q(T,\Sigma,\mu)$ such that

$$u_i(x) = \int_T f_i(t)x(t)\,d\mu(t)\,, \quad x \in L_p^+(T,\Sigma,\mu)\,.$$

Also, assume that there exist pairwise disjoint measurable sets $A_1, \ldots, A_m$ satisfying $T = \bigcup_{i=1}^{m} A_i$ and

$$\max\{f_1(t), f_2(t), \ldots, f_m(t)\} = f_i(t)$$

for each $t \in A_i$ $(i = 1, \ldots, m)$.

Then show that the allocation $(\chi_{A_1}, \chi_{A_2}, \ldots, \chi_{A_m})$ is a Walrasian equilibrium supported by the price $\mathbf{p}$ defined by

$$\mathbf{p}(t) = \max\{f_1(t), f_2(t), \ldots, f_m(t)\}, \quad t \in T.$$

8. The material in this exercise is taken from an example of L. E. Jones [35]. Consider an exchange economy with Riesz dual system $\langle \ell_2, \ell_2 \rangle$ and one consumer with initial endowment $\omega = (1, \frac{1}{2^2}, \frac{1}{3^2}, \ldots)$ and utility function $u: \ell_2^+ \longrightarrow \mathcal{R}$ defined by

$$u(x_1, x_2, \ldots) = \sum_{n=1}^{\infty} \frac{1-e^{-n^2 x_n}}{n^2}.$$

a) Show that the utility function u is strictly monotone, strictly concave and weakly continuous.

b) Show that the economy has an Edgeworth equilibrium—and hence (ω) must be the only Edgeworth equilibrium.

c) Show that the price $0 \ll p = (1, 1, 1, \ldots) \in A'_\omega$ supports the allocation (ω) on A_ω as a Walrasian equilibrium.
[HINT: Start by observing that $x \geq 2 - e^{1-x}$ holds for each $x \in \mathcal{R}$. Now if $x = (x_1, x_2, \ldots) \succeq \omega$ holds in A_ω^+ (i.e, if $\sum_{n=1}^{\infty} \frac{1-e^{-n^2 x_n}}{n^2} \geq \sum_{n=1}^{\infty} \frac{1-e^{-1}}{n^2}$ holds), then note that

$$\begin{aligned} p \cdot x &= \sum_{n=1}^{\infty} x_n = \sum_{n=1}^{\infty} \frac{n^2 x_n}{n^2} \\ &\geq \sum_{n=1}^{\infty} \frac{2-e^{1-n^2 x_n}}{n^2} = \sum_{n=1}^{\infty} \frac{2-e+e(1-e^{-n^2 x_n})}{n^2} \\ &\geq \sum_{n=1}^{\infty} \frac{2-e+e(1-e^{-1})}{n^2} = \sum_{n=1}^{\infty} \frac{1}{n^2} = p \cdot \omega . \text{]} \end{aligned}$$

d) Show that aside from a scalar multiple, the only price that supports (ω) on A_ω^+ as a Walrasian equilibrium is the strictly positive price $p = (1, 1, 1, \ldots)$.
[HINT: Assume that $0 < p = (p_1, p_2, \ldots) \in A'_\omega$ is a price that supports (ω). Then the price $(p_1, p_2, \ldots, p_\ell)$ supports the allocation $(1, \frac{1}{2^2}, \ldots, \frac{1}{2^{\ell-1}})$ in $\mathcal{R}_+^\ell$, where the utility function is now $U_\ell(x_1, x_2, \ldots, x_\ell) = \sum_{n=1}^{\ell} \frac{1-e^{-n^2 x_n}}{n^2}$. Since U_ℓ is differentiable and strictly concave, it follows that

$$(p_1, p_2, \ldots, p_\ell) = \lambda \nabla U_\ell(1, \tfrac{1}{2^2}, \ldots, \tfrac{1}{2^{\ell-1}}) = \lambda e^{-1}(1, 1, \ldots, 1).$$

Hence, $p_1 = p_2 = \cdots = p_\ell$ for each ℓ. This shows that the price p must be a scalar multiple of $(1, 1, \ldots)$.]

e) Show that the preference $\succeq$ represented by the utility function u is not uniformly ℓ_2-norm proper.
[HINT: If $\succeq$ is uniformly ℓ_2-norm proper, then in view of $\overline{A_\omega} = \ell_2$ (why?), any price supporting (ω) on A_ω^+ must extend to a supporting continuous price of (ω) on ℓ_2^+; see Exercise 11 below. To obtain a contradiction invoke part (d).]

f) Study this problem when the Riesz dual system $\langle \ell_2, \ell_2 \rangle$ is replaced by the Riesz dual system $\langle \ell_p, \ell_q \rangle$; $1 \le p,\, q \le \infty$, $\frac{1}{p} + \frac{1}{q} = 1$.

9. Consider an exchange economy with Riesz dual system $\langle C[0,1], \mathrm{ca}[0,1] \rangle$ having two consumers with initial endowments $\omega_1 = \omega_2 = \mathbf{1}$ and utility functions given by

$$u_1(x) = \lambda \int_0^{\frac{1}{2}} \sqrt{x(t)}\, dt + (1 - \lambda) \int_{\frac{1}{2}}^1 \sqrt{x(t)}\, dt$$

and

$$u_2(x) = (1 - \lambda) \int_0^{\frac{1}{2}} \sqrt{x(t)}\, dt + \lambda \int_{\frac{1}{2}}^1 \sqrt{x(t)}\, dt\,,$$

where $0 \le \lambda \le 1$ is a fixed real number.

a) Show that for $\lambda \ne \frac{1}{2}$ the economy does not have any core allocations.

b) Show that for $\lambda = \frac{1}{2}$ the allocation (ω_1, ω_2) is a Walrasian equilibrium.

10. Consider an exchange economy with Riesz dual system $\langle L_p[0,1], L_q[0,1] \rangle$—where, as usual, $1 \le p,\, q \le \infty$; $\frac{1}{p} + \frac{1}{q} = 1$—and two consumers having the characteristics of Exercise 9. Show that the allocation (x_1, x_2) given by

$$x_1 = \tfrac{2\lambda^2}{\lambda^2 + (1-\lambda)^2}\, \chi_{[0,\frac{1}{2}]} + \tfrac{2(1-\lambda)^2}{\lambda^2 + (1-\lambda)^2}\, \chi_{(\frac{1}{2},1]}$$

and

$$x_2 = \tfrac{2(1-\lambda)^2}{\lambda^2 + (1-\lambda)^2}\, \chi_{[0,\frac{1}{2}]} + \tfrac{2\lambda^2}{\lambda^2 + (1-\lambda)^2}\, \chi_{(\frac{1}{2},1]}\,,$$

is a Walrasian equilibrium supported by the Lebesgue integral.
[HINT: Observe that if $f = \lambda\chi_{[0,\frac{1}{2}]} + (1-\lambda)\chi_{(\frac{1}{2},1]}$ and $x \succeq_1 x_1$ holds in $L_p^+[0,1]$, then

$$\begin{aligned}\sqrt{\tfrac{\lambda^2 + (1-\lambda)^2}{2}} = u_1(x_1) \le u_1(x) &= \int_0^1 f(t)\sqrt{x(t)}\, dt \\ &\le \Big[\int_0^1 f^2(t)\, dt\Big]^{\frac{1}{2}} \cdot \Big[\int_0^1 x(t)\, dt\Big]^{\frac{1}{2}} \\ &= \sqrt{\tfrac{\lambda^2 + (1-\lambda)^2}{2}} \cdot \Big[\int_0^1 x(t)\, dt\Big]^{\frac{1}{2}}.\end{aligned}$$

Use a similar argument for the second consumer.]

11. Consider an allocation $(x_1, \ldots, x_m)$ in an exchange economy that is supported on A_ω by a price $0 < p \in A'_\omega$. If preferences are uniformly τ-proper on A_ω and each preference has an extremely desirable bundle on $\overline{A_\omega}$, then show that the price p extends to a τ-continuous price on $\overline{A_\omega}$ that supports the allocation $(x_1, \ldots, x_m)$.
[HINT: Apply Theorem 3.4.22.]

12. If $(x_1, \ldots, x_m)$ is a quasiequilibrium, then show that each preference relation $\succeq_i$ is τ-proper at x_i.
[HINT: Pick a price $0 < p \in E'$ such that $x \succeq_i x_i$ implies $p \cdot x \geq p \cdot \omega_i = p \cdot x_i$ and then choose a τ-neighborhood V of zero such that $|p \cdot y| < 1$ holds for all $y \in V$. Now choose some $v \in E^+$ with $p \cdot v = 1$ and note that $x_i - \alpha v + z \succeq_i x_i$ in E^+ implies $z \notin \alpha V$.]

3.5. PARETO OPTIMALITY

The main idea in Mas-Colell's approach to existence of Walrasian equilibria in an exchange economy with infinitely many commodities is to support Pareto optimal allocations with prices. This approach to proving existence first appeared in T. Negishi's proof of the Arrow–Debreu existence theorem [50] and was later extended to L_∞ by M. Magill [43]. Of course, this approach requires that Pareto optimal allocations exist. The weak compactness of the order interval $[0, \omega]$ guarantees their existence, but A. Mas-Colell introduced a weaker condition which he called "closedness." The name derives from the fact that for this condition to be satisfied it is necessary and sufficient that the set of all feasible utility levels of the economy be closed. Weak compactness of $[0, \omega]$ implies "closedness" but the converse is not true.

The results in this section on supporting Pareto optimal allocations are due to A. Mas-Colell [46]. We start by restating the various optimality properties of allocations.

Definition 3.5.1. *An allocation $(x_1, \ldots, x_m)$ in an exchange economy is said to be:*

a) **Individually Rational,** *whenever $x_i \succeq_i \omega_i$ holds for each consumer i;*
b) **Weakly Pareto Optimal,** *if there is no other allocation $(y_1, \ldots, y_m)$ such that $y_i \succ_i x_i$ holds for each consumer i; and*
c) **Pareto Optimal,** *whenever there is no other allocation $(y_1, \ldots, y_m)$ such that $y_i \succeq_i x_i$ holds for each consumer i and $y_i \succ_i x_i$ holds for at least one consumer i.*

Every Pareto optimal allocation is weakly Pareto optimal. The converse is also true for pure exchange economies. For a proof of the next result repeat the proof of Theorem 1.5.2.

Theorem 3.5.2. *In a pure exchange economy an allocation is Pareto optimal if and only if it is weakly Pareto optimal.*

Individually rational Pareto optimal allocations exist as long as the order interval $[0, \omega]$ is weakly compact.

Theorem 3.5.3. *If in an exchange economy the order interval $[0, \omega]$ is weakly compact, then the set of all individually rational Pareto optimal allocations is a non-empty and weakly compact subset of E^m.*

Proof. Since E^+ is τ-closed, it follows that the convex set $\{x \in E^+ \colon\ x \succeq_i y\}$ is τ-closed, and hence weakly closed. Now to complete the proof repeat the proof of Theorem 1.5.3 and take into account the above observations. ■

We saw before (in Example 3.3.7) that if the order interval $[0,\omega]$ is not weakly compact, then individually rational Pareto optimal allocations need not exist.

The next result—due to A. Mas-Colell [46]—presents an important supportability property of weakly Pareto optimal allocations. It can be viewed as a version of the second welfare theorem for economies with infinitely many commodities.

Theorem 3.5.4. (Mas-Colell) *If in an exchange economy preferences are monotone, convex and uniformly τ-proper, then every weakly Pareto optimal allocation can be supported by a non-zero price.*

Moreover, if for each i we pick a convex solid τ-neighborhood V_i of zero and a vector $v_i > 0$ that satisfy the definition of uniform properness for $\succeq_i$, then every weakly Pareto optimal allocation can be supported by a price $p > 0$ that satisfies

$$p\cdot\Big(\sum_{i=1}^m v_i\Big) = 1 \quad \textit{and} \quad |p\cdot z| \le 1 \quad \textit{for all} \quad z \in V = \bigcap_{i=1}^m V_i .$$

Proof. Let $(x_1,\dots,x_m)$ be a weakly Pareto optimal allocation in an exchange economy with monotone, convex and uniformly τ-proper preferences. As usual, for each i consider the convex set $F_i = \{x \in E^+\colon\ x \succeq_i x_i\}$ and let

$$F = \sum_{i=1}^m (F_i - x_i) = F_1 + \cdots + F_m - \omega .$$

Clearly, F is a convex set and $0 \in F$.

Now for each i pick a vector $v_i \in E^+$ and a convex solid τ-neighborhood V_i of zero such that

$$x - \alpha v_i + z \succeq_i x \quad \text{in} \quad E^+ \quad \text{implies} \quad z \notin \alpha V_i .$$

Put $v = \sum_{i=1}^m v_i$ and $V = \bigcap_{i=1}^m V_i$. Clearly, V is a convex and solid τ-neighborhood of zero. Next, let Γ be the convex cone generated by $v + V$, i.e., let

$$\Gamma = \{\alpha(v+w)\colon\ \alpha > 0 \ \text{and} \ w \in V\} .$$

We claim that $F \cap (-\Gamma) = \emptyset$.

To see this, assume by way of contradiction that $F\cap(-\Gamma) \ne \emptyset$. Then there exist $z_i \in F_i\,(i = 1,\dots,m)$, $\alpha > 0$ and $w \in V$ such that $\sum_{i=1}^m (z_i - x_i) = -\alpha(v+w)$. This implies

$$\sum_{i=1}^m (z_i - x_i) + \alpha v = \sum_{i=1}^m (z_i - x_i + \alpha v_i) = -\alpha w .$$

Let

$$f = \sum_{i=1}^m (z_i - x_i + \alpha v_i) .$$

From $f = \sum_{i=1}^m (z_i - x_i + \alpha v_i) \le \sum_{i=1}^m (z_i + \alpha v_i)$, it follows that

$$f^+ \le \sum_{i=1}^m (z_i + \alpha v_i).$$

Therefore, by the Riesz Decomposition Property, there exist $f_i \in E^+$ $(i = 1, \ldots, m)$ with $0 \le f_i \le z_i + \alpha v_i$ and $f^+ = \sum_{i=1}^m f_i$. Now let

$$h_i = z_i + \alpha v_i - f_i \ge 0,$$

and note that $h_i \succ_i z_i$ holds for each i. Indeed, if for some i we have $z_i = h_i - \alpha v_i + f_i \succeq_i h_i$, then (by the uniform τ-properness) we must also have $f_i \notin \alpha V_i$. However,

$$0 \le f_i \le f^+ \le |f| = \alpha|w| \in \alpha V,$$

implies $f_i \in \alpha V$ and so $f_i \in \alpha V_i$, a contradiction. Hence, $h_i \succ_i z_i \succeq_i x_i$ holds for each i. Next, note that

$$\begin{aligned}\sum_{i=1}^m h_i &= \sum_{i=1}^m (z_i + \alpha v_i - f_i) \\ &= \sum_{i=1}^m (z_i - x_i + \alpha v_i) + \omega - \sum_{i=1}^m f_i \\ &= f - f^+ + \omega \le \omega,\end{aligned}$$

and so if $h_1^* = h_1 + \omega - \sum_{i=1}^m h_i$ and $h_i^* = h_i$ $(i = 2, \ldots, m)$, then $(h_1^*, \ldots, h_m^*)$ is an allocation satisfying $h_i^* \succ_i x_i$ for each i, contradicting the weak Pareto optimality of the allocation $(x_1, \ldots, x_m)$. Hence, $F \cap (-\Gamma) = \emptyset$.

Since the convex cone $-\Gamma$ has interior points (note that $-v + V \subseteq -\Gamma$), it follows from the classical separation theorem that there exist a non-zero price p and a constant c such that $p \cdot g \ge c \ge -p \cdot \gamma$ holds for all $g \in F$ and all $\gamma \in \Gamma$. Since Γ is a cone, we see that $c \ge 0$. On the other hand, $0 \in F$ implies $p \cdot 0 = 0 \ge c$, and so $c = 0$. Thus, $p \cdot g \ge 0$ for all $g \in F$ and $p \cdot h \le 0$ for all $h \in -\Gamma$.

Now if $x \succeq_i x_i$ holds, then $x - x_i \in F$ and so $p \cdot x \ge p \cdot x_i$ must hold. This implies that the price p supports the allocation $(x_1, \ldots, x_m)$. In particular, note that $p \ge 0$.

Next, we claim that $p \cdot v > 0$. To see this, assume that $p \cdot v = 0$. Since $w \in V$ implies $-v \pm w \in -\Gamma$, we see that $p \cdot (-v \pm w) = \pm p \cdot w \le 0$ holds for all $w \in V$, and so $p \cdot w = 0$ for each $w \in V$. This implies $p = 0$, a contradiction—and so, $p \cdot v > 0$ must hold. Replacing p by $\frac{p}{p \cdot v}$, we can suppose that the supporting price satisfies $p \cdot v = 1$. Finally, note that if $z \in V$, then we have $-v \pm z \in -\Gamma$, and so from $p \cdot (-v \pm z) = -p \cdot v \pm p \cdot z = -1 \pm p \cdot z \le 0$, we see that $|p \cdot z| \le 1$ holds for each $z \in V$. The proof of the theorem is now complete. ■

The rest of our discussion in this section will be devoted to establishing an existence result for quasiequilibria in exchange economies. We shall assume (without loss of generality) that

a) $u_i(0) = 0$ holds for each i; and

b) the total endowment ω is extremely desirable by each consumer.

An m-tuple $(x_1, \ldots, x_m)$ is called a **feasible allocation** whenever $x_i \geq 0$ holds for each i and $\sum_{i=1}^m x_i \leq \omega$. A **utility allocation** is any vector of $\mathcal{R}_+^m$ of the form $\big(u_1(x_1), \ldots, u_m(x_m)\big)$, where $(x_1, \ldots, x_m)$ is a feasible allocation. The set of all utility allocations is referred to as the utility space of the economy.

Definition 3.5.5. *The* **utility space U** *of an exchange economy is the set of all utility allocations, i.e.,*

$$\mathbf{U} = \big\{\big(u_1(x_1), \ldots, u_m(x_m)\big)\colon\ (x_1, \ldots, x_m) \text{ is a feasible allocation}\big\}\,.$$

Since $0 \leq u_i(x) \leq u_i(\omega)$ holds for each $0 \leq x \leq \omega$, it follows that the utility space $\mathbf{U}$ is always a non-empty bounded subset of $\mathcal{R}_+^m$. The utility space of an exchange economy is a "relatively comprehensive" set.

Lemma 3.5.6. *The utility space* $\mathbf{U}$ *of an exchange economy satisfies the following properties:*

1) *If* $\mathbf{0} \leq (z_1, \ldots, z_m) \leq (z_1^*, \ldots, z_m^*)$ *holds in* $\mathcal{R}^m$ *and* $(z_1^*, \ldots, z_m^*) \in \mathbf{U}$, *then we have* $(z_1, \ldots, z_m) \in \mathbf{U}$.

2) *If the total endowment is extremely desirable by each consumer, then there exists some* $r > 0$ *such that* $\mathbf{0} \leq \mathbf{z} \in \mathcal{R}^m$ *and* $\|\mathbf{z}\| \leq r$ *imply* $\mathbf{z} \in \mathbf{U}$.

Proof. (1) Assume that $\mathbf{0} \leq (z_1, \ldots, z_m) \leq (z_1^*, \ldots, z_m^*) \in \mathbf{U}$. Pick a feasible allocation $(x_1^*, \ldots, x_m^*)$ such that $z_i^* = u_i(x_i^*)$ holds for each i. Since for each i the real-valued function $f_i(\lambda) = u_i(\lambda x_i^*)$, $\lambda \in [0,1]$, is continuous, it follows from the intermediate value theorem that there exist $0 \leq \lambda_i \leq 1$ such that $u_i(\lambda_i x_i^*) = z_i$. Put $x_i = \lambda_i x_i^* \geq 0$ and note that $\sum_{i=1}^m x_i = \sum_{i=1}^m \lambda_i x_i^* \leq \sum_{i=1}^m x_i^* \leq \omega$. Therefore, $(z_1, \ldots, z_m) \in \mathbf{U}$.

(2) Since the total endowment ω is extremely desirable by each consumer, it follows that $u_i(\frac{1}{n}\omega) > 0$ for each i—and moreover $\big(u_1(\frac{1}{n}\omega), \ldots, u_m(\frac{1}{n}\omega)\big) \in \mathbf{U}$. Now note that the positive real number $r = \min\{u_i(\frac{1}{n}\omega)\colon\ i = 1, \ldots, m\}$ satisfies the desired property. ■

A possible utility space for an exchange economy with two consumers is shown in Figure 3.5-1.

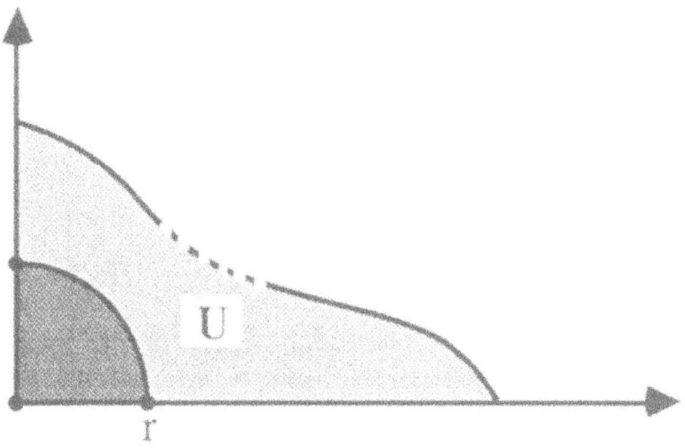

Fig. 3.5-1

There is an important real-valued function ρ with domain the closed $m-1$ simplex Δ associated with the utility space $\mathbf{U}$ of an exchange economy—where, as usual,

$$\Delta = \{\mathbf{s} = (s_1, \ldots, s_m) \in \mathcal{R}^m_+ \colon\ s_1 + s_2 + \cdots + s_m = 1\}.$$

If $\mathbf{U}$ is the utility space of an exchange economy, then the function $\rho\colon \Delta \to (0, \infty)$ is defined by

$$\rho(\mathbf{s}) = \sup\{\alpha > 0\colon\ \alpha\mathbf{s} \in \mathbf{U}\},\ \ \mathbf{s} \in \Delta.$$

Note that the function ρ is well defined. Indeed, since $\mathbf{U}$ contains the positive part of a ball about zero and is bounded from above, it follows that for each $\mathbf{s} \in \Delta$ the set $\{\alpha > 0\colon\ \alpha\mathbf{s} \in \mathbf{U}\}$ is non-empty and bounded from above in $\mathcal{R}$.

The function ρ—which will play a crucial role in our discussion—is a continuous function.

Theorem 3.5.7. *If the total endowment is extremely desirable by each consumer, then the function* $\rho\colon \Delta \longrightarrow (0, \infty)$ *defined by*

$$\rho(\mathbf{s}) = \sup\{\alpha > 0\colon\ \alpha\mathbf{s} \in \mathbf{U}\},\ \ \mathbf{s} \in \Delta,$$

is a continuous function.

Proof. Assume that $\mathbf{s}_n \to \mathbf{s}$ holds in Δ. We have to establish that $\rho(\mathbf{s}_n) \to \rho(\mathbf{s})$.

Let $\alpha > 0$ satisfy $\alpha\mathbf{s} \in \mathbf{U}$ and let $0 < \beta < \alpha$. Pick a feasible allocation $(x_1, \ldots, x_m)$ such that $\alpha\mathbf{s} = \big(u_1(x_1), u_2(x_2), \ldots, u_m(x_m)\big) > \beta\mathbf{s}$. By the continuity of the utility functions there exists some $0 < \delta < 1$ such that

$$\big(u_1(\delta x_1), u_2(\delta x_2), \ldots, u_m(\delta x_m)\big) > \beta\mathbf{s}.$$

Now note that $\big(\delta x_1 + \frac{1-\delta}{m}\omega, \delta x_2 + \frac{1-\delta}{m}\omega, \ldots, \delta x_m + \frac{1-\delta}{m}\omega\big)$ is a feasible allocation which—by the extreme desirability of ω—satisfies $u_i(\delta x_i + \frac{1-\delta}{m}\omega) > u_i(\delta x_i) \geq \beta s_i$ for each i. In view of $\mathbf{s}_n \to \mathbf{s}$, we see that

$$\big(u_1(\delta x_1 + \tfrac{1-\delta}{m}\omega), u_2(\delta x_2 + \tfrac{1-\delta}{m}\omega), \ldots, u_m(\delta x_m + \tfrac{1-\delta}{m}\omega)\big) > \beta\mathbf{s}_n$$

holds for all sufficiently large n. This implies $\beta\mathbf{s}_n \in \mathbf{U}$ for all sufficiently large n, and so $\beta \leq \rho(\mathbf{s}_n)$ holds for all sufficiently large n. Consequently, $\beta \leq \liminf_{n\to\infty} \rho(\mathbf{s}_n)$ holds for all $0 < \beta < \alpha$ and thus $\alpha \leq \liminf_{n\to\infty} \rho(\mathbf{s}_n)$ for all $\alpha > 0$ with $\alpha\mathbf{s} \in \mathbf{U}$. We conclude that

$$\rho(\mathbf{s}) \leq \liminf_{n\to\infty} \rho(\mathbf{s}_n)\,. \qquad (\star)$$

Now let $\rho(\mathbf{s}) < \beta$. Fix some γ with $\rho(\mathbf{s}) < \gamma < \beta$. From $\mathbf{s}_n \to \mathbf{s}$ and $\gamma s_i < \beta s_i$ for each i with $s_i > 0$, we infer that $\gamma\mathbf{s} \leq \beta\mathbf{s}_n$ holds for all sufficiently large n. Now note that if $\beta\mathbf{s}_n \in \mathbf{U}$, then (by Lemma 3.5.6(1)) $\gamma\mathbf{s} \in \mathbf{U}$, contrary to $\rho(\mathbf{s}) < \gamma$. Thus, $\beta\mathbf{s}_n \notin \mathbf{U}$ holds for all sufficiently large n, and so $\rho(\mathbf{s}_n) \leq \beta$ holds for all sufficiently large n. Therefore, $\limsup_{n\to\infty} \rho(\mathbf{s}_n) \leq \beta$ holds for all β with $\rho(\mathbf{s}) < \beta$, and consequently

$$\limsup_{n\to\infty} \rho(\mathbf{s}_n) \leq \rho(\mathbf{s})\,. \qquad (\star\star)$$

Finally, from $(\star)$ and $(\star\star)$, we see that $\lim_{n\to\infty} \rho(\mathbf{s}_n) = \rho(\mathbf{s})$ holds, as desired. ■

When is the utility space a closed set? The next result provides the answer.

Theorem 3.5.8. *For the utility space* $\mathbf{U}$ *of an exchange economy the following statements are equivalent.*

1. $\mathbf{U}$ *is a closed subset of* $\mathcal{R}^m_+$.
2. $\mathbf{U}$ *is a compact subset of* $\mathcal{R}^m_+$.
3. *If* $\{(x_1^n, \ldots, x_m^n)\}$ *is a sequence of feasible allocations satisfying* $x_i^{n+1} \succeq_i x_i^n$ *for all* i *and all* n, *then there exists a feasible allocation* $(x_1, \ldots, x_m)$ *such that* $x_i \succeq_i x_i^n$ *holds for all* i *and all* n.

Proof. (1)$\Longrightarrow$(2) Since the utility space $\mathbf{U}$ is bounded, notice that $\mathbf{U}$ is compact if and only if it is closed.

(2)$\Longrightarrow$(3) Consider a sequence $\{(x_1^n, \ldots, x_m^n)\}$ of feasible allocations such that $x_i^{n+1} \succeq_i x_i^n$ (i.e., $u_i(x_i^{n+1}) \geq u_i(x_i^n)$) holds for all i and all n. This implies that the sequence $\{(u_1(x_1^n), \ldots, u_m(x_m^n))\}$ of $\mathbf{U}$ is increasing. By the compactness of $\mathbf{U}$, the sequence converges to an element of $\mathbf{U}$, say $(u_1(x_1), \ldots, u_m(x_m))$. Now an easy argument shows that $x_i \succeq_i x_i^n$ holds for each i and each n.

(3)$\Longrightarrow$(1) Let $\{(z_1^n, \ldots, z_m^n)\}$ be a sequence of $\mathbf{U}$ satisfying

$$\mathbf{z}_n = (z_1^n, \ldots, z_m^n) \longrightarrow \mathbf{z} = (z_1, \ldots, z_m)$$

in $\mathcal{R}^m$. By passing to a subsequence, we can suppose that $|z_i^n - z_i| \leq \frac{1}{n}$ holds for each n and all i. Thus, $\mathbf{z} - \mathbf{z}_n \leq |\mathbf{z}_n - \mathbf{z}| \leq \frac{1}{n}\mathbf{e}$ holds for each n, where $\mathbf{e} = (1, 1, \ldots, 1)$. From $\mathbf{0} \leq (\mathbf{z} - \frac{1}{n}\mathbf{e})^+ \leq \mathbf{z}_n$ and Lemma 3.5.6(1), we see that $(\mathbf{z} - \frac{1}{n}\mathbf{e})^+ \in \mathbf{U}$ holds for all n, and from $(\mathbf{z} - \frac{1}{n}\mathbf{e})^+ \uparrow \mathbf{z}$ and our hypothesis, we easily infer that $\mathbf{z} \in \mathbf{U}$. The proof of the theorem is now complete. ■

An exchange economy for which the equivalent statements of Theorem 3.5.8 are true is referred to as an exchange economy that satisfies *the closedness condition.*

Definition 3.5.9. *An exchange economy is said to satisfy the* **closedness condition** *whenever it satisfies the three equivalent statements of Theorem 3.5.8, i.e., whenever its utility space* $\mathbf{U}$ *is a closed set.*

If the order interval $[0, \omega]$ is weakly compact, then it should be clear that the exchange economy satisfies the closedness condition. However, an exchange economy can satisfy the closedness condition without the order interval $[0, \omega]$ being weakly compact; see Exercise 6 at the end of this section.

For economies with the closedness condition the values of the function ρ are intimately related to the weakly Pareto optimal allocations. It turns out that the boundary points of the utility space correspond to weakly Pareto optimal allocations. The precise relation is described in the next theorem.

Theorem 3.5.10. *If an exchange economy satisfies the closedness condition, then for each* $\mathbf{s} \in \Delta$ *there exists an allocation* $(x_1^{\mathbf{s}}, x_2^{\mathbf{s}}, \ldots, x_m^{\mathbf{s}})$*—which is necessarily weakly Pareto optimal—such that*

$$\rho(\mathbf{s})\mathbf{s} = \big(u_1(x_1^{\mathbf{s}}), u_2(x_2^{\mathbf{s}}), \ldots, u_m(x_m^{\mathbf{s}})\big).$$

Proof. Consider an exchange economy satisfying the closedness condition and let $\mathbf{s} \in \Delta$. Pick a feasible allocation $(x_1, x_2, \ldots, x_m)$ such that

$$\rho(\mathbf{s})\mathbf{s} = \big(u_1(x_1), u_2(x_2), \ldots, u_m(x_m)\big).$$

If $\sum_{i=1}^m x_i = \omega$, then there is nothing to prove. So, assume that $\sum_{i=1}^m x_i < \omega$ holds and let $z = \omega - \sum_{i=1}^m x_i > 0$.

By the monotonicity of the preferences, we have $x_i + \frac{1}{m}z \succeq_i x_i$ for each i. On the other hand, if $x_i + \frac{1}{m}z \succ_i x_i$ holds for each i (i.e., if $u_i(x_i + \frac{1}{m}z) > u_i(x_i)$ for each i), then there exists some $\varepsilon > 0$ such that

$$[\rho(\mathbf{s}) + \varepsilon]\mathbf{s} \le \big(u_1(x_1 + \tfrac{1}{m}z), u_2(x_2 + \tfrac{1}{m}z), \ldots, u_m(x_m + \tfrac{1}{m}z)\big) \in \mathbf{U},$$

which is a contradiction. Thus, $u_i(x_i + \frac{1}{m}z) = u_i(x_i)$ must hold for some i. Now let $(x_1^1, x_2^1, \ldots, x_m^1)$ be a feasible allocation with $x_i^1 = x_i$ for all but one i and for that exceptional i we have $x_i^1 = x_i + \frac{1}{m}z$ with $u_i(x_i + \frac{1}{m}z) = u_i(x_i)$. Clearly,

$$\omega - \sum_{i=1}^m x_i^1 = (1 - \tfrac{1}{m})z = z_1 > 0.$$

Now repeat the above argument with z_1 in place of z and continue on by repeating the above process. Thus, we can obtain a sequence $\{(x_{n,1}, x_{n,2}, \ldots, x_{n,m})\}$ of feasible allocations with the following properties.

a) $x_{n+1,i} = x_{n,i}$ holds for all but one i and for that exceptional i we have

$$x_{n+1,i} = x_{n,i} + \tfrac{1}{m}(1 - \tfrac{1}{m})^{n-1}z;$$

b) $u_i(x_{n,i}) = u_i(x_i)$ for all $i = 1, \ldots, m$ and all n; and

c) $\omega - \sum_{i=1}^m x_{n,i} = (1 - \frac{1}{m})^n z$.

Clearly, $x_{n,i} \uparrow_n$ holds for each i and moreover (in view of $\sum_{n=1}^\infty (1 - \frac{1}{m})^n < \infty$), it follows that each sequence $\{x_{n,i}\}$ is τ-convergent in E. If $\lim_{n\to\infty} x_{n,i} = x_i^{\mathbf{s}}$, then from (c), we see that $\sum_{i=1}^m x_i^{\mathbf{s}} = \omega$, i.e., that $(x_1^{\mathbf{s}}, \ldots, x_m^{\mathbf{s}})$ is an allocation. From (b) and the continuity of the utility functions, we infer that $u_i(x_i^{\mathbf{s}}) = u_i(x_i)$ holds for each i, and consequently

$$\rho(\mathbf{s})\mathbf{s} = \big(u_1(x_1^{\mathbf{s}}), u_2(x_2^{\mathbf{s}}), \ldots, u_m(x_m^{\mathbf{s}})\big)$$

holds, as desired. Also, it should be clear (from the definition of $\rho(\mathbf{s})$) that the allocation $(x_1^{\mathbf{s}}, x_2^{\mathbf{s}}, \ldots, x_m^{\mathbf{s}})$ is necessarily weakly Pareto optimal. ■

An immediate consequence of the preceding result is that an exchange economy with the closedness condition has plenty of weakly Pareto optimal allocations. Geometrically, the weakly Pareto optimal allocations correspond to the part of the boundary of the utility space that lies in the interior of $\mathcal{R}_+^m$; see Figure 3.5-2.

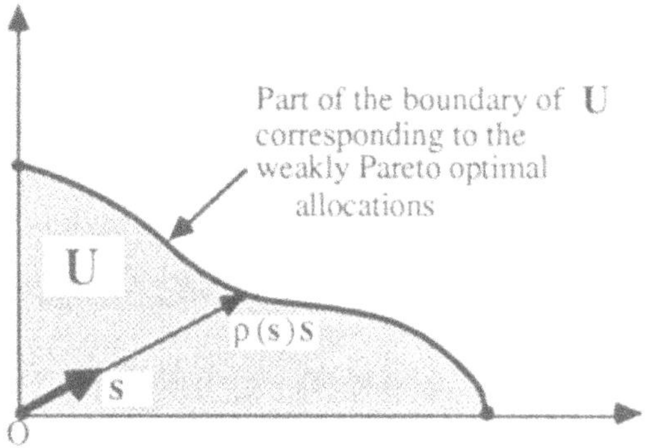

Fig. 3.5-2

Our next objective is to prove that exchange economies with the closedness condition have quasiequilibria. The next simple result tells us where the search for quasiequilibria should be confined.

Lemma 3.5.11. *If in an exchange economy a quasiequilibrium is supported by a price $p > 0$ with $p \cdot \omega > 0$, then the quasiequilibrium is a weakly Pareto optimal allocation.*

Proof. Assume that $(x_1, \ldots, x_m)$ is a quasiequilibrium in an exchange economy supported by a price $p > 0$ with $p \cdot \omega > 0$. Suppose by way of contradiction that there exists another allocation $(z_1, \ldots, z_m)$ satisfying $z_i \succ_i x_i$ for each i. By the supportability of p, we see that $p \cdot z_i \geq p \cdot \omega_i = p \cdot x_i$ holds for each i, and in view of $\sum_{i=1}^m z_i = \sum_{i=1}^m \omega_i$, we infer that $p \cdot z_i = p \cdot \omega_i$ holds for each i.

Now $p \cdot \omega > 0$ implies $p \cdot \omega_i > 0$ for at least one i. However, for any such i the bundle x_i is a maximal element in the budget set $\mathcal{B}_i(p) = \{x \in E^+ \colon\ p \cdot x \leq p \cdot \omega_i\}$, which contradicts $z_i \in \mathcal{B}_i(p)$ and $z_i \succ_i x_i$. Hence $(x_1, \ldots, x_m)$ is a weakly Pareto optimal allocation. ■

We now come to a basic existence theorem for quasiequilibria due to A. Mas-Colell [46].

Theorem 3.5.12. (Mas-Colell) *If an exchange economy satisfies the closedness condition, preferences are uniformly τ-proper and the total endowment is extremely desirable by each consumer, then the economy has a quasiequilibrium.*

Proof. Consider an exchange economy that satisfies the hypotheses of the theorem. For each i pick a vector $v_i > 0$ and a convex solid τ-neighborhood V_i of zero that satisfy the definition of uniform properness for the preference $\succeq_i$ and let $v = \sum_{i=1}^m v_i$ and $V = \bigcap_{i=1}^m V_i$. As usual, Δ will denote the $m-1$ closed simplex.

For each $\mathbf{s} \in \Delta$ pick (by using Theorem 3.5.10) an allocation $(x_1^{\mathbf{s}}, x_2^{\mathbf{s}}, \ldots, x_m^{\mathbf{s}})$ such that

$$\rho(\mathbf{s})\mathbf{s} = \big(u_1(x_1^{\mathbf{s}}), u_2(x_2^{\mathbf{s}}), \ldots, u_m(x_m^{\mathbf{s}})\big), \tag{1}$$

and then define the set

$$P(\mathbf{s}) = \{p \in E'_+ \colon\ p \text{ supports } (x_1^{\mathbf{s}}, \ldots, x_m^{\mathbf{s}}),\ p \cdot v = 1 \text{ and } |p \cdot z| \le 1\ \forall\ z \in V\}.$$

Since $(x_1^{\mathbf{s}}, x_2^{\mathbf{s}}, \ldots, x_m^{\mathbf{s}})$ is weakly Pareto optimal, it follows from Theorem 3.5.4 that $P(\mathbf{s})$ is non-empty. Clearly, each $P(\mathbf{s})$ is also a convex set.

Now for each $\mathbf{s} \in \Delta$ define the set

$$\Phi(\mathbf{s}) = \{\mathbf{z} = (z_1, \ldots, z_m) \in \mathcal{R}^m \colon\ \exists\ p \in P(\mathbf{s}) \text{ with } z_i = p \cdot (\omega_i - x_i^{\mathbf{s}})\ \forall\ i\}.$$

Since $P(\mathbf{s})$ is non-empty and convex, $\Phi(\mathbf{s})$ is non-empty and convex. In addition, $\Phi(\mathbf{s})$ is a bounded subset of $\mathcal{R}^m$. Indeed, note that there exists some $\delta > 0$ such that $[-\omega, \omega] \subseteq \delta V$, and so $|p \cdot z| \le \delta$ holds for each $z \in [-\omega, \omega]$ and all $p \in P(\mathbf{s})$. Thus,

$$\mathbf{z} = (z_1, \ldots, z_m) \in \Phi(\mathbf{s}) \text{ implies } |z_i| \le \delta \text{ for each } i \text{ and all } \mathbf{s} \in \Delta. \tag{2}$$

Next, we claim that the correspondence $\Phi \colon \Delta \longrightarrow 2^{\mathcal{R}^m}$ has a closed graph. To see this, let $\mathbf{s}_n \to \mathbf{s}$, $\mathbf{z}_n = (z_1^n, \ldots, z_m^n) \in \Phi(\mathbf{s}_n)$ for each n and $\mathbf{z}_n \to \mathbf{z}$ in $\mathcal{R}^m$; we must verify that $\mathbf{z} = (z_1, \ldots, z_n) \in \Phi(\mathbf{s})$. For each n pick some $p_n \in P(\mathbf{s}_n)$ such that $z_i^n = p_n \cdot (\omega_i - x_i^{\mathbf{s}_n})$. Since the sequence $\{p_n\}$ belongs to the polar V° of V and V° is by Alaoglu's theorem w*-compact (see [8, Theorem 9.20, p. 141]), there exists a subnet $\{p_{n_\alpha}\}$ of $\{p_n\}$—where, of course, $\{n_\alpha\}$ is a subnet of $\{n\}$—such that $p_{n_\alpha} \xrightarrow{w^*} p$ in E'. Clearly, $p \cdot v = 1$ and $|p \cdot z| \le 1$ for all $z \in V$.

Now assume that $x \succeq_i x_i^{\mathbf{s}}$. Clearly, $x + \varepsilon\omega \succ_i x_i^{\mathbf{s}}$ holds for each $\varepsilon > 0$. By the continuity of the function ρ (Theorem 3.5.7), we have $\rho(\mathbf{s}_{n_\alpha})\mathbf{s}_{n_\alpha} \longrightarrow \rho(\mathbf{s})\mathbf{s}$ and so there exists some α_0 such that $x + \varepsilon\omega \succ_i x_i^{\mathbf{s}_{n_\alpha}}$ holds for all $\alpha \ge \alpha_0$. The supportability of p_{n_α} implies

$$p_{n_\alpha} \cdot (x + \varepsilon\omega) \ge p_{n_\alpha} \cdot x_i^{\mathbf{s}_{n_\alpha}} = p_{n_\alpha} \cdot \omega_i - z_i^{n_\alpha}$$

for all $\alpha \geq \alpha_0$. Passing to the limit, we see that $p \cdot x + \varepsilon p \cdot \omega \geq p \cdot \omega_i - z_i$ holds for all $\varepsilon > 0$. This implies that

$$p \cdot x \geq p \cdot \omega_i - z_i \tag{3}$$

holds for each i. In particular, letting $x = x_i^{\mathbf{s}}$, we see that $p \cdot x_i^{\mathbf{s}} \geq p \cdot \omega_i - z_i$ for each i. From $\sum_{i=1}^m x_i^{\mathbf{s}} = \sum_{i=1}^m \omega_i$ and $\sum_{i=1}^m z_i = 0$, we infer that $p \cdot x_i^{\mathbf{s}} = p \cdot \omega_i - z_i$ for each i and so $z_i = p \cdot (\omega_i - x_i^{\mathbf{s}})$ for each i.

To complete the proof that $\mathbf{z} \in \Phi(\mathbf{s})$, it remains to be shown that the price p supports the allocation $(x_1^{\mathbf{s}}, \ldots, x_m^{\mathbf{s}})$. To this end, assume $x \succeq_i x_i^{\mathbf{s}}$. Then, from (**3**), it follows that $p \cdot x \geq p \cdot \omega_i - z_i = p \cdot x_i^{\mathbf{s}}$ holds. Therefore, p supports $(x_1^{\mathbf{s}}, \ldots, x_m^{\mathbf{s}})$, and so $\mathbf{z} \in \Phi(\mathbf{s})$. In other words, the correspondence Φ has a closed graph.

Next, consider the non-empty, compact and convex subset of $\mathcal{R}^m$

$$T = \{\mathbf{t} = (t_1, \ldots, t_m) \in \mathcal{R}^m \colon \ \|\mathbf{t}\|_1 = \sum_{i=1}^m |t_i| \leq m\delta\}.$$

By (**2**), we have $\Phi(\mathbf{s}) \subseteq T$ for each $\mathbf{s} \in \Delta$. Now fix some $\eta > m\delta$ and define the function $f \colon \Delta \times T \longrightarrow \Delta$ by

$$f(\mathbf{s}, \mathbf{t}) = \left(\frac{(s_1 + \frac{t_1}{\eta})^+}{\sum_{i=1}^m (s_i + \frac{t_i}{\eta})^+}, \frac{(s_2 + \frac{t_2}{\eta})^+}{\sum_{i=1}^m (s_i + \frac{t_i}{\eta})^+}, \ldots, \frac{(s_m + \frac{t_m}{\eta})^+}{\sum_{i=1}^m (s_i + \frac{t_i}{\eta})^+} \right), \ (\mathbf{s}, \mathbf{t}) \in \Delta \times T,$$

where, as usual, $r^+ = \max\{r, 0\}$ for each real number r. Since

$$\textstyle\sum_{i=1}^m \big(s_i + \frac{t_i}{\eta}\big)^+ \geq \sum_{i=1}^m \big(s_i + \frac{t_i}{\eta}\big) = 1 + \frac{1}{\eta} \sum_{i=1}^m t_i \geq 1 - \frac{m\delta}{\eta} > 0$$

holds for each $(\mathbf{s}, \mathbf{t}) \in \Delta \times T$, it follows that the function f is well defined and continuous.

Finally, we define the non-empty correspondence $\phi \colon \Delta \times T \longrightarrow 2^{\Delta \times T}$ by

$$\phi(\mathbf{s}, \mathbf{t}) = \{f(\mathbf{s}, \mathbf{t})\} \times \Phi(\mathbf{s}).$$

Clearly, ϕ is convex-valued. The continuity of f coupled with the fact that $\mathbf{s} \mapsto \Phi(\mathbf{s})$ has a closed graph implies that ϕ has also a closed graph. Thus, by Kakutani's fixed point theorem (Theorem 1.4.7), the correspondence ϕ has a fixed point, say $(\mathbf{s}, \mathbf{t})$. That is, there exists some $(\mathbf{s}, \mathbf{t}) \in \Delta \times T$ such that $\mathbf{s} = f(\mathbf{s}, \mathbf{t})$ and $\mathbf{t} \in \Phi(\mathbf{s})$. Pick some $p \in P(\mathbf{s})$ such that

$$t_i = p \cdot \omega_i - p \cdot x_i^{\mathbf{s}} \quad \text{for all} \quad i. \tag{4}$$

To complete the proof, we shall establish that $t_i = 0$ for each i.

If $s_i = 0$, then from (**1**) we see that $x_i^{\mathbf{s}} \sim_i 0$. So, by the supportability of p, we obtain $0 = p \cdot 0 \geq p \cdot x_i^{\mathbf{s}} \geq 0$, i.e., $p \cdot x_i^{\mathbf{s}} = 0$. Now note that from $\mathbf{s} = f(\mathbf{s}, \mathbf{t})$, it follows that $(s_i + \frac{t_i}{\eta})^+ = (\frac{t_i}{\eta})^+ = 0$ and so $t_i \leq 0$. From (**4**), we conclude that $0 \leq p \cdot \omega_i = t_i$. That is, $s_i = 0$ implies $t_i = 0$, and so $\big(s_i + \frac{t_i}{\eta}\big)^+ = s_i + \frac{t_i}{\eta} = 0$.

Now if $s_i > 0$ holds, then from $\mathbf{s} = f(\mathbf{s}, \mathbf{t})$, we see that $\left(s_i + \frac{t_i}{\eta}\right)^+ > 0$ and so $\left(s_i + \frac{t_i}{\eta}\right)^+ = s_i + \frac{t_i}{\eta}$ must hold. Thus, for each i we have $\left(s_i + \frac{t_i}{\eta}\right)^+ = s_i + \frac{t_i}{\eta}$. Consequently,

$$\sum_{i=1}^m \left(s_i + \tfrac{t_i}{\eta}\right)^+ = \sum_{i=1}^m \left(s_i + \tfrac{t_i}{\eta}\right) = \sum_{i=1}^m s_i + \tfrac{1}{\eta}\sum_{i=1}^m (p\cdot\omega_i - p\cdot x_i^{\mathbf{s}}) = 1\,.$$

Finally, using once more the equation $\mathbf{s} = f(\mathbf{s}, \mathbf{t})$, we see that $s_i = s_i + \frac{t_i}{\eta}$ holds for each i, which yields $t_i = 0$ for each i and the proof of the theorem is complete. ■

As a consequence of the preceding result, we have the following generalization of Theorem 3.3.9.

Corollary 3.5.13. *If an exchange economy satisfies the closedness condition and preferences are strictly monotone on A_ω^+, then the economy has an Edgeworth equilibrium.*

Proof. Consider an exchange economy satisfying the closedness condition having strictly monotone preferences on A_ω^+. With respect to the Riesz dual system $\langle A_\omega, A'_\omega\rangle$, each utility function is $\|\cdot\|_\infty$-continuous—see the discussion after Theorem 3.4.12—and (by Theorem 3.2.4) uniformly $\|\cdot\|_\infty$-proper.

Now, according to Theorem 3.5.12, the economy has a quasiequilibrium with respect to the Riesz dual system $\langle A_\omega, A'_\omega\rangle$. Since each preference is strictly monotone on A_ω^+, it follows (how?) that the quasiequilibrium is supported by a strictly positive price of A'_ω. This implies that the exchange economy has a Walrasian equilibrium with respect to the Riesz dual system $\langle A_\omega, A'_\omega\rangle$, which (by Theorem 3.4.18) is an Edgeworth equilibrium for the original exchange economy. ■

It is interesting to know that when preferences are represented by myopic utility functions, the closedness condition is always satisfied.

Theorem 3.5.14. *If the commodity space E is a normal Riesz space, then every exchange economy whose preferences are represented by myopic utility functions satisfies the closedness condition.*

Proof. Assume that in an exchange economy the Riesz space E is normal and that the preference of each consumer is represented by a myopic utility function u_i. Consider a sequence $\{(x_{n,1}, \ldots, x_{n,m})\}$ of feasible allocations such that $x_{n+1,i} \succeq_i x_{n,i}$ holds for all n and all i. We have to show that there exists a feasible allocation $(x_1, \ldots, x_m)$ satisfying $x_i \succeq_i x_{n,i}$ for all n and all i.

To this end, consider the order interval $[0, \omega]$ equipped with the topology $\sigma(E, E_n^\sim)$ and let t denote the product topology on $[0,\omega]^m$. Since $[0,\omega]$ is $\sigma(E, E_n^\sim)$-compact, it follows that $[0,\omega]^m$ is t-compact. Now the sequence $\{(x_{n,1}, \ldots, x_{n,m})\}$ is a sequence of $[0,\omega]^m$, and so it has a t-accumulation point, say $(x_1, \ldots, x_m)$. Clearly, $(x_1, \ldots, x_m)$ is a feasible allocation, and each x_i is a $\sigma(E, E_n^\sim)$-accumulation point of the sequence $\{x_{n,i}\}$. By Theorem 3.2.12 we have

$$u_i(x_i) \geq \liminf_{n\to\infty} u_i(x_{n,i}) = \sup\{u_i(x_{n,i}) \colon n = 1, 2, \ldots\}\,,$$

and so $x_i \succeq_i x_{n,i}$ holds for all n and all i, as desired. ∎

And now we come to a remarkable application of Theorem 3.5.12 to exchange economies having preferences represented by myopic utility functions.

Theorem 3.5.15. *Assume that the commodity space of an exchange economy is a normal Riesz space and that preferences are represented by myopic utility functions. If $a \geq \omega$ and the total endowment ω is extremely desirable by each consumer on A_a, then the exchange economy has a quasiequilibrium with respect to the Riesz dual system $\langle A_a, A'_a \rangle$.*

Proof. Let $a \geq \omega$ be fixed and consider the exchange economy with respect to the Riesz dual system $\langle A_a, A'_a \rangle$ and with the original agents' characteristics restricted to A_a. By Theorem 3.2.11 we know that every utility function is $\|\cdot\|_\infty$-continuous on A_a and Theorem 3.2.4 guarantees that all preferences are uniformly $\|\cdot\|_\infty$-proper on A_a. In addition, by Theorem 3.5.14 the exchange economy satisfies the closedness condition with respect to the Riesz dual system $\langle A_a, A'_a \rangle$, and our conclusion follows from Theorem 3.5.12.

It should be noted that the supporting prices can be normalized with respect to a, i.e., if $p \in A'_a$ supports an allocation with respect to $\langle A_a, A'_a \rangle$, then we can choose p to satisfy $p \cdot a = 1$. ∎

EXERCISES

1. If in an exchange economy the order interval $[0, \omega]$ is weakly compact, then show that the economy satisfies the closedness condition.
[HINT: Use Exercise 8 of Section 1.2.]

2. Complete the details in the proof of Theorem 3.5.3.

3. Show that every exchange economy with the closedness condition has individually rational Pareto optimal allocations.
[HINT: Repeat the proof of Theorem 1.5.3 and use the closedness condition instead of the weak compactness of the set of all allocations.]

4. Consider the exchange economy with Riesz dual system $\langle L_\infty[0,1], L_1[0,1] \rangle$ having two consumers with utility functions

$$u_1(x) = \int_0^1 x(t)\,dt \quad \text{and} \quad u_2(x) = \int_0^1 \sqrt{x(t)}\,dt\,,$$

and total endowment $\omega = \mathbf{1}$ (the constant function one). Show that the utility space $\mathbf{U}$ of this economy is $\mathbf{U} = \{(x, y) \in \mathcal{R}^2_+ \colon\ x + y^2 \leq 1\}$; see Figure 3.5-3.

[HINT: For $0 \le x \le \omega$ let $\varepsilon = \int_0^1 x(t)\,dt$, and note that by Hölder's inequality we have

$$u_2(\omega - x) = \int_0^1 \sqrt{1 - x(t)}\,dt \le \Big[\int_0^1 (1 - x(t))\,dt\Big]^{\frac{1}{2}} = \sqrt{1-\varepsilon}\,.$$

Now note that $(\varepsilon, \sqrt{1-\varepsilon}) \in \mathbf{U}$ holds for each $0 \le \varepsilon \le 1$.]

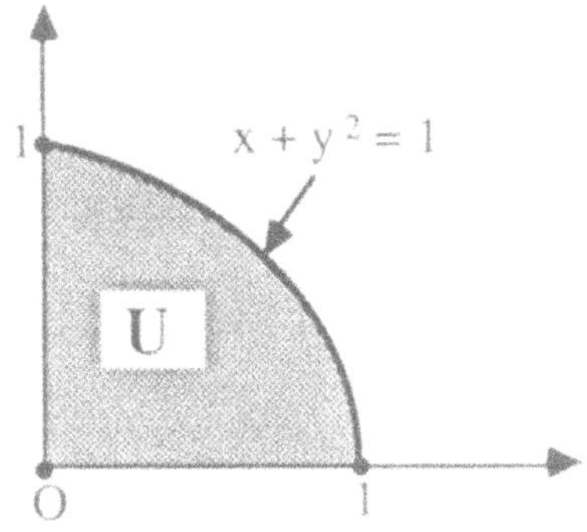

Fig. 3.5-3

5. Assume that an exchange economy with Riesz dual system $\langle L_\infty[0,1], L_1[0,1]\rangle$ has m consumers with utility functions $u_i(x) = \int_0^1 \sqrt[i]{x(t)}\,dt$ $(i = 1, \ldots, m)$ and total endowment $\omega = \mathbf{1}$ (the constant function one). Find the utility space of the economy.
Answer: $\mathbf{U} = \{(x_1, \ldots, x_m) \in \mathcal{R}^m_+ \colon\ x_1 + (x_2)^2 + \cdots + (x_m)^m \le 1\}$

6. Consider an exchange economy with Riesz dual system $\langle C[0,1], \mathrm{ca}[0,1]\rangle$ and two consumers having utility functions

$$u_1(x) = \int_0^1 x(t)\,dt \quad \text{and} \quad u_2(x) = \int_0^1 \sqrt{x(t)}\,dt\,,$$

and initial endowments $\omega_1(t) = t$ and $\omega_2(t) = 1 - t$. (Keep in mind that $\mathrm{ca}[0,1]$ is the norm dual of $C[0,1]$ equipped with the sup norm.)

a) Show that both utility functions are continuous, concave (in fact, u_2 is strictly concave), strictly monotone and uniformly $\|\cdot\|_\infty$-proper.
[HINT: For the uniform $\|\cdot\|_\infty$-properness use Theorem 3.2.4.]

b) Show that the order interval $[0, \omega]$ is not weakly compact and that the economy satisfies the closedness condition.
[HINT: Argue as in Exercise 4 and show that $\mathbf{U} = \{(x,y) \in \mathcal{R}^2_+ \colon\ x + y^2 \le 1\}$; see Figure 3.5-3.]

c) Show that the economy has quasiequilibria—which are, in fact, Walrasian equilibria (why?).

d) If $x_1 = x_2 = \frac{1}{2}\chi_{[0,1]}$, then show directly that the allocation (x_1, x_2) is a Walrasian equilibrium supported by the Lebesgue integral.

[HINT: If $x \succeq_2 x_2$, then

$$\tfrac{1}{\sqrt{2}} = u_2(x_2) \le u_2(x) = \int_0^1 \sqrt{x(t)}\,dt \le \Big(\int_0^1 x(t)\,dt\Big)^{\frac{1}{2}}$$

and so $\int_0^1 x(t)\,dt \ge \frac{1}{2} = \int_0^1 \omega_2(t)\,dt$.]

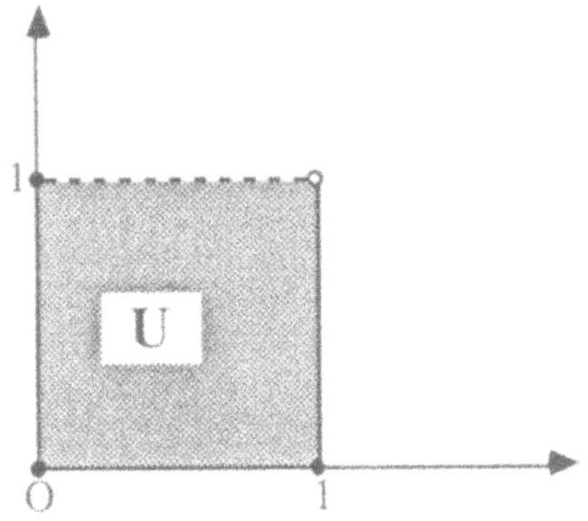

Fig. 3.5-4

7. The example presented in this exercise is due to A. Araujo [10]. Consider an exchange economy with Riesz dual system $\langle \ell_\infty, \ell_1 \rangle$ having two consumers with utility functions

$$u_1(x_1, x_2, \ldots) = \liminf_{n\to\infty} x_n \qquad \text{and} \qquad u_2(x_1, x_2, \ldots) = \sum_{n=1}^{\infty} \frac{x_n}{2^n},$$

and total endowment $\omega = (1, 1, 1, \ldots)$.

a) Show that the utility function u_1 is monotone, concave, has ω as an extremely desirable bundle but fails to be Mackey continuous.
[HINT: For the Mackey continuity of u_1 let $\mathbf{x}_n = (0, \ldots, 0, 1, 1, 1, \ldots)$, where the zeros occupy the first n positions, and note that $\mathbf{x}_n \xrightarrow{\tau(\ell_\infty, \ell_1)} \mathbf{0}$ while $\lim_{n\to\infty} u_1(\mathbf{x}_n) \ne u_1(\mathbf{0})$.]

b) Show that the utility function u_2 is strictly monotone, concave and Mackey continuous.
[HINT: Note that if $\mathbf{p} = (\frac{1}{2}, \frac{1}{2^2}, \frac{1}{2^3}, \ldots) \in \ell_1$, then $u_2(\mathbf{x}) = \mathbf{p} \cdot \mathbf{x}$.]

c) Show that the utility space of this economy is $\mathbf{U} = [0,1] \times [0,1) \cup \{(0,1)\}$; see Figure 3.5.4.

d) If $\omega_1 > 0$ and $\omega_2 > 0$ hold, then show that the economy has no quasiequilibria.
[HINT: Assume $(\mathbf{x}_1, \mathbf{x}_2)$ is a quasiequilibrium supported by a price $\mathbf{0} < \mathbf{p} \in \ell_1$. Now note that if $\mathbf{x}_1 = (x_1^1, x_2^1, x_3^1, \ldots) \in \ell_\infty$ and

$$\mathbf{z}_n = (0, 0, \ldots, 0, x_{n+1}^1, x_{n+2}^1, \ldots),$$

where the zeros occupy the first n positions, then $\mathbf{z}_n \sim_1 \mathbf{x}_1$ for each n. This implies $\mathbf{p} \cdot \mathbf{z}_n \geq \mathbf{p} \cdot \omega_1 \geq 0$ for all n. Therefore, $\mathbf{p} \cdot \omega_1 = \lim_{n \to \infty} \mathbf{p} \cdot \mathbf{z}_n = 0$. The latter implies $\mathbf{p} \cdot \omega_2 > 0$ and since u_2 is strictly monotone, we see that $\mathbf{p} \gg \mathbf{0}$ must hold. However, the latter conclusion contradicts $\mathbf{p} \cdot \omega_1 = 0$.]

8. Show that the exchange economy of Example 3.3.7 satisfies the closedness condition with respect to the Riesz dual system $\langle L_\infty[0,1], L_1[0,1] \rangle$ but it fails to satisfy the closedness condition with respect to $\langle C[0,1], \text{ca}[0,1] \rangle$.

3.6. EXAMPLES OF EXCHANGE ECONOMIES

The main objective of this section is to illustrate the results of the preceding sections with several examples. We start with an example demonstrating that in the infinite dimensional case demand functions need not exist.

Example 3.6.1. Let $E = C[0,1]$, $\omega = \mathbf{1}$ (the constant function one) and let p be the strictly positive price defined by the Lebesgue integral, i.e.,

$$p \cdot x = \int_0^1 x(t)\,dt, \quad x \in C[0,1].$$

Let $\{r_0, r_1, r_2, \ldots\}$ be an enumeration of the rational numbers of $[0,1]$ with $r_0 = 0$, and consider the utility function $u: (C[0,1])^+ \longrightarrow \mathcal{R}$ defined by

$$u(x) = \sum_{i=0}^{\infty} 2^{-i}\sqrt{x(r_i)}.$$

Clearly, u is strictly concave, strictly monotone and continuous and we claim that the preference relation defined by u does not have any maximal element in the budget set

$$\mathcal{B} = \{x \in C[0,1]\colon\ x \geq 0 \text{ and } p \cdot x \leq p \cdot \omega = 1\}.$$

To see this, let x_n be the function defined by

$$x_n(t) = \begin{cases} -n^2t + n, & \text{if } 0 \leq t \leq \frac{1}{n}; \\ 0, & \text{if } \frac{1}{n} \leq t \leq 1, \end{cases}$$

and note that $x_n \in \mathcal{B}$ and $u(x_n) \geq \sqrt{x_n(0)} = \sqrt{n}$. Hence, $\sup\{u(x)\colon\ x \in \mathcal{B}\} = \infty$, and so the preference relation defined by u does not have any maximal element in the budget set $\mathcal{B}$. ■

The next finite dimensional example illustrates the role of the ideal generated by the total endowment and is a variation of an example presented by A. Mas-Colell [46].

Example 3.6.2. Start by observing that if the exchange economy has only one consumer, then the set of all allocations consists of one element—the initial endowment of the consumer.

Suppose that there are two goods in the economy (i.e., the commodity-price duality is $\langle E, E' \rangle = \langle \mathcal{R}^2, \mathcal{R}^2 \rangle$) and one consumer with initial endowment $\omega = (1,0)$ and utility function

$$u(x,y) = \sqrt{x} + \sqrt{y}.$$

Clearly, u is a strictly monotone, strictly concave and continuous utility function defined on $\mathcal{R}^2_+$. The situation is illustrated geometrically in Figure 3.6-1.

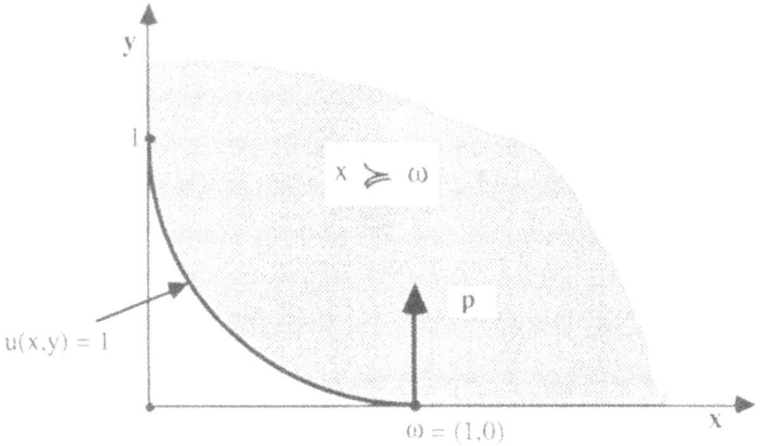

Fig. 3.6-1

By Theorem 3.3.9, the economy has Edgeworth equilibria and so (since ω is the only allocation) ω is an Edgeworth equilibrium. (The reader should stop and verify directly as an exercise that ω is indeed an Edgeworth equilibrium.) Since the preference is uniformly proper (Theorem 3.2.4), we know that ω is also a quasiequilibrium (Theorem 3.4.6). Notice that the positive prices $\mathbf{p} = \lambda(0,1)$, $\lambda > 0$, are the only prices supporting the allocation ω; see Figure 3.6-1. It is not difficult to see that ω is not a Walrasian equilibrium, and so the economy does not have Walrasian equilibria.

Now by Theorem 3.4.18, the allocation ω is a Walrasian equilibrium on the ideal generated by ω. A moment's thought reveals that

$$A_\omega = \{(x,0)\colon\ x \in \mathcal{R}\},$$

i.e., A_ω is the x-axis, and so $A'_\omega = \{(p,0)\colon\ p \in \mathcal{R}\}$. The price $\mathbf{p} = (1,0)$ is a strictly positive price on A_ω supporting ω as a Walrasian equilibrium. Also, note that for the price $\mathbf{p} = (1,0)$ the budget set in A_ω is the compact set $[0,1]$, while in $\mathcal{R}^2$ is the unbounded "strip" $\{(x,y)\colon\ 0 \le x \le 1 \text{ and } y \ge 0\}$. ■

Before presenting more examples of exchange economies, let us present two examples of utility functions on infinite dimensional spaces. The first one deals with utility functions in L_p-spaces.

Example 3.6.3. Let (X, Σ, μ) be a finite measure space. For simplicity we shall write L_p instead of $L_p(X, \Sigma, \mu)$. In this case, we know that $L_p \subseteq L_1$ holds for each $1 \le p \le \infty$.

Fix $0 < \alpha \le 1$ and let $1 \le p \le \infty$. Now define the function $u\colon L_p^+ \longrightarrow \mathcal{R}$ by

$$u(f) = \int_X f^\alpha \, d\mu .$$

Note that—in view of $f^\alpha \in L_{\frac{p}{\alpha}} \subseteq L_1$—the value $u(f)$ is well defined.

Thus, u is a utility function defined on the positive cone of L_p. This type of utility function has the following properties.

1. *The utility function u is additively separable, that is, $f \wedge g = 0$ implies $u(f+g) = u(f) + u(g)$.*

If $f \wedge g = 0$ holds, then $(f+g)^\alpha = f^\alpha + g^\alpha$ and so $u(f+g) = u(f) + u(g)$ also holds.

2. *The utility function u is strictly monotone.*

If $0 \le f < g$ holds in L_p^+, then $0 \le f^\alpha < g^\alpha$ also holds, and so

$$u(f) = \int_X f^\alpha \, d\mu < \int_X g^\alpha \, d\mu = u(g).$$

3. *The utility function u is strictly concave for each $0 < \alpha < 1$.*

Assume $0 < \alpha < 1$. Note first that the function $\phi(t) = t^\alpha$, $t > 0$, satisfies $\phi''(t) < 0$ for all $t > 0$. This implies that ϕ is strictly concave on $[0, \infty)$; see the proof of Theorem 1.1.7.

Thus, if $f, g \in L_p^+$ satisfy $f \neq g$, then $[\lambda f + (1-\lambda) g]^\alpha > \lambda f^\alpha + (1-\lambda) g^\alpha$ holds for each $0 < \lambda < 1$, and so by integrating, we see that

$$u(\lambda f + (1-\lambda) g) > \lambda u(f) + (1-\lambda) u(g).$$

4. *The utility function u is norm continuous (i.e., $\|\cdot\|_p$-continuous).*

Let $\|f_n - f\|_p = \left(\int_X |f_n - f|^p \, d\mu\right)^{\frac{1}{p}} \longrightarrow 0$ hold in L_p^+. Let $1 \le r \le \infty$ be the unique extended real number such that $\frac{\alpha}{p} + \frac{1}{r} = 1$. Then, from Hölder's inequality, we have

$$\begin{aligned}|u(f_n) - u(f)| &= \left|\int_X (f_n)^\alpha \, d\mu - \int_X f^\alpha \, d\mu\right| \le \int_X |f_n - f|^\alpha \, d\mu \\ &\le \left[\int_X \left(|f_n - f|^\alpha\right)^{\frac{p}{\alpha}} d\mu\right]^{\frac{\alpha}{p}} \cdot \left[\int_X 1^r \, d\mu\right]^{\frac{1}{r}} \\ &= [\mu(X)]^{\frac{1}{r}} \cdot \left[\int_X |f_n - f|^p \, d\mu\right]^{\frac{\alpha}{p}} = [\mu(X)]^{\frac{1}{r}} \cdot (\|f_n - f\|_p)^\alpha,\end{aligned}$$

and so $\lim_{n\to\infty} u(f_n) = u(f)$.

5. *If X is a compact Hausdorff topological space and u is considered defined on $(C(X))^+$, then u is weakly sequentially continuous.*

Note that by the Riesz Representation Theorem—see, for example, [7, Section 28]—we know that $f_n \xrightarrow{w} f$ holds in $(C(X))^+$ if and only if the sequence $\{f_n\}$ is uniformly bounded and satisfies $f_n(x) \longrightarrow f(x)$ for each $x \in X$. Thus, if $f_n \xrightarrow{w} f$, then by the Lebesgue Dominated Convergence Theorem, we infer that

$$u(f_n) = \int_X (f_n)^\alpha \, d\mu \longrightarrow \int_X f^\alpha \, d\mu = u(f).$$

6. *The special utility function* $u\colon L_1^+[0,1] \longrightarrow \mathcal{R}$ *is not weakly continuous.*

Let $\{r_n\}$ denote the sequence of Rademacher functions on the interval $[0,1]$, i.e., $r_n(x) = \operatorname{Sgn}\sin(2^n\pi x)$. It is well known that $r_n \xrightarrow{w} 0$ holds in $L_1[0,1]$, and so the sequence $\{\mathbf{1}+r_n\} \subseteq L_1^+[0,1]$ satisfies $\mathbf{1}+r_n \xrightarrow{w} \mathbf{1}$. Now observe that

$$u(\mathbf{1}+r_n) = \int_0^1 (1+r_n)^\alpha\,dx = \frac{2^\alpha}{2} \longrightarrow \frac{2^\alpha}{2} \neq 1 = \int_0^1 1^\alpha\,dx = u(\mathbf{1})\,. \ \blacksquare$$

Next, we shall present examples of utility functions on ℓ_p-spaces. The examples below are variations of the examples presented by K. D. Stroyan in [65].

Example 3.6.4. Fix a sequence $(w_1, w_2, \ldots)$ in ℓ_1^+ such that $w_n > 0$ holds for each n. For each $1 \le p \le \infty$ and each $0 < \alpha \le 1$ define the function $u\colon \ell_p^+ \longrightarrow \mathcal{R}$ by

$$u(x_1, x_2, \ldots) = \sum_{n=1}^{\infty} w_n[x_n]^\alpha\,.$$

Then, u is a utility function on ℓ_p^+ satisfying the following properties.

1. *For each* $0 < \alpha < 1$ *the utility function* u *is strictly concave.*

Indeed, if $\mathbf{x} = (x_1, x_2, \ldots)$ and $\mathbf{y} = (y_1, y_2, \ldots)$ in ℓ_p^+ satisfy $\mathbf{x} \neq \mathbf{y}$ and $0 < \lambda < 1$, then we have

$$\begin{aligned} u(\lambda\mathbf{x}+(1-\lambda)\mathbf{y}) &= \sum_{n=1}^{\infty} w_n[\lambda x_n + (1-\lambda)y_n]^\alpha \\ &> \sum_{n=1}^{\infty} w_n[\lambda(x_n)^\alpha + (1-\lambda)(y_n)^\alpha] \\ &= \lambda\sum_{n=1}^{\infty} w_n[x_n]^\alpha + (1-\lambda)\sum_{n=1}^{\infty} w_n[y_n]^\alpha \\ &= \lambda u(\mathbf{x}) + (1-\lambda)u(\mathbf{y})\,. \end{aligned}$$

2. *The utility function* u *is strictly monotone.*

If $\mathbf{0} \le \mathbf{x} = (x_1, x_2, \ldots) < \mathbf{y} = (y_1, y_2, \ldots)$ holds, then $0 \le x_n \le y_n$ holds for all n and $0 \le x_n < y_n$ must hold for at least one n. Thus,

$$u(\mathbf{x}) = \sum_{n=1}^{\infty} w_n[x_n]^\alpha < \sum_{n=1}^{\infty} w_n[y_n]^\alpha = u(\mathbf{y})\,.$$

3. *The utility function* u *is sequentially weakly continuous (and hence it is norm continuous).*

Let $\mathbf{x}^n = (x_1^n, x_2^n, \ldots) \xrightarrow{w} \mathbf{x} = (x_1, x_2, \ldots)$ in ℓ_p. Then there exists some $M > 0$ such that $\|\mathbf{x}^n\|_p \le M$ holds for all n, and so $|x_i^n| \le M$ and $|x_i| \le M$ hold for all n and all i.

Now let $\delta > 0$. Pick some s such that $2M^\alpha \sum_{i=s}^{\infty} w_i < \delta$, and then (in view of $\lim_{n\to\infty} x_i^n = x_i$ for each i) pick some n_0 such that $\sum_{i=1}^{s} w_i|(x_i^n)^\alpha - (x_i)^\alpha| < \delta$ for all $n \geq n_0$. Thus, if $n \geq n_0$, then

$$\begin{aligned}|u(\mathbf{x}^n) - u(\mathbf{x})| &\leq \sum_{i=1}^{s} w_i|(x_i^n)^\alpha - (x_i)^\alpha| + \sum_{i=s}^{\infty} w_i|(x_i^n)^\alpha - (x_i)^\alpha| \\ &< \delta + 2M^\alpha \sum_{i=s}^{\infty} w_i < 2\delta\,,\end{aligned}$$

which means that $\lim_{n\to\infty} u(\mathbf{x}^n) = u(\mathbf{x})$.

4. *If $1 < p < \infty$, then u restricted to any norm bounded subset of ℓ_p is weakly continuous.*

In this case the norm dual of ℓ_p is ℓ_q which is a separable Banach space. This implies—see, for instance, [8, Theorem 10.8, p. 153]—that the weak topology on the norm bounded subsets of ℓ_p is metrizable. The conclusion now follows from part (3) and the fact that the closed balls of ℓ_p are weakly compact sets.

5. *For $p = 1$ the utility function u is weakly continuous (and hence, norm continuous) on every weakly compact subset of ℓ_1.*

The weak topology is metrizable on every weakly compact subset of ℓ_1—see [8, Theorem 10.11, p. 154]—and the conclusion follows from part (3).

6. *The utility function is additively separable.*

Observe that $\mathbf{x} \wedge \mathbf{y} = \mathbf{0}$ implies $x_n = 0$ or $y_n = 0$ for each n, and consequently

$$(x_n + y_n)^\alpha = (x_n)^\alpha + (y_n)^\alpha$$

holds for each n. The latter easily implies that $u(\mathbf{x} + \mathbf{y}) = u(\mathbf{x}) + u(\mathbf{y})$. ■

We are now ready to present a few more examples of exchange economies with infinite dimensional commodity spaces.

Example 3.6.5. Let (X, Σ, μ) be a σ-finite measure space and let $L_p = L_p(X, \Sigma, \mu)$, $1 \leq p \leq \infty$. We shall consider the Riesz dual system $\langle L_\infty, L_1 \rangle$ which was first studied by T. F. Bewley [16]. The Riesz dual system $\langle L_\infty, L_1 \rangle$ is symmetric, i.e., the order intervals of L_∞ are weakly compact. In addition, the Mackey topology is a locally convex-solid topology.

Consider now a pure exchange economy with Riesz dual system $\langle L_\infty, L_1 \rangle$ such that the total endowment ω is "bounded away from zero," i.e., there exists some constant $c > 0$ such that $\omega(x) \geq c$ holds for μ-almost all x. By Theorem 3.3.9 such an exchange economy has an Edgeworth equilibrium.

In this model, the assumption on ω implies that $A_\omega = L_\infty$. Thus, by Theorem 3.4.18, every Edgeworth equilibrium is a Walrasian equilibrium with respect to the Riesz dual system $\langle L_\infty, L'_\infty \rangle$. Let $0 < p \in L'_\infty$ be a price supporting an

Edgeworth equilibrium. By Theorem 3.4.21, the price p is order continuous on $A_\omega = L_\infty$. Since the order continuous dual of L_∞ is L_1 (i.e., $(L_\infty)_n^\sim = L_1$; see [8, Theorem 14.12, p. 226]), we infer that $p \in L_1$. Consequently, every pure exchange economy with Riesz dual system $\langle L_\infty, L_1 \rangle$ has a Walrasian equilibrium—a conclusion obtained first by T. F. Bewley [16]. ■

Example 3.6.6. Consider a pure exchange economy with respect to the Riesz dual system $\langle L_1(\mu), L_\infty(\mu)\rangle$, where μ is a σ-finite measure. Since $L_\infty(\mu)$ is the norm dual of $L_1(\mu)$ and $L_1(\mu)$ has order continuous norm, the Riesz dual system $\langle L_1(\mu), L_\infty(\mu)\rangle$ is symmetric.

If $\omega \gg 0$ holds and the preferences are uniformly norm-proper, then—according to Corollary 3.4.9—the economy has a Walrasian equilibrium. ■

Example 3.6.7. Consider a pure exchange economy with respect to the symmetric Riesz dual system $\langle L_p(\mu), L_q(\mu)\rangle$, $1 < p,\ q < \infty$; $\frac{1}{p} + \frac{1}{q} = 1$, where μ is an arbitrary measure—for an application of this model when $p = 2$ see [25].

If $\omega \gg 0$ holds and preferences are uniformly norm-proper, then—according to Corollary 3.4.9—the economy has Walrasian equilibria. ■

Example 3.6.8. Consider a σ-algebra Σ of subsets of a set X. Then, the symbol $\mathrm{ca}(\Sigma)$ will denote the vector space of all signed (countably additive) measures on Σ with finite total variation. The vector space $\mathrm{ca}(\Sigma)$ under the ordering $\mu \le \nu$ whenever $\mu(A) \le \nu(A)$ holds for each $A \in \Sigma$ is a Dedekind complete Riesz space; see [7, Sections 26 & 27]. If X is a topological space, then we shall write $\mathrm{ca}(X)$ instead of $\mathrm{ca}(\mathcal{B})$, where $\mathcal{B}$ is the σ-algebra of all Borel sets of X, i.e., $\mathcal{B}$ is the σ-algebra generated by the open sets of X. In addition, the Riesz space $\mathrm{ca}(\Sigma)$ under the norm

$$\|\mu\| = |\mu|(X)$$

is a Banach lattice with order continuous norm. In fact, $\mathrm{ca}(\Sigma)$ is an AL-space; see, for example, [7, Theorem 26.10, p. 224]. Therefore, if $\mathrm{ca}'(\Sigma)$ denotes the norm dual of $\mathrm{ca}(\Sigma)$, then $\langle \mathrm{ca}(\Sigma), \mathrm{ca}'(\Sigma)\rangle$ is a symmetric Riesz dual system. In particular, this implies that a measure $0 < \omega \in \mathrm{ca}(\Sigma)$ is strictly positive if and only if it is a weak order unit, i.e., if and only if $\omega \wedge \mu = 0$ implies $\mu = 0$. We remind the reader that $\mu \wedge \nu = 0$ holds in $\mathrm{ca}(\Sigma)$ if and only if there exists some $A \in \Sigma$ such that $\mu(A) = \nu(X \setminus A) = 0$; see [7, Theorem 27.5, p. 228].

Now assume that X is a Hausdorff compact topological space with X an uncountable set. Then, $\mathrm{ca}(X)$ does not have any strictly positive elements. Indeed, if $0 \ll \omega \in \mathrm{ca}(X)$, then $\omega(\{x\}) > 0$ holds for each $x \in X$—otherwise, $\omega(\{x\}) = 0$ implies $\omega \wedge \delta_x = 0$ ($\delta_x =$ the Dirac measure supported at x), contrary to $\omega \gg 0$—and so X must be at most countable. Thus, for each $\omega > 0$ we have $\overline{A_\omega} \neq \mathrm{ca}(X)$.

Now assume that we have a pure exchange economy with respect to the Riesz dual system $\langle \mathrm{ca}(X), \mathrm{ca}'(X)\rangle$. By Theorem 3.3.9 the economy has an Edgeworth equilibrium. If preferences are uniformly τ-proper, then—according to Theorem 3.4.6—every Edgeworth equilibrium is a quasiequilibrium with respect to the Riesz dual system $\langle \mathrm{ca}(X), \mathrm{ca}'(X)\rangle$. On the other hand, if preferences are uniformly τ-proper on $\overline{A_\omega}$, then every Edgeworth equilibrium is a Walrasian equilibrium with respect to the Riesz dual system $\langle \overline{A_\omega}, (\overline{A_\omega})' \rangle$ (Theorem 3.4.20). For an application of this model see [34]. ∎

Example 3.6.9. Let $\mathcal{R}_\infty$ denote the Dedekind complete Riesz space of all real valued sequences (i.e., $\mathcal{R}_\infty = \mathcal{R}^{\mathcal{N}}$) and let τ be the product topology. Then τ is an order continuous locally convex-solid topology, and so $\langle \mathcal{R}_\infty \mathcal{R}'_\infty \rangle$ is a symmetric Riesz dual system.

Now consider a pure exchange economy with Riesz dual system $\langle \mathcal{R}_\infty \mathcal{R}'_\infty \rangle$. We assume that $\omega \gg 0$ (which in this case means $\omega_n > 0$ for each n) and so $\overline{A_\omega} = \mathcal{R}_\infty$. By Theorem 3.3.9 the economy has Edgeworth equilibria. However, since there are no strictly positive linear functionals on $\mathcal{R}_\infty$—the dual $\mathcal{R}'_\infty$ coincides with the vector space of all real-valued sequences that are eventually zero—it follows from Theorem 3.4.4 that this type of economy does not have any Walrasian equilibrium.

The latter conclusion, coupled with Corollary 3.4.9, reveals that there are no utility functions on $\mathcal{R}^+_\infty$ which are strictly monotone, quasi-concave, τ-continuous and uniformly τ-proper. In contrast to this, Theorem 3.4.18 guarantees that the economy has an extended quasiequilibrium—a result obtained first by B. Peleg and M. E. Yaari [53]. ∎

If we change the Riesz dual system, then the equilibrium behavior of the economy is radically altered. Example 3.3.7 exhibited an economy with no core allocations and hence without Walrasian equilibria. The next example uses the utility functions and endowments of Example 3.3.7. Remarkably, a Walrasian equilibrium will exist when the commodity space is altered.

Example 3.6.10. The symbol $L_p (1 \le p \le \infty)$ will denote $L_p[0,1]$. We consider a two consumer exchange economy with the following characteristics. Its Riesz dual system will be $\langle L_p, L_q \rangle (1 \le p, q \le \infty$; and $\frac{1}{p} + \frac{1}{q} = 1)$. The consumers' initial endowments are $\omega_1 = \omega_2 = \mathbf{1}$, where $\mathbf{1}$ denotes the constant function one on $[0,1]$. Let $\omega = \omega_1 + \omega_2 = \mathbf{2} \gg 0$, then the order interval $[0, \omega]$ is weakly compact. Each consumer has the positive cone as her consumption set and their preferences are represented by the utility functions

$$u_1(x) = \int_0^{\frac{1}{2}} \sqrt{x(t)}\, dt + \tfrac{1}{2} \int_{\frac{1}{2}}^1 \sqrt{x(t)}\, dt \quad \text{and} \quad u_2(x) = \tfrac{1}{2} \int_0^{\frac{1}{2}} \sqrt{x(t)}\, dt + \int_{\frac{1}{2}}^1 \sqrt{x(t)}\, dt\,.$$

It is easy to see that the utility functions are strictly monotone and strictly concave. In Example 3.3.7 it was established that the utility functions are continuous for the $\|\cdot\|_p$-norm. Next, we exhibit a Walrasian equilibrium for the economy with Riesz dual system $\langle L_p, L_q \rangle$. We claim that:

The allocation (x_1, x_2) *given by*

$$x_1 = \tfrac{8}{5}\chi_{[0,\frac{1}{2}]} + \tfrac{2}{5}\chi_{(\frac{1}{2},1]} \qquad \textit{and} \qquad x_2 = \tfrac{2}{5}\chi_{[0,\frac{1}{2}]} + \tfrac{8}{5}\chi_{(\frac{1}{2},1]}\,,$$

is a Walrasian equilibrium for the economy whose Riesz dual system is $\langle L_p, L_q\rangle$*;* $1 \le p, q \le \infty$, $\frac{1}{p}+\frac{1}{q}=1$. *Moreover, in this case, the Lebesgue integral is a strictly positive price that supports the Walrasian equilibrium* (x_1, x_2).

To see this, note first that $u_1(x_1) = u_2(x_2) = \sqrt{\frac{5}{8}}$. Also, let $f = \chi_{[0,\frac{1}{2}]} + \frac{1}{2}\chi_{(\frac{1}{2},1]}$ and note that $u_1(x) = \int_0^1 f(t)\sqrt{x(t)}\,dt$. Therefore, if $x \succeq_1 x_1$, then from Hölder's inequality it follows that

$$\sqrt{\tfrac{5}{8}} = u_1(x_1) \le u_1(x) = \int_0^1 f(t)\sqrt{x(t)}\,dt$$
$$\le \Big(\int_0^1 [f(t)]^2\,dt\Big)^{\frac{1}{2}} \cdot \Big(\int_0^1 x(t)\,dt\Big)^{\frac{1}{2}} = \sqrt{\tfrac{5}{8}}\cdot\Big(\int_0^1 x(t)\,dt\Big)^{\frac{1}{2}},$$

and so $\big(\int_0^1 x(t)\,dt\big)^{\frac{1}{2}} \ge 1$, i.e.,

$$\int_0^1 x(t)\,dt \ge 1 = \int_0^1 \omega_1(t)\,dt\,.$$

Similarly, $x \succeq_2 x_2$ implies $\int_0^1 x(t)\,dt \ge \int_0^1 \omega_2(t)\,dt$. This establishes that the Lebesgue integral is a price that supports (x_1, x_2), and therefore (x_1, x_2) is a Walrasian equilibrium with respect to the Riesz dual system $\langle L_p, L_q\rangle$. ■

Finally, we close this section by observing—in view of Example 3.3.7—that in case the order interval $[0, \omega]$ is not weakly compact, the economy need not have Edgeworth equilibria.

EXERCISES

1. Show that the utility function u defined in Example 3.6.1 is sequentially $\sigma(C[0,1], ca[0,1])$-continuous, i.e., show that $x_n \xrightarrow{w} x$ in $(C[0,1])^+$ implies $u(x_n) \longrightarrow u(x)$.
2. Let $\{r_n\}$ denote the sequence of Rademacher functions on the interval $[0,1]$, i.e., $r_n(x) = \operatorname{Sgn}\sin(2^n \pi x)$.
   a) Sketch the graphs of the functions r_n; and
   b) Show that $\{r_n\}$ converges weakly to zero in $L_1[0,1]$.
   [HINT: To establish that $r_n \xrightarrow{w} 0$ holds in $L_1[0,1]$ note that it suffices to show that $\lim_{n\to\infty} \int_a^b r_n(x)\,dx = 0$ holds for every closed subinterval $[a,b]$ of $[0,1]$.]
3. If (X, Σ, μ) is a σ-finite measure space, then show that the Riesz dual system $\langle L_\infty(\mu), L_1(\mu)\rangle$ is a symmetric Riesz dual system.
   [HINT: Use the fact that $(L_\infty)\tilde{_n} = L_1$.]

4. This exercise presents some examples of utility functions on $\mathcal{R}_\infty$—the vector space of all real-valued sequences. The product topology τ on $\mathcal{R}_\infty$ is an order continuous locally convex-solid topology and $(\mathcal{R}_\infty, \tau)$ is a Fréchet lattice. We know that $(\mathcal{R}_\infty, \tau)'$ consists of all sequences that are eventually zero.

   Let $\mathcal{F}$ denote the collection of all strictly monotone, strictly concave and continuous functions $u\colon [0,\infty) \to \mathcal{R}$ with $u(0) = 0$—for instance, if $u(x) = \frac{x}{1+x}$ and $v(x) = 1 - e^{-\beta x^\alpha}$ ($\beta > 0$; $\alpha \geq 1$), then $u, v \in \mathcal{F}$. Now consider a uniformly bounded sequence $\{u_n\}$ of $\mathcal{F}$, i.e., there exists some $M > 0$ such that $u_n(x) \leq M$ holds for all n and each $x \in [0,\infty)$. Also, let $\{\lambda_n\}$ be a sequence of strictly positive real numbers such that $\sum_{n=1}^{\infty} \lambda_n < \infty$ and define $U\colon \mathcal{R}_\infty^+ \longrightarrow \mathcal{R}$ by

$$U(x_1, x_2, \ldots) = \sum_{n=1}^{\infty} \lambda_n u_n(x_n), \quad (x_1, x_2, \ldots) \in \mathcal{R}_\infty^+ .$$

   Establish the following properties for the utility function U.

   a) U is strictly monotone, strictly concave and τ-continuous; and
   b) U is not uniformly τ-proper.

5. Study the uniform properness property for the preferences defined by the utility functions in Examples 3.6.3 and 3.6.4.

6. This exercise presents another example showing that in the infinite dimensional case demand functions need not exist even when the order interval $[0,\omega]$ is compact. Consider the symmetric Riesz dual system $\langle \ell_2, \ell_2 \rangle$ and define the utility function $u\colon \ell_2^+ \longrightarrow \mathcal{R}$ by

$$u(x_1, x_2, \ldots) = \sum_{i=1}^{\infty} \left(\tfrac{2}{3}\right)^{\frac{i}{2}} \sqrt{x_i} .$$

   Also, let $\omega = \left(\frac{3}{2}, \frac{3}{2^2}, \frac{3}{2^3}, \ldots\right)$ and $\mathbf{p} = \left(\frac{1}{2}, \frac{1}{2^2}, \frac{1}{2^3}, \ldots\right)$.

   a) Show that the order interval $[0,\omega]$ is norm compact.
   b) Show that the price $\mathbf{p}$ is strictly positive.
   c) Show that the utility function u is strictly monotone, strictly concave and norm continuous.
   d) Show that the preference relation represented by the utility function u does not have any maximal element in the budget set

$$\mathcal{B} = \{\mathbf{x} = (x_1, x_2, \ldots) \in \ell_2^+ \colon\ \mathbf{p} \cdot \mathbf{x} \leq \mathbf{p} \cdot \omega = 1\} .$$

   [HINT: If $\mathbf{x}_n = (0, \ldots, 0, 2^n, 0, 0, \ldots)$, where the number 2^n occupies the nth position, then $\mathbf{x}_n \in \mathcal{B}$ and $u(\mathbf{x}_n) = \left(\frac{4}{3}\right)^{\frac{n}{2}}$ holds.]

CHAPTER 4:

PRODUCTION WITH INFINITELY MANY COMMODITIES

The existence and optimality of competitive equilibria in pure exchange economies with finitely many agents and infinitely many commodities was extensively investigated in the previous chapter. We now extend this analysis to production economies. Equilibrium analysis is technically more demanding for production economies, than for exchange economies, even in the finite dimensional case. In the standard Arrow–Debreu model, the feasible (or attainable) sets of agent's consumption plans or production plans are shown to be compact as a consequence of economically defensible assumptions on tastes and technology. In the infinite dimensional analysis, we, in essence, must assume compactness of the relevant sets.

The seminal paper on production economies in infinite-dimensional commodity space is again due to T. F. Bewley [16] where the commodity space is L_∞. An essential feature in the model examined by Bewley (which extends the classical Arrow–Debreu finite dimensional model discussed in Chapter 1) is that the positive cone has a non-empty interior. As observed earlier in our analysis, many important commodity spaces such as L_2, L_1, and the space $\mathrm{ca}(X)$ of all the countably additive measures on a compact Hausdorff topological space X, do not enjoy this property. Consequently, in these spaces some additional conditions must be placed on preferences and technologies to bound the marginal rates of substitution and the marginal rates of transformation in production. Hence, the general case requires more complex methods, and stronger assumptions on both individual household characteristics and the aggregate characteristics of the technology.

A. Mas-Colell [47] building on his previous contributions to the literature on exchange economies with infinite-dimensional commodity spaces, has investigated the existence and supportability of Pareto optima in production economies with infinite-dimensional commodity spaces where the positive cone has an empty interior. This generalizes the work of G. Debreu [22] who assumes that the positive cone has a non-empty interior. A. Mas-Colell's approach is to extend his notion of uniform properness of preferences to uniform properness of technologies. The intuitions one should have about uniform properness is that it bounds the marginal rates of substitution and transformation. W. R. Zame's paper [71] gives several examples of non-existence of equilibria where either the marginal rates of substitution or the marginal rates of transformation is unbounded. In addition, W. R. Zame proves the existence of competitive equilibria in production economies for a large class of normed Riesz spaces. S. F. Richard has also established the existence of equilibria in production economies with a Riesz space of commodities [55].

The principal economic model in this chapter is the now standard private ownership model of Arrow–Debreu where households hold limited liability shares in firms, entitling them to a share of the firm's profit. The firms, in turn, take market prices as fixed and maximize profits subject to their technology. In this chapter we present the theory of existence and optimality of Walrasian equilibrium in production economies with a finite number of households and firms, and infinitely many commodities. This is a continuation of the investigation of Edgeworth equilibria due to the authors [3]. Our first major result (Theorem 4.2.7) proves the existence of a core allocation for a compact economy. Compact economies satisfy quite weak conditions comparable to those in Bewley [16], but for economic models with Riesz dual systems of commodities and prices. In particular, we do not assume that the positive cone of the commodity space has a non-empty interior.

To demonstrate the existence of Edgeworth equilibria, each agent's consumption set is assumed to be the positive cone and the preferences are assumed to be strictly monotone. These assumptions are needed to show that in every replica of the economy, there exists a core allocation with the equal treatment property. To compensate for the emptiness of the interior of the positive cone, we must assume that the firm's technology is proper. Using the notion of uniformly proper economies, the next major result (Theorem 4.3.5) is that in a uniformly proper economy, every Edgeworth equilibrium can be supported as a quasiequilibrium. In addition, we show that Walrasian equilibrium exist for uniformly proper compact economies. We, also, present Mas-Colell's results [47] extending the Debreu versions of the welfare theorems. Recall that the Debreu versions of the two fundamental theorems of welfare economics can be stated (under appropriate assumptions) as follows.

The First Welfare Theorem: *An allocation which is supported by a non-zero price (in particular a Walrasian equilibrium) is Pareto optimal.*

The Second Welfare Theorem: *A Pareto optimal allocation can be supported by a non-zero price.*

Finally, in the absence of uniform properness, the best one can expect is that a weakly Pareto optimal allocation can be approximately supported by prices. This was first demonstrated in the works of M. A. Khan and R. Vohra [39] and C. D. Aliprantis and O. Burkinshaw [9]. We shall show that in production economies with infinitely many commodities, the notion of "approximate supportability" characterizes the weakly Pareto optimal allocations. Here, we do not require agent's characteristics to be proper nor the interior of the positive cone of the commodity space to be non-empty.

4.1. THE MODEL OF A PRODUCTION ECONOMY

In the economic model for a production economy, the commodity price duality will be described by a Riesz dual system $\langle E, E' \rangle$. The Riesz space E will always represent the commodity space and the Riesz space E' will be the price space. The production model will consist of m consumers indexed by i and k production firms indexed by j.

The characteristics that describe the production economy are as follows.

1. Consumers

There are m consumers indexed by i such that:

a) Each consumer i has E^+ as her consumption set.

b) Each consumer i has an initial endowment $\omega_i > 0$. As usual, the total endowment will be denoted by ω, i.e., $\omega = \sum_{i=1}^{m} \omega_i$.

c) The preferences of each consumer i are represented by a monotone quasi-concave utility function $u_i: E^+ \longrightarrow \mathcal{R}$.

d) There is a locally convex-solid topology τ on E consistent with the dual system $\langle E, E' \rangle$ for which every utility function u_i is τ-continuous. (Equivalently, we can say that every utility function is continuous for the absolute Mackey topology $|\tau|(E, E')$; this implies, of course, that every utility function is Mackey continuous.)

2. Producers

There are k production firms indexed by j. Each production firm is characterized by its production set Y_j, the elements of which are called the *production plans* for the producer. For a production plan $y = y^+ - y^- \in Y_j$ the negative part y^- is interpreted as the input and the positive part y^+ as the output. The production sets are assumed to satisfy the following property.

e) Each production set Y_j is a weakly closed convex set and $Y_j \cap E^+ = \{0\}$.

The above properties will characterize the production economies in this chapter. Formally, we have the following general definition of a production economy.

Definition 4.1.1. *A production economy $\mathcal{E}$ is a 3-tuple*

$$\mathcal{E} = \big(\langle E, E'\rangle,\ \{\omega_i, u_i\}_{i=1}^m,\ \{Y_j\}_{j=1}^k\big),$$

where

α) the Riesz dual system $\langle E, E'\rangle$ represents the commodity-price duality;
*β) each consumer i has the characteristics (ω_i, u_i) satisfying property (**1**) above; and*
γ) there are k producers indexed by j each of whom has a production set Y_j.

In the private ownership model of Arrow–Debreu the households hold limited liability shares in firms entitling them to a share of the firm's profit. The model for a private ownership production economy is now defined as follows.

Definition 4.1.2. *A private ownership production economy $\mathcal{E}$ is a 4-tuple*

$$\mathcal{E} = \big(\langle E, E'\rangle,\ \{\omega_i, u_i\}_{i=1}^m,\ \{Y_j\}_{j=1}^k,\ \{\theta_{ij}\colon i = 1, \ldots, m;\ j = 1, \ldots, k\}\big),$$

where

α) The Riesz dual system $\langle E, E'\rangle$ represents the commodity-price duality.
*β) There are m consumers indexed by i such that each consumer has a strictly monotone preference $\succeq_i$ and the characteristics (ω_i, u_i) satisfying property (**1**) above.*
γ) There are k producers indexed by j each of whom has a production set Y_j.
δ) The economy is a private ownership economy. That is for each (i, j) the real number θ_{ij} represents the share of consumer i to the profit of producer j; $0 \le \theta_{ij} \le 1$ holds for all i and j and $\sum_{i=1}^m \theta_{ij} = 1$ for all $j = 1, \ldots, k$.

It should be noted that by assigning the production sets $Y_j = \{0\}$ and arbitrary shares, every exchange economy can be considered as a private ownership production economy with any desired number of producers.

We remind the reader that if in a private ownership production economy the prevailing price vector is $p \in E'$ and each producer j chooses a production plan y_j, then the *income* of the ith consumer is

$$w_i(p) = p \cdot \omega_i + \sum_{j=1}^{m} \theta_{ij} p \cdot y_j .$$

4.2. EDGEWORTH EQUILIBRIA AND THE CORE

The objective of this section is to study core allocations in production economies. So, for our discussion $\mathcal{E}$ will denote an arbitrary (private ownership or not) production economy as introduced in Section 4.1. We start with the definition of the *aggregate production set* for a production economy.

> **Definition 4.2.1.** *If $\mathcal{E}$ is a production economy, then the non-empty and convex set*
> $$Y = Y_1 + \cdots + Y_k$$
> *is called the* **aggregate production set** *of $\mathcal{E}$.*

An (m+k)-tuple $(x_1, \ldots, x_m, y_1, \ldots, y_k)$, where $x_i \in E^+$ for $i = 1, \ldots, m$ and $y_j \in Y_j$ for $j = 1, \ldots, k$, is said to be an **allocation** whenever

$$\sum_{i=1}^{m} x_i = \sum_{i=1}^{m} \omega_i + \sum_{j=1}^{k} y_j .$$

The set of all allocations will be denoted—as before—by $\mathcal{A}$. That is,

$$\mathcal{A} = \Big\{(x_1, \ldots, x_m, y_1, \ldots, y_k)\colon\ x_i \in E^+,\ y_j \in Y_j \text{ and } \sum_{i=1}^{m} x_i = \sum_{i=1}^{m} \omega_i + \sum_{j=1}^{k} y_j \Big\} .$$

It should be obvious that the set $\mathcal{A}$ of all allocations is a convex and weakly closed subset of E^{m+k}.

A commodity bundle $x \in E^+$ is said to be *feasible* for the ith consumer whenever there exists an allocation $(x_1, \ldots, x_m, y_1, \ldots, y_k)$ with $x_i = x$. Similarly, a production plan $y \in Y_j$ is said to be *feasible* for the jth producer whenever there exists an allocation $(x_1, \ldots, x_m, y_1, \ldots, y_k)$ such that $y_j = y$. The feasible consumption and production sets are defined as follows.

Definition 4.2.2. *The* **feasible consumption set** $\hat{X}_i$ *of the* i^{th} *consumer is the convex set of all of its feasible consumption bundles, i.e.,*

$$\hat{X}_i = \{x \in E^+ \colon \exists\ (x_1, \ldots, x_m, y_1, \ldots, y_k) \in \mathcal{A} \ \text{ such that } \ x_i = x\}.$$

Similarly, the **feasible production set** $\hat{Y}_j$ *for the* j^{th} *producer is the convex set of all of its feasible production plans, i.e.,*

$$\hat{Y}_j = \{y \in Y_j \colon \exists\ (x_1, \ldots, x_m, y_1, \ldots, y_k) \in \mathcal{A} \ \text{ such that } \ y_j = y\}.$$

In order to discuss the properties of the feasible consumption and production sets we need a mathematical result. (Recall that a Riesz dual system $\langle E, E' \rangle$ is said to be symmetric whenever the order intervals of E are weakly compact.)

Lemma 4.2.3. *Assume that* $\langle E, E' \rangle$ *is a symmetric Riesz dual system. If* A *is a relatively weakly compact subset of* E^+, *then* sol(A)—*the solid hull of* A—*is also a relatively weakly compact subset of* E.

Proof. Since $\langle E, E' \rangle$ is a symmetric Riesz dual system, we know that E "sits" as an ideal in E''; see [8, Theorem 11.13, p. 170].

Now let A be a relatively weakly compact subset of E^+, and let

$$\text{sol}(A) = \{x \in E \colon \exists\ y \in A \ \text{ with } \ |x| \le y\}.$$

Then A is a $\sigma(E'', E')$-bounded subset of E'' and therefore sol(A) is likewise a $\sigma(E'', E')$-bounded subset of E''. Hence, if B denotes the $\sigma(E'', E')$-closure of sol(A) in E'', then B is a $\sigma(E'', E')$-compact subset of E''. We claim that B is a subset of E. If this is established, then—since $\sigma(E'', E')$ and $\sigma(E, E')$ agree on E—it will follow that B is a weakly compact subset of E, and consequently that sol(A) is a relatively weakly compact subset of E.

To see that B is a subset of E, let $\{x_\alpha\} \subseteq$ sol(A) satisfy $x_\alpha \xrightarrow{\sigma(E'', E')} x''$ in E''. For each α choose some $y_\alpha \in A$ such that $-y_\alpha \le x_\alpha \le y_\alpha$. Since A is relatively weakly compact in E, we can assume (by passing to a subnet) that $y_\alpha \xrightarrow{w} y$ holds in E. The latter and $-y_\alpha \le x_\alpha \le y_\alpha$ for all α imply $-y \le x'' \le y$. Since E is an ideal of E'' (and $y \in E$), it follows that $x'' \in E$. Thus, $B \subseteq E$ holds, and the proof of the theorem is finished. ■

Now we can state some of the basic properties of the feasible consumption and production sets.

Theorem 4.2.4. *For a production economy with a symmetric Riesz dual system the following statements hold.*

1. *If all production sets are order bounded from above, then each feasible production set is weakly compact.*
2. *If each feasible production set is weakly compact, then the set* $(Y+\omega)\cap E^+$ *is weakly compact—where* $Y = Y_1 + \cdots + Y_k$ *is the aggregate production set.*
3. *If* $(Y+\omega)\cap E^+$ *is weakly compact, then the feasible consumption sets* $\hat{X}_i$ *are all weakly compact subsets of* E^+.

Proof. (1) Pick some $a \in E^+$ such that $z \in Y_j\,(j = 1,\dots,k)$ implies $z \le a$. Let $y \in \hat{Y}_j$. Choose an allocation $(x_1,\dots,x_m,y_1,\dots,y_k)$ with $y_j = y$. Then, we have

$$0 \le y^- \le \sum_{j=1}^{k} y_j^- + \sum_{i=1}^{m} x_i = \sum_{j=1}^{k} y_j^+ + \omega \le ka + \omega = b \in E^+\,,$$

and so

$$-b \le -y^- \le y^+ - y^- = y \le a \le b\,.$$

Therefore, $\hat{Y}_j \subseteq [-b,b]$. Since the order interval $[-b,b]$ is weakly compact, we infer that $\hat{Y}_j$ is relatively weakly compact. Thus, in order to establish that $\hat{Y}_j$ is weakly compact, it suffices to show that $\hat{Y}_j$ is weakly closed.

To this end, let $\{y^\alpha\} \subseteq \hat{Y}_j$ satisfy $y^\alpha \xrightarrow{w} y$ in E. For each α pick an allocation $(x_1^\alpha,\dots,x_m^\alpha,y_1^\alpha,\dots,y_k^\alpha)$ with $y_j^\alpha = y^\alpha$. Since each $\hat{Y}_j$ is relatively weakly compact, by passing to an appropriate subnet, we can assume that $y_j^\alpha \xrightarrow{w} y_j \in Y_j$ holds for each j. From

$$0 \le x_i^\alpha \le \sum_{r=1}^{m} x_r^\alpha = \sum_{j=1}^{k} y_j^\alpha + \omega \in \hat{Y}_1 + \cdots + \hat{Y}_k + \omega\,,$$

we see that each x_i^α belongs—by Lemma 4.2.3—to the relatively weakly compact set $\mathrm{sol}[(\hat{Y}_1+\cdots+\hat{Y}_k+\omega)\cap E^+]$. Thus, each net $\{x_i^\alpha\}$ has a weakly convergent subnet, and so (by passing to an appropriate subnet again), we can assume that $x_i^\alpha \xrightarrow{w} x_i \in E^+$ holds for each i. From

$$\sum_{i=1}^{m} x_i^\alpha = \sum_{i=1}^{m} \omega_i + \sum_{j=1}^{k} y_j^\alpha\,,$$

we get $\sum_{i=1}^{m} x_i = \sum_{i=1}^{m} \omega_i + \sum_{j=1}^{k} y_j$. This implies $y \in \hat{Y}_j$, and so $\hat{Y}_j$ is a weakly closed set, as desired.

(2) Note that

$$(Y+\omega)\cap E^+ \subseteq (\hat{Y}_1 + \cdots + \hat{Y}_k + \omega)\cap E^+\,.$$

Therefore, $(Y+\omega)\cap E^+$ is a relatively weakly compact set.

Now assume that a net $\{(y_1^\alpha + \cdots + y_k^\alpha + \omega)\}$ of $(Y+\omega)\cap E^+$ satisfies

$$y_1^\alpha + \cdots + y_k^\alpha + \omega \xrightarrow{w} z\,.$$

Since $\{y_j^\alpha\} \subseteq \hat{Y}_j$ holds for all j, we can assume that $y_j^\alpha \xrightarrow{w} y_j \in Y_j$ holds for all j. This implies $z = y_1 + \cdots + y_k + \omega \in (Y+\omega) \cap E^+$, and so $(Y+\omega) \cap E^+$ is weakly closed. Consequently, $(Y+\omega) \cap E^+$ is weakly compact.

(3) Fix some i, and let $x \in \hat{X}_i$. Pick an allocation $(x_1, \ldots, x_m, y_1, \ldots, y_k)$ with $x_i = x$. From

$$0 \le x \le \sum_{r=1}^{m} x_r = \omega + \sum_{j=1}^{k} y_j \in (Y+\omega) \cap E^+ ,$$

we see that $x \in \mathrm{sol}[(Y+\omega) \cap E^+]$, and so $\hat{X}_i \subseteq \mathrm{sol}[(Y+\omega) \cap E^+]$. Since the set $\mathrm{sol}[(Y+\omega) \cap E^+]$ is a relatively weakly compact subset of E (Lemma 4.2.3), it follows that each $\hat{X}_i$ is a relatively weakly compact subset of E^+.

Next, we assume that a net $\{x^\alpha\}$ of $\hat{X}_i$ satisfies $x^\alpha \xrightarrow{w} x$. For each α pick an allocation $(x_1^\alpha, \ldots, x_m^\alpha, y_1^\alpha, \ldots, y_k^\alpha)$ with $x_i^\alpha = x^\alpha$. By the preceding conclusion, we can assume (by passing to a subnet) that $x_r^\alpha \xrightarrow{w} x_r$ holds for each r. Let $y^\alpha = \sum_{j=1}^k y_j^\alpha$. From $y^\alpha + \omega = \sum_{j=1}^k y_j^\alpha + \omega \in (Y+\omega) \cap E^+$, we can assume (by passing to a subnet again!) that $y^\alpha \xrightarrow{w} z \in Y$ holds. If $z = z_1 + \cdots + z_k \in Y$, then $(x_1, \ldots, x_m, z_1, \ldots, z_k)$ is an allocation, and so $x = x_i \in \hat{X}_i$. Thus, $\hat{X}_i$ is weakly closed, and hence each $\hat{X}_i$ is a weakly compact subset of E^+. ■

We now come to the definition of a compact production economy.

Definition 4.2.5. *A production economy is said to be a* **compact production economy** *whenever*

1) *its Riesz dual system is symmetric; and*
2) *if $Y = Y_1 + \cdots + Y_k$ is its aggregate production set, then $(Y+\omega) \cap E^+$ is a weakly compact set.*

You should keep in mind that in a compact production economy all feasible consumption sets are (by Theorem 4.2.4) weakly compact subsets of E^+.

Now let $\mathcal{E}$ be a private ownership production economy and let S be a coalition of consumers. Then a subset $\{z_i\colon\ i \in S\}$ of E^+ is said to be a *feasible assignment for the coalition* S whenever there exist production plans $h_j \in Y_j\, (j = 1, \ldots, k)$ such that

$$\sum_{i \in S} z_i = \sum_{i \in S} \omega_i + \sum_{j=1}^{k} \Big(\sum_{i \in S} \theta_{ij} \Big) h_j .$$

In case $\mathcal{E}$ is a general production economy, then a subset $\{z_i\colon\ i \in S\}$ of E^+ is said to be a *feasible assignment for the coalition* S whenever there exist production plans $h_j \in Y_j\, (j = 1, \ldots, k)$ such that

$$\sum_{i \in S} z_i = \sum_{i \in S} \omega_i + \sum_{j=1}^{k} h_j .$$

A coalition S **improves upon an allocation** $(x_1, \ldots, x_m, y_1, \ldots, y_k)$ whenever there exists a feasible assignment $\{z_i\colon\ i \in S\}$ for S such that $z_i \succ_i x_i$ holds for each $i \in S$.

It should be noted that in a private ownership production economy a coalition S improves upon an allocation $(x_1, \ldots, y_m, y_1, \ldots, y_k)$ if and only if there exist consumption bundles $z_i \in E^+ \, (i \in S)$ and production plans $h_j \in Y_j \, (j = 1, \ldots, k)$ such that

i) $z_i \succ_i x_i$ for each $i \in S$; and

ii) $\displaystyle\sum_{i\in S} z_i \le \sum_{i\in S} \omega_i + \sum_{j=1}^{k} \Big(\sum_{i\in S} \theta_{ij}\Big) h_j$.

As usual, a **core allocation** is an allocation that cannot be improved upon by any coalition. The **core** Core($\mathcal{E}$) of a production economy $\mathcal{E}$ is the set of all core allocations. *Do core allocations exist?* The answer is yes for compact production economies. The discussion below will clarify the situation.

Lemma 4.2.6. *If the Riesz dual system of a private ownership production economy is symmetric and each production set is order bounded from above, then its core is non-empty.*

Proof. Define an m-person game V by

$$V(S) = \{(z_1, \ldots, z_m) \in \mathcal{R}^m\colon \text{ There exists a feasible assignment } \{x_i\colon\ i \in S\} \text{ with } u_i(x_i) \ge z_i \text{ for all } i \in S\}.$$

We claim that the m-person game V satisfies the hypotheses of Scarf's theorem (Theorem 1.5.9). Indeed, assumptions (b) and (c) of Scarf's theorem are trivially true. Fix some $a \in E^+$ such that $y \in Y_j$ $(j = 1, \ldots, k)$ implies $y \le a$. To verify assumption (d), observe that $\hat{X}_i \subseteq [0, \omega + ka]$, holds. Thus, if $\{x_i\colon\ i \in S\}$ is a feasible assignment, then we have $x_i \in \hat{X}_i \subseteq [0, \omega + ka]$. Since each utility function is monotone, it follows that $V(S)$ is bounded from above in $\mathcal{R}^S$.

The closedness of the sets $V(S)$ and the balancedness of the game need special verification. Let S be a coalition. Since $\big(u_1(\omega_1), \ldots, u_m(\omega_m)\big) \in V(S)$, we see that $V(S)$ is non-empty. Also, since $V(S)$ is bounded from above relative to $\mathcal{R}^S$, we infer that $V(S)$ is a proper subset of $\mathcal{R}^m$. To see that $V(S)$ is closed, assume that a net $\{(z_1^\alpha, \ldots, z_m^\alpha)\}$ of $V(S)$ satisfies $(z_1^\alpha, \ldots, z_m^\alpha) \longrightarrow (z_1, \ldots, z_m)$ in $\mathcal{R}^m$. For each α pick $x_i^\alpha \in E^+$ $(i \in S)$ and $y_j^\alpha \in Y_j$ $(j = 1, \ldots, k)$ such that

$$\sum_{i\in S} x_i^\alpha = \sum_{i\in S} \omega_i + \sum_{j=1}^{k} \Big(\sum_{i\in S} \theta_{ij}\Big) y_j^\alpha \quad \text{and} \quad z_i^\alpha \le u_i(x_i^\alpha) \quad \text{for all } i \in S.$$

In case $\sum_{i\in S} \theta_{ij} = 0$, we can assume without loss of generality that $y_j^\alpha = 0$. Since for each j we have $(\sum_{i\in S} \theta_{ij}) y_j^\alpha \in \hat{Y}_j$ and $\hat{Y}_j$ is weakly compact (Theorem 4.2.4(1)), it follows—by passing to a subnet if necessary—that $y_j^\alpha \longrightarrow y_j \in Y_j$ holds for all $j = 1, \ldots, k$. Also, $0 \le x_i^\alpha \le \omega + ka$ holds for all $i \in S$, and so by the weak compactness of the order interval $[0, \omega + ka]$—by passing to a subnet again—we can assume that $x_i^\alpha \longrightarrow x_i \in E^+$ holds for all $i \in S$. Consequently,

$$\sum_{i \in S} x_i = \sum_{i \in S} \omega_i + \sum_{j=1}^{k} \Big(\sum_{i \in S} \theta_{ij}\Big) y_j .$$

By Lemma 1.2.4 each utility function is weakly upper semicontinuous. From Exercise 8 of Section 1.2 (p. 18), it follows that

$$z_i = \lim_\alpha z_i^\alpha \le \limsup_\alpha u_i(x_i^\alpha) \le u_i(x_i)$$

for each $i \in S$, and so $(z_1, \ldots, z_m) \in V(S)$. Hence, each $V(S)$ is a closed subset of $\mathcal{R}^m$.

To see that the game is balanced, consider a balanced family $\mathcal{B}$ of coalitions with weights $\{w_S\colon\ S \in \mathcal{B}\}$. That is, $\sum_{S \in \mathcal{B}_i} w_S = 1$ holds for all i, where $\mathcal{B}_i = \{S \in \mathcal{B}\colon\ i \in S\}$. Now let $(z_1, \ldots, z_m) \in \bigcap_{S \in \mathcal{B}} V(S)$. We have to show that $(z_1, \ldots, z_m) \in V(\{1, \ldots, m\})$.

Let $S \in \mathcal{B}$. Since $(z_1, \ldots, z_m) \in V(S)$, there exist $x_i^S \in E^+$ $(i \in S)$ and $y_j^S \in Y_j$ $(j = 1, \ldots, k)$ with

$$\sum_{i \in S} x_i^S = \sum_{i \in S} \omega_i + \sum_{j=1}^{k} \Big(\sum_{i \in S} \theta_{ij}\Big) y_j^S$$

and $u_i(x_i^S) \ge z_i$ for all $i \in S$. Now put

$$x_i = \sum_{S \in \mathcal{B}_i} w_S x_i^S \in E^+ ,\ i = 1, \ldots, m$$

and

$$y_j = \sum_{S \in \mathcal{B}_i} \sum_{i \in S} w_S \theta_{ij} y_j^S = \sum_{i=1}^{m} \theta_{ij} \Big(\sum_{S \in \mathcal{B}_i} w_s y_j^S\Big) \in Y_j ,\ j = 1, \ldots, k .$$

Since each x_i is a convex combination, it follows from the quasi-concavity of u_i that $z_i \le u_i(x_i)$ holds for each $i = 1, \ldots, m$. Moreover, we have

$$\begin{aligned}
\sum_{i=1}^{m} x_i &= \sum_{i=1}^{m} \sum_{S \in \mathcal{B}_i} w_S x_i^S = \sum_{S \in \mathcal{B}} w_S \Big(\sum_{i \in S} x_i^S\Big) \\
&= \sum_{S \in \mathcal{B}} w_S \Big[\sum_{i \in S} \omega_i + \sum_{j=1}^{k} \Big(\sum_{i \in S} \theta_{ij}\Big) y_j^S\Big] \\
&= \sum_{i=1}^{m} \sum_{S \in \mathcal{B}_i} w_S \omega_i + \sum_{j=1}^{k} \sum_{S \in \mathcal{B}} \sum_{i \in S} w_S \theta_{ij} y_j^S = \sum_{i=1}^{m} \omega_i + \sum_{j=1}^{k} y_j ,
\end{aligned}$$

which proves that $(z_1, \ldots, z_m) \in V(\{1, \ldots, m\})$, as desired.

Now by Scarf's theorem the m-person game V has a non-empty core (that is, the set $V(\{1,\ldots,m\}) \setminus \bigcup_{S\in\mathcal{N}} \mathrm{Int}V(S)$ is non-empty, where $\mathcal{N}$ denotes the set of all coalitions). Let $(z_1,\ldots,z_m)$ be a core vector. Pick $x_i \in E^+$ $(i = 1,\ldots,m)$ and $y_j \in Y_j$ $(j = 1,\ldots,k)$ such that

a) $\sum_{i=1}^m x_i = \sum_{i=1}^m \omega_i + \sum_{j=1}^k y_j$; and

b) $u_i(x_i) \geq z_i$ for each $i = 1,\ldots,m$.

Clearly, $(x_1,\ldots,x_m,y_1,\ldots,y_k)$ is an allocation, and we claim that it is a core allocation. To see the latter, assume by way of contradiction that there exists a coalition S and a feasible assignment $\{x_i^*\colon\ i \in S\}$ satisfying $x_i^* \succ_i x_i$ for all $i \in S$. Then $u_i(x_i^*) > u_i(x_i) \geq z_i$ holds for each $i \in S$, and from this, we see that $(z_1,\ldots,z_m) \in \mathrm{Int}V(S)$, which is a contradiction. Hence, $(x_1,\ldots,x_m,y_1,\ldots,y_k)$ is a core allocation, and therefore the economy has a non-empty core. ∎

We are now in the position to establish that every compact private ownership production economy has always a core allocation.

Theorem 4.2.7. *The core of a compact private ownership production economy is non-empty and weakly closed.*

Proof. Put $\hat{Y} = (Y + \omega) \cap E^+ - \omega$, where $Y = Y_1 + \cdots + Y_k$ is the aggregate production set of a compact private ownership production economy $\mathcal{E}$, and note that $\hat{Y}$ is a weakly compact set. Also, define the set $\hat{\mathcal{A}}$ by

$$\hat{\mathcal{A}} = \Big\{(x_1,\ldots,x_m,y) \in E^{m+1}\colon\ y = \sum_{j=1}^k y_j \ \text{ with } \ (x_1,\ldots,x_m,y_1,\ldots,y_k) \in \mathcal{A}\Big\}.$$

Clearly, $\hat{\mathcal{A}} \subseteq \hat{X}_1 \times \cdots \times \hat{X}_m \times \hat{Y}$ and so from Theorem 4.2.4(3), it follows that $\hat{\mathcal{A}}$ is a weakly compact subset of E^{m+1}. The proof of the theorem will be completed in two steps.

1. *The core is non-empty.*

For each $a \in E^+$ we shall denote by $\mathcal{E}_a$ the private ownership production economy which is obtained from the original production economy $\mathcal{E}$ by replacing each production set Y_j by the production set $Y_j^a = \{y \in Y_j\colon\ y \leq a\}$; the set Y_j^a is represented geometrically by the darkened region in Figure 4.2-1.

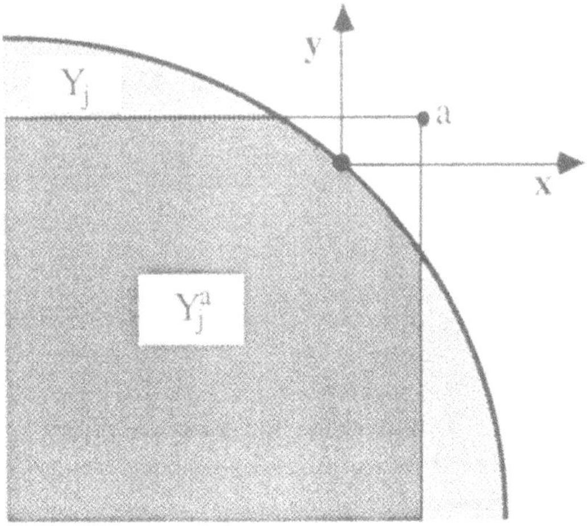

Fig. 4.2-1

By Lemma 4.2.6, we know that $\text{Core}(\mathcal{E}_a) \neq \emptyset$. For each $a \in E^+$ pick some allocation $(x_1^a, \ldots, x_m^a, y_1^a, \ldots, y_k^a)$ in the core of $\mathcal{E}_a$ and let $y^a = \sum_{j=1}^k y_j^a$. Then $(x_1^a, \ldots, x_m^a, y^a)$ lies in $\hat{\mathcal{A}}$ for each $a \in E^+$. Since $\hat{\mathcal{A}}$ is weakly compact, the net $\{(x_1^a, \ldots, x_m^a, y^a)\colon\ a \in E^+\}$ has a weak accumulation point in $\hat{\mathcal{A}}$, say $(x_1, \ldots, x_m, y)$; clearly, $x_1 + \cdots + x_m = \omega + y$ and $y \in Y$. Pick $y_j \in Y_j\,(j = 1, \ldots, k)$ with $y = y_1 + \cdots + y_k$. We claim that the allocation $(x_1, \ldots, x_m, y_1, \ldots, y_k)$ is a core allocation for the production economy $\mathcal{E}$.

To see this, assume by way of contradiction that there exist a coalition S, consumption bundles $z_i \in E^+\,(i \in S)$ and production plans $h_j \in Y_j\,(j = 1, \ldots, k)$ such that

a) $z_i \succ_i x_i$ for all $i \in S$; and

b) $\displaystyle\sum_{i\in S} z_i = \sum_{i\in S} \omega_i + \sum_{j=1}^{k}\Big(\sum_{i\in S} \theta_{ij}\Big) h_j\,.$

Now note that for each $i \in S$ the set

$$V_i = \{(f_1, \ldots, f_m, g) \in \hat{\mathcal{A}}\colon\ f_i \succeq_i z_i\}$$

is a weakly closed subset of E^{m+1}, and so $V = \bigcup_{i\in S} V_i$ is also weakly closed. Thus, its complement $V^c = E^{m+1} \setminus V$ is weakly open. Since $(x_1, \ldots, x_m, y) \in V^c$ and $(x_1, \ldots, x_m, y)$ is a weak accumulation point of the net $\{(x_1^a, \ldots, x_m^a, y^a)\}_{a\in E^+}$, there exists some $a \geq \sum_{j=1}^k |h_j|$ such that $(x_1^a, \ldots, x_m^a, y^a) \in V^c$. Clearly, $h_j \in Y_j^a$ for each j. Also, $z_i \succ_i x_i^a$ holds for all $i \in S$, and so from (b), we conclude that $(x_1^a, \ldots, x_m^a, y_1^a, \ldots, y_k^a) \notin \text{Core}(\mathcal{E}_a)$, a contradiction. Therefore, the allocation $(x_1, \ldots, x_m, y_1, \ldots, y_k)$ is a core allocation for $\mathcal{E}$.

2. *The core is a weakly closed set.*

Denote by $\mathcal{C}$ the (non-empty) set of all core allocations, and let an allocation $(x_1, \ldots, x_m, y_1, \ldots, y_k)$ lie in the weak closure of $\mathcal{C}$. Assume by way of contradiction that there exist a coalition S, consumption bundles $z_i \in E^+$ $(i \in S)$ and production plans $h_j \in Y_j$ $(j = 1, \ldots, k)$ such that

$$z_i \succ_i x_i \quad \text{for all } i \in S \text{ and } \sum_{i \in S} z_i = \sum_{i \in S} \omega_i + \sum_{j=1}^{k} \Big(\sum_{i \in S} \theta_{ij}\Big) h_j .$$

For each $i \in S$ the set of allocations

$$W_i = \{(b_1, \ldots, b_m, g_1, \ldots, g_k) \in \mathcal{A}: \; b_i \succeq_i z_i\}$$

is a weakly closed subset of E^{m+k}. Thus, the set $W = \bigcup_{i \in S} W_i$ is weakly closed, and so its complement $W^c = E^{m+k} \setminus W$ is weakly open. Since $(x_1, \ldots, x_m, y_1, \ldots, y_k)$ belongs to W^c, we infer that $W^c \bigcap \mathcal{C} \neq \emptyset$. If $(b_1, \ldots, b_m, g_1, \ldots, g_k) \in W^c \bigcap \mathcal{C}$, then we have

$$z_i \succ_i b_i \quad \text{for all } i \in S \text{ and } \sum_{i \in S} z_i = \sum_{i \in S} \omega_i + \sum_{j=1}^{k} \Big(\sum_{i \in S} \theta_{ij}\Big) h_j ,$$

which contradicts the fact that $(b_1, \ldots, b_m, g_1, \ldots, g_k)$ is a core allocation. Hence, the allocation $(x_1, \ldots, x_m, y_1, \ldots, y_k)$ belongs to $\mathcal{C}$, and so $\mathcal{C}$ is weakly closed. ■

We continue with the introduction of the replication concept of a private ownership production economy. If n is a natural number, then the n-**fold replica** of a private ownership production economy $\mathcal{E}$ is a new private ownership production economy $\mathcal{E}_n$ with the following characteristics.

1. The production economy $\mathcal{E}_n$ has the same Riesz dual system $\langle E, E' \rangle$ as $\mathcal{E}$.
2. There are mn consumers indexed by (i, s) $(i = 1, \ldots, m;\; s = 1, \ldots, n)$ such that the consumers (i, s) $(s = 1, \ldots, n)$ are of the "same type" as the consumer i of $\mathcal{E}$. That is, each consumer (i, s) has:
   a) E^+ as a consumption set;
   b) an initial endowment ω_{is} equal to ω_i, i.e., $\omega_{is} = \omega_i$ (and so the total endowment of $\mathcal{E}_n$ is $\sum_{i=1}^{m} \sum_{s=1}^{n} \omega_{is} = n\omega$); and
   c) a utility function u_{is} equal to u_i, i.e., $u_{is} = u_i$.
3. There are kn producers indexed by (j, t) $(j = 1, \ldots, k;\; t = 1, \ldots, n)$ with the following properties.
   i) The production set of the (j, t) producer is Y_j, i.e., $Y_{jt} = Y_j$; and
   ii) The share θ_{isjt} of the (i, s) consumer to the profit of the (j, t) producer is

$$\theta_{isjt} = \begin{cases} 0, & \text{if } s \neq t; \\ \theta_{ij}, & \text{if } s = t. \end{cases}$$

Theorem 4.2.8. *Every replica of a compact private ownership production economy is itself a compact private ownership production economy.*

Proof. Let $\mathcal{E}$ be a compact private ownership production economy. If n is a natural number, then the aggregate production set of $\mathcal{E}_n$ is

$$Y_n^* = \sum_{j=1}^{k}\sum_{t=1}^{n} Y_{jt} = \sum_{j=1}^{k}\sum_{t=1}^{n} Y_j = nY$$

where $Y = Y_1 + \cdots + Y_k$ is the aggregate production set of $\mathcal{E}$. Therefore, we see that

$$(Y_n^* + n\omega) \cap E^+ = n\big[(Y + \omega) \cap E^+\big]$$

is a weakly compact subset of E^+. This implies that $\mathcal{E}_n$ is a compact private ownership production economy. ■

Now let $(x_1, \ldots, x_m, y_1, \ldots, y_k)$ be an allocation of a private ownership production economy $\mathcal{E}$. If n is a natural number, then by assigning the consumption bundle x_i to each consumer (i, s) (i.e., $x_{is} = x_i$ for $s = 1, \ldots, n$) and the production plan y_j to each producer (j, t) (i.e., $y_{jt} = y_j$ for $t = 1, \ldots, n$), it is easy to see that this assignment defines an allocation for the n-fold replica economy $\mathcal{E}_n$. Thus, every allocation of $\mathcal{E}$ defines (in the above manner) an allocation in every n-fold replica economy of $\mathcal{E}$. Any allocation of this type is known as an *equal treatment* allocation. The Edgeworth equilibria for production economies are now defined in the usual manner.

Definition 4.2.9. *An allocation in a private ownership production economy is said to be an* **Edgeworth equilibrium** *whenever it belongs to the core of every n-fold replica of the economy.*

Do Edgeworth equilibria exist? The final result of this section provides an affirmative answer.

Theorem 4.2.10. *In a compact private ownership production economy the set of all Edgeworth equilibria is a non-empty weakly closed subset of E^{m+k}.*

Proof. Let $\mathcal{E}$ be a compact private ownership production economy. For each n let

$$\mathcal{C}_n = \mathcal{A} \cap \text{Core}(\mathcal{E}_n),$$

where $\mathcal{E}_n$ is the n-fold replica of $\mathcal{E}$. Clearly, the set of all Edgeworth equilibria is precisely the set $\bigcap_{n=1}^{\infty} \mathcal{C}_n$. The proof will be based upon the following properties of the sets $\mathcal{C}_n$.

1. *Each $\mathcal{C}_n$ is non-empty.*

Note first that (by Theorem 4.2.8) the economy $\mathcal{E}_n$ is a compact economy and so by Theorem 4.2.7 we know that $\text{Core}(\mathcal{E}_n) \neq \emptyset$. Let

$$(x_{11}, \ldots, x_{1n}, x_{21}, \ldots, x_{2n}, \ldots, x_{m1}, \ldots, x_{mn}, y_{11}, \ldots, y_{1n}, \ldots, y_{k1}, \ldots, y_{kn})$$

be a core allocation for $\mathcal{E}_n$. Then, we claim that

$$x_{ir} \sim_i x_{is} \quad \text{for} \quad r,s = 1,\ldots,n \quad \text{and} \quad i = 1,\ldots,m\,,$$

i.e., no consumer prefers his bundle to that of another consumer of the same type.

To see this, note first that by rearranging the consumers of each type, we can suppose that $x_{is} \succeq_i x_{i1}$ holds for all i and s. Put

$$z_i = \tfrac{1}{n}\sum_{s=1}^{n} x_{is}\,, \quad i = 1,\ldots,m \quad \text{and} \quad y_j = \tfrac{1}{n}\sum_{t=1}^{n} y_{jt} \in Y_j\,, \quad j = 1,\ldots,k\,.$$

Then, we have

$$\sum_{i=1}^{m} z_i = \tfrac{1}{n}\sum_{i=1}^{m}\sum_{s=1}^{n} x_{is} = \tfrac{1}{n}\Big(\sum_{i=1}^{m}\sum_{s=1}^{n}\omega_{is} + \sum_{j=1}^{k}\sum_{t=1}^{n} y_{jt}\Big) = \omega + \sum_{j=1}^{k} y_j\,,$$

and so $(z_1,\ldots,z_m,y_1,\ldots,y_k) \in \mathcal{A}$. Also, by the convexity of the preferences, we see that $z_i \succeq_i x_{i1}$ holds for each $i = 1,\ldots,m$. Now assume by way of contradiction that there exists some (i,r) such that $x_{ir} \succ_i x_{i1}$. The latter, in view of the convexity of $\succeq_i$, implies (as in Lemma 1.6.13) $z_i \succ_i x_{i1}$. Now if each consumer $(i,1)$ is assigned the bundle z_i and each producer (j,t) chooses the production plan y_j (i.e., $y_{jt} = y_j$), then it is easy to see—by arguing as in the proof of Lemma 1.6.14—that $\{z_i\colon\ i = 1,\ldots,m\}$ is a feasible assignment for the coalition $\{(i,1)\colon\ i = 1,\ldots,m\}$ that improves upon the original core allocation, which is impossible. This contradiction establishes the validity of our claim.

Next, note that by the quasi-concavity of the utility functions we have $z_i \succeq_i x_{ir}$ for $r = 1,\ldots,n$ and $i = 1,\ldots,m$. The latter easily implies that the allocation $(z_1,\ldots,z_m,y_1,\ldots,y_k)$ belongs to $\mathcal{C}_n$, and thus $\mathcal{C}_n$ is a non-empty set.

2. *For each n we have $\mathcal{C}_{n+1} \subseteq \mathcal{C}_n$.*

This follows easily from the fact that if a coalition S of consumers of $\mathcal{E}_n$ improves upon an allocation of $\mathcal{A}$, then S also improves upon the same allocation in $\mathcal{E}_{n+1}$.

3. *Each $\mathcal{C}_n$ is weakly closed.*

This follows easily from the fact that $\mathcal{A}$ and Core($\mathcal{E}_n$) are both weakly closed sets.

4. *The set of Edgeworth equilibria is weakly closed.*

This follows from (3) by observing that the set of all Edgeworth equilibria is precisely the set $\bigcap_{n=1}^{\infty} \mathcal{C}_n$.

5. *Edgeworth equilibria exist.*

For each n define the set

$$\hat{\mathcal{C}}_n = \Big\{(x_1,\ldots,x_m,y) \in E^{m+1}\colon\ y = \sum_{j=1}^{k} y_j \quad \text{with} \quad (x_1,\ldots,x_m,y_1,\ldots,y_k) \in \mathcal{C}_n\Big\}\,.$$

Since each $\mathcal{C}_n$ is non-empty, we see that each $\hat{\mathcal{C}}_n$ is likewise non-empty. From the inclusion $\mathcal{C}_{n+1} \subseteq \mathcal{C}_n$, it follows that $\hat{\mathcal{C}}_{n+1} \subseteq \hat{\mathcal{C}}_n$. In addition, we claim that each $\hat{\mathcal{C}}_n$ is a weakly compact subset of E^{m+1}. To see this, note first that from

$$\hat{\mathcal{C}}_n \subseteq \hat{X}_1 \times \cdots \times \hat{X}_m \times \big[(Y+\omega)\cap E^+ - \omega\big]$$

and Theorem 4.2.4(3), we infer that each $\hat{\mathcal{C}}_n$ is a relatively weakly compact subset of E^{m+1}. Now let a net $\{(x_1^\alpha,\ldots,x_m^\alpha,y^\alpha)\} \subseteq \hat{\mathcal{C}}_n$ satisfy

$$(x_1^\alpha,\ldots,x_m^\alpha,y^\alpha) \xrightarrow{w} (x_1,\ldots,x_m,y)\,.$$

Pick $y_j^\alpha \in Y_j\,(j=1,\ldots,k)$ with $y^\alpha = \sum_{j=1}^k y_j^\alpha$ and $(x_1^\alpha,\ldots,x_m^\alpha,y_1^\alpha,\ldots,y_k^\alpha)$ in $\mathcal{C}_n$. An easy argument shows that there exist $y_j \in Y_j\,(j=1,\ldots,k)$ such that $y=\sum_{j=1}^k y_j$ and $(x_1,\ldots,x_m,y_1,\ldots,y_k) \in \mathcal{A}$. If $(x_1,\ldots,x_m,y_1,\ldots,y_k) \notin \mathcal{C}_n$, then some coalition S of the n-fold replica economy $\mathcal{E}_n$ improves upon the allocation $(x_1,\ldots,x_m,y_1,\ldots,y_k)$ in $\mathcal{E}_n$. Since $(x_1^\alpha,\ldots,x_m^\alpha,y^\alpha) \xrightarrow{w} (x_1,\ldots,x_m,y)$ and each set $\{z \in E^+\colon\ z \succ_i x_i\}$ is weakly open relative to E^+, it is easy to see that the coalition S improves upon $(x_1^\alpha,\ldots,x_m^\alpha,y_1^\alpha,\ldots,y_k^\alpha)$ in $\mathcal{E}_n$ for some α, which is a contradiction. Hence, $(x_1,\ldots,x_m,y) \in \hat{\mathcal{C}}_n$. This implies that $\hat{\mathcal{C}}_n$ is weakly closed, and hence weakly compact.

From the finite intersection property we have $\bigcap_{n=1}^\infty \hat{\mathcal{C}}_n \neq \emptyset$. Fix some element $(x_1,\ldots,x_m,y) \in \bigcap_{n=1}^\infty \hat{\mathcal{C}}_n$, and then pick $y_j \in Y_j\,(j=1,\ldots,k)$ with $y=\sum_{j=1}^k y_j$. We claim that the allocation $(x_1,\ldots,x_m,y_1,\ldots,y_k)$ is an Edgeworth equilibrium. To see this, assume by way of contradiction that $(x_1,\ldots,x_m,y_1,\ldots,y_k)$ can be improved upon by a coalition S in the r-fold replica economy. Since $(x_1,\ldots,x_m,y)$ is in $\hat{\mathcal{C}}_r$, there exist $h_j \in Y_j\,(j=1,\ldots,k)$ such that $(x_1,\ldots,x_m,h_1,\ldots,h_k) \in \mathcal{C}_r$, and an easy argument shows that $(x_1,\ldots,x_m,h_1,\ldots,h_k)$ can be improved upon by the coalition S in the r-fold replica of the economy, which is impossible. The proof of the theorem is now complete. ■

EXERCISES

1. Show that the weak compactness of $(Y+\omega)\cap E^+$ does not imply the weak compactness of the feasible production sets.
   [HINT: Consider the production economy with Riesz dual system $\langle \mathcal{R}^2,\mathcal{R}^2\rangle$ having one consumer with initial endowment $\omega=(1,1)$ and two producers with production sets $Y_1=Y_2=\{(x,y)\in\mathcal{R}^2\colon\ y\le -x\}$.]

2. Consider an allocation $(x_1,\ldots,x_m,y_1,\ldots,y_k)$ in a private ownership production economy with monotone preferences. Show that a coalition S improves

upon the allocation $(x_1, \ldots, x_m, y_1, \ldots, y_k)$ if and only if there exist consumption bundles $z_i \in E^+ (i \in S)$ and production plans $h_j (j = 1, \ldots, k)$ such that

a) $z_i \succ_i x_i$ holds for each $i \in S$; and

b) $\sum_{i \in S} z_i \leq \sum_{i \in S} \omega_i + \sum_{j=1}^{k} \Big(\sum_{i \in S} \theta_{ij} \Big) h_j$.

Prove a similar result for an arbitrary production economy.

3. Prove that the set $\hat{\mathcal{A}}$ defined in the proof of Theorem 4.2.7 is weakly compact.

4. Prove Theorem 4.2.7 for an arbitrary production economy.

5. Consider an allocation $(x_1, \ldots, x_m, y_1, \ldots, y_k)$ in a private ownership production economy. If the allocation $(x_1, \ldots, x_m, y_1, \ldots, y_k)$ is a Walrasian equilibrium, i.e., if there exists a non-zero price $p \in E'$ such that
   a) $x \succ_i x_i$ in E^+ implies $p \cdot x > p \cdot \omega_i + \sum_{j=1}^{k} \theta_{ij} p \cdot y_j$; and
   b) $p \cdot y_j = \max\{p \cdot y \colon\ y \in Y_j\}$ for each j,

   then show that $(x_1, \ldots, x_m, y_1, \ldots, y_k)$ is an Edgeworth equilibrium.

6. Formulate the notion of an r-fold replica production economy and show that every compact production economy has an Edgeworth equilibrium.

4.3. WALRASIAN EQUILIBRIA AND QUASIEQUILIBRIA

The main objective of this section is to establish for private ownership production economies the analogue of Theorem 3.4.6—that every Edgeworth equilibrium is a quasiequilibrium. To do this, we need some preliminary discussion.

We shall start our discussion by presenting the notion of uniform properness for production sets. The notion of uniform properness for production sets was introduced first by A. Mas-Colell [47]. Notions of properness for production sets were also presented by N. C. Yannelis and W. R. Zame [69] and W. R. Zame [71]. The definition of uniform properness for production sets below is due to S. F. Richard [55].

Definition 4.3.1. *A production set Y is said to be* **uniformly τ-proper** *whenever there exists a vector $w > 0$ and a convex τ-neighborhood W of zero such that the convex cone Γ generated by $w + W$, i.e., the cone*

$$\Gamma = \{\alpha(w + x)\colon\ \alpha > 0 \ \text{ and } \ x \in W\},$$

satisfies

$$(z + \Gamma) \cap \{y \in Y\colon\ y^+ \geq z^+\} = \emptyset$$

for all $z \notin Y$.

The geometrical interpretations of the sets involved in the above definition are depicted in Figure 4.3-1.

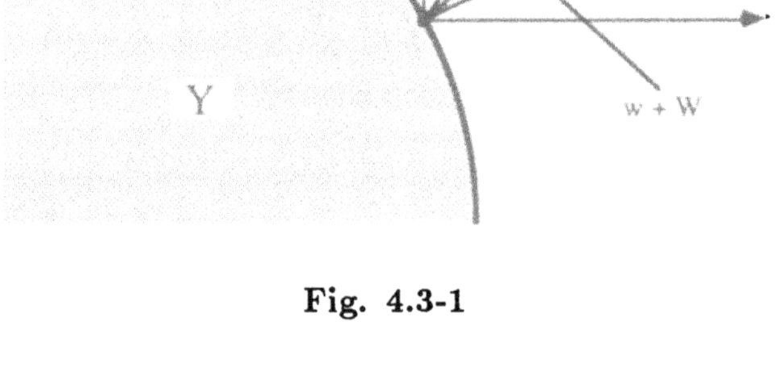

Fig. 4.3-1

Definition 4.3.2. *In a private ownership production economy the* **share set** *of consumer i is the convex set*

$$Z_i = \sum_{j=1}^{k} \theta_{ij} Y_j .$$

If $(x_1, \ldots, x_m, y_1, \ldots, y_k)$ is an allocation in a production economy, then the *strictly better set* F_i^* of consumer i is the set

$$F_i^* = \{x \in E^+ \colon\ x \succ_i x_i\} .$$

If the preference $\succeq_i$ is non-satiated—in particular, if ω is extremely desirable by consumer i—then the strictly better set F_i^* of consumer i is non-empty. In case $\succeq_i$ is also strictly convex, the set F_i^* is clearly a convex set.

With any allocation $(x_1, \ldots, x_m, y_1, \ldots, y_k)$ we associate the set

$$\begin{aligned} H^* &= \operatorname{co}\Big[\bigcup_{i=1}^{m} (F_i^* - Z_i - \omega_i)\Big] \\ &= \Big\{\sum_{i=1}^{m} \lambda_i (f_i - z_i - \omega_i) \colon\ \lambda_i \geq 0,\ f_i \succ_i x_i,\ z_i \in Z_i \text{ and } \sum_{i=1}^{m} \lambda_i = 1\Big\} . \end{aligned}$$

The set H^* will play an important role in our discussion. Its first property is described in the next theorem.

Theorem 4.3.3. *Assume that in a private ownership production economy preferences are strictly convex and the total endowment is extremely desirable by each consumer. If $(x_1, \ldots, x_m, y_1, \ldots, y_k)$ is an Edgeworth equilibrium, then for each $h \geq 0$ the zero vector does not belong to the set $h + H^*$, i.e., $0 \notin h + H^*$.*

Proof. Let $h \geq 0$ and assume that $0 \in h + H^*$. Then, there exist $f_i \in F_i^*$, $z_i \in Z_i$ and $\lambda_i \geq 0$ with $\sum_{i=1}^{m} \lambda_i = 1$ such that $h + \sum_{i=1}^{m} \lambda_i (f_i - z_i - \omega_i) = 0$, and so

$$\sum_{i=1}^{m} \lambda_i (f_i - z_i - \omega_i) \leq 0 . \qquad (\star)$$

Next, let $S = \{i\colon\ \lambda_i > 0\}$, and note that from $(\star)$ it follows that

$$\sum_{i \in S} \lambda_i f_i \leq \sum_{i \in S} \lambda_i z_i + \sum_{i \in S} \lambda_i \omega_i . \qquad (\star\star)$$

Now if n is a positive integer and $i \in S$, let n_i be the smallest integer greater than or equal to $n\lambda_i$ (i.e., $0 \leq n_i - n\lambda_i \leq 1$). Since $f_i \succ_i x_i$ and $\lim_{n\to\infty} \frac{n\lambda_i}{n_i} = 1$

for each $i \in S$, we can choose (by the continuity of the utility functions) n large enough so that

$$g_i = \tfrac{n\lambda_i}{n_i} f_i \succ_i x_i \quad \text{for all} \quad i \in S\,. \qquad (\star\star\star)$$

Taking into account ($\star\star$), we infer that

$$\sum_{i\in S} n_i g_i = \sum_{i\in S} n\lambda_i f_i \le \sum_{i\in S} n\lambda_i z_i + \sum_{i\in S} n\lambda_i \omega_i \le \sum_{i\in S} n_i \tfrac{n\lambda_i}{n_i} z_i + \sum_{i\in S} n_i \omega_i\,.$$

Since $0 \le \frac{n\lambda_i}{n_i} \le 1$, we see that $h_i = \frac{n\lambda_i}{n_i} z_i \in Z_i$, and from the preceding inequality, we conclude that

$$\sum_{i\in S} n_i g_i \le \sum_{i\in S} n_i h_i + \sum_{i\in S} n_i \omega_i\,.$$

By rearranging the consumers, we can assume that $S = \{1, \ldots, \ell\}$, where $1 \le \ell \le m$. For each $i \in S$ pick $h_{ij} \in Y_j\, (j = 1, \ldots, k)$ such that

$$h_i = \sum_{j=1}^{k} \theta_{ij} h_{ij}\,.$$

Let $n = n_1 + \cdots + n_\ell$, and let $\mathcal{E}_n$ denote the n-fold replica of our economy. For each $i \in S$, let T_i be the set of consumers of $\mathcal{E}_n$ defined by

$$T_i = \{(i, s)\colon\ n_0 + n_1 + \cdots + n_{i-1} + 1 \le s \le n_1 + \cdots + n_i\}\,,$$

where $n_0 = 0$. Clearly, $T_i \cap T_r = \emptyset$ for $i \ne r$. Now consider the coalition T of $\mathcal{E}_n$ given by $T = \bigcup_{i\in S} T_i$. Next, for each consumer $(i, s) \in T_i$ we assign the bundle $\xi_{is} = g_i$, and to each producer $(j, t)\, (j = 1, \ldots, k;\ n_0 + n_1 + \cdots + n_{i-1} + 1 \le t \le n_1 + \cdots + n_i)$ we assign the production plan $\zeta_{jt} = h_{ij}$; see Figure 4.3-2.

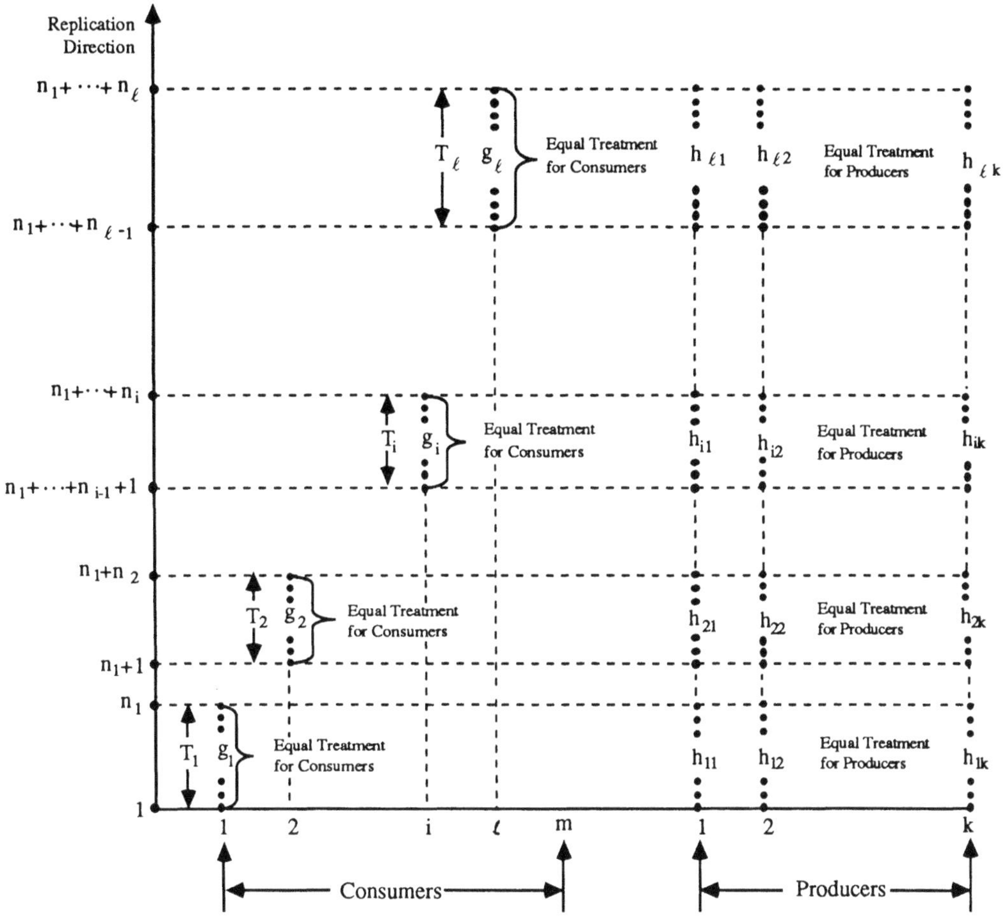

Fig. 4.3-2

Now note that $\xi_{is} \succ_{(i,s)} x_{is}$ for all $(i,s) \in T$, and moreover

$$\begin{aligned}\sum_{(i,s)\in T} \xi_{is} &= \sum_{i\in S} n_i g_i \\ &\leq \sum_{i\in S} n_i \omega_i + \sum_{i\in S} n_i h_i \\ &= \sum_{(i,s)\in T} \omega_{is} + \sum_{i\in S} n_i \Big(\sum_{j=1}^{k} \theta_{ij} h_{ij}\Big) \\ &= \sum_{(i,s)\in T} \omega_{is} + \sum_{j=1}^{k}\sum_{t=1}^{n}\Big(\sum_{(i,s)\in T} \theta_{isjt}\Big)\zeta_{jt}\,.\end{aligned}$$

The above show that the allocation $(x_1, \ldots, x_m, y_1, \ldots, y_k)$ is improved upon by the coalition T in the n-fold replica of the economy, which is impossible. Consequently, $0 \notin h + H^*$ must hold, as desired. ■

In order to to continue our study of Edgeworth equilibria in private ownership production economies we need a lemma.

Lemma 4.3.4. *Let Y be a uniformly τ-proper production set and let the vector $w > 0$ and the symmetric τ-neighborhood W of zero satisfy the definition of uniform properness for Y. If a vector $z = y + \alpha(t - w)$, where $y \in Y$, $\alpha > 0$ and $t \in W$, satisfies $z^+ \leq y^+$, then $z \in Y$.*

Proof. Assume that Y, $w > 0$ and W are as in the statement of the lemma, and let the vector $z = y + \alpha(t - w)$, where $y \in Y$, $\alpha > 0$ and $t \in W$, satisfy $z^+ \leq y^+$.

Suppose by way of contradiction that $z \notin Y$. If we consider the cone $\Gamma = \{\alpha(w + x)\colon\ \alpha > 0 \text{ and } x \in W\}$, then we have $y = z + \alpha(w - t) \in (z + \Gamma) \cap Y$. However, the inequality $z^+ \leq y^+$ implies

$$y \in (z + \Gamma) \cap \{f \in Y\colon\ f^+ \geq z^+\},$$

contrary to the uniform τ-properness of Y. Thus, $z \in Y$, and the proof of the lemma is finished. ■

We are now ready to establish the analogue of Theorem 3.4.6 for private ownership production economies. The result is due to the authors [3].

Theorem 4.3.5. *If in a private ownership production economy preferences and production sets are uniformly τ-proper, then every Edgeworth equilibrium is a quasiequilibrium.*

Proof. Let $(x_1, \ldots, x_m, y_1, \ldots, y_k)$ be an Edgeworth equilibrium in a private ownership production economy whose preferences and production sets are uniformly τ-proper. For each $i = 1, \ldots, m$ pick some $v_i > 0$ and a convex solid τ-neighborhood V_i of zero that satisfy the definition of properness for the preference $\succeq_i$. Similarly, for each $j = 1, \ldots, k$ pick some $w_j > 0$ and a convex solid τ-neighborhood W_j of zero that satisfy the definition of uniform properness for the production set Y_j. Put

$$v = \sum_{i=1}^{m} v_i + \sum_{j=1}^{k} w_j \quad \text{and} \quad W = V_1 \cap \cdots \cap V_m \cap W_1 \cap \cdots \cap W_k\,,$$

and consider the cone

$$\Gamma = \big\{\alpha(-v + \tfrac{1}{m}w)\colon\ \alpha > 0 \text{ and } w \in W\big\}.$$

In view of $-v \in \Gamma$ and $-v + \frac{1}{m}W \subseteq \Gamma$, we see that Γ has a non-empty interior. We claim that $H^* \cap \Gamma = \emptyset$, where $H^* = \text{co}\big[\bigcup_{i=1}^{m}(F_i^* - Z_i - \omega_i)\big]$; see the discussion preceding Theorem 4.3.3.

To see this, assume by way of contradiction that $H^* \cap \Gamma \neq \emptyset$. Then there exist $f_i \geq 0$ with $f_i \succ_i x_i$, $\lambda_i \geq 0$ with $\sum_{i=1}^m \lambda_i = 1$, $y_{ij} \in Y_j\,(i = 1, \ldots, m;\ j = 1, \ldots, k)$ and some $\varepsilon > 0$ such that

$$\sum_{i=1}^{m} \lambda_i \Big(f_i - \sum_{j=1}^{k} \theta_{ij} y_{ij} - \omega_i \Big) + \varepsilon v \in \tfrac{\varepsilon}{m} W\,. \tag{a}$$

Note that the set $S = \{i\colon\ \lambda_i > 0\}$ is non-empty.

Now consider the positive elements

$$y = \sum_{i=1}^{m} \lambda_i \Big[\omega_i + \sum_{j=1}^{k} \theta_{ij} (y_{ij})^+ \Big]$$

and

$$z = \sum_{i=1}^{m} \lambda_i \Big[f_i + \sum_{j=1}^{k} \theta_{ij} (y_{ij})^- \Big] + \varepsilon v = \sum_{i=1}^{m} (\lambda_i f_i + \varepsilon v_i) + \sum_{i=1}^{m} \sum_{j=1}^{k} \big[\lambda_i \theta_{ij} (y_{ij})^- + \tfrac{\varepsilon}{m} w_j \big]\,.$$

From (**a**), we see that

$$z - y = \sum_{i=1}^{m} \lambda_i \Big(f_i - \sum_{j=1}^{k} \theta_{ij} y_{ij} - \omega_i \Big) + \varepsilon v \in \tfrac{\varepsilon}{m} W\,. \tag{b}$$

Moreover, we have

$$0 \leq (z-y)^+ \leq z = \sum_{i=1}^{m} (\lambda_i f_i + \varepsilon v_i) + \sum_{i=1}^{m} \sum_{j=1}^{k} \big[\lambda_i \theta_{ij} (y_{ij})^- + \tfrac{\varepsilon}{m} w_j \big]\,. \tag{c}$$

From $z - y \in \frac{\varepsilon}{m} W$ and the solidness of W, we see that

$$(z-y)^+ \in \tfrac{\varepsilon}{m} W\,. \tag{d}$$

Applying the Riesz Decomposition Property to (**c**), we can write

$$(z-y)^+ = s + t\,, \tag{e}$$

where

$$0 \leq s \leq \sum_{i=1}^{m} (\lambda_i f_i + \varepsilon v_i) \tag{f}$$

and

$$0 \leq t \leq \sum_{i=1}^{m} \sum_{j=1}^{k} \big[\lambda_i \theta_{ij} (y_{ij})^- + \tfrac{\varepsilon}{m} w_j \big]\,. \tag{g}$$

Now applying the Riesz Decomposition Property to (**f**), we can write $s = \sum_{i=1}^{m} s_i$ with $0 \le s_i \le \lambda_i f_i + \varepsilon v_i$ for each i. From $0 \le s_i \le s \le (z-y)^+ \in \frac{\varepsilon}{m}W$ and the solidness of W, we see that

$$s_i \in \tfrac{\varepsilon}{m}W \subseteq \varepsilon W \quad \text{for} \quad i = 1, \dots, m. \tag{h}$$

Let

$$g_i = \begin{cases} f_i, & \text{if } i \notin S; \\ f_i + \frac{\varepsilon}{\lambda_i}v_i - \frac{1}{\lambda_i}s_i, & \text{if } i \in S. \end{cases}$$

Clearly, $g_i \ge 0$ for each i. Also, $g_i \succeq_i f_i$ holds for each $i \notin S$ and we claim that $g_i \succ_i f_i$ for each $i \in S$. Indeed, if for some $i \in S$ we have

$$f_i = g_i - \tfrac{\varepsilon}{\lambda_i}v_i + \tfrac{1}{\lambda_i}s_i \succeq_i g_i\,,$$

then by the uniform properness of the preferences we must have $\frac{1}{\lambda_i}s_i \notin \frac{\varepsilon}{\lambda_i}W$, i.e., $s_i \notin \varepsilon W$, which contradicts (**h**).

Next, using (**g**) and the Riesz Decomposition Property, we can write $t = \sum_{i=1}^{m}\sum_{j=1}^{k} t_{ij}$ with $0 \le t_{ij} \le \lambda_i\theta_{ij}(y_{ij})^- + \frac{\varepsilon}{m}w_j$. Let $T = \{(i,j)\colon\ \lambda_i\theta_{ij} > 0\}$, and define

$$z_{ij} = \begin{cases} y_{ij} - \frac{\varepsilon}{m}(\lambda_i\theta_{ij})^{-1}w_j + (\lambda_i\theta_{ij})^{-1}t_{ij}, & \text{if } (i,j) \in T; \\ 0, & \text{if } (i,j) \notin T. \end{cases}$$

Fix $(i,j) \in T$. From $0 \le t_{ij} \le t \le (z-y)^+ \in \frac{\varepsilon}{m}W$ and the solidness of W, we infer that $t_{ij} \in \frac{\varepsilon}{m}W$, or $\frac{m}{\varepsilon}t_{ij} \in W$. Also, note that

$$\begin{aligned} (z_{ij})^+ &= \tfrac{1}{\lambda_i\theta_{ij}}(\lambda_i\theta_{ij}y_{ij} - \tfrac{\varepsilon}{m}w_j + t_{ij})^+ \\ &\le \tfrac{1}{\lambda_i\theta_{ij}}[\lambda_i\theta_{ij}y_{ij} + \lambda_i\theta_{ij}(y_{ij})^-] = \tfrac{\lambda_i\theta_{ij}}{\lambda_i\theta_{ij}}(y_{ij})^+ = (y_{ij})^+\,. \end{aligned}$$

In view of $z_{ij} = y_{ij} + \frac{\varepsilon}{m}(\lambda_i\theta_{ij})^{-1}\big(\frac{m}{\varepsilon}t_{ij} - w_j\big)$ and Lemma 4.3.4, we see that $z_{ij} \in Y_j$ for all $(i,j) \in T$, and, of course, $z_{ij} \in Y_j$ is trivially true for $(i,j) \notin T$.

Now for $\lambda_i = 0$, we have $s_i \le \varepsilon v_i$, and so $\varepsilon v_i - s_i \ge 0$ for all $i \notin S$. Similarly, for $\lambda_i\theta_{ij} = 0$, we have $t_{ij} \le \frac{\varepsilon}{m}w_j$, and so $\frac{\varepsilon}{m}w_j - t_{ij} \ge 0$ for all $(i,j) \notin T$. Taking into account these observations, we see that

$$\begin{aligned}
&\sum_{i=1}^{m}\lambda_i\Big(g_i-\sum_{j=1}^{k}\theta_{ij}z_{ij}-\omega_i\Big)\\
&=\sum_{i=1}^{m}\lambda_i\Big(f_i-\sum_{j=1}^{k}\theta_{ij}y_{ij}-\omega_i\Big)+\varepsilon\sum_{i\in S}v_i-\sum_{i\in S}s_i+\tfrac{\varepsilon}{m}\sum_{(i,j)\in T}w_j-\sum_{(i,j)\in T}t_{ij}\\
&\le\sum_{i=1}^{m}\lambda_i\Big(f_i-\sum_{j=1}^{k}\theta_{ij}y_{ij}-\omega_i\Big)+\varepsilon\sum_{i\in S}v_i-\sum_{i\in S}s_i+\sum_{i\notin S}(\varepsilon v_i-s_i)+\tfrac{\varepsilon}{m}\sum_{(i,j)\in T}w_j\\
&\qquad+\sum_{(i,j)\in T}t_{ij}+\sum_{(i,j)\notin T}\big(\tfrac{\varepsilon}{m}w_j-t_{ij}\big)\\
&=\sum_{i=1}^{m}\lambda_i\Big(f_i-\sum_{j=1}^{k}\theta_{ij}y_{ij}-\omega_i\Big)+\varepsilon\sum_{i=1}^{m}v_i-\sum_{i=1}^{m}s_i+\tfrac{\varepsilon}{m}\sum_{i=1}^{m}\sum_{j=1}^{k}w_j-\sum_{i=1}^{m}\sum_{j=1}^{k}t_{ij}\\
&=\sum_{i=1}^{m}\lambda_i\Big(f_i-\sum_{j=1}^{k}\theta_{ij}y_{ij}-\omega_i\Big)+\varepsilon v-(s+t)\\
&=z-y-(s+t)=z-y-(z-y)^+=-(z-y)^-\le 0\,.
\end{aligned}$$

Therefore, the element

$$g=\sum_{i=1}^{m}\lambda_i\Big(g_i-\sum_{j=1}^{k}\theta_{ij}z_{ij}-\omega_i\Big)\in H^*$$

satisfies $g\le 0$. Now let $h=-g\ge 0$. Then, from $h+g=0$, we see that $0\in h+H^*$, which contradicts Theorem 4.3.3. Thus, $H^*\cap\Gamma=\emptyset$ holds, as claimed.

Finally, by the separation theorem there exist a non-zero price p and some constant c such that

$$p\cdot h\ge c\ge p\cdot g$$

holds for all $h\in H^*$ and all $g\in\Gamma$. Since Γ is a cone, we see that $c\ge 0$. Now if $x\succ_i x_i$ holds in E^+, then $x-\sum_{j=1}^{k}\theta_{ij}y_j-\omega_i\in H^*$, and so $p\cdot x\ge p\cdot\omega_i+\sum_{j=1}^{k}\theta_{ij}p\cdot y_j$. On the other hand, we know that each v_i is an extremely desirable vector for $\succeq_i$. If $y\in Y_r$, then put $w=\sum_{i=1}^{m}v_i$, $z_j=y_j$ for $j\ne r$ and $z_r=y$, and note that

$$\tfrac{1}{m}(y_r-y+\alpha w)=\sum_{i=1}^{m}\tfrac{1}{m}\Big[(x_i+\alpha v_i)-\sum_{j=1}^{k}\theta_{ij}z_j-\omega_i\Big]\in H^*$$

holds for all $\alpha>0$. Hence, $p\cdot y_r-p\cdot y+\alpha p\cdot w\ge 0$ holds for all $\alpha>0$, and so $p\cdot y_r\ge p\cdot y$ for all $y\in Y_r$. Consequently, the Edgeworth equilibrium $(x_1,\dots,x_m,y_1,\dots,y_k)$ is a quasiequilibrium, and the proof is finished. ■

An immediate consequence of the preceding result is the following version of the Debreu–Scarf theorem (Theorem 1.6.16) for private ownership production economies.

Corollary 4.3.6. *If in a private ownership production economy preferences and production sets are uniformly τ-proper and $\omega \gg 0$, then an allocation is an Edgeworth equilibrium if and only if it is a Walrasian equilibrium.*

In particular, in this case, if the private ownership production economy is also compact, then Walrasian equilibria exist.

Thus, by the above corollary, in a private ownership production economy with uniformly proper preferences and production sets every Edgeworth equilibrium is a quasiequilibrium—and hence, it can be decentralized by a price. In the absence of uniform properness, one can only expect that an Edgeworth equilibrium can be decentralized "approximately" by a price. Our next objective is to establish that without uniform properness an Edgeworth equilibrium can be approximately price supported in the sense that expenditures are approximately minimized and profits are approximately maximized.

For each fixed $a \in E^+$ and each consumer i, we define **the a-truncated share set Z_i^a** by

$$Z_i^a = \Big\{\sum_{j=1}^k \theta_{ij} y_j\colon\ y_j \in Y_j \text{ and } y_j \le a\Big\} = \sum_{j=1}^k \theta_{ij} Y_j^a\,.$$

Clearly, each truncated share set Z_i^a is convex. In case the Riesz dual system for a private ownership production economy is symmetric, the convex sets Z_i^a are also weakly closed. The details follow.

Lemma 4.3.7. *If the Riesz dual system of a private ownership production economy is symmetric, then for each i and each $a \in E^+$ the convex set Z_i^a is weakly closed.*

Proof. Consider a private ownership production economy with symmetric Riesz dual system, fix i and $a \in E^+$ and let f be an element in the weak closure of the convex set Z_i^a. Then f belongs also in the τ-closure of Z_i^a. Pick a net $\{f_\alpha\}$ of Z_i^a with $f_\alpha \xrightarrow{\tau} f$. For each α choose $y_j^\alpha \in Y_j$ with $y_j^\alpha \le a$ and $f_\alpha = \sum_{j=1}^k \theta_{ij} y_j^\alpha$. (In case we have $\theta_{ij} = 0$, we shall assume that $y_j^\alpha = 0$.)

Since $0 \le (y_j^\alpha)^+ \le a$ holds for all α and j and the order interval $[0, a]$ is weakly compact, we can suppose (by passing to an appropriate subnet) that for each j we have

$$(y_j^\alpha)^+ \xrightarrow{w} y_j^1\,. \qquad (\star)$$

Also, from the relation

$$\begin{aligned} 0 \le \theta_{ij}(y_j^\alpha)^- &\le \sum_{t=1}^k \theta_{it}(y_t^\alpha)^- \\ &= -\sum_{t=1}^k \theta_{it} y_t^\alpha + \sum_{t=1}^k \theta_{it}(y_t^\alpha)^+ \\ &\le -f_\alpha + a \le (f - f_\alpha)^+ + f^+ + a \xrightarrow{\tau} f^+ + a \end{aligned}$$

and Lemma 3.3.10, it follows—by passing to a subnet again—that for each j we have

$$(y_j^\alpha)^- \xrightarrow{w} y_j^2 . \qquad (\star\star)$$

From ($\star$) and ($\star\star$), we infer that

$$y_j^\alpha = (y_j^\alpha)^+ - (y_j^\alpha)^- \xrightarrow{w} y_j^1 - y_j^2 = y_j$$

for each j. Since each Y_j is weakly closed, we see that $y_j \in Y_j$, and moreover, from $y_j^\alpha \leq a$, we infer that $y_j \leq a$. Finally, taking weak limits, we see that

$$f = \lim_\alpha f_\alpha = \lim_\alpha \sum_{j=1}^k \theta_{ij} y_j^\alpha = \sum_{j=1}^k \theta_{ij} y_j \in Z_i^\alpha ,$$

and the proof is finished. ■

Consider m consumption bundles $x_i \in E^+ \, (i = 1, \ldots, m)$. For each i we shall denote by F_i the "better set" of x_i, i.e., F_i is the weakly closed convex set defined by

$$F_i = \{x \in E^+ \colon \; x \succeq_i x_i\} .$$

With the above convex sets we shall associate for each $a \in E^+$ the convex set

$$\begin{aligned} H_a &= \operatorname{co}\Big[\bigcup_{i=1}^m (F_i - Z_i^a - \omega_i)\Big] \\ &= \Big\{\sum_{i=1}^k \lambda_i(f_i - z_i - \omega_i) \colon \; \lambda_i \geq 0, \; f_i \succeq_i x_i, \; z_i \in Z_i^a \text{ and } \sum_{i=1}^m \lambda_i = 1\Big\} . \end{aligned}$$

When the Riesz dual system is symmetric, the convex sets H_a are weakly closed.

Lemma 4.3.8. *Assume that Riesz dual system of a private ownership production economy is symmetric. If $x_i \in E^+ \, (i = 1, \ldots, m)$ are consumption bundles, then for each $a \in E^+$ the convex set*

$$H_a = \operatorname{co}\Big[\bigcup_{i=1}^m (F_i - Z_i^a - \omega_i)\Big]$$

is a weakly closed subset of E.

Proof. Fix $x_i \in E^+ \, (i = 1, \ldots, m)$ and $a \in E^+$, and let g be in the weak closure of H_a. Then g belongs to the τ-closure of H_a, and so there exists a net $\{g_\alpha\}$ of H_a with $g_\alpha \xrightarrow{\tau} g$. For each α let $f_i^\alpha \succeq_i x_i$, $z_i^\alpha \in Z_i^a$, $\lambda_i^\alpha \geq 0$ with $\sum_{i=1}^m \lambda_i^\alpha = 1$ such that

$$g_\alpha = \sum_{i=1}^m \lambda_i^\alpha (f_i^\alpha - z_i^\alpha - \omega_i) .$$

By passing to a subnet, we can assume that $\lambda_i^\alpha \to \lambda_i \geq 0$ holds in $\mathcal{R}$ for each i. Clearly, $\sum_{i=1}^m \lambda_i = 1$. Let $S = \{i\colon\ \lambda_i > 0\}$, and note that $S \neq \emptyset$. From

$$0 \leq \sum_{i=1}^m \lambda_i^\alpha f_i^\alpha + \sum_{i=1}^m \lambda_i^\alpha (z_i^\alpha)^- = \sum_{i=1}^m \lambda_i^\alpha (f_i^\alpha - z_i^\alpha - \omega_i) + \sum_{i=1}^m \lambda_i^\alpha \omega_i + \sum_{i=1}^m \lambda_i^\alpha (z_i^\alpha)^+$$
$$\leq g_\alpha + \omega + a\,,$$

we see that

$$0 \leq \lambda_i^\alpha f_i^\alpha \leq g_\alpha + \omega + a \qquad \text{and} \qquad 0 \leq \lambda_i^\alpha (z_i^\alpha)^- \leq g_\alpha + \omega + a$$

hold for all i and all α. Thus, by Lemma 3.3.10, we can assume—by passing to a subnet again—that for each $i \in S$ we have

$$f_i^\alpha \xrightarrow{w} f_i \in F_i \qquad \text{and} \qquad (z_i^\alpha)^- \xrightarrow{w} z_i^1\,.$$

From $0 \leq (z_i^\alpha)^+ \leq a$ and the weak compactness of $[0, a]$, we can assume (by passing to a subnet once more) that for each i we have $(z_i^\alpha)^+ \xrightarrow{w} z_i^2$. Thus, taking into account that each Z_i^a is weakly closed (Lemma 4.3.7), we see that

$$z_i^\alpha = (z_i^\alpha)^+ - (z_i^\alpha)^- \xrightarrow{w} z_i^2 - z_i^1 = z_i \in Z_i^a\,.$$

In addition, from $0 \leq \lambda_i^\alpha (z_i^\alpha)^+ \leq \lambda_i^\alpha a$, it follows that $\lambda_i^\alpha (z_i^\alpha)^+ \xrightarrow{w} 0$ for all $i \notin S$.

Now from the weak closedness of E^+ and the inequality

$$g_\alpha = \sum_{i=1}^m \lambda_i^\alpha [f_i^\alpha - (z_i^\alpha)^+ + (z_i^\alpha)^- - \omega_i]$$
$$\geq \sum_{i\in S} \lambda_i^\alpha f_i^\alpha - \sum_{i=1}^m \lambda_i^\alpha (z_i^\alpha)^+ + \sum_{i\in S} \lambda_i^\alpha (z_i^\alpha)^- - \sum_{i=1}^m \lambda_i^\alpha \omega_i\,,$$

we infer by taking weak limits that

$$g = \lim_\alpha g_\alpha \geq \sum_{i\in S} \lambda_i f_i - \sum_{i\in S} \lambda_i z_i^2 + \sum_{i\in S} \lambda_i z_i^1 - \sum_{i\in S} \lambda_i \omega_i = \sum_{i\in S} \lambda_i (f_i - z_i - \omega_i) = h\,.$$

For $i \notin S$, let $f_i = x_i$ and $z_i = 0$. Then $f_i + g - h \succeq_i x_i$, and

$$g = (g - h) + h = \sum_{i=1}^m \lambda_i [(f_i + g - h) - z_i - \omega_i] \in H_\alpha\,,$$

and the proof of the lemma is finished. ■

Edgeworth equilibria in private ownership production economies are characterized by the following "approximate" supportability property.

Theorem 4.3.9. *Assume that the Riesz dual system of a private ownership production economy is symmetric. Then an allocation* $(x_1, \ldots, x_m, y_1, \ldots, y_k)$ *is an Edgeworth equilibrium if and only if for each* $f > 0$, *each* $\varepsilon > 0$ *and each* $a \in E^+$ *there exists a price* $p \in E'$ *such that:*

1. $p \cdot f = 1$;
2. $x \succeq_i x_i$ *in* E^+ *implies* $p \cdot x \geq p \cdot \omega_i + \sum_{j=1}^k \theta_{ij} p \cdot y_j - \varepsilon$; *and*
3. $p \cdot y_j \geq p \cdot y - \varepsilon$ *holds for each* $y \in Y_j$ *with* $y \leq a$.

Proof. Assume that $(x_1, \ldots, x_m, y_1, \ldots, y_k)$ is an Edgeworth equilibrium. Fix $f > 0$, $\varepsilon > 0$ and $a \in E^+$. We can suppose that $a \geq \bigvee_{j=1}^k y_j$. From

$$\tfrac{\varepsilon}{m} f + H_a = \tfrac{\varepsilon}{2m} f + \left(\tfrac{\varepsilon}{2m} f + H_a\right) \subseteq \tfrac{\varepsilon}{2m} f + H^*,$$

and Theorem 4.3.3, we see that $0 \notin \frac{\varepsilon}{m} f + H_a$. Since—by Lemma 4.3.8—the set H_a is weakly closed, it follows from the separation theorem that there exists some $p \in E'$ such that

$$p \cdot \left(\tfrac{\varepsilon}{m} f + g\right) > 0 \tag{$\star$}$$

holds for all $g \in H_a$. Since $h_i = \sum_{j=1}^k \theta_{ij} y_j \in Z_i^a$, it follows that

$$0 = \sum_{i=1}^m \frac{1}{m}(x_i - h_i - \omega_i) \in H_a,$$

and from $(\star)$ we see that $p \cdot f > 0$. Thus, replacing p by $\frac{p}{p \cdot f}$, we can assume that $p \cdot f = 1$. Now let $x \succeq_i x_i$ hold in E^+. Then $x - \sum_{j=1}^k \theta_{ij} y_j - \omega_i \in H_a$, and so $p \cdot \left(\frac{\varepsilon}{m} f + x - \sum_{j=1}^k \theta_{ij} y_j - \omega_i\right) > 0$. This implies

$$p \cdot x \geq p \cdot \omega_i + \sum_{j=1}^k \theta_{ij} p \cdot y_j - \tfrac{\varepsilon}{m} > p \cdot \omega_i + \sum_{j=1}^k \theta_{ij} p \cdot y_j - \varepsilon.$$

Next, let $y \in Y_j$ satisfy $y \leq a$. Put $h_t = y_t$ for $t \neq j$ and $h_j = y$. From

$$\tfrac{1}{m}(y_j - y) = \tfrac{1}{m}\Big(\sum_{i=1}^m x_i - \sum_{i=1}^m \omega_i - \sum_{t=1}^k h_t\Big) = \sum_{i=1}^m \tfrac{1}{m}\Big(x_i - \sum_{t=1}^k \theta_{it} h_t - \omega_i\Big) \in H_a$$

and $(\star)$, we see that $p \cdot \left[\frac{\varepsilon}{m} f + \frac{1}{m}(y_j - y)\right] > 0$. Therefore, $p \cdot y_j \geq p \cdot y - \varepsilon$ holds for all $y \in Y_j$ with $y \leq a$.

For the converse, assume that an allocation $(x_1, \ldots, x_m, y_1, \ldots, y_k)$ satisfies properties (1), (2) and (3). Also, assume by way of contradiction that there exists an n-fold replica of the economy, a coalition S of consumers of the n-fold replica, a subset $\{f_{is}\colon (i,s) \in S\}$ of E^+ and production plans $z_{jt} \in Y_{jt}$ $(j = 1, \ldots, k;\ t = 1, \ldots, n)$ such that

$$f_{is} \succ_{(i,s)} x_{is} = x_i \qquad \text{for all} \quad (i,s) \in S \tag{1}$$

and

$$\sum_{(i,s)\in S} f_{is} = \sum_{(i,s)\in S} \omega_{is} + \sum_{j=1}^{k}\sum_{t=1}^{n}\Big(\sum_{(i,s)\in S} \theta_{isjt}\Big) z_{jt}\,. \tag{2}$$

Now let $f = \sum_{(i,s)\in S} f_{is} > 0$ and let $a = \sum_{j=1}^{k} |y_j| + \sum_{j=1}^{k}\sum_{t=1}^{n} |z_{jt}|$. Then for each ℓ there exists some $p_\ell \in E'$ such that

$$p_\ell \cdot f = 1\,, \tag{3}$$

$$x \succeq_i x_i \ \text{ in } E^+ \ \text{ implies } \ p_\ell \cdot x \geq p_\ell \cdot \omega_i + \sum_{j=1}^{k} \theta_{ij} p_\ell \cdot y_j - \tfrac{1}{\ell}\,, \tag{4}$$

and

$$p_\ell \cdot y_j \geq p_\ell \cdot y - \tfrac{1}{\ell} \ \text{ for all } \ y \in Y_j \ \text{ with } \ y \leq a\,. \tag{5}$$

Choose $0 < \delta < 1$ such that $\delta f_{is} \succ_{(i,s)} x_{is} = x_i$ holds for all $(i,s) \in S$. By (4) and (5) for each $(i,s) \in S$, we have

$$\begin{aligned} p_\ell \cdot (\delta f_{is}) &\geq p_\ell \cdot \omega_{is} + p_\ell \cdot \Big(\sum_{j=1}^{k} \theta_{ij} y_j\Big) - \tfrac{1}{\ell} \\ &= p_\ell \cdot \omega_{is} + p_\ell \cdot \Big(\sum_{j=1}^{k}\sum_{t=1}^{n} \theta_{isjt} y_j\Big) - \tfrac{1}{\ell} \\ &\geq p_\ell \cdot \omega_{is} + p_\ell \cdot \Big(\sum_{j=1}^{k}\sum_{t=1}^{n} \theta_{isjt} z_{jt}\Big) - \tfrac{2}{\ell}\,, \end{aligned} \tag{6}$$

and so

$$p_\ell \cdot \Big(\delta \sum_{(i,s)\in S} f_{is}\Big) \geq p_\ell \cdot \Big(\sum_{(i,s)\in S} \omega_{is}\Big) + p_\ell \cdot \Big[\sum_{j=1}^{k}\sum_{t=1}^{n}\Big(\sum_{(i,s)\in S} \theta_{isjt}\Big) z_{jt}\Big] - \tfrac{2m}{\ell}\,. \tag{7}$$

Combining (2) and (7), we obtain

$$\delta = \delta p_\ell \cdot \Big(\sum_{(i,s)\in S} f_{is}\Big) \geq p_\ell \cdot \Big(\sum_{(i,s)\in S} f_{is}\Big) - \tfrac{2mn}{\ell} = 1 - \tfrac{2mn}{\ell}$$

for each ℓ, and so $\delta \geq 1$, which is a contradiction. Therefore, $(x_1, \ldots, x_m, y_1, \ldots, y_k)$ is an Edgeworth equilibrium. ■

EXERCISES

1. Prove Corollary 4.3.6.

2. A subset Y of a vector space E is said to be **continuous** for a linear topology ξ on E (briefly, ξ-continuous) whenever $\{y_\alpha\} \subseteq Y$ and $y_\alpha^- \xrightarrow{\xi} 0$ imply $y_\alpha^+ \xrightarrow{\xi} 0$. The continuity of a production set captures the economic intuition according to which a decrease in the input must cause a decrease in the output.

   If a production set Y is a cone in the dual of an AM-space with unit (in particular, in a finite dimensional space), then show that Y is norm continuous. [HINT: Assume that a cone Y is a production set in the dual of an AM-space with unit and let $\{z_n\} \subseteq Y$ satisfy $\|z_n^-\| \to 0$. Assume by way of contradiction that $\|z_n^+\| > \varepsilon > 0$ holds for all n and some $\varepsilon > 0$. Now let

$$x_n = \frac{z_n}{\|z_n^+\|} = \frac{z_n^+}{\|z_n^+\|} - \frac{z_n^-}{\|z_n^+\|}. \tag{$\star$}$$

   Since Y is a cone, we have $x_n \in Y$ for each n. From

$$\left\|\frac{z_n^-}{\|z_n^+\|}\right\| = \frac{\|z_n^-\|}{\|z_n^+\|} \leq \frac{\|z_n^-\|}{\varepsilon} \longrightarrow 0,$$

   we see that $\lim_{n\to\infty} \frac{z_n^-}{\|z_n^+\|} = 0$. On the other hand, we have $\left\|\frac{z_n^+}{\|z_n^+\|}\right\| = 1$ for each n. Since the set $\{y \in E^+ \colon \|y\| = 1\}$ is weak* compact, it follows that $\left\{\frac{z_n^+}{\|z_n^+\|}\right\}$ has a weak* accumulation point $z > 0$. From ($\star$), we conclude that $z \in Y \cap E^+ = \{0\}$, which is impossible.]

3. Assume that the Riesz dual system for a production economy is symmetric, preferences are strictly monotone and that the aggregate production set $Y = Y_1 + \cdots + Y_k$ is a cone. If the economy has a Walrasian equilibrium, then show that $\{y_n\} \subseteq Y$ and $y_n^- \xrightarrow{\tau} 0$ imply $y_n^+ \wedge a \xrightarrow{\tau} 0$ for each $a \in E^+$. In particular, if in this case E is also finite dimensional, then $\{y_n\} \subseteq Y$ and $\|y_n^-\| \to 0$ imply $\|y_n^+\| \to 0$.
   [HINT: Let $(x_1, \ldots, x_m, h_1, \ldots, h_k)$ be a Walrasian equilibrium supported by a price p, and let $y = h_1 + \cdots + h_k \in Y$. Since Y is a cone, we have (why?)

$$\max\{p \cdot z \colon\ z \in Y\} = p \cdot y = 0.$$

   Now let $\{y_n\} \subseteq Y$ satisfy $y_n^- \xrightarrow{\tau} 0$, and let $a \in E^+$. From

$$p \cdot y_n^+ - p \cdot y_n^- = p \cdot y_n \leq 0,$$

   we see that $p \cdot y_n^+ \leq p \cdot y_n^-$, and so in view of $0 \leq p \cdot (y_n^+ \wedge a) \leq p \cdot y_n^+ \leq p \cdot y_n^- \to 0$, we conclude that

$$p \cdot (y_n^+ \wedge a) \longrightarrow 0. \tag{$\star\star$}$$

Since preferences are strictly monotone, we have $p \gg 0$, and so the function

$$\|x\| = p \cdot x\,, \quad x \in E\,,$$

defines an order continuous norm on E. By [6, Theorem 12.9, p. 87] the topology generated by the lattice norm $\|\cdot\|$ and τ agree on the order interval $[0,a]$, and in view of $(\star\star)$, we see that $y_n^+ \wedge a \xrightarrow{\tau} 0$.]

4. Assume that for a private ownership production economy:
a) Its Riesz dual system $\langle E, E' \rangle$ is given by a reflexive Banach lattice;
b) There is only one producer whose production set Y is a norm continuous closed cone (see Exercise 2 for the definition); and
c) The share θ_i of each consumer to the profit of the producer is positive, i.e., $\theta_i > 0$ holds for each $i = 1, \ldots, m$.

If $(x_1, \ldots, x_m, y_1, \ldots, y_k)$ is an allocation, then show that the convex set

$$H = \operatorname{co}\Big[\bigcup_{i=1}^{m}(F_i - \theta_i Y - \omega_i)\Big] = G - Y\,,$$

where $G = \operatorname{co}\big[\bigcup_{i=1}^m (F_i - \omega_i)\big]$, is weakly closed.
[HINT: We have $\theta_i Y = Y$ for each i and so $H = G - Y$. From Lemma 4.3.8 it follows (how?) that G is a weakly closed set. To see that $G - Y$ is also weakly closed, let f be in the weak closure of $G - Y$. Then there exists a sequence $\{g_n - y_n\}$ of $G - Y$ with $\lim_{n\to\infty} \|g_n - y_n - f\| = 0$.

For each n write $g_n = \sum_{i=1}^n \lambda_i^n (f_i^n - \omega_i)$, $f_i^n \succeq_i x_i$, $\lambda_i^n \geq 0$ with $\sum_{i=1}^m \lambda_i^n = 1$ for each n. Then $g_n + \omega \geq g_n + \sum_{i=1}^m \lambda_i^n \omega_i = \sum_{i=1}^m \lambda_i^n f_i^n \geq 0$, and so from

$$0 \leq y_n^- = (-y_n)^+ \leq (g_n - y_n + \omega)^+ \text{ and } \lim_{n\to\infty} \|(g_n - y_n + \omega)^+ - (f+\omega)^+\| = 0\,,$$

we see that $\{y_n^-\}$ is a norm bounded sequence.

Next, we claim that the sequence $\{y_n\}$ is a norm bounded sequence. To see this, assume (by passing to a subsequence if necessary) that $\|y_n\| \to \infty$. Since $\{y_n^-\}$ is norm bounded, we see that $\lim_{n\to\infty} \big\| \frac{y_n^-}{\|y_n\|} \big\| = 0$. The norm continuity of Y implies $\lim_{n\to\infty} \big\| \frac{y_n^+}{\|y_n\|} \big\| = 0$ and so

$$1 = \Big\| \frac{y_n}{\|y_n\|} \Big\| \leq \Big\| \frac{y_n^+}{\|y_n\|} \Big\| + \Big\| \frac{y_n^-}{\|y_n\|} \Big\| \longrightarrow 0\,,$$

which is a contradiction. Thus, $\{y_n\}$ is a bounded sequence. Since E is reflexive, we can assume (by passing to a subsequence) that $y_n \xrightarrow{w} y \in Y$. Finally, from the relation $g_n = (g_n - y_n) + y_n \xrightarrow{w} f + y = g \in G$, we see that $f = g - y \in G - Y$.]

5. Let us say that an allocation $(x_1, \ldots, x_m, y_1, \ldots, y_k)$ in a private ownership production economy is an **approximate Walrasian equilibrium** whenever for each $\varepsilon > 0$ there exists some price p such that:

a) $p \cdot e = 1$ (where $e = \sum_{i=1}^{m} x_i$);
b) $x \succeq_i x_i$ in E^+ implies $p \cdot x \geq p \cdot \omega_i + \sum_{j=1}^{k} \theta_{ij} p \cdot y_j - \varepsilon$; and
c) $p \cdot y_j \geq p \cdot y - \varepsilon$ for each $y \in Y_j$.

Assume that for a compact private ownership production economy the following statements hold.

1. Its Riesz dual system $\langle E, E' \rangle$ is given by a reflexive Banach lattice;
2. Its aggregate production set $Y = Y_1 + \cdots + Y_k$ is a norm continuous closed cone—see Exercise 2 above for the definition; and
3. The total endowment is strictly positive, i.e., $\omega \gg 0$ holds.

Show that the economy has an approximate Walrasian equilibrium. [HINT: Consider a new economy with Riesz dual system $\langle E, E' \rangle$ having the same consumers, endowments and preferences but having one producer whose production set is Y. Also, assume that each consumer has the share $\theta_i = \frac{1}{m}\,(i = 1, \ldots, m)$ to the profit of the producer. This new production economy is compact and (by Corollary 4.3.6) it has an Edgeworth equilibrium, say $(x_1, \ldots, x_m, y)$. Write $y = y_1 + \cdots + y_k \in Y$, and we claim that $(x_1, \ldots, x_m, y_1, \ldots, y_k)$ is an approximate Walrasian equilibrium.

To see this, let $G = \mathrm{co}\big[\bigcup_{i=1}^{m} (F_i - \omega_i)\big]$, where $F_i = \{x \in E^+\colon\ x \succeq_i x_i\}$, and let $\varepsilon > 0$. Clearly, G is weakly closed (why?). Now put $H = G - Y$, and note that (by the previous exercise) the convex set H is weakly closed. Now for $e = \sum_{i=1}^{m} x_i > 0$, we have

$$\tfrac{\varepsilon}{m} e + G - Y = \tfrac{\varepsilon}{2m} e + \big(\tfrac{\varepsilon}{2m} e + H\big) \subseteq \tfrac{\varepsilon}{2m} e + H^*\,,$$

and so from Theorem 4.3.3, we infer that $0 \notin \frac{\varepsilon}{m} e + G - Y$. Then, by the separation theorem, there exists some $p \in E'$ such that

$$p \cdot \big(\tfrac{\varepsilon}{m} e + g - y\big) > 0 \qquad (\star\star\star)$$

holds for all $g \in G$ and all $y \in Y$. Since $0 = \sum_{i=1}^{m} \frac{1}{m}(x_i - \omega_i) - \frac{1}{m} y \in G - Y$, we see that $p \cdot e > 0$, and so, replacing p by $\frac{p}{p \cdot e}$, we can assume that $p \cdot e = 1$.

Now assume $x \succeq_i x_i$. Then $x - \omega_i \in G$ and $\sum_{j=1}^{k} \theta_{ij} y_j \in Y$. Thus, from $(\star\star\star)$, we see that

$$p \cdot x \geq p \cdot \omega_i + p \cdot \Big(\sum_{j=1}^{k} \theta_{ij} y_j\Big) - \tfrac{\varepsilon}{m} \geq p \cdot \omega_i + \sum_{j=1}^{k} \theta_{ij} p \cdot y_j - \varepsilon\,.$$

Next, note that

$$\sum_{i=1}^{m} \tfrac{1}{m}(x_i - \omega_i) \in G\,.$$

For $y \in Y_j$, put $z_t = y_t$ for $t \neq j$ and $z_j = y$, and note that

$$\tfrac{1}{m}(y_j - y) = \sum_{i=1}^{m} \tfrac{1}{m}(x_i - \omega_i) - \tfrac{1}{m} \sum_{t=1}^{k} z_t \in G - Y\,.$$

Therefore, from $(\star\star\star)$, we see that $p \cdot \big(\frac{\varepsilon}{m} e + \frac{1}{m}(y_j - y)\big) > 0$, and so $p \cdot y_j \geq p \cdot y - \varepsilon$ for all $y \in Y_j$.]

4.4. APPROXIMATE SUPPORTABILITY

The core properties of allocations in production economies were studied in section 4.2. In this section, we shall discuss the welfare theorems for production economies in the infinite dimensional setting. The major results of this section are due to C. D. Aliprantis and O. Burkinshaw [9]. Recall that an allocation in a production economy is an $(m+k)$-tuple $(x_1,\ldots,x_m,y_1,\ldots,y_k)$ such that $x_i \in E^+$ for all i, $y_j \in Y_j$ for all j and

$$\sum_{i=1}^{m} x_i = \sum_{i=1}^{m} \omega_i + \sum_{j=1}^{k} y_j\,.$$

The notion of supportability of an allocation in a production economy by prices is as follows.

Definition 4.4.1. *An allocation* $(x_1,\ldots,x_m,y_1,\ldots,y_k)$ *in a production economy is said to be supported by a non-zero price* $p \in E'$ *whenever*

a) $x \succeq_i x_i$ *implies* $p\cdot x \geq p\cdot x_i$ (cost minimization by consumers); *and*

b) $p\cdot y_j \geq p\cdot y$ *holds for all* $y \in Y_j$ (profit maximization by producers).

The geometrical meaning of supportability is shown in Figure 4.4-1.

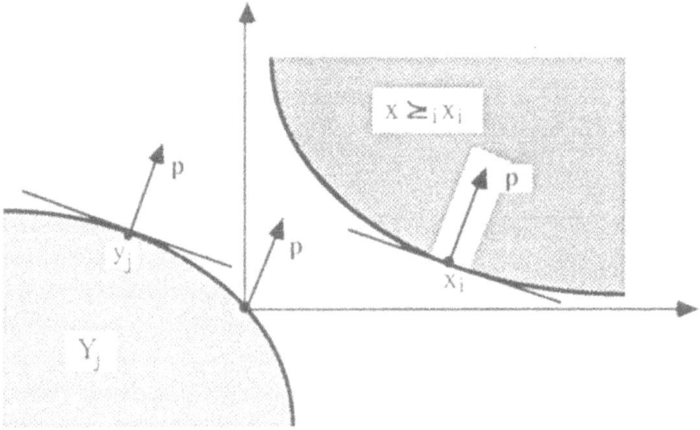

Fig. 4.4-1

Let $(x_1,\ldots,x_m,y_1,\ldots,y_k)$ be an allocation. We shall use the letter e to designate the total commodity assigned by the allocation, i.e.,

$$e := \sum_{i=1}^{m} x_i = \sum_{i=1}^{m} \omega_i + \sum_{j=1}^{k} y_j .$$

If the prevailing price vector is p, then $p \cdot e$ represents the total income of the consumers with respect to the allocation $(x_1, \ldots, x_m, y_1, \ldots, y_k)$.

The notion of an allocation approximately supported by prices conveys the idea that expenditures are approximately minimized and profits are approximately maximized. This concept will be introduced next. It is intuitive that the total income should always be positive. This intuition leads us to normalize prices with respect to the total income. (Recall that if $a \in E^+$, then $Y_j^a = \{y \in Y_j\colon\ y \leq a\}$; see Figure 4.2-1.)

Definition 4.4.2. *An allocation* $(x_1, \ldots, x_m, y_1, \ldots, y_k)$ *is said to be* **approximately supported by prices** *whenever for each* $\varepsilon > 0$ *and each* $a \in E^+$ *there exists a price* p *such that:*

i) $p \cdot e = 1$ *(the total income of the consumers is positive);*
ii) $x \succeq_i x_i$ *implies* $p \cdot x \geq p \cdot x_i - \varepsilon$*; and*
iii) $p \cdot y_j \geq p \cdot y - \varepsilon$ *for all* $y \in Y_j^a$.

If E is a Banach lattice, then the normalization with respect to the total income is not the same as the normalization with respect to the norm. The next result clarifies the situation.

Lemma 4.4.3. *Assume that the commodity space* E *is a Banach lattice (and* E' *its norm dual). If an allocation* $(x_1, \ldots, x_m, y_1, \ldots, y_k)$ *is approximately supported by prices, then for each* $\varepsilon > 0$ *and each* $a \in E^+$ *there exists a price* $p \in E'$ *such that:*

1. $\|p\| = 1$ *and* $p \cdot e > 0$*;*
2. $x \succeq_i x_i$ *implies* $p \cdot x \geq p \cdot x_i - \varepsilon$*; and*
3. $p \cdot y_j \geq p \cdot y - \varepsilon$ *for all* $y \in Y_j^a$.

Proof. Let $(x_1, \ldots, x_m, y_1, \ldots, y_k)$ be an allocation approximately supported by prices. Fix $\varepsilon > 0$ and $a \in E^+$. Put $\delta = \frac{\varepsilon}{\|e\|}$, and then select a non-zero price $q \in E'$ such that:

a) $q \cdot e = 1$;
b) $x \succeq_i x_i$ implies $q \cdot x \geq q \cdot x_i - \delta$; and
c) $q \cdot y_j \geq q \cdot y - \delta$ for all $y \in Y_j^a$.

Now consider the non-zero price $p = \frac{q}{\|q\|}$, and note that

$$\frac{\delta}{\|q\|} = \frac{\varepsilon}{\|q\| \cdot \|e\|} = \varepsilon \cdot \frac{q \cdot e}{\|q\| \cdot \|e\|} \leq \varepsilon .$$

Thus, using (b) above, we see that if $x \succeq_i x_i$ holds in E^+, then

$$p \cdot x = \frac{q \cdot x}{\|q\|} \geq \frac{q \cdot x_i}{\|q\|} - \frac{\delta}{\|q\|} \geq p \cdot x_i - \varepsilon\,.$$

Similarly, if $y \in Y_j^a$, then from (c) we have

$$p \cdot y_j \geq \frac{q \cdot y}{\|q\|} - \frac{\delta}{\|q\|} \geq p \cdot y - \varepsilon,$$

and the proof is finished. ■

We are now in the position to show that for finite dimensional commodity spaces the notions of price supportability and approximate price supportability coincide. Recall that an economy is said to be **a free disposal economy** whenever

$$-E^+ \subseteq \sum_{j=1}^{k} Y_j\,.$$

Theorem 4.4.4. *If the commodity space of a free disposal production economy is finite dimensional and the total endowment ω is strictly positive, then an allocation is price supported if and only if it is approximately price supported.*

Proof. Let $(x_1, \ldots, x_m, y_1, \ldots, y_k)$ be an allocation supported by a price q. To see that q is a positive price, let $x \geq 0$. Then $-\frac{x}{\lambda} \in -E^+$ holds for each $\lambda > 0$ and from the free disposal hypothesis $-E^+ \subseteq \sum_{j=1}^{k} Y_j$, we see that $-q \cdot x \leq \lambda\big(\sum_{j=1}^{k} q \cdot y_j\big)$ holds for all $\lambda > 0$. This implies $q \cdot x \geq 0$ and so $q > 0$. From $\omega \gg 0$, we infer that $q \cdot \omega > 0$. On the other hand, we have $q \cdot y_j \geq 0$ for each j, and so

$$q \cdot e = q \cdot \omega + \sum_{j=1}^{k} q \cdot y_j > 0\,.$$

Now note that the price $p = \frac{q}{q \cdot e}$ satisfies $p \cdot e = 1$ and supports the allocation—and hence, p approximately supports the allocation.

For the converse assume that $(x_1, \ldots, x_m, y_1, \ldots, y_k)$ is approximately supported by prices and that $\langle E, E' \rangle = \langle \mathcal{R}^\ell, \mathcal{R}^\ell \rangle$. Fix a strictly positive vector $v \in E$ and let $a_n = nv$. By Lemma 4.4.3, for each n there exists a price $p_n \in E'$ such that:

1. $\|p_n\| = 1$;
2. $x \succeq_i x$ in E^+ implies $p_n \cdot x \geq p_n \cdot x_i - \frac{1}{n}$; and
3. $p_n \cdot y_j \geq p_n \cdot y - \frac{1}{n}$ for all $y \in Y_j^{a_n}$.

Since the closed unit ball of $\mathcal{R}^\ell$ is norm compact, we can assume (by passing to a subsequence) that $p_n \to p$ holds in $\mathcal{R}^\ell$. Clearly, $\|p\| = 1$, and so $p \neq 0$. We claim that p supports $(x_1, \ldots, x_m, y_1, \ldots, y_k)$. Indeed, note first that if $x \succeq_i x_i$ holds, then $p_n \cdot x \geq p_n \cdot x_i - \frac{1}{n}$ holds for all n, which implies $p \cdot x \geq p \cdot x_i$. On the other hand, if $y \in Y_j$, then $y \leq a_n$ holds eventually for all n, and so $p_n \cdot y_j \geq p_n \cdot y - \frac{1}{n}$ also holds eventually for all n. This implies $p \cdot y_j \geq p \cdot y$, and the proof of the theorem is finished. ■

When the commodity space is infinite dimensional, approximate supportability does not imply supportability. The next example presents an allocation approximately supported by prices that fails to be supported by prices.

Example 4.4.5. We consider a two consumer pure exchange economy with respect to the symmetric Riesz dual system $\langle \ell_1, \ell_\infty \rangle$. The initial endowments of the consumers are given by

$$\omega_1 = \omega_2 = \left(\tfrac{1}{2^3}, \tfrac{1}{2^5}, \ldots, \tfrac{1}{2^{2n+1}}, \ldots \right),$$

and so $\omega = \omega_1 + \omega_2$ is a strictly positive element of ℓ_1. Both consumers will have the same utility function $U: \ell_1^+ \longrightarrow \mathcal{R}$ defined by

$$U(\mathbf{x}) = \sum_{n=1}^{\infty} u_n(x_n), \quad \mathbf{x} = (x_1, x_2, \ldots) \in \ell_1^+,$$

where

$$u_n(t) = \begin{cases} 2^n t, & \text{if } t \leq \frac{1}{2^{2n}}; \\ \frac{1}{2^n} - \frac{1}{2^{2n}} + t, & \text{if } t > \frac{1}{2^{2n}}; \end{cases}$$

see Exercise 6 of Section 3.2. Clearly, the utility function U is concave, strictly monotone and norm continuous.

The rest of the discussion is devoted to establishing that (ω_1, ω_2) is a Pareto optimal allocation approximately supported by prices which cannot be supported by any non-zero price.

1. *The allocation* (ω_1, ω_2) *is Pareto optimal.*

Observe that if $\mathbf{x} = (x_1, x_2, \ldots)$ and $\mathbf{y} = (y_1, y_2, \ldots)$ are two arbitrary positive sequences satisfying $0 \leq x_n + y_n \leq 2^{-2n}$ for all n, then

$$U(\mathbf{x} + \mathbf{y}) = U(\mathbf{x}) + U(\mathbf{y}).$$

Now assume that $(\mathbf{x}_1, \mathbf{x}_2)$ is an allocation satisfying $\mathbf{x}_1 \succeq_1 \omega_1$ and $\mathbf{x}_2 \succeq_2 \omega_2$. From $\mathbf{x}_1 + \mathbf{x}_2 = \omega_1 + \omega_2$ and the above observation, we see that

$$U(\mathbf{x}_1) + U(\mathbf{x}_2) = U(\mathbf{x}_1 + \mathbf{x}_2) = U(\omega_1 + \omega_2) = U(\omega_1) + U(\omega_2).$$

From $U(\mathbf{x}_1) \geq U(\omega_1)$ and $U(\mathbf{x}_2) \geq U(\omega_2)$, we infer that $U(\mathbf{x}_1) = U(\omega_1)$ and $U(\mathbf{x}_2) = U(\omega_2)$. This implies that the allocation (ω_1, ω_2) is Pareto optimal.

2. *The allocation* (ω_1, ω_2) *cannot be supported by prices.*

Let $\mathbf{p} \in \ell_\infty$ be a price that supports (ω_1, ω_2). By the monotonicity of the utility function U, it follows that $\mathbf{p} \geq 0$. Denote by $\mathbf{e}_k$ the sequence whose k^{th}

component is one and every other zero, i.e., $\mathbf{e}_k = (0,\ldots,0,1,0,0,\ldots)$. Now a direct computation shows that

$$(1-2^{-k})\omega_1 + 2^{-2k}\mathbf{e}_k \succ_1 \omega_1,$$

and so by the supportability of $\mathbf{p}$ we get

$$(1-2^{-k})\mathbf{p}\cdot\omega_1 + 2^{-2k}\mathbf{p}\cdot\mathbf{e}_k \geq \mathbf{p}\cdot\omega_1.$$

This implies

$$0 \leq 2^k\mathbf{p}\cdot\omega_1 \leq \mathbf{p}\cdot\mathbf{e}_k \leq \|\mathbf{p}\|_\infty < \infty$$

for all k. Therefore, $\mathbf{p}\cdot\omega_1 = 0$, and since all components of ω_1 are positive, we see that $\mathbf{p} = \mathbf{0}$. Consequently, (ω_1,ω_2) cannot be supported by any non-zero price.

3. *The allocation (ω_1,ω_2) is approximately supported by prices.*

Let $\varepsilon > 0$. Fix some k such that $\sum_{n=k}^{\infty} 2^{-n} < \frac{\varepsilon}{2}$, and consider the ℓ_∞-price

$$\mathbf{q} = (2, 2^2, \ldots, 2^k, 1, 1, 1, \ldots).$$

The price $\mathbf{q}$ satisfies the following properties.

a) *For each i we have $U(\omega_i) \geq \mathbf{q}\cdot\omega_i$.*

To see this, note that

$$U(\omega_i) = \sum_{n=1}^{\infty} \frac{1}{2^{n+1}} \geq \sum_{n=1}^{k} \frac{1}{2^{n+1}} + \sum_{n=k+1}^{\infty} \frac{1}{2^{2n+1}} = \mathbf{q}\cdot\omega_i.$$

b) *If $\mathbf{x} = (x_1, x_2, \ldots) \in \ell_1^+$, then $\mathbf{q}\cdot\mathbf{x} \geq U(\mathbf{x}) - \frac{\varepsilon}{2}$ holds.*

To see this, fix $\mathbf{x} = (x_1, x_2, \ldots) \in \ell_1^+$. First, we claim that

$$2^n x_n \geq u_n(x_n) \quad \text{for each} \quad n.$$

Indeed, for $x_n \leq \frac{1}{2^{2n}}$ we have $u_n(x_n) = 2^n x_n$. On the other hand, if $x_n > \frac{1}{2^{2n}}$, then note that

$$2^n x_n = x_n + (2^n - 1)x_n > x_n + (2^n - 1)\cdot\tfrac{1}{2^{2n}} = x_n + \tfrac{1}{2^n} - \tfrac{1}{2^{2n}} = u_n(x_n).$$

Moreover, an easy argument shows that

$$x_n + \tfrac{1}{2^n} \geq u_n(x_n) \quad \text{for all} \quad n.$$

Now note that the above inequalities yield

$$\begin{aligned}
\mathbf{q}\cdot\mathbf{x} &= \sum_{n=1}^{k} 2^n x_n + \sum_{n=k+1}^{\infty} x_n \\
&= \sum_{n=1}^{k} 2^n x_n + \sum_{n=k+1}^{\infty}\Big(x_n + \frac{1}{2^n}\Big) - \sum_{n=k+1}^{\infty}\frac{1}{2^n} \\
&\geq \sum_{n=1}^{k} u_n(x_n) + \sum_{n=k+1}^{\infty} u_n(x_n) - \frac{\varepsilon}{2} \\
&= U(\mathbf{x}) - \frac{\varepsilon}{2}.
\end{aligned}$$

c) *If* $\mathbf{x} \succeq_i \omega_i$, *then* $\mathbf{q}\cdot\mathbf{x} \geq \mathbf{q}\cdot\omega_i - \frac{\varepsilon}{2}$.

Let $\mathbf{x} \succeq_i \omega_i$, i.e., $U(\mathbf{x}) \geq U(\omega_i)$. Using (b) and then (a), we see that

$$\mathbf{q}\cdot\mathbf{x} \geq U(\mathbf{x}) - \tfrac{\varepsilon}{2} \geq U(\omega_i) - \tfrac{\varepsilon}{2} \geq \mathbf{q}\cdot\omega_i - \tfrac{\varepsilon}{2}.$$

Finally, to see that (ω_1, ω_2) is approximately supported by prices, let $\mathbf{p} = \frac{\mathbf{q}}{\mathbf{q}\cdot\omega}$, where $\omega = \omega_1 + \omega_2$. Then $\mathbf{p}\cdot\omega = 1$ and moreover, if $\mathbf{x} \succeq_i \omega_i$, then by (c) and the fact that $2\mathbf{q}\cdot\omega > 1$ we have

$$\mathbf{p}\cdot\mathbf{x} = \frac{\mathbf{q}\cdot\mathbf{x}}{\mathbf{q}\cdot\omega} \geq \frac{\mathbf{q}\cdot\omega_i}{\mathbf{q}\cdot\omega} - \frac{\varepsilon}{2\mathbf{q}\cdot\omega} \geq \mathbf{p}\cdot\omega_i - \varepsilon.$$

Therefore, (ω_1, ω_2) can be approximately supported by prices. ∎

The Pareto optimality properties of allocations in production economies are defined in the usual manner.

Definition 4.4.6. *An allocation* $(x_1, \ldots, x_m, y_1, \ldots, y_k)$ *in a production economy is said to be:*

1) **Pareto optimal,** *whenever no other allocation* $(z_1, \ldots, z_m, h_1, \ldots, h_k)$ *satisfies* $z_i \succeq_i x_i$ *for all* i *and* $z_i \succ_i x_i$ *for at least one* i; *and*
2) **weakly Pareto optimal,** *whenever there exists no other allocation* $(z_1, \ldots, z_m, h_1, \ldots, h_k)$ *satisfying* $z_i \succ_i x_i$ *for all* i.

The first fundamental theorem of welfare economics can be formulated in the general case as follows.

Theorem 4.4.7. *If an allocation in a production economy is approximately supported by prices, then the allocation is weakly Pareto optimal.*

Proof. Consider a production economy and let $(x_1, \ldots, x_m, y_1, \ldots, y_k)$ be an allocation approximately supported by prices. Assume by way of contradiction that there exists another allocation $(z_1, \ldots, z_m, h_1, \ldots, h_k)$ with $z_i \succ_i x_i$ for each i. Choose $0 < \delta < 1$ such that $\delta z_i \succ_i x_i$ holds for each i.

Now let $\varepsilon > 0$. Put $a = \sum_{j=1}^{k} |h_j|$ and then pick a price p such that

a) $p \cdot e = 1$, where $e = \sum_{i=1}^{m} x_i$;
b) $x \succeq_i x_i$ implies $p \cdot x \geq p \cdot x_i - \varepsilon$; and
c) $p \cdot y_j \geq p \cdot y - \varepsilon$ for all $y \in Y_j$ with $y \leq a$.

From $\delta z_i \succ_i x_i$ and (b), we infer that $p \cdot (\delta z_i) \geq p \cdot x_i - \varepsilon$, and so

$$\delta p \cdot \Big(\sum_{i=1}^{m} z_i\Big) \geq p \cdot \Big(\sum_{i=1}^{m} x_i\Big) - m\varepsilon = 1 - m\varepsilon\,. \qquad (\star)$$

Using $(\star)$ and taking into account (c), we infer that

$$\begin{aligned}
\delta p \cdot \Big(\sum_{i=1}^{m} z_i\Big) &\geq p \cdot \Big(\sum_{i=1}^{m} x_i\Big) - m\varepsilon \\
&= p \cdot \Big(\sum_{i=1}^{m} \omega_i\Big) + \sum_{j=1}^{k} p \cdot y_j - m\varepsilon \\
&\geq p \cdot \Big(\sum_{i=1}^{m} \omega_i\Big) + \sum_{j=1}^{k} p \cdot h_j - k\varepsilon - m\varepsilon \\
&= p \cdot \Big(\sum_{i=1}^{m} z_i\Big) - (k+m)\varepsilon.
\end{aligned}$$

Hence, $(k+m)\varepsilon \geq (1-\delta)p \cdot (\sum_{i=1}^{m} z_i)$, and so from $(\star)$, it follows that $(k+m)\varepsilon \geq \frac{(1-\delta)(1-m\varepsilon)}{\delta}$, i.e., $\delta(k+m)\varepsilon \geq (1-\delta)(1-m\varepsilon)$. This implies

$$\delta \geq 1 - (m + \delta k)\varepsilon\,.$$

Since $\varepsilon > 0$ is arbitrary, the latter inequality shows that $\delta \geq 1$, which is impossible. This contradiction shows that $(x_1, \ldots, x_m, y_1, \ldots, y_k)$ is weakly Pareto optimal. ■

In the sequel the following notation will be employed. If $a \in E^+$, then we shall put

$$Y^a = Y_1^a + \cdots + Y_k^a\,,$$

where as usual $Y_j^a = \{y \in Y_j\colon\ y \leq a\}$. In order to state the second welfare theorem in a general context, we need a lemma. (Recall that a Riesz dual system $\langle E, E' \rangle$ is symmetric if and only if each order interval of E is weakly compact.)

Lemma 4.4.8. *Assume that the Riesz dual system for a production economy is symmetric and let $x_i \in E^+$ $(i = 1, \ldots, m)$ be arbitrary consumption bundles. If $F_i = \{x \in E^+\colon\ ,x \succeq_i x_i\}$, then for each $a \in E^+$ the convex set*

$$F = F_1 + \cdots + F_m - Y^a$$

is weakly closed.

Proof. Fix $a \in E^+$, and let z be in the weak closure of F. Since F is convex, z also belongs to the τ-closure of F. Thus, there exists a net $\{z_\alpha\}$ of F with $z_\alpha \xrightarrow{\tau} z$. Write

$$z_\alpha = \sum_{i=1}^{m} x_\alpha^i - \sum_{j=1}^{k} y_\alpha^j, \tag{$\star\star$}$$

where $x_\alpha^i \in E^+$ and $y_\alpha^j \in Y_j$ satisfy $x_\alpha^i \succeq_i x_i$ and $y_\alpha^j \leq a$.

Clearly, $(y_\alpha^j)^+ \leq a$ and so, since the order interval $[0, a]$ is weakly compact, every subnet of $\{(y_\alpha^j)^+\}$ has a weakly convergent subnet. Now from

$$0 \leq \sum_{i=1}^{m} x_\alpha^i + \sum_{j=1}^{k} (y_\alpha^j)^- = z_\alpha + \sum_{j=1}^{k} (y_\alpha^j)^+ \leq z_\alpha + ka,$$

we see that

$$0 \leq x_\alpha^i \leq z_\alpha + ka \qquad \text{and} \qquad 0 \leq (y_\alpha^j)^- \leq z_\alpha + ka$$

hold for all i and j. Thus, by Lemma 3.3.10, we can assume (by passing to an appropriate subnet) that all nets are weakly convergent. That is, we can assume that $x_\alpha^i \xrightarrow{w} v_i$ and $y_\alpha^j \xrightarrow{w} y_j$ hold for all i and j. Since E^+ and the Y_j^a are weakly closed sets, we see that $v_i \in F_i\,(i = 1, \ldots, m)$ and $y_j \in Y_j^a (j = 1, \ldots, k)$. Now taking weak limits in ($\star\star$), we see that

$$z = \lim_\alpha z_\alpha = \lim_\alpha \Bigl(\sum_{i=1}^{m} x_\alpha^i - \sum_{j=1}^{k} y_\alpha^j \Bigr) = \sum_{i=1}^{m} v_i - \sum_{j=1}^{k} y_j \in F,$$

and the proof is finished. ∎

We are now in the position to state the second fundamental theorem of welfare economics in a general context.

Theorem 4.4.9. *Assume that the Riesz dual system for a production economy is symmetric and that the total endowment is extremely desirable by each consumer. Then every weakly Pareto optimal allocation is approximately supported by prices.*

Proof. Let $(x_1, \ldots, x_m, y_1, \ldots, y_k)$ be a weakly Pareto optimal allocation and let $a \in E^+$ and $\varepsilon > 0$ be fixed. We have to show that there exists some price p that satisfies the three properties of Definition 4.4.2.

To this end, start by letting $b = a + \sum_{j=1}^{k} |y_j|$ and $F_i = \{x \in E^+ \colon\ x \succeq x_i\}$ for all i. Next, choose some $0 < t < 1$ such that $0 < 1 - t < \varepsilon$ and $\frac{1-t}{t} < \varepsilon$. By Lemma 4.4.8, the convex set

$$F = F_1 + \cdots + F_m - Y^b - t\omega$$

is weakly closed.

We claim that $0 \notin F$. To see this, assume that $0 \in F$. Then there are $v_i \in F_i\,(i = 1,\ldots,m)$ and $h_j \in Y_j\,(j = 1,\ldots,k)$ with $\sum_{i=1}^m v_i - \sum_{j=1}^k h_j - t\omega = 0$. This implies

$$\sum_{i=1}^m \left(v_i + \tfrac{1-t}{m}\omega\right) = \sum_{i=1}^m \omega_i + \sum_{j=1}^k h_j.$$

Since ω is extremely desirable by each consumer, we see that $v_i + \frac{1-t}{m}\omega \succ_i v_i \succeq_i x_i$ for each i, which contradicts the weak Pareto optimality of $(x_1,\ldots,x_m,y_1,\ldots,y_k)$. Hence $0 \notin F$.

Now by the separation theorem there exists a price $q \in E'$ satisfying $q \cdot f > 0$ for each $f \in F$. From

$$(1-t)e = \sum_{i=1}^m x_i - \sum_{j=1}^k t y_j - t\omega \in F\,,$$

we see that $q \cdot e > 0$. Put $p = \frac{q}{q \cdot e} \in E'$ and note that $p \cdot f > 0$ holds for all $f \in F$. The rest of the proof is devoted to proving that the price p approximately supports the allocation $(x_1,\ldots,x_m,y_1,\ldots,y_k)$.

1. $p \cdot e = 1$.

This is immediate from the definition of p.

2. *If $x \succeq_r x_r$, then $p \cdot x \geq p \cdot x_r - \varepsilon$ holds.*

To see this, let $x \in E^+$ satisfy $x \succeq_r x_r$. Define $z_i \in E^+$ by $z_i = x$ if $i = r$ and $z_i = x_i$ if $i \neq r$. Then

$$\begin{aligned} x - x_r + (1-t)e &= \sum_{i=1}^m z_i - \sum_{j=1}^k y_j - \omega + (1-t)e \\ &= \sum_{i=1}^m z_i - \sum_{j=1}^k t y_j - t\omega \in F\,, \end{aligned}$$

and so $p \cdot [x - x_r + (1-t)e] > 0$. Therefore, $p \cdot x \geq p \cdot x_r - \varepsilon$.

3. *If $y \in Y_s^a$, then $p \cdot y_s \geq p \cdot y - \varepsilon$ holds.*

To see this, let $y \in Y_s$ satisfy $y \leq a$. Define $h_j \in Y_j^b$ by $h_j = y$ if $j = s$ and $h_j = y_j$ if $j \neq s$. Then we have

$$\begin{aligned} (1-t)e + t(y_s - y) &= \left(\sum_{i=1}^m x_i - \sum_{j=1}^k t y_j - t\omega\right) + t(y_s - y) \\ &= \sum_{i=1}^m x_i - \sum_{j=1}^k t h_j - t\omega \in F, \end{aligned}$$

and so $p \cdot [(1-t)e + t(y_s - y)] > 0$. This implies $p \cdot (y_s - y) \geq -\frac{1-t}{t} > -\varepsilon$, and so $p \cdot y_s \geq p \cdot y - \varepsilon$. The proof of the theorem is now complete. ■

EXERCISES

1. Show that every price that satisfies property (2) of Definition 4.4.2 is necessarily a positive price.
[HINT: Use Theorem 3.4.11.]

2. If the total endowment is strictly positive (i.e., if $\omega \gg 0$ holds) in a production economy, then show that every allocation supported by prices is also approximately supported by prices.

3. Assume that in a production economy an allocation $(x_1, \ldots, x_m, y_1, \ldots, y_k)$ is supported by a price p. If a production set Y_j is also a cone, then show that $p \cdot y_j = 0$.

4. If an allocation $(x_1, \ldots, x_m, y_1, \ldots, y_k)$ in a production economy is approximately supported by prices, then show that for each $a \geq \sum_{i=1}^m \omega_i + \sum_{j=1}^k |y_j|$ the allocation can be supported by a price with respect to the Riesz dual system $\langle A_a, A_a' \rangle$, i.e., show that for every $a \geq \sum_{i=1}^m \omega_i + \sum_{j=1}^k |y_j|$ there exists a price $0 < p \in A_a'$ such that

1) $x \succeq_i x_i$ in A_a^+ implies $p \cdot x \geq p \cdot x_i$; and
2) $p \cdot y_j \geq p \cdot y$ for all $y \in A_a \cap Y_j$.

[HINT: Assume that $(x_1, \ldots, x_m, y_1, \ldots, y_k)$ is an allocation approximately supported by prices and let $a \geq \sum_{i=1}^m \omega_i + \sum_{j=1}^k |y_j|$ be fixed. Then for each n there exists a price $0 < q_n \in E'$ such that

i) $q_n \cdot e = 1$;
ii) $x \succeq_i x_i$ in E^+ implies $q_n \cdot x \geq q_n \cdot x_i - \frac{1}{n}$; and
iii) $q_n \cdot y_j \geq q_n \cdot y - \frac{1}{n}$ for all $y \in Y_j$ with $y \leq a$.

In view of $a \geq e$ and the positivity of each q_n, we see that $q_n \cdot a \geq q_n \cdot e = 1$. Thus, if $p_n = \frac{q_n}{q_n \cdot a}$, then $p_n \cdot a = 1$ holds for each n. Moreover, an easy argument shows that

α) $x \succeq_i x_i$ in E^+ implies $p_n \cdot x \geq p_n \cdot x - \frac{1}{n}$, and
β) $p_n \cdot y_j \geq p_n \cdot y - \frac{1}{n}$ for all $y \in Y_j$ with $y \leq a$.

Next, note that each p_n considered as a positive functional on the AM-space A_a has $\|\cdot\|_\infty$-norm equal to one. Thus, the sequence $\{p_n\}$ lies in the w*-compact set $\{p \in A_a' \colon \|p\|_\infty = |p| \cdot a = 1\}$. Now note that any w*-accumulation point p of $\{p_n\}$ supports the allocation $(x_1, \ldots, x_m, y_1, \ldots, y_k)$ on A_a.]

5. Assume that the Riesz dual system for a production economy is symmetric and that the total endowment is extremely desirable by each consumer. Then show that an allocation is weakly Pareto optimal if and only if it is approximately supported by prices.

4.5. PROPERNESS AND THE WELFARE THEOREMS

In this section, we shall discuss the welfare properties and the existence of quasiequilibria in production economies in the presence of properness. When preferences and production sets are uniformly proper A. Mas-Colell [47] obtained the following version of the second welfare theorem.

Theorem 4.5.1. (Mas-Colell) *If in a production economy preferences and production sets are uniformly τ-proper, then every weakly Pareto optimal allocation can be supported by a price.*

Moreover, if $v_i > 0$ and the convex solid τ-neighborhood V_i of zero (resp. $w_j > 0$ and the convex solid τ-neighborhood W_j of zero) satisfy the definition of uniform properness for $\succeq_i$ (resp. for Y_j), then every weakly Pareto optimal allocation can be supported by a price $p > 0$ that satisfies

$$p\cdot\Big(\sum_{i=1}^m v_i+\sum_{j=1}^k w_j\Big)=1 \quad \textit{and} \quad |p\cdot z|\le 1 \quad \textit{for all} \quad z\in V_1\cap\cdots\cap V_m\cap W_1\cap\cdots\cap W_k\,.$$

Proof. The proof is along the lines of that of Theorem 3.5.4. Consider a production economy that satisfies the hypotheses of our theorem and let $(v_i, V_i)\,(i = 1,\ldots,m)$ and $(w_j, W_j)\,(j = 1,\ldots,k)$ satisfy the definition of uniform properness for the preferences and production sets respectively. Put

$$v=\sum_{i=1}^m v_i+\sum_{j=1}^k w_j>0 \quad \text{and} \quad V=V_1\cap\cdots\cap V_m\cap W_1\cap\cdots\cap W_k\,.$$

Also, let $(x_1,\ldots,x_m,y_1,\ldots,y_k)$ be a weakly Pareto optimal allocation.

For each i consider the non-empty convex set $F_i = \{x \in E^+\colon\ x \succeq_i x_i\}$, and then define the non-empty convex set

$$G=\sum_{i=1}^m F_i-\sum_{j=1}^k Y_j-\omega\,.$$

Also, define the non-empty convex cone Γ by

$$\Gamma=\{\alpha(v+w)\colon\ \alpha>0 \text{ and } w\in V\}\,.$$

Clearly, Γ has interior points (note that $v+V\subseteq\Gamma$), and we claim that $G\cap(-\Gamma)=\emptyset$.

To verify our claim, assume by way of contradiction that $G\cap(-\Gamma)\neq\emptyset$. Then there exist $z_i\in F_i\,(i=1,\ldots,m)$, $y_j\in Y_j\,(j=1,\ldots,k)$ and $\alpha>0$ such that

$$z=\sum_{i=1}^m z_i-\sum_{j=1}^k y_j-\omega+\alpha v\in\alpha V\,. \qquad (\star)$$

From the identity $y_j = y_j^+ - y_j^-$ and $(\star)$, it follows that

$$z = \sum_{i=1}^{m} z_i - \sum_{j=1}^{k} y_j^+ + \sum_{j=1}^{k} y_j^- - \omega + \alpha v \leq \sum_{i=1}^{m} z_i + \sum_{j=1}^{k} y_j^- + \alpha v .$$

Since $z^+ = z \vee 0$, we see that

$$0 \leq z^+ \leq \sum_{i=1}^{m} z_i + \sum_{j=1}^{k} y_j^- + \alpha v = \sum_{i=1}^{m} (z_i + \alpha v_i) + \sum_{j=1}^{k} (y_j^- + \alpha w_j) .$$

By the Riesz Decomposition Property there exist vectors $0 \leq s_i \leq z_i + \alpha v_i \, (i = 1, \ldots, m)$ and $0 \leq t_j \leq y_j^- + \alpha w_j \, (j = 1, \ldots, k)$ such that $\sum_{i=1}^{m} s_i + \sum_{j=1}^{k} t_j = z^+$. From $0 \leq s_i \leq z^+$ and $0 \leq t_j \leq z^+$ and $(\star)$ and the solidness of V, we see that

$$s_i \in \alpha V_i \text{ for } i = 1, \ldots, m \quad \text{and} \quad t_j \in \alpha W_j \text{ for } j = 1, \ldots, k . \qquad (\star\star)$$

Let Γ_j be the convex cone generated by $w_j + W_j$, i.e.,

$$\Gamma_j = \{\lambda(w_j + x) \colon \ \lambda > 0 \ \text{ and } \ x \in W_j\} .$$

If $f_j = y_j - \alpha w_j + t_j$, then $f_j \in Y_j$. Indeed, if $f_j \notin Y_j$, then $y_j = f_j + \alpha w_j - t_j$ belongs to $f_j + \Gamma_j$ and $f_j^+ = (y_j - \alpha w_j + t_j)^+ \leq (y_j + y_j^-)^+ = y_j^+$ contradict the uniform properness of the production set Y_j. Next, note that

$$\begin{aligned} \omega + \sum_{j=1}^{k} f_j &= \omega + \sum_{j=1}^{k} y_j - \alpha \sum_{j=1}^{k} w_j + \sum_{j=1}^{k} t_j \\ &= \omega + \sum_{j=1}^{k} y_j - \alpha v + \alpha \sum_{i=1}^{m} v_i + z^+ - \sum_{i=1}^{m} s_i \\ &= \sum_{i=1}^{m} z_i - z + \alpha \sum_{i=1}^{m} v_i + z^+ - \sum_{i=1}^{m} s_i \\ &= z^- + \sum_{i=1}^{m} (z_i + \alpha v_i - s_i) \\ &= \sum_{i=1}^{m} (z_i + \alpha v_i + \tfrac{1}{m} z^- - s_i) = \sum_{i=1}^{m} g_i , \end{aligned}$$

where $g_i = z_i + \alpha v_i + \frac{1}{m} z^- - s_i$. Put $z_i^* = z_i + \alpha v_i - s_i \geq 0$ and note that $z_i^* \succ_i z_i$ holds for all i. Indeed, if $z_i = z_i^* - \alpha v_i + s_i \succeq_i z_i^*$, then from the uniform properness of $\succeq_i$ it follows that $s_i \notin \alpha V_i$, contrary to $(\star\star)$. From the monotonicity of the preferences and $g_i \geq z_i^*$, we see that $g_i \succ_i z_i$ holds for each i. However, since $(g_1, \ldots, g_m, f_1, \ldots, f_k)$ is an allocation, the latter conclusion contradicts the weak Pareto optimality of $(x_1, \ldots, x_m, y_1, \ldots, y_k)$. Therefore, $G \cap (-\Gamma) = \emptyset$.

Now, by the separation theorem, there exists a non-zero price $p \in E'$ and some constant c such that $p \cdot g \geq c \geq -p \cdot \gamma$ holds for each $g \in G$ and each $\gamma \in \Gamma$. Since Γ is a cone and $0 \in G$, we see that $c = 0$. Therefore, $p \cdot g \geq 0$ and $p \cdot \gamma \geq 0$ hold for all $g \in G$ and all $\gamma \in \Gamma$.

If $x \succeq_r x_r$ holds, then from

$$x - x_r = \sum_{i \neq r} x_i + x - \sum_{j=1}^{k} y_j - \omega \in G\,,$$

we infer that $p \cdot x \geq p \cdot x_r$. On the other hand, if $y \in Y_r$, then from

$$y_r - y = \sum_{i=1}^{m} x_i - \sum_{j \neq r} y_j - y - \omega \in G\,,$$

we also infer that $p \cdot y_r \geq p \cdot y$. Finally, to see that $p \cdot v = 1$ and $|p \cdot z| \leq 1$ for each $z \in V$, repeat the last part of the proof of Theorem 3.5.4. Also, it should be noted that necessarily $p > 0$. ■

The rest of the section is devoted to proving the analogue of Theorem 3.5.12 for production economies. To do this, we need to introduce the utility space for production economies. As before, we shall say that an $(m+k)$-tuple $(x_1, \ldots, x_m, y_1, \ldots, y_k)$ is a *feasible allocation* whenever $x_i \geq 0$ holds for each i, $y_j \in Y_j$ for each j and $\sum_{i=1}^{m} x_i \leq \omega + \sum_{j=1}^{k} y_j$. A *utility allocation* is any vector of $\mathcal{R}_+^m$ of the form $(u_1(x_1), \ldots, u_m(x_m))$, where $(x_1, \ldots, x_m)$ is a part of a feasible allocation. In the sequel, we shall assume that $u_i(0) = 0$ and that ω is extremely desirable by each consumer i. The **utility space** $\mathbf{U}$ of a production economy is the set of all utility allocations, i.e.,

$$\mathbf{U} = \big\{(u_1(x_1), \ldots, u_m(x_m))\colon\ (x_1, \ldots, x_m) \text{ is a part of a feasible allocation}\big\}\,.$$

Clearly, the utility space $\mathbf{U}$ is always a non-empty subset of $\mathcal{R}_+^m$. Unlike the exchange case, $\mathbf{U}$ need not be bounded; see Exercise 3 at the end of this section. However, the two properties of Lemma 3.5.6 are still true in this case. Namely,

a) If $\mathbf{0} \leq (z_1, \ldots, z_m) \leq (z_1^*, \ldots, z_m^*)$ holds in $\mathcal{R}^m$ and $(z_1^*, \ldots, z_m^*) \in \mathbf{U}$, then the vector $(z_1, \ldots, z_m)$ belongs to $\mathbf{U}$; and
b) There exists some $r > 0$ such that $\mathbf{0} \leq \mathbf{z} \in \mathcal{R}^m$ and $\|\mathbf{z}\| \leq r$ imply $\mathbf{z} \in \mathbf{U}$.

Definition 4.5.2. A production economy is said to satisfy

1) **the boundedness condition**, whenever its utility space is a bounded set of $\mathcal{R}_+^m$; and
2) **the compactness condition**, whenever its utility space is a compact subset of $\mathcal{R}_+^m$.

Here are some conditions that guarantee the boundedness and compactness conditions. Recall that—according to Definition 4.2.5—a production economy is said to be a **compact production economy** whenever

i) its Riesz dual system is symmetric; and
ii) $(Y+\omega)\cap E^+$ is a weakly compact set, where $Y=Y_1+\cdots+Y_k$ is the aggregate production set of the economy.

Theorem 4.5.3. *For a production economy the following statements hold.*

1) *If $(Y+\omega)\cap E^+$ is a relatively weakly compact set, then the economy satisfies the boundedness condition.*
2) *If the economy is compact, then the economy satisfies the compactness condition.*

Proof. (1) Let $(Y+\omega)\cap E^+$ be relatively weakly compact, and assume by way of contradiction that $\mathbf{U}$ is not bounded in $\mathcal{R}^m_+$. Then there exists some i and a sequence of feasible allocations $(x_1^n,\ldots,x_m^n,y_1^n,\ldots,y_k^n)$ such that $\limsup_{n\to\infty} u_i(x_i^n)=\infty$. Note that $0\le x_i^n\le \omega+\sum_{i=1}^k y_j^n = z_n\in (Y+\omega)\cap E^+$. Since the set $(Y+\omega)\cap E^+$ is relatively weakly compact, the sequence $\{z_n\}$ has a weakly convergent subnet, say $z_{n_\alpha}\xrightarrow{w} z$. However, by Lemma 1.2.4 each utility function is weakly upper semicontinuous. Therefore, by Exercise 8 of Section 1.2, we have

$$\infty=\limsup_\alpha u_i(x_i^{n_\alpha})\le \limsup_\alpha u_i(z_{n_\alpha})\le u_i(z)<\infty\,,$$

which is a contradiction. Hence, in this case, $\mathbf{U}$ is a bounded set.

(2) Assume that the production economy is compact. By part (1), we know that $\mathbf{U}$ is bounded. So, it remains to be shown that $\mathbf{U}$ is closed. For this, it suffices to establish that if $\{\mathbf{z}_n\}\subseteq \mathbf{U}$ and $\mathbf{z}_n\longrightarrow \mathbf{z}$ in $\mathcal{R}^m$ imply $\mathbf{z}\in\mathbf{U}$.

To this end, for each n write $z_i^n=u_i(x_i^n)$, where $(x_1^n,\ldots,x_m^n,y_1^n\ldots,y_k^n)$ is a feasible allocation. Since $\{x_i^n\}$ lies in the solid hull of the weakly compact subset $(Y+\omega)\cap E^+$ of E^+, it follows from Lemma 4.2.3 that there exists a subnet n_α of $\{1,2,3,\ldots\}$ such that $x_i^{n_\alpha}\xrightarrow{w} x_i$ for each i and $\sum_{i=1}^m x_i\le\omega+\sum_{j=1}^k y_j$, where $\sum_{j=1}^k y_j^{n_\alpha}\xrightarrow{w}\sum_{j=1}^k y_j\in Y$. By Exercise 8 of Section 1.2, we see that

$$z_i\le \lim_\alpha u_i(x_i^{n_\alpha})\le u_i(x_i)$$

holds for each i. From $(u_1(x_1),\ldots,u_m(x_m))\in\mathbf{U}$, we infer that $\mathbf{z}\in\mathbf{U}$, and consequently, $\mathbf{U}$ is a compact set. ■

When a production economy satisfies the boundedness condition, then the function $\rho\colon\Delta\longrightarrow(0,\infty)$ defined by

$$\rho(\mathbf{s})=\sup\{\alpha>0\colon\ \alpha\mathbf{s}\in\mathbf{U}\}$$

is well defined, and by repeating the proof of Theorem 3.5.7, we infer that ρ is also a continuous function. In addition, if the economy satisfies the compactness condition, then—by repeating the proof of Theorem 3.5.10—we see that for each $\mathbf{s} \in \Delta$ there exists an allocation $(x_1^{\mathbf{s}}, \ldots, x_m^{\mathbf{s}}, y_1^{\mathbf{s}}, \ldots, y_k^{\mathbf{s}})$ such that

$$\rho(\mathbf{s})\mathbf{s} = \big(u_1(x_1^{\mathbf{s}}), \ldots, u_m(x_m^{\mathbf{s}})\big)\,.$$

Clearly, any allocation $(x_1^{\mathbf{s}}, \ldots, x_m^{\mathbf{s}}, y_1^{\mathbf{s}}, \ldots, y_k^{\mathbf{s}})$ that satisfies the above equality is automatically weakly Pareto optimal. Also, recall that in a private ownership production economy an allocation $(x_1, \ldots, x_m, y_1, \ldots, y_m)$ is said to be a *quasiequilibrium* whenever there exists a non-zero price p—which is necessarily positive—such that

a) $x \succeq_i x_i$ implies $p \cdot x \geq p \cdot \omega_i + \sum_{j=1}^k \theta_{ij} p \cdot y_j$; and
b) $p \cdot y_j \geq p \cdot y$ for each $y \in Y_j$.

Of course, in this case we have $p \cdot x_i = p \cdot \omega_i + \sum_{j=1}^k \theta_{ij} p \cdot y_j$.

We are now in the position to establish the analogue of Theorem 3.5.12 for the production case. The result is essentially due to S. F. Richard [55].

Theorem 4.5.4. *If a private ownership production economy is compact, preferences and production sets are uniformly τ-proper and the total endowment is extremely desirable by each consumer, then the economy has a quasiequilibrium.*

Proof. Consider a private ownership production economy that satisfies the properties of the theorem. Also, let (v_i, V_i) and (w_j, W_j) satisfy the properties of τ-properness for preferences and production sets, respectively. Put

$$v = \sum_{i=1}^m v_i + \sum_{j=1}^k w_j \qquad \text{and} \qquad V = V_1 \cap \cdots \cap V_m \cap W_1 \cap \cdots \cap W_k\,.$$

The proof of the theorem is similar to that of Theorem 3.5.12.

For each $\mathbf{s} \in \Delta$ pick an allocation $(x_1^{\mathbf{s}}, \ldots, x_m^{\mathbf{s}}, y_1^{\mathbf{s}}, \ldots, y_k^{\mathbf{s}})$ such that

$$\rho(\mathbf{s})\mathbf{s} = \big(u_1(x_1^{\mathbf{s}}), u_2(x_2^{\mathbf{s}}), \ldots, u_m(x_m^{\mathbf{s}})\big)\,, \tag{1}$$

and then define the set

$$P(\mathbf{s}) = \big\{p \in E'_+\colon\ p \text{ supports } (x_1^{\mathbf{s}}, \ldots, x_m^{\mathbf{s}}, y_1^{\mathbf{s}}, \ldots, y_k^{\mathbf{s}}),\ p \cdot v = 1 \text{ and } |p \cdot z| \leq 1\ \forall\ z \in V\big\}\,.$$

Since $(x_1^{\mathbf{s}}, \ldots, x_m^{\mathbf{s}}, y_1^{\mathbf{s}}, \ldots, y_k^{\mathbf{s}})$ is weakly Pareto optimal, it follows from Theorem 4.5.1 that $P(\mathbf{s})$ is non-empty. Clearly, each $P(\mathbf{s})$ is also a convex set.

Now for each $\mathbf{s} \in \Delta$ define the set

$$\Phi(\mathbf{s}) = \Big\{(z_1, \ldots, z_m) \in \mathcal{R}^m\colon\ \exists\ p \in P(\mathbf{s}) \text{ with } z_i = p \cdot \Big(\omega_i + \sum_{j=1}^k \theta_{ij} y_j^{\mathbf{s}} - x_i^{\mathbf{s}}\Big)\ \forall\ i\Big\}\,.$$

Since $P(\mathbf{s})$ is non-empty and convex, $\Phi(\mathbf{s})$ is non-empty and convex. In addition, $\Phi(\mathbf{s})$ is a bounded subset of $\mathcal{R}^m$. Indeed, note first that since $(Y + \omega) \cap E^+$ is

τ-bounded, there exists some $\delta > 0$ such that $(Y + \omega) \cap E^+ \subseteq \delta V$. Now let $\mathbf{z} = (z_1, \ldots, z_m) \in \Phi(\mathbf{s})$. Pick some $p \in P(\mathbf{s})$ such that $z_i = p \cdot \left(\omega_i + \sum_{j=1}^k \theta_{ij} y_j^{\mathbf{s}} - x_i^{\mathbf{s}}\right)$ holds for all i. Clearly, $\sum_{i=1}^m x_i^{\mathbf{s}} = \omega + \sum_{j=1}^k y_j^{\mathbf{s}} \in (Y + \omega) \cap E^+$. Since $p \cdot y_j^{\mathbf{s}} \geq p \cdot 0 = 0$, we see that

$$z_i = p \cdot \Big(\omega_i + \sum_{j=1}^k \theta_{ij} y_j^{\mathbf{s}} - x_i^{\mathbf{s}}\Big) \leq p \cdot \Big(\omega + \sum_{j=1}^k \theta_{ij} y_j^{\mathbf{s}}\Big) \leq p \cdot \Big(\omega + \sum_{j=1}^k y_j^{\mathbf{s}}\Big) \leq \delta\,.$$

Likewise, we have

$$z_i = p \cdot \Big(\omega_i + \sum_{j=1}^k \theta_{ij} y_j^{\mathbf{s}} - x_i^{\mathbf{s}}\Big) \geq -p \cdot x_i^{\mathbf{s}} \geq -p \cdot \Big(\sum_{r=1}^m x_r^{\mathbf{s}}\Big) \geq -\delta\,.$$

Consequently,

$$\mathbf{z} = (z_1, \ldots, z_m) \in \Phi(\mathbf{s}) \text{ implies } |z_i| \leq \delta \text{ for each } i \text{ and all } \mathbf{s} \in \Delta\,. \qquad (\mathbf{2})$$

Next, we claim that the correspondence $\Phi \colon \Delta \longrightarrow 2^{\mathcal{R}^m}$ has a closed graph. To see this, let $\mathbf{s}_n \to \mathbf{s}$, $\mathbf{z}_n = (z_1^n, \ldots, z_m^n) \in \Phi(\mathbf{s}_n)$ for each n and $\mathbf{z}_n \to \mathbf{z}$ in $\mathcal{R}^m$; we must verify that $\mathbf{z} = (z_1, \ldots, z_n) \in \Phi(\mathbf{s})$. For each n pick some $p_n \in P(\mathbf{s}_n)$ such that $z_i^n = p_n \cdot \left(\omega_i + \sum_{j=1}^k \theta_{ij} y_j^{\mathbf{s}_n} - x_i^{\mathbf{s}_n}\right)$. Since the sequence $\{p_n\}$ belongs to the polar V° of V and V° is by Alaoglu's theorem w*-compact (see [8, Theorem 9.20, p. 141]), there exists a subnet $\{p_{n_\alpha}\}$ of $\{p_n\}$—where, of course, $\{n_\alpha\}$ is a subnet of $\{n\}$—such that $p_{n_\alpha} \xrightarrow{w^*} p$ in E'. Clearly, $p \cdot v = 1$, and $|p \cdot z| \leq 1$ for all $z \in V$.

Now let $x_i \succeq_i x_i^{\mathbf{s}}$ for each i and $h_j \in Y_j$ for all j. Fix $\varepsilon > 0$ and note that $x_i + \varepsilon\omega \succ_i x_i^{\mathbf{s}}$. By the continuity of the function ρ, we have $\rho(\mathbf{s}_{n_\alpha})\mathbf{s}_{n_\alpha} \longrightarrow \rho(\mathbf{s})\mathbf{s}$ and so there exists some α_0 such that $x_i + \varepsilon\omega \succ_i x_i^{\mathbf{s}_{n_\alpha}}$ holds for all $\alpha \geq \alpha_0$. The supportability of p_{n_α} implies

$$\begin{aligned} p_{n_\alpha} \cdot (x_i + \varepsilon\omega) \geq p_{n_\alpha} \cdot x_i^{\mathbf{s}_{n_\alpha}} &= p_{n_\alpha} \cdot \omega_i + \sum_{j=1}^k \theta_{ij} p_{n_\alpha} \cdot y_j^{\mathbf{s}_{n_\alpha}} - z_i^{n_\alpha} \\ &\geq p_{n_\alpha} \cdot \omega_i + \sum_{j=1}^k \theta_{ij} p_{n_\alpha} \cdot h_j - z_i^{n_\alpha} \end{aligned}$$

for all $\alpha \geq \alpha_0$. Passing to the limit, we see that $p \cdot x_i + \varepsilon p \cdot \omega \geq p \cdot \omega_i + \sum_{j=1}^k \theta_{ij} p \cdot h_j - z_i$ holds for all $\varepsilon > 0$. This implies that

$$p \cdot x_i \geq p \cdot \omega_i + \sum_{j=1}^k \theta_{ij} p \cdot h_j - z_i \qquad (\mathbf{3})$$

for each i. Letting $x_i = x_i^{\mathbf{s}}\,(i = 1, \ldots, m)$ and $h_j = y_j^{\mathbf{s}}\,(j = 1, \ldots, k)$ in (**3**) and taking into account the equalities $\sum_{i=1}^m x_i^{\mathbf{s}} = \sum_{i=1}^m \omega_i + \sum_{j=1}^k y_j^{\mathbf{s}}$ and $\sum_{i=1}^m z_i = 0$, we conclude that $p \cdot x_i^s = p \cdot \omega_i + \sum_{j=1}^k \theta_{ij} p \cdot y_j^s - z_i$. Thus, $z_i = p \cdot \big(\omega_i + \sum_{j=1}^k \theta_{ij} y_j^s - x_i^s\big)$ for each i.

To complete the proof that $\mathbf{z} \in \Phi(\mathbf{s})$, it remains to be shown that the price p supports the allocation $(x_1^s, \ldots, x_m^s, y_1^s, \ldots, y_k^s)$. First, note that if $x \succsim_i x_i^s$, then by letting $x_i = x$ and $y_j = y_j^s\ (j = 1, \ldots, k)$ in (3) we get

$$p \cdot x \geq p \cdot \omega_i + \sum_{j=1}^k \theta_{ij} p \cdot y_j^s - z_i = p \cdot x_i^s .$$

On the other hand, if we put $x_i = x_i^s\ (i = 1, \ldots, m)$ and $h_j = y_j^s$ for $j \neq r$ and $h_r = y \in Y_r$, then from (3) it follows that

$$\begin{aligned} p \cdot y_r^s - p \cdot y &= \Big[\sum_{i=1}^m p \cdot \omega_i + \sum_{j=1}^k p \cdot y_j^s\Big] - \Big[\sum_{i=1}^m p \cdot \omega_i + \sum_{j=1}^k p \cdot h_j + \sum_{i=1}^m z_i\Big] \\ &= \sum_{i=1}^m p \cdot x_i^s - \Big[\sum_{i=1}^m p \cdot \omega_i + \sum_{i=1}^m \sum_{j=1}^k \theta_{ij} p \cdot h_j + \sum_{i=1}^m z_i\Big] \\ &= \sum_{i=1}^m \Big(p \cdot x_i^s - p \cdot \omega_i - \sum_{j=1}^k \theta_{ij} p \cdot h_j + z_i\Big) \geq 0 , \end{aligned}$$

i.e., $p \cdot y_r^s \geq p \cdot y$ holds for each $y \in Y_r\ (r = 1, \ldots, k)$. Therefore, p supports the allocation $(x_1^s, \ldots, x_m^s, y_1^s, \ldots, y_k^s)$, and so $\mathbf{z} \in \Phi(\mathbf{s})$. In other words, the correspondence Φ has a closed graph.

Next, consider the non-empty, compact and convex subset of $\mathcal{R}^m$

$$T = \{\mathbf{t} = (t_1, \ldots, t_m) \in \mathcal{R}^m \colon\ \|\mathbf{t}\|_1 = \sum_{i=1}^m |t_i| \leq m\delta\} .$$

By (2), we have $\Phi(\mathbf{s}) \subseteq T$ for each $\mathbf{s} \in \Delta$. Now fix some $\eta > m\delta$ and define the function $f \colon \Delta \times T \longrightarrow \Delta$ by

$$f(\mathbf{s}, \mathbf{t}) = \left(\frac{(s_1 + \frac{t_1}{\eta})^+}{\sum_{i=1}^m (s_i + \frac{t_i}{\eta})^+}, \frac{(s_2 + \frac{t_2}{\eta})^+}{\sum_{i=1}^m (s_i + \frac{t_i}{\eta})^+}, \ldots, \frac{(s_m + \frac{t_m}{\eta})^+}{\sum_{i=1}^m (s_i + \frac{t_i}{\eta})^+} \right), \quad (\mathbf{s}, \mathbf{t}) \in \Delta \times T ,$$

where, as usual, $r^+ = \max\{r, 0\}$ for each real number r. Since

$$\textstyle\sum_{i=1}^m \big(s_i + \frac{t_i}{\eta}\big)^+ \geq \sum_{i=1}^m \big(s_i + \frac{t_i}{\eta}\big) = 1 + \frac{1}{\eta} \sum_{i=1}^m t_i \geq 1 - \frac{m\delta}{\eta} > 0$$

holds for each $(\mathbf{s}, \mathbf{t}) \in \Delta \times T$, it follows that the function f is well defined and continuous.

Finally, we define the non-empty correspondence $\phi \colon \Delta \times T \longrightarrow 2^{\Delta \times T}$ by

$$\phi(\mathbf{s}, \mathbf{t}) = \{f(\mathbf{s}, \mathbf{t})\} \times \Phi(\mathbf{s}) .$$

Clearly, ϕ is convex-valued. The continuity of f coupled with the fact that $\mathbf{s} \mapsto \Phi(\mathbf{s})$ has a closed graph implies that ϕ has also a closed graph. Thus, by Kakutani's fixed point theorem (Theorem 1.4.7), the correspondence ϕ has a fixed point, say $(\mathbf{s}, \mathbf{t})$. That is, there exists some $(\mathbf{s}, \mathbf{t}) \in \Delta \times T$ such that $\mathbf{s} = f(\mathbf{s}, \mathbf{t})$ and $\mathbf{t} \in \Phi(\mathbf{s})$. Pick some $p \in P(\mathbf{s})$ such that

$$t_i = p \cdot \omega_i + \sum_{j=1}^{k} \theta_{ij} p \cdot y_j^{\mathbf{s}} - p \cdot x_i^{\mathbf{s}} \quad \text{for all} \quad i \,. \tag{4}$$

To complete the proof, we shall establish that $t_i = 0$ for each i.

If $s_i = 0$, then from (1) we see that $x_i^{\mathbf{s}} \sim_i 0$. So, by the supportability of p, we obtain $0 = p \cdot 0 \geq p \cdot x_i^{\mathbf{s}} + \sum_{j=1}^{k} \theta_{ij} p \cdot y_j^{\mathbf{s}} \geq 0$ and so $p \cdot x_i^{\mathbf{s}} = 0$. Now note that from $\mathbf{s} = f(\mathbf{s}, \mathbf{t})$, it follows that $(s_i + \frac{t_i}{\eta})^+ = (\frac{t_i}{\eta})^+ = 0$ and so $t_i \leq 0$. From (4), we conclude that $0 \leq p \cdot \omega_i + \sum_{j=1}^{k} \theta_{ij} p \cdot y_j^{\mathbf{s}} = t_i$. That is, $s_i = 0$ implies $t_i = 0$, and so $\left(s_i + \frac{t_i}{\eta}\right)^+ = s_i + \frac{t_i}{\eta} = 0$.

Now if $s_i > 0$ holds, then from $\mathbf{s} = f(\mathbf{s}, \mathbf{t})$, we see that $\left(s_i + \frac{t_i}{\eta}\right)^+ > 0$ and so $\left(s_i + \frac{t_i}{\eta}\right)^+ = s_i + \frac{t_i}{\eta}$ must hold. Thus, for each i we have $\left(s_i + \frac{t_i}{\eta}\right)^+ = s_i + \frac{t_i}{\eta}$. Consequently,

$$\sum_{i=1}^{m} \left(s_i + \tfrac{t_i}{\eta}\right)^+ = \sum_{i=1}^{m} \left(s_i + \tfrac{t_i}{\eta}\right) = \sum_{i=1}^{m} s_i + \tfrac{1}{\eta} \sum_{i=1}^{m} \Big(p \cdot \omega_i + \sum_{j=1}^{k} \theta_{ij} p \cdot y_j^{\mathbf{s}} - p \cdot x_i^{\mathbf{s}}\Big) = 1 \,.$$

Finally, using once more the equation $\mathbf{s} = f(\mathbf{s}, \mathbf{t})$, we see that $s_i = s_i + \frac{t_i}{\eta}$ holds for each i, which yields $t_i = 0$ for each i and the proof of the theorem is complete. ■

EXERCISES

1. (A. Mas-Colell [47]) A set Z is said to be a *pre-technology set* for a production set Y whenever Z is comprehensive from below (i.e., $Z - E^+ = Z$ holds), $Y \subseteq Z$ and $z \in Z$ implies $z^+ = z \vee 0 \in Z$.

   Assume that for a production set Y there exists a pre-technology set Z, a vector $w > 0$ and a τ-neighborhood W of zero such that $z \in Z \setminus Y$ and $z + \alpha w + y \in Z$ with $\alpha > 0$ imply $y \notin \alpha W$. Show that the production set Y is uniformly τ-proper.

   [HINT: Let $\Gamma = \{\alpha(w + x)\colon\ \alpha > 0 \text{ and } x \in W\}$. If

   $$(z + \Gamma) \cap \{y \in Y\colon\ y^+ \geq z^+\} \neq \emptyset$$

   holds for some $z \notin Y$, then there exist $\alpha > 0$ and $x \in W$ such that $z + \alpha(w + x) \in Y \subseteq Z$ and $[z + \alpha(w + x)]^+ \geq z^+$. This implies $z^+ \in Z$ and from $z \leq z^+$ we see that $z \in Z$. On the other hand, from $z \notin Y$ and $z + \alpha(w + x) = z + \alpha w + \alpha x \in Y \subseteq Z$, it follows that $\alpha x \notin \alpha W$ (i.e., $x \notin W$), which is impossible.]

2. Let E be an AM-space with unit—in particular, let E be a finite dimensional vector space. If a production set Y is comprehensive from below (that is, if $Y - E^+ = Y$), then show that Y is a uniformly $\|\cdot\|_\infty$-proper production set.

3. Consider a production economy with Riesz dual system $\langle \mathcal{R}^2, \mathcal{R}^2 \rangle$ having two producers with production sets

$$Y_1 = \{(x, y) \in \mathcal{R}^2\colon\ x \leq 0 \text{ and } y \leq -2x\},$$
$$Y_2 = \{(x, y) \in \mathcal{R}^2\colon\ y \leq 0 \text{ and } x \leq -y\},$$

and one consumer with utility function $u(x, y) = x + y$ and initial endowment $\omega = (1, 1)$.

Show that $Y_1 + Y_2 = \mathcal{R}^2$ and conclude from this that $\mathbf{U} = [0, \infty)$—and so, $\mathbf{U}$ is an unbounded set.

4. If a production economy satisfies the boundedness condition, then show that the function $\rho\colon \Delta \longrightarrow (0, \infty)$ defined by

$$\rho(\mathbf{s}) = \sup\{\alpha > 0\colon\ \alpha\mathbf{s} \in \mathbf{U}\}$$

is a continuous function.
[HINT: Repeat the proof of Theorem 3.5.7.]

5. If a production economy satisfies the compactness condition, then show that for each $\mathbf{s} \in \Delta$ there exists an allocation $(x_1^{\mathbf{s}}, \ldots, x_m^{\mathbf{s}}, y_1^{\mathbf{s}}, \ldots, y_k^{\mathbf{s}})$ such that

$$\rho(\mathbf{s})\mathbf{s} = \big(u_1(x_1^{\mathbf{s}}), \ldots, u_m(x_m^{\mathbf{s}})\big).$$

[HINT: Repeat the proof of Theorem 3.5.10.]

CHAPTER 5:

THE OVERLAPPING GENERATIONS MODEL

In this final chapter, we turn to the other major paradigm in general equilibrium theory: the overlapping generations (OLG) model. The OLG models are extensions and elaborations of P. A. Samuelson's celebrated pure consumption loan model [59]. Unlike the Arrow–Debreu model which has its genesis in the work of L. Walras [67], Samuelson's model derives from I. Fisher's classic monograph *The Theory of Interest* [28]. As such it shares its origins with the models of T. F. Bewley [16] and B. Peleg and M. E. Yaari [53].

In our framework, we can view I. Fisher's "first approximation" as a standard Arrow–Debreu pure exchange economy with the additional behavioral assumption that agents are "impatient." Consequently, the equilibrium rate of interest will be positive. The work of T. F. Bewley and B. Peleg and M. E. Yaari can be considered as infinite horizon versions of Fisher's "first approximation." The weaker (topological) notion of impatience assumed by these authors only guarantees that the rate of interest is asymptotically positive, but this is still consistent with Fisher's intuition that impatience (together with the other standard assumptions on agents' characteristics) suffices for the existence of a positive market clearing rate of interest. Surprisingly, there is no discussion of optimality in *The Theory of Interest*, but we already know from the analysis in the previous chapters that competitive allocations are Pareto optimal in both the finite horizon model of Arrow–Debreu and the infinite horizon models of T. F. Bewley and B. Peleg and M. E. Yaari.

The OLG model of P. A. Samuelson has quite a different structure. There are a countable number of overlapping generations and each generation consists of a finite number of finitely lived agents. In the simplest case, a generation consists of a single agent who lives for two periods. Each agent is endowed with an infinite consumption stream which is zero in every period except (possibly) in the two periods in which she is alive. In addition, each agent has a utility function over the space of infinite consumption streams that depends only on the consumption they provide during her lifetime. Samuelson goes beyond Fisher in his concern about the optimality of competitive allocations.

Certainly, one of the most memorable aspects of Samuelson's paper [59] is his simple example of an OLG model where the initial endowments constitute a competitive equilibrium that is Pareto suboptimal. As an aside, we note that the rate of interest is zero in Samuelson's example—more about impatience and the rate of interest in OLG models can be found in D. Gale's penetrating study [29]. D. Cass and M. E. Yaari argue in [21] that "infinity" is not the cause of the inefficiency. It is obvious that in the OLG model, the failure of the proof of the first welfare theorem—given in earlier chapters—must have something to do with the "double infinity" of agents and commodities, an observation first made by K. Shell [64]. But what exactly is the role of the "double infinity?"

To answer this question, we first identify the commodity and price spaces which appear in the literature on existence and optimality of competitive equilibria in the OLG model. In most papers (see, for example, [14, 15, 20, 68]) the commodity space is $\mathcal{R}_\infty$ with the product topology and the price space is also $\mathcal{R}_\infty$. Of course, these two spaces do not form a dual pair. In these models the proof of the first welfare theorem fails because the equilibrium prices for Pareto suboptimal competitive allocations give infinite valuation to the social endowment. A notable exception is the work of S. F. Richard and S. Srivastava [56] where they consider the dual pair of spaces $\langle \ell_\infty, \mathrm{ba} \rangle$ as the commodity and price spaces for the OLG model. In their model, equilibrium prices may be purely finitely additive linear functionals. Hence, the value of each agent's endowment can be zero and the value of the social endowment can be positive. That is, the sum of the values (of the initial endowments) is not equal to the value of the sum (of the initial endowments). Of course, there are prices in ba which do not allow "arbitrage at infinity," i.e., ℓ_1 prices. If the equilibrium prices are in ℓ_1, then the resulting allocation is Pareto optimal. Unfortunately, the converse is not true. There are Pareto optimal competitive allocations in the OLG model where the equilibrium prices define a purely finitely additive linear functional. This important result is a consequence of the characterization of Pareto optimality in smooth OLG models due to Y. Balasko and K. Shell [15].

Although the $\langle \ell_\infty, \mathrm{ba} \rangle$ duality illuminates the difficulty in extending the first welfare theorem to economies with both a countable number of agents and commodities, it gives rise to difficulties in interpretation, since—as mentioned previously—purely finitely additive linear functionals cannot be interpreted as defining interest rates between periods. This is the reason that the other authors, following Samuelson, have defined prices as elements of $\mathcal{R}_\infty$. In this chapter, we shall present a new commodity-price space duality for the OLG model that also allows for an interpretation of prices as rates of interest. A novel feature of our model—which was presented in [5]—is that the social endowment does not belong to the commodity space. If the domain of the equilibrium prices can be extended to include the social endowment, then the allocation which they support is Pareto optimal, but in general the social endowment may have "infinite valuation" with respect to prices supporting an equilibrium allocation.

In the OLG model, each generation has (implicitly) its own commodity space. Our construction of the commodity space for the whole economy consists of "gluing" together these overlapping commodity spaces in a coherent fashion. The natural construction is to form the direct sum (or more generally the inductive limit) of the individual spaces. Each generation's commodity space has its own topology, hence the topology that we impose on the economy-wide commodity space should be consistent with the existing topologies. One notion of consistency is to require that a linear functional is continuous in the economy-wide topology if and only if its restriction to every generation's commodity space is continuous. The inductive limit topology is the finest such topology and it is this topology which we impose on the direct sum (or inductive limit) of the individual spaces. The price space in our commodity-price duality is now the space of linear functionals, on the inductive limit of the individual commodity spaces, that are continuous with respect to the inductive limit topology. For the OLG models considered in the literature—where each generation's commodity space is a copy of $\mathcal{R}^\ell$—our duality specializes to $\langle \phi, \mathcal{R}_\infty \rangle$, where as usual ϕ denotes the vector space of all sequences that are eventually zero. In this case the inductive limit topology coincides with the "fine" topology.

Given the failure of the first welfare theorem in the OLG model, we consider a weaker notion of optimality—referred to as Malinvaud optimality. This optimality notion was introduced by Y. Balasko and K. Shell in [15] where they called it weak Pareto optimality—which already has a standard definition in the general equilibrium literature. Balasko and Shell showed that the first and second welfare theorems hold for the notion of Malinvaud optimality if each generation has a finite dimensional commodity space. We extend their result to infinite dimensional commodity spaces for each generation.

Finally, we prove the existence of competitive equilibria in OLG models where each generation may have an infinite dimensional commodity space. This is technically the most difficult theorem in the monograph and depends crucially on a lemma first proved by C. A. Wilson in [68]. In addition to the authors cited above, we have been much influenced by the published and unpublished research of J. Geanakoplos—see [30] and the references cited there.

5.1. THE SETTING OF THE OLG MODEL

In the overlapping generations model the index t will denote the time period. The commodity-price duality at period t will be represented by a Riesz dual system $\langle E_t, E'_t \rangle$. Consequently, we have a sequence $(\langle E_1, E'_1 \rangle, \langle E_2, E'_2 \rangle, \ldots)$ of Riesz dual systems each member of which designates the commodity-price duality at the corresponding time period. Each Riesz space E_t is assumed equipped with a locally convex-solid topology that is consistent with the dual system $\langle E_t, E'_t \rangle$. As usual, the terms "consumer" and "agent" will be used interchangeably in our discussion of exchange.

For simplicity of exposition, we assume that only one consumer is born in each period and has a two-period lifetime. Thus, consumer t is born at period t and is alive in periods t and $t+1$. Each consumer trades and has tastes for commodities only during her life-time. We suppose that consumer t gets an initial endowment $0 < \omega_t^t \in E_t$ at period t and $0 < \omega_t^{t+1} \in E_{t+1}$ at period $t+1$ (and, of course, nothing else in any other periods). Consequently, her initial endowment ω_t is represented by the vector

$$\omega_t = (0, \ldots, 0, \omega_t^t, \omega_t^{t+1}, 0, 0, \ldots),$$

where ω_t^t and ω_t^{t+1} occupy the positions t and $t+1$, respectively. Also, for mathematical convenience, we shall assume that the "mother" of consumer 1 (i.e., consumer 0) is present in the model at period 1. She will be designated as consumer 0 and her endowment will be taken to be of the form

$$\omega_0 = (\omega_0^1, 0, 0, \ldots)$$

with $0 < \omega_0^1 \in E_1$. Thus, the vectors of the Riesz space $E_1 \times E_2 \times \cdots$ given by

$$\begin{array}{lcllllllll} \omega_{t-1} & = & (0, & \ldots, & 0, & \omega_{t-1}^{t-1}, & \omega_{t-1}^{t}, & 0, & 0, & 0, \ \ldots) \\ \omega_t & = & (0, & \ldots, & 0, & 0, & \omega_t^t, & \omega_t^{t+1}, & 0, & 0, \ \ldots) \end{array}$$

represent the initial endowments of the two consecutive consumers $t-1$ and t. Consequently, the commodity bundle

$$\omega_{t-1}^t + \omega_t^t$$

represents the total endowment in period t. An illustration of the overlapping generations model is shown in Figure 5.1-1.

The vectors of the form

$$\mathbf{x}_t = (0, \ldots, 0, x_t^t, x_t^{t+1}, 0, 0, \ldots),$$

where $x_t^t \in E_t^+$ and $x_t^{t+1} \in E_{t+1}^+$ represent the commodity bundles for consumer t during her life-time. Each consumer t maximizes a utility function u_t defined on her commodity space, i.e., u_t is a function from $E_t^+ \times E_{t+1}^+$ into $\mathcal{R}$. The value of u_t at the commodity bundle $\mathbf{x}_t = (0, \ldots, 0, x_t^t, x_t^{t+1}, 0, 0, \ldots)$ will be denoted by $u_t(x_t^t, x_t^{t+1})$. We shall consider u_t defined everywhere on $E_1^+ \times E_2^+ \times \cdots$ by the formula

$$u_t(\mathbf{x}) = u_t(x^1, x^2, \ldots) = u_t(x^t, x^{t+1}).$$

The utility functions will be assumed to satisfy the following properties.

1. *Each u_t is quasi-concave;*
2. *Each u_t is strictly monotone on $E_t^+ \times E_{t+1}^+$, that is, if $(x, y) > (x_1, y_1)$ holds in $E_t^+ \times E_{t+1}^+$, then $u_t(x, y) > u_t(x_1, y_1)$; and*
3. *Each u_t is continuous on $E_t^+ \times E_{t+1}^+$, where each E_t is now equipped with a locally convex-solid topology consistent with the Riesz dual system $\langle E_t, E_t' \rangle$.*

The case $t = 0$ is a special case. The utility function u_0 is a function of one variable defined on E_1^+. It is also assumed to satisfy properties (1), (2) and (3) above.

Generation \ Period	1	2	3	4	• • •	t	t+1	• • •
0	ω_0^1							
1	ω_1^1	ω_1^2						
2		ω_2^2	ω_2^3					
3			ω_3^3	ω_3^4				
⋮ t-1					• • • ω_{t-1}^{t-1}	ω_{t-1}^{t}		
t						ω_t^t	ω_t^{t+1}	
t+1							ω_{t+1}^{t+1}	ω_{t+1}^{t+2}
⋮								• • •

Fig. 5.1-1

Example 5.1.1. Here are two utility functions that satisfy the above properties (whose straightforward verifications are left for the reader).

1. Consider two (symmetric) Riesz dual systems of the form $\langle \ell_p, \ell_q \rangle$ and $\langle \ell_r, \ell_s \rangle$, where $1 \le p, q \le \infty$ and $1 \le r, s \le \infty$ satisfy $\frac{1}{p} + \frac{1}{q} = \frac{1}{r} + \frac{1}{s} = 1$. Then the utility function $u: \ell_p^+ \times \ell_r^+ \longrightarrow \mathcal{R}$ defined by

$$u(\mathbf{x}, \mathbf{y}) = \sum_{n=1}^{\infty} \frac{\sqrt[n]{x_n + y_n}}{n^2}, \quad \mathbf{x} = (x_1, x_2, \ldots) \in \ell_p^+, \quad \mathbf{y} = (y_1, y_2, \ldots) \in \ell_r^+,$$

   satisfies the above three properties.

2. Consider the two (symmetric) Riesz dual systems $\langle \ell_p, \ell_q \rangle$ and $\langle L_r[0,1], L_s[0,1] \rangle$, where $1 \le p, q \le \infty$ and $1 \le r, s \le \infty$ satisfy $\frac{1}{p} + \frac{1}{q} = \frac{1}{r} + \frac{1}{s} = 1$. Fix some strictly positive function $h \in L_s[0,1]$—for instance, consider the function $h(x) = x^2$. Then the utility function $u: \ell_p^+ \times L_r^+[0,1] \longrightarrow \mathcal{R}$ defined by

$$u(\mathbf{x}, f) = \int_0^1 f(x)h(x)\,dx + \sum_{n=1}^{\infty} \frac{\sqrt{x_n}}{n^2}, \quad \mathbf{x} = (x_1, x_2, \ldots) \in \ell_p^+, \quad f \in L_r^+[0,1],$$

   satisfies properties (1), (2), and (3). ■

We continue with the concept of an allocation for the OLG model.

Definition 5.1.2. *A sequence* $(\mathbf{x}_0, \mathbf{x}_1, \mathbf{x}_2, \ldots)$, *where*

$$\mathbf{0} \le \mathbf{x}_0 = (x_0^1, 0, 0, \ldots) \quad \textit{and} \quad \mathbf{0} \le \mathbf{x}_t = (0, \ldots, 0, x_t^t, x_t^{t+1}, 0, 0, \ldots), \quad t \ge 1,$$

is said to be an **allocation** *whenever*

$$x_{t-1}^t + x_t^t = \omega_{t-1}^t + \omega_t^t$$

holds for each $t = 1, 2, \ldots$ *—or equivalently, whenever* $\sum_{t=0}^{\infty} \mathbf{x}_t = \sum_{t=0}^{\infty} \omega_t$.

An allocation $(\mathbf{x}_0, \mathbf{x}_1, \mathbf{x}_2, \ldots)$ will be denoted for brevity by the symbol $(\mathbf{x}_t)$. A **price system** of the overlapping generations model is any sequence $\mathbf{p} = (p^1, p^2, \ldots)$, where $p^t \in E_t'$ for each $t \ge 1$; the linear functional p^t should be interpreted as representing the prices prevailing at period t.

Next, we define the Riesz dual system for the overlapping generations model. We shall denote by boldface $\mathbf{E}$ the ideal of $E_1 \times E_2 \times \cdots$ consisting of all sequences that vanish eventually, i.e.,

$$\mathbf{E} = \{(x_1, x_2, \ldots) \in E_1 \times E_2 \times \cdots : \exists\ k \text{ such that } x_i = 0 \text{ for all } i > k\}.$$

By $\mathbf{E}'$ we shall denote the product Riesz space of the sequence of Riesz spaces $(E_1', E_2', \ldots)$, i.e.,

$$\mathbf{E}' = E_1' \times E_2' \times \cdots.$$

Thus, the prices for the OLG model are the elements of the Riesz space $\mathbf{E}'$. Now the pair $\langle \mathbf{E}, \mathbf{E}' \rangle$, under the duality

$$\mathbf{p} \cdot \mathbf{x} = \sum_{t=1}^{\infty} p^t \cdot x_t$$

for all $\mathbf{x} = (x_1, x_2, \ldots) \in \mathbf{E}$ and all $\mathbf{p} = (p^1, p^2, \ldots) \in \mathbf{E}'$, is a Riesz dual system. In this context, the overlapping generations model defines a pure exchange economy with a countable number of agents having $\langle \mathbf{E}, \mathbf{E}' \rangle$ as its Riesz dual system.

The supportability of allocations by prices in the overlapping generations model takes the following form.

Definition 5.1.3. *A non-zero price* $\mathbf{p} = (p^1, p^2, \ldots)$ *is said to* **support an allocation** $(\mathbf{x}_0, \mathbf{x}_1, \mathbf{x}_2, \ldots)$ *whenever*

a) $x \succeq_0 x_0^1$ *in* E_1^+ *implies* $p^1 \cdot x \geq p^1 \cdot x_0^1$*; and*

b) $(x, y) \succeq_t (x_t^t, x_t^{t+1})$ *in* $E_t^+ \times E_{t+1}^+$ *implies*

$$p^t \cdot x + p^{t+1} \cdot y \geq p^t \cdot x_t^t + p^{t+1} \cdot x_t^{t+1}$$

for all $t = 1, 2, \ldots$.

It should be noted that if a price $\mathbf{p} = (p^1, p^2, \ldots)$ supports an allocation $(\mathbf{x}_0, \mathbf{x}_1, \mathbf{x}_2, \ldots)$, then $\mathbf{x} \succeq_t \mathbf{x}_t$ implies $\mathbf{p} \cdot \mathbf{x} \geq \mathbf{p} \cdot \mathbf{x}_t$. Supporting prices are necessarily positive prices. To see this, let a price $\mathbf{p} = (p^1, p^2, \ldots)$ support an allocation $(\mathbf{x}_t)$ and let $\mathbf{x} \geq 0$. Then $\mathbf{x}_t + \mathbf{x} \succeq_t \mathbf{x}_t$ holds, and so $\mathbf{p} \cdot (\mathbf{x}_t + \mathbf{x}) \geq \mathbf{p} \cdot \mathbf{x}_t$. This implies $\mathbf{p} \cdot \mathbf{x} \geq 0$, and thus $\mathbf{p} = (p^1, p^2, \ldots)$ is a positive price, which means, of course, that $p^t \geq 0$ holds for all $t \geq 1$.

The notion of a competitive equilibrium for the overlapping generations model is now defined as follows.

Definition 5.1.4. *An allocation* $(\mathbf{x}_0, \mathbf{x}_1, \mathbf{x}_2, \ldots)$ *is said to be a* **competitive equilibrium** *for the overlapping generations model, whenever there exists a price* $\mathbf{p} = (p^1, p^2, \ldots) > \mathbf{0}$ *such that each* $\mathbf{x}_t$ *is a maximal element in the* t^{th} *consumer's budget set* $\mathcal{B}_t(\mathbf{p})$*—where, as usual, the budget set is defined by* $\mathcal{B}_t(\mathbf{p}) = \{\mathbf{x} \in E^+ \colon \mathbf{p} \cdot \mathbf{x} \leq \mathbf{p} \cdot \omega_t\}$.

As expected, the competitive equilibria can be supported by prices. The details are included in the next result.

Theorem 5.1.5. *If an allocation* $(\mathbf{x}_0, \mathbf{x}_1, \mathbf{x}_2, \ldots)$ *is a competitive equilibrium with respect to a price* $\mathbf{p} = (p^1, p^2, \ldots) > \mathbf{0}$*, then it can be supported by* $\mathbf{p}$*. Moreover, we have the budget equalities*

a) $p^1 \cdot x_0^1 = p^1 \cdot \omega_0^1$ *(or* $\mathbf{p} \cdot \mathbf{x}_0 = \mathbf{p} \cdot \omega_0$*); and*

b) $p^t \cdot x_t^t + p^{t+1} \cdot x_t^{t+1} = p^t \cdot \omega_t^t + p^{t+1} \cdot \omega_t^{t+1}$ *(or* $\mathbf{p} \cdot \mathbf{x}_t = \mathbf{p} \cdot \omega_t$*) for* $t \geq 1$.

Proof. Let $(\mathbf{x}_0, \mathbf{x}_1, \mathbf{x}_2, \ldots)$ be a competitive equilibrium with respect to the price $\mathbf{p} = (p^1, p^2, \ldots) > \mathbf{0}$. Note that $\omega_t \succ_t 0$ holds. Thus, if $\mathbf{x}_t = 0$, then—in view of $\omega_t \in \mathcal{B}_t(\mathbf{p})$—the element $\mathbf{x}_t$ cannot be a maximal element in the budget set $\mathcal{B}_t(\mathbf{p})$. Therefore, $\mathbf{x}_t > \mathbf{0}$ must hold for all t. Since $\mathbf{x}_t$ belongs to $\mathcal{B}_t(\mathbf{p})$, we see that $\mathbf{p} \cdot \mathbf{x}_t \leq \mathbf{p} \cdot \omega_t$ holds. On the other hand, if $\mathbf{p} \cdot \mathbf{x}_t < \mathbf{p} \cdot \omega_t$ is true, then choose some

$\delta > 1$ such that

$$\mathbf{p}\cdot(\delta\mathbf{x}_t) = \delta\mathbf{p}\cdot\mathbf{x}_t < \mathbf{p}\cdot\omega_t\,,$$

and note that $\delta\mathbf{x}_t \in \mathcal{B}_t(\mathbf{p})$ and $\delta\mathbf{x}_t \succ_t \mathbf{x}_t$ hold, contrary to the maximality property of $\mathbf{x}_t$ in $\mathcal{B}_t(\mathbf{p})$. Consequently, $\mathbf{p}\cdot\mathbf{x}_t = \mathbf{p}\cdot\omega_t$ holds for all t. ∎

A few remarks regarding the *general overlapping generations model* are in order. This is the OLG model, where

a) r consumers are born in each period; and
b) each consumer lives ℓ periods.

In this OLG model the consumers are identified by the periods of their births. A consumer i (where $1 \le i \le r$) born at period t will live all her life in periods $t, t+1, \ldots, t+\ell-1$ and her initial endowment is

$$\omega_{i,t} = (0,0,\ldots,0,\omega_{i,t}^t,\omega_{i,t}^{t+1},\ldots,\omega_{i,t}^{t+\ell-1},0,0,\ldots)\,.$$

Thus, a consumer in the general OLG model is identified by the pair (i,t), where $1 \le i \le r$ and t designates the period of her birth. For mathematical convenience, the consumers of the form (i,t), where $1 \le i \le r$ and $2-\ell \le t \le 0$, will be assumed to be present in the general OLG model.

A commodity bundle for consumer (i,t) is any vector $\mathbf{x}_{i,t} \in \mathbf{E}$ of the form

$$\mathbf{x}_{i,t} = (0,0,\ldots,0,x_{i,t}^t,x_{i,t}^{t+1},\ldots,x_{i,t}^{t+\ell-1},0,0,\ldots)\,.$$

Each consumer (i,t) in the OLG model is assumed to have a utility function $u_{i,t}\colon E_t^+ \times E_{t+1}^+ \times \cdots \times E_{t+\ell-1}^+ \longrightarrow \mathcal{R}$ that satisfies the above described properties (1), (2) and (3).

EXERCISES

1. Verify that the utility functions of Example 5.1.1 satisfy the stated properties.

2. If $(\mathbf{x}_0,\mathbf{x}_1,\mathbf{x}_2,\ldots)$ is an allocation of the overlapping generations model, then for each non-negative integer k show that $\sum_{t=0}^k \mathbf{x}_t \le \sum_{t=0}^{k+1}\omega_t$ and $\sum_{t=0}^k \omega_t \le \sum_{t=0}^{k+1}\mathbf{x}_t$ both hold.

3. Consider the overlapping generations model having the following characteristics.
Commodity Spaces: $E_t = \mathcal{R}$ for each t.
Initial Endowments: $\omega_0 = (\frac{1}{2},0,0,\ldots)$ and $\omega_t = (0,\ldots,0,\frac{1}{2},\frac{1}{3},0,0,\ldots)$ for $t \ge 1$—where the numbers $\frac{1}{2}$ and $\frac{1}{3}$ occupy the t and $t+1$ positions.
Find an allocation $(\mathbf{x}_t)$ satisfying $\mathbf{x}_t \ne \omega_t$ for all t.

4. Consider the overlapping generations model having the following characteristics.
Commodity Spaces: $E_t = \mathcal{R}$ for each t.
Utility Functions: $u_0(x^0) = x^0$ and $u_t(x^t, x^{t+1}) = \sqrt{x^t} + \sqrt{x^{t+1}}$.
Initial Endowments: $\omega_0 = (\frac{1}{4}, 0, 0, \ldots)$ and $\omega_t = (0, \ldots, 0, \frac{1}{4}, \frac{1}{4}, 0, 0, \ldots)$ for $t \geq 1$—where the number $\frac{1}{4}$ occupies the t and $t+1$ positions.
   a) Find an allocation $(\mathbf{x}_t)$ such that $\mathbf{x}_0 \succ \omega_0$ and $\mathbf{x}_1 \succ \omega_1$.
   b) For each fixed integer k find an allocation $(\mathbf{x}_t)$ such that $\mathbf{x}_t \succ \omega_t$ holds for $0 \leq t \leq k$.

5. Show that in the overlapping generations model for each fixed k there exists an allocation $(\mathbf{x}_t)$ satisfying $\mathbf{x}_t \succ \omega_t$ for each $t > k$.

6. If a price $\mathbf{0} < \mathbf{p} \in \mathbf{E}'$ supports an allocation $(\mathbf{x}_0, \mathbf{x}_1, \ldots)$ and satisfies $\mathbf{p} \cdot \mathbf{x}_t > 0$ for each t, then show that the price $\mathbf{p}$ is strictly positive.

5.2. THE OLG COMMODITY-PRICE DUALITY

In this section, we shall construct the Riesz dual system that defines the commodity-price duality for the overlapping generations model. Our construction uses the ideas from the theory of inductive and projective limits of locally convex spaces, developed in the early 1950's by L. Schwartz, J. Dieudonné and A. Grothendieck. For our purposes, we shall present the theory of inductive limits in the setting of Riesz spaces and for the general theory we shall refer the reader to the books [31,33,58,62].

Consider the overlapping generations model where the commodity space for each period t is E_t. As mentioned before, we shall assume (for simplicity) that only one consumer is born in each period and has a two-period lifetime. We shall employ the notation

$$\theta_t = \omega_{t-1}^t + \omega_t^t, \quad t = 1, 2, \ldots \ .$$

Clearly, the commodity bundle $\theta_t = \omega_{t-1}^t + \omega_t^t \in E_t^+$, $t = 1, 2, \ldots$, represents the total endowment present at period t.

It will be useful to consider the overlapping generations model when the commodity space at period t is the ideal generated by the total endowment present at period t. The ideal generated by θ_t in E_t will be denoted by Θ_t. That is,

$$\Theta_t = \big\{x \in E_t\colon \text{ There exists } \lambda > 0 \text{ with } |x| \leq \lambda\theta_t\big\}.$$

The ideal Θ_t under the norm $\|x\|_\infty = \inf\{\lambda > 0\colon\ |x| \leq \lambda\theta_t\}$ is an M-space having θ_t as a unit. As usual, the norm dual of Θ_t will be denoted by Θ_t'.

Let $\mathbf{\Theta}$ denote the ideal of $\Theta_1 \times \Theta_2 \times \cdots$ consisting of all sequences having at most a finite number of non-zero coordinates, i.e.,

$$\mathbf{\Theta} = \{(x_1, x_2, \ldots) \in \Theta_1 \times \Theta_2 \times \cdots\colon\ \exists\ k \text{ such that } x_i = 0 \text{ for all } i > k\}.$$

Clearly, $\mathbf{\Theta}$ is an ideal of $\mathbf{E}$. Also, let

$$\mathbf{\Theta}' = \Theta_1' \times \Theta_2' \times \cdots$$

be the product Riesz space of the sequence $(\Theta_1', \Theta_2', \ldots)$. It should be clear that the pair of Riesz spaces $\langle \mathbf{\Theta}, \mathbf{\Theta}' \rangle$, under the duality

$$\mathbf{p} \cdot \mathbf{x} = \sum_{t=1}^{\infty} p^t \cdot x_t$$

for all $\mathbf{x} = (x_1, x_2, \ldots) \in \mathbf{\Theta}$ and all $\mathbf{p} = (p^1, p^2, \ldots) \in \mathbf{\Theta}'$, is a Riesz dual system.

We shall need to consider the overlapping generations model when the commodity price duality at each period is given by the Riesz dual pair $\langle \Theta_t, \Theta_t' \rangle$. A **price vector** (or simply a **price**) for this OLG model is any sequence of the form

$$\mathbf{p} = (p^1, p^2, \ldots),$$

where $p^t \in \Theta'_t$ for each t. Therefore, in order to understand the economic properties of the OLG model, we need to study the mathematical structures of the Riesz dual systems $\langle \mathbf{E}, \mathbf{E}' \rangle$ and $\langle \Theta, \Theta' \rangle$. To do this, we shall invoke the theory of "inductive limits."

For the discussion in this section, E will denote a fixed Archimedean Riesz space*. Also, we shall fix a sequence $\{a_n\}$ of E and we shall denote by A the ideal generated by the sequence $\{a_n\}$. Clearly, A coincides with the ideal generated by the sequence $\{\hat{a}_n\}$, where $\hat{a}_n = \sum_{i=1}^{n} |a_i|$, $n = 1, 2, \ldots$. Thus, replacing each a_n by $\hat{a}_n$, we can assume without loss of generality that $0 \le a_n \uparrow$ holds in E, i.e., we can suppose that the sequence $\{a_n\}$ is an increasing sequence. Note that

$$A = \{x \in E\colon \text{ There exists } \lambda > 0 \text{ and some } n \text{ with } |x| \le \lambda a_n\}.$$

For each n we shall denote by A_n the principal ideal generated by a_n, i.e.,

$$A_n = \{x \in E : \text{ There exists some } \lambda > 0 \text{ with } |x| \le \lambda a_n\}.$$

The ideal A_n equipped with the lattice norm

$$\|x\|_n = \inf\{\, \lambda > 0 : \ |x| \le \lambda a_n \,\}, \ x \in A_n ,$$

is a normed Riesz space. In case E is also a uniformly complete Riesz space (in particular, a Dedekind complete Riesz space), then the normed Riesz space A_n is also a Banach lattice—in fact, A_n under $\|\cdot\|_n$ is an AM-space having a_n as a unit. Clearly, $|x| \le \|x\|_n a_n$ holds for each $x \in A_n$, and from this it follows that the closed unit ball of A_n is the order interval $[-a_n, a_n]$, i.e.,

$$\{x \in A_n\colon \ \|x\|_n \le 1\} = [-a_n, a_n].$$

In particular, a subset of A_n is norm bounded (i.e., $\|\cdot\|_n$-bounded) if and only if it is order bounded, and consequently the order dual coincides with the norm dual. We state this property as a lemma.

Lemma 5.2.1. *The norm dual of A_k coincides with its order dual, i.e., $A'_k = A^{\sim}_k$ holds for each k.*

From $0 \le a_n \uparrow$ in E, we see that $A_n \subseteq A_{n+1}$ holds for all n and $A = \bigcup_{n=1}^{\infty} A_n$. We shall denote by ξ_n the norm topology induced on A_n by $\|\cdot\|_n$. From the norm inequality $\|x\|_{n+1} \le \|x\|_n$, $x \in A_n$, it follows that $\xi_{n+1} \subseteq \xi_n$ holds on A_n. The subsets of A of the form

$$V = \operatorname{co}\Big(\bigcup_{n=1}^{\infty} V_n\Big),$$

* Recall that a Riesz space E is said to be Archimedean whenever $x, y \in E^+$ and $nx \le y$ for each n imply $x = 0$—equivalently, whenever $\frac{1}{n}x \downarrow 0$ holds in E for each $x \in E^+$.

where $V_n \subseteq A_n$ is a ξ_n-neighborhood of zero form a base for a locally convex topology ξ on A—see Exercise 1 at the end of this section. Recall that the (natural) embedding $i_n: A_n \hookrightarrow A$ is the function defined by $i_n(x) = x$ for all $x \in A_n$.

Theorem 5.2.2. *The locally convex topology ξ is the finest locally convex topology on A for which all the embeddings $i_n: (A_n, \xi_n) \hookrightarrow (A, \xi)$ are continuous.*

Proof. First, let us show that each embedding $i_n: (A_n, \xi_n) \hookrightarrow (A, \xi)$ is continuous. Indeed, if $V = \operatorname{co}\bigl(\bigcup_{n=1}^{\infty} V_n\bigr)$ is a basic ξ-neighborhood of zero, then from the inclusion $V_n \subseteq i_n^{-1}(V)$, we see that $i_n^{-1}(V)$ is a ξ_n-neighborhood of zero, and consequently $i_n: (A_n, \xi_n) \hookrightarrow (A, \xi)$ is continuous.

Now let τ be a locally convex topology on A such that every natural embedding $i_n: (A_n, \xi_n) \hookrightarrow (A, \tau)$ is continuous, and let W be a convex τ-neighborhood of zero. Then $V_n = i_n^{-1}(W) = W \cap A_n \subseteq W$ is a ξ_n-neighborhood, and $\bigcup_{n=1}^{\infty} V_n = \bigcup_{n=1}^{\infty} W \cap A_n = W$ implies that W is also a ξ-neighborhood of zero. That is, $\tau \subseteq \xi$ holds, and the proof of the theorem is finished. ■

The unique locally convex topology ξ on A is known as the *inductive limit topology* of the topologies ξ_n. Precisely, we have the following definition.

Definition 5.2.3. *The* **inductive limit topology** *ξ is the finest locally convex topology on A for which all the embeddings $i_n: (A_n, \xi_n) \hookrightarrow (A, \xi)$ are continuous.*

The locally convex topology ξ is also uniquely determined in the following sense. If $\{b_n\}$ is another sequence that generates A (we can suppose $0 \le b_n \uparrow$ in E) and B_n denotes the principal ideal generated by b_n, then the inductive limit topology of the sequence $\{B_n\}$ on A is precisely ξ. To see this, consider B_n equipped with the lattice norm

$$|||x|||_n = \inf\{\, \lambda > 0 \colon\ |x| \le \lambda b_n \,\},\ \ x \in B_n\,,$$

and let η_n denote the topology induced by $|||\cdot|||_n$ on B_n. Also, denote by η the finest locally convex topology on A such that all embeddings $j_n: (B_n, \eta_n) \hookrightarrow (A, \eta)$ are continuous. Now if k is fixed, then there exist some n and some $M > 0$ satisfying $a_k \le M b_n$. This implies $A_k \subseteq B_n$ and $|x| \le \|x\|_k a_k \le M\|x\|_k b_n$ for all $x \in A_k$. Hence, $|||x|||_n \le M\|x\|_k$ holds for all $x \in A_k$, and so the natural embedding $i_{nk}: (A_k, \xi_k) \hookrightarrow (B_n, \eta_n)$ is continuous. Since $j_n: (B_n, \eta_n) \hookrightarrow (A, \eta)$ is also continuous, we see that each $i_k = j_n \circ i_{nk}: (A_k, \xi_k) \hookrightarrow (A, \eta)$ is continuous. Therefore, $\eta \subseteq \xi$. By the symmetry of the situation, $\xi \subseteq \eta$ must also hold, and hence $\eta = \xi$.

The next result presents a characterization of the continuous (linear) operators with domain (A, ξ).

Theorem 5.2.4. *If X is a locally convex space, then an operator $T: (A, \xi) \longrightarrow X$ is continuous if and only if its restriction to each ideal A_n (i.e., each operator $T: (A_n, \xi_n) \longrightarrow X$) is continuous.*

Proof. Let X be a locally convex space and let $T: A \to X$ be an operator. If the operator $T:(A,\xi) \longrightarrow X$ is continuous, then—in view of the continuity of $i_n:(A_n,\xi_n) \hookrightarrow (A,\xi)$—the operator $T:(A_n,\xi_n) \longrightarrow X$ is continuous for each n.

For the converse, assume that $T:(A_n,\xi_n) \longrightarrow X$ is continuous for each n. If W is a convex neighborhood of zero for X, then $V_n = T^{-1}(W) \cap A_n$ is a convex ξ_n-neighborhood of zero and from

$$\operatorname{co}\Big(\bigcup_{n=1}^{\infty} V_n\Big) = \operatorname{co}\Big(\bigcup_{n=1}^{\infty} T^{-1}(W) \cap A_n\Big) = \operatorname{co}\big(T^{-1}(W)\big) = T^{-1}(W),$$

it follows that $T^{-1}(W)$ is ξ-neighborhood of zero. Therefore, $T:(A,\xi) \longrightarrow X$ is a continuous operator. ■

Next, we shall list the basic properties of the inductive limit topology ξ.

Theorem 5.2.5. *The locally convex space (A,ξ) is a locally convex-solid Riesz space whose topological dual coincides with the order dual of A, i.e., $(A,\xi)' = A^{\sim}$ holds.*

In particular, ξ is a Hausdorff topology if and only if the order dual $A^{\sim}$ separates the points of A (and hence, in this case, $\langle A, A'\rangle$ is a Riesz dual system).

Proof. If V_n is a solid ξ_n-neighborhood of A_n, then $\bigcup_{n=1}^{\infty} V_n$ is a solid subset of A, and hence $\operatorname{co}(\bigcup_{n=1}^{\infty} V_n)$ is a solid ξ-neighborhood of A—it is well known that the convex hull of a solid set is also a solid set; see Theorem 2.1.4 or [6, Theorem 1.3, p. 4]. This implies that ξ is also a locally solid topology.

Next, note that a linear functional $f: A \to \mathcal{R}$ is order bounded (i.e., $f \in A^{\sim}$) if and only if f restricted to each A_n is order bounded. The latter—in view of Lemma 5.2.1—says that f is order bounded if and only if f restricted to each A_n is continuous. Invoking Theorem 5.2.4, we see that f is order bounded if and only if $f:(A,\xi) \to \mathcal{R}$ is continuous, i.e., $(A,\xi)' = A^{\sim}$ holds. ■

It should be kept in mind that if $E^{\sim}$ separates the points of E, then $A^{\sim}$ also separates the points of A, and hence the inductive limit topology ξ is always a Hausdorff locally convex-solid topology on A. For the rest of the discussion in this section we shall assume that $A^{\sim}$ separates the points of A so that the inductive limit topology ξ is a Hausdorff locally convex-solid topology. Recall that a (Hausdorff) locally convex space (X,τ) is said to be a **bornological space** whenever

a) the topology τ coincides with the Mackey topology, i.e., $\tau = \tau(X,X')$ holds; and
b) every linear functional on X that maps τ-bounded subsets of X onto bounded subsets of $\mathcal{R}$ is necessarily τ-continuous.

Theorem 5.2.6. *The inductive limit topology ξ on A is Mackey and bornological.*

Proof. First, we shall prove that $\xi = \tau(A, A^{\sim})$ holds. By Theorem 5.2.5 the inductive limit topology ξ on A is consisted with the duality $\langle A, A^{\sim}\rangle$. Therefore, $\xi \subseteq \tau(A,A^{\sim})$. To establish that $\tau(A,A^{\sim}) \subseteq \xi$ also holds, it suffices to show that each natural embedding $i_n:(A_n,\xi_n) \hookrightarrow \big(A,\tau(A,A^{\sim})\big)$ is continuous. So, let a sequence

$\{x_k\}$ of some A_n satisfy $\lim_{k\to\infty} \|x_k\|_n = 0$. We have to show that the sequence $\{x_k\}$ converges uniformly to zero on every balanced, convex and w*-compact (i.e., $\sigma(A, A^{\sim})$-compact) subset of $A^{\sim}$.

To this end, let S be a balanced, convex and w*-compact subset of $A^{\sim}$. If S_n denotes the set of the restrictions of the functionals of S to A_n, then S_n is a balanced, convex and $\sigma(A_n, A'_n)$-compact subset of A'_n —see Theorem 5.2.5 and Lemma 5.2.1. Since A_n is a normed space, we know that its norm topology coincides with the Mackey topology $\tau(A_n, A'_n)$. Consequently, the sequence $\{x_k\}$ converges uniformly to zero on S_n (and hence on S), as desired.

To see that (A, ξ) is a bornological space, consider a linear functional $f: A \to \mathcal{R}$ that carries ξ-bounded subsets of A onto bounded subsets of $\mathcal{R}$. In particular, $f([-a_n, a_n])$ is a bounded subset of $\mathcal{R}$ for each n, i.e., $f: (A_n, \xi_n) \longrightarrow \mathcal{R}$ is a continuous linear functional. By Theorem 5.2.4, we see that f is ξ-continuous, and so (A, ξ) is a bornological space. ■

A locally convex space X is said to be a **barrelled space** whenever every absorbing, balanced, convex and closed subset of X (referred to as a *barrel*) is a neighborhood of zero.

Theorem 5.2.7. *If E is uniformly complete, then (A, ξ) is a barrelled space.*

Proof. Note first that when E is a uniformly complete Riesz space, each A_n is a Banach lattice—in fact, an AM-space with unit. Let V be an absorbing, balanced, convex and ξ-closed subset of A. Then the set $V_n = V \cap A_n$ is an absorbing, balanced, convex and—by the continuity of the embedding $i_n: (A_n, \xi_n) \longrightarrow (A, \xi)$—a ξ_n-closed subset of A_n. Since A_n is (as a Banach space) a barrelled space, we see that V_n is a ξ_n-neighborhood of A_n. From

$$\bigcup_{n=1}^{\infty} V_n = \bigcup_{n=1}^{\infty} V \cap A_n = V\,,$$

we see that V is a ξ-neighborhood of zero, and so (A, ξ) is a barrelled space. ■

Remarkably, the order dual $A^{\sim}$ of A with the strong topology is a Fréchet lattice, i.e., the order dual $A^{\sim}$ with the strong topology is a complete metrizable locally convex-solid Riesz space.

Theorem 5.2.8. *The order dual $A^{\sim}$ with the strong topology $\beta(A^{\sim}, A)$ is a Fréchet lattice.*

Proof. Combine [31, Proposition 5, p. 171] with [31, Corollary 4, p. 166]. ■

Next, we shall discuss the case when ξ is a "strict inductive limit." As mentioned before, the inductive limit topology ξ on A is independent of the generating sequence $\{a_n\}$. Now assume that there exists a disjoint sequence $\{\omega_n\}$ of E^+ (i.e., $\omega_n \wedge \omega_m = 0$ for $n \neq m$) that generates the ideal A; we can assume that $\omega_n > 0$ holds for all n. Put $\hat{\omega}_n = \sum_{i=1}^{n} \omega_i$ and let C_n denote the principal ideal generated by $\hat{\omega}_n$. Note that $\hat{\omega}_n \wedge \omega_{n+1} = 0$ holds for all n. Let $x \in C_n$. If $\lambda > 0$ satisfies $|x| \leq \lambda\hat{\omega}_n$, then clearly $|x| \le \lambda\hat{\omega}_{n+1}$ holds. On the other hand, if $\lambda > 0$ satisfies $|x| \le \lambda\hat{\omega}_{n+1}$, then we have

$$\begin{aligned}|x| = |x| \wedge \lambda\hat{\omega}_{n+1} &\le |x| \wedge \lambda\hat{\omega}_n + |x| \wedge \lambda\omega_{n+1}\\ &= |x| \wedge \lambda\hat{\omega}_n \le \lambda\hat{\omega}_n.\end{aligned}$$

Thus, a constant $\lambda > 0$ satisfies $|x| \le \lambda\hat{\omega}_n$ if and only if $|x| \le \lambda\hat{\omega}_{n+1}$. This shows that $\|x\|_n = \|x\|_{n+1}$ holds for all $x \in C_n$, i.e., $\|\cdot\|_{n+1}$ restricted to C_n is precisely $\|\cdot\|_n$. The latter implies (see Exercise 2 at the end of the section) that C_n is ξ_{n+1}-closed in C_{n+1}, where ξ_n now denotes the topology generated by $\|\cdot\|_n$ on C_n. In this case (A,ξ) is called the **strict inductive limit** of the sequence $\{(C_n,\xi_n)\}$.

It is interesting to note that when ξ is the strict inductive limit, the ideal A has a nice representation; see [37, Theorem 6.6, p. 311] for details.

Theorem 5.2.9. (Kawai) *If ξ is a strict inductive limit, then there exists a locally compact and σ-compact Hausdorff topological space Ω such that A is lattice isomorphic to $C_c(\Omega)$ (the Riesz space of all continuous real-valued functions on Ω with compact support).*

In addition, if $H = \{h \in C(\Omega)\colon\ h(\omega) > 0$ for all $\omega \in \Omega\}$, then the sets

$$V_h = \{\, f \in C_c(\Omega)\colon\ |f(\omega)| \le h(\omega) \text{ for all } \omega \in \Omega \,\},\ \ h \in H\,,$$

form a base for the ξ-neighborhoods at zero.

When ξ is the strict inductive limit, then it also has a number of additional properties—proofs can be found in any standard book on locally convex spaces; for instance, see [33, pp. 157–165].

Theorem 5.2.10. *If ξ is the strict inductive limit, then:*

1. *The topology ξ induces ξ_n on each A_n and each A_n is ξ-closed in A.*
2. *A subset of A is ξ-bounded if and only if it is contained in some A_n and is ξ_n-bounded there.*
3. *When E is uniformly complete, the locally convex-solid Riesz space (A,ξ) is topologically complete and non-metrizable.*

Recall that a topological vector space (X,τ) is said to have the **Dunford-Pettis property** if $x_n \xrightarrow{w} x$ in X and $f_n \xrightarrow{w} f$ in X' (the topological dual of (X,τ)) imply $f_n(x_n) \longrightarrow f(x)$. The reader will notice here that the Dunford-Pettis property is nothing else than a joint sequential continuity property of the evaluation map $(x,p) \mapsto p\cdot x$. The lack of joint continuity of the evaluation map is one of the major differences between economies with finite and infinite dimensional commodity spaces. For more about the Dunford-Pettis property see [8, Section 19].

Theorem 5.2.11. *If E is Dedekind complete and ξ is the strict inductive limit, then (A,ξ) has the Dunford-Pettis property.*

Proof. Assume $x_n \xrightarrow{w} x$ in A and $p_n \xrightarrow{w} p$ in A'. Then the set $\{x, x_1, x_2, \ldots\}$ is weakly bounded, and hence ξ-bounded. By Theorem 5.2.10(2) there exists some k such that $\{x, x_1, x_2, \ldots\} \subseteq A_k$.

Now consider each p_n restricted to A_k. Clearly, $p_n \in A'_k$ for each n, and moreover, $p_n \xrightarrow{w} p$ in A' implies $p_n \xrightarrow{w^*} p$ in A'_k. By a theorem of A. Grothendieck [8, Theorem 13.13, p. 211], we see that $p_n \xrightarrow{w} p$ also holds in A'_k. Since A_k has the Dunford-Pettis property [8, Theorem 19.6, p. 336], we infer that $p_n \cdot x_n \longrightarrow p \cdot x$, as desired. ■

By Theorem 5.2.8 we know that the strong dual of A is a Fréchet lattice. When ξ is the strict inductive limit, then the strong dual of A is, in fact, an order continuous Fréchet lattice.

Theorem 5.2.12. *If ξ is the strict inductive limit, then $A^{\sim}$ with the strong topology $\beta(A^{\sim}, A)$ is an order continuous Fréchet lattice*.*

Proof. Assume that ξ is the strict inductive limit. Let $f_\alpha \downarrow 0$ hold in $A^{\sim}$ and let B be a ξ-bounded subset of A. We have to show that $\{f_\alpha\}$ converges to zero uniformly on B.

By Theorem 5.2.10(2) there exists some n such that $B \subseteq A_n$. If we consider each f_α restricted to A_n, then $\{f_\alpha\}$ as a net of A'_n satisfies $f_\alpha \downarrow 0$. Since A_n is an M-space, its norm dual A'_n is an AL-space—see [6 or 8]—and so A'_n has order continuous norm [8, p. 187]. Therefore, $\|f_\alpha\| \downarrow 0$ holds, and from this we see that $\{f_\alpha\}$ converges to zero uniformly on the set B. ■

Now assume that A is generated by a disjoint sequence $\{\omega_n\}$ of non-zero positive elements, so that ξ is the strict inductive limit topology. We shall also assume one extra condition; namely that $\omega = \sup\{\omega_n\colon n = 1, 2, \ldots\}$ exists in E, i.e., we shall assume that

$$\hat{\omega}_n = \sum_{i=1}^{n} \omega_i \uparrow \omega$$

holds in E.

If A_ω denotes the principal ideal generated by ω in E, then we have the following ideal inclusions

$$A \subseteq A_\omega \subseteq E,$$

where the ideal A is order dense in A_ω. We shall denote by τ_∞ the locally convex-solid topology on A_ω generated by the lattice norm

$$\|x\|_\infty = \inf\{\, \lambda > 0\colon\ |x| \le \lambda\omega \,\},\ x \in A_\omega .$$

Notice that the lattice norm $\|\cdot\|_\infty$ restricted to each A_n (the principal ideal generated by $\hat{\omega}_n$) satisfies $\|x\|_\infty \le \|x\|_n$ for all $x \in A_n$, and so the inclusions $i_n\colon (A_n, \xi_n) \hookrightarrow (A, \tau_\infty)$ are all continuous. This implies that on A we have $\tau_\infty \subseteq \xi$, where the inclusion is proper by Theorem 5.2.10(3). Since any locally convex-solid topology τ on A_ω satisfies $\tau \subseteq \tau_\infty$ [6, Theorem 16.7, p. 112], we see that

$$\tau \subseteq \tau_\infty \subseteq \xi$$

* In this case, it turns out that $\big(A^{\sim}, \beta(A^{\sim}, A)\big)$ is also the projective limit of the sequence $\{A'_n\}$. For details see [58, Proposition 15, p. 85].

holds on A. In addition, it should be noted that ξ cannot be extended to a locally convex-solid topology on A_ω. Indeed, if ξ extends to a locally convex-solid topology on A_ω, say $\hat{\xi}$, then $\hat{\xi} \subseteq \tau_\infty$ must hold on A_ω. Therefore, $\xi = \tau_\infty$ on A, which means that ξ is metrizable on A, contrary to Theorem 5.2.10(3).

The following example—which is the one considered (implicitly) in the important papers of P. A. Samuelson [59] and D. Gale [29]—illustrates all the preceding spaces and topologies.

Example 5.2.13. Let $E = \mathcal{R}_\infty$, the vector space of all real sequences, and let τ be the locally convex-solid topology of pointwise convergence. For each n let $\omega_n = (0, \ldots, 0, 1, 0, 0, \ldots)$, where the 1 occupies the nth position. Clearly, $\{\omega_n\}$ is a disjoint sequence of positive elements, such that

$$\omega = \sup\{\omega_n\colon\ n = 1, 2, \ldots\} = (1, 1, 1, \ldots)\,.$$

It is easily seen that

1. $A_\omega = \ell_\infty$;
2. $A = \{\,(x_1, x_2, \ldots) \in \mathcal{R}_\infty\colon$ There exists k with $x_n = 0$ for all $n \geq k\}$;
3. $A' = A^\sim = \mathcal{R}_\infty$; and
4. the topology ξ is the locally convex-solid topology on A having a basis at zero consisting of the sets of the form

$$V = \{\,(x_1, x_2, \ldots) \in A\colon\ |x_i| \leq y_i \ \text{ for all } i\}\,,$$

where $(y_1, y_2, \ldots) \in \mathcal{R}_\infty$ satisfies $y_i > 0$ for each i. ■

One more remark is in order. If $\{\omega_n\}$ is a disjoint sequence, then

$$\omega = \sup\{\omega_n\colon\ n = 1, 2, \ldots\}$$

exists in the universal completion E^u of E. This means that A_ω can be defined as the ideal generated by ω in E^u, and so the $\|\cdot\|_\infty$ norm on A_ω always induces the locally convex-solid topology τ_∞ on A. For the concept of the "*universal completion*" of a Riesz space see [42] and [6].

We now return to the overlapping generations model. We shall denote the ideal generated by $\{\omega_t\colon\ t = 0, 1, \ldots, n\}$ in $\mathbf{E}$ by $\mathbf{A}_n$. Clearly,

$$\mathbf{A}_n = \Theta_1 \times \Theta_2 \times \cdots \times \Theta_n \times \Omega_n \times \mathbf{0} \times \mathbf{0} \times \cdots\,,$$

where $\mathbf{0} = \{0\}$ and Ω_n denotes the ideal generated by ω_n^{n+1} in E_{n+1}. Obviously, each $\mathbf{A}_n$ is an M-space having $(\theta_1, \ldots, \theta_n, \omega_n^{n+1}, 0, 0, \ldots)$ as a unit. Note that for each n we have the proper inclusion $\mathbf{A}_n \subseteq \mathbf{A}_{n+1}$. In addition, note that $\boldsymbol{\Theta}$ coincides with $\mathbf{A}$ (the ideal generated in $\mathbf{E}$ by the sequence $\{\omega_n\colon\ n = 0, 1, 2, \ldots\}$). That is, we have

$$\boldsymbol{\Theta} = \mathbf{A} = \bigcup_{n=1}^{\infty} \mathbf{A}_n.$$

Let ξ denote the inductive limit topology generated by the sequence $\{\mathbf{A}_n\}$ on $\mathbf{\Theta}$. Since the ideal $\mathbf{\Theta}$ is also generated by the disjoint sequence $\{\mathbf{a}_n\}$, where

$$\mathbf{a}_n = (0, \ldots, 0, \theta_n, 0, 0, \ldots), \quad n = 1, 2, \ldots,$$

we see that ξ is also the strict inductive limit topology. The topological dual of $(\mathbf{\Theta}, \xi)$ is described in the next theorem.

Theorem 5.2.14. *The topological dual of* $(\mathbf{\Theta}, \xi)$ *is*

$$\mathbf{\Theta}' = \Theta_1' \times \Theta_2' \times \cdots,$$

where the duality between $\mathbf{\Theta}$ *and* $\mathbf{\Theta}'$ *is given by*

$$\mathbf{p} \cdot \mathbf{x} = \sum_{t=1}^{\infty} p^t \cdot x_t,$$

for all $\mathbf{x} = (x_1, x_2, \ldots)$ *and all* $\mathbf{p} = (p^1, p^2, \ldots)$.

Proof. By Theorem 5.2.5 we know that $\mathbf{\Theta}' = \mathbf{\Theta}^{\sim}$. Consequently, it suffices to show that $\mathbf{\Theta}^{\sim} = \Theta_1' \times \Theta_2' \times \cdots$.

Note first that if $\mathbf{p} = (p^1, p^2, \ldots) \in \Theta_1' \times \Theta_2' \times \cdots$, then the formula

$$\mathbf{p} \cdot \mathbf{x} = \sum_{t=1}^{\infty} p^t \cdot x_t, \;\; \mathbf{x} = (x_1, x_2, \ldots) \in \mathbf{\Theta},$$

defines clearly an order bounded linear functional on $\mathbf{\Theta}$.

Now let $\mathbf{p} \in \mathbf{\Theta}^{\sim}$. For each t define $p^t \in \Theta_t'$ by

$$p^t \cdot x = \mathbf{p} \cdot (0, \ldots, 0, x, 0, 0, \ldots), \;\; x \in \Theta_t,$$

where x occupies the tth position. If $\mathbf{x} = (x_1, x_2, \ldots) \in \mathbf{\Theta}$, then $x_t \in \Theta_t$ for each t and $x_t = 0$ for all but a finite number of t. Thus,

$$\mathbf{p} \cdot \mathbf{x} = \sum_{t=1}^{\infty} \mathbf{p} \cdot (0, \ldots, 0, x_t, 0, 0, \ldots) = \sum_{t=1}^{\infty} p^t \cdot x_t,$$

and so $\mathbf{p}$ can be identified with the sequence $(p^1, p^2, \ldots)$, as desired. ■

A consequence of the preceding theorem and Theorem 5.2.6 is that for the Riesz dual system $\langle \mathbf{\Theta}, \mathbf{\Theta}' \rangle$ the Mackey topology $\tau(\mathbf{\Theta}, \mathbf{\Theta}')$ coincides with the inductive limit topology generated by the sequence of ideals $\{\mathbf{A}_n\}$.

EXERCISES

1. From the theory of locally convex spaces it is well known that a locally convex topology on a vector space is completely determined by a non-empty family $\mathcal{U}$ of subsets with the following properties:

a) $0 \in V$ for each $V \in \mathcal{U}$;

b) for each U and V in $\mathcal{U}$ there exists some $W \in \mathcal{U}$ such that $W \subseteq V \cap U$;

c) each $V \in \mathcal{U}$ is absorbing (i.e, for each x there exists some $\lambda > 0$ with $\lambda x \in V$), balanced (i.e., $\lambda x \in V$ for all $|\lambda| \leq 1$ and all $x \in V$) and convex; and

d) for each $V \in \mathcal{U}$ there exists some $U \in \mathcal{U}$ such that $U + U \subseteq V$.

In this case the family $\mathcal{U}$ is a base for the neighborhood system at zero.

Assume that $0 \leq a_n \uparrow$ holds in a Riesz space, let A_n denote the ideal generated by the sequence $\{a_n\}$ and let $A = \bigcup_{n=1}^{\infty} A_n$. Show that the family $\mathcal{U}$ of subsets of A consisting of all sets of the form

$$V = \mathrm{co}\Big(\bigcup_{n=1}^{\infty} V_n\Big)$$

where V_n is a balanced ξ_n-neighborhood of A_n satisfies the above properties. (The locally convex topology generated by $\mathcal{U}$ is, of course, the inductive limit topology ξ.)

2. Assume that the ideal A is generated by a disjoint sequence $\{\omega_n\}$ of E^+. Let C_n be the ideal generated by $\hat{\omega}_n = \sum_{i=1}^{n} \omega_i$ and let ξ_n denote the locally convex-solid topology generated on C_n by $\|\cdot\|_n$. Show that C_n is ξ_{n+1}-closed in C_{n+1}.

[HINT: Let $\{x_k\}$ be a sequence of C_n satisfying $\lim_{k\to\infty} \|x_k - x\|_{n+1} = 0$ for some $x \in C_{n+1}$. Note that

$$\begin{aligned}|x| \leq |x - x_k| + |x_k| &\leq \|x - x_k\|_{n+1} \cdot \hat{\omega}_{n+1} + \|x_k\|_n \cdot \hat{\omega}_n \\ &= \|x - x_k\|_{n+1} \cdot \hat{\omega}_{n+1} + \|x_k\|_{n+1} \cdot \hat{\omega}_n .\end{aligned}$$

On the other hand, $\|x - x_k\|_{n+1} \cdot \omega_{n+1} + \|x_k\|_{n+1}\hat{\omega}_n \xrightarrow{o} \|x\|_{n+1} \cdot \hat{\omega}_n$ holds, where the convergence is now in order. It follows that $|x| \leq \|x\|_{n+1} \cdot \hat{\omega}_n$, and so $x \in C_n$.]

3. Verify the assertions of Example 5.2.13.

5.3. MALINVAUD OPTIMALITY

Given the failure of the first welfare theorem in the overlapping generations model, as first demonstrated by P. A. Samuelson [59], we shall consider a weaker notion of optimality—referred to as *Malinvaud optimality*—for which the first welfare theorem does hold. That is, we shall show that every competitive equilibrium is Malinvaud optimal. Moreover, we shall establish that the second welfare theorem also holds, i.e., we shall show that every Malinvaud optimal allocation can be supported (subject to transfers) by a price as a competitive equilibrium.

We shall begin our discussion by introducing the concept of Pareto optimality in the overlapping generations model.

Definition 5.3.1. *An allocation* $(\mathbf{x}_t)$ *in an OLG model is said to be* **Pareto optimal** *whenever there is no other allocation* $(\mathbf{y}_t)$ *satisfying* $\mathbf{y}_t \succeq_t \mathbf{x}_t$ *for all* t *and* $\mathbf{y}_t \succ_t \mathbf{x}_t$ *for at least one* t.

Next, we present a variant of Samuelson's observation that a competitive equilibrium may fail to be Pareto optimal. The following example is essentially due to K. Shell [64].

Example 5.3.2. Consider an overlapping generations model with the following characteristics.
Commodity Spaces: $E_t = \mathcal{R}$ for each t.
Utility Functions: $u_0(x^0) = x^0$ and $u_t(x^t, x^{t+1}) = x^t + x^{t+1}$.
Initial Endowments: $\omega_0 = (2, 0, 0, \ldots)$ and $\omega_t = (0, \ldots, 0, 2, 2, 0, 0, \ldots)$ for $t \geq 1$.

We claim that the allocation $(\omega_0, \omega_1, \omega_2, \ldots)$ is a competitive equilibrium supported by the price $\mathbf{p} = (1, 1, 1, 1, \ldots)$. To see this, let $\mathbf{x} \succeq \omega_t$, i.e., assume that $u_t(\mathbf{x}) = x^t + x^{t+1} \geq u_t(\omega_t)$. Therefore,

$$\mathbf{p} \cdot \mathbf{x} = x^t + x^{t+1} \geq u_t(\omega_t) = \mathbf{p} \cdot \omega_t\,,$$

which means that the strictly positive price $\mathbf{p}$ supports the allocation (ω_t). Now an easy argument shows that ω_t is a maximal element in the budget set $\mathcal{B}_t(\mathbf{p})$.

However, we shall show next that the competitive equilibrium (ω_t) is not Pareto optimal. To see this, consider the allocation:

$$\begin{aligned}
\mathbf{y}_0 &= (2,0,0,0,\ldots)\\
\mathbf{y}_1 &= (2,3,0,0,0,\ldots)\\
\mathbf{y}_2 &= (0,1,3,0,0,\ldots)\\
\mathbf{y}_3 &= (0,0,1,3,0,0,\ldots)\\
&\ \vdots\\
\mathbf{y}_t &= (0,0,0,\ldots,1,3,0,0,\ldots)\\
&\ \vdots
\end{aligned}$$

A simple calculation shows that $\mathbf{y}_t \succeq_t \omega_t$ holds for all t and that $\mathbf{y}_1 \succ_1 \omega_1$—and therefore, the competitive equilibrium (ω_t) is not a Pareto optimal allocation. ■

In E. Malinvaud's work on capital accumulation in infinite horizon models [44, 45], a notion of efficiency in production was proposed that—following Y. Balasko and K. Shell [15]—we have transcribed as a notion of optimality in consumption. It is defined as follows.

Definition 5.3.3. *An allocation* $(\mathbf{x}_t)$ *in an OLG model is said to be* **Malinvaud optimal** *if there is no other allocation* $(\mathbf{y}_t)$ *such that*

a) $\mathbf{y}_t = \mathbf{x}_t$ *for all but a finite number of* t,

b) $\mathbf{y}_t \succeq_t \mathbf{x}_t$ *for all* t, *and*

c) $\mathbf{y}_t \succ_t \mathbf{x}_t$ *for at least one* t.

Every Pareto optimal allocation is clearly Malinvaud optimal. However, the notion of Malinvaud optimality is weaker than the concept of Pareto optimality—see Exercise 2 at the end of this section. As we shall see, the notion of Malinvaud optimality is the key to establishing the two welfare theorems in the overlapping generations model. One can show directly that Pareto optimal allocations exist and conclude that Malinvaud optimal allocations always exist.

Now the first fundamental theorem of welfare economics in an OLG model takes the following form; it guarantees that a competitive equilibrium is a Malinvaud optimal allocation.

Theorem 5.3.4. *If an allocation* $(\mathbf{x}_t)$ *in an overlapping generations model satisfies* $x_{t-1}^t > 0$ *and* $x_t^t > 0$ *for each* $t \geq 1$ *and is supported on* $\boldsymbol{\Theta}$ *by a non-zero price of* $\boldsymbol{\Theta}'$, *then it is Malinvaud optimal.*

Proof. Let $(\mathbf{x}_t)$ be an allocation such that $x_{t_1}^t > 0$ and $x_t^t > 0$ hold for each $t \geq 1$. Also, let a price $\mathbf{0} < \mathbf{p} = (p^1, p^2, \ldots) \in \boldsymbol{\Theta}'$ support the allocation. We claim that the price $\mathbf{p}$ is strictly positive on $\boldsymbol{\Theta}$. To see this, notice first that $\mathbf{p} \cdot \omega_t > 0$ must hold for some t and therefore $\mathbf{p} \cdot \mathbf{x}_t > 0$ must also hold for some t. Hence, by the strict monotonicity of preferences, $\mathbf{p}\cdot\mathbf{x}_{t-1}>0$ and $\mathbf{p}\cdot\mathbf{x}_{t+1}>0$ are also true and an easy inductive argument guarantees that $\mathbf{p}\cdot\mathbf{x}_t>0$ holds for each t. The latter easily implies (how?) that $\mathbf{p}\gg\mathbf{0}$.

Now, assume by way of contradiction that $(\mathbf{x}_0,\mathbf{x}_1,\ldots)$ is not Malinvaud optimal. Then, there exists another allocation $(\mathbf{y}_t)$ such that

a) $\mathbf{y}_t=\mathbf{x}_t$ for all but a finite number of t,
b) $\mathbf{y}_t\succeq_t\mathbf{x}_t$ for all t, and
c) $\mathbf{y}_t\succ_t\mathbf{x}_t$ for at least one t.

Choose an integer k such that $\mathbf{y}_t\succ_t\mathbf{x}_t$ for at least one $t\le k$ and $\mathbf{y}_t=\mathbf{x}_t$ for all $t>k$. Clearly,

$$\begin{aligned}\sum_{t=0}^{k}\mathbf{y}_t+\sum_{t=k+1}^{\infty}\mathbf{y}_t&=\sum_{t=0}^{\infty}\mathbf{y}_t\\&=\sum_{t=0}^{\infty}\mathbf{x}_t\\&=\sum_{t=0}^{k}\mathbf{x}_t+\sum_{t=k+1}^{\infty}\mathbf{x}_t\,,\end{aligned}$$

and so $\sum_{t=0}^{k}\mathbf{y}_t=\sum_{t=0}^{k}\mathbf{x}_t$. Therefore,

$$\sum_{t=0}^{k}\mathbf{p}\cdot\mathbf{y}_t=\sum_{t=0}^{k}\mathbf{p}\cdot\mathbf{x}_t\,.$$

On the other hand, $\mathbf{y}_t\succeq\mathbf{x}_t$ and the supportability of $\mathbf{p}$ imply $\mathbf{p}\cdot\mathbf{y}_t\ge\mathbf{p}\cdot\mathbf{x}_t$ and from the above equality, we see that $\mathbf{p}\cdot\mathbf{y}_t=\mathbf{p}\cdot\mathbf{x}_t>0$ holds for $0\le t\le k$. Now pick some $0\le i\le k$ with $\mathbf{y}_i\succ_i\mathbf{x}_i$ and use the continuity of the utility functions to select some $0<\delta<1$ such that $\delta\mathbf{y}_i\succ_i\mathbf{x}_i$. This (in view of $\mathbf{p}\cdot\mathbf{y}_i>0$) implies

$$\mathbf{p}\cdot\mathbf{y}_i>\delta\mathbf{p}\cdot\mathbf{y}_i=\mathbf{p}\cdot(\delta\mathbf{y}_i)\ge\mathbf{p}\cdot\mathbf{x}_i=\mathbf{p}\cdot\mathbf{y}_i\,,$$

which is impossible, and the desired conclusion follows. ■

Next we shall prove a version of the second fundamental theorem of welfare economics for the overlapping generations model. Actually, we shall establish two versions of the second welfare theorem; one with proper preferences and one without proper preferences. Recall that Θ_t denotes the ideal generated by the total endowment θ_t present in period t. First, we shall consider the case where the commodity-price duality at each period is given by the Riesz dual pair $\langle\Theta_t,\Theta_t'\rangle$.

Theorem 5.3.5. *Every Malinvaud optimal allocation $(\mathbf{x}_t)$, in an overlapping generations model, that satisfies $x_{t-1}^t>0$ and $x_t^t>0$ for each $t\ge 1$ can be supported on the ideal $\boldsymbol{\Theta}$ by a strictly positive price of $\boldsymbol{\Theta}'$.*

The proof of this theorem is quite involved and it will be accomplished by a series of steps in the form of lemmas. Before proving Theorem 5.3.5, we shall use the theorem to derive another version of the second fundamental theorem of welfare economics in the overlapping generations model.

In the overlapping generations model each consumer $t \geq 1$ lives in periods t and $t+1$ and her utility function u_t is defined on $E_t^+ \times E_{t+1}^+$. Let us say that the preference $\succeq_t$ induced by u_t is *uniformly proper* whenever each preference $\succeq_t$ is uniformly proper with respect to the product topology on $E_t \times E_{t+1}$. The preference $\succeq_0$ is said to be *uniformly proper* whenever it is uniformly proper on E_1.

Recall that the element θ_t is said to be *strictly positive* whenever $q \cdot \theta_t > 0$ holds for all $0 < q \in E'_t$—equivalently, whenever Θ_t is $\sigma(E_t, E'_t)$-dense in E_t. Now consider the overlapping generations model having the Riesz dual system $\langle \mathbf{E}, \mathbf{E}' \rangle$. In this case, the second fundamental theorem of welfare economics for proper overlapping generations model can be formulated as follows.

Theorem 5.3.6. *If a Malinvaud optimal allocation* $(\mathbf{x}_t)$ *in an overlapping generations model with uniformly proper preferences satisfies* $x_{t-1}^t > 0$ *and* $x_t^t > 0$ *for each* $t \geq 1$, *then* $(\mathbf{x}_t)$ *can be supported on* $\mathbf{E}$ *by a non-zero price of* $\mathbf{E}'$.

Proof. Let $(\mathbf{x}_t)$ be a Malinvaud optimal allocation in an overlapping generations model with uniformly proper preferences such that $x_{t-1}^t > 0$ and $x_t^t > 0$ hold for each $t \geq 1$. By Theorem 5.3.5 there exists a price $\mathbf{p} = (p^1, p^2, \ldots) \in \boldsymbol{\Theta}'$ supporting the allocation $(\mathbf{x}_0, \mathbf{x}_1, \mathbf{x}_2, \ldots)$ on $\boldsymbol{\Theta}$ and satisfying $\mathbf{p} \cdot \mathbf{x}_t > 0$ for $t = 0, 1, 2, \ldots$. We have $p^t \in \Theta'_t$ for each t, where Θ_t is the ideal generated by θ_t in E_t.

Now since the utility functions are proper it follows from Theorem 3.4.22, that each linear functional $p^t \colon \Theta_t \longrightarrow \mathcal{R}$ is continuous. Since Θ_t is dense in E_t, it follows that p^t has a unique continuous positive extension, say q^t, to all of E_t. Clearly, $\mathbf{q} = (q^1, q^2, \ldots) \in \mathbf{E}'$, and we claim that the price $\mathbf{q}$ supports $(\mathbf{x}_0, \mathbf{x}_1, \mathbf{x}_2, \ldots)$ on $\mathbf{E}$.

To see this, let $\mathbf{y} \succeq_t \mathbf{x}_t$ in $E_t^+ \times E_{t+1}^+$. Fix $\delta > 0$ and note that $\mathbf{y} + \delta\omega_t \succ_t \mathbf{x}_t$. Since each Θ_i is $\sigma(E_i, E'_i)$-dense in E_i, it follows that Θ_i is also dense in E_i for the locally convex-solid topology on $E_i \times E_{i+1}$ for which u_i is continuous. Thus, there exists a net $\{\mathbf{y}_\alpha\} \subseteq \Theta_t^+ \times \Theta_{t+1}^+$ that converges topologically to $\mathbf{y} + \delta\omega_t$. In view of $\mathbf{y} + \delta\omega_t \succ_t \mathbf{x}_t$ and the continuity of u_t, we can assume that $\mathbf{y}_\alpha \succ_t \mathbf{x}_t$ holds for all α. Taking into account that $\mathbf{p}$ supports the allocation on $\boldsymbol{\Theta}$, we get $\mathbf{p} \cdot \mathbf{y}_\alpha \geq \mathbf{p} \cdot \mathbf{x}_t$ for all α, and by the continuity of $\mathbf{q}$ on $E_t \times E_{t+1}$, we see that $\mathbf{q} \cdot \mathbf{y} + \delta\mathbf{q} \cdot \omega_t \geq \mathbf{q} \cdot \mathbf{x}_t$ for all $\delta > 0$. Therefore, $\mathbf{y} \succeq_t \mathbf{x}_t$ in $E_t^+ \times E_{t+1}^+$ implies $\mathbf{q} \cdot \mathbf{y} \geq \mathbf{q} \cdot \mathbf{x}_t$, and the proof of the theorem is finished. ∎

We are now ready to start the discussion about the proof of Theorem 5.3.5. Throughout the proof, $(\mathbf{x}_t)$ will denote a fixed Malinvaud optimal allocation. Our objective is to construct a sequence of prices that support the given allocation in *the short run* and then take an "appropriate" limit of the sequence to obtain a supporting price.

Definition 5.3.7. *A* **sequence of short run supporting prices** *for an allocation* $(\mathbf{x}_t)$ *in an overlapping generations model is a sequence of prices* $(\mathbf{p}_n)$ *such that:*

a) $\mathbf{p}_n = (p_n^1, p_n^2, \ldots, p_n^n, p_n^{n+1}, 0, 0, 0, \ldots)$;

b) $0 < p_n^k \in \Theta_k'$ *holds for each* k *and* n *with* $1 \le k \le n+1$; *and*

c) $\mathbf{x} \succeq_t \mathbf{x}_t$ *in* $\boldsymbol{\Theta}$ *implies* $\mathbf{p}_n \cdot \mathbf{x} \ge \mathbf{p}_n \cdot \mathbf{x}_t$ *for each* $n \ge t$.

Our first goal is to establish that a Malinvaud optimal allocation admits a sequence of short run supporting prices.

Lemma 5.3.8. *Let* $(\mathbf{x}_t)$ *be a Malinvaud optimal allocation satisfying* $x_{t-1}^t > 0$ *and* $x_t^t > 0$ *for each* $t \ge 1$. *Then for every natural number* n *there exists a price* $\mathbf{p} = (p^1, p^2, \ldots, p^n, p^{n+1}, 0, 0, 0, \ldots)$ *such that*

a) $0 < p^t \in \Theta_t'$;

b) $\mathbf{p} \cdot \mathbf{x}_t > 0$; *and*

c) $\mathbf{x} \succeq_t \mathbf{x}_t$ *in* $\boldsymbol{\Theta}$ *and* $0 \le t \le n$ *imply* $\mathbf{p} \cdot \mathbf{x} \ge \mathbf{p} \cdot \mathbf{x}_t$.

Proof. Assume that $(\mathbf{x}_t)$ is a Malinvaud optimal allocation satisfying $x_{t-1}^t > 0$ and $x_t^t > 0$ for each $t \ge 1$. Let $\mathbf{I}$ denote the ideal generated by $\sum_{t=0}^{n+1} \mathbf{x}_t$; clearly, all coordinates of the vectors of $\mathbf{I}$ greater than $n+2$ are zero. Also, note that

$$\mathbf{I} = \Theta_1 \times \Theta_2 \times \cdots \times \Theta_{n+1} \times \Omega_{n+2} \times \mathbf{0} \times \mathbf{0} \times \cdots,$$

where $\mathbf{0} = \{0\}$ and Ω_{n+2} denotes the ideal generated by x_{n+1}^{n+2} in E_{n+2}. Now for each i consider the non-empty convex set $G_i = \{\mathbf{x} \in \mathbf{I}^+ \colon \mathbf{x} \succeq_i \mathbf{x}_i\}$ and let

$$G = \sum_{i=0}^{n+1} (G_i - \mathbf{x}_i).$$

If $K = \operatorname{Int}(\mathbf{I}^+)$ with respect to the $\|\cdot\|_\infty$-norm of $\mathbf{I}$, then $K \ne \emptyset$, and we claim that $G \cap (-K) = \emptyset$. To see this, assume by way of contradiction that $G \cap (-K) \ne \emptyset$. Then there exists some $\mathbf{f} \in K$ with $-\mathbf{f} \in G$. Pick elements $\mathbf{y}_i \in G_i$ such that $-\mathbf{f} = \sum_{i=0}^{n+1} (\mathbf{y}_i - \mathbf{x}_i)$, and note that

$$\sum_{i=0}^{n+1} (\mathbf{y}_i + \tfrac{1}{n+2}\mathbf{f}) = \sum_{i=0}^{n+1} \mathbf{x}_i.$$

Since $\mathbf{f} \in \operatorname{Int}(\mathbf{I}^+)$, we must have $\mathbf{y}_i + \frac{1}{n+2}\mathbf{f} \gg \mathbf{y}_i$. Now put

$$\mathbf{z}_i = \mathbf{y}_i + \tfrac{1}{n+2}\mathbf{f} \quad \text{for} \quad 0 \le i \le n+1 \quad \text{and} \quad \mathbf{z}_i = \mathbf{x}_i \quad \text{for} \quad i > n+1,$$

and note that $(\mathbf{z}_0, \mathbf{z}_1, \ldots)$ is an allocation. In addition, for $0 \le i \le n$ we have

$$\mathbf{z}_i = \mathbf{y}_i + \tfrac{1}{n+2}\mathbf{f} \succ_i \mathbf{y}_i \succeq_i \mathbf{x}_i,$$

and $\mathbf{z}_i \succeq_i \mathbf{x}_i$ for $i > n+1$, contrary to the Malinvaud optimality of $(\mathbf{x}_0, \mathbf{x}_1, \ldots)$. Hence $G \cap (-K) = \emptyset$.

Since G and $-K$ are both non-empty convex sets and $-K$ is an $\|\cdot\|_\infty$-open cone, it follows from the classical separation theorem (Theorem 2.3.3) that there exists some non-zero price

$$\mathbf{p} = (p^1, p^2, \ldots, p^{n+1}, p^{n+2}, 0, 0, 0, \ldots)$$

with $p^t \in \Theta_t'$ for $1 \le t \le n+1$ and $p^{n+2} \in \Omega_{n+2}'$ such that $\mathbf{g} \in G$ implies $\mathbf{p} \cdot \mathbf{g} \ge 0$. Since $\mathbf{p} > 0$ must hold, we infer that $\mathbf{p} \cdot \mathbf{x}_i > 0$ must also hold for some $0 \le i \le n+1$.

We claim that $\mathbf{p} \cdot \mathbf{x}_t > 0$ holds for all $0 \le t \le n+1$. To see this, assume by way of contradiction that $\mathbf{p} \cdot \mathbf{x}_t = 0$ for some $0 \le t \le n+1$. Then the two sets

$$C_1 = \{i \in C\colon\ 0 \le i \le n+1 \text{ and } \mathbf{p} \cdot \mathbf{x}_i > 0\}$$

and

$$C_2 = \{i \in C\colon\ 0 \le i \le n+1 \text{ and } \mathbf{p} \cdot \mathbf{x}_i = 0\}$$

are both non-empty. Thus, there exist two consecutive integers $i \in C_1$ and $j \in C_2$. Since preferences are strictly monotone, we see that

$$\mathbf{y} = \mathbf{x}_i + \mathbf{x}_j \succ_i \mathbf{x}_i\,.$$

Clearly, $\mathbf{p} \cdot \mathbf{y} = \mathbf{p} \cdot \mathbf{x}_i > 0$. Now by the continuity of the utility functions there exists some $0 < \delta < 1$ with $\delta \mathbf{y} \succ_i \mathbf{x}_i$. From $\delta \mathbf{y} - \mathbf{x}_i \in G$, it follows that

$$\mathbf{p} \cdot \mathbf{y} > \delta \mathbf{p} \cdot \mathbf{y} = \mathbf{p} \cdot (\delta \mathbf{y}) \ge \mathbf{p} \cdot \mathbf{x}_i = \mathbf{p} \cdot \mathbf{y}\,,$$

which is impossible. Hence, $\mathbf{p} \cdot \mathbf{x}_t > 0$ holds for all $0 \le t \le n+1$. To complete the proof, note that by dropping the p^{n+2} term from $\mathbf{p}$ we obtain a price

$$\mathbf{p} = (p^1, p^2, \ldots, p^n, p^{n+1}, 0, 0, 0, \ldots)$$

that satisfies the desired properties. ■

An immediate consequence of the preceding lemma is the following result.

Lemma 5.3.9. *If a Malinvaud optimal allocation* $(\mathbf{x}_t)$ *satisfies* $x_{t-1}^t > 0$ *and* $x_t^t > 0$ *for each* $t \ge 1$, *then* $(\mathbf{x}_t)$ *admits a sequence of short run supporting prices* $(\mathbf{p}_n)$ *such that* $\mathbf{p}_n \cdot \mathbf{x}_i > 0$ *holds for all* n *and all* i *with* $n \ge i$.

Proof. Let $(\mathbf{x}_t)$ be a Malinvaud optimal allocation satisfying $x_{t-1}^t > 0$ and $x_t^t > 0$ for each $t \ge 1$ and let n be fixed. By Lemma 5.3.8, there exists a price $0 < \mathbf{p}_n \in \Theta'$ such that $\mathbf{p}_n \cdot \mathbf{x}_i > 0$ holds for all $0 \le i \le n$ and $\mathbf{x} \succeq_i \mathbf{x}_i$ in Θ^+ implies $\mathbf{p}_n \cdot \mathbf{x} \ge \mathbf{p}_n \cdot \mathbf{x}_i$. Note that the sequence of prices $(\mathbf{p}_n)$ is a sequence of short run supporting prices that satisfies the desired properties. ■

The next lemma presents a growth estimate for a sequence of short run supporting prices and is the analogue of C. A. Wilson's Lemma 3 in [68].

Lemma 5.3.10. *Let* $(\mathbf{x}_t)$ *be an allocation satisfying* $x^t_{t-1} > 0$ *and* $x^t_t > 0$ *for each* $t \geq 1$ *and let* $(\mathbf{p}_n)$ *be a sequence of short run supporting prices for the allocation such that* $\mathbf{p}_n \cdot \mathbf{x}_i > 0$ *holds for all* n *and all* i *with* $n \geq i$. *Then for each fixed pair of non-negative integers* k *and* m *there exists some constant* $M > 0$ *(depending only upon* k *and* m*) such that*

$$0 < \mathbf{p}_n \cdot \mathbf{x}_k \leq M\, \mathbf{p}_n \cdot \mathbf{x}_m$$

holds for all $n \geq \max\{k, m\}$.

Proof. Let $(\mathbf{x}_0, \mathbf{x}_1, \ldots)$ be an allocation satisfying $x^t_{t-1} > 0$ and $x^t_t > 0$ for each $t \geq 1$ and let $(\mathbf{p}_n)$ be a short run sequence of prices satisfying $\mathbf{p}_n \cdot \mathbf{x}_i > 0$ for $n \geq i$. Let k and m be fixed and suppose by way of contradiction that our claim is not true. That is, assume that $\liminf_{n \geq t} \frac{\mathbf{p}_n \cdot \mathbf{x}_m}{\mathbf{p}_n \cdot \mathbf{x}_k} = 0$, where $t = \max\{k, m\}$. Let $\mathcal{N}$ denote the set of all non-negative integers. Put

$$C_1 = \Big\{ i \in \mathcal{N}\colon \liminf_{n \to \infty} \tfrac{\mathbf{p}_n \cdot \mathbf{x}_i}{\mathbf{p}_n \cdot \mathbf{x}_k} = 0 \Big\} \text{ and } C_2 = \Big\{ i \in \mathcal{N}\colon \liminf_{n \to \infty} \tfrac{\mathbf{p}_n \cdot \mathbf{x}_i}{\mathbf{p}_n \cdot \mathbf{x}_k} > 0 \Big\}.$$

Clearly, $\mathcal{N} = C_1 \cup C_2$, $k \in C_2$ and $m \in C_1$. Since $\mathcal{N} = C_1 \cup C_2$, there exist two consecutive integers i and j with $j \in C_1$ and $i \in C_2$. Note that $\mathbf{x}_i + \mathbf{x}_j \succ_i \mathbf{x}_i$. Since the utility function u_i is continuous, there exists some $0 < \delta < 1$ with

$$\delta \mathbf{x}_i + \mathbf{x}_j \succ_i \mathbf{x}_i \,.$$

Therefore, by the supportability of $\mathbf{p}_n$, we see that

$$\delta \mathbf{p}_n \cdot \mathbf{x}_i + \mathbf{p}_n \cdot \mathbf{x}_j \geq \mathbf{p}_n \cdot \mathbf{x}_i$$

holds for all sufficiently large n. Thus, $\mathbf{p}_n \cdot \mathbf{x}_j \geq (1 - \delta)\mathbf{p}_n \cdot \mathbf{x}_i$, and hence

$$\tfrac{\mathbf{p}_n \cdot \mathbf{x}_j}{\mathbf{p}_n \cdot \mathbf{x}_k} \geq (1 - \delta) \tfrac{\mathbf{p}_n \cdot \mathbf{x}_i}{\mathbf{p}_n \cdot \mathbf{x}_k}\,,$$

holds for all sufficiently large n. Consequently,

$$\liminf_{n \to \infty} \tfrac{\mathbf{p}_n \cdot \mathbf{x}_j}{\mathbf{p}_n \cdot \mathbf{x}_k} \geq (1 - \delta) \liminf_{n \to \infty} \tfrac{\mathbf{p}_n \cdot \mathbf{x}_i}{\mathbf{p}_n \cdot \mathbf{x}_k}\,,$$

which implies $\liminf_{n \to \infty} \frac{\mathbf{p}_n \cdot \mathbf{x}_i}{\mathbf{p}_n \cdot \mathbf{x}_k} = 0$, contrary to $i \in C_2$, and the proof of the lemma is finished. ■

To complete the proof of Theorem 5.3.5, fix a Malinvaud optimal allocation $(\mathbf{x}_t)$ such that $x^t_{t-1} > 0$ and $x^t_t > 0$ hold for each $t \geq 1$. By Lemma 5.3.9, there exists a short run sequence of prices $(\mathbf{p}_n)$, where

$$\mathbf{p}_n = (p^1_n, p^2_n, \ldots, p^n_n, p^{n+1}_n, 0, 0, 0, \ldots)\,,$$

such that $\mathbf{p}_n \cdot \mathbf{x}_t > 0$ holds for all $n \geq t$. Replacing each $\mathbf{p}_n$ by $\frac{\mathbf{p}_n}{\mathbf{p}_n \cdot \mathbf{x}_0}$, we can suppose without loss of generality that

$$\mathbf{p}_n \cdot \mathbf{x}_0 = 1$$

holds for each n. In addition, by Lemma 5.3.10, for each k there exists some $M_k > 0$ such that

$$0 < \mathbf{p}_n \cdot \mathbf{x}_k \leq M_k \mathbf{p}_n \cdot \mathbf{x}_0 = M_k$$

holds for all $n \geq k$. The latter implies that the sequence of linear functionals $\{p_k^n\colon n \geq k\}$ is a norm bounded sequence of Θ_k', and so it forms a relatively weak* compact subset of Θ_k'. For each k, let $\mathcal{C}_k$ be a closed ball of Θ_k' centered at zero containing the sequence $\{p_k^n\colon n \geq k\}$, and let

$$\mathcal{C} = \mathcal{C}_1 \times \mathcal{C}_2 \times \mathcal{C}_3 \times \cdots$$

be equipped with the product topology—where, of course, each $\mathcal{C}_i$ is endowed with the weak* topology. By Tychonoff's classical compactness theorem, $\mathcal{C}$ is a compact topological space. Now for each n, note that

$$\mathbf{p}_n = (p_n^1, p_n^2, \ldots, p_n^n, p_n^{n+1}, 0, 0, 0, \ldots) \in \mathcal{C}\,.$$

Pick a convergent subnet $\{\mathbf{p}_{n_\lambda}\}$ of the sequence $\{\mathbf{p}_n\}$—where $\{n_\lambda\}$ is a subnet of the sequence of natural numbers—such that $\mathbf{p}_{n_\lambda} \longrightarrow \mathbf{p}$ holds in $\mathcal{C}$.

Clearly, the price $\mathbf{p} = (p^1, p^2, \ldots)$ is a positive linear functional and $p^k \in \Theta_k'$ for all k. Since, by Lemma 5.3.10, the sequence of real numbers $\{\mathbf{p}_n \cdot \mathbf{x}_t\colon n = 1, 2, \ldots\}$ is bounded away from zero, we see that $\mathbf{p} \cdot \mathbf{x}_t > 0$ holds for each t.

We claim that $\mathbf{p}$ is a price that supports $(\mathbf{x}_0, \mathbf{x}_1, \ldots)$ on $\mathbf{\Theta}$. To see this, let some $\mathbf{x} \in \mathbf{\Theta}^+$ satisfy $\mathbf{x} \succeq_t \mathbf{x}_t$. Note that $n \geq t$ implies $\mathbf{p}_n \cdot \mathbf{x} \geq \mathbf{p}_n \cdot \mathbf{x}_t$, and so by taking limits, we see that

$$\mathbf{p} \cdot \mathbf{x} = \lim_\lambda \mathbf{p}_{n_\lambda} \cdot \mathbf{x} \geq \lim_\lambda \mathbf{p}_{n_\lambda} \cdot \mathbf{x}_t = \mathbf{p} \cdot \mathbf{x}_t > 0\,.$$

That is, the allocation is supported on $\mathbf{\Theta}$ by the price $\mathbf{p} = (p^1, p^2, \ldots)$. To complete the proof of Theorem 5.3.5 note that—as in the proof of Theorem 5.3.4—the price $\mathbf{p}$ is also a strictly positive linear functional of $\mathbf{\Theta}$.

The two fundamental theorems of welfare economics (Theorems 5.3.4 and 5.3.5) can be combined as follows.

Theorem 5.3.11. *An allocation $(\mathbf{x}_t)$, in an overlapping generations model, that satisfies $x_{t-1}^t > 0$ and $x_t^t > 0$ for each $t \geq 1$ is Malinvaud optimal if and only it is supported on $\mathbf{\Theta}$ by a non-zero price of $\mathbf{\Theta}'$.*

Finally, summing up the major conclusions of this section, we have: *Every competitive equilibrium is Malinvaud optimal. Conversely, every Malinvaud optimal allocation is a competitive equilibrium with respect to some suitably assigned initial endowments.*

EXERCISES

1. Show that every Pareto optimal allocation is Malinvaud optimal.

2. Show that the allocation (ω_t) of Example 5.3.2 is Malinvaud optimal—and hence, this is an example of a Malinvaud optimal allocation which is not Pareto optimal. More generally, show that every competitive equilibrium is a Malinvaud optimal allocation.

3. Complete the details of the assertion used in the proof of Theorem 5.3.4: *If a non-zero price of* Θ' *supports an allocation* $(\mathbf{x}_t)$ *with* $x_{t-1}^t > 0$ *and* $x_t^t > 0$ *for each* $t \geq 1$, *then the price is strictly positive.*

4. An allocation $(\mathbf{x}_0, \mathbf{x}_1, \ldots)$ in an overlapping generations model is said to be **weakly Pareto optimal** whenever there is no other allocation $(\mathbf{y}_0, \mathbf{y}_1, \ldots)$ such that $\mathbf{y}_t \succ_t \mathbf{x}_t$ holds for all t. Give an example of a weakly Pareto optimal allocation.

5. Consider two allocations $(\mathbf{x}_0, \mathbf{x}_1, \ldots)$ and $(\mathbf{y}_0, \mathbf{y}_1, \ldots)$ in an overlapping generations model. If there exists a finite set B of natural numbers such that $\mathbf{x}_t = \mathbf{y}_t$ for all $t \notin B$, then show that there exists some integer k such that $\sum_{t=0}^k \mathbf{x}_t = \sum_{t=0}^k \mathbf{y}_t$ holds.

6. In an OLG model show that for each positive integer k there exists an allocation $(\mathbf{x}_t)$ such that $\mathbf{x}_t \succ \omega_t$ holds for all $t \neq k$.

7. Consider an overlapping generations model where each commodity price system $\langle E_t, E_t' \rangle$ is a symmetric Riesz dual system. Show that every Malinvaud optimal allocation $(\mathbf{x}_t)$ that satisfies $x_{t-1}^t > 0$ and $x_t^t > 0$ for each $t \geq 1$ is supported on Θ by an order continuous price.

8. Consider the overlapping generations model with the following characteristics.
   Commodity Spaces: $E_t = \mathcal{R}$ for each t.
   Utility Functions: $u_0(x^0) = x^0$ and $u_t(x^t, x^{t+1}) = x^t + x^{t+1}$.
   Initial Endowments: $\omega_t = (0, \ldots, 0, \frac{1}{4}, \frac{3}{4}, 0, 0, \ldots)$ for $t \geq 2$—where the numbers $\frac{1}{4}$ and $\frac{3}{4}$ occupy the t and $t+1$ positions—$\omega_0 = (\frac{1}{2}, 0, 0, \ldots)$ and $\omega_1 = (\frac{1}{2}, \frac{3}{4}, 0, 0, \ldots)$.
   Establish that the allocation $(\mathbf{x}_0, \mathbf{x}_1, \mathbf{x}_2, \ldots)$, where $\mathbf{x}_0 = (\frac{1}{2}, 0, 0, \ldots)$ and $\mathbf{x}_t = (0, \ldots, 0, \frac{1}{2}, \frac{1}{2}, 0, 0, \ldots)$ for $t \geq 1$, is Malinvaud optimal.

9. Consider the overlapping generations model with the following characteristics.
   Commodity Spaces: $E_t = \mathcal{R}$ for each t.
   Utility Functions: $u_0(x^0) = x^0$ and $u_t(x^t, x^{t+1}) = x^t + 2x^{t+1}$.
   Initial Endowments: $\omega_0 = (\frac{1}{2}, 0, 0, \ldots)$ and $\omega_t = (0, \ldots, 0, \frac{1}{2}, \frac{1}{2}, 0, 0, \ldots)$ for $t \geq 1$—where the number $\frac{1}{2}$ occupies the t and $t+1$ positions.
   Establish that the allocation (ω_t) is not Malinvaud optimal.

10. In the overlapping generations model, a *finite coalition* S of consumers is simply a non-empty finite subset of $\mathcal{N} = \{0, 1, 2, \ldots\}$. As usual, let us say that a coalition S **improves upon** an allocation $(\mathbf{x}_0, \mathbf{x}_1, \ldots)$ whenever there exists another allocation $(\mathbf{y}_0, \mathbf{y}_1, \ldots)$ such that

a) $\sum_{i \in S} \mathbf{y}_i = \sum_{i \in S} \omega_i$; and

b) $\mathbf{y}_i \succ_i \mathbf{x}_i$ holds for each $i \in S$.

1. Define the r-fold replica of the overlapping generations model and show that every allocation defines an "equal treatment" allocation for every r-fold replica of the overlapping generations model.
2. The **finite core** (or simply the **f-core**) consists of all allocations that cannot be improved upon by any finite coalition of $\mathcal{N}$. An allocation in the overlapping generations model is said to be **an Edgeworth equilibrium** whenever it belongs to the f-core of every replica of the OLG model.

   Show that in an overlapping generations model every competitive equilibrium is an Edgeworth equilibrium.

5.4. EXISTENCE OF COMPETITIVE EQUILIBRIA

The purpose of this section is to establish the existence of equilibria in the overlapping generations model. We must first establish the existence of a competitive equilibrium for the Riesz dual system $\langle \mathbf{\Theta}, \mathbf{\Theta}' \rangle$. That is, we shall first consider the overlapping generations model where the commodity space at each period t is the ideal Θ_t generated by the total endowment of that period. This will then be used to establish that competitive equilibrium exists for the Riesz dual system $\langle \mathbf{E}, \mathbf{E}' \rangle$ when the preferences are uniformly proper. The first major result of this section can be stated as follows.

Theorem 5.4.1. *Every overlapping generations model with symmetric Riesz dual systems has a competitive equilibrium with respect to the Riesz dual system $\langle \mathbf{\Theta}, \mathbf{\Theta}' \rangle$ that can be supported by an order continuous strictly positive price.*

Before proving Theorem 5.4.1, we shall present a condition which guarantees the existence of equilibria for the overlapping generations model with respect to the Riesz dual system $\langle \mathbf{E}, \mathbf{E}' \rangle$. Recall that an overlapping generations model has a **competitive equilibrium** with respect to the Riesz dual system $\langle \mathbf{E}, \mathbf{E}' \rangle$ whenever there exists an allocation $(\mathbf{x}_0, \mathbf{x}_1, \mathbf{x}_2, \ldots)$ and some non-zero price $\mathbf{p} = (p^1, p^2, \ldots)$ in $\mathbf{E}'$ such that

1) $x \succeq_0 x_0^1$ in E_1^+ implies $p_1 \cdot x \geq p_1 \cdot \omega_0^1$;
2) $(x, y) \succeq_t (x_t^t, x_t^{t+1})$ in $E_t^+ \times E_{t+1}^+$ implies $p_t \cdot x + p_{t+1} \cdot y \geq p_t \cdot \omega_t^t + p_{t+1} \cdot \omega_t^{t+1}$; and
3) $\mathbf{p} \cdot \mathbf{x}_t = \mathbf{p} \cdot \omega_t$ holds for $t = 0, 1, 2, \ldots$.

Note that $\mathbf{E}$ is a Riesz space containing $\mathbf{\Theta}$ as an ideal. In general, $\mathbf{\Theta}$ is a proper ideal of $\mathbf{E}$. Observe that under the duality

$$\mathbf{p} \cdot \mathbf{y} = \sum_{i=1}^{\infty} p^i \cdot y_i\,,$$

the dual system $\langle \mathbf{E}, \mathbf{E}' \rangle$ is a Riesz dual system—which is symmetric if and only if each Riesz dual system $\langle E_t, E_t' \rangle$ is symmetric.

Theorem 5.4.2. *Every overlapping generations model with uniformly proper preferences and symmetric Riesz dual systems has a competitive equilibrium with respect to the symmetric Riesz dual system $\langle \mathbf{E}, \mathbf{E}' \rangle$.*

Proof. Assume that an overlapping generations model has uniformly proper preferences and symmetric Riesz dual systems. By Theorem 5.4.1, we know that there exists a competitive equilibrium with respect to the Riesz dual system $\langle \mathbf{\Theta}, \mathbf{\Theta}' \rangle$, where

$$(\mathbf{x}_0, \mathbf{x}_1, \mathbf{x}_2, \ldots) \in \mathbf{\Theta} \quad \text{and} \quad \mathbf{p} = (p^1, p^2, \ldots) \in \mathbf{\Theta}'\,.$$

Let t be fixed. Note that the price $\mathbf{p} = (p^1, p^2, \ldots) \in \mathbf{\Theta}'$ "supports" the vectors $\mathbf{x}_0, \mathbf{x}_1, \ldots, \mathbf{x}_t$ on $\mathbf{\Theta}$. Since the preferences are uniformly proper on $\mathbf{E}$ with respect to the product topology τ and $\mathbf{\Theta}$ is τ-dense in $\mathbf{E}$, it follows from Theorem 3.2.6 that the preferences are also uniformly τ-proper on $\mathbf{\Theta}$. Thus, by Theorem 3.4.22, the price $\mathbf{p}$ is τ-continuous on $\mathbf{A}_a$, where $a = \sum_{i=0}^{t} \mathbf{x}_i$. Since $\Theta_1 \times \Theta_2 \times \cdots \times \Theta_t \times \mathbf{0} \times \mathbf{0} \cdots$ is an ideal of $\mathbf{A}_a$, we see that each individual price p^t is continuous on Θ_t.

Since Θ_t is dense in E_t, the price $p^t\colon \Theta_t \longrightarrow \mathcal{R}$ has a unique continuous extension q^t on E_t. We claim that the price $\mathbf{q} = (q^1, q^2, \ldots) \in \mathbf{E}'$ supports $(\mathbf{x}_t)$ on $\mathbf{E}$. To see this, let $\mathbf{y} \succeq_t \mathbf{x}_t$ in $E_t^+ \times E_{t+1}^+$. Fix $\delta > 0$ and then pick a net $\{\mathbf{y}_\alpha\} \subseteq \Theta_t^+ \times \Theta_{t+1}^+$ with $\mathbf{y}_\alpha \xrightarrow{\tau} \mathbf{y} + \delta\omega_t$. In view of $\mathbf{y}_\alpha \xrightarrow{\tau} \mathbf{y} + \delta\omega_t$, and $\mathbf{y} + \delta\omega_t \succ_i \mathbf{x}_i$ it follows from the continuity of the utility functions, that we can also assume $\mathbf{y}_\alpha + \delta\omega_t \succ_t \mathbf{x}_t$ holds for all α. Thus, by the supportability of $\mathbf{p}$ on $\mathbf{\Theta}$, we get $\mathbf{p} \cdot \mathbf{y}_\alpha + \delta \mathbf{p} \cdot \omega_t \geq \mathbf{p} \cdot \omega_t$ for all α, and by the continuity of $\mathbf{q}$ on $E_t \times E_{t+1}$, we see that $\mathbf{q} \cdot \mathbf{y} + \delta \mathbf{p} \cdot \omega_t \geq \mathbf{q} \cdot \omega_t$ for all $\delta > 0$. Thus, $\mathbf{y} \succeq_t \mathbf{x}_t$ in $E_t^+ \times E_{t+1}^+$ implies $\mathbf{q} \cdot \mathbf{y} \geq \mathbf{q} \cdot \omega_t$, and the proof of the theorem is finished. ■

The proof of Theorem 5.4.1 is quite involved and it will be accomplished by a series of lemmas. Let $\mathbf{A}_n$ denote the ideal generated by $\sum_{t=0}^{n} \omega_t$. From Section 5.2 we know that $\mathbf{A}_n$ is a Banach lattice—in fact, an AM-space. Its norm dual will be denoted by $\mathbf{A}_n'$. We shall first focus our attention to the underlying exchange economies with a finite number of agents associated with the OLG model.

Definition 5.4.3. *For each n we shall denote by $\mathcal{E}_n$ the pure exchange economy having Riesz dual system $\langle \mathbf{A}_n, \mathbf{A}_n' \rangle$ and set of agents $\{0, 1, \ldots, n\}$ with their original characteristics.*

Intuitively speaking, the overlapping generations model is the "limit" of the sequence $\{\mathcal{E}_n\}$ of exchange economies. This intuitive idea underlies the mathematically delicate proof of Theorem 5.4.1. Before passing to a "limit" of the sequence $\{\mathcal{E}_n\}$ we study its properties.

Our first result is that each exchange economy $\mathcal{E}_n$ has a Walrasian equilibrium.

Lemma 5.4.4. *In an OLG model with symmetric Riesz dual systems every exchange economy $\mathcal{E}_n$ has a Walrasian equilibrium $(\mathbf{x}_0, \mathbf{x}_1, \ldots, \mathbf{x}_n)$ of the form*

$$\mathbf{x}_0 = (x_0^1, 0, 0, \ldots) \quad \textit{and} \quad \mathbf{x}_t = (0, \ldots, 0, x_t^t, x_t^{t+1}, 0, 0, \ldots), \quad 1 \leq t \leq n\,.$$

Moreover, every non-zero price

$$\mathbf{p} = (p^1, p^2, \ldots, p^n, p^{n+1}, 0, 0, \ldots) \in \mathbf{A}_n'$$

that supports $(\mathbf{x}_0, \mathbf{x}_1, \ldots, \mathbf{x}_n)$ as a Walrasian equilibrium is strictly positive on $\mathbf{A}_n$. In particular, we have

$$\mathbf{p} \cdot \omega_t > 0 \qquad \textit{for each} \qquad 0 \leq t \leq n\,.$$

Proof. From our previous discussion, we know that $\mathbf{A}_n$ coincides with the ideal generated in $\mathbf{E}$ by $(\theta_1, \theta_2, \ldots, \theta_n, \omega_n^{n+1}, 0, 0, \ldots)$, and so $\mathbf{A}_n$ is an AM-space with unit. Also, we know that every utility function is $\|\cdot\|_\infty$-continuous on $\mathbf{A}_n$ and Theorem 3.2.4 guarantees that all preferences are uniformly $\|\cdot\|_\infty$-proper on $\mathbf{A}_n$. In addition, we claim that the exchange economy $\mathcal{E}_n$ satisfies the closedness condition.

To see this, let $\{(\mathbf{x}_0^k, \mathbf{x}_1^k, \ldots, \mathbf{x}_n^k)\colon k = 1, 2, \ldots\}$ be a sequence of feasible allocations for the exchange economy $\mathcal{E}_n$ satisfying $\mathbf{x}_t^{k+1} \succeq_t \mathbf{x}_t^k$ for all k and all $0 \le t \le n$. Let

$$\mathcal{Z}_0 = [0, \theta_1] \quad \text{and} \quad \mathcal{Z}_t = [0, \theta_t] \times [0, \theta_{t+1}] \quad \text{for} \quad 1 \le t \le n\,.$$

If each order interval $[0, \theta_t]$ is equipped with the weak topology (i.e., with the topology $\sigma(E_t, E_t')$), then each $\mathcal{Z}_t$ is a compact topological space and consequently the product topological space

$$\mathcal{Z} = \mathcal{Z}_0 \times \mathcal{Z}_1 \times \cdots \mathcal{Z}_n$$

is likewise a compact topological space. Since $(\mathbf{x}_0^k, \mathbf{x}_1^k, \ldots, \mathbf{x}_n^k) \in \mathcal{Z}$ holds for each k, it follows that there exists a subnet $\{(\mathbf{x}_0^{k_\alpha}, \mathbf{x}_1^{k_\alpha}, \ldots, \mathbf{x}_n^{k_\alpha})\}$ of the sequence of feasible allocations $\{(\mathbf{x}_0^k, \mathbf{x}_1^k, \ldots, \mathbf{x}_n^k)\}$ satisfying

$$(\mathbf{x}_0^{k_\alpha}, \mathbf{x}_1^{k_\alpha}, \ldots, \mathbf{x}_n^{k_\alpha}) \longrightarrow (\mathbf{x}_0, \mathbf{x}_1, \ldots, \mathbf{x}_n)$$

in $\mathcal{Z}$. Clearly, $(\mathbf{x}_0, \mathbf{x}_1, \ldots, \mathbf{x}_n)$ is a feasible allocation and $\mathbf{x}_t^{k_\alpha} \xrightarrow{w} \mathbf{x}_t$ holds for each $0 \le t \le n$. Invoking Exercise 8 of Section 1.2, we see that $u_t(\mathbf{x}_t) \ge \limsup_\alpha u_t(\mathbf{x}_t^{k_\alpha})$ holds for each $0 \le t \le n$. The latter easily implies that $\mathbf{x}_t \succeq_t \mathbf{x}_t^k$ holds for each k and each $0 \le t \le n$, and so the economy $\mathcal{E}_n$ satisfies the closedness condition.

Now by Theorem 3.5.12 there exists a quasiequilibrium $(\mathbf{x}_0, \mathbf{x}_1, \ldots, \mathbf{x}_n)$ supported by a price $\mathbf{0} < \mathbf{p} \in \mathbf{A}_n'$ such that $\mathbf{p}\cdot(\sum_{t=0}^n \omega_t) = 1$. Thus, $\mathbf{p}\cdot\omega_t > 0$ must hold for some $0 \le t \le n$. We claim that $\mathbf{p}\cdot\omega_t > 0$ actually holds for each $0 \le t \le n$. To see this, assume that $\mathbf{p}\cdot\omega_t = 0$ holds for some $0 \le t \le n$. Then there exist two consecutive integers $0 \le r, s \le n$ such that $\mathbf{p}\cdot\omega_r > 0$ and $\mathbf{p}\cdot\omega_s = 0$. Clearly, $\mathbf{x}_r$ is a maximal element in the budget set of consumer r. However, this conclusion is contrary to $\mathbf{x}_r + \omega_s \succ_r \mathbf{x}_r$ and $\mathbf{p}\cdot(\mathbf{x}_r + \omega_s) = \mathbf{p}\cdot\mathbf{x}_r = \mathbf{p}\cdot\omega_r$. Therefore, $\mathbf{p}\cdot\omega_t > 0$ holds for each $0 \le t \le n$ and so $(\mathbf{x}_0, \mathbf{x}_1, \ldots, \mathbf{x}_n)$ is a Walrasian equilibrium with respect to the price $\mathbf{p}$.

To see that $\mathbf{p}$ is strictly positive, let $\mathbf{0} < \mathbf{x} = (x_1, \ldots, x_n, x_{n+1}, 0, 0, \ldots) \in \mathbf{A}_n$. Then $x_t > 0$ must hold for some $1 \le t \le n+1$. So, if $\mathbf{p}\cdot\mathbf{x} = 0$ holds, then $\mathbf{x}_{t-1} + \mathbf{x} \succ_{t-1} \mathbf{x}_{t-1}$ and $\mathbf{p}\cdot(\mathbf{x}_{t-1} + \mathbf{x}) = \mathbf{p}\cdot\mathbf{x}_{t-1} = \mathbf{p}\cdot\omega_{t-1}$ contradict the maximality of $\mathbf{x}_{t-1}$ in the budget set of consumer $t-1$. Hence, $\mathbf{p}\cdot\mathbf{x} > 0$ must hold proving that $\mathbf{p}$ is strictly positive.

By the special nature of the utility functions, it easily follows that the vectors $\mathbf{x}_t$ are of the form

$$\mathbf{x}_0 = (x_0^1, 0, 0, \ldots) \quad \text{and} \quad \mathbf{x}_t = (0, \ldots, 0, x_t^t, x_t^{t+1}, 0, 0, \ldots) \quad \text{for} \quad 1 \le t \le n\,.$$

Also, it should be noted that the price $\mathbf{p}$ above is of the form

$$\mathbf{p} = (p^1, p^2, \ldots, p^n, p^{n+1}, 0, 0, \ldots)\,,$$

where $0 \ll p^t \in \Theta'_t$ $(1 \le t \le n)$ and $0 \ll p^{n+1} \in \Omega'_{n+1}$. ■

In the sequel a Walrasian equilibrium $(\mathbf{x}_0, \mathbf{x}_1, \ldots, \mathbf{x}_n)$ for the exchange economy $\mathcal{E}_n$ supported by a price $0 < \mathbf{p} \in \mathbf{A}'_n$ will be denoted by $(\mathbf{x}_0, \mathbf{x}_1, \ldots, \mathbf{x}_n; \mathbf{p})$. Also, as mentioned above, every Walrasian equilibrium $(\mathbf{x}_0, \mathbf{x}_1, \ldots, \mathbf{x}_n; \mathbf{p})$ for the economy $\mathcal{E}_n$ is necessarily of the form

$$\mathbf{x}_0 = (x_0^1, 0, 0, \ldots) \quad \text{and} \quad \mathbf{x}_t = (0, \ldots, 0, x_t^t, x_t^{t+1}, 0, 0, \ldots) \quad \text{for} \quad 1 \le t \le n\,.$$

We continue our discussion with an important property of nets. Recall that a net $\{y_\lambda\}_{\lambda \in \Lambda}$ is said to be a *subnet* of another net $\{x_\alpha\}_{\alpha \in A}$ whenever there exists a function $\sigma: \Lambda \longrightarrow A$ such that

a) $y_\lambda = x_{\sigma_\lambda}$ holds for all $\lambda \in \Lambda$; and
b) given $\alpha_0 \in A$ there exists some $\lambda_0 \in \Lambda$ so that $\lambda \ge \lambda_0$ implies $\sigma_\lambda \ge \alpha_0$.

Now if $\{y_\alpha\}$ is a subnet of a sequence $\{x_n\}$, then for any α_0, we see that the set $S = \{y_\alpha\colon \alpha \ge \alpha_0\}$ contains infinitely many terms of the sequence $\{x_n\}$ (i.e., $x_n \in S$ holds for infinitely many n), and so there exists a subsequence $\{y_n\}$ of $\{x_n\}$ satisfying $y_n \in S$ for each n. This observation will be employed quite often in the proofs of this section.

The next lemma presents a "growth" estimate for a sequence of Walrasian equilibria for the finite economies $\mathcal{E}_n$. It is the analogue of C. A. Wilson's Lemma 3 in [68].

Lemma 5.4.5. *If* $\{(\mathbf{x}_0^n, \mathbf{x}_1^n, \ldots, \mathbf{x}_n^n; \mathbf{p}_n)\}$ *is a sequence of Walrasian equilibria for the exchange economies* $\mathcal{E}_n\,(n = 1, 2, \ldots)$, *then for each pair* (k, m) *of non-negative integers there exists a constant* $M > 0$ *(depending upon* k *and* m*) such that*

$$0 < \mathbf{p}_n \cdot \omega_k \le M\, \mathbf{p}_n \cdot \omega_m$$

holds for all $n \ge \max\{k, m\}$.

Proof. Fix m and suppose by way of contradiction that there exists some non-negative integer k satisfying $\liminf_{n \ge k_1} \frac{\mathbf{p}_n \cdot \omega_m}{\mathbf{p}_n \cdot \omega_k} = 0$, where $k_1 = \max\{\, k, m\,\}$. Thus, the sets

$$\Big\{i\colon \liminf_{n\to\infty} \frac{\mathbf{p}_n \cdot \omega_i}{\mathbf{p}_n \cdot \omega_k} > 0\Big\} \quad \text{and} \quad \Big\{i\colon \liminf_{n\to\infty} \frac{\mathbf{p}_n \cdot \omega_i}{\mathbf{p}_n \cdot \omega_k} = 0\Big\}$$

are both non-empty—k belongs to the first set and m to the second. It follows that there exist two consecutive integers r and s such that

$$\liminf_{n\to\infty} \frac{\mathbf{p}_n \cdot \omega_r}{\mathbf{p}_n \cdot \omega_k} > 0 \quad \text{and} \quad \liminf_{n\to\infty} \frac{\mathbf{p}_n \cdot \omega_s}{\mathbf{p}_n \cdot \omega_k} = 0\,.$$

By passing to a subsequence, we can assume that

$$\liminf_{n\to\infty} \frac{\mathbf{p}_n \cdot \omega_r}{\mathbf{p}_n \cdot \omega_k} > 0 \quad \text{and} \quad \lim_{n\to\infty} \frac{\mathbf{p}_n \cdot \omega_s}{\mathbf{p}_n \cdot \omega_k} = 0\,. \qquad (\star)$$

In view of $\mathbf{x}_r^n \in [0,\theta_r] \times [0,\theta_{r+1}]$ $(n \geq r)$ and the weak compactness of the order intervals, we see that the sequence $\{\mathbf{x}_r^n\colon n = 1,2,\dots\}$ has a weakly convergent subnet $\{\mathbf{y}_\alpha\}$, say $\mathbf{y}_\alpha \xrightarrow{w} \mathbf{y}$ holds in $E_r^+ \times E_{r+1}^+$.

From $\mathbf{y} + \omega_s \succ_r \mathbf{y}$ and the continuity of the utility function u_r, there exists some $0 < \delta < 1$ such that $\delta(\mathbf{y} + \omega_s) \succ_r \mathbf{y}$. Using the continuity of u_r once again and Lemma 1.2.4, we see that there is some α_0 satisfying $\delta(\mathbf{y}_\alpha + \omega_s) \succ_r \mathbf{y}_\alpha$ for infinitely many $\alpha \geq \alpha_0$. Consequently, there exists a strictly increasing sequence k_n of natural numbers satisfying $\delta(\mathbf{x}_r^{k_n} + \omega_s) \succ_r \mathbf{x}_r^{k_n}$; see the discussion preceding the lemma. Since $(\star)$ remains true if we replace $\mathbf{p}_n$ by $\mathbf{p}_{k_n}$, we can assume without loss of generality that $\delta(\mathbf{x}_r^n + \omega_s) \succ_r \mathbf{x}_r^n$ holds for all $n \geq r$. Therefore, by the supportability of $\mathbf{p}_n$, we have $\delta\mathbf{p}_n\cdot(\omega_r + \omega_s) = \mathbf{p}_n\cdot[\delta(\mathbf{x}_r^n + \omega_s)] \geq \mathbf{p}_n\cdot\omega_r$ for all $n \geq r$. Now note that

$$\begin{aligned}\delta \liminf_{n\to\infty} \frac{\mathbf{p}_n\cdot\omega_r}{\mathbf{p}_n\cdot\omega_k} &= \delta \liminf_{n\to\infty}\left(\frac{\mathbf{p}_n\cdot\omega_r}{\mathbf{p}_n\cdot\omega_k} + \frac{\mathbf{p}_n\cdot\omega_s}{\mathbf{p}_n\cdot\omega_k}\right)\\ &= \liminf_{n\to\infty} \frac{\delta\mathbf{p}_n\cdot(\omega_r + \omega_s)}{\mathbf{p}_n\cdot\omega_k}\\ &\geq \liminf_{n\to\infty} \frac{\mathbf{p}_n\cdot\omega_r}{\mathbf{p}_n\cdot\omega_k} > 0\,,\end{aligned}$$

which is impossible, and our conclusion follows. ■

Now consider each interval $[0,\theta_t]$ equipped with the weak topology $\sigma(E_t, E_t')$ and let

$$\mathcal{X}_0 = [0,\theta_1] \times \mathbf{0} \times \mathbf{0} \times \cdots$$

and

$$\mathcal{X}_t = \mathbf{0} \times \cdots \times \mathbf{0} \times [0,\theta_t] \times [0,\theta_{t+1}] \times \mathbf{0} \times \mathbf{0} \times \cdots \quad (t = 1,2,\dots),$$

where $\mathbf{0} = \{0\}$ and the order intervals $[0,\theta_t]$ and $[0,\theta_{t+1}]$ occupy the t and $t+1$ factors. Clearly, each $\mathcal{X}_t$ is a compact topological space, and so by Tychonoff's classical compactness theorem the product topological space

$$\mathcal{X} = \prod_{t=0}^{\infty} \mathcal{X}_t$$

is a compact topological space.

The topological space $\mathcal{X}$ will play an important role in our proofs. At this point, let us illustrate briefly its role. By Lemma 5.4.4 we know that every exchange economy $\mathcal{E}_n$ has a Walrasian equilibrium. For each n, let $(\mathbf{x}_0^n, \mathbf{x}_1^n, \dots, \mathbf{x}_n^n)$ be a Walrasian equilibrium for $\mathcal{E}_n$, where

$$\mathbf{x}_0^n = (x_{0,n}^1, 0, 0, \dots) \quad\text{and}\quad \mathbf{x}_t^n = (0,\dots,0, x_{t,n}^t, x_{t,n}^{t+1}, 0, 0, \dots) \quad\text{for}\quad t \geq 1\,.$$

If we let

$$\mathbf{f}_n = (\mathbf{x}_0^n, \mathbf{x}_1^n, \dots, \mathbf{x}_n^n, 0, 0, \dots)\,,$$

then $\{\mathbf{f}_n\}$ is a sequence of $\mathcal{X}$, and so since $\mathcal{X}$ is compact, it has an accumulation point $\mathbf{x} = (\mathbf{x}_0, \mathbf{x}_1, \ldots)$. Clearly, the accumulation point $\mathbf{x}$ is an allocation (why?). It will turn out that the allocation $\mathbf{x}$ is, in fact, an equilibrium for our overlapping generations model. The objective of our next goal is the establishment of this claim.

Definition 5.4.6. *A sequence* $\{(\mathbf{x}_0^n, \mathbf{x}_1^n, \ldots, \mathbf{x}_n^n; \mathbf{p}_n)\}$ *of Walrasian equilibria for the sequence of exchange economies* $\{\mathcal{E}_n\}$ *is said to be a* **sequence of short run equilibria** *for the overlapping generations model whenever* $\mathbf{p}_n \cdot \omega_0 = 1$ *holds for all* n.

The reader should notice that (by Lemma 5.4.4) every overlapping generations model with symmetric Riesz dual systems admits a sequence of short run equilibria. As mentioned before, our next objective is to show that an appropriate "limit" of any sequence of short run equilibria yields a competitive equilibrium for the overlapping generations model.

Now fix a sequence of short run equilibria $\{(\mathbf{x}_0^n, \mathbf{x}_1^n, \ldots, \mathbf{x}_n^n; \mathbf{p}_n)\}$ for an overlapping generations model with symmetric Riesz dual systems. As above, let

$$\mathbf{f}_n = (\mathbf{x}_0^n, \mathbf{x}_1^n, \ldots, \mathbf{x}_n^n, 0, 0, \ldots) \in \mathcal{X}.$$

Letting $m = 0$ in Lemma 5.4.5 and taking into account that $\mathbf{p}_n \cdot \omega_0 = 1$ for each n, we see that there exists a constant M_k such that

$$0 < \mathbf{p}_n \cdot \omega_k \le M_k$$

holds for each pair (n, k) with $n \ge k$. In particular, if for each $n > k$ the linear functional $\mathbf{p}_n$ is restricted to $\mathbf{A}_k$, then the sequence $\{\mathbf{p}_n\colon n > k\}$ is a norm bounded sequence of $\mathbf{A}'_k$. Let C_k be a closed ball of $\mathbf{A}'_k$ with center at zero that contains the sequence $\{\mathbf{p}_n\colon n > k\}$—clearly, the ball C_k is a w*-compact subset of $\mathbf{A}'_k$.

Now for each $k = 1, 2, \ldots$ consider the sequence $\{\mathbf{q}_n^k\}$ of positive linear functionals on $\mathbf{A}_k$ defined by $\mathbf{q}_n^k = \mathbf{0}$ if $1 \le n \le k$ and $\mathbf{q}_n^k = \mathbf{p}_n$ (the restriction of $\mathbf{p}_n$ to $\mathbf{A}_k$) for $n > k$. Note that $\{\mathbf{q}_k^n\}$ is a sequence of the w*-compact set C_k. Next, consider the product topological space (with the product topology)

$$\mathcal{C} = \mathcal{X} \times C_1 \times C_2 \times C_3 \times \cdots,$$

and note that—by Tychonoff's classical compactness theorem—$\mathcal{C}$ is a compact topological space. Clearly,

$$(\mathbf{f}_n, \mathbf{q}_n^1, \mathbf{q}_n^2, \mathbf{q}_n^3, \ldots) \in \mathcal{C}$$

holds for all n. Therefore, there exists a subnet $\{n_\lambda\}$ of the sequence of natural numbers $\{n\}$ such that

$$(\mathbf{f}_{n_\lambda}, \mathbf{q}_{n_\lambda}^1, \mathbf{q}_{n_\lambda}^2, \mathbf{q}_{n_\lambda}^3, \ldots) \longrightarrow (\mathbf{x}, \mathbf{q}^1, \mathbf{q}^2, \mathbf{q}^3, \ldots)$$

holds in $\mathcal{C}$. Notice that $\mathbf{q}^k_{n_\lambda} = \mathbf{p}_{n_\lambda}$ holds on $\mathbf{A}_k$ for all λ sufficiently large. The latter implies that for each $\mathbf{y} \in \mathbf{\Theta}$ the value $\mathbf{p}_{n_\lambda}\cdot\mathbf{y}$ is eventually well defined and, in addition, $\lim_\lambda \mathbf{p}_{n_\lambda}\cdot\mathbf{y}$ exists in $\mathcal{R}$. Therefore, a positive linear functional (i.e., a price) $\mathbf{p}: \mathbf{\Theta} \longrightarrow \mathcal{R}$ can be defined via the formula

$$\mathbf{p}\cdot\mathbf{y} = \lim_\lambda \mathbf{p}_{n_\lambda}\cdot\mathbf{y}\,, \quad \mathbf{y} \in \mathbf{\Theta}\,.$$

This price is very important for the overlapping generations model.

Definition 5.4.7. *An* **asymptotic limit** *for a sequence of short run equilibria* $\{(\mathbf{x}^n_0, \mathbf{x}^n_1, \ldots, \mathbf{x}^n_n; \mathbf{p}_n)\}$ *is a pair* $(\mathbf{x}, \mathbf{p})$, *where* $\mathbf{x} = (\mathbf{x}_0, \mathbf{x}_1, \mathbf{x}_2, \ldots)$ *is an allocation and* $\mathbf{p}$ *is a price, such that there exists a subnet* $\{n_\lambda\}$ *of the sequence of natural numbers satisfying*

a) $\mathbf{x}^{n_\lambda}_i \xrightarrow{w} \mathbf{x}_i$ *for all* $i = 0, 1, \ldots$; *and*

b) $\mathbf{p}\cdot\mathbf{y} = \lim_\lambda \mathbf{p}_{n_\lambda}\cdot\mathbf{y}$ *for all* $\mathbf{y} \in \mathbf{\Theta}$.

The preceding discussion guarantees that in an overlapping generations model with symmetric Riesz dual systems asymptotic limits always exist.

Lemma 5.4.8. *In an OLG model with symmetric Riesz dual systems every sequence of short run equilibria has an asymptotic limit.*

Prices associated with asymptotic limits are necessarily order continuous.

Lemma 5.4.9. *If* $(\mathbf{x}, \mathbf{p})$ *is an asymptotic limit of an OLG model with symmetric Riesz dual systems, then the price* $\mathbf{p}$ *is order continuous on the ideal* $\mathbf{\Theta}$.

Proof. Suppose that $(\mathbf{x}, \mathbf{p})$ is an asymptotic limit for a sequence of short run equilibria $\{(\mathbf{x}^n_0, \mathbf{x}^n_1, \ldots, \mathbf{x}^n_n; \mathbf{p}_n)\}$ corresponding to a subnet $\{n_\lambda\}$ of the sequence of natural numbers $\{n\}$. Also, let $\mathbf{y}_\alpha \downarrow \mathbf{0}$ hold in $\mathbf{\Theta}$. We have to show that $\mathbf{p}\cdot\mathbf{y}_\alpha \downarrow 0$.

Without loss of generality, we can assume that for some $k > 1$ we have $\mathbf{y}_\alpha$ in $\mathbf{A}_{k-1}$ for each α and $\mathbf{p}\cdot\left(\sum_{i=0}^k \omega_i\right) = 1$. Moreover, by scaling appropriately, we can suppose that $\mathbf{y}_\alpha \le \sum_{i=0}^k \mathbf{x}^{n_\lambda}_i$ holds for each α and each λ. Thus, by the Riesz Decomposition Theorem, we can write $\mathbf{y}_\alpha = \sum_{i=0}^k \mathbf{y}^i_{\alpha,\lambda}$, where $\mathbf{0} \le \mathbf{y}^i_{\alpha,\lambda} \le \mathbf{x}^{n_\lambda}_i$ for each $i = 0, 1, \ldots, k$. From $\mathbf{0} \le \mathbf{y}^i_{\alpha,\lambda} \le \mathbf{y}_\alpha \downarrow \mathbf{0}$ and the fact that each Riesz dual system $\langle E_t, E'_t\rangle$ is symmetric, it follows that $\mathbf{y}^i_{\alpha,\lambda} \xrightarrow{w} \mathbf{0}$ holds with respect to (α, λ).

Now fix $\varepsilon > 0$ and note that $\mathbf{x}_i + \varepsilon\omega_i \succ_i \mathbf{x}_i$ holds for each i. From $\mathbf{x}^{n_\lambda}_i \xrightarrow{w} \mathbf{x}_i$, $\mathbf{0} \le \mathbf{x}^{n_\lambda}_i - \mathbf{y}^i_{\alpha,\lambda} \xrightarrow{w} \mathbf{x}_i$ and Lemma 1.2.4, we can assume (by passing to a subnet if necessary) that there exist α_0 and λ_0 such that

$$\mathbf{x}^{n_\lambda}_i + \varepsilon\omega_i - \mathbf{y}^i_{\alpha,\lambda} \succ_i \mathbf{x}^{n_\lambda}_i \quad \text{and} \quad n_\lambda \ge k$$

hold for all $\alpha \geq \alpha_0$ all $\lambda \geq \lambda_0$ and each $i = 0, 1, \ldots, k$. By the supportability of the price $\mathbf{p}_{n_\lambda}$, we infer that $\mathbf{p}_{n_\lambda} \cdot \mathbf{x}_i^{n_\lambda} + \varepsilon \mathbf{p}_{n_\lambda} \cdot \omega_i - \mathbf{p}_{n_\lambda} \cdot \mathbf{y}_{\alpha,\lambda}^i \geq \mathbf{p}_{n_\lambda} \cdot \mathbf{x}_i^{n_\lambda}$, and so $0 \leq \mathbf{p}_{n_\lambda} \cdot \mathbf{y}_{\alpha,\lambda}^i \leq \varepsilon \mathbf{p}_{n_\lambda} \cdot \omega_i$ holds for all $\alpha \geq \alpha_0$ all $\lambda \geq \lambda_0$ and each $i = 0, 1, \ldots, k$. Therefore,

$$0 \leq \mathbf{p}_{n_\lambda} \cdot \mathbf{y}_\alpha = \sum_{i=0}^{k} \mathbf{p}_{n_\lambda} \cdot \mathbf{y}_{\alpha,\lambda}^i \leq \varepsilon \mathbf{p}_{n_\lambda} \cdot \Big(\sum_{i=0}^{k} \omega_i \Big)$$

for all $\alpha \geq \alpha_0$ and all $\lambda \geq \lambda_0$. Taking limits with respect to λ, we get

$$0 \leq \mathbf{p} \cdot \mathbf{y}_\alpha \leq \varepsilon \mathbf{p} \cdot \Big(\sum_{i=0}^{k} \omega_i \Big) = \varepsilon$$

for all $\alpha \geq \alpha_0$. Hence, $\mathbf{p} \cdot \mathbf{y}_\alpha \downarrow 0$ and so the price $\mathbf{p}$ is order continuous on Θ. ■

The next lemma presents a supportability property of the asymptotic limits.

Lemma 5.4.10. *If $(\mathbf{x}, \mathbf{p})$ is an asymptotic limit for a sequence of short run equilibria, then $\mathbf{y} \succeq_i \mathbf{x}_i$ in Θ implies $\mathbf{p} \cdot \mathbf{y} \geq \mathbf{p} \cdot \omega_i$.*

Proof. Suppose that $(\mathbf{x}, \mathbf{p})$ is an asymptotic limit of a sequence of short run equilibria $\{ (\mathbf{x}_0^n, \mathbf{x}_1^n, \ldots, \mathbf{x}_n^n; \mathbf{p}_n) \}$. Pick a subnet $\{n_\lambda\}$ of the sequence of natural numbers such that

a) $\mathbf{x}_i^{n_\lambda} \xrightarrow{w} \mathbf{x}_i$ for all $i = 0, 1, 2, \ldots$; and
b) $\mathbf{p} \cdot \mathbf{y} = \lim_\lambda \mathbf{p}_{n_\lambda} \cdot \mathbf{y}$ for all $\mathbf{y} \in \Theta$.

Now let $\mathbf{y} \succeq_i \mathbf{x}_i$ hold in Θ^+. Fix some $k \geq i$ with $\mathbf{y} \in \mathbf{A}_k$ and let $\varepsilon > 0$. Clearly, $\mathbf{y} + \varepsilon \omega_i \succ_i \mathbf{x}_i$. Invoking Lemma 1.2.4 and passing to a subnet if necessary, we can assume that there exists some λ_0 such that

$$\mathbf{y} + \varepsilon \omega_i \succ_i \mathbf{x}_i^{n_\lambda} \quad \text{and} \quad n_\lambda \geq k$$

hold for all $\lambda \geq \lambda_0$. By the supportability of the price $\mathbf{p}_{n_\lambda}$, we see that

$$\mathbf{p}_{n_\lambda} \cdot \mathbf{y} + \varepsilon \mathbf{p}_{n_\lambda} \cdot \omega_i \geq \mathbf{p}_{n_\lambda} \cdot \mathbf{x}_i^{n_\lambda} = \mathbf{p}_{n_\lambda} \cdot \omega_i$$

holds for all $\lambda \geq \lambda_0$. Passing to the limit, we obtain $\mathbf{p} \cdot \mathbf{y} + \varepsilon \mathbf{p} \cdot \omega_i \geq \mathbf{p} \cdot \omega_i$ for all $\varepsilon > 0$, and so $\mathbf{p} \cdot \mathbf{y} \geq \mathbf{p} \cdot \omega_i$, as desired. ■

It is not difficult to see that (with some appropriate modifications) the arguments in this section up to this point are valid for the general overlapping generations model as was introduced in Section 5.1. Our next objective is to establish—in the next four lemmas—that budget equalities hold, i.e, to establish that if $(\mathbf{x}, \mathbf{p})$ is an asymptotic limit, then $\mathbf{p} \cdot \mathbf{x}_t = \mathbf{p} \cdot \omega_t$ holds for each t.

For simplicity, we shall assume that $r = 1$, i.e., we shall assume that exactly one person is born in each period and that he lives ℓ periods. The initial endowment of person t is given by

$$\omega_t = (0, 0, \ldots, 0, \omega_t^t, \omega_t^{t+1}, \ldots, \omega_t^{t+\ell-1}, 0, 0, \ldots).$$

Also, we shall assume that the $\ell - 1$ "ancestors" of consumer 1—labelled with the non-positive integers $2-\ell, 1-\ell, \ldots, -1, 0$—are present in the model. Their initial endowments are of the form

$$\omega_t = (\omega_t^1, \omega_t^2, \ldots, \omega_t^{\ell+t-1}, 0, 0, \ldots), \quad 2-\ell \le t \le 0 .$$

For each $k \ge 1$, we shall denote by P_k the projection of $E_1 \times E_2 \times E_3 \cdots$ defined by

$$P_k(x_1, x_2, x_3, \ldots) = (x_1, x_2, \ldots, x_k, 0, 0, \ldots) .$$

Also, we shall denote by Q_k the complementary projection of P_k defined by

$$Q_k(x_1, x_2, \ldots) = (0, 0, \ldots, 0, x_{k+1}, x_{k+2}, x_{k+3}, \ldots) .$$

Clearly, $P_k + Q_k = I$, the identity operator on $\mathbf{E}$.

As mentioned above, our next objective is to prove that if $(\mathbf{x}, \mathbf{p})$ is an asymptotic limit, then

$$\mathbf{p} \cdot \mathbf{x}_t = \mathbf{p} \cdot \omega_t$$

holds for each t, where

$$\mathbf{x}_t = (0, \ldots, 0, x_t^t, x_t^{t+1}, \ldots, x_t^{t+\ell-1}, 0, 0, \ldots) \quad \text{for} \quad t \ge 1$$

and

$$\mathbf{x}_t = (x_t^1, x_t^2, \ldots, x_t^{\ell+t-1}, 0, 0, \ldots) \quad \text{for} \quad 2-\ell \le t \le 0 .$$

Start by observing that—according to Lemma 5.4.10—we have $\mathbf{p} \cdot \mathbf{x}_t \ge \mathbf{p} \cdot \omega_t$ for each t. Moreover, note that

$$P_k\Big(\sum_{t=2-\ell}^{n} \mathbf{x}_t\Big) = P_k\Big(\sum_{t=2-\ell}^{n} \omega_t\Big) \qquad \text{for all} \qquad 1 \le k \le n , \tag{1}$$

$$Q_k(\mathbf{x}_t) = Q_k(\omega_t) = \mathbf{0} \qquad \text{for all} \qquad t \le k-\ell+1 , \text{ and} \tag{2}$$

$$Q_k\Big(\sum_{t=2-\ell}^{k} \mathbf{x}_t\Big) = Q_k\Big(\sum_{t=k-\ell+1}^{k} \mathbf{x}_t\Big) \qquad \text{for all} \qquad k \ge 1 . \tag{3}$$

Lemma 5.4.11. *If $(\mathbf{x}, \mathbf{p})$ is an asymptotic limit, then for each $k \ge 1$ we have*

$$\mathbf{p} \cdot \Big[Q_k\Big(\sum_{t=k-\ell+1}^{k} \mathbf{x}_t\Big)\Big] \ge \mathbf{p} \cdot \Big[Q_k\Big(\sum_{t=k-\ell+1}^{k} \omega_t\Big)\Big] .$$

Proof. From $\mathbf{p} \cdot \mathbf{x}_t \ge \mathbf{p} \cdot \omega_t$, we see that

$$\mathbf{p} \cdot \Big(\sum_{t=2-\ell}^{k} \mathbf{x}_t\Big) \ge \mathbf{p} \cdot \Big(\sum_{t=2-\ell}^{k} \omega_t\Big) . \tag{$\star$}$$

Also, from (**1**), we have

$$P_k\Big(\sum_{t=2-\ell}^{k} \mathbf{x}_t\Big) = P_k\Big(\sum_{t=2-\ell}^{k} \omega_t\Big),$$

and so

$$\mathbf{p}\cdot\Big[P_k\Big(\sum_{t=2-\ell}^{k} \mathbf{x}_t\Big)\Big] = \mathbf{p}\cdot\Big[P_k\Big(\sum_{t=2-\ell}^{k} \omega_t\Big)\Big].$$

To obtain the desired inequality subtract the latter equation from ($\star$) and take into consideration (**3**). ■

Lemma 5.4.12. *If* $(\mathbf{x}, \mathbf{p})$ *is an asymptotic limit, then for each* $k \geq 1$ *we have*

$$\mathbf{p}\cdot\Big[P_k\Big(\sum_{t=k-\ell+1}^{k} \mathbf{x}_t\Big)\Big] \geq \mathbf{p}\cdot\Big[P_k\Big(\sum_{t=k-\ell+1}^{k} \omega_t\Big)\Big].$$

Proof. From $P_k(\mathbf{x}_t) + Q_k(\mathbf{x}_t) + \varepsilon\omega_t \succ_t \mathbf{x}_t$ ($\varepsilon > 0$; $k-\ell+1 \leq t \leq k$), it follows that

$$P_k(\mathbf{x}_t) + Q_k(\mathbf{x}_t^n) + \varepsilon\omega_t \succ_t \mathbf{x}_t^n \quad \text{for all} \quad k-\ell+1 \leq t \leq k$$

and infinitely many n. Consequently,

$$\mathbf{p}_n\cdot\Big[P_k\Big(\sum_{t=k-\ell+1}^{k} \mathbf{x}_t\Big) + Q_k\Big(\sum_{t=k-\ell+1}^{k} \mathbf{x}_t^n\Big) + \varepsilon\mathbf{v}\Big] \geq \mathbf{p}_n\cdot\Big(\sum_{t=k-\ell+1}^{k} \mathbf{x}_t^n\Big)$$

holds for infinitely many n, where $\mathbf{v} = \sum_{t=k-\ell+1}^{k} \omega_t$. By addition, the latter combined with the identity

$$Q_k\Big(\sum_{t=k+1}^{n} \mathbf{x}_t^n\Big) = \sum_{t=k+1}^{n} \mathbf{x}_t^n,$$

implies

$$\mathbf{p}_n\cdot\Big[P_k\Big(\sum_{t=k-\ell+1}^{k} \mathbf{x}_t\Big) + Q_k\Big(\sum_{t=k-\ell+1}^{n} \mathbf{x}_t^n\Big) + \varepsilon\mathbf{v}\Big] \geq \mathbf{p}_n\cdot\Big(\sum_{t=k-\ell+1}^{n} \mathbf{x}_t^n\Big) \geq \mathbf{p}_n\cdot\Big(\sum_{t=k-\ell+1}^{n} \omega_t\Big)$$

for infinitely many $n > k$. Now from $\sum_{t=2-\ell}^{n} \mathbf{x}_t^n = \sum_{t=2-\ell}^{n} \omega_t$ and (3), we see that

$$Q_k\Big(\sum_{t=k-\ell+1}^{n} \mathbf{x}_t^n\Big) = Q_k\Big(\sum_{t=k-\ell+1}^{n} \omega_t\Big),$$

and consequently

$$\mathbf{p}_n \cdot \Big[P_k\Big(\sum_{t=k-\ell+1}^{k} \mathbf{x}_t\Big)\Big] + \varepsilon \mathbf{p}_n \cdot \mathbf{v} \ge \mathbf{p}_n \cdot \Big[P_k\Big(\sum_{t=k-\ell+1}^{n} \omega_t\Big)\Big] = \mathbf{p}_n \cdot \Big[P_k\Big(\sum_{t=k-\ell+1}^{k} \omega_t\Big)\Big]$$

holds for infinitely many $n > k$. This implies

$$\mathbf{p} \cdot \Big[P_k\Big(\sum_{t=k-\ell+1}^{k} \mathbf{x}_t\Big)\Big] + \varepsilon \mathbf{p} \cdot \mathbf{v} \ge \mathbf{p} \cdot \Big[P_k\Big(\sum_{t=k-\ell+1}^{k} \omega_t\Big)\Big]$$

holds for all $\varepsilon > 0$, and the desired conclusion follows. ■

Lemma 5.4.13. *If* $(\mathbf{x}, \mathbf{p})$ *is an asymptotic limit, then for each* $k \ge 1$ *we have*

$$P_{k+\ell}\Big(\sum_{t=k+1}^{k+\ell} \mathbf{x}_t\Big) + Q_k\Big(\sum_{t=k-\ell+1}^{k} \mathbf{x}_t\Big) = P_{k+\ell}\Big(\sum_{t=k+1}^{k+\ell} \omega_t\Big) + Q_k\Big(\sum_{t=k-\ell+1}^{k} \omega_t\Big).$$

Proof. Note that

$$\begin{aligned}
&P_{k+\ell}\Big(\sum_{t=k+1}^{k+\ell} \mathbf{x}_t\Big) + Q_k\Big(\sum_{t=k-\ell+1}^{k} \mathbf{x}_t\Big) \\
&= P_{k+\ell}\Big(\sum_{t=k+1}^{k+\ell} \mathbf{x}_t\Big) + \Big(\sum_{t=k-\ell+1}^{k} \mathbf{x}_t\Big) - P_k\Big(\sum_{t=k-\ell+1}^{k} \mathbf{x}_t\Big) \\
&= P_{k+\ell}\Big(\sum_{t=k-\ell+1}^{k+\ell} \mathbf{x}_t\Big) - P_k\Big(\sum_{t=k-\ell+1}^{k} \mathbf{x}_t\Big) \\
&= \Big[P_{k+\ell}\Big(\sum_{t=k-\ell+1}^{k+\ell} \mathbf{x}_t\Big) + \sum_{t=2-\ell}^{k-\ell} \mathbf{x}_t\Big] - \Big[P_k\Big(\sum_{t=k-\ell+1}^{k} \mathbf{x}_t\Big) + \sum_{t=2-\ell}^{k-\ell} \mathbf{x}_t\Big] \\
&= P_{k+\ell}\Big(\sum_{t=2-\ell}^{k+\ell} \mathbf{x}_t\Big) - P_k\Big(\sum_{t=2-\ell}^{k} \mathbf{x}_t\Big).
\end{aligned}$$

Using (3), the desired equality now follows from

$$P_{k+\ell}\Big(\sum_{t=2-\ell}^{k+\ell} \mathbf{x}_t\Big) = P_{k+\ell}\Big(\sum_{t=2-\ell}^{k+\ell} \omega_t\Big) \quad \text{and} \quad P_k\Big(\sum_{t=2-\ell}^{k} \mathbf{x}_t\Big) = P_k\Big(\sum_{t=2-\ell}^{k} \omega_t\Big). \quad ■$$

Lemma 5.4.14. *If* $(\mathbf{x}, \mathbf{p})$ *is an asymptotic limit, then for each* t *we have the budget equality* $\mathbf{p} \cdot \mathbf{x}_t = \mathbf{p} \cdot \omega_t$.

Proof. Applying Lemma 5.4.11, we get

$$\mathbf{p}\cdot\Big[Q_k\Big(\sum_{t=k-\ell+1}^{k}\mathbf{x}_t\Big)\Big]\geq\mathbf{p}\cdot\Big[Q_k\Big(\sum_{t=k-\ell+1}^{k}\omega_t\Big)\Big].$$

Similarly, Lemma 5.4.12 applied with $k+\ell$ instead of k gives

$$\mathbf{p}\cdot\Big[P_{k+\ell}\Big(\sum_{t=k+1}^{k+\ell}\mathbf{x}_t\Big)\Big]\geq\mathbf{p}\cdot\Big[P_{k+\ell}\Big(\sum_{t=k+1}^{k+\ell}\omega_t\Big)\Big].$$

The above two inequalities combined with Lemma 5.4.13 show that the inequalities in Lemmas 5.4.11 and 5.4.12 are, in fact, both equalities. In particular, from the first equality, we obtain

$$\mathbf{p}\cdot\Big[Q_k\Big(\sum_{t=k-\ell+1}^{k}\mathbf{x}_t\Big)\Big]=\mathbf{p}\cdot\Big[Q_k\Big(\sum_{t=2-\ell}^{k}\mathbf{x}_t\Big)\Big]=\mathbf{p}\cdot\Big[Q_k\Big(\sum_{t=2-\ell}^{k}\omega_t\Big)\Big].$$

Now using (**1**), we see that

$$\begin{aligned}\sum_{t=2-\ell}^{k}\mathbf{x}_t&=P_k\Big(\sum_{t=2-\ell}^{k}\mathbf{x}_t\Big)+Q_k\Big(\sum_{t=2-\ell}^{k}\mathbf{x}_t\Big)\\&=P_k\Big(\sum_{t=2-\ell}^{k}\omega_t\Big)+Q_k\Big(\sum_{t=2-\ell}^{k}\mathbf{x}_t\Big).\end{aligned}$$

Consequently,

$$\begin{aligned}\sum_{t=2-\ell}^{k}\mathbf{p}\cdot\mathbf{x}_t&=\mathbf{p}\cdot\Big[P_k\Big(\sum_{t=2-\ell}^{k}\omega_t\Big)\Big]+\mathbf{p}\cdot\Big[Q_k\Big(\sum_{t=2-\ell}^{k}\mathbf{x}_t\Big)\Big]\\&=\mathbf{p}\cdot\Big[P_k\Big(\sum_{t=2-\ell}^{k}\omega_t\Big)\Big]+\mathbf{p}\cdot\Big[Q_k\Big(\sum_{t=2-\ell}^{k}\omega_t\Big)\Big]\\&=\mathbf{p}\cdot\Big(\sum_{t=2-\ell}^{k}\omega_t\Big)\\&=\sum_{t=2-\ell}^{k}\mathbf{p}\cdot\omega_t\,,\end{aligned}$$

holds for each $k\geq 1$. This implies that $\mathbf{p}\cdot\mathbf{x}_t=\mathbf{p}\cdot\omega_t$ holds for each t. ■

To complete the proof of Theorem 5.4.1, it remains to be shown that the prices of asymptotic limits are strictly positive. This will be taken care by the next lemma.

Lemma 5.4.15. *If* $(\mathbf{x},\mathbf{p})$ *is an asymptotic limit of a sequence of short run equilibria, then* $\mathbf{p}$ *is strictly positive, i.e., for each* $\mathbf{0} < \mathbf{y} \in \mathbf{\Theta}$ *we have* $0 < \mathbf{p}\cdot\mathbf{y}$.

Proof. Let $(\mathbf{x},\mathbf{p})$ be an asymptotic limit of a sequence of short run equilibria. We shall establish first that $\mathbf{p}\cdot\omega_t > 0$ holds for each t. For $t=0$, we have $\mathbf{p}\cdot\omega_0 = 1 > 0$. Therefore, for the inductive argument, assume that $\mathbf{p}\cdot\omega_t > 0$. If $\mathbf{p}\cdot\omega_{t+1} = 0$, then $\mathbf{x}_t + \omega_{t+1} \succ_t \mathbf{x}_t$ and $\mathbf{x}_t + \omega_{t+1}$ belongs to the budget set of consumer t, contradicting the maximality of $\mathbf{x}_t$ in the budget set. Hence, $\mathbf{p}\cdot\omega_{t+1} > 0$ must hold, and consequently $\mathbf{p}\cdot\omega_t > 0$ holds for each $t = 0,1,2,\ldots$.

Now for the general case, let $\mathbf{0} < \mathbf{y} = (y_1, y_2, \ldots) \in \mathbf{\Theta}$ and assume that $\mathbf{p}\cdot\mathbf{y} = 0$. Pick some t such that $y_t > 0$. Then $\mathbf{x}_t + \mathbf{y} \succ_t \mathbf{x}_t$ and $\mathbf{x}_t + \mathbf{y}$ lies in the budget set of consumer t, contradicting the maximality of $\mathbf{x}_t$ in that budget set. Hence, $\mathbf{p}\cdot\mathbf{y} > 0$ holds for each $\mathbf{0} < \mathbf{y} \in \mathbf{\Theta}$. ■

EXERCISES

1. Verify the assertion used in the proof of Lemma 5.4.4: If $(\mathbf{x}_0, \mathbf{x}_1, \ldots, \mathbf{x}_n; \mathbf{p})$ is a Walrasian equilibrium for the exchange economy $\mathcal{E}_n$, then the vectors $\mathbf{x}_i$ are of the form

$$\mathbf{x}_0 = (x_0^1, 0, 0, \ldots) \quad \text{and} \quad \mathbf{x}_t = (0, \ldots, 0, x_t^t, x_t^{t+1}, 0, 0, \ldots) \quad \text{for} \quad 1 \le t \le n.$$

2. Show that if $(\mathbf{x}_0, \mathbf{x}_1, \ldots, \mathbf{x}_n; \mathbf{p})$ is a Walrasian equilibrium for the exchange economy $\mathcal{E}_n$, then the strictly positive price $\mathbf{p}$ is also order continuous on $\mathbf{A}_n$. [HINT: We can assume that $\mathbf{p}\cdot(\sum_{t=0}^{n+1}\omega_t) = 1$. Let $\mathbf{y}_\alpha \downarrow \mathbf{0}$ in $\mathbf{A}_n$ and let $\varepsilon > 0$ be fixed. Without loss of generality we can suppose that $0 \le \mathbf{y}_\alpha \le \sum_{t=0}^{n+1}\mathbf{x}_t$ holds for all α. Thus, by the Riesz Decomposition Property, we can write $\mathbf{y}_\alpha = \sum_{t=0}^{n+1}\mathbf{y}_\alpha^t$ with $0 \le \mathbf{y}_\alpha^t \le \mathbf{x}_t$ for $t = 0,1,2,\ldots,n+1$. From $\mathbf{x}_t + \varepsilon\omega_t \succ_t \mathbf{x}_t$, $\mathbf{y}_\alpha^t \xrightarrow{w} \mathbf{0}$ and the continuity of the utility functions, we see that there exists some β such that $\mathbf{x}_t + \varepsilon\omega_t - \mathbf{y}_\alpha^t \succ_t \mathbf{x}_t$ for all $\alpha \ge \beta$ and all $t = 0,1,\ldots,n+1$— note that, in view of $\mathbf{y}_\alpha^t \le \mathbf{x}_t$, we indeed have $\mathbf{x}_t + \varepsilon\omega_t - \mathbf{y}_\alpha^t \ge \mathbf{0}$. By the supportability of $\mathbf{p}$, we infer that

$$\mathbf{p}\cdot(\mathbf{x}_t + \varepsilon\omega_t - \mathbf{y}_\alpha^t) = \mathbf{p}\cdot\mathbf{x}_t + \varepsilon\mathbf{p}\cdot\omega_t - \mathbf{p}\cdot\mathbf{y}_\alpha^t \ge \mathbf{p}\cdot\omega_t = \mathbf{p}\cdot\mathbf{x}_t,$$

and so $0 \le \mathbf{p}\cdot\mathbf{y}_\alpha^t \le \varepsilon\mathbf{p}\cdot\omega_t$ for all $\alpha \ge \beta$ and all $0 \le t \le n+1$. Thus, for $\alpha \ge \beta$ we have

$$0 \le \mathbf{p}\cdot\mathbf{y}_\alpha = \sum_{t=0}^{n+1}\mathbf{p}\cdot\mathbf{y}_\alpha^t \le \sum_{t=0}^{n+1}\varepsilon\mathbf{p}\cdot\omega_t = \varepsilon,$$

proving that $\lim_\alpha \mathbf{p} \cdot \mathbf{y}_\alpha = 0$.]

3. Consider a sequence $\{(\mathbf{x}_0^n, \mathbf{x}_1^n, \ldots, \mathbf{x}_n^n; \mathbf{p}_n)\}$ of Walrasian equilibria for the sequence of economies $\mathcal{E}_n$ and let $\mathbf{f}_n = (\mathbf{x}_0^n, \mathbf{x}_1^n, \ldots, \mathbf{x}_n^n, 0, 0, \ldots) \in \mathcal{X}$. If $\mathbf{x}$ is an accumulation point of the sequence $\{\mathbf{f}_n\}$, then show that $\mathbf{x}$ is an allocation for the overlapping generations model.

4. Verify that the discussion and conclusions up to (and including) Lemma 5.4.10 are valid for the general overlapping generations model—as it was introduced at the end of Section 5.1.

5. Verify properties (**1**), (**2**) and (**3**) listed just before Lemma 5.4.11 (p. 266).

6. Prove Lemmas 5.4.11–5.4.14 for the general overlapping generations model, i.e., establish the validity of the lemmas for an arbitrary r.

7. Consider the one-consumer two-period OLG model and let $(\mathbf{x}, \mathbf{p})$ be an asymptotic limit. Then

$$\mathbf{y}_t = (0, \ldots, 0, x_t^t, 0, 0, \ldots) \quad \text{and} \quad \mathbf{z}_t = (0, \ldots, 0, x_t^{t+1}, 0, 0, \ldots)$$

represent the allocations that consumer t is receiving at periods t and $t+1$, while

$$\mathbf{e}_t = (0, \ldots, 0, \omega_t^t, 0, 0, \ldots) \quad \text{and} \quad \mathbf{f}_t = (0, \ldots, 0, \omega_t^{t+1}, 0, 0, \ldots),$$

are her initial endowments at periods t and $t+1$, respectively. Show that

$$\mathbf{p} \cdot \mathbf{y}_t = \mathbf{p} \cdot \mathbf{e}_t \quad \text{and} \quad \mathbf{p} \cdot \mathbf{z}_t = \mathbf{p} \cdot \mathbf{f}_t .$$

8. Consider the overlapping generations model with the following characteristics.
Commodity Spaces: $E_t = \mathcal{R}$ for each t.
Utility Functions: $u_0(x^0) = x^0$ and $u_t(x^t, x^{t+1}) = x^t + x^{t+1}$.
Initial Endowments: $\omega_t = (0, \ldots, 0, \frac{1}{4}, \frac{3}{4}, 0, 0, \ldots)$ for $t \geq 2$—where the numbers $\frac{1}{4}$ and $\frac{3}{4}$ occupy the t and $t+1$ positions—$\omega_0 = (\frac{1}{2}, 0, 0, \ldots)$ and $\omega_1 = (\frac{1}{2}, \frac{3}{4}, 0, 0, \ldots)$.
Establish the following properties.
   1) $\mathbf{\Theta}$=the vector space of all real sequences that are eventually zero;
   2) $\mathbf{\Theta}' = \mathcal{R}_\infty$=the vector space of all real sequences;
   3) The allocation $(\mathbf{x}_0, \mathbf{x}_1, \mathbf{x}_2, \ldots)$, where $\mathbf{x}_t = (0, \ldots, 0, \frac{1}{2}, \frac{1}{2}, 0, 0, \ldots)$ for $t \geq 1$ and $\mathbf{x}_0 = (\frac{1}{2}, 0, 0, \ldots)$, is not a competitive equilibrium.
   4) Find a competitive equilibrium—whose existence is guaranteed by Theorem 5.4.1—for this overlapping generations model.

9. Show that the Riesz dual system $\langle \mathbf{E}, \mathbf{E}' \rangle$ is symmetric if and only if every Riesz dual system $\langle E_t, E_t' \rangle$ is symmetric.

10. Show that in an OLG model every competitive equilibrium with respect to the Riesz dual system $\langle \mathbf{\Theta}, \mathbf{\Theta}' \rangle$ is Malinvaud optimal—and conclude that, in an OLG model with symmetric Riesz dual systems, Malinvaud optimal allocations exist.

REFERENCES

1. C. D. ALIPRANTIS AND D. J. BROWN, Equilibria in markets with a Riesz space of commodities, *J. Math. Econom.* **11** (1983), 189–207. **MR 85**d:90021.
2. C. D. ALIPRANTIS, D. J. BROWN AND O. BURKINSHAW, Edgeworth equilibria, *Econometrica* **55** (1987), 1109–1137.
3. C. D. ALIPRANTIS, D. J. BROWN AND O. BURKINSHAW, Edgeworth equilibria in production economies, *J. Econom. Theory* **43** (1987), 252–291.
4. C. D. ALIPRANTIS, D. J. BROWN AND O. BURKINSHAW, An economy with infinite dimensional commodity space and empty core, *Econom. Lett.* **23** (1987), 1–4. **MR 88**f:90036.
5. C. D. ALIPRANTIS, D. J. BROWN AND O. BURKINSHAW, Equilibria in exchange economies with a countable number of agents, *J. Math. Anal. Appl.*, forthcoming.
6. C. D. ALIPRANTIS AND O. BURKINSHAW, *Locally Solid Riesz Spaces*, Pure and Applied Mathematics Series # 76, Academic Press, New York & London, 1978. **MR 58** # 12271.
7. C. D. ALIPRANTIS AND O. BURKINSHAW, *Principles of Real Analysis*, Elsevier North-Holland, New York, 1981. **MR 82**j:28001.
8. C. D. ALIPRANTIS AND O. BURKINSHAW, *Positive Operators*, Pure and Applied Mathematics Series # 119, Academic Press, New York & London, 1985. **MR 87**h:47086.
9. C. D. ALIPRANTIS AND O. BURKINSHAW, The fundamental theorems of welfare economics without proper preferences, *J. Math. Econom.* **17** (1988), 41–54.
10. A. ARAUJO, Lack of Pareto optimal allocations in economies with infinitely many commodities: The need for impatience, *Econometrica* **53** (1985), 455-461. **MR 86**h:90017.
11. K. J. ARROW, An extension of the basic theorems of classical welfare economics, in: J. Neyman, Ed., *Proceedings of the Second Berkeley Symposium on Mathematical Statistics and Probability* (University of California Press, Berkeley and Los Angeles, 1951), pp. 507–532. **MR 13**, 482.
12. K. J. ARROW AND G. DEBREU, Existence of an equilibrium for a competitive economy, *Econometrica* **22** (1954), 265–290. **MR 17**, 985.
13. K. J. ARROW AND F. H. HAHN, *General Competitive Analysis*, Holden-Day, San Francisco, CA; Oliver & Boyd, Edinburg, 1971. **MR 55** # 11958.

14. Y. BALASKO, D. CASS AND K. SHELL, Existence of competitive equilibrium in a general overlapping-generations model, *J. Economic Theory* **23** (1980), 307–322. **MR 84**e:90017e.

15. Y. BALASKO AND K. SHELL, The overlapping-generations model, I: The case of pure exchange without money, *J. Econom. Theory* **23** (1980), 281–306. **MR 84**e:90017a.

16. T. F. BEWLEY, Existence of equilibria in economies with infinitely many commodities, *J. Econom. Theory* **4** (1972), 514–540. **MR 56** # 10785.

17. O. N. BONDAREVA, Kernel theory in n-person games, *Vestnik Leningrad Univ. Math.* **17** (1962), 141–142. **MR 26** # 7450.

18. D. J. BROWN AND L. M. LEWIS, Myopic economic agents, *Econometrica* **49** (1981), 359–368. **MR 82**f:90022.

19. D. J. BROWN AND S. A. ROSS, Spanning, valuation and options, Cowles Foundation Discussion Paper, No. 873, June, 1988.

20. J. BURKE, On the existence of price equilibria in dynamic economies, *J. Econom. Theory* **44** (1988), 281–300.

21. D. CASS AND M. E. YAARI, A re-examination of the pure consumption loans model, *J. Pol. Econom.* **74** (1966), 353–367.

22. G. DEBREU, Valuation equilibrium and Pareto Optimum, *Proc. Nat. Acad. Sci. U.S.A.* **40** (1954), 588–592. **MR 16**, 500.

23. G. DEBREU, *Theory of Value*, Yale University Press, New Haven, CT, 1959. **MR 22** # 1447.

24. G. DEBREU AND H. E. SCARF, A limit theorem on the core of an economy, *Internat. Econom. Rev.* 4 (1963), 235–246. **Zbl 122**, 377.

25. D. DUFFIE AND C. F. HUANG, Implementing Arrow–Debreu equilibria by continuous trading of few long-lived securities, *Econometrica* **53** (1985), 1337–1356. **MR 88**b:90021.

26. F. Y. EDGEWORTH, *Mathematical Psychics*, Kegan Paul, London, 1881.

27. K. FAN, A generalization of Tychonoff's fixed point theorem, *Math, Ann.* **142** (1961), 305–310. **MR 24** #*A*1120.

28. I. FISHER, *The Theory of Interest*, Macmillan, New York, 1930. Reprinted in *Reprints of Economic Classics*, A. M. Kelley, Publisher, New York, 1965.

29. D. GALE, Pure exchange equilibrium of dynamic economic models, *J. Econom. Theory* **6**(1973), 12–36. **MR 56** # 7831.

30. J. GEANAKOPLOS, The overlapping generations model of general equilibrium, *The New Palgrave*, Macmillan, New York & London, pp. 767–779.

31. A. GROTHENDIECK, *Topological Vector Spaces*, Gordon and Breach, New York & London, 1973. **MR 17**, 1110.

32. W. HILDENBRAND AND A. P. KIRMAN, *Introduction to Equilibrium Analysis*, Advanced Textbooks in Economics # 6, North-Holland, Amsterdam, 1976. **MR 57** # 4992.

33. J. HORVÁTH, *Topological Vector Spaces and Distributions*, Addison-Wesley, Reading, MA, 1966. **MR 34** # 4863.

34. L. E. JONES, A competitive model of commodity differentiation, *Econometrica* **52** (1984), 507–530. **Zbl 544**, 90006.

35. L. E. JONES, Special problems arising in the study of economies with infinitely many commodities, in: H. F. Sonnenschein, Ed., *Models of Economic Dynamics* (Springer-Verlag Lecture Notes in Economics and Mathem. Systems # 264, Berlin-New York, 1986), 184–205. **MR 88**a:90042.

36. S. KAKUTANI, A generalization of Brouwer's fixed point theorem, *Duke Math. J.* **8** (1941), 457–459. **MR 3**, 60.

37. I. KAWAI, Locally convex lattices, *J. Math. Soc. Japan* **9** (1957), 281–314. **MR 20** # 1902.

38. J. L. KELLEY, *General Topology*, D. Van Nostrand Co., New York & London, 1955. **MR 16**, 1136.

39. M. A. KHAN AND R. VOHRA, On approximate decentralization of Pareto optimal allocations in locally convex spaces, *J. Approx. Theory* **52** (1988), 149–161.

40. B. KNASTER, C. KURATOWSKI AND S. MAZURKIEWICZ, Ein Beweis des Fixpunktsatzes für n-dimensionale simplexe, *Fund. Math.* **14** (1926), 132–137.

41. D. M. KREPS, Arbitrage and equilibrium in economies with infinitely many commodities, *J. Math. Econom.* **8** (1981), 15–35. **MR 82**m:90038.

42. W. A. J. LUXEMBURG AND A. C. ZAANEN, *Riesz Spaces I*, North-Holland, Amsterdam, 1971. **MR 58** # 23483.

43. M. MAGILL, An equilibrium existence theorem, *J. Mathematical Analysis Appl.* **84** (1981), 162–169. **MR 83**b:90018.

44. E. MALINVAUD, Capital accumulation and efficient allocation of resources, *Econometrica* **21** (1953), 233–268. **MR 15**, 48.

45. E. MALINVAUD, Efficient capital accumulation: A Corrigendum, *Econometrica* **30** (1962), 570–573.

46. A. MAS-COLELL, The price equilibrium existence problem in topological vector lattices, *Econometrica* **54** (1986), 1039–1053. **MR 87**m:90038.

47. A. MAS-COLELL, Valuation equilibrium and Pareto optimum revisited, in: W. Hildenbrand and A. Mas-Colell Eds., *Contributions to Mathematical Economics* (North-Holland, New York, 1986), Chapter 17, pp. 317–331. **MR 88**k:90036.

48. L. W. McKENZIE, On the existence of general equilibrium for a competitive market, *Econometrica* **27** (1959), 54–71. **MR 21** # 5507.

49. L. W. McKENZIE, The classical theorem on existence of competitive equilibrium, *Econometrica* **49** (1981), 819–841. **MR 83**b:90019.

50. T. NEGISHI, Welfare economics and existence of an equilibrium for a competitive economy, *Metroeconomica* **12** (1960), 92–97.

51. W. NEUEFEIND, Notes on existence of equilibrium proofs and the boundary behavior of supply, *Econometrica* **48** (1980), 1831–1837. **MR 83**k:90026.

52. H. NIKAIDO, *Convex Structures and Economic Theory*, Mathematics in Science and Engineering Vol. 51, Academic Press, New York & London, 1968. **MR 43** # 2970.

53. B. PELEG AND M. E. YAARI, Markets with countably many commodities, *Internat. Econom. Rev.* **11** (1970), 369–377. **Zbl 211**, 230.

54. L. K. RAUT, Myopic topologies on general commodity spaces, *J. Econom. Theory* **39** (1986), 358–367. **MR 88**h:90011.

55. S. F. RICHARD, Competitive equilibrium in Riesz spaces, *J. Math. Econom.*, forthcoming.

56. S. F. RICHARD AND S. SRIVASTAVA, Equilibrium in economies with infinitely many consumers and infinitely many commodities, *J. Math. Econom.* **17** (1988), 9–21.

57. S. F. RICHARD AND W. R. ZAME, Proper preferences and quasi-concave utility functions, *J. Math. Econom.* **15** (1986), 231–247. **MR 88**b:90037.

58. A. P. ROBERTSON AND W. ROBERTSON, *Topological Vector Spaces*, Cambridge University Press, London, 1973. **MR 28** # 5318.

59. P. A. SAMUELSON, An exact consumption-loan model of interest with or without the social contrivance of money, *J. Pol. Econom.* **66** (1958), 467–482.

60. H. E. SCARF, The core of an N person game, *Econometrica* **35** (1967), 50–69. **MR 38** # 3051.

61. H. E. SCARF, *The Computation of Economic Equilibria*, Yale Univ. Press, New Haven, CT, 1973.

62. H. H. SCHAEFER, *Topological Vector Spaces*, Springer-Verlag, New York & Berlin, 1971. **MR 33** # 1689.

63. H. H. SCHAEFER, *Banach Lattices and Positive Operators*, Springer-Verlag, New York & Berlin, 1974. **MR 54** # 11023.

64. K. SHELL, Notes on the economics of infinity, *J. Pol. Econ.* **79** (1971), 1002–1011.

65. K. D. STROYAN, Myopic utility functions on sequential economies, *J. Math. Econom.* **11** (1983), 267–276. **MR 85**h:90025.

66. R. VOHRA, On Scarf's theorem on the non-emptiness of the core: A direct proof through Kakutani's fixed point theorem, Brown University Working Paper, January, 1987.

67. L. WALRAS, *Eléments d' économie politique pure*, L. Corbaz, Lausanne, 1874. Reprinted in *Reprints of Economic Classics*, A. M. Kelley, Publisher, New York, 1954.

68. C. A. WILSON, Equilibrium in dynamic models with an infinity of agents, *J. Econom. Theory* **24** (1981), 95–111. **MR 84**a:90018.

69. N. C. YANNELIS AND W. R. ZAME, Equilibria in Banach lattices without ordered preferences, *J. Math. Econom.* **15** (1986), 85–110. **MR 88**a:90047.

70. A. C. ZAANEN, *Riesz Spaces II*, North-Holland, Amsterdam, 1983. **MR 86**b:46001.

71. W. R. ZAME, Competitive equilibria in production economies with an infinite-dimensional commodity space, *Econometrica* **55** (1987), 1075–1108.

INDEX

D

E

I

K

L

M

N

O

P

T

U

V

W

GPSR Compliance
The European Union's (EU) General Product Safety Regulation (GPSR) is a set of rules that requires consumer products to be safe and our obligations to ensure this.

If you have any concerns about our products, you can contact us on

ProductSafety@springernature.com

In case Publisher is established outside the EU, the EU authorized representative is:

Springer Nature Customer Service Center GmbH
Europaplatz 3
69115 Heidelberg, Germany

www.ingramcontent.com/pod-product-compliance
Ingram Content Group UK Ltd.
Pitfield, Milton Keynes, MK11 3LW, UK
UKHW050722170926
15229UKWH00010B/38
* 9 7 8 3 6 6 2 2 1 8 9 4 5 *